A COMPUTATIONAL INTRODUCTION
TO NUMBER THEORY AND ALGEBRA

A COMPUTATIONAL INTRODUCTION TO NUMBER THEORY AND ALGEBRA

VICTOR SHOUP

CAMBRIDGE
UNIVERSITY PRESS

CAMBRIDGE UNIVERSITY PRESS
Cambridge, New York, Melbourne, Madrid, Cape Town, Singapore, São Paulo

Cambridge University Press
The Edinburgh Building, Cambridge CB2 2RU, UK

Published in the United States of America by Cambridge University Press, New York

www.cambridge.org
Information on this title: www.cambridge.org/9780521851541

© V. Shoup 2005

First published 2005
Reprinted 2006

Printed in the United Kingdom at the University Press, Cambridge

A catalog record for this book is available from the British Library

ISBN-13   978-0-521-85154-1 hardback
ISBN-10   0-521-85154-8 hardback

ISBN-13   978-0-521-61725-3 paperback
ISBN-10   0-521-61725-1 paperback

Contents

Preface

Number theory and algebra play an increasingly significant role in computing and communications, as evidenced by the striking applications of these subjects to such fields as cryptography and coding theory. My goal in writing this book was to provide an introduction to number theory and algebra, with an emphasis on algorithms and applications, that would be accessible to a broad audience. In particular, I wanted to write a book that would be accessible to typical students in computer science or mathematics who have a some amount of *general* mathematical experience, but without presuming too much *specific* mathematical knowledge.

Prerequisites. The mathematical prerequisites are minimal: no particular mathematical concepts beyond what is taught in a typical undergraduate calculus sequence are assumed.

The computer science prerequisites are also quite minimal: it is assumed that the reader is proficient in programming, and has had some exposure to the analysis of algorithms, essentially at the level of an undergraduate course on algorithms and data structures.

Even though it is mathematically quite self contained, the text does presuppose that the reader is comfortable with mathematical formalism and has some experience in reading and writing mathematical proofs. Readers may have gained such experience in computer science courses such as algorithms, automata or complexity theory, or some type of "discrete mathematics for computer science students" course. They also may have gained such experience in undergraduate mathematics courses, such as abstract or linear algebra—these courses overlap with some of the material presented here, but even if the reader already has had some exposure to this material, it nevertheless may be convenient to have all of the relevant material easily accessible in one place, and moreover, the emphasis and perspective here will no doubt be different than in a typical mathematics course on these subjects.

Structure of the text. All of the mathematics required beyond basic calculus is developed "from scratch." Moreover, the book generally alternates between "theory" and "applications": one or two chapters on a particular set of purely mathematical concepts are followed by one or two chapters on algorithms and applications—the mathematics provides the theoretical underpinnings for the applications, while the applications both motivate and illustrate the mathematics. Of course, this dichotomy between theory and applications is not perfectly maintained: the chapters that focus mainly on applications include the development of some of the mathematics that is specific to a particular application, and very occasionally, some of the chapters that focus mainly on mathematics include a discussion of related algorithmic ideas as well.

In developing the mathematics needed to discuss certain applications, I tried to strike a reasonable balance between, on the one hand, presenting the absolute minimum required to understand and rigorously analyze the applications, and on the other hand, presenting a full-blown development of the relevant mathematics. In striking this balance, I wanted to be fairly economical and concise, while at the same time, I wanted to develop enough of the theory so as to present a fairly well-rounded account, giving the reader more of a feeling for the mathematical "big picture."

The mathematical material covered includes the basics of number theory (including unique factorization, congruences, the distribution of primes, and quadratic reciprocity) and abstract algebra (including groups, rings, fields, and vector spaces). It also includes an introduction to discrete probability theory—this material is needed to properly treat the topics of probabilistic algorithms and cryptographic applications. The treatment of all these topics is more or less standard, except that the text only deals with commutative structures (i.e., abelian groups and commutative rings with unity)—this is all that is really needed for the purposes of this text, and the theory of these structures is much simpler and more transparent than that of more general, non-commutative structures.

The choice of topics covered in this book was motivated primarily by their applicability to computing and communications, especially to the specific areas of cryptography and coding theory. For example, the book may be useful for reference or self-study by readers who want to learn about cryptography. The book could also be used as a textbook in a graduate or upper-division undergraduate course on (computational) number theory and algebra, perhaps geared towards computer science students.

Since this is an introductory textbook, and not an encyclopedic reference for specialists, some topics simply could not be covered. One such topic whose exclusion will undoubtedly be lamented by some is the theory of lattices, along with algorithms for and applications of lattice basis reduction. Another such topic is that of fast algorithms for integer and polynomial arithmetic—although some of the basic ideas of this topic are developed in the exercises, the main body of the text deals only with classical, quadratic-time algorithms for integer and polynomial arithmetic. As an introductory text, some topics just had to go; moreover, there are more advanced texts that cover these topics perfectly well, and these texts should be readily accessible to students who have mastered the material in this book.

Note that while continued fractions are not discussed, the closely related problem of "rational reconstruction" is covered, along with a number of interesting applications (which could also be solved using continued fractions).

Using the text. Here are a few tips on using the text.

- There are a few sections that are marked with a "(∗)," indicating that the material covered in that section is a bit technical, and is not needed elsewhere.

- There are many examples in the text. These form an integral part of the text, and should not be skipped.

- There are a number of exercises in the text that serve to reinforce, as well as to develop important applications and generalizations of, the material presented in the text. In solving exercises, the reader is free to use any *previously* stated results in the text, including those in previous exercises. However, except where otherwise noted, any result in a section marked with a "(∗)," or in §5.5, need not and should not be used outside the section in which it appears.

- There is a very brief "Preliminaries" chapter, which fixes a bit of notation and recalls a few standard facts. This should be skimmed over by the reader.

- There is an appendix that contains a few useful facts; where such a fact is used in the text, there is a reference such as "see §An," which refers to the item labeled "An" in the appendix.

Feedback. I welcome comments on the book (suggestions for improvement, error reports, etc.) from readers. Please send your comments to

`victor@shoup.net`.

There is also web site where further material and information relating to the book (including a list of errata and the latest electronic version of the book) may be found:

www.shoup.net/ntb.

Acknowledgments. I would like to thank a number of people who volunteered their time and energy in reviewing one or more chapters: Siddhartha Annapureddy, John Black, Carl Bosley, Joshua Brody, Jan Camenisch, Ronald Cramer, Alex Dent, Nelly Fazio, Mark Giesbrecht, Stuart Haber, Alfred Menezes, Antonio Nicolosi, Roberto Oliveira, and Louis Salvail. Thanks to their efforts, the "bug count" has been significantly reduced, and the readability of the text much improved. I am also grateful to the National Science Foundation for their support provided under grant CCR-0310297. Thanks to David Tranah and his colleagues at Cambridge University Press for their progressive attitudes regarding intellectual property and open access.

New York, January 2005 *Victor Shoup*

Preliminaries

We establish here a few notational conventions used throughout the text.

Arithmetic with ∞

We shall sometimes use the symbols "∞" and "$-\infty$" in simple arithmetic expressions involving real numbers. The interpretation given to such expressions is the usual, natural one; for example, for all real numbers x, we have $-\infty < x < \infty$, $x + \infty = \infty$, $x - \infty = -\infty$, $\infty + \infty = \infty$, and $(-\infty) + (-\infty) = -\infty$. Some such expressions have no sensible interpretation (e.g., $\infty - \infty$).

Logarithms and exponentials

We denote by $\log x$ the natural logarithm of x. The logarithm of x to the base b is denoted $\log_b x$.

We denote by e^x the usual exponential function, where $e \approx 2.71828$ is the base of the natural logarithm. We may also write $\exp[x]$ instead of e^x.

Sets and relations

We use the symbol $\emptyset$ to denote the empty set. For two sets A, B, we use the notation $A \subseteq B$ to mean that A is a subset of B (with A possibly equal to B), and the notation $A \subsetneq B$ to mean that A is a proper subset of B (i.e., $A \subseteq B$ but $A \neq B$); further, $A \cup B$ denotes the union of A and B, $A \cap B$ the intersection of A and B, and $A \setminus B$ the set of all elements of A that are not in B.

For sets $S_1, \ldots, S_n$, we denote by $S_1 \times \cdots \times S_n$ the **Cartesian product** of $S_1, \ldots, S_n$, that is, the set of all n-tuples $(a_1, \ldots, a_n)$, where $a_i \in S_i$ for $i = 1, \ldots, n$.

We use the notation $S^{\times n}$ to denote the Cartesian product of n copies of a set S, and for $x \in S$, we denote by $x^{\times n}$ the element of $S^{\times n}$ consisting of n copies of x. (We shall reserve the notation S^n to denote the set of all nth powers of S, assuming a multiplication operation on S is defined.)

Two sets A and B are **disjoint** if $A \cap B = \emptyset$. A collection $\{C_i\}$ of sets is called **pairwise disjoint** if $C_i \cap C_j = \emptyset$ for all i, j with $i \neq j$.

A **partition** of a set S is a pairwise disjoint collection of non-empty subsets of S whose union is S. In other words, each element of S appears in exactly one subset.

A **binary relation** on a set S is a subset R of $S \times S$. Usually, one writes $a \sim b$ to mean that $(a, b) \in R$, where $\sim$ is some appropriate symbol, and rather than refer to the relation as R, one refers to it as $\sim$.

A binary relation $\sim$ on a set S is called an **equivalence relation** if for all $x, y, z \in S$, we have

- $x \sim x$ (reflexive property),
- $x \sim y$ implies $y \sim x$ (symmetric property), and
- $x \sim y$ and $y \sim z$ implies $x \sim z$ (transitive property).

If $\sim$ is an equivalence relation on S, then for $x \in S$ one defines the set $[x] := \{y \in S : x \sim y\}$. Such a set $[x]$ is an **equivalence class**. It follows from the definition of an equivalence relation that for all $x, y \in S$, we have

- $x \in [x]$, and
- either $[x] \cap [y] = \emptyset$ or $[x] = [y]$.

In particular, the collection of all distinct equivalence classes partitions the set S. For any $x \in S$, the set $[x]$ is called the the **equivalence class containing** x, and x is called a **representative** of $[x]$.

Functions

For any function f from a set A into a set B, if $A' \subseteq A$, then $f(A') := \{f(a) \in B : a \in A'\}$ is the **image** of A' under f, and $f(A)$ is simply referred to as the **image** of f; if $B' \subseteq B$, then $f^{-1}(B') := \{a \in A : f(a) \in B'\}$ is the **pre-image** of B' under f.

A function $f : A \to B$ is called **one-to-one** or **injective** if $f(a) = f(b)$ implies $a = b$. The function f is called **onto** or **surjective** if $f(A) = B$. The function f is called **bijective** if it is both injective and surjective; in this case, f is called a **bijection**. If f is bijective, then we may define the

inverse function $f^{-1} : B \to A$, where for $b \in B$, $f^{-1}(b)$ is defined to be the unique $a \in A$ such that $f(a) = b$.

If $f : A \to B$ and $g : B \to C$ are functions, we denote by $g \circ f$ their composition, that is, the function that sends $a \in A$ to $g(f(a)) \in C$. Function composition is associative; that is, for functions $f : A \to B$, $g : B \to C$, and $h : C \to D$, we have $(h \circ g) \circ f = h \circ (g \circ f)$. Thus, we can simply write $h \circ g \circ f$ without any ambiguity. More generally, if we have functions $f_i : A_i \to A_{i+1}$ for $i = 1, \ldots, n$, where $n \geq 2$, then we may write their composition as $f_n \circ \cdots \circ f_1$ without any ambiguity. As a special case of this, if $A_i = A$ and $f_i = f$ for $i = 1, \ldots, n$, then we may write $f_n \circ \cdots \circ f_1$ as f^n. It is understood that $f^1 = f$, and that f^0 is the identity function on A. If f is a bijection, then so is f^n for any non-negative integer n, the inverse function of f^n being $(f^{-1})^n$, which one may simply write as f^{-n}.

Binary operations

A **binary operation** $\star$ on a set S is a function from $S \times S$ to S, where the value of the function at $(a, b) \in S \times S$ is denoted $a \star b$.

A binary operation $\star$ on S is called **associative** if for all $a, b, c \in S$, we have $(a \star b) \star c = a \star (b \star c)$. In this case, we can simply write $a \star b \star c$ without any ambiguity. More generally, for $a_1, \ldots, a_n \in S$, where $n \geq 2$, we can write $a_1 \star \cdots \star a_n$ without any ambiguity.

A binary operation $\star$ on S is called **commutative** if for all $a, b \in S$, we have $a \star b = b \star a$. If the binary operation $\star$ is both associative and commutative, then not only is the expression $a_1 \star \cdots \star a_n$ unambiguous, but its value remains unchanged even if we re-order the a_i.

1

Basic properties of the integers

This chapter discusses some of the basic properties of the integers, including the notions of divisibility and primality, unique factorization into primes, greatest common divisors, and least common multiples.

1.1 Divisibility and primality

Consider the integers $\mathbb{Z} := \{\ldots, -2, -1, 0, 1, 2, \ldots\}$. For $a, b \in \mathbb{Z}$, we say that b **divides** a, or alternatively, that a is **divisible by** b, if there exists $c \in \mathbb{Z}$ such that $a = bc$. If b divides a, then b is called a **divisor** of a, and we write $b \mid a$. If b does not divide a, then we write $b \nmid a$.

We first state some simple facts:

Theorem 1.1. *For all $a, b, c \in \mathbb{Z}$, we have*

  (i) $a \mid a$, $1 \mid a$, and $a \mid 0$;

  (ii) $0 \mid a$ if and only if $a = 0$;

  (iii) $a \mid b$ and $a \mid c$ implies $a \mid (b + c)$;

  (iv) $a \mid b$ implies $a \mid -b$;

  (v) $a \mid b$ and $b \mid c$ implies $a \mid c$.

Proof. These properties can be easily derived from the definition using elementary facts about the integers. For example, $a \mid a$ because we can write $a = a \cdot 1$; $1 \mid a$ because we can write $a = 1 \cdot a$; $a \mid 0$ because we can write $0 = a \cdot 0$. We leave it as an easy exercise for the reader to verify the remaining properties. $\square$

Another simple but useful fact is the following:

Theorem 1.2. *For all $a, b \in \mathbb{Z}$, we have $a \mid b$ and $b \mid a$ if and only if $a = \pm b$.*

Proof. Clearly, if $a = \pm b$, then $a \mid b$ and $b \mid a$. So let us assume that $a \mid b$ and $b \mid a$, and prove that $a = \pm b$. If either of a or b are zero, then part (ii) of the previous theorem implies that the other is zero. So assume that neither is zero. Now, $b \mid a$ implies $a = bc$ for some $c \in \mathbb{Z}$. Likewise, $a \mid b$ implies $b = ad$ for some $d \in \mathbb{Z}$. From this, we obtain $b = ad = bcd$, and canceling b from both sides of the equation $b = bcd$, we obtain $1 = cd$. The only possibility is that either $c = d = -1$, in which case $a = -b$, or $c = d = 1$, in which case $a = b$. $\square$

Any integer n is trivially divisible by ± 1 and $\pm n$. We say that an integer p is **prime** if $p > 1$ and the only divisors of p are the trivial divisors ± 1 and $\pm p$. Conversely, an integer n is called **composite** if $n > 1$ and it is not prime. So an integer $n > 1$ is composite if and only if $n = ab$ for some integers a, b with $1 < a < n$ and $1 < b < n$. The first few primes are

$$2, 3, 5, 7, 11, 13, 17, \ldots.$$

The number 1 is not considered to be either prime or composite. Also, we do not consider the negative of a prime (e.g., -2) to be prime (although one can, and some authors do so).

A basic fact is that any non-zero integer can be expressed as a signed product of primes in an essentially unique way. More precisely:

Theorem 1.3 (Fundamental theorem of arithmetic). *Every non-zero integer n can be expressed as*

$$n = \pm p_1^{e_1} \cdots p_r^{e_r},$$

where the p_i are distinct primes and the e_i are positive integers. Moreover, this expression is unique, up to a reordering of the primes.

Note that if $n = \pm 1$ in the above theorem, then $r = 0$, and the product of zero terms is interpreted (as usual) as 1.

To prove this theorem, we may clearly assume that n is positive, since otherwise, we may multiply n by -1 and reduce to the case where n is positive.

The proof of the existence part of Theorem 1.3 is easy. This amounts to showing that every positive integer n can be expressed as a product (possibly empty) of primes. We may prove this by induction on n. If $n = 1$, the statement is true, as n is the product of zero primes. Now let $n > 1$, and assume that every positive integer smaller than n can be expressed as a product of primes. If n is a prime, then the statement is true, as n is the product of one prime; otherwise, n is composite, and so there exist $a, b \in \mathbb{Z}$ with $1 < a < n$, $1 < b < n$, and $n = ab$; by the induction hypothesis, both a and b can be expressed as a product of primes, and so the same holds for n.

The uniqueness part of Theorem 1.3 is by no means obvious, and most of the rest of this section and the next section are devoted to developing a proof of this. We give a quite leisurely proof, introducing a number of other very important tools and concepts along the way that will be useful later. An essential ingredient in this proof is the following:

Theorem 1.4 (Division with remainder property). *For $a, b \in \mathbb{Z}$ with $b > 0$, there exist unique $q, r \in \mathbb{Z}$ such that $a = bq + r$ and $0 \le r < b$.*

Proof. Consider the set S of non-negative integers of the form $a - zb$ with $z \in \mathbb{Z}$. This set is clearly non-empty, and so contains a minimum. Let r be the smallest integer in this set, with $r = a - qb$ for $q \in \mathbb{Z}$. By definition, we have $r \ge 0$. Also, we must have $r < b$, since otherwise, we would have $0 \le r - b < r$ and $r - b = a - (q+1)b \in S$, contradicting the minimality of r.

That proves the existence of r and q. For uniqueness, suppose that $a = bq + r$ and $a = bq' + r'$, where $0 \le r < b$ and $0 \le r' < b$. Then subtracting these two equations and rearranging terms, we obtain

$$r' - r = b(q - q'). \tag{1.1}$$

Now observe that by assumption, the left-hand side of (1.1) is less than b in absolute value. However, if $q \ne q'$, then the right-hand side of (1.1) would be at least b in absolute value; therefore, we must have $q = q'$. But then by (1.1), we must have $r = r'$. $\square$

In the above theorem, it is easy to see that $q = \lfloor a/b \rfloor$, where for any real number x, $\lfloor x \rfloor$ denotes the greatest integer less than or equal to x. We shall write $r = a \bmod b$; that is, $a \bmod b$ denotes the remainder in dividing a by b. It is clear that $b \mid a$ if and only if $a \bmod b = 0$.

One can generalize the notation $a \bmod b$ to all integers a and b, with $b \ne 0$: we define $a \bmod b := a - bq$, where $q = \lfloor a/b \rfloor$.

In addition to the "floor" function $\lfloor \cdot \rfloor$, the "ceiling" function $\lceil \cdot \rceil$ is also useful: for any real number x, $\lceil x \rceil$ is defined as the smallest integer greater than or equal to x.

EXERCISE 1.1. Let n be a composite integer. Show that there exists a prime p dividing n, such that $p \le |n|^{1/2}$.

EXERCISE 1.2. For integer n and real x, show that $n \leq x$ if and only if $n \leq \lfloor x \rfloor$.

EXERCISE 1.3. For real x and positive integer n, show that $\lfloor \lfloor x \rfloor / n \rfloor = \lfloor x/n \rfloor$. In particular, for positive integers a, b, c, $\lfloor \lfloor a/b \rfloor / c \rfloor = \lfloor a/(bc) \rfloor$.

EXERCISE 1.4. For real x, show that $2\lfloor x \rfloor \leq \lfloor 2x \rfloor \leq 2\lfloor x \rfloor + 1$.

EXERCISE 1.5. For positive integers m and n, show that the number of multiples of m among $1, 2, \ldots, n$ is $\lfloor n/m \rfloor$. More generally, for integer $m \geq 1$ and real $x \geq 0$, show that the number of multiples of m in the interval $[1, x]$ is $\lfloor x/m \rfloor$.

EXERCISE 1.6. For integers a, b with $b < 0$, show that $b < a \bmod b \leq 0$.

1.2 Ideals and greatest common divisors

To carry on with the proof of Theorem 1.3, we introduce the notion of an **ideal of** $\mathbb{Z}$, which is a non-empty set of integers that is closed under addition, and under multiplication by an arbitrary integer. That is, a non-empty set $I \subseteq \mathbb{Z}$ is an ideal if and only if for all $a, b \in I$ and all $z \in \mathbb{Z}$, we have

$$a + b \in I \quad \text{and} \quad az \in I.$$

Note that for an ideal I, if $a \in I$, then so is $-a$, since $-a = a \cdot (-1) \in I$. It is easy to see that any ideal must contain 0: since an ideal I must contain some element a, and by the closure properties of ideals, we must have $0 = a + (-a) \in I$. It is clear that $\{0\}$ and $\mathbb{Z}$ are ideals. Moreover, an ideal I is equal to $\mathbb{Z}$ if and only if $1 \in I$—to see this, note that $1 \in I$ implies that for all $z \in \mathbb{Z}$, $z = 1 \cdot z \in I$, and hence $I = \mathbb{Z}$; conversely, if $I = \mathbb{Z}$, then in particular, $1 \in I$.

For $a \in \mathbb{Z}$, define $a\mathbb{Z} := \{az : z \in \mathbb{Z}\}$; that is, $a\mathbb{Z}$ is the set of all integer multiples of a. It is easy to see that $a\mathbb{Z}$ is an ideal: for $az, az' \in a\mathbb{Z}$ and $z'' \in \mathbb{Z}$, we have $az + az' = a(z + z') \in a\mathbb{Z}$ and $(az)z'' = a(zz'') \in a\mathbb{Z}$. The set $a\mathbb{Z}$ is called the **ideal generated by** a, and any ideal of the form $a\mathbb{Z}$ for some $a \in \mathbb{Z}$ is called a **principal ideal**.

We observe that for all $a, b \in \mathbb{Z}$, we have $a \in b\mathbb{Z}$ if and only if $b \mid a$. We also observe that for any ideal I, we have $a \in I$ if and only if $a\mathbb{Z} \subseteq I$. Both of these observations are simple consequences of the definitions, as the reader may verify. Combining these two observations, we see that $a\mathbb{Z} \subseteq b\mathbb{Z}$ if and only if $b \mid a$.

We can generalize the above method of constructing ideals. For

$a_1, \ldots, a_k \in \mathbb{Z}$, define

$$a_1\mathbb{Z} + \cdots + a_k\mathbb{Z} := \{a_1 z_1 + \cdots + a_k z_k : z_1, \ldots, z_k \in \mathbb{Z}\}.$$

That is, $a_1\mathbb{Z} + \cdots + a_k\mathbb{Z}$ consists of all linear combinations, with integer coefficients, of $a_1, \ldots, a_k$. We leave it to the reader to verify that $a_1\mathbb{Z} + \cdots + a_k\mathbb{Z}$ is an ideal and contains $a_1, \ldots, a_k$; it is called the **ideal generated by** $a_1, \ldots, a_k$. In fact, this ideal is the "smallest" ideal containing $a_1, \ldots, a_k$, in the sense that any other ideal that contains $a_1, \ldots, a_k$ must already contain this ideal (verify).

***Example* 1.1.** Let $a := 3$ and consider the ideal $a\mathbb{Z}$. This consists of all integer multiples of 3; that is, $a\mathbb{Z} = \{\ldots, -9, -6, -3, 0, 3, 6, 9, \ldots\}$. $\square$

***Example* 1.2.** Let $a_1 := 3$ and $a_2 := 5$, and consider the ideal $a_1\mathbb{Z} + a_2\mathbb{Z}$. This ideal contains $2a_1 - a_2 = 1$. Since it contains 1, it contains all integers; that is, $a_1\mathbb{Z} + a_2\mathbb{Z} = \mathbb{Z}$. $\square$

***Example* 1.3.** Let $a_1 := 4$ and $a_2 := 6$, and consider the ideal $a_1\mathbb{Z} + a_2\mathbb{Z}$. This ideal contains $a_2 - a_1 = 2$, and therefore, it contains all even integers. It does not contain any odd integers, since the sum of two even integers is again even. $\square$

The following theorem says that all ideals of $\mathbb{Z}$ are principal.

Theorem 1.5. *For any ideal $I \subseteq \mathbb{Z}$, there exists a unique non-negative integer d such that $I = d\mathbb{Z}$.*

Proof. We first prove the existence part of the theorem. If $I = \{0\}$, then $d = 0$ does the job, so let us assume that $I \neq \{0\}$. Since I contains non-zero integers, it must contain positive integers, since if $z \in I$ then so is $-z$. Let d be the smallest positive integer in I. We want to show that $I = d\mathbb{Z}$.

We first show that $I \subseteq d\mathbb{Z}$. To this end, let c be any element in I. It suffices to show that $d \mid c$. Using the division with remainder property, write $c = qd + r$, where $0 \leq r < d$. Then by the closure properties of ideals, one sees that $r = c - qd$ is also an element of I, and by the minimality of the choice of d, we must have $r = 0$. Thus, $d \mid c$.

We next show that $d\mathbb{Z} \subseteq I$. This follows immediately from the fact that $d \in I$ and the closure properties of ideals.

That proves the existence part of the theorem. As for uniqueness, note that if $d\mathbb{Z} = d'\mathbb{Z}$, we have $d \mid d'$ and $d' \mid d$, from which it follows by Theorem 1.2 that $d' = \pm d$. $\square$

For $a, b \in \mathbb{Z}$, we call $d \in \mathbb{Z}$ a **common divisor** of a and b if $d \mid a$ and

$d \mid b$; moreover, we call such a d a **greatest common divisor** of a and b if d is non-negative and all other common divisors of a and b divide d.

Theorem 1.6. *For any $a, b \in \mathbb{Z}$, there exists a unique greatest common divisor d of a and b, and moreover, $a\mathbb{Z} + b\mathbb{Z} = d\mathbb{Z}$.*

Proof. We apply the previous theorem to the ideal $I := a\mathbb{Z} + b\mathbb{Z}$. Let $d \in \mathbb{Z}$ with $I = d\mathbb{Z}$, as in that theorem. We wish to show that d is a greatest common divisor of a and b. Note that $a, b, d \in I$ and d is non-negative.

Since $a \in I = d\mathbb{Z}$, we see that $d \mid a$; similarly, $d \mid b$. So we see that d is a common divisor of a and b.

Since $d \in I = a\mathbb{Z} + b\mathbb{Z}$, there exist $s, t \in \mathbb{Z}$ such that $as + bt = d$. Now suppose $a = a'd'$ and $b = b'd'$ for $a', b', d' \in \mathbb{Z}$. Then the equation $as + bt = d$ implies that $d'(a's + b't) = d$, which says that $d' \mid d$. Thus, any common divisor d' of a and b divides d.

That proves that d is a greatest common divisor of a and b. As for uniqueness, note that if d'' is a greatest common divisor of a and b, then $d \mid d''$ and $d'' \mid d$, and hence $d'' = \pm d$, and the requirement that d'' is non-negative implies that $d'' = d$. $\square$

For $a, b \in \mathbb{Z}$, we denote by $\gcd(a, b)$ the greatest common divisor of a and b. Note that as we have defined it, $\gcd(a, 0) = |a|$. Also note that when at least one of a or b are non-zero, $\gcd(a, b)$ is the largest positive integer that divides both a and b.

An immediate consequence of Theorem 1.6 is that for all $a, b \in \mathbb{Z}$, there exist $s, t \in \mathbb{Z}$ such that $as + bt = \gcd(a, b)$, and that when at least one of a or b are non-zero, $\gcd(a, b)$ is the smallest positive integer that can be expressed as $as + bt$ for some $s, t \in \mathbb{Z}$.

We say that $a, b \in \mathbb{Z}$ are **relatively prime** if $\gcd(a, b) = 1$, which is the same as saying that the only common divisors of a and b are ± 1. It is immediate from Theorem 1.6 that a and b are relatively prime if and only if $a\mathbb{Z} + b\mathbb{Z} = \mathbb{Z}$, which holds if and only if there exist $s, t \in \mathbb{Z}$ such that $as + bt = 1$.

Theorem 1.7. *For $a, b, c \in \mathbb{Z}$ such that $c \mid ab$ and $\gcd(a, c) = 1$, we have $c \mid b$.*

Proof. Suppose that $c \mid ab$ and $\gcd(a, c) = 1$. Then since $\gcd(a, c) = 1$, by Theorem 1.6 we have $as + ct = 1$ for some $s, t \in \mathbb{Z}$. Multiplying this equation by b, we obtain

$$abs + cbt = b. \tag{1.2}$$

Since c divides ab by hypothesis, and since c clearly divides cbt, it follows that c divides the left-hand side of (1.2), and hence that c divides b. $\square$

As a consequence of this theorem, we have:

Theorem 1.8. *Let p be prime, and let $a, b \in \mathbb{Z}$. Then $p \mid ab$ implies that $p \mid a$ or $p \mid b$.*

Proof. Assume that $p \mid ab$. The only divisors of p are ± 1 and $\pm p$. Thus, $\gcd(p, a)$ is either 1 or p. If $p \mid a$, we are done; otherwise, if $p \nmid a$, we must have $\gcd(p, a) = 1$, and by the previous theorem, we conclude that $p \mid b$. $\square$

An obvious corollary to Theorem 1.8 is that if $a_1, \ldots, a_k$ are integers, and if p is a prime that divides the product $a_1 \cdots a_k$, then $p \mid a_i$ for some $i = 1, \ldots, k$. This is easily proved by induction on k. For $k = 1$, the statement is trivially true. Now let $k > 1$, and assume that statement holds for $k - 1$. Then by Theorem 1.8, either $p \mid a_1$ or $p \mid a_2 \cdots a_{k-1}$; if $p \mid a_1$, we are done; otherwise, by induction, p divides one of $a_2, \ldots, a_{k-1}$.

We are now in a position to prove the uniqueness part of Theorem 1.3, which we can state as follows: if $p_1, \ldots, p_r$ and $p_1', \ldots, p_s'$ are primes (with duplicates allowed among the p_i and among the p_j') such that

$$p_1 \cdots p_r = p_1' \cdots p_s', \tag{1.3}$$

then $(p_1, \ldots, p_r)$ is just a reordering of $(p_1', \ldots, p_s')$. We may prove this by induction on r. If $r = 0$, we must have $s = 0$ and we are done. Now suppose $r > 0$, and that the statement holds for $r - 1$. Since $r > 0$, we clearly must have $s > 0$. Also, as p_1 is obviously divides the left-hand side of (1.3), it must also divide the right-hand side of (1.3); that is, $p_1 \mid p_1' \cdots p_s'$. It follows from (the corollary to) Theorem 1.8 that $p_1 \mid p_j'$ for some $j = 1, \ldots, s$, and indeed, since p_i and p_j' are both prime, we must have $p_i = p_j'$. Thus, we may cancel p_i from the left-hand side of (1.3) and p_j' from the right-hand side of (1.3), and the statement now follows from the induction hypothesis. That proves the uniqueness part of Theorem 1.3.

EXERCISE 1.7. Let I be a non-empty set of integers that is closed under addition, that is, $a + b \in I$ for all $a, b \in I$. Show that the condition

$$-a \in I \quad \text{for all } a \in I$$

holds if and only if

$$az \in I \quad \text{for all } a \in I, \, z \in \mathbb{Z}.$$

EXERCISE 1.8. Let a, b, c be positive integers, with $\gcd(a, b) = 1$ and $c \geq ab$. Show that there exist *non-negative* integers s, t such that $c = as + bt$.

EXERCISE 1.9. Show that for any integers a, b with $d := \gcd(a, b) \neq 0$, we have $\gcd(a/d, b/d) = 1$.

1.3 Some consequences of unique factorization

The following theorem is a consequence of just the existence part of Theorem 1.3:

Theorem 1.9. *There are infinitely many primes.*

Proof. By way of contradiction, suppose that there were only finitely many primes; call them $p_1, \ldots, p_k$. Then set $n := 1 + \prod_{i=1}^{k} p_i$, and consider a prime p that divides n. There must be at least one such prime p, since $n \geq 2$, and every positive integer can be written as a product of primes. Clearly, p cannot equal any of the p_i, since if it did, then p would divide $n - \prod_{i=1}^{k} p_i = 1$, which is impossible. Therefore, the prime p is not among $p_1, \ldots, p_k$, which contradicts our assumption that these are the only primes. $\square$

For a prime p, we may define the function ν_p, mapping non-zero integers to non-negative integers, as follows: for integer $n \neq 0$, if $n = p^e m$, where $p \nmid m$, then $\nu_p(n) := e$. We may then write the factorization of n into primes as

$$n = \pm \prod_{p} p^{\nu_p(n)},$$

where the product is over all primes p, with all but finitely many of the terms in the product equal to 1.

It is also convenient to extend the domain of definition of ν_p to include 0, defining $\nu_p(0) := \infty$. Following standard conventions for arithmetic with infinity (see Preliminaries), it is easy to see that for all $a, b \in \mathbb{Z}$, we have

$$\nu_p(a \cdot b) = \nu_p(a) + \nu_p(b) \quad \text{for all } p. \tag{1.4}$$

From this, it follows that for all $a, b \in \mathbb{Z}$, we have

$$b \mid a \quad \text{if and only if} \quad \nu_p(b) \leq \nu_p(a) \quad \text{for all } p, \tag{1.5}$$

and

$$\nu_p(\gcd(a, b)) = \min(\nu_p(a), \nu_p(b)) \quad \text{for all } p. \tag{1.6}$$

For $a, b \in \mathbb{Z}$ a **common multiple** of a and b is an integer m such that

$a \mid m$ and $b \mid m$; moreover, such an m is the **least common multiple** of a and b if m is non-negative and m divides all common multiples of a and b. In light of Theorem 1.3, it is clear that the least common multiple exists and is unique, and we denote the least common multiple of a and b by $\mathrm{lcm}(a,b)$. Note that as we have defined it, $\mathrm{lcm}(a,0) = 0$, and that when both a and b are non-zero, $\mathrm{lcm}(a,b)$ is the smallest positive integer divisible by both a and b. Also, for all $a, b \in \mathbb{Z}$, we have

$$\nu_p(\mathrm{lcm}(a,b)) = \max(\nu_p(a), \nu_p(b)) \quad \text{for all } p, \tag{1.7}$$

and

$$\gcd(a,b) \cdot \mathrm{lcm}(a,b) = |ab|. \tag{1.8}$$

It is easy to generalize the notions of greatest common divisor and least common multiple from two integers to many integers. For $a_1, \ldots, a_k \in \mathbb{Z}$, with $k \geq 1$, we call $d \in \mathbb{Z}$ a common divisor of $a_1, \ldots, a_k$ if $d \mid a_i$ for $i = 1, \ldots, k$; moreover, we call such a d the greatest common divisor of $a_1, \ldots, a_k$ if d is non-negative and all other common divisors of $a_1, \ldots, a_k$ divide d. It is clear that the greatest common divisor of $a_1, \ldots, a_k$ exists and is unique, and moreover, we have

$$\nu_p(\gcd(a_1, \ldots, a_k)) = \min(\nu_p(a_1), \ldots, \nu_p(a_k)) \quad \text{for all } p. \tag{1.9}$$

Analogously, for $a_1, \ldots, a_k \in \mathbb{Z}$, with $k \geq 1$, we call $m \in \mathbb{Z}$ a common multiple of $a_1, \ldots, a_k$ if $a_i \mid m$ for $i = 1, \ldots, k$; moreover, such an m is called the least common multiple of $a_1, \ldots, a_k$ if m divides all common multiples of $a_1, \ldots, a_k$. It is clear that the least common multiple of $a_1, \ldots, a_k$ exists and is unique, and moreover, we have

$$\nu_p(\mathrm{lcm}(a_1, \ldots, a_k)) = \max(\nu_p(a_1), \ldots, \nu_p(a_k)) \quad \text{for all } p. \tag{1.10}$$

We say that integers $a_1, \ldots, a_k$ are **pairwise relatively prime** if $\gcd(a_i, a_j) = 1$ for all i, j with $i \neq j$. Note that if $a_1, \ldots, a_k$ are pairwise relatively prime, then $\gcd(a_1, \ldots, a_k) = 1$; however, $\gcd(a_1, \ldots, a_k) = 1$ does not imply that $a_1, \ldots, a_k$ are pairwise relatively prime.

Consider now the rational numbers $\mathbb{Q} := \{a/b : a, b \in \mathbb{Z},\ b \neq 0\}$. Because of the unique factorization property for $\mathbb{Z}$, given any rational number a/b, if we set $d := \gcd(a,b)$, and define the integers $a' := a/d$ and $b' := b/d$, then we have $a/b = a'/b'$ and $\gcd(a',b') = 1$. Moreover, if $\tilde{a}/\tilde{b} = a'/b'$, then we have $\tilde{a}b' = a'\tilde{b}$, and so $b' \mid a'\tilde{b}$, and since $\gcd(a',b') = 1$, we see that $b' \mid \tilde{b}$; if $\tilde{b} = \tilde{d}b'$, it follows that $\tilde{a} = \tilde{d}a'$. Thus, we can represent every rational number as a fraction in **lowest terms**, that is, a fraction of the form a'/b'

where a' and b' are relatively prime; moreover, the values of a' and b' are uniquely determined up to sign, and every other fraction that represents the same rational number is of the form $(\tilde{d}a')/(\tilde{d}b')$, for some non-zero integer $\tilde{d}$.

EXERCISE 1.10. Let n be a positive integer. Show that if a, b are relatively prime integers, each of which divides n, then ab divides n. More generally, show that if $a_1, \ldots, a_k$ are pairwise relatively prime integers, each of which divides n, then their product $a_1 \cdots a_k$ divides n.

EXERCISE 1.11. For positive integer n, let $\mathcal{D}(n)$ denote the set of positive divisors of n. For relatively prime, positive integers n_1, n_2, show that the sets $\mathcal{D}(n_1) \times \mathcal{D}(n_2)$ and $\mathcal{D}(n_1 \cdot n_2)$ are in one-to-one correspondence, via the map that sends $(d_1, d_2) \in \mathcal{D}(n_1) \times \mathcal{D}(n_2)$ to $d_1 \cdot d_2$.

EXERCISE 1.12. Let p be a prime and k an integer $0 < k < p$. Show that the binomial coefficient

$$\binom{p}{k} = \frac{p!}{k!(p-k)!},$$

which is an integer, of course, is divisible by p.

EXERCISE 1.13. An integer $a \in \mathbb{Z}$ is called **square-free** if it is not divisible by the square of any integer greater than 1. Show that any integer $n \in \mathbb{Z}$ can be expressed as $n = ab^2$, where $a, b \in \mathbb{Z}$ and a is square-free.

EXERCISE 1.14. Show that any non-zero $x \in \mathbb{Q}$ can be expressed as

$$x = \pm p_1^{e_1} \cdots p_r^{e_r},$$

where the p_i are distinct primes and the e_i are non-zero integers, and that this expression in unique up to a reordering of the primes.

EXERCISE 1.15. Show that if an integer cannot be expressed as a square of an integer, then it cannot be expressed as a square of any rational number.

EXERCISE 1.16. Show that for all integers a, b, and all primes p, we have $\nu_p(a+b) \geq \min\{\nu_p(a), \nu_p(b)\}$, and that if $\nu_p(a) < \nu_p(b)$, then $\nu_p(a+b) = \nu_p(a)$.

EXERCISE 1.17. For a prime p, we may extend the domain of definition of ν_p from $\mathbb{Z}$ to $\mathbb{Q}$: for non-zero integers a, b, let us define $\nu_p(a/b) := \nu_p(a) - \nu_p(b)$.

(a) Show that this definition of $\nu_p(a/b)$ is unambiguous, in the sense that it does not depend on the particular choice of a and b.

(b) Show that for all $x, y \in \mathbb{Q}$, we have $\nu_p(xy) = \nu_p(x) + \nu_p(y)$.

(c) Show that for all $x, y \in \mathbb{Q}$, we have $\nu_p(x + y) \geq \min\{\nu_p(x), \nu_p(y)\}$, and that if $\nu_p(x) < \nu_p(y)$, then $\nu_p(x + y) = \nu_p(x)$.

(d) Show that for all non-zero $x \in \mathbb{Q}$, we have

$$x = \pm \prod_p p^{\nu_p(x)},$$

where the product is over all primes, and all but a finite number of terms in the product is 1.

EXERCISE 1.18. Let n be a positive integer, and let C_n denote the number of pairs of integers (a, b) such that $1 \leq a \leq n$, $1 \leq b \leq n$ and $\gcd(a, b) = 1$, and let F_n be the number of *distinct* rational numbers a/b, where $0 \leq a < b \leq n$.

(a) Show that $F_n = (C_n + 1)/2$.

(b) Show that $C_n \geq n^2/4$. Hint: first show that $C_n \geq n^2(1 - \sum_{d \geq 2} 1/d^2)$, and then show that $\sum_{d \geq 2} 1/d^2 \leq 3/4$.

EXERCISE 1.19. This exercise develops a characterization of least common multiples in terms of ideals.

(a) Arguing directly from the definition of an ideal, show that if I and J are ideals of $\mathbb{Z}$, then so is $I \cap J$.

(b) Let $a, b \in \mathbb{Z}$, and consider the ideals $I := a\mathbb{Z}$ and $J := b\mathbb{Z}$. By part (a), we know that $I \cap J$ is an ideal. By Theorem 1.5, we know that $I \cap J = m\mathbb{Z}$ for some uniquely determined non-negative integer m. Show that $m = \text{lcm}(a, b)$.

EXERCISE 1.20. For $a_1, \ldots, a_k \in \mathbb{Z}$, with $k > 1$, show that

$$\gcd(a_1, \ldots, a_k) = \gcd(\gcd(a_1, \ldots, a_{k-1}), a_k)$$

and

$$\text{lcm}(a_1, \ldots, a_k) = \text{lcm}(\text{lcm}(a_1, \ldots, a_{k-1}), a_k).$$

EXERCISE 1.21. Show that for any $a_1, \ldots, a_k \in \mathbb{Z}$, if $d := \gcd(a_1, \ldots, a_k)$, then $d\mathbb{Z} = a_1\mathbb{Z} + \cdots + a_k\mathbb{Z}$; in particular, there exist integers $s_1, \ldots, s_k$ such that

$$d = a_1 s_1 + \cdots + a_k s_k.$$

EXERCISE 1.22. Show that for all integers a, b, we have

$$\gcd(a + b, \text{lcm}(a, b)) = \gcd(a, b).$$

EXERCISE 1.23. Show that for integers $c, a_1, \ldots, a_k$, we have

$$\gcd(ca_1, \ldots, ca_k) = |c| \gcd(a_1, \ldots, a_k).$$

2

Congruences

This chapter introduces the basic properties of congruences modulo n, along with the related notion of congruence classes modulo n. Other items discussed include the Chinese remainder theorem, Euler's phi function, arithmetic functions and Möbius inversion, and Fermat's little theorem.

2.1 Definitions and basic properties

For positive integer n, and for $a, b \in \mathbb{Z}$, we say that a **is congruent to** b **modulo** n if $n \mid (a - b)$, and we write $a \equiv b \pmod{n}$. If $n \nmid (a - b)$, then we write $a \not\equiv b \pmod{n}$. The relation $a \equiv b \pmod{n}$ is called a **congruence relation**, or simply, a **congruence**. The number n appearing in such congruences is called the **modulus** of the congruence. This usage of the "mod" notation as part of a congruence is not to be confused with the "mod" operation introduced in §1.1.

A simple observation is that $a \equiv b \pmod{n}$ if and only if there exists an integer c such that $a = b + cn$. From this, and Theorem 1.4, the following is immediate:

Theorem 2.1. *Let n be a positive integer. For every integer a, there exists a unique integer b such that $a \equiv b \pmod{n}$ and $0 \leq b < n$, namely, $b :=$ $a \bmod n$.*

If we view the modulus n as fixed, then the following theorem says that the binary relation "$\cdot \equiv \cdot \pmod{n}$" is an equivalence relation on the set $\mathbb{Z}$:

Theorem 2.2. *Let n be a positive integer. For all $a, b, c \in \mathbb{Z}$, we have:*

   (i) $a \equiv a \pmod{n}$;

   (ii) $a \equiv b \pmod{n}$ implies $b \equiv a \pmod{n}$;

   (iii) $a \equiv b \pmod{n}$ and $b \equiv c \pmod{n}$ implies $a \equiv c \pmod{n}$.

Proof. For (i), observe that n divides $0 = a - a$. For (ii), observe that if n divides $a - b$, then it also divides $-(a - b) = b - a$. For (iii), observe that if n divides $a - b$ and $b - c$, then it also divides $(a - b) + (b - c) = a - c$. $\square$

A key property of congruences is that they are "compatible" with integer addition and multiplication, in the following sense:

Theorem 2.3. *For all positive integers n, and all $a, a', b, b' \in \mathbb{Z}$, if $a \equiv a' \pmod{n}$ and $b \equiv b' \pmod{n}$, then*

$$a + b \equiv a' + b' \pmod{n}$$

and

$$a \cdot b \equiv a' \cdot b' \pmod{n}.$$

Proof. Suppose that $a \equiv a' \pmod{n}$ and $b \equiv b' \pmod{n}$. This means that there exist integers c and d such that $a' = a + cn$ and $b' = b + dn$. Therefore,

$$a' + b' = a + b + (c + d)n,$$

which proves the first congruence of the theorem, and

$$a'b' = (a + cn)(b + dn) = ab + (ad + bc + cdn)n,$$

which proves the second congruence. $\square$

Theorems 2.2 and 2.3 allow one to work with congruence relations modulo n much as one would with ordinary equalities: one can add to, subtract from, or multiply both sides of a congruence modulo n by the same integer; also, if x is congruent to y modulo n, one may substitute y for x in any simple arithmetic expression (more precisely, any polynomial in x with integer coefficients) appearing in a congruence modulo n.

***Example* 2.1.** Observe that

$$3 \cdot 5 \equiv 1 \pmod{7}. \tag{2.1}$$

Using this fact, let us find the set of solutions z to the congruence

$$3z + 4 \equiv 6 \pmod{7}. \tag{2.2}$$

Suppose that z is a solution to (2.2). Subtracting 4 from both sides of (2.2), we see that

$$3z \equiv 2 \pmod{7}. \tag{2.3}$$

Now, multiplying both sides of (2.3) by 5, and using (2.1), we obtain

$$z \equiv 1 \cdot z \equiv (3 \cdot 5) \cdot z \equiv 2 \cdot 5 \equiv 3 \pmod{7}.$$

Thus, if z is a solution to (2.2), we must have $z \equiv 3 \pmod 7$; conversely, one can verify that if $z \equiv 3 \pmod 7$, then (2.2) holds. We conclude that the integers z that are solutions to (2.2) are precisely those integers that are congruent to 3 modulo 7, which we can list as follows:

$$\ldots, -18, -11, -4, 3, 10, 17, 24, \ldots \quad \square$$

In the next section, we shall give a systematic treatment of the problem of solving linear congruences, such as the one appearing in the previous example.

EXERCISE 2.1. Let $x, y, n \in \mathbb{Z}$ with $n > 0$ and $x \equiv y \pmod n$. Also, let $a_0, a_1, \ldots, a_k$ be integers. Show that

$$a_0 + a_1 x + \cdots + a_k x^k \equiv a_0 + a_1 y + \cdots + a_k y^k \pmod n.$$

EXERCISE 2.2. Let $a, b, n, n' \in \mathbb{Z}$ with $n > 0$ and $n' \mid n$. Show that if $a \equiv b \pmod n$, then $a \equiv b \pmod{n'}$.

EXERCISE 2.3. Let $a, b, n, n' \in \mathbb{Z}$ with $n > 0$, $n' > 0$, and $\gcd(n, n') = 1$. Show that if $a \equiv b \pmod n$ and $a \equiv b \pmod{n'}$, then $a \equiv b \pmod{nn'}$.

EXERCISE 2.4. Let $a, b, n \in \mathbb{Z}$ such that $n > 0$ and $a \equiv b \pmod n$. Show that $\gcd(a, n) = \gcd(b, n)$.

EXERCISE 2.5. Prove that for any prime p and integer x, if $x^2 \equiv 1 \pmod p$ then $x \equiv 1 \pmod p$ or $x \equiv -1 \pmod p$.

EXERCISE 2.6. Let a be a positive integer whose base-10 representation is $a = (a_{k-1} \cdots a_1 a_0)_{10}$. Let b be the sum of the decimal digits of a; that is, let $b := a_0 + a_1 + \cdots + a_{k-1}$. Show that $a \equiv b \pmod 9$. From this, justify the usual "rules of thumb" for determining divisibility by 9 and 3: a is divisible by 9 (respectively, 3) if and only if the sum of the decimal digits of a is divisible by 9 (respectively, 3).

EXERCISE 2.7. Show that there are 14 distinct, possible, yearly (Gregorian) calendars, and show that all 14 calendars actually occur.

2.2 Solving linear congruences

For a positive integer n, and $a \in \mathbb{Z}$, we say that $a' \in \mathbb{Z}$ is a **multiplicative inverse of a modulo n** if $aa' \equiv 1 \pmod n$.

Theorem 2.4. *Let $a, n \in \mathbb{Z}$ with $n > 0$. Then a has a multiplicative inverse modulo n if and only if a and n are relatively prime.*

Proof. This follows immediately from Theorem 1.6: a and n are relatively prime if and only if there exist $s, t \in \mathbb{Z}$ such that $as + nt = 1$, if and only if there exists $s \in \mathbb{Z}$ such that $as \equiv 1 \pmod{n}$. $\square$

Note that the existence of a multiplicative inverse of a modulo n depends only on the value of a modulo n; that is, if $b \equiv a \pmod{n}$, then a has an inverse if and only if b does. Indeed, by Theorem 2.3, if $b \equiv a \pmod{n}$, then for any integer a', $aa' \equiv 1 \pmod{n}$ if and only if $ba' \equiv 1 \pmod{n}$. (This fact is also implied by Theorem 2.4 together with Exercise 2.4.)

We now prove a simple "cancellation law" for congruences:

Theorem 2.5. *Let $a, n, z, z' \in \mathbb{Z}$ with $n > 0$. If a is relatively prime to n, then $az \equiv az' \pmod{n}$ if and only if $z \equiv z' \pmod{n}$. More generally, if $d := \gcd(a, n)$, then $az \equiv az' \pmod{n}$ if and only if $z \equiv z' \pmod{n/d}$.*

Proof. For the first statement, assume that $\gcd(a, n) = 1$, and let a' be a multiplicative inverse of a modulo n. Then, $az \equiv az' \pmod{n}$ implies $a'az \equiv a'az' \pmod{n}$, which implies $z \equiv z' \pmod{n}$, since $a'a \equiv 1 \pmod{n}$. Conversely, if $z \equiv z' \pmod{n}$, then trivially $az \equiv az' \pmod{n}$. That proves the first statement.

For the second statement, let $d = \gcd(a, n)$. Simply from the definition of congruences, one sees that in general, $az \equiv az' \pmod{n}$ holds if and only if $(a/d)z \equiv (a/d)z' \pmod{n/d}$. Moreover, since a/d and n/d are relatively prime (see Exercise 1.9), the first statement of the theorem implies that $(a/d)z \equiv (a/d)z' \pmod{n/d}$ holds if and only if $z \equiv z' \pmod{n/d}$. That proves the second statement. $\square$

Theorem 2.5 implies that multiplicative inverses modulo n are uniquely determined modulo n; indeed, if a is relatively prime to n, and if $aa' \equiv 1 \equiv aa'' \pmod{n}$, then we may cancel a from the left- and right-hand sides of this congruence, obtaining $a' \equiv a'' \pmod{n}$.

***Example* 2.2.** Observe that

$$5 \cdot 2 \equiv 5 \cdot (-4) \pmod{6}. \tag{2.4}$$

Theorem 2.5 tells us that since $\gcd(5, 6) = 1$, we may cancel the common factor of 5 from both sides of (2.4), obtaining $2 \equiv -4 \pmod{6}$, which one can also verify directly.

Next observe that

$$3 \cdot 5 \equiv 3 \cdot 3 \pmod{6}. \tag{2.5}$$

We cannot simply cancel the common factor of 3 from both sides of (2.5);

indeed, $5 \not\equiv 3 \pmod 6$. However, $\gcd(3,6) = 3$, and as Theorem 2.5 guarantees, we do indeed have $5 \equiv 3 \pmod 2$. $\square$

Next, we consider the problem of determining the solutions z to congruences of the form $az + c \equiv b \pmod n$, for given integers a, b, c, n. Since we may both add and subtract c from both sides of a congruence modulo n, it is clear that z is a solution to the above congruence if and only if $az \equiv b - c \pmod n$. Therefore, it suffices to consider the problem of determining the solutions z to congruences of the form $az \equiv b \pmod n$, for given integers a, b, n.

Theorem 2.6. *Let $a, b, n \in \mathbb{Z}$ with $n > 0$. If a is relatively prime to n, then the congruence $az \equiv b \pmod n$ has a solution z; moreover, any integer z' is a solution if and only if $z \equiv z' \pmod n$.*

Proof. The integer $z := ba'$, where a' is a multiplicative inverse of a modulo n, is clearly a solution. For any integer z', we have $az' \equiv b \pmod n$ if and only if $az' \equiv az \pmod n$, which by Theorem 2.5 holds if and only if $z \equiv z' \pmod n$. $\square$

Suppose that $a, b, n \in \mathbb{Z}$ with $n > 0$, $a \neq 0$, and $\gcd(a, n) = 1$. This theorem says that there exists a unique integer z satisfying

$$az \equiv b \pmod n \quad \text{and} \quad 0 \le z < n.$$

Setting $s := b/a \in \mathbb{Q}$, we may generalize the "mod" operation, defining $s \bmod n$ to be this value z. As the reader may easily verify, this definition of $s \bmod n$ does not depend on the particular choice of fraction used to represent the rational number s. With this notation, we can simply write $a^{-1} \bmod n$ to denote the unique multiplicative inverse of a modulo n that lies in the interval $0, \dots, n - 1$.

Theorem 2.6 may be generalized as follows:

Theorem 2.7. *Let $a, b, n \in \mathbb{Z}$ with $n > 0$, and let $d := \gcd(a, n)$. If $d \mid b$, then the congruence $az \equiv b \pmod n$ has a solution z, and any integer z' is also a solution if and only if $z \equiv z' \pmod{n/d}$. If $d \nmid b$, then the congruence $az \equiv b \pmod n$ has no solution z.*

Proof. For the first statement, suppose that $d \mid b$. In this case, by Theorem 2.5, we have $az \equiv b \pmod n$ if and only if $(a/d)z \equiv (b/d) \pmod{n/d}$, and so the statement follows immediately from Theorem 2.6, and the fact that a/d and n/d are relatively prime.

For the second statement, we show that if $az \equiv b \pmod n$ for some integer z, then d must divide b. To this end, assume that $az \equiv b \pmod{n}$ for some integer z. Then since $d \mid n$, we have $az \equiv b \pmod{d}$. However, $az \equiv 0 \pmod{d}$, since $d \mid a$, and hence $b \equiv 0 \pmod{d}$; that is, $d \mid b$. $\square$

Example 2.3. The following table illustrates what the above theorem says for $n = 15$ and $a = 1, 2, 3, 4, 5, 6$.

z	0	1	2	3	4	5	6	7	8	9	10	11	12	13	14
$2z \bmod 15$	0	2	4	6	8	10	12	14	1	3	5	7	9	11	13
$3z \bmod 15$	0	3	6	9	12	0	3	6	9	12	0	3	6	9	12
$4z \bmod 15$	0	4	8	12	1	5	9	13	2	6	10	14	3	7	11
$5z \bmod 15$	0	5	10	0	5	10	0	5	10	0	5	10	0	5	10
$6z \bmod 15$	0	6	12	3	9	0	6	12	3	9	0	6	12	3	9

In the second row, we are looking at the values $2z \bmod 15$, and we see that this row is just a permutation of the first row. So for every b, there exists a unique z such that $2z \equiv b \pmod{15}$. We could have inferred this fact from the theorem, since $\gcd(2, 15) = 1$.

In the third row, the only numbers hit are the multiples of 3, which follows from the theorem and the fact that $\gcd(3, 15) = 3$. Also note that the pattern in this row repeats every five columns; that is also implied by the theorem; that is, $3z \equiv 3z' \pmod{15}$ if and only if $z \equiv z' \pmod{5}$.

In the fourth row, we again see a permutation of the first row, which follows from the theorem and the fact that $\gcd(4, 15) = 1$.

In the fifth row, the only numbers hit are the multiples of 5, which follows from the theorem and the fact that $\gcd(5, 15) = 5$. Also note that the pattern in this row repeats every three columns; that is also implied by the theorem; that is, $5z \equiv 5z' \pmod{15}$ if and only if $z \equiv z' \pmod{3}$.

In the sixth row, since $\gcd(6, 15) = 3$, we see a permutation of the third row. The pattern repeats after five columns, although the pattern is a permutation of the pattern in the third row. $\square$

Next, we consider systems of linear congruences with respect to moduli that are relatively prime in pairs. The result we state here is known as the Chinese remainder theorem, and is extremely useful in a number of contexts.

Theorem 2.8 (Chinese remainder theorem). *Let $n_1, \ldots, n_k$ be pairwise relatively prime, positive integers, and let $a_1, \ldots, a_k$ be arbitrary integers. Then there exists an integer z such that*

$$z \equiv a_i \pmod{n_i} \quad (i = 1, \ldots, k).$$

Moreover, any other integer z' is also a solution of these congruences if and only if $z \equiv z' \pmod{n}$, where $n := \prod_{i=1}^{k} n_i$.

Proof. Let $n := \prod_{i=1}^{k} n_i$, as in the statement of the theorem. Let us also define

$$n'_i := n/n_i \quad (i = 1, \ldots, k).$$

From the fact that $n_1, \ldots, n_k$ are pairwise relatively prime, it is clear that $\gcd(n_i, n'_i) = 1$ for $i = 1, \ldots, k$. Therefore, let

$$m_i := (n'_i)^{-1} \bmod n_i \quad \text{and} \quad w_i := n'_i m_i \quad (i = 1, \ldots, k).$$

By construction, one sees that for $i = 1, \ldots, k$, we have

$$w_i \equiv 1 \pmod{n_i}$$

and

$$w_i \equiv 0 \pmod{n_j} \quad \text{for } j = 1, \ldots, k \text{ with } j \neq i.$$

That is to say, for $i, j = 1, \ldots, k$, we have $w_i \equiv \delta_{ij} \pmod{n_j}$, where

$$\delta_{ij} := \begin{cases} 1 & \text{if } i = j, \\ 0 & \text{if } i \neq j. \end{cases}$$

Now define

$$z := \sum_{i=1}^{k} w_i a_i.$$

One then sees that

$$z \equiv \sum_{i=1}^{k} w_i a_i \equiv \sum_{i=1}^{k} \delta_{ij} a_i \equiv a_j \pmod{n_j} \quad \text{for } j = 1, \ldots, k.$$

Therefore, this z solves the given system of congruences.

Moreover, if $z' \equiv z \pmod{n}$, then since $n_i \mid n$ for $i = 1, \ldots, k$, we see that $z' \equiv z \equiv a_i \pmod{n_i}$ for $i = 1, \ldots, k$, and so z' also solves the system of congruences.

Finally, if z' solves the system of congruences, then $z' \equiv z \pmod{n_i}$ for $i = 1, \ldots, k$. That is, $n_i \mid (z' - z)$ for $i = 1, \ldots, k$. Since $n_1, \ldots, n_k$ are pairwise relatively prime, this implies that $n \mid (z' - z)$, or equivalently, $z' \equiv z \pmod{n}$. $\square$

Example 2.4. The following table illustrates what the above theorem says for $n_1 = 3$ and $n_2 = 5$.

z	0	1	2	3	4	5	6	7	8	9	10	11	12	13	14
$z \bmod 3$	0	1	2	0	1	2	0	1	2	0	1	2	0	1	2
$z \bmod 5$	0	1	2	3	4	0	1	2	3	4	0	1	2	3	4

We see that as z ranges from 0 to 14, the pairs $(z \bmod 3, z \bmod 5)$ range over all pairs (a_1, a_2) with $a_1 \in \{0, 1, 2\}$ and $a_2 \in \{0, \ldots, 4\}$, with every pair being hit exactly once. $\square$

EXERCISE 2.8. Let $a_1, \ldots, a_k, n, b$ be integers with $n > 0$, and let $d :=$ $\gcd(a_1, \ldots, a_k, n)$. Show that the congruence

$$a_1 z_1 + \cdots + a_k z_k \equiv b \,(\mathrm{mod}\ n)$$

has a solution $z_1, \ldots, z_k$ if and only if $d \mid b$.

EXERCISE 2.9. Find an integer z such that $z \equiv -1$ (mod 100), $z \equiv 1$ (mod 33), and $z \equiv 2$ (mod 7).

EXERCISE 2.10. If you want to show that you are a real nerd, here is an age-guessing game you might play at a party. First, prepare 2 cards as follows:

$$
\begin{array}{cccccc}
1 & 4 & 7 & 10 & \cdots & 94 \quad 97 \\
2 & 5 & 8 & 11 & \cdots & 95 \quad 98
\end{array}
$$

and 4 cards as follows:

$$
\begin{array}{cccccc}
1 & 6 & 11 & 16 & \cdots & 91 \quad 96 \\
2 & 7 & 12 & 17 & \cdots & 92 \quad 97 \\
3 & 8 & 13 & 18 & \cdots & 93 \quad 98 \\
4 & 9 & 14 & 19 & \cdots & 94 \quad 99
\end{array}
$$

At the party, ask a person to tell you if their age is odd or even, and then ask them to tell you on which of the six cards their age appears. Show how to use this information (and a little common sense) to determine their age.

2.3 Residue classes

As we already observed in Theorem 2.2, for any fixed positive integer n, the binary relation "$\cdot \equiv \cdot$ (mod n)" is an equivalence relation on the set $\mathbb{Z}$. As such, this relation partitions the set $\mathbb{Z}$ into equivalence classes. We denote the equivalence class containing the integer a by $[a]_n$, or when n is clear from context, we may simply write $[a]$. Historically, these equivalence classes are called **residue classes modulo** n, and we shall adopt this terminology here as well.

It is easy to see from the definitions that

$$[a]_n = a + n\mathbb{Z} := \{a + nz : z \in \mathbb{Z}\}.$$

Note that a given residue class modulo n has many different "names"; for example, the residue class $[1]_n$ is the same as the residue class $[1 + n]_n$. For any integer a in a residue class, we call a a **representative** of that class.

The following is simply a restatement of Theorem 2.1:

Theorem 2.9. *For a positive integer n, there are precisely n distinct residue classes modulo n, namely, $[a]_n$ for $a = 0, \ldots, n - 1$.*

Fix a positive integer n. Let us define $\mathbb{Z}_n$ as the set of residue classes modulo n. We can "equip" $\mathbb{Z}_n$ with binary operations defining addition and multiplication in a natural way as follows: for $a, b \in \mathbb{Z}$, we define

$$[a]_n + [b]_n := [a + b]_n,$$

and we define

$$[a]_n \cdot [b]_n := [a \cdot b]_n.$$

Of course, one has to check this definition is unambiguous, in the sense that the sum or product of two residue classes should not depend on which particular representatives of the classes are chosen in the above definitions. More precisely, one must check that if $[a]_n = [a']_n$ and $[b]_n = [b']_n$, then $[a \text{ op } b]_n = [a' \text{ op } b']_n$, for op $\in \{+, \cdot\}$. However, this property follows immediately from Theorem 2.3.

It is also convenient to define a negation operation on $\mathbb{Z}_n$, defining

$$-[a]_n := [-1]_n \cdot [a]_n = [-a]_n.$$

Having defined addition and negation operations on $\mathbb{Z}_n$, we naturally define a subtraction operation on $\mathbb{Z}_n$ as follows: for $a, b \in \mathbb{Z}$,

$$[a]_n - [b]_n := [a]_n + (-[b]_n) = [a - b]_n.$$

Example **2.5.** Consider the residue classes modulo 6. These are as follows:

$$[0] = \{\ldots, -12, -6, 0, 6, 12, \ldots\}$$
$$[1] = \{\ldots, -11, -5, 1, 7, 13, \ldots\}$$
$$[2] = \{\ldots, -10, -4, 2, 8, 14, \ldots\}$$
$$[3] = \{\ldots, -9, -3, 3, 9, 15, \ldots\}$$
$$[4] = \{\ldots, -8, -2, 4, 10, 16, \ldots\}$$
$$[5] = \{\ldots, -7, -1, 5, 11, 17, \ldots\}$$

Let us write down the addition and multiplication tables for $\mathbb{Z}_6$. The addition table looks like this:

+	[0]	[1]	[2]	[3]	[4]	[5]
[0]	[0]	[1]	[2]	[3]	[4]	[5]
[1]	[1]	[2]	[3]	[4]	[5]	[0]
[2]	[2]	[3]	[4]	[5]	[0]	[1]
[3]	[3]	[4]	[5]	[0]	[1]	[2]
[4]	[4]	[5]	[0]	[1]	[2]	[3]
[5]	[5]	[0]	[1]	[2]	[3]	[4]

The multiplication table looks like this:

·	[0]	[1]	[2]	[3]	[4]	[5]
[0]	[0]	[0]	[0]	[0]	[0]	[0]
[1]	[0]	[1]	[2]	[3]	[4]	[5]
[2]	[0]	[2]	[4]	[0]	[2]	[4]
[3]	[0]	[3]	[0]	[3]	[0]	[3]
[4]	[0]	[4]	[2]	[0]	[4]	[2]
[5]	[0]	[5]	[4]	[3]	[2]	[1]

□

These operations on $\mathbb{Z}_n$ yield a very natural algebraic structure whose salient properties are as follows:

Theorem 2.10. *Let n be a positive integer, and consider the set $\mathbb{Z}_n$ of residue classes modulo n with addition and multiplication of residue classes as defined above. For all $\alpha, \beta, \gamma \in \mathbb{Z}_n$, we have*

(i) $\alpha + \beta = \beta + \alpha$ (addition is commutative),

(ii) $(\alpha + \beta) + \gamma = \alpha + (\beta + \gamma)$ (addition is associative),

(iii) $\alpha + [0]_n = \alpha$ (existence of additive identity),

(iv) $\alpha - \alpha = [0]_n$ (existence of additive inverses),

(v) $\alpha \cdot \beta = \beta \cdot \alpha$ (multiplication is commutative),

(vi) $(\alpha \cdot \beta) \cdot \gamma = \alpha \cdot (\beta \cdot \gamma)$ (multiplication is associative),

(vii) $\alpha \cdot (\beta + \gamma) = \alpha \cdot \beta + \alpha \cdot \gamma$ (multiplication distributes over addition)

(viii) $\alpha \cdot [1]_n = \alpha$ (existence of multiplicative identity).

Proof. All of these properties follow easily from the corresponding properties for the integers, together with the definitions of addition, subtraction, and multiplication of residue classes. For example, for (i), we have

$$[a]_n + [b]_n = [a+b]_n = [b+a]_n = [b]_n + [a]_n,$$

where the first and third equalities follow from the definition of addition of residue classes, and the second equality follows from the commutativity property of integer addition. The reader may verify the other properties using similar arguments. $\square$

An algebraic structure satisfying the conditions in the above theorem is known more generally as a "commutative ring with unity," a notion that we will discuss in Chapter 9.

Note that while all elements of $\mathbb{Z}_n$ have an additive inverses, not all elements of $\mathbb{Z}_n$ have a multiplicative inverse. Indeed, for $a \in \mathbb{Z}$, the residue class $[a]_n \in \mathbb{Z}_n$ has a multiplicative inverse in $\mathbb{Z}_n$ if and only if a has a multiplicative inverse modulo n, which by Theorem 2.4, holds if and only if $\gcd(a, n) = 1$. Since multiplicative inverses modulo n are uniquely determined modulo n (see discussion following Theorem 2.5), it follows that if $\alpha \in \mathbb{Z}_n$ has a multiplicative inverse in $\mathbb{Z}_n$, then this inverse is unique, and we may denote it by α^{-1}.

One denotes by $\mathbb{Z}_n^*$ the set of all residue classes that have a multiplicative inverse. It is easy to see that $\mathbb{Z}_n^*$ is closed under multiplication; indeed, if $\alpha, \beta \in \mathbb{Z}_n^*$, then $(\alpha\beta)^{-1} = \alpha^{-1}\beta^{-1}$. Also, note that for $\alpha \in \mathbb{Z}_n^*$ and $\beta, \beta' \in \mathbb{Z}_n$, if $\alpha\beta = \alpha\beta'$, we may effectively cancel α from both sides of this equation, obtaining $\beta = \beta'$—this is just a restatement of the first part of Theorem 2.5 in the language of residue classes.

For $\alpha \in \mathbb{Z}_n$ and positive integer k, the expression α^k denotes the product $\alpha \cdot \alpha \cdots \alpha$, where there are k terms in the product. One may extend this definition to $k = 0$, defining α^0 to be the multiplicative identity $[1]_n$. If α has a multiplicative inverse, then it is easy to see that for any integer $k \geq 0$, α^k has a multiplicative inverse as well, namely, $(\alpha^{-1})^k$, which we may naturally write as α^{-k}.

In general, one has a choice between working with congruences modulo n, or with the algebraic structure $\mathbb{Z}_n$; ultimately, the choice is one of taste and convenience, and it depends on what one prefers to treat as "first class objects": integers and congruence relations, or elements of $\mathbb{Z}_n$.

An alternative, and somewhat more concrete, approach to defining $\mathbb{Z}_n$ is to simply define it to consist of the n "symbols" $\overline{0}, \overline{1}, \ldots, \overline{n-1}$, with addition and multiplication defined as

$$\overline{a} + \overline{b} := \overline{(a + b) \bmod n}, \quad \overline{a} \cdot \overline{b} := \overline{(a \cdot b) \bmod n},$$

for $a, b = 0, \ldots, n-1$. Such a definition is equivalent to the one we have given here, with the symbol $\overline{a}$ corresponding to the residue class $[a]_n$. One should keep this alternative characterization of $\mathbb{Z}_n$ in mind; however, we prefer the characterization in terms of residue classes, as it is mathematically more elegant, and is usually more convenient to work with.

EXERCISE 2.11. Show that for any positive integer n, and any integer k, the residue classes $[k + a]_n$, for $a = 0, \ldots, n - 1$, are distinct and therefore include all residue classes modulo n.

EXERCISE 2.12. Verify the following statements for $\mathbb{Z}_n$:

(a) There is only one element of $\mathbb{Z}_n$ that acts as an additive identity; that is, if $\alpha \in \mathbb{Z}_n$ satisfies $\alpha + \beta = \beta$ for all $\beta \in \mathbb{Z}_n$, then $\alpha = [0]_n$.

(b) Additive inverses in $\mathbb{Z}_n$ are unique; that is, for all $\alpha \in \mathbb{Z}_n$, if $\alpha + \beta = [0]_n$, then $\beta = -\alpha$.

(c) If $\alpha \in \mathbb{Z}_n^*$ and $\gamma, \delta \in \mathbb{Z}_n$, then there exists a unique $\beta \in \mathbb{Z}_n$ such that $\alpha\beta + \gamma = \delta$.

EXERCISE 2.13. Verify the usual "rules of exponent arithmetic" for $\mathbb{Z}_n$. That is, show that for $\alpha \in \mathbb{Z}_n$, and non-negative integers k_1, k_2, we have

$$(\alpha^{k_1})^{k_2} = \alpha^{k_1 k_2} \quad \text{and} \quad \alpha^{k_1}\alpha^{k_2} = \alpha^{k_1 + k_2}.$$

Moreover, show that if $\alpha \in \mathbb{Z}_n^*$, then these identities hold for all integers k_1, k_2.

2.4 Euler's phi function

Euler's phi function $\phi(n)$ is defined for positive integer n as the number of elements of $\mathbb{Z}_n^*$. Equivalently, $\phi(n)$ is equal to the number of integers between 0 and $n - 1$ that are relatively prime to n. For example, $\phi(1) = 1$, $\phi(2) = 1$, $\phi(3) = 2$, and $\phi(4) = 2$.

A fact that is sometimes useful is the following:

Theorem 2.11. *For any positive integer n, we have*

$$\sum_{d \mid n} \phi(d) = n,$$

where the sum is over all positive divisors d of n.

Proof. Consider the list of n rational numbers $0/n, 1/n, \ldots, (n-1)/n$. For any divisor d of n and for any integer a with $0 \leq a < d$ and $\gcd(a, d) = 1$, the fraction a/d appears in the list exactly once, and moreover, every number in the sequence, when expressed as a fraction in lowest terms, is of this form. $\square$

Using the Chinese remainder theorem, it is easy to get a nice formula for $\phi(n)$ in terms for the prime factorization of n, as we establish in the following sequence of theorems.

Theorem 2.12. *For positive integers n, m with $\gcd(n, m) = 1$, we have*
$$\phi(nm) = \phi(n)\phi(m).$$

Proof. Consider the map
$$\rho: \quad \mathbb{Z}_{nm} \to \mathbb{Z}_n \times \mathbb{Z}_m$$
$$[a]_{nm} \mapsto ([a]_n, [a]_m).$$

First, note that the definition of ρ is unambiguous, since $a \equiv a' \pmod{nm}$ implies $a \equiv a' \pmod{n}$ and $a \equiv a' \pmod{m}$. Second, according to the Chinese remainder theorem, the map ρ is one-to-one and onto. Moreover, it is easy to see that $\gcd(a, nm) = 1$ if and only if $\gcd(a, n) = 1$ and $\gcd(a, m) = 1$ (verify). Therefore, the map ρ carries $\mathbb{Z}_{nm}^*$ injectively onto $\mathbb{Z}_n^* \times \mathbb{Z}_m^*$. In particular, $|\mathbb{Z}_{nm}^*| = |\mathbb{Z}_n^* \times \mathbb{Z}_m^*|$. $\square$

Theorem 2.13. *For a prime p and a positive integer e, we have $\phi(p^e) = p^{e-1}(p-1)$.*

Proof. The multiples of p among $0, 1, \ldots, p^e - 1$ are
$$0 \cdot p, 1 \cdot p, \ldots, (p^{e-1} - 1) \cdot p,$$
of which there are precisely p^{e-1}. Thus, $\phi(p^e) = p^e - p^{e-1} = p^{e-1}(p-1)$. $\square$

As an immediate consequence of the above two theorems, we have:

Theorem 2.14. *If $n = p_1^{e_1} \cdots p_r^{e_r}$ is the factorization of n into primes, then*
$$\phi(n) = \prod_{i=1}^{r} p_i^{e_i - 1}(p_i - 1) = n \prod_{i=1}^{r} (1 - 1/p_i).$$

EXERCISE 2.14. Show that $\phi(nm) = \gcd(n, m) \cdot \phi(\mathrm{lcm}(n, m))$.

2.5 Fermat's little theorem

Let n be a positive integer, and let $a \in \mathbb{Z}$ with $\gcd(a, n) = 1$. Consider the sequence of powers of $\alpha := [a]_n \in \mathbb{Z}_n^*$:
$$[1]_n = \alpha^0, \alpha^1, \alpha^2, \ldots.$$

Since each such power is an element of $\mathbb{Z}_n^*$, and since $\mathbb{Z}_n^*$ is a finite set, this sequence of powers must start to repeat at some point; that is, there must be a positive integer k such that $\alpha^k = \alpha^i$ for some $i = 0, \ldots, k - 1$. Let us assume that k is chosen to be the smallest such positive integer. We claim that $i = 0$, or equivalently, $\alpha^k = [1]_n$. To see this, suppose by way of contradiction that $\alpha^k = \alpha^i$, for some $i = 1, \ldots, k - 1$. Then we can cancel α from both sides of the equation $\alpha^k = \alpha^i$, obtaining $\alpha^{k-1} = \alpha^{i-1}$, and this contradicts the minimality of k.

From the above discussion, we see that the first k powers of α, that is, $[1]_n = \alpha^0, \alpha^1, \ldots, \alpha^{k-1}$, are distinct, and subsequent powers of α simply repeat this pattern. More generally, we may consider both positive and negative powers of α—it is easy to see (verify) that for all $i, j \in \mathbb{Z}$, we have $\alpha^i = \alpha^j$ if and only if $i \equiv j \pmod{k}$. In particular, we see that for any integer i, we have $\alpha^i = [1]_n$ if and only if k divides i.

This value k is called the **multiplicative order of** α or the **multiplicative order of** a **modulo** n. It can be characterized as the smallest positive integer k such that

$$a^k \equiv 1 \pmod{n}.$$

***Example* 2.6.** Let $n = 7$. For each value $a = 1, \ldots, 6$, we can compute successive powers of a modulo n to find its multiplicative order modulo n.

i	1	2	3	4	5	6
$1^i \bmod 7$	1	1	1	1	1	1
$2^i \bmod 7$	2	4	1	2	4	1
$3^i \bmod 7$	3	2	6	4	5	1
$4^i \bmod 7$	4	2	1	4	2	1
$5^i \bmod 7$	5	4	6	2	3	1
$6^i \bmod 7$	6	1	6	1	6	1

So we conclude that modulo 7: 1 has order 1; 6 has order 2; 2 and 4 have order 3; and 3 and 5 have order 6. $\square$

Theorem 2.15 (Euler's Theorem). *For any positive integer n, and any integer a relatively prime to n, we have $a^{\phi(n)} \equiv 1 \pmod{n}$. In particular, the multiplicative order of a modulo n divides $\phi(n)$.*

Proof. Let $\alpha := [a]_n \in \mathbb{Z}_n^*$. Consider the map $f : \mathbb{Z}_n^* \to \mathbb{Z}_n^*$ that sends $\beta \in \mathbb{Z}_n^*$ to $\alpha\beta$. Observe that f is injective, since if $\alpha\beta = \alpha\beta'$, we may cancel α from both sides of this equation, obtaining $\beta = \beta'$. Since f maps $\mathbb{Z}_n^*$ injectively into itself, and since $\mathbb{Z}_n^*$ is a finite set, it must be the case that f is surjective as well. Thus, as β ranges over the set $\mathbb{Z}_n^*$, so does $\alpha\beta$, and we have

$$\prod_{\beta \in \mathbb{Z}_n^*} \beta = \prod_{\beta \in \mathbb{Z}_n^*} (\alpha\beta) = \alpha^{\phi(n)} \left(\prod_{\beta \in \mathbb{Z}_n^*} \beta \right). \tag{2.6}$$

Canceling the common factor $\prod_{\beta \in \mathbb{Z}_n^*} \beta \in \mathbb{Z}_n^*$ from the left- and right-hand side of (2.6), we obtain

$$\alpha^{\phi(n)} = [1]_n.$$

That proves the first statement of the theorem. The second follows from the observation made above that $\alpha^i = [1]_n$ if and only if the multiplicative order of α divides i. $\square$

As a consequence of this, we obtain:

Theorem 2.16 (Fermat's little theorem). *For any prime p, and any integer $a \not\equiv 0 \pmod{p}$, we have $a^{p-1} \equiv 1 \pmod{p}$. Moreover, for any integer a, we have $a^p \equiv a \pmod{p}$.*

Proof. The first statement follows from Theorem 2.15, and the fact that $\phi(p) = p - 1$. The second statement is clearly true if $a \equiv 0 \pmod{p}$, and if $a \not\equiv 0 \pmod{p}$, we simply multiply both sides of the congruence $a^{p-1} \equiv 1 \pmod{p}$ by a. $\square$

For a positive integer n, we say that $a \in \mathbb{Z}$ with $\gcd(a, n) = 1$ is a **primitive root modulo** n if the multiplicative order of a modulo n is equal to $\phi(n)$. If this is the case, then for $\alpha := [a]_n$, the powers α^i range over all elements of $\mathbb{Z}_n^*$ as i ranges over the interval $0, \ldots, \phi(n) - 1$. Not all positive integers have primitive roots—we will see in §10.2 that the only positive integers n for which there exists a primitive root modulo n are

$$n = 1, 2, 4, p^e, 2p^e,$$

where p is an odd prime and e is a positive integer.

EXERCISE 2.15. Find an integer whose multiplicative order modulo 101 is 100.

EXERCISE 2.16. Suppose $\alpha \in \mathbb{Z}_n^*$ has multiplicative order k. Show that for any $m \in \mathbb{Z}$, the multiplicative order of α^m is $k/\gcd(m, k)$.

EXERCISE 2.17. Suppose $\alpha \in \mathbb{Z}_n^*$ has multiplicative order k, $\beta \in \mathbb{Z}_n^*$ has multiplicative order ℓ, and $\gcd(k, \ell) = 1$. Show that $\alpha\beta$ has multiplicative order $k\ell$. Hint: use the previous exercise.

EXERCISE 2.18. Prove that for any prime p, we have

$$(p-1)! \equiv -1 \pmod{p}.$$

Hint: using the result of Exercise 2.5, we know that the only elements of $\mathbb{Z}_p^*$ that act as their own multiplicative inverse are $[\pm 1]_n$; rearrange the terms in the product $\prod_{\beta \in \mathbb{Z}_p^*} \beta$ so that except for $[\pm 1]_n$, the terms are arranged in pairs, where each pair consists of some $\beta \in \mathbb{Z}_p^*$ and its multiplicative inverse.

2.6 Arithmetic functions and Möbius inversion

A function, such as Euler's function ϕ, from the positive integers into the reals is sometimes called an **arithmetic function** (actually, one usually considers complex-valued functions as well, but we shall not do so here). An arithmetic function f is called **multiplicative** if $f(1) = 1$ and for all positive integers n, m with $\gcd(n, m) = 1$, we have $f(nm) = f(n)f(m)$. Theorem 2.12 simply says that ϕ is multiplicative.

In this section, we develop some of the theory of arithmetic functions that is pertinent to number theory; however, the results in this section will play only a very minor role in the remainder of the text.

We begin with a simple observation, which the reader may easily verify:

if f is a multiplicative function, and if $n = p_1^{e_1} \cdots p_r^{e_r}$ is the prime factorization of n, then

$$f(n) = f(p_1^{e_1}) \cdots f(p_r^{e_r}).$$

Next, we define a binary operation on arithmetic functions that has a number of interesting properties and applications. Let f and g be arithmetic functions. The **Dirichlet product** of f and g, denoted $f \star g$, is the arithmetic function whose value at n is defined by the formula

$$(f \star g)(n) := \sum_{d \mid n} f(d)g(n/d),$$

the sum being over all positive divisors d of n. Another, more symmetric, way to write this is

$$(f \star g)(n) = \sum_{n = d_1 d_2} f(d_1)g(d_2),$$

the sum being over all pairs (d_1, d_2) of positive integers with $d_1 d_2 = n$. The Dirichlet product is clearly commutative (i.e., $f \star g = g \star f$), and is associative as well, which one can see by checking that

$$(f \star (g \star h))(n) = \sum_{n=d_1 d_2 d_3} f(d_1)g(d_2)h(d_3) = ((f \star g) \star h)(n),$$

the sum being over all triples (d_1, d_2, d_3) of positive integers with $d_1 d_2 d_3 = n$.

We now introduce three special arithmetic functions: I, J, and μ. The function $I(n)$ is defined to be 1 when $n = 1$ and 0 when $n > 1$. The function $J(n)$ is defined to be 1 for all n.

The **Möbius function** μ is defined for positive integers n as follows:

$$\mu(n) := \begin{cases} 0 & \text{if } n \text{ is divisible by a square other than 1;} \\ (-1)^r & \text{if } n \text{ is the product of } r \geq 0 \text{ distinct primes.} \end{cases}$$

Thus, if $n = p_1^{e_1} \cdots p_r^{e_r}$ is the prime factorization of n, then $\mu(n) = 0$ if $e_i > 1$ for some i, and otherwise, $\mu(n) = (-1)^r$. Here are some examples:

$$\mu(1) = 1, \ \mu(2) = -1, \ \mu(3) = -1, \ \mu(4) = 0, \ \mu(5) = -1, \ \mu(6) = 1.$$

It is easy to see (verify) that for any arithmetic function f, we have

$$I \star f = f \ \text{ and } \ (J \star f)(n) = \sum_{d|n} f(d).$$

Also, the functions I, J, and μ are multiplicative (verify). A useful property of the Möbius function is the following:

Theorem 2.17. *For any multiplicative function f, if $n = p_1^{e_1} \cdots p_r^{e_r}$ is the prime factorization of n, we have*

$$\sum_{d|n} \mu(d)f(d) = (1 - f(p_1)) \cdots (1 - f(p_r)). \tag{2.7}$$

In case $r = 0$ (i.e., $n = 1$), the product on the right-hand side of (2.7) is interpreted (as usual) as 1.

Proof. The non-zero terms in the sum on the left-hand side of (2.7) are those corresponding to divisors d of the form $p_{i_1} \cdots p_{i_\ell}$, where $p_{i_1}, \ldots, p_{i_\ell}$ are distinct; the value contributed to the sum by such a term is $(-1)^\ell f(p_{i_1} \cdots p_{i_\ell}) = (-1)^\ell f(p_{i_1}) \cdots f(p_{i_\ell})$. These are the same as the terms in the expansion of the product on the right-hand side of (2.7). $\square$

For example, suppose $f(d) = 1/d$ in the above theorem, and let $n = p_1^{e_1} \cdots p_r^{e_r}$ be the prime factorization of n. Then we obtain:

$$\sum_{d|n} \mu(d)/d = (1 - 1/p_1) \cdots (1 - 1/p_r). \tag{2.8}$$

As another example, suppose $f = J$. Then we obtain

$$(\mu \star J)(n) = \sum_{d|n} \mu(d) = \prod_{i=1}^{r}(1 - 1),$$

which is 1 if $n = 1$, and is zero if $n > 1$. Thus, we have

$$\mu \star J = I. \tag{2.9}$$

Theorem 2.18 (Möbius inversion formula). *Let f and F be arithmetic functions. Then we have $F = J \star f$ if and only if $f = \mu \star F$.*

Proof. If $F = J \star f$, then

$$\mu \star F = \mu \star (J \star f) = (\mu \star J) \star f = I \star f = f,$$

and conversely, if $f = \mu \star F$, then

$$J \star f = J \star (\mu \star F) = (J \star \mu) \star F = I \star F = F. \quad \Box$$

The Möbius inversion formula says this:

$$F(n) = \sum_{d|n} f(d) \quad \text{for all positive integers } n$$

if and only if

$$f(n) = \sum_{d|n} \mu(d)F(n/d) \quad \text{for all positive integers } n.$$

As an application of the Möbius inversion formula, we can get a different proof of Theorem 2.14, based on Theorem 2.11. Let $F(n) := n$ and $f(n) := \phi(n)$. Theorem 2.11 says that $F = J \star f$. Applying Möbius inversion to this yields $f = \mu \star F$, and using (2.8), we obtain

$$\phi(n) = \sum_{d|n} \mu(d)n/d = n\sum_{d|n} \mu(d)/d$$
$$= n(1 - 1/p_1)\cdots(1 - 1/p_r).$$

Of course, one could turn the above argument around, using Möbius inversion and (2.8) to derive Theorem 2.11 from Theorem 2.14.

EXERCISE 2.19. In our definition of a multiplicative function f, we made the requirement that $f(1) = 1$. Show that if we dropped this requirement, the only other function that would satisfy the definition would be the zero function (i.e., the function that is everywhere zero).

EXERCISE 2.20. Let f be a polynomial with integer coefficients, and for positive integer n define $\omega_f(n)$ to be the number of integers $z \in \{0, \ldots, n-1\}$ such that $f(z) \equiv 0 \pmod{n}$. Show that ω_f is multiplicative.

EXERCISE 2.21. Show that if f and g are multiplicative, then so is $f \star g$.

EXERCISE 2.22. Define $\tau(n)$ to be the number of positive divisors of n.

(a) Show that τ is a multiplicative function.

(b) Show that

$$\tau(n) = (e_1 + 1) \cdots (e_r + 1),$$

where $n = p_1^{e_1} \cdots p_r^{e_r}$ is the prime factorization of n.

(c) Show that

$$\sum_{d \mid n} \mu(d) \tau(n/d) = 1.$$

(d) Show that

$$\sum_{d \mid n} \mu(d) \tau(d) = (-1)^r,$$

where $n = p_1^{e_1} \cdots p_r^{e_r}$ is the prime factorization of n.

EXERCISE 2.23. Define $\sigma(n) := \sum_{d \mid n} d$.

(a) Show that σ is a multiplicative function.

(b) Show that

$$\sigma(n) = \prod_{i=1}^{r} \frac{p_i^{e_i+1} - 1}{p_i - 1},$$

where $n = p_1^{e_1} \cdots p_r^{e_r}$ is the prime factorization of n.

(c) Show that

$$\sum_{d \mid n} \mu(d) \sigma(n/d) = n.$$

(d) Show that

$$\sum_{d \mid n} \mu(d) \sigma(d) = (-1)^r p_1 \cdots p_r,$$

where $n = p_1^{e_1} \cdots p_r^{e_r}$ is the prime factorization of n.

EXERCISE 2.24. The **Mangoldt function** $\Lambda(n)$ is defined for all positive integers n by

$$\Lambda(n) := \begin{cases} \log p & \text{if } n = p^k, \text{ where } p \text{ is prime and } k \text{ is a positive integer;} \\ 0 & \text{otherwise.} \end{cases}$$

(a) Show that

$$\sum_{d|n} \Lambda(d) = \log n.$$

(b) Using part (a), show that

$$\Lambda(n) = -\sum_{d|n} \mu(d) \log d.$$

EXERCISE 2.25. Show that if f is multiplicative, and if $n = p_1^{e_1} \cdots p_r^{e_r}$ is the prime factorization of n, then

$$\sum_{d|n} (\mu(d))^2 f(d) = (1 + f(p_1)) \cdots (1 + f(p_r)).$$

EXERCISE 2.26. Show that n is square-free (see Exercise 1.13) if and only if $\sum_{d|n} (\mu(d))^2 \phi(d) = n$.

EXERCISE 2.27. Show that for any arithmetic function f with $f(1) \neq 0$, there is a unique arithmetic function g, called the **Dirichlet inverse** of f, such that $f \star g = I$. Also, show that if $f(1) = 0$, then f has no Dirichlet inverse.

EXERCISE 2.28. Show that if f is a multiplicative function, then so is its Dirichlet inverse (as defined in the previous exercise).

3

Computing with large integers

In this chapter, we review standard asymptotic notation, introduce the formal computational model we shall use throughout the rest of the text, and discuss basic algorithms for computing with large integers.

3.1 Asymptotic notation

We review some standard notation for relating the rate of growth of functions. This notation will be useful in discussing the running times of algorithms, and in a number of other contexts as well.

Suppose that x is a variable taking non-negative integer or real values, and let g denote a real-valued function in x that is positive for all sufficiently large x; also, let f denote any real-valued function in x. Then

- $f = O(g)$ means that $|f(x)| \leq cg(x)$ for some positive constant c and all sufficiently large x (read, "f is big-O of g"),

- $f = \Omega(g)$ means that $f(x) \geq cg(x)$ for some positive constant c and all sufficiently large x (read, "f is big-Omega of g"),

- $f = \Theta(g)$ means that $cg(x) \leq f(x) \leq dg(x)$, for some positive constants c and d and all sufficiently large x (read, "f is big-Theta of g"),

- $f = o(g)$ means that $f/g \to 0$ as $x \to \infty$ (read, "f is little-o of g"), and

- $f \sim g$ means that $f/g \to 1$ as $x \to \infty$ (read, "f is asymptotically equal to g").

Example 3.1. Let $f(x) := x^2$ and $g(x) := 2x^2 - x + 1$. Then $f = O(g)$ and $f = \Omega(g)$. Indeed, $f = \Theta(g)$. $\square$

Example 3.2. Let $f(x) := x^2$ and $g(x) := x^2 - 2x + 1$. Then $f \sim g$. $\square$

***Example* 3.3.** Let $f(x) := 1000x^2$ and $g(x) := x^3$. Then $f = o(g)$. $\square$

Let us call a function in x **eventually positive** if it takes positive values for all sufficiently large x. Note that by definition, if we write $f = \Omega(g)$, $f = \Theta(g)$, or $f \sim g$, it must be the case that f (in addition to g) is eventually positive; however, if we write $f = O(g)$ or $f = o(g)$, then f need not be eventually positive.

When one writes "$f = O(g)$," one should interpret "$\cdot = O(\cdot)$" as a binary relation between f with g. Analogously for "$f = \Omega(g)$," "$f = \Theta(g)$," and "$f = o(g)$."

One may also write "$O(g)$" in an expression to denote an anonymous function f such that $f = O(g)$. As an example, one could write $\sum_{i=1}^{n} i = n^2/2 + O(n)$. Analogously, $\Omega(g)$, $\Theta(g)$, and $o(g)$ may denote anonymous functions. The expression $O(1)$ denotes a function bounded in absolute value by a constant, while the expression $o(1)$ denotes a function that tends to zero in the limit.

As an even further use (abuse?) of the notation, one may use the big-O, -Omega, and -Theta notation for functions on an arbitrary domain, in which case the relevant bound should hold throughout the entire domain.

EXERCISE 3.1. Show that

    (a) $f = o(g)$ implies $f = O(g)$ and $g \neq O(f)$;

    (b) $f = O(g)$ and $g = O(h)$ implies $f = O(h)$;

    (c) $f = O(g)$ and $g = o(h)$ implies $f = o(h)$;

    (d) $f = o(g)$ and $g = O(h)$ implies $f = o(h)$.

EXERCISE 3.2. Let f and g be eventually positive functions in x. Show that

    (a) $f \sim g$ if and only if $f = (1 + o(1))g$;

    (b) $f \sim g$ implies $f = \Theta(g)$;

    (c) $f = \Theta(g)$ if and only if $f = O(g)$ and $f = \Omega(g)$;

    (d) $f = \Omega(g)$ if and only if $g = O(f)$.

EXERCISE 3.3. Let f and g be eventually positive functions in x, and suppose f/g tends to a limit L (possibly $L = \infty$) as $x \to \infty$. Show that

    (a) if $L = 0$, then $f = o(g)$;

    (b) if $0 < L < \infty$, then $f = \Theta(g)$;

    (c) if $L = \infty$, then $g = o(f)$.

EXERCISE 3.4. Order the following functions in x so that for each adjacent pair f, g in the ordering, we have $f = O(g)$, and indicate if $f = o(g)$, $f \sim g$, or $g = O(f)$:

$$x^3, \ e^x x^2, \ 1/x, \ x^2(x + 100) + 1/x, \ x + \sqrt{x}, \ \log_2 x, \ \log_3 x, \ 2x^2, \ x,$$
$$e^{-x}, \ 2x^2 - 10x + 4, \ e^{x + \sqrt{x}}, \ 2^x, \ 3^x, \ x^{-2}, \ x^2(\log x)^{1000}.$$

EXERCISE 3.5. Suppose that x takes non-negative integer values, and that $g(x) > 0$ for all $x \geq x_0$ for some x_0. Show that $f = O(g)$ if and only if $|f(x)| \leq cg(x)$ for some positive constant c and all $x \geq x_0$.

EXERCISE 3.6. Give an example of two non-decreasing functions f and g, both mapping positive integers to positive integers, such that $f \neq O(g)$ and $g \neq O(f)$.

EXERCISE 3.7. Show that

(a) the relation "$\sim$" is an equivalence relation on the set of eventually positive functions;

(b) for eventually positive functions f_1, f_2, g_2, g_2, if $f_1 \sim f_2$ and $g_1 \sim g_2$, then $f_1 \star g_1 \sim f_2 \star g_2$, where "$\star$" denotes addition, multiplication, or division;

(c) for eventually positive functions f_1, f_2, and any function g that tends to infinity as $x \to \infty$, if $f_1 \sim f_2$, then $f_1 \circ g \sim f_2 \circ g$, where "$\circ$" denotes function composition.

EXERCISE 3.8. Show that all of the claims in the previous exercise also hold when the relation "$\sim$" is replaced with the relation "$\cdot = \Theta(\cdot)$."

EXERCISE 3.9. Let f_1, f_2 be eventually positive functions. Show that if $f_1 \sim f_2$, then $\log(f_1) = \log(f_2) + o(1)$, and in particular, if $\log(f_1) = \Omega(1)$, then $\log(f_1) \sim \log(f_2)$.

EXERCISE 3.10. Suppose that f and g are functions defined on the integers $k, k + 1, \ldots$, and that g is eventually positive. For $n \geq k$, define $F(n) := \sum_{i=k}^{n} f(i)$ and $G(n) := \sum_{i=k}^{n} g(i)$. Show that if $f = O(g)$ and G is eventually positive, then $F = O(G)$.

EXERCISE 3.11. Suppose that f and g are functions defined on the integers $k, k+1, \ldots$, both of which are eventually positive. For $n \geq k$, define $F(n) := \sum_{i=k}^{n} f(i)$ and $G(n) := \sum_{i=k}^{n} g(i)$. Show that if $f \sim g$ and $G(n) \to \infty$ as $n \to \infty$, then $F \sim G$.

The following two exercises are continuous variants of the previous two exercises. To avoid unnecessary distractions, we shall only consider functions that are quite "well behaved." In particular, we restrict ourselves to piece-wise continuous functions (see §A3).

EXERCISE 3.12. Suppose that f and g are piece-wise continuous on $[a, \infty)$, and that g is eventually positive. For $x \geq a$, define $F(x) := \int_a^x f(t)dt$ and $G(x) := \int_a^x g(t)dt$. Show that if $f = O(g)$ and G is eventually positive, then $F = O(G)$.

EXERCISE 3.13. Suppose that f and g are piece-wise continuous $[a, \infty)$, both of which are eventually positive. For $x \geq a$, define $F(x) := \int_a^x f(t)dt$ and $G(x) := \int_a^x g(t)dt$. Show that if $f \sim g$ and $G(x) \to \infty$ as $x \to \infty$, then $F \sim G$.

3.2 Machine models and complexity theory

When presenting an algorithm, we shall always use a high-level, and some-what informal, notation. However, all of our high-level descriptions can be routinely translated into the machine-language of an actual computer. So that our theorems on the running times of algorithms have a precise mathe-matical meaning, we formally define an "idealized" computer: the **random access machine** or **RAM**.

A RAM consists of an unbounded sequence of **memory cells**

$$m[0], m[1], m[2], \ldots$$

each of which can store an arbitrary integer, together with a **program**. A program consists of a finite sequence of instructions $I_0, I_1, \ldots$, where each instruction is of one of the following types:

arithmetic This type of instruction is of the form $\alpha \leftarrow \beta \star \gamma$, where $\star$ represents one of the operations addition, subtraction, multiplication, or integer division (i.e., $\lfloor \cdot / \cdot \rfloor$). The values β and γ are of the form c, $m[a]$, or $m[m[a]]$, and α is of the form $m[a]$ or $m[m[a]]$, where c is an integer constant and a is a non-negative integer constant. Execution of this type of instruction causes the value $\beta \star \gamma$ to be evaluated and then stored in α.

branching This type of instruction is of the form IF $\beta \diamond \gamma$ GOTO i, where i is the index of an instruction, and where $\diamond$ is one of the comparison operations $=, \neq, <, >, \leq, \geq$, and β and γ are as above. Execution of this type of instruction causes the "flow of control" to pass condi-tionally to instruction I_i.

halt The HALT instruction halts the execution of the program.

A RAM executes by executing instruction I_0, and continues to execute instructions, following branching instructions as appropriate, until a HALT instruction is executed.

We do not specify input or output instructions, and instead assume that the input and output are to be found in memory at some prescribed location, in some standardized format.

To determine the running time of a program on a given input, we charge 1 unit of time to each instruction executed.

This model of computation closely resembles a typical modern-day computer, except that we have abstracted away many annoying details. However, there are two details of real machines that cannot be ignored; namely, any real machine has a finite number of memory cells, and each cell can store numbers only in some fixed range.

The first limitation must be dealt with by either purchasing sufficient memory or designing more space-efficient algorithms.

The second limitation is especially annoying, as we will want to perform computations with quite large integers—much larger than will fit into any single memory cell of an actual machine. To deal with this limitation, we shall represent such large integers as vectors of digits to some fixed base, so that each digit is bounded so as to fit into a memory cell. This is discussed in more detail in the next section. Using this strategy, the only other numbers we actually need to store in memory cells are "small" numbers representing array indices, addresses, and the like, which hopefully will fit into the memory cells of actual machines.

Thus, whenever we speak of an algorithm, we shall mean an algorithm that can be implemented on a RAM, such that all numbers stored in memory cells are "small" numbers, as discussed above. Admittedly, this is a bit imprecise. For the reader who demands more precision, we can make a restriction such as the following: there exist positive constants c and d, such that at any point in the computation, if k memory cells have been written to (including inputs), then all numbers stored in memory cells are bounded by $k^c + d$ in absolute value.

Even with these caveats and restrictions, the running time as we have defined it for a RAM is still only a rough predictor of performance on an actual machine. On a real machine, different instructions may take significantly different amounts of time to execute; for example, a division instruction may take much longer than an addition instruction. Also, on a real machine, the behavior of the cache may significantly affect the time it takes to load or store the operands of an instruction. Finally, the precise running time of an algorithm given by a high-level description will depend on the quality of the translation of this algorithm into "machine code." However, despite all of these problems, it still turns out that measuring the running time on a RAM as we propose here is nevertheless a good "first order" predictor of performance on real machines in many cases. Also, we shall only state the running time of an algorithm using a big-O estimate, so that implementation-specific constant factors are anyway "swept under the rug."

If we have an algorithm for solving a certain type of problem, we expect that "larger" instances of the problem will require more time to solve than "smaller" instances. Theoretical computer scientists sometimes equate the notion of an "efficient" algorithm with that of a **polynomial-time algorithm** (although not everyone takes theoretical computer scientists very seriously, especially on this point). A polynomial-time algorithm is one whose running time on inputs of length n is bounded by $n^c + d$ for some constants c and d (a "real" theoretical computer scientist will write this as $n^{O(1)}$). To make this notion mathematically precise, one needs to define the *length* of an algorithm's input.

To define the length of an input, one chooses a "reasonable" scheme to encode all possible inputs as a string of symbols from some finite alphabet, and then defines the length of an input as the number of symbols in its encoding.

We will be dealing with algorithms whose inputs consist of arbitrary integers, or lists of such integers. We describe a possible encoding scheme using the alphabet consisting of the six symbols '0', '1', '-', ',', '(', and ')'. An integer is encoded in binary, with possibly a negative sign. Thus, the length of an integer x is approximately equal to $\log_2 |x|$. We can encode a list of integers $x_1, \ldots, x_n$ as "$(\bar{x}_1, \ldots, \bar{x}_n)$", where $\bar{x}_i$ is the encoding of x_i. We can also encode lists of lists, and so on, in the obvious way. All of the mathematical objects we shall wish to compute with can be encoded in this way. For example, to encode an $n \times n$ matrix of rational numbers, we may encode each rational number as a pair of integers (the numerator and denominator), each row of the matrix as a list of n encodings of rational numbers, and the matrix as a list of n encodings of rows.

It is clear that other encoding schemes are possible, giving rise to different definitions of input length. For example, we could encode inputs in some base other than 2 (but not unary!) or use a different alphabet. Indeed, it is typical to assume, for simplicity, that inputs are encoded as bit strings. However, such an alternative encoding scheme would change the definition of input length by at most a constant multiplicative factor, and so would not affect the notion of a polynomial-time algorithm.

Note that algorithms may use data structures for representing mathematical objects that look quite different from whatever encoding scheme one might choose. Indeed, our mathematical objects may never actually be written down using our encoding scheme (either by us or our programs)— the encoding scheme is a purely conceptual device that allows us to express the running time of an algorithm as a function of the length of its input.

Also note that in defining the notion of polynomial time on a RAM, it is essential that we restrict the sizes of numbers that may be stored in the machine's memory cells, as we have done above. Without this restriction, a program could perform arithmetic on huge numbers, being charged just one unit of time for each arithmetic operation—not only is this intuitively "wrong," it is possible to come up with programs that solve some problems using a polynomial number of arithmetic operations on huge numbers, and these problems cannot otherwise be solved in polynomial time (see §3.6).

3.3 Basic integer arithmetic

We will need algorithms to manipulate integers of arbitrary length. Since such integers will exceed the word-size of actual machines, and to satisfy the formal requirements of our random access model of computation, we shall represent large integers as vectors of digits to some base B, along with a bit indicating the sign. That is, for $a \in \mathbb{Z}$, if we write

$$a = \pm \sum_{i=0}^{k-1} a_i B^i = \pm(a_{k-1} \cdots a_1 a_0)_B,$$

where $0 \le a_i < B$ for $i = 0, \ldots, k-1$, then a will be represented in memory as a data structure consisting of the vector of base-B digits $a_0, \ldots, a_{k-1}$, along with a "sign bit" to indicate the sign of a. When a is non-zero, the high-order digit a_{k-1} in this representation should be non-zero.

For our purposes, we shall consider B to be a constant, and moreover, a power of 2. The choice of B as a power of 2 is convenient for a number of technical reasons.

A note to the reader: *If you are not interested in the low-level details of algorithms for integer arithmetic, or are willing to take them on faith, you may safely skip ahead to §3.3.5, where the results of this section are summarized.*

We now discuss in detail basic arithmetic algorithms for unsigned (i.e., non-negative) integers—these algorithms work with vectors of base-B digits, and except where explicitly noted, we do not assume the high-order digits of the input vectors are non-zero, nor do these algorithms ensure that the high-order digit of the output vector is non-zero. These algorithms can be very easily adapted to deal with arbitrary signed integers, and to take proper care that the high-order digit of the vector representing a non-zero number is non-zero (the reader is asked to fill in these details in some of the exercises below). All of these algorithms can be implemented directly in a programming language that provides a "built-in" signed integer type that can represent all integers of absolute value less than B^2, and that provides the basic arithmetic operations (addition, subtraction, multiplication, integer division). So, for example, using the C or *Java* programming language's `int` type on a typical 32-bit computer, we could take $B = 2^{15}$. The resulting software would be reasonably efficient, but certainly not the best possible.

Suppose we have the base-B representations of two unsigned integers a and b. We present algorithms to compute the base-B representation of $a+b$, $a - b$, $a \cdot b$, $\lfloor a/b \rfloor$, and $a \bmod b$. To simplify the presentation, for integers x, y with $y \neq 0$, we write $\mathrm{divmod}(x, y)$ to denote $(\lfloor x/y \rfloor, x \bmod y)$.

3.3.1 Addition

Let $a = (a_{k-1} \cdots a_0)_B$ and $b = (b_{\ell-1} \cdots b_0)_B$ be unsigned integers. Assume that $k \geq \ell \geq 1$ (if $k < \ell$, then we can just swap a and b). The sum $c := a+b$ is of the form $c = (c_k c_{k-1} \cdots c_0)_B$. Using the standard "paper-and-pencil" method (adapted from base-10 to base-B, of course), we can compute the base-B representation of $a + b$ in time $O(k)$, as follows:

> $carry \leftarrow 0$
> for $i \leftarrow 0$ to $\ell - 1$ do
> $tmp \leftarrow a_i + b_i + carry$, $(carry, c_i) \leftarrow \mathrm{divmod}(tmp, B)$
> for $i \leftarrow \ell$ to $k - 1$ do
> $tmp \leftarrow a_i + carry$, $(carry, c_i) \leftarrow \mathrm{divmod}(tmp, B)$
> $c_k \leftarrow carry$

Note that in every loop iteration, the value of $carry$ is 0 or 1, and the value tmp lies between 0 and $2B - 1$.

3.3.2 Subtraction

Let $a = (a_{k-1} \cdots a_0)_B$ and $b = (b_{\ell-1} \cdots b_0)_B$ be unsigned integers. Assume that $k \geq \ell \geq 1$. To compute the difference $c := a - b$, we may use the same algorithm as above, but with the expression "$a_i + b_i$" replaced by "$a_i - b_i$." In every loop iteration, the value of *carry* is 0 or -1, and the value of *tmp* lies between $-B$ and $B-1$. If $a \geq b$, then $c_k = 0$ (i.e., there is no carry out of the last loop iteration); otherwise, $c_k = -1$ (and $b - a = B^k - (c_{k-1} \cdots c_0)_B$, which can be computed with another execution of the subtraction routine).

3.3.3 Multiplication

Let $a = (a_{k-1} \cdots a_0)_B$ and $b = (b_{\ell-1} \cdots b_0)_B$ be unsigned integers, with $k \geq 1$ and $\ell \geq 1$. The product $c := a \cdot b$ is of the form $(c_{k+\ell-1} \cdots c_0)_B$, and may be computed in time $O(k\ell)$ as follows:

> for $i \leftarrow 0$ to $k + \ell - 1$ do $c_i \leftarrow 0$
> for $i \leftarrow 0$ to $k - 1$ do
> $\quad$ *carry* $\leftarrow 0$
> $\quad$ for $j \leftarrow 0$ to $\ell - 1$ do
> $\quad\quad$ *tmp* $\leftarrow a_i b_j + c_{i+j} + carry$
> $\quad\quad$ $(carry, c_{i+j}) \leftarrow \mathrm{divmod}(tmp, B)$
> $\quad$ $c_{i+\ell} \leftarrow carry$

Note that at every step in the above algorithm, the value of *carry* lies between 0 and $B - 1$, and the value of *tmp* lies between 0 and $B^2 - 1$.

3.3.4 Division with remainder

Let $a = (a_{k-1} \cdots a_0)_B$ and $b = (b_{\ell-1} \cdots b_0)_B$ be unsigned integers, with $k \geq 1$, $\ell \geq 1$, and $b_{\ell-1} \neq 0$. We want to compute q and r such that $a = bq + r$ and $0 \leq r < b$. Assume that $k \geq \ell$; otherwise, $a < b$, and we can just set $q \leftarrow 0$ and $r \leftarrow a$. The quotient q will have at most $m := k - \ell + 1$ base-B digits. Write $q = (q_{m-1} \cdots q_0)_B$.

At a high level, the strategy we shall use to compute q and r is the following:

> $r \leftarrow a$
> for $i \leftarrow m - 1$ down to 0 do
> $\quad$ $q_i \leftarrow \lfloor r / B^i b \rfloor$
> $\quad$ $r \leftarrow r - B^i \cdot q_i b$

One easily verifies by induction that at the beginning of each loop iteration, we have $0 \leq r < B^{i+1} b$, and hence each q_i will be between 0 and $B - 1$, as required.

Turning the above strategy into a detailed algorithm takes a bit of work.

In particular, we want an easy way to compute $\lfloor r/B^i b \rfloor$. Now, we could in theory just try all possible choices for q_i — this would take time $O(B\ell)$, and viewing B as a constant, this is $O(\ell)$. However, this is not really very desirable from either a practical or theoretical point of view, and we can do much better with just a little effort.

We shall first consider a special case; namely, the case where $\ell = 1$. In this case, the computation of the quotient $\lfloor r/B^i b \rfloor$ is facilitated by the following, which essentially tells us that this quotient is determined by the two high-order digits of r:

Theorem 3.1. *Let x and y be integers such that*

$$0 \le x = x'2^n + s \quad and \quad 0 < y = y'2^n$$

for some integers n, s, x', y', with $n \ge 0$ and $0 \le s < 2^n$. Then $\lfloor x/y \rfloor = \lfloor x'/y' \rfloor$.

Proof. We have

$$\frac{x}{y} = \frac{x'}{y'} + \frac{s}{y'2^n} \ge \frac{x'}{y'}.$$

It follows immediately that $\lfloor x/y \rfloor \ge \lfloor x'/y' \rfloor$.

We also have

$$\frac{x}{y} = \frac{x'}{y'} + \frac{s}{y'2^n} < \frac{x'}{y'} + \frac{1}{y'} \le \left(\left\lfloor \frac{x'}{y'} \right\rfloor + \frac{y'-1}{y'} \right) + \frac{1}{y'}.$$

Thus, we have $x/y < \lfloor x'/y' \rfloor + 1$, and hence, $\lfloor x/y \rfloor \le \lfloor x'/y' \rfloor$. $\square$

From this theorem, one sees that the following algorithm correctly computes the quotient and remainder in time $O(k)$ (in the case $\ell = 1$):

$$carry \leftarrow 0$$
for $i \leftarrow k - 1$ down to 0 do
    $tmp \leftarrow carry \cdot B + a_i$
    $(carry, q_i) \leftarrow \mathrm{divmod}(tmp, b_0)$
output the quotient $q = (q_{k-1} \cdots q_0)_B$ and the remainder $carry$

Note that in every loop iteration, the value of $carry$ lies between 0 and $b_0 \le B - 1$, and the value of tmp lies between 0 and $B \cdot b_0 + (B - 1) \le B^2 - 1$.

That takes care of the special case where $\ell = 1$. Now we turn to the general case $\ell \ge 1$. In this case, we cannot so easily get the digits q_i of the quotient, but we can still fairly easily estimate these digits, using the following:

Theorem 3.2. *Let x and y be integers such that*

$$0 \le x = x'2^n + s \quad and \quad 0 < y = y'2^n + t$$

for some integers n, s, t, x', y' with $n \ge 0$, $0 \le s < 2^n$, and $0 \le t < 2^n$. Further suppose that $2y' \ge x/y$. Then we have

$$\lfloor x/y \rfloor \le \lfloor x'/y' \rfloor \le \lfloor x/y \rfloor + 2.$$

Proof. For the first inequality, note that $x/y \le x/(y'2^n)$, and so $\lfloor x/y \rfloor \le \lfloor x/(y'2^n) \rfloor$, and by the previous theorem, $\lfloor x/(y'2^n) \rfloor = \lfloor x'/y' \rfloor$. That proves the first inequality.

For the second inequality, first note that from the definitions, $x/y \ge x'/(y'+1)$, which is equivalent to $x'y - xy' - x \le 0$. Now, the inequality $2y' \ge x/y$ is equivalent to $2yy' - x \ge 0$, and combining this with the inequality $x'y - xy' - x \le 0$, we obtain $2yy' - x \ge x'y - xy' - x$, which is equivalent to $x/y \ge x'/y' - 2$. It follows that $\lfloor x/y \rfloor \ge \lfloor x'/y' \rfloor - 2$. That proves the second inequality. $\square$

Based on this theorem, we first present an algorithm for division with remainder that works assuming that b is appropriately "normalized," meaning that $b_{\ell-1} \ge 2^{w-1}$, where $B = 2^w$. This algorithm is shown in Fig. 3.1.

Some remarks are in order:

1. In line 4, we compute q_i, which by Theorem 3.2 is greater than or equal to the true quotient digit, but exceeds this value by at most 2.

2. In line 5, we reduce q_i if it is obviously too big.

3. In lines 6–10, we compute

$$(r_{i+\ell} \cdots r_i)_B \leftarrow (r_{i+\ell} \cdots r_i)_B - q_i b.$$

In each loop iteration, the value of *tmp* lies between $-(B^2 - B)$ and $B - 1$, and the value *carry* lies between $-(B - 1)$ and 0.

4. If the estimate q_i is too large, this is manifested by a negative value of $r_{i+\ell}$ at line 10. Lines 11–17 detect and correct this condition: the loop body here executes at most twice; in lines 12–16, we compute

$$(r_{i+\ell} \cdots r_i)_B \leftarrow (r_{i+\ell} \cdots r_i)_B + (b_{\ell-1} \cdots b_0)_B.$$

Just as in the algorithm in §3.3.1, in every iteration of the loop in lines 13–15, the value of *carry* is 0 or 1, and the value *tmp* lies between 0 and $2B - 1$.

It is quite easy to see that the running time of the above algorithm is $O(\ell \cdot (k - \ell + 1))$.

1. for $i \leftarrow 0$ to $k - 1$ do $r_i \leftarrow a_i$
2. $r_k \leftarrow 0$
3. for $i \leftarrow k - \ell$ down to 0 do
4. $\quad q_i \leftarrow \lfloor (r_{i+\ell}B + r_{i+\ell-1})/b_{\ell-1} \rfloor$
5. $\quad$ if $q_i \geq B$ then $q_i \leftarrow B - 1$
6. $\quad carry \leftarrow 0$
7. $\quad$ for $j \leftarrow 0$ to $\ell - 1$ do
8. $\quad\quad tmp \leftarrow r_{i+j} - q_i b_j + carry$
9. $\quad\quad (carry, r_{i+j}) \leftarrow \mathrm{divmod}(tmp, B)$
10. $\quad r_{i+\ell} \leftarrow r_{i+\ell} + carry$
11. $\quad$ while $r_{i+\ell} < 0$ do
12. $\quad\quad carry \leftarrow 0$
13. $\quad\quad$ for $j \leftarrow 0$ to $\ell - 1$ do
14. $\quad\quad\quad tmp \leftarrow r_{i+j} + b_i + carry$
15. $\quad\quad\quad (carry, r_{i+j}) \leftarrow \mathrm{divmod}(tmp, B)$
16. $\quad\quad r_{i+\ell} \leftarrow r_{i+\ell} + carry$
17. $\quad\quad q_i \leftarrow q_i - 1$
18. output the quotient $q = (q_{k-\ell} \cdots q_0)_B$
    $\quad\quad$ and the remainder $r = (r_{\ell-1} \cdots r_0)_B$

Fig. 3.1. Division with Remainder Algorithm

Finally, consider the general case, where b may not be normalized. We multiply both a and b by an appropriate value $2^{w'}$, with $0 \leq w' < w$, obtaining $a' := a2^{w'}$ and $b' := 2^{w'}$, where b' is normalized; alternatively, we can use a more efficient, special-purpose "left shift" algorithm to achieve the same effect. We then compute q and r' such that $a' = b'q + r'$, using the above division algorithm for the normalized case. Observe that $q = \lfloor a'/b' \rfloor = \lfloor a/b \rfloor$, and $r' = r2^{w'}$, where $r = a \bmod b$. To recover r, we simply divide r' by $2^{w'}$, which we can do either using the above "single precision" division algorithm, or by using a special-purpose "right shift" algorithm. All of this normalizing and denormalizing takes time $O(k + \ell)$. Thus, the total running time for division with remainder is still $O(\ell \cdot (k - \ell + 1))$.

EXERCISE 3.14. Work out the details of algorithms for arithmetic on *signed* integers, using the above algorithms for unsigned integers as subroutines. You should give algorithms for addition, subtraction, multiplication, and division with remainder of arbitrary signed integers (for division with remainder, your algorithm should compute $\lfloor a/b \rfloor$ and $a \bmod b$). Make sure your algorithm correctly computes the sign bit of the result, and also strips leading zero digits from the result.

EXERCISE 3.15. Work out the details of an algorithm that compares two *signed* integers a and b, determining which of $a < b$, $a = b$, or $a > b$ holds.

EXERCISE 3.16. Suppose that we run the division with remainder algorithm in Fig. 3.1 for $\ell > 1$ without normalizing b, but instead, we compute the value q_i in line 4 as follows:

$$q_i \leftarrow \lfloor (r_{i+\ell}B^2 + r_{i+\ell-1}B + r_{i+\ell-2})/(b_{\ell-1}B + b_{\ell-2}) \rfloor.$$

Show that q_i is either equal to the correct quotient digit, or the correct quotient digit plus 1. Note that a limitation of this approach is that the numbers involved in the computation are larger than B^2.

EXERCISE 3.17. Work out the details for an algorithm that shifts a given unsigned integer a to the left by a specified number of bits s (i.e., computes $b := a \cdot 2^s$). The running time of your algorithm should be linear in the number of digits of the output.

EXERCISE 3.18. Work out the details for an algorithm that shifts a given unsigned integer a to the right by a specified number of bits s (i.e., computes $b := \lfloor a/2^s \rfloor$). The running time of your algorithm should be linear in the number of digits of the output. Now modify your algorithm so that it correctly computes $\lfloor a/2^s \rfloor$ for *signed* integers a.

EXERCISE 3.19. This exercise is for *C/Java* programmers. Evaluate the *C/Java* expressions

   (-17) % 4;   (-17) & 3;

and compare these values with $(-17) \bmod 4$. Also evaluate the *C/Java* expressions

   (-17) / 4;   (-17) >> 2;

and compare with $\lfloor -17/4 \rfloor$. Explain your findings.

EXERCISE 3.20. This exercise is also for *C/Java* programmers. Suppose that values of type int are stored using a 32-bit 2's complement representation, and that all basic arithmetic operations are computed correctly modulo 2^{32}, even if an "overflow" happens to occur. Also assume that double precision floating point has 53 bits of precision, and that all basic arithmetic operations give a result with a relative error of at most 2^{-53}. Also assume that conversion from type `int` to `double` is exact, and that conversion from `double` to `int` truncates the fractional part. Now, suppose we are given `int` variables `a`, `b`, and `n`, such that $1 < n < 2^{30}$, $0 \le a < n$, and $0 \le b < n$. Show that after the following code sequence is executed, the value of `r` is equal to $(a \cdot b) \bmod n$:

```
int q;
q  = (int) ((((double) a) * ((double) b)) / ((double) n));
r = a*b - q*n;
if (r >= n)
   r = r - n;
else if (r < 0)
   r = r + n;
```

3.3.5 Summary

We now summarize the results of this section. For an integer a, we define $\text{len}(a)$ to be the number of bits in the binary representation of $|a|$; more precisely,

$$\text{len}(a) := \begin{cases} \lfloor \log_2 |a| \rfloor + 1 & \text{if } a \neq 0, \\ 1 & \text{if } a = 0. \end{cases}$$

Notice that for $a > 0$, if $\ell := \text{len}(a)$, then we have $\log_2 a < \ell \le \log_2 a + 1$, or equivalently, $2^{\ell-1} \le a < 2^{\ell}$.

Assuming that arbitrarily large integers are represented as described at the beginning of this section, with a sign bit and a vector of base-B digits, where B is a constant power of 2, we may state the following theorem.

Theorem 3.3. *Let a and b be arbitrary integers.*

(i) *We can compute $a \pm b$ in time $O(\text{len}(a) + \text{len}(b))$.*

(ii) *We can compute $a \cdot b$ in time $O(\text{len}(a)\,\text{len}(b))$.*

(iii) *If $b \neq 0$, we can compute the quotient $q := \lfloor a/b \rfloor$ and the remainder $r := a \bmod b$ in time $O(\text{len}(b)\,\text{len}(q))$.*

Note the bound $O(\text{len}(b)\,\text{len}(q))$ in part (iii) of this theorem, which may be significantly less than the bound $O(\text{len}(a)\,\text{len}(b))$. A good way to remember this bound is as follows: the time to compute the quotient and remainder is roughly the same as the time to compute the product bq appearing in the equality $a = bq + r$.

This theorem does not explicitly refer to the base B in the underlying implementation. The choice of B affects the values of the implied big-O constants; while in theory, this is of no significance, it does have a significant impact in practice.

From now on, we shall (for the most part) not worry about the implementation details of long-integer arithmetic, and will just refer directly this theorem. However, we will occasionally exploit some trivial aspects of our data structure for representing large integers. For example, it is clear that in constant time, we can determine the sign of a given integer a, the bit length of a, and any particular bit of the binary representation of a; moreover, as discussed in Exercises 3.17 and 3.18, multiplications and divisions by powers of 2 can be computed in linear time via "left shifts" and "right shifts." It is also clear that we can convert between the base-2 representation of a given integer and our implementation's internal representation in linear time (other conversions may take longer—see Exercise 3.25).

> **A note on notation: "len" and "log."** In expressing the running times of algorithms, we generally prefer to write, for example, $O(\mathrm{len}(a)\,\mathrm{len}(b))$, rather than $O((\log a)(\log b))$. There are two reasons for this. The first is esthetic: the function "len" stresses the fact that running times should be expressed in terms of the bit length of the inputs. The second is technical: big-O estimates involving expressions containing several independent parameters, like $O(\mathrm{len}(a)\,\mathrm{len}(b))$, should be valid for *all* possible values of the parameters, since the notion of "sufficiently large" does not make sense in this setting; because of this, it is very inconvenient to have functions, like log, that vanish or are undefined on some inputs.

EXERCISE 3.21. Let $n_1, \ldots, n_k$ be positive integers. Show that

$$\sum_{i=1}^{k} \mathrm{len}(n_i) - k \le \mathrm{len}\left(\prod_{i=1}^{k} n_i\right) \le \sum_{i=1}^{k} \mathrm{len}(n_i).$$

EXERCISE 3.22. Show that the product n of integers $n_1, \ldots, n_k$, with each $n_i > 1$, can be computed in time $O(\mathrm{len}(n)^2)$. Do not assume that k is a constant.

EXERCISE 3.23. Show that given integers $n_1, \ldots, n_k$, with each $n_i > 1$, and an integer z, where $0 \le z < n$ and $n := \prod_i n_i$, we can compute the k integers $z \bmod n_i$, for $i = 1, \ldots, k$, in time $O(\mathrm{len}(n)^2)$.

EXERCISE 3.24. Consider the problem of computing $\lfloor n^{1/2} \rfloor$ for a given non-negative integer n.

(a) Using binary search, give an algorithm for this problem that runs in time $O(\operatorname{len}(n)^3)$. Your algorithm should discover the bits of $\lfloor n^{1/2} \rfloor$ one at a time, from high- to low-order bit.

(b) Refine your algorithm from part (a), so that it runs in time $O(\operatorname{len}(n)^2)$.

EXERCISE 3.25. Show how to convert (in both directions) between the base-10 representation and our implementation's internal representation of an integer n in time $O(\operatorname{len}(n)^2)$.

3.4 Computing in $\mathbb{Z}_n$

Let $n > 1$. For $\alpha \in \mathbb{Z}_n$, there exists a unique integer $a \in \{0, \ldots, n-1\}$ such that $\alpha = [a]_n$; we call this integer a the **canonical representative of** α, and denote it by $\operatorname{rep}(\alpha)$. For computational purposes, we represent elements of $\mathbb{Z}_n$ by their canonical representatives.

Addition and subtraction in $\mathbb{Z}_n$ can be performed in time $O(\operatorname{len}(n))$: given $\alpha, \beta \in \mathbb{Z}_n$, to compute $\operatorname{rep}(\alpha + \beta)$, we simply compute the integer sum $\operatorname{rep}(\alpha) + \operatorname{rep}(\beta)$, subtracting n if the result is greater than or equal to n; similarly, to compute $\operatorname{rep}(\alpha - \beta)$, we compute the integer difference $\operatorname{rep}(\alpha) - \operatorname{rep}(\beta)$, adding n if the result is negative. Multiplication in $\mathbb{Z}_n$ can be performed in time $O(\operatorname{len}(n)^2)$: given $\alpha, \beta \in \mathbb{Z}_n$, we compute $\operatorname{rep}(\alpha \cdot \beta)$ as $\operatorname{rep}(\alpha) \operatorname{rep}(\beta) \bmod n$, using one integer multiplication and one division with remainder.

> **A note on notation: "rep," "mod," and "$[\cdot]_n$."** In describing algorithms, as well as in other contexts, if α, β are elements of $\mathbb{Z}_n$, we may write, for example, $\gamma \leftarrow \alpha + \beta$ or $\gamma \leftarrow \alpha\beta$, and it is understood that elements of $\mathbb{Z}_n$ are represented by their canonical representatives as discussed above, and arithmetic on canonical representatives is done modulo n. Thus, we have in mind a "strongly typed" language for our pseudo-code that makes a clear distinction between integers in the set $\{0, \ldots, n-1\}$ and elements of $\mathbb{Z}_n$. If $a \in \mathbb{Z}$, we can convert a to an object $\alpha \in \mathbb{Z}_n$ by writing $\alpha \leftarrow [a]_n$, and if $a \in \{0, \ldots, n-1\}$, this type conversion is purely conceptual, involving no actual computation. Conversely, if $\alpha \in \mathbb{Z}_n$, we can convert α to an object $a \in \{0, \ldots, n-1\}$, by writing $a \leftarrow \operatorname{rep}(\alpha)$; again, this type conversion is purely conceptual, and involves no actual computation. It is perhaps also worthwhile to stress the distinction between $a \bmod n$ and $[a]_n$—the former denotes an element of the set $\{0, \ldots, n-1\}$, while the latter denotes an element of $\mathbb{Z}_n$.

Another interesting problem is exponentiation in $\mathbb{Z}_n$: given $\alpha \in \mathbb{Z}_n$ and a non-negative integer e, compute $\alpha^e \in \mathbb{Z}_n$. Perhaps the most obvious way to do this is to iteratively multiply by α a total of e times, requiring time $O(e \operatorname{len}(n)^2)$. A much faster algorithm, the **repeated-squaring algorithm**, computes α^e using just $O(\operatorname{len}(e))$ multiplications in $\mathbb{Z}_n$, thus taking time $O(\operatorname{len}(e) \operatorname{len}(n)^2)$.

This method works as follows. Let $e = (b_{\ell-1} \cdots b_0)_2$ be the binary expansion of e (where b_0 is the low-order bit). For $i = 0, \ldots, \ell$, define $e_i := \lfloor e/2^i \rfloor$; the binary expansion of e_i is $e_i = (b_{\ell-1} \cdots b_i)_2$. Also define $\beta_i := \alpha^{e_i}$ for $i = 0, \ldots, \ell$, so $\beta_\ell = 1$ and $\beta_0 = \alpha^e$. Then we have

$$e_i = 2e_{i+1} + b_i \quad \text{and} \quad \beta_i = \beta_{i+1}^2 \cdot \alpha^{b_i} \quad \text{for } i = 0, \ldots, \ell - 1.$$

This idea yields the following algorithm:

$\beta \leftarrow [1]_n$
for $i \leftarrow \ell - 1$ down to 0 do
$\quad \beta \leftarrow \beta^2$
$\quad$ if $b_i = 1$ then $\beta \leftarrow \beta \cdot \alpha$
output β

It is clear that when this algorithm terminates, we have $\beta = \alpha^e$, and that the running-time estimate is as claimed above. Indeed, the algorithm uses ℓ squarings in $\mathbb{Z}_n$, and at most ℓ additional multiplications in $\mathbb{Z}_n$.

The following exercises develop some important efficiency improvements to the basic repeated-squaring algorithm.

EXERCISE 3.26. The goal of this exercise is to develop a "2^t-ary" variant of the above repeated-squaring algorithm, in which the exponent is effectively treated as a number in base 2^t, rather than in base 2.

(a) Show how to modify the repeated squaring so as to compute α^e using $\ell + O(1)$ squarings in $\mathbb{Z}_n$, and an additional $2^t + \ell/t + O(1)$ multiplications in $\mathbb{Z}_n$. As above, $\alpha \in \mathbb{Z}_n$ and $\operatorname{len}(e) = \ell$, while t is a parameter that we are free to choose. Your algorithm should begin by building a table of powers $[1], \alpha, \ldots, \alpha^{2^t-1}$, and after that, it should process the bits of e from left to right in blocks of length t (i.e., as base-2^t digits).

(b) Show that by appropriately choosing the parameter t, we can bound the number of additional multiplications in $\mathbb{Z}_n$ by $O(\ell/\operatorname{len}(\ell))$. Thus, from an asymptotic point of view, the cost of exponentiation is essentially the cost of ℓ squarings in $\mathbb{Z}_n$.

(c) Improve your algorithm from part (a), so that it only uses $\ell + O(1)$ squarings in $\mathbb{Z}_n$, and an additional $2^{t-1} + \ell/t + O(1)$ multiplications in $\mathbb{Z}_n$. Hint: build a table that contains only the *odd* powers of α among $[1], \alpha, \ldots, \alpha^{2^t-1}$.

EXERCISE 3.27. Suppose we are given $\alpha_1, \ldots, \alpha_k \in \mathbb{Z}_n$, along with non-negative integers $e_1, \ldots, e_k$, where $\operatorname{len}(e_i) \leq \ell$ for $i = 1, \ldots, k$. Show how to compute

$$\beta := \alpha_1^{e_1} \cdots \alpha_k^{e_k}$$

using $\ell + O(1)$ squarings in $\mathbb{Z}_n$ and an additional $\ell + 2^k + O(1)$ multiplications in $\mathbb{Z}_n$. Your algorithm should work in two phases: in the first phase, the algorithm uses just the values $\alpha_1, \ldots, \alpha_k$ to build a table of all possible products of subsets of $\alpha_1, \ldots, \alpha_k$; in the second phase, the algorithm computes β, using the exponents $e_1, \ldots, e_k$, and the table computed in the first phase.

EXERCISE 3.28. Suppose that we are to compute α^e, where $\alpha \in \mathbb{Z}_n$, for many ℓ-bit exponents e, but with α fixed. Show that for any positive integer parameter k, we can make a pre-computation (depending on α, ℓ, and k) that uses $\ell + O(1)$ squarings in $\mathbb{Z}_n$ and $2^k + O(1)$ multiplications in $\mathbb{Z}_n$, so that after the pre-computation, we can compute α^e for any ℓ-bit exponent e using just $\ell/k + O(1)$ squarings and $\ell/k + O(1)$ multiplications in $\mathbb{Z}_n$. Hint: use the algorithm in the previous exercise.

EXERCISE 3.29. Let k be a *constant*, positive integer. Suppose we are given $\alpha_1, \ldots, \alpha_k \in \mathbb{Z}_n$, along with non-negative integers $e_1, \ldots, e_k$, where $\operatorname{len}(e_i) \leq \ell$ for $i = 1, \ldots, k$. Show how to compute

$$\beta := \alpha_1^{e_1} \cdots \alpha_k^{e_k}$$

using $\ell + O(1)$ squarings in $\mathbb{Z}_n$ and an additional $O(\ell/\operatorname{len}(\ell))$ multiplications in $\mathbb{Z}_n$. Hint: develop a 2^t-ary version of the algorithm in Exercise 3.27.

EXERCISE 3.30. Let $m_1, \ldots, m_r$ be integers, each greater than 1, and let $m := m_1 \cdots m_r$. Also, for $i = 1, \ldots, r$, define $m_i' := m/m_i$. Given $\alpha \in \mathbb{Z}_n$, show how to compute all of the quantities

$$\alpha^{m_1'}, \ldots, \alpha^{m_r'}$$

using a total of $O(\operatorname{len}(r) \operatorname{len}(m))$ multiplications in $\mathbb{Z}_n$. Hint: divide and conquer.

EXERCISE 3.31. The repeated-squaring algorithm we have presented here processes the bits of the exponent from left to right (i.e., from high order to low order). Develop an algorithm for exponentiation in $\mathbb{Z}_n$ with similar complexity that processes the bits of the exponent from right to left.

3.5 Faster integer arithmetic (∗)

The quadratic-time algorithms presented in §3.3 for integer multiplication and division are by no means the fastest possible. The next exercise develops a faster multiplication algorithm.

EXERCISE 3.32. Suppose we have two positive, ℓ-bit integers a and b such that $a = a_1 2^k + a_0$ and $b = b_1 2^k + b_0$, where $0 \leq a_0 < 2^k$ and $0 \leq b_0 < 2^k$. Then

$$ab = a_1 b_1 2^{2k} + (a_0 b_1 + a_1 b_0) 2^k + a_0 b_0.$$

Show how to compute the product ab in time $O(\ell)$, given the products $a_0 b_0$, $a_1 b_1$, and $(a_0 - a_1)(b_0 - b_1)$. From this, design a recursive algorithm that computes ab in time $O(\ell^{\log_2 3})$. (Note that $\log_2 3 \approx 1.58$.)

The algorithm in the previous is also not the best possible. In fact, it is possible to multiply ℓ-bit integers *on a RAM* in time $O(\ell)$, but we do not explore this any further here (see §3.6).

The following exercises explore the relationship between integer multiplication and related problems. We assume that we have an algorithm that multiplies two integers of at most ℓ bits in time $M(\ell)$. It is convenient (and reasonable) to assume that M is a **well-behaved complexity function**. By this, we mean that M maps positive integers to positive real numbers, and

- for all positive integers a and b, we have $M(a + b) \geq M(a) + M(b)$, and

- for all real $c > 1$ there exists real $d > 1$, such that for all positive integers a and b, if $a \leq cb$, then $M(a) \leq dM(b)$.

EXERCISE 3.33. Let $\alpha > 0$, $\beta \geq 1$, $\gamma \geq 0$, $\delta \geq 0$ be real constants. Show that

$$M(\ell) := \alpha \ell^\beta \operatorname{len}(\ell)^\gamma \operatorname{len}(\operatorname{len}(\ell))^\delta$$

is a well-behaved complexity function.

EXERCISE 3.34. Give an algorithm for Exercise 3.22 that runs in time

$$O(M(\operatorname{len}(n)) \operatorname{len}(k)).$$

Hint: divide and conquer.

EXERCISE 3.35. We can represent a "floating point" number $\hat{z}$ as a pair (a, e), where a and e are integers—the value of $\hat{z}$ is the rational number

$a2^e$, and we call len(a) the **precision** of $\hat{z}$. We say that $\hat{z}$ is a k-**bit approximation** of a real number z if $\hat{z}$ has precision k and $\hat{z} = (1 + \epsilon)z$ for some $|\epsilon| \leq 2^{-k+1}$. Show how to compute — given positive integers b and k — a k-bit approximation of $1/b$ in time $O(M(k))$. Hint: using Newton iteration, show how to go from a t-bit approximation of $1/b$ to a $(2t - 2)$-bit approximation of $1/b$, making use of just the high-order $O(t)$ bits of b, in time $O(M(t))$. **Newton iteration** is a general method of iteratively approximating a root of an equation $f(x) = 0$ by starting with an initial approximation x_0, and computing subsequent approximations by the formula $x_{i+1} = x_i - f(x_i)/f'(x_i)$, where $f'(x)$ is the derivative of $f(x)$. For this exercise, apply Newton iteration to the function $f(x) = x^{-1} - b$.

EXERCISE 3.36. Using the result of the previous exercise, given positive integers a and b of bit length at most ℓ, show how to compute $\lfloor a/b \rfloor$ and $a \bmod b$ in time $O(M(\ell))$. From this, we see that up to a constant factor, division with remainder is no harder that multiplication.

EXERCISE 3.37. Using the result of the previous exercise, give an algorithm for Exercise 3.23 that runs in time $O(M(\mathrm{len}(n)) \, \mathrm{len}(k))$. Hint: divide and conquer.

EXERCISE 3.38. Give an algorithm for Exercise 3.24 that runs in time $O(M(\mathrm{len}(n)))$. Hint: Newton iteration.

EXERCISE 3.39. Give algorithms for Exercise 3.25 that run in time $O(M(\ell) \, \mathrm{len}(\ell))$, where $\ell := \mathrm{len}(n)$. Hint: divide and conquer.

EXERCISE 3.40. Suppose we have an algorithm that computes the square of an ℓ-bit integer in time $S(\ell)$, where S is a well-behaved complexity function. Show how to use this algorithm to compute the product of two arbitrary integers of at most ℓ bits in time $O(S(\ell))$.

3.6 Notes

Shamir [84] shows how to factor an integer in polynomial time on a RAM, but where the numbers stored in the memory cells may have exponentially many bits. As there is no known polynomial-time factoring algorithm on any realistic machine, Shamir's algorithm demonstrates the importance of restricting the sizes of numbers stored in the memory cells of our RAMs to keep our formal model realistic.

The most practical implementations of algorithms for arithmetic on large integers are written in low-level "assembly language," specific to a particular machine's architecture (e.g., the GNU Multi-Precision library GMP, available at www.swox.com/gmp). Besides the general fact that such hand-crafted code is more efficient than that produced by a compiler, there is another, more important reason for using such code. A typical 32-bit machine often comes with instructions that allow one to compute the 64-bit product of two 32-bit integers, and similarly, instructions to divide a 64-bit integer by a 32-bit integer (obtaining both the quotient and remainder). However, high-level programming languages do not (as a rule) provide any access to these low-level instructions. Indeed, we suggested in §3.3 using a value for the base B of about half the word-size of the machine, so as to avoid overflow. However, if one codes in assembly language, one can take B to be much closer to, or even equal to, the word-size of the machine. Since our basic algorithms for multiplication and division run in time quadratic in the number of base-B digits, the effect of doubling the bit-length of B is to decrease the running time of these algorithms by a factor of *four*. This effect, combined with the improvements one might typically expect from using assembly-language code, can easily lead to a five- to ten-fold decrease in the running time, compared to an implementation in a high-level language. This is, of course, a significant improvement for those interested in serious "number crunching."

The "classical," quadratic-time algorithms presented here for integer multiplication and division are by no means the best possible: there are algorithms that are asymptotically faster. We saw this in the algorithm in Exercise 3.32, which was originally invented by Karatsuba [52] (although Karatsuba is one of two authors on this paper, the paper gives exclusive credit for this particular result to Karatsuba). That algorithm allows us to multiply two ℓ-bit integers in time $O(\ell^{\log_2 3})$. The fastest known algorithm for multiplying two ℓ-bit integers on a RAM runs in time $O(\ell)$. This algorithm is due to Schönhage, and actually works on a very restricted type of RAM called a "pointer machine" (see Problem 12, Section 4.3.3 of Knuth [54]). See Exercise 18.27 later in this text for a much simpler (but heuristic) $O(\ell)$ multiplication algorithm.

Another model of computation is that of **Boolean circuits**. In this model of computation, one considers families of Boolean circuits (with, say, the usual "and," "or," and "not" gates) that compute a particular function — for every input length, there is a different circuit in the family that computes the function on inputs of that length. One natural notion of complexity for such circuit families is the **size** of the circuit (i.e., the number of gates and wires in the circuit), which is measured as a function of the input length. The smallest known Boolean circuit that multiplies two ℓ-bit numbers has size $O(\ell \operatorname{len}(\ell) \operatorname{len}(\operatorname{len}(\ell)))$. This result is due to Schönhage and Strassen [82].

It is hard to say which model of computation, the RAM or circuits, is "better." On the one hand, the RAM very naturally models computers as we know them today: one stores small numbers, like array indices, counters, and pointers, in individual words of the machine, and processing such a number typically takes a single "machine cycle." On the other hand, the RAM model, as we formally defined it, invites a certain kind of "cheating," as it allows one to stuff $O(\operatorname{len}(\ell))$-bit integers into memory cells. For example, even with the simple, quadratic-time algorithms for integer arithmetic discussed in §3.3, we can choose the base B to have $\operatorname{len}(\ell)$ bits, in which case these algorithms would run in time $O((\ell / \operatorname{len}(\ell))^2)$. However, just to keep things simple, we have chosen to view B as a constant (from a formal, asymptotic point of view).

In the remainder of this text, unless otherwise specified, we shall always use the classical $O(\ell^2)$ bounds for integer multiplication and division, which have the advantage of being both simple and reasonably reliable predictors of actual performance for small to moderately sized inputs. For relatively large numbers, experience shows that the classical algorithms are definitely not the best—Karatsuba's multiplication algorithm, and related algorithms for division, start to perform significantly better than the classical algorithms on inputs of a thousand bits or so (the exact crossover depends on myriad implementation details). The even "faster" algorithms discussed above are typically not interesting unless the numbers involved are truly huge, of bit length around 10^5–10^6. Thus, the reader should bear in mind that for serious computations involving very large numbers, the faster algorithms are very important, even though this text does not discuss them at great length.

For a good survey of asymptotically fast algorithms for integer arithmetic, see Chapter 9 of Crandall and Pomerance [30], as well as Chapter 4 of Knuth [54].

4

Euclid's algorithm

In this chapter, we discuss Euclid's algorithm for computing greatest common divisors. It turns out that Euclid's algorithm has a number of very nice properties, and has applications far beyond that purpose.

4.1 The basic Euclidean algorithm

We consider the following problem: given two non-negative integers a and b, compute their greatest common divisor, $\gcd(a, b)$. We can do this using the well-known **Euclidean algorithm**, also called **Euclid's algorithm**.

The basic idea of Euclid's algorithm is the following. Without loss of generality, we may assume that $a \geq b \geq 0$. If $b = 0$, then there is nothing to do, since in this case, $\gcd(a, 0) = a$. Otherwise, if $b > 0$, we can compute the integer quotient $q := \lfloor a/b \rfloor$ and remainder $r := a \bmod b$, where $0 \leq r < b$. From the equation

$$a = bq + r,$$

it is easy to see that if an integer d divides both b and r, then it also divides a; likewise, if an integer d divides a and b, then it also divides r. From this observation, it follows that $\gcd(a, b) = \gcd(b, r)$, and so by performing a division, we reduce the problem of computing $\gcd(a, b)$ to the "smaller" problem of computing $\gcd(b, r)$.

The following theorem develops this idea further:

Theorem 4.1. *Let a, b be integers, with $a \geq b \geq 0$. Using the division with remainder property, define the integers $r_0, r_1, \ldots, r_{\ell+1}$, and $q_1, \ldots, q_\ell$, where $\ell \geq 0$, as follows:*

$$a = r_0,$$
$$b = r_1,$$
$$r_0 = r_1 q_1 + r_2 \quad (0 < r_2 < r_1),$$
$$\vdots$$
$$r_{i-1} = r_i q_i + r_{i+1} \quad (0 < r_{i+1} < r_i),$$
$$\vdots$$
$$r_{\ell-2} = r_{\ell-1} q_{\ell-1} + r_\ell \quad (0 < r_\ell < r_{\ell-1}),$$
$$r_{\ell-1} = r_\ell q_\ell \quad (r_{\ell+1} = 0).$$

Note that by definition, $\ell = 0$ if $b = 0$, and $\ell > 0$, otherwise.

Then we have $r_\ell = \gcd(a, b)$. Moreover, if $b > 0$, then $\ell \leq \log b / \log \phi + 1$, where $\phi := (1 + \sqrt{5})/2 \approx 1.62$.

Proof. For the first statement, one sees that for $i = 1, \ldots, \ell$, we have $r_{i-1} = r_i q_i + r_{i+1}$, from which it follows that the common divisors of r_{i-1} and r_i are the same as the common divisors of r_i and r_{i+1}, and hence $\gcd(r_{i-1}, r_i) = \gcd(r_i, r_{i+1})$. From this, it follows that

$$\gcd(a, b) = \gcd(r_0, r_1) = \gcd(r_\ell, r_{\ell+1}) = \gcd(r_\ell, 0) = r_\ell.$$

To prove the second statement, assume that $b > 0$, and hence $\ell > 0$. If $\ell = 1$, the statement is obviously true, so assume $\ell > 1$. We claim that for $i = 0, \ldots, \ell - 1$, we have $r_{\ell-i} \geq \phi^i$. The statement will then follow by setting $i = \ell - 1$ and taking logarithms.

We now prove the above claim. For $i = 0$ and $i = 1$, we have

$$r_\ell \geq 1 = \phi^0 \quad \text{and} \quad r_{\ell-1} \geq r_\ell + 1 \geq 2 \geq \phi^1.$$

For $i = 2, \ldots, \ell - 1$, using induction and applying the fact the $\phi^2 = \phi + 1$, we have

$$r_{\ell-i} \geq r_{\ell-(i-1)} + r_{\ell-(i-2)} \geq \phi^{i-1} + \phi^{i-2} = \phi^{i-2}(1 + \phi) = \phi^i,$$

which proves the claim. $\square$

Example 4.1. Suppose $a = 100$ and $b = 35$. Then the numbers appearing in Theorem 4.1 are easily computed as follows:

i	0	1	2	3	4
r_i	100	35	30	5	0
q_i			2	1	6

So we have $\gcd(a, b) = r_3 = 5$. $\Box$

We can easily turn the scheme described in Theorem 4.1 into a simple algorithm, taking as input integers a, b, such that $a \geq b \geq 0$, and producing as output $d = \gcd(a, b)$:

$r \leftarrow a, \ r' \leftarrow b$
while $r' \neq 0$ do
$\quad r'' \leftarrow r \bmod r'$
$\quad (r, r') \leftarrow (r', r'')$
$d \leftarrow r$
output d

We now consider the running time of Euclid's algorithm. Naively, one could estimate this as follows. Suppose a and b are k-bit numbers. The algorithm performs $O(k)$ divisions on numbers with at most k-bits. As each such division takes time $O(k^2)$, this leads to a bound on the running time of $O(k^3)$. However, as the following theorem shows, this cubic running time bound is well off the mark.

Theorem 4.2. *Euclid's algorithm runs in time $O(\mathrm{len}(a)\,\mathrm{len}(b))$.*

Proof. We may assume that $b > 0$. The running time is $O(\tau)$, where $\tau := \sum_{i=1}^{\ell} \mathrm{len}(r_i)\,\mathrm{len}(q_i)$. Since $r_i \leq b$ for $i = 1, \ldots, \ell$, we have

$$\tau \leq \mathrm{len}(b) \sum_{i=1}^{\ell} \mathrm{len}(q_i) \leq \mathrm{len}(b) \sum_{i=1}^{\ell} (\log_2 q_i + 1) = \mathrm{len}(b)(\ell + \log_2(\prod_{i=1}^{\ell} q_i)).$$

Note that

$$a = r_0 \geq r_1 q_1 \geq r_2 q_2 q_1 \geq \cdots \geq r_\ell q_\ell \cdots q_1 \geq q_\ell \cdots q_1.$$

We also have $\ell \leq \log b / \log \phi + 1$. Combining this with the above, we have

$$\tau \leq \mathrm{len}(b)(\log b / \log \phi + 1 + \log_2 a) = O(\mathrm{len}(a)\,\mathrm{len}(b)),$$

which proves the theorem. $\Box$

EXERCISE 4.1. This exercise looks at an alternative algorithm for computing $\gcd(a, b)$, called the **binary gcd algorithm**. This algorithm avoids complex operations, such as division and multiplication; instead, it relies only on division and multiplication by powers of 2, which assuming a binary representation of integers (as we are) can be very efficiently implemented using "right shift" and "left shift" operations. The algorithm takes positive integers a and b as input, and runs as follows:

$r \leftarrow a, \ r' \leftarrow b, \ e \leftarrow 0$
while $2 \mid r$ and $2 \mid r'$ do $r \leftarrow r/2, \ r' \leftarrow r'/2, \ e \leftarrow e+1$
repeat
      while $2 \mid r$ do $r \leftarrow r/2$
      while $2 \mid r'$ do $r' \leftarrow r'/2$
      if $r' < r$ then $(r, r') \leftarrow (r', r)$
      $r' \leftarrow r' - r$
until $r' = 0$
$d \leftarrow 2^e \cdot r$
output d

Show that this algorithm correctly computes $\gcd(a, b)$, and runs in time $O(\ell^2)$, where $\ell := \max(\operatorname{len}(a), \operatorname{len}(b))$.

4.2 The extended Euclidean algorithm

Let a and b be non-negative integers, and let $d := \gcd(a, b)$. We know by Theorem 1.6 that there exist integers s and t such that $as + bt = d$. The **extended Euclidean algorithm** allows us to efficiently compute s and t. The following theorem describes the algorithm, and also states a number of important facts about the relative sizes of the numbers that arise during the computation—these size estimates will play a crucial role, both in the analysis of the running time of the algorithm, as well as in applications of the algorithm that we will discuss later.

Theorem 4.3. *Let a, b, $r_0, r_1, \ldots, r_{\ell+1}$ and $q_1, \ldots, q_\ell$ be as in Theorem 4.1. Define integers $s_0, s_1, \ldots, s_{\ell+1}$ and $t_0, t_1, \ldots, t_{\ell+1}$ as follows:*

$$s_0 := 1, \quad t_0 := 0,$$
$$s_1 := 0, \quad t_1 := 1,$$

and for $i = 1, \ldots, \ell$,

$$s_{i+1} := s_{i-1} - s_i q_i, \quad t_{i+1} := t_{i-1} - t_i q_i.$$

Then

(i) *for $i = 0, \ldots, \ell+1$, we have $s_i a + t_i b = r_i$; in particular, $s_\ell a + t_\ell b = \gcd(a, b)$;*

(ii) *for $i = 0, \ldots, \ell$, we have $s_i t_{i+1} - t_i s_{i+1} = (-1)^i$;*

(iii) *for $i = 0, \ldots, \ell+1$, we have $\gcd(s_i, t_i) = 1$;*

(iv) *for $i = 0, \ldots, \ell$, we have $t_i t_{i+1} \le 0$ and $|t_i| \le |t_{i+1}|$; for $i = 1, \ldots, \ell$, we have $s_i s_{i+1} \le 0$ and $|s_i| \le |s_{i+1}|$;*

(v) *for $i = 1, \ldots, \ell+1$, we have $r_{i-1}|t_i| \le a$ and $r_{i-1}|s_i| \le b$.*

Proof. (i) is easily proved by induction on i. For $i = 0, 1$, the statement is clear. For $i = 2, \ldots, \ell + 1$, we have

$$
\begin{aligned}
s_i a + t_i b &= (s_{i-2} - s_{i-1} q_{i-1}) a + (t_{i-2} - t_{i-1} q_{i-1}) b \\
&= (s_{i-2} a + t_{i-2} b) - (s_{i-1} a + t_{i-1} b) q_i \\
&= r_{i-2} - r_{i-1} q_{i-1} \quad \text{(by induction)} \\
&= r_i.
\end{aligned}
$$

(ii) is also easily proved by induction on i. For $i = 0$, the statement is clear. For $i = 1, \ldots, \ell$, we have

$$
\begin{aligned}
s_i t_{i+1} - t_i s_{i+1} &= s_i (t_{i-1} - t_i q_i) - t_i (s_{i-1} - s_i q_i) \\
&= -(s_{i-1} t_i - t_{i-1} s_i) \quad \text{(after expanding and simplifying)} \\
&= -(-1)^{i-1} = (-1)^i \quad \text{(by induction)}.
\end{aligned}
$$

(iii) follows directly from (ii).

For (iv), one can easily prove both statements by induction on i. The statement involving the t_i is clearly true for $i = 0$; for $i = 1, \ldots, \ell$, we have $t_{i+1} = t_{i-1} - t_i q_i$, and since by the induction hypothesis t_{i-1} and t_i have opposite signs and $|t_i| \geq |t_{i-1}|$, it follows that $|t_{i+1}| = |t_{i-1}| + |t_i| q_i \geq |t_i|$, and that the sign of t_{i+1} is the opposite of that of t_i. The proof of the statement involving the s_i is the same, except that we start the induction at $i = 1$.

For (v), one considers the two equations:

$$
\begin{aligned}
s_{i-1} a + t_{i-1} b &= r_{i-1}, \\
s_i a + t_i b &= r_i.
\end{aligned}
$$

Subtracting t_{i-1} times the second equation from t_i times the first, applying (ii), and using the fact that t_i and t_{i-1} have opposite sign, we obtain

$$
a = |t_i r_{i-1} - t_{i-1} r_i| \geq |t_i| r_{i-1},
$$

from which the inequality involving t_i follows. The inequality involving s_i follows similarly, subtracting s_{i-1} times the second equation from s_i times the first. $\square$

Suppose that $a > 0$ in the above theorem. Then for $i = 1, \ldots, \ell + 1$, the value r_{i-1} is a positive integer, and so part (v) of the theorem implies that $|t_i| \leq a/r_{i-1} \leq a$ and $|s_i| \leq b/r_{i-1} \leq b$. Moreover, if $a > 1$ and $b > 0$, then $\ell > 0$ and $r_{\ell-1} \geq 2$, and hence $|t_\ell| \leq a/2$ and $|s_\ell| \leq b/2$.

***Example* 4.2.** We continue with Example 4.1. The numbers s_i and t_i are easily computed from the q_i:

i	0	1	2	3	4
r_i	100	35	30	5	0
q_i		2	1	6	
s_i	1	0	1	-1	7
t_i	0	1	-2	3	-20

So we have $\gcd(a, b) = 5 = -a + 3b$. $\square$

We can easily turn the scheme described in Theorem 4.3 into a simple algorithm, taking as input integers a, b, such that $a \geq b \geq 0$, and producing as output integers d, s, and t, such that $d = \gcd(a, b)$ and $as + bt = d$:

$$r \leftarrow a, \ r' \leftarrow b$$
$$s \leftarrow 1, \ s' \leftarrow 0$$
$$t \leftarrow 0, \ t' \leftarrow 1$$
while $r' \neq 0$ do
$$q \leftarrow \lfloor r/r' \rfloor, \ r'' \leftarrow r \bmod r'$$
$$(r, s, t, r', s', t') \leftarrow (r', s', t', r'', s - s'q, t - t'q)$$
$$d \leftarrow r$$
output d, s, t

Theorem 4.4. *The extended Euclidean algorithm runs in time*

$$O(\operatorname{len}(a) \operatorname{len}(b)).$$

Proof. We may assume that $b > 0$. It suffices to analyze the cost of computing the sequences $\{s_i\}$ and $\{t_i\}$. Consider first the cost of computing all of the t_i, which is $O(\tau)$, where $\tau := \sum_{i=1}^{\ell} \operatorname{len}(t_i) \operatorname{len}(q_i)$. We have $t_1 = 1$ and, by part (v) of Theorem 4.3, we have $|t_i| \leq a$ for $i = 2, \ldots, \ell$. Arguing as in the proof of Theorem 4.2, we have

$$\tau \leq \operatorname{len}(q_1) + \operatorname{len}(a) \sum_{i=2}^{\ell} \operatorname{len}(q_i) \leq \operatorname{len}(q_1) + \operatorname{len}(a)(\ell - 1 + \log_2(\prod_{i=2}^{\ell} q_i))$$
$$= O(\operatorname{len}(a) \operatorname{len}(b)),$$

where we have used the fact that $\prod_{i=2}^{\ell} q_i \leq b$. An analogous argument shows that one can also compute all of the s_i in time $O(\operatorname{len}(a) \operatorname{len}(b))$, and in fact, in time $O(\operatorname{len}(b)^2)$. $\square$

Another, instructive way to view Theorem 4.3 is as follows. For $i = 1, \ldots, \ell$, we have

$$\begin{pmatrix} r_i \\ r_{i+1} \end{pmatrix} = \begin{pmatrix} 0 & 1 \\ 1 & -q_i \end{pmatrix} \begin{pmatrix} r_{i-1} \\ r_i \end{pmatrix}.$$

Recursively expanding the right-hand side of this equation, we have for $i = 0, \ldots, \ell$,

$$\begin{pmatrix} r_i \\ r_{i+1} \end{pmatrix} = M_i \begin{pmatrix} a \\ b \end{pmatrix},$$

where for $i = 1, \ldots, \ell$, the matrix M_i is defined as

$$M_i := \begin{pmatrix} 0 & 1 \\ 1 & -q_i \end{pmatrix} \cdots \begin{pmatrix} 0 & 1 \\ 1 & -q_1 \end{pmatrix}.$$

If we define M_0 to be the 2×2 identity matrix, then it is easy to see that

$$M_i = \begin{pmatrix} s_i & t_i \\ s_{i+1} & t_{i+1} \end{pmatrix},$$

for $i = 0, \ldots, \ell$. From this observation, part (i) of Theorem 4.3 is immediate, and part (ii) follows from the fact that M_i is the product of i matrices, each of determinant -1, and the determinant of M_i is evidently $s_i t_{i+1} - t_i s_{i+1}$.

EXERCISE 4.2. One can extend the binary gcd algorithm discussed in Exercise 4.1 so that in addition to computing $d = \gcd(a, b)$, it also computes s and t such that $as + bt = d$. Here is one way to do this (again, we assume that a and b are positive integers):

> $r \leftarrow a, \; r' \leftarrow b, \; e \leftarrow 0$
> while $2 \mid r$ and $2 \mid r'$ do $r \leftarrow r/2, \; r' \leftarrow r'/2, \; e \leftarrow e + 1$
> $\tilde{a} \leftarrow r, \; \tilde{b} \leftarrow r', \; s \leftarrow 1, \; t \leftarrow 0, \; s' \leftarrow 0, \; t' \leftarrow 1$
> repeat
> > while $2 \mid r$ do
> > > $r \leftarrow r/2$
> > > if $2 \mid s$ and $2 \mid t$ then $s \leftarrow s/2, \; t \leftarrow t/2$
> > >   else $s \leftarrow (s + \tilde{b})/2, \; t \leftarrow (t - \tilde{a})/2$
> >
> > while $2 \mid r'$ do
> > > $r' \leftarrow r'/2$
> > > if $2 \mid s'$ and $2 \mid t'$ then $s' \leftarrow s'/2, \; t' \leftarrow t'/2$
> > >   else $s' \leftarrow (s' + \tilde{b})/2, \; t' \leftarrow (t' - \tilde{a})/2$
> >
> > if $r' < r$ then $(r, s, t, r', s', t') \leftarrow (r', s', t', r, s, t)$
> > $r' \leftarrow r' - r, \; s' \leftarrow s' - s, \; t' \leftarrow t' - t$
> until $r' = 0$
> $d \leftarrow 2^e \cdot r$,   output d, s, t

Show that this algorithm is correct and runs in time $O(\ell^2)$, where $\ell := \max(\mathrm{len}(a), \mathrm{len}(b))$. In particular, you should verify that all of the divisions by 2 performed by the algorithm yield integer results. Moreover, show that the outputs s and t are of length $O(\ell)$.

4.3 Computing modular inverses and Chinese remaindering

One application of the extended Euclidean algorithm is to the problem of computing multiplicative inverses in $\mathbb{Z}_n$, where $n > 1$.

Given $y \in \{0, \ldots, n-1\}$, in time $O(\operatorname{len}(n)^2)$, we can determine if y is relatively prime to n, and if so, compute $y^{-1} \bmod n$, as follows. We run the extended Euclidean algorithm on inputs $a := n$ and $b := y$, obtaining integers d, s, and t, such that $d = \gcd(n, y)$ and $ns + yt = d$. If $d \neq 1$, then y does not have a multiplicative inverse modulo n. Otherwise, if $d = 1$, then t is a multiplicative inverse of y modulo n; however, it may not lie in the range $\{0, \ldots, n-1\}$, as required. Based on Theorem 4.3 (and the discussion immediately following it), we know that $|t| \leq n/2 < n$; therefore, either $t \in \{0, \ldots, n-1\}$, or $t < 0$ and $t + n \in \{0, \ldots, n-1\}$. Thus, $y^{-1} \bmod n$ is equal to either t or $t + n$.

We also observe that the Chinese remainder theorem (Theorem 2.8) can be made computationally effective:

Theorem 4.5. *Given integers $n_1, \ldots, n_k$ and $a_1, \ldots, a_k$, where $n_1, \ldots, n_k$ are pairwise relatively prime, and where $n_i > 1$ and $0 \leq a_i < n_i$ for $i = 1, \ldots, k$, we can compute the integer z, such that $0 \leq z < n$ and $z \equiv a_i \pmod{n_i}$ for $i = 1, \ldots, k$, where $n := \prod_i n_i$, in time $O(\operatorname{len}(n)^2)$.*

Proof. Exercise (just use the formulas in the proof of Theorem 2.8, and see Exercises 3.22 and 3.23). $\square$

EXERCISE 4.3. In this exercise and the next, you are to analyze an "incremental Chinese remaindering algorithm." Consider the following algorithm, which takes as input integers z, n, z', n', such that

$$n' > 1, \quad \gcd(n, n') = 1, \quad 0 \leq z < n, \quad \text{and} \quad 0 \leq z' < n'.$$

It outputs integers z'', n'', such that

$$n'' = nn', \quad 0 \leq z'' < n'', \quad z'' \equiv z \pmod{n}, \quad \text{and} \quad z'' \equiv z' \pmod{n'}.$$

It runs as follows:

    1. Set $\tilde{n} \leftarrow n^{-1} \bmod n'$.

    2. Set $h \leftarrow ((z' - z)\tilde{n}) \bmod n'$.

3. Set $z'' \leftarrow z + nh$.

4. Set $n'' \leftarrow nn'$.

5. Output z'', n''.

Show that the output z'', n'' of the algorithm satisfies the conditions stated above, and estimate the running time of the algorithm.

EXERCISE 4.4. Using the algorithm in the previous exercise as a subroutine, give a simple $O(\operatorname{len}(n)^2)$ algorithm that takes as input integers $n_1, \ldots, n_k$ and $a_1, \ldots, a_k$, where $n_1, \ldots, n_k$ are pairwise relatively prime, and where $n_i > 1$ and $0 \le a_i < n_i$ for $i = 1, \ldots, k$, and outputs integers z and n such that $0 \le z < n$, $n = \prod_i n_i$, and $z \equiv a_i \pmod{n_i}$ for $i = 1, \ldots, k$. The algorithm should be "incremental," in that it processes the pairs (n_i, a_i) one at a time, using time $O(\operatorname{len}(n) \operatorname{len}(n_i))$ to process each such pair.

EXERCISE 4.5. Suppose you are given $\alpha_1, \ldots, \alpha_k \in \mathbb{Z}_n^*$. Show how to compute $\alpha_1^{-1}, \ldots, \alpha_k^{-1}$ by computing *one* multiplicative inverse modulo n, and performing less than $3k$ multiplications modulo n. This result is useful, as in practice, if n is several hundred bits long, it may take 10–20 times longer to compute multiplicative inverses modulo n than to multiply modulo n.

4.4 Speeding up algorithms via modular computation

An important practical application of the above "computational" version (Theorem 4.5) of the Chinese remainder theorem is a general algorithmic technique that can significantly speed up certain types of computations involving long integers. Instead of trying to describe the technique in some general form, we simply illustrate the technique by means of a specific example: integer matrix multiplication.

Suppose we have two $m \times m$ matrices A and B whose entries are large integers, and we want to compute the product matrix $C := AB$. If the entries of A are (a_{rs}) and the entries of B are (b_{st}), then the entries (c_{rt}) of C are given by the usual rule for matrix multiplication:

$$c_{rt} = \sum_{s=1}^{m} a_{rs} b_{st}.$$

Suppose further that H is the maximum absolute value of the entries in A and B, so that the entries in C are bounded in absolute value by $H' := H^2 m$. Then by just applying the above formula, we can compute the entries of C using m^3 multiplications of numbers of length at most $\operatorname{len}(H)$, and m^3 additions of numbers of length at most $\operatorname{len}(H')$, where

$\mathrm{len}(H') \le 2\,\mathrm{len}(H) + \mathrm{len}(m)$. This yields a running time of

$$O(m^3 \,\mathrm{len}(H)^2 + m^3 \,\mathrm{len}(m)). \tag{4.1}$$

If the entries of A and B are large relative to m, specifically, if $\mathrm{len}(m) = O(\mathrm{len}(H)^2)$, then the running time is dominated by the first term above, namely

$$O(m^3 \,\mathrm{len}(H)^2).$$

Using the Chinese remainder theorem, we can actually do much better than this, as follows.

For any integer $n > 1$, and for all $r, t = 1, \ldots, m$, we have

$$c_{rt} \equiv \sum_{s=1}^{m} a_{rs} b_{st} \pmod{n}. \tag{4.2}$$

Moreover, if we compute integers c'_{rt} such that

$$c'_{rt} \equiv \sum_{s=1}^{m} a_{rs} b_{st} \pmod{n} \tag{4.3}$$

and if we also have

$$-n/2 \le c'_{rt} < n/2 \quad \text{and} \quad n > 2H', \tag{4.4}$$

then we must have

$$c_{rt} = c'_{rt}. \tag{4.5}$$

To see why (4.5) follows from (4.3) and (4.4), observe that (4.2) and (4.3) imply that $c_{rt} \equiv c'_{rt} \pmod{n}$, which means that n divides $(c_{rt} - c'_{rt})$. Then from the bound $|c_{rt}| \le H'$ and from (4.4), we obtain

$$|c_{rt} - c'_{rt}| \le |c_{rt}| + |c'_{rt}| \le H' + n/2 < n/2 + n/2 = n.$$

So we see that the quantity $(c_{rt} - c'_{rt})$ is a multiple of n, while at the same time this quantity is strictly less than n in absolute value; hence, this quantity must be zero. That proves (4.5).

So from the above discussion, to compute C, it suffices to compute the entries of C modulo n, where we have to make sure that we compute "balanced" remainders in the interval $[-n/2, n/2)$, rather than the more usual "least non-negative" remainders.

To compute C modulo n, we choose a number of small integers $n_1, \ldots, n_k$, relatively prime in pairs, and such that the product $n := n_1 \cdots n_k$ is just a bit larger than $2H'$. In practice, one would choose the n_i to be small primes, and a table of such primes could easily be computed in advance, so that all problems up to a given size could be handled. For example, the product of all primes of at most 16 bits is a number that has more than $90,000$ bits. Thus, by simply pre-computing and storing such a table of small primes, we can handle input matrices with quite large entries (up to about $45,000$ bits).

Let us assume that we have pre-computed appropriate small primes $n_1, \ldots, n_k$. Further, we shall assume that addition and multiplication modulo any of the n_i can be done in *constant* time. This is reasonable, both from a practical and theoretical point of view, since such primes easily "fit" into a memory cell. Finally, we assume that we do not use more of the numbers n_i than are necessary, so that $\text{len}(n) = O(\text{len}(H'))$ and $k = O(\text{len}(H'))$.

To compute C, we execute the following steps:

1. For each $i = 1, \ldots, k$, do the following:

   (a) compute $\hat{a}_{rs}^{(i)} \leftarrow a_{rs} \bmod n_i$ for $r, s = 1, \ldots, m$,

   (b) compute $\hat{b}_{st}^{(i)} \leftarrow b_{st} \bmod n_i$ for $s, t = 1, \ldots, m$,

   (c) For $r, t = 1, \ldots, m$, compute

   $$\hat{c}_{rt}^{(i)} \leftarrow \sum_{s=1}^{m} \hat{a}_{rs}^{(i)} \hat{b}_{st}^{(i)} \bmod n_i.$$

2. For each $r, t = 1, \ldots, m$, apply the Chinese remainder theorem to $\hat{c}_{rt}^{(1)}, \hat{c}_{rt}^{(2)}, \ldots, \hat{c}_{rt}^{(k)}$, obtaining an integer c_{rt}, which should be computed as a balanced remainder modulo n, so that $n/2 \le c_{rt} < n/2$.

3. Output $(c_{rt} : r, t = 1, \ldots, m)$.

Note that in Step 2, if our Chinese remainder algorithm happens to be implemented to return an integer z with $0 \le z < n$, we can easily get a balanced remainder by just subtracting n from z if $z \ge n/2$.

The correctness of the above algorithm has already been established. Let us now analyze its running time. The running time of Steps 1a and 1b is easily seen (see Exercise 3.23) to be $O(m^2 \text{len}(H')^2)$. Under our assumption about the cost of arithmetic modulo small primes, the cost of Step 1c is $O(m^3 k)$, and since $k = O(\text{len}(H')) = O(\text{len}(H) + \text{len}(m))$, the cost of this step is $O(m^3 (\text{len}(H) + \text{len}(m)))$. Finally, by Theorem 4.5, the cost of Step 2 is $O(m^2 \text{len}(H')^2)$. Thus, the total running time of this algorithm is easily calculated (discarding terms that are dominated by others) as

$$O(m^2 \text{len}(H)^2 + m^3 \text{len}(H) + m^3 \text{len}(m)).$$

Compared to (4.1), we have essentially replaced the term $m^3 \text{len}(H)^2$ by $m^2 \text{len}(H)^2 + m^3 \text{len}(H)$. This is a significant improvement: for example, if $\operatorname{len}(H) \approx m$, then the running time of the original algorithm is $O(m^5)$, while the running time of the modular algorithm is $O(m^4)$.

EXERCISE 4.6. Apply the ideas above to the problem of computing the product of two polynomials whose coefficients are large integers. First, determine the running time of the "obvious" algorithm for multiplying two such polynomials, then design and analyze a "modular" algorithm.

4.5 Rational reconstruction and applications

We next state a theorem whose immediate utility may not be entirely obvious, but we quickly follow up with several very neat applications. The general problem we consider here, called **rational reconstruction**, is as follows. Suppose that there is some rational number $\hat{y}$ that we would like to get our hands on, but the only information we have about $\hat{y}$ is the following:

- First, suppose that we know that $\hat{y}$ may be expressed as r/t for integers r, t, with $|r| \leq r^*$ and $|t| \leq t^*$ —we do not know r or t, but we do know the bounds r^* and t^*.

- Second, suppose that we know integers y and n such that n is relatively prime to t, and $y = rt^{-1} \bmod n$.

It turns out that if n is sufficiently large relative to the bounds r^* and t^*, then we can virtually "pluck" $\hat{y}$ out of the extended Euclidean algorithm applied to n and y. Moreover, the restriction that n is relatively prime to t is not really necessary; if we drop this restriction, then our assumption is that $r \equiv ty \pmod{n}$, or equivalently, $r = sn + ty$ for some integer s.

Theorem 4.6. *Let r^*, t^*, n, y be integers such that $r^* > 0$, $t^* > 0$, $n \geq 4r^*t^*$, and $0 \leq y < n$. Suppose we run the extended Euclidean algorithm with inputs $a := n$ and $b := y$. Then, adopting the notation of Theorem 4.3, the following hold:*

(i) *There exists a unique index $i = 1, \ldots, \ell+1$ such that $r_i \leq 2r^* < r_{i-1}$; note that $t_i \neq 0$ for this i.*

Let $r' := r_i$, $s' := s_i$, and $t' := t_i$.

(ii) *Furthermore, for any integers r, s, t such that*

$$r = sn + ty, \quad |r| \leq r^*, \quad and \quad 0 < |t| \leq t^*, \tag{4.6}$$

we have

$$r = r'\alpha, \quad s = s'\alpha, \quad and \quad t = t'\alpha,$$

for some non-zero integer α.

Proof. By hypothesis, $2r^* < n = r_0$. Moreover, since $r_0, \dots, r_\ell, r_{\ell+1} = 0$ is a decreasing sequence, and $1 = |t_1|, |t_2|, \dots, |t_{\ell+1}|$ is a non-decreasing sequence, the first statement of the theorem is clear.

Now let i be defined as in the first statement of the theorem. Also, let r, s, t be as in (4.6).

From part (v) of Theorem 4.3 and the inequality $2r^* < r_{i-1}$, we have

$$|t_i| \leq \frac{n}{r_{i-1}} < \frac{n}{2r^*}.$$

From the equalities $r_i = s_i n + t_i y$ and $r = sn + ty$, we have the two congruences:

$$r \equiv ty \pmod{n},$$
$$r_i \equiv t_i y \pmod{n}.$$

Subtracting t_i times the first from t times the second, we obtain

$$rt_i \equiv r_i t \pmod{n}.$$

This says that n divides $rt_i - r_i t$. Using the bounds $|r| \leq r^*$ and $|t_i| < n/(2r^*)$, we see that $|rt_i| < n/2$, and using the bounds $|r_i| \leq 2r^*$, $|t| \leq t^*$, and $4r^* t^* \leq n$, we see that $|r_i t| \leq n/2$. It follows that

$$|rt_i - r_i t| \leq |rt_i| + |r_i t| < n/2 + n/2 = n.$$

Since n divides $rt_i - r_i t$ and $|rt_i - r_i t| < n$, the only possibility is that

$$rt_i - r_i t = 0. \tag{4.7}$$

Now consider the two equations:

$$r = sn + ty$$
$$r_i = s_i n + t_i y.$$

Subtracting t_i times the first from t times the second, and using the identity (4.7), we obtain $n(st_i - s_i t) = 0$, and hence

$$st_i - s_i t = 0. \tag{4.8}$$

From (4.8), we see that $t_i \mid s_i t$, and since from part (iii) of Theorem 4.3, we know that $\gcd(s_i, t_i) = 1$, we must have $t_i \mid t$. So $t = t_i \alpha$ for some α, and we must have $\alpha \neq 0$ since $t \neq 0$. Substituting $t_i \alpha$ for t in equations (4.7) and (4.8) yields $r = r_i \alpha$ and $s = s_i \alpha$. That proves the second statement of the theorem. $\square$

4.5.1 Application: Chinese remaindering with errors

One interpretation of the Chinese remainder theorem is that if we "encode" an integer z, with $0 \le z < n$, as the sequence $(a_1, \dots, a_k)$, where $a_i = z \bmod n_i$ for $i = 1, \dots, k$, then we can efficiently recover z from this encoding. Here, of course, $n = n_1 \cdots n_k$, and the integers $n_1, \dots, n_k$ are pairwise relatively prime.

But now suppose that Alice encodes z as $(a_1, \dots, a_k)$, and sends this encoding to Bob; however, during the transmission of the encoding, some (but hopefully not too many) of the values $a_1, \dots, a_k$ may be corrupted. The question is, can Bob still efficiently recover the original z from its corrupted encoding?

To make the problem more precise, suppose that the original, correct encoding of z is $(a_1, \dots, a_k)$, and the corrupted encoding is $(\tilde{a}_1, \dots, \tilde{a}_k)$. Let us define $G \subseteq \{1, \dots, k\}$ to be the set of "good" positions i with $\tilde{a}_i = a_i$, and $B \subseteq \{1, \dots, k\}$ to be the set of "bad" positions i with $\tilde{a}_i \ne a_i$. We shall assume that $|B| \le \ell$, where ℓ is some specified parameter.

Of course, if Bob hopes to recover z, we need to build some redundancy into the system; that is, we must require that $0 \le z \le Z$ for some Z that is somewhat smaller than n. Now, if Bob knew the location of bad positions, and if the product of the integers n_i at the good positions exceeds Z, then Bob could simply discard the errors, and reconstruct z by applying the Chinese remainder theorem to the values a_i and n_i at the good positions. However, in general, Bob will not know a priori the location of the bad positions, and so this approach will not work.

Despite these apparent difficulties, Theorem 4.6 may be used to solve the problem quite easily, as follows. Let P be an upper bound on the product of any ℓ of the integers $n_1, \dots, n_k$ (e.g., we could take P to be the product of the ℓ largest n_i). Further, let us assume that $n \ge 4P^2 Z$.

Now, suppose Bob obtains the corrupted encoding $(\tilde{a}_1, \dots, \tilde{a}_k)$. Here is what Bob does to recover z:

1. Apply the Chinese remainder theorem, obtaining an integer y, with $0 \le y < n$ and $y \equiv \tilde{a}_i \pmod{n_i}$ for $i = 1, \dots, k$.

2. Run the extended Euclidean algorithm on $a := n$ and $b := y$, and let r', t' be the values obtained from Theorem 4.6 applied with $r^* := ZP$ and $t^* := P$.

3. If $t' \mid r'$, output r'/t'; otherwise, output "error."

We claim that the above procedure outputs z, under our assumption that the set B of bad positions is of size at most ℓ. To see this, let $t := \prod_{i \in B} n_i$. By construction, we have $1 \le t \le P$. Also, let $r := tz$, and note that

$0 \le r \le r^*$ and $0 < t \le t^*$. We claim that

$$r \equiv ty \pmod{n}. \tag{4.9}$$

To show that (4.9) holds, it suffices to show that

$$tz \equiv ty \pmod{n_i} \tag{4.10}$$

for all $i = 1, \dots, k$. To show this, for each index i we consider two cases:

Case 1: $i \in G$. In this case, we have $a_i = \tilde{a}_i$, and therefore,

$$tz \equiv ta_i \equiv t\tilde{a}_i \equiv ty \pmod{n_i}.$$

Case 2: $i \in B$. In this case, we have $n_i \mid t$, and therefore,

$$tz \equiv 0 \equiv ty \pmod{n_i}.$$

Thus, (4.10) holds for all $i = 1, \dots, k$, and so it follows that (4.9) holds. Therefore, the values r', t' obtained from Theorem 4.6 satisfy

$$\frac{r'}{t'} = \frac{r}{t} = \frac{tz}{t} = z.$$

One easily checks that both the procedures to encode and decode a value z run in time $O(\mathrm{len}(n)^2)$. If one wanted a practical implementation, one might choose $n_1, \dots, n_k$ to be, say, 16-bit primes, so that the encoding of a value z consisted of a sequence of k 16-bit words.

The above scheme is an example of an **error correcting code**, and is actually the integer analog of a **Reed–Solomon code**.

4.5.2 Application: recovering fractions from their decimal expansions

Suppose Alice knows a rational number $z := s/t$, where s and t are integers with $0 \le s < t$, and tells Bob some of the high-order digits in the decimal expansion of z. Can Bob determine z? The answer is yes, provided Bob knows an upper bound T on t, and provided Alice gives Bob enough digits. Of course, from grade school, Bob probably remembers that the decimal expansion of z is ultimately periodic, and that given enough digits of z so as to include the periodic part, he can recover z; however, this technique is quite useless in practice, as the length of the period can be huge—$\Theta(T)$ in the worst case (see Exercises 4.8–4.10 below). The method we discuss here requires only $O(\mathrm{len}(T))$ digits.

To be a bit more general, suppose that Alice gives Bob the high-order k

digits in the d-ary expansion of z, for some base $d > 1$. Now, we can express z in base d as

$$z = z_1 d^{-1} + z_2 d^{-2} + z_3 d^{-3} + \cdots ,$$

and the sequence of digits $z_1, z_2, z_3, \ldots$ is uniquely determined if we require that the sequence does not terminate with an infinite run of $(d-1)$-digits. Suppose Alice gives Bob the first k digits $z_1, \ldots, z_k$. Define

$$y := z_1 d^{k-1} + \cdots + z_{k-1} d + z_k = \lfloor z d^k \rfloor .$$

Let us also define $n := d^k$, so that $y = \lfloor zn \rfloor$.

Now, if n is much smaller than T^2, the number z is not even uniquely determined by y, since there are $\Omega(T^2)$ distinct rational numbers of the form s/t, with $0 \le s < t \le T$ (see Exercise 1.18). However, if $n \ge 4T^2$, then not only is z uniquely determined by y, but using Theorem 4.6, we can compute it as follows:

1. Run the extended Euclidean algorithm on inputs $a := n$ and $b := y$, and let s', t' be as in Theorem 4.6, using $r^* := t^* := T$.

2. Output s', t'.

We claim that $z = -s'/t'$. To prove this, observe that since $y = \lfloor zn \rfloor = \lfloor (ns)/t \rfloor$, if we set $r := (ns) \bmod t$, then we have

$$r = sn - ty \quad \text{and} \quad 0 \le r < t \le t^* .$$

It follows that the integers s', t' from Theorem 4.6 satisfy $s = s'\alpha$ and $-t = t'\alpha$ for some non-zero integer α. Thus, $s'/t' = -s/t$, which proves the claim.

We may further observe that since the extended Euclidean algorithm guarantees that $\gcd(s', t') = 1$, not only do we obtain z, but we obtain z expressed as a fraction in lowest terms.

It is clear that the running time of this algorithm is $O(\text{len}(n)^2)$.

***Example* 4.3.** Alice chooses numbers $0 \le s < t \le 1000$, and tells Bob the high-order seven digits y in the decimal expansion of $z := s/t$, from which Bob should be able to compute z. Suppose $s = 511$ and $t = 710$. Then $s/t \approx 0.71971830985915492958$, and so $y = 7197183$ and $n = 10^7$. Running the extended Euclidean algorithm on inputs $a := n$ and $b := y$, Bob obtains the following data:

i	r_i	q_i	s_i	t_i
0	10000000		1	0
1	7197183	1	0	1
2	2802817	2	1	-1
3	1591549	1	-2	3
4	1211268	1	3	-4
5	380281	3	-5	7
6	70425	5	18	-25
7	28156	2	-95	132
8	14113	1	208	-289
9	14043	1	-303	421
10	70	200	511	-710
11	43	1	-102503	142421
12	27	1	103014	-143131
13	16	1	-205517	285552
14	11	1	308531	-428683
15	5	2	-514048	714235
16	1	5	1336627	-1857153
17	0		-7197183	10000000

The first r_i that meets or falls below the threshold $2r^* = 2000$ is at $i = 10$, and Bob reads off $s' = 511$ and $t' = -710$, from which he obtains $z = -s'/t' = 511/710$. $\square$

EXERCISE 4.7. Show that given integers s, t, k, with $0 \leq s < t$, and $k > 0$, we can compute the kth digit in the decimal expansion of s/t in time $O(\text{len}(k) \, \text{len}(t)^2)$.

For the following exercises, we need a definition: a sequence $S := (z_1, z_2, z_3, \ldots)$ of elements drawn from some arbitrary set is called (k, ℓ)-**periodic** for integers $k \geq 0$ and $\ell \geq 1$ if $z_i = z_{i+\ell}$ for all $i > k$. S is called **ultimately periodic** if it is (k, ℓ)-periodic for some (k, ℓ).

EXERCISE 4.8. Show that if a sequence S is ultimately periodic, then it is (k^*, ℓ^*)-periodic for some uniquely determined pair (k^*, ℓ^*) for which the following holds: for any pair (k, ℓ) such that S is (k, ℓ)-periodic, we have $k^* \leq k$ and $\ell^* \leq \ell$.

The value ℓ^* in the above exercise is called the **period** of S, and k^* is called the **pre-period** of S. If its pre-period is zero, then S is called **purely periodic**.

EXERCISE 4.9. Let z be a real number whose base-d expansion is an ultimately periodic sequence. Show that z is rational.

EXERCISE 4.10. Let $z = s/t \in \mathbb{Q}$, where s and t are relatively prime integers
with $0 \le s < t$, and let $d > 1$ be an integer.

(a) Show that there exist integers k, k' such that $0 \le k < k'$ and $sd^k \equiv sd^{k'} \pmod{t}$.

(b) Show that for integers k, k' with $0 \le k < k'$, the base-d expansion of
z is $(k, k' - k)$-periodic if and only if $sd^k \equiv sd^{k'} \pmod{t}$.

(c) Show that if $\gcd(t, d) = 1$, then the base-d expansion of z is purely
periodic with period equal to the multiplicative order of d modulo t.

(d) More generally, show that if k is the smallest non-negative integer
such that d and $t' := t/\gcd(d^k, t)$ are relatively prime, then the base-
d expansion of z is ultimately periodic with pre-period k and period
equal to the multiplicative order of d modulo t'.

A famous conjecture of Artin postulates that for any integer d, not equal
to -1 or to the square of an integer, there are infinitely many primes t such
that d has multiplicative order $t - 1$ modulo t. If Artin's conjecture is true,
then by part (c) of the previous exercise, for any $d > 1$ that is not a square,
there are infinitely many primes t such that the base-d expansion of s/t, for
any $0 < s < t$, is a purely periodic sequence of period $t - 1$. In light of these
observations, the "grade school" method of computing a fraction from its
decimal expansion using the period is hopelessly impractical.

4.5.3 Applications to symbolic algebra

Rational reconstruction also has a number of applications in symbolic algebra. We briefly sketch one such application here. Suppose that we want to
find the solution v to the equation

$$vA = w,$$

where we are given as input a non-singular square integer matrix A and an
integer vector w. The solution vector v will, in general, have rational entries. We stress that we want to compute the *exact* solution v, and not some
floating point approximation to it. Now, we could solve for v directly using Gaussian elimination; however, the intermediate quantities computed by
that algorithm would be rational numbers whose numerators and denominators might get quite large, leading to a rather lengthy computation (however,

it is possible to show that the overall running time is still polynomial in the input length).

Another approach is to compute a solution vector modulo n, where n is a power of a prime that does not divide the determinant of A. Provided n is large enough, one can then recover the solution vector v using rational reconstruction. With this approach, all of the computations can be carried out using arithmetic on integers not too much larger than n, leading to a more efficient algorithm. More of the details of this procedure are developed later, in Exercise 15.13.

4.6 Notes

The Euclidean algorithm as we have presented it here is not the fastest known algorithm for computing greatest common divisors. The asymptotically fastest known algorithm for computing the greatest common divisor of two numbers of bit length at most ℓ runs in time $O(\ell \operatorname{len}(\ell))$ on a RAM, and the smallest Boolean circuits are of size $O(\ell \operatorname{len}(\ell)^2 \operatorname{len}(\operatorname{len}(\ell)))$. This algorithm is due to Schönhage [81]. The same complexity results also hold for the extended Euclidean algorithm, as well as Chinese remaindering and rational reconstruction.

Experience suggests that such fast algorithms for greatest common divisors are not of much practical value, unless the integers involved are *very* large—at least several tens of thousands of bits in length. The extra "log" factor and the rather large multiplicative constants seem to slow things down too much.

The binary gcd algorithm (Exercise 4.1) is due to Stein [95]. The extended binary gcd algorithm (Exercise 4.2) was first described by Knuth [54], who attributes it to M. Penk. Our formulation of both of these algorithms closely follows that of Menezes, van Oorschot, and Vanstone [62]. Experience suggests that the binary gcd algorithm is faster in practice than Euclid's algorithm.

Our exposition of Theorem 4.6 is loosely based on Bach [11]. A somewhat "tighter" result is proved, with significantly more effort, by Wang, Guy, and Davenport [97]. However, for most practical purposes, the result proved here is just as good. The application of Euclid's algorithm to computing a rational number from the first digits of its decimal expansion was observed by Blum, Blum, and Shub [17], where they considered the possibility of using such sequences of digits as a pseudo-random number generator—the conclusion, of course, is that this is not such a good idea.

5

The distribution of primes

This chapter concerns itself with the question: how many primes are there? In Chapter 1, we proved that there are infinitely many primes; however, we are interested in a more quantitative answer to this question; that is, we want to know how "dense" the prime numbers are.

This chapter has a bit more of an "analytical" flavor than other chapters in this text. However, we shall not make use of any mathematics beyond that of elementary calculus.

5.1 Chebyshev's theorem on the density of primes

The natural way of measuring the density of primes is to count the number of primes up to a bound x, where x is a real number. For a real number $x \geq 0$, the function $\pi(x)$ is defined to be the number of primes up to x. Thus, $\pi(1) = 0$, $\pi(2) = 1$, $\pi(7.5) = 4$, and so on. The function π is an example of a "step function," that is, a function that changes values only at a discrete set of points. It might seem more natural to define π only on the integers, but it is the tradition to define it over the real numbers (and there are some technical benefits in doing so).

Let us first take a look at some values of $\pi(x)$. Table 5.1 shows values of $\pi(x)$ for $x = 10^{3i}$ and $i = 1, \ldots, 6$. The third column of this table shows the value of $x/\pi(x)$ (to five decimal places). One can see that the differences between successive rows of this third column are roughly the same—about 6.9—which suggests that the function $x/\pi(x)$ grows logarithmically in x. Indeed, as $\log(10^3) \approx 6.9$, it would not be unreasonable to guess that $x/\pi(x) \approx \log x$, or equivalently, $\pi(x) \approx x/\log x$.

The following theorem is a first—and important—step towards making the above guesswork more rigorous:

Table 5.1. *Some values of $\pi(x)$*

x	$\pi(x)$	$x/\pi(x)$
10^3	168	5.95238
10^6	78498	12.73918
10^9	50847534	19.66664
10^{12}	37607912018	26.59015
10^{15}	29844570422669	33.50693
10^{18}	24739954287740860	40.42045

Theorem 5.1 (Chebyshev's theorem). *We have*

$$\pi(x) = \Theta(x/\log x).$$

It is not too difficult to prove this theorem, which we now proceed to do in several steps. Recalling that $\nu_p(n)$ denotes the power to which a prime p divides an integer n, we begin with the following observation:

Theorem 5.2. *Let n be a positive integer. For any prime p, we have*

$$\nu_p(n!) = \sum_{k \geq 1} \lfloor n/p^k \rfloor.$$

Proof. This follows immediately from the observation that the numbers $1, 2, \ldots, n$ include exactly $\lfloor n/p \rfloor$ multiplies of p, $\lfloor n/p^2 \rfloor$ multiplies of p^2, and so on (see Exercise 1.5). $\square$

The following theorem gives a lower bound on $\pi(x)$.

Theorem 5.3. $\pi(n) \geq \frac{1}{2}(\log 2)n/\log n$ *for all integers $n \geq 2$.*

Proof. For positive integer m, consider the binomial coefficient

$$N := \binom{2m}{m} = \frac{(2m)!}{(m!)^2}.$$

Note that

$$N = \left(\frac{m+1}{1}\right)\left(\frac{m+2}{2}\right)\cdots\left(\frac{m+m}{m}\right),$$

from which it is clear that $N \geq 2^m$ and that N is divisible only by primes p not exceeding $2m$. Applying Theorem 5.2 to the identity $N = (2m)!/(m!)^2$, we have

$$\nu_p(N) = \sum_{k \geq 1}(\lfloor 2m/p^k \rfloor - 2\lfloor m/p^k \rfloor).$$

Each term in this sum is either 0 or 1 (see Exercise 1.4), and for $k > \log(2m)/\log p$, each term is zero. Thus, $\nu_p(N) \leq \log(2m)/\log p$.

So we have

$$\pi(2m)\log(2m) = \sum_{p \leq 2m} \frac{\log(2m)}{\log p}\log p$$

$$\geq \sum_{p \leq 2m} \nu_p(N)\log p = \log N \geq m\log 2,$$

where the summations are over the primes p up to $2m$. Therefore,

$$\pi(2m) \geq \tfrac{1}{2}(\log 2)(2m)/\log(2m).$$

That proves the theorem for even n. Now consider odd $n \geq 3$, so $n = 2m - 1$ for $m \geq 2$. Since the function $x/\log x$ is increasing for $x \geq 3$ (verify), and since $\pi(2m - 1) = \pi(2m)$ for $m \geq 2$, we have

$$\pi(2m - 1) = \pi(2m)$$

$$\geq \tfrac{1}{2}(\log 2)(2m)/\log(2m)$$

$$\geq \tfrac{1}{2}(\log 2)(2m - 1)/\log(2m - 1).$$

That proves the theorem for odd n. $\square$

As a consequence of the above theorem, we have $\pi(x) = \Omega(x/\log x)$ for real $x \to \infty$. Indeed, for real $x \geq 2$, setting $c := \tfrac{1}{2}(\log 2)$, we have

$$\pi(x) = \pi(\lfloor x \rfloor) \geq c\lfloor x \rfloor/\log\lfloor x \rfloor \geq c(x - 1)/\log x = \Omega(x/\log x).$$

To obtain a corresponding upper bound for $\pi(x)$, we introduce an auxiliary function, called Chebyshev's theta function:

$$\vartheta(x) := \sum_{p \leq x} \log p,$$

where the sum is over all primes p up to x.

Chebyshev's theta function is an example of a summation over primes, and in this chapter, we will be considering a number of functions that are defined in terms of sums or products over primes. To avoid excessive tedium, we adopt the usual convention used by number theorists: if not explicitly stated, summations and products over the variable p are always understood to be over primes. For example, we may write $\pi(x) = \sum_{p \leq x} 1$.

The next theorem relates $\pi(x)$ and $\vartheta(x)$. Recall the "$\sim$" notation from §3.1: for two functions f and g such that $f(x)$ and $g(x)$ are positive for all sufficiently large x, we write $f \sim g$ to mean that $\lim_{x \to \infty} f(x)/g(x) = 1$, or equivalently, for all $\epsilon > 0$ there exists x_0 such that $(1 - \epsilon)g(x) < f(x) < (1 + \epsilon)g(x)$ for all $x > x_0$.

Theorem 5.4. *We have*

$$\pi(x) \sim \frac{\vartheta(x)}{\log x}.$$

Proof. On the one hand, we have

$$\vartheta(x) = \sum_{p \leq x} \log p \leq \log x \sum_{p \leq x} 1 = \pi(x) \log x.$$

So we have

$$\pi(x) \geq \frac{\vartheta(x)}{\log x}.$$

On the other hand, for every $x > 1$ and δ with $0 < \delta < 1$, we have

$$\vartheta(x) \geq \sum_{x^\delta < p \leq x} \log p$$

$$\geq \delta \log x \sum_{x^\delta < p \leq x} 1$$

$$= \delta \log x \left(\pi(x) - \pi(x^\delta) \right)$$

$$\geq \delta \log x \left(\pi(x) - x^\delta \right).$$

Hence,

$$\pi(x) \leq x^\delta + \frac{\vartheta(x)}{\delta \log x}.$$

Since by the previous theorem, the term x^δ is $o(\pi(x))$, we have for all sufficiently large x (depending on δ), $x^\delta \leq (1 - \delta)\pi(x)$, and so

$$\pi(x) \leq \frac{\vartheta(x)}{\delta^2 \log x}.$$

Now, for any $\epsilon > 0$, we can choose δ sufficiently close to 1 so that $1/\delta^2 < 1 + \epsilon$, and for this δ, and for all sufficiently large x, we have $\pi(x) < (1 + \epsilon)\vartheta(x)/\log x$, and the theorem follows. $\square$

Theorem 5.5. $\vartheta(x) < 2x \log 2$ *for all real numbers* $x \geq 1$.

Proof. It suffices to prove that $\vartheta(n) < 2n \log 2$ for integers $n \geq 1$, since then $\vartheta(x) = \vartheta(\lfloor x \rfloor) < 2\lfloor x \rfloor \log 2 \leq 2x \log 2$.

For positive integer m, consider the binomial coefficient

$$M := \binom{2m + 1}{m} = \frac{(2m + 1)!}{m!(m + 1)!}.$$

One sees that M is divisible by all primes p with $m + 1 < p \leq 2m + 1$. As M occurs twice in the binomial expansion of $(1 + 1)^{2m+1}$, one sees that $M < 2^{2m+1}/2 = 2^{2m}$. It follows that

$$\vartheta(2m + 1) - \vartheta(m + 1) = \sum_{m+1 < p \leq 2m+1} \log p \leq \log M < 2m \log 2.$$

We now prove the theorem by induction. For $n = 1$ and $n = 2$, the theorem is trivial. Now let $n > 2$. If n is even, then we have

$$\vartheta(n) = \vartheta(n - 1) < 2(n - 1) \log 2 < 2n \log 2.$$

If $n = 2m + 1$ is odd, then we have

$$\vartheta(n) = \vartheta(2m + 1) - \vartheta(m + 1) + \vartheta(m + 1)$$
$$< 2m \log 2 + 2(m + 1) \log 2 = 2n \log 2. \quad \square$$

Another way of stating the above theorem is:

$$\prod_{p \leq x} p < 4^x.$$

Theorem 5.1 follows immediately from Theorems 5.3, 5.4 and 5.5. Note that we have also proved:

Theorem 5.6. *We have*

$$\vartheta(x) = \Theta(x).$$

EXERCISE 5.1. If p_n denotes the nth prime, show that $p_n = \Theta(n \log n)$.

EXERCISE 5.2. For integer $n > 1$, let $\omega(n)$ denote the number of distinct primes dividing n. Show that $\omega(n) = O(\log n / \log \log n)$.

EXERCISE 5.3. Show that for positive integers a and b,

$$\binom{a + b}{b} \geq 2^{\min(a,b)}.$$

5.2 Bertrand's postulate

Suppose we want to know how many primes there are of a given bit length, or more generally, how many primes there are between m and $2m$ for a given integer m. Neither the statement, nor the proof, of Chebyshev's theorem imply that there are *any* primes between m and $2m$, let alone a useful density estimate of such primes.

Bertrand's postulate is the assertion that for all positive integers m, there exists a prime between m and $2m$. We shall in fact prove a stronger result, namely, that not only is there one prime, but the number of primes between m and $2m$ is $\Omega(m/\log m)$.

Theorem 5.7 (Bertrand's postulate). *For any positive integer m, we have*

$$\pi(2m) - \pi(m) > \frac{m}{3\log(2m)}.$$

The proof uses Theorem 5.5, along with a more careful re-working of the proof of Theorem 5.3. The theorem is clearly true for $m \leq 2$, so we may assume that $m \geq 3$. As in the proof of the Theorem 5.3, define $N := \binom{2m}{m}$, and recall that N is divisible only by primes strictly less than $2m$, and that we have the identity

$$\nu_p(N) = \sum_{k \geq 1} (\lfloor 2m/p^k \rfloor - 2\lfloor m/p^k \rfloor), \tag{5.1}$$

where each term in the sum is either 0 or 1. We can characterize the values $\nu_p(N)$ a bit more precisely, as follows:

Lemma 5.8. *Let $m \geq 3$ and $N = \binom{2m}{m}$ as above. For all primes p, we have*

$$p^{\nu_p(N)} \leq 2m; \tag{5.2}$$

$$\text{if } p > \sqrt{2m}, \text{ then } \nu_p(N) \leq 1; \tag{5.3}$$

$$\text{if } 2m/3 < p \leq m, \text{ then } \nu_p(N) = 0; \tag{5.4}$$

$$\text{if } m < p < 2m, \text{ then } \nu_p(N) = 1. \tag{5.5}$$

Proof. For (5.2), all terms with $k > \log(2m)/\log p$ in (5.1) vanish, and hence $\nu_p(N) \leq \log(2m)/\log p$, from which it follows that $p^{\nu_p(N)} \leq 2m$.

(5.3) follows immediately from (5.2).

For (5.4), if $2m/3 < p \leq m$, then $2m/p < 3$, and we must also have $p \geq 3$, since $p = 2$ implies $m < 3$. We have $p^2 > p(2m/3) = 2m(p/3) \geq 2m$, and hence all terms with $k > 1$ in (5.1) vanish. The term with $k = 1$ also vanishes, since $1 \leq m/p < 3/2$, from which it follows that $2 \leq 2m/p < 3$, and hence $\lfloor m/p \rfloor = 1$ and $\lfloor 2m/p \rfloor = 2$.

For (5.5), if $m < p < 2m$, it follows that $1 < 2m/p < 2$, so $\lfloor 2m/p \rfloor = 1$. Also, $m/p < 1$, so $\lfloor m/p \rfloor = 0$. It follows that the term with $k = 1$ in (5.1) is 1, and it is clear that $2m/p^k < 1$ for all $k > 1$, and so all the other terms vanish. $\square$

We need one more technical fact, namely, a somewhat better lower bound on N than that used in the proof of Theorem 5.3:

Lemma 5.9. *Let $m \geq 3$ and $N = \binom{2m}{m}$ as above. We have*

$$N > 4^m/(2m). \tag{5.6}$$

Proof. We prove this for all $m \geq 3$ by induction on m. One checks by direct calculation that it holds for $m = 3$. For $m > 3$, by induction we have

$$\binom{2m}{m} = 2\frac{2m-1}{m}\binom{2(m-1)}{m-1} > \frac{(2m-1)4^{m-1}}{m(m-1)}$$

$$= \frac{2m-1}{2(m-1)}\frac{4^m}{2m} > \frac{4^m}{2m}. \quad \square$$

We now have the necessary technical ingredients to prove Theorem 5.7. Define

$$P_m := \prod_{m<p<2m} p,$$

and define Q_m so that

$$N = Q_m P_m.$$

By (5.4) and (5.5), we see that

$$Q_m = \prod_{p \leq 2m/3} p^{\nu_p(N)}.$$

Moreover, by (5.3), $\nu_p(N) > 1$ for at most those $p \leq \sqrt{2m}$, so there are at most $\sqrt{2m}$ such primes, and by (5.2), the contribution of each such prime to the above product is at most $2m$. Combining this with Theorem 5.5, we obtain

$$Q_m < (2m)^{\sqrt{2m}} \cdot 4^{2m/3}.$$

We now apply (5.6), obtaining

$$P_m = NQ_m^{-1} > 4^m(2m)^{-1}Q_m^{-1} > 4^{m/3}(2m)^{-(1+\sqrt{2m})}.$$

It follows that

$$\pi(2m) - \pi(m) \geq \log P_m/\log(2m) > \frac{m\log 4}{3\log(2m)} - (1+\sqrt{2m})$$

$$= \frac{m}{3\log(2m)} + \frac{m(\log 4 - 1)}{3\log(2m)} - (1+\sqrt{2m}). \tag{5.7}$$

Clearly, the term $(m(\log 4 - 1))/(3\log(2m))$ in (5.7) dominates the term $1 + \sqrt{2m}$, and so Theorem 5.7 holds for all sufficiently large m. Indeed, a simple calculation shows that (5.7) implies the theorem for $m \geq 13,000$, and one can verify by brute force (with the aid of a computer) that the theorem holds for $m < 13,000$.

5.3 Mertens' theorem

Our next goal is to prove the following theorem, which turns out to have a number of applications.

Theorem 5.10. *We have*

$$\sum_{p \leq x} \frac{1}{p} = \log \log x + O(1).$$

The proof of this theorem, while not difficult, is a bit technical, and we proceed in several steps.

Theorem 5.11. *We have*

$$\sum_{p \leq x} \frac{\log p}{p} = \log x + O(1).$$

Proof. Let $n := \lfloor x \rfloor$. By Theorem 5.2, we have

$$\log(n!) = \sum_{p \leq n} \sum_{k \geq 1} \lfloor n/p^k \rfloor \log p = \sum_{p \leq n} \lfloor n/p \rfloor \log p + \sum_{k \geq 2} \sum_{p \leq n} \lfloor n/p^k \rfloor \log p.$$

We next show that the last sum is $O(n)$. We have

$$\sum_{p \leq n} \log p \sum_{k \geq 2} \lfloor n/p^k \rfloor \leq n \sum_{p \leq n} \log p \sum_{k \geq 2} p^{-k}$$

$$= n \sum_{p \leq n} \frac{\log p}{p^2} \cdot \frac{1}{1 - 1/p} = n \sum_{p \leq n} \frac{\log p}{p(p-1)}$$

$$\leq n \sum_{k \geq 2} \frac{\log k}{k(k-1)} = O(n).$$

Thus, we have shown that

$$\log(n!) = \sum_{p \leq n} \lfloor n/p \rfloor \log p + O(n).$$

Further, since $\lfloor n/p \rfloor = n/p + O(1)$, applying Theorem 5.5, we have

$$\log(n!) = \sum_{p \leq n} (n/p) \log p + O(\sum_{p \leq n} \log p) + O(n) = n \sum_{p \leq n} \frac{\log p}{p} + O(n). \quad (5.8)$$

We can also estimate $\log(n!)$ using a little calculus (see §A2). We have

$$\log(n!) = \sum_{k=1}^{n} \log k = \int_1^n \log t \, dt + O(\log n) = n \log n - n + O(\log n). \quad (5.9)$$

Combining (5.8) and (5.9), and noting that $\log x - \log n = o(1)$, we obtain

$$\sum_{p \leq x} \frac{\log p}{p} = \log n + O(1) = \log x + O(1),$$

which proves the theorem. □

We shall also need the following theorem, which is a very useful tool in its own right:

Theorem 5.12 (Abel's identity). *Suppose that $c_k, c_{k+1}, \ldots$ is a sequence of numbers, that*

$$C(t) := \sum_{k \leq i \leq t} c_i,$$

and that $f(t)$ has a continuous derivative $f'(t)$ on the interval $[k, x]$. Then

$$\sum_{k \leq i \leq x} c_i f(i) = C(x) f(x) - \int_k^x C(t) f'(t)\, dt.$$

Note that since $C(t)$ is a step function, the integrand $C(t)f'(t)$ is piecewise continuous on $[k, x]$, and hence the integral is well defined (see §A3).

Proof. Let $n := \lfloor x \rfloor$. We have

$$\begin{aligned}
\sum_{i=k}^n c_i f(i) &= C(k) f(k) + [C(k+1) - C(k)] f(k+1) + \cdots \\
&\quad + [C(n) - C(n-1)] f(n) \\
&= C(k)[f(k) - f(k+1)] + \cdots + C(n-1)[f(n-1) - f(n)] \\
&\quad + C(n) f(n) \\
&= C(k)[f(k) - f(k+1)] + \cdots + C(n-1)[f(n-1) - f(n)] \\
&\quad + C(n)[f(n) - f(x)] + C(x) f(x).
\end{aligned}$$

Observe that for $i = k, \ldots, n-1$, we have $C(t) = C(i)$ for $t \in [i, i+1)$, and so

$$C(i)[f(i) - f(i+1)] = -\int_i^{i+1} C(t) f'(t)\, dt;$$

likewise,

$$C(n)[f(n) - f(x)] = -\int_n^x C(t) f'(t)\, dt,$$

from which the theorem directly follows. □

Proof of Theorem 5.10. For $i \geq 2$, set

$$c_i := \begin{cases} (\log i)/i & \text{if } i \text{ is prime,} \\ 0 & \text{otherwise.} \end{cases}$$

By Theorem 5.11, we have

$$C(t) := \sum_{2 \leq i \leq t} c_i = \sum_{p \leq t} \frac{\log p}{p} = \log t + O(1).$$

Applying Theorem 5.12 with $f(t) = 1/\log t$, we obtain

$$\sum_{p \leq x} \frac{1}{p} = \frac{C(x)}{\log x} + \int_2^x \frac{C(t)}{t(\log t)^2} dt$$

$$= \left(1 + O(1/\log x)\right) + \left(\int_2^x \frac{dt}{t \log t} + O\left(\int_2^x \frac{dt}{t(\log t)^2}\right)\right)$$

$$= 1 + O(1/\log x) + (\log \log x - \log \log 2) + O(1/\log 2 - 1/\log x)$$

$$= \log \log x + O(1). \quad \square$$

Using Theorem 5.10, we can easily show the following:

Theorem 5.13 (Mertens' theorem). *We have*

$$\prod_{p \leq x}(1 - 1/p) = \Theta(1/\log x).$$

Proof. Using parts (i) and (iii) of §A1, for any fixed prime p, we have

$$-\frac{1}{p^2} \leq \frac{1}{p} + \log(1 - 1/p) \leq 0. \tag{5.10}$$

Moreover, since

$$\sum_{p \leq x} \frac{1}{p^2} \leq \sum_{i \geq 2} \frac{1}{i^2} < \infty,$$

summing the inequality (5.10) over all primes $p \leq x$ yields

$$-C \leq \sum_{p \leq x} \frac{1}{p} + \log U(x) \leq 0,$$

where C is a positive constant, and $U(x) := \prod_{p \leq x}(1 - 1/p)$. From this, and from Theorem 5.10, we obtain

$$\log \log x + \log U(x) = O(1).$$

This means that

$$-D \leq \log \log x + \log U(x) \leq D$$

for some positive constant D and all sufficiently large x, and exponentiating this yields

$$e^{-D} \leq (\log x)U(x) \leq e^{D},$$

and hence, $U(x) = \Theta(1/\log x)$, and the theorem follows. $\square$

EXERCISE 5.4. Let $\omega(n)$ be the number of distinct prime factors of n, and define $\overline{\omega}(x) = \sum_{n \leq x} \omega(n)$, so that $\overline{\omega}(x)/x$ represents the "average" value of ω. First, show that $\overline{\omega}(x) = \sum_{p \leq x} \lfloor x/p \rfloor$. From this, show that $\overline{\omega}(x) \sim x \log \log x$.

EXERCISE 5.5. Analogously to the previous exercise, show that $\sum_{n \leq x} \tau(n) \sim x \log x$, where $\tau(n)$ is the number of positive divisors of n.

EXERCISE 5.6. Define the sequence of numbers $n_1, n_2, \ldots$, where n_k is the product of all the primes up to k. Show that as $k \to \infty$, $\phi(n_k) = \Theta(n_k/\log \log n_k)$. Hint: you will want to use Mertens' theorem, and also Theorem 5.6.

EXERCISE 5.7. The previous exercise showed that $\phi(n)$ could be as small as (about) $n/\log \log n$ for infinitely many n. Show that this is the "worst case," in the sense that $\phi(n) = \Omega(n/\log \log n)$ as $n \to \infty$.

EXERCISE 5.8. Show that for any positive integer constant k,

$$\int_2^x \frac{dt}{(\log t)^k} = \frac{x}{(\log x)^k} + O\left(\frac{x}{(\log x)^{k+1}}\right).$$

EXERCISE 5.9. Use Chebyshev's theorem and Abel's identity to show that

$$\sum_{p \leq x} \frac{1}{\log p} = \frac{\pi(x)}{\log x} + O(x/(\log x)^3).$$

EXERCISE 5.10. Use Chebyshev's theorem and Abel's identity to prove a stronger version of Theorem 5.4:

$$\vartheta(x) = \pi(x) \log x + O(x/\log x).$$

EXERCISE 5.11. Show that

$$\prod_{2 < p \leq x} (1 - 2/p) = \Theta(1/(\log x)^2).$$

EXERCISE 5.12. Show that if $\pi(x) \sim cx/\log x$ for some constant c, then we must have $c = 1$. Hint: use either Theorem 5.10 or 5.11.

EXERCISE 5.13. Strengthen Theorem 5.10, showing that $\sum_{p \leq x} 1/p \sim \log \log x + A$ for some constant A. (Note: $A \approx 0.261497212847643$.)

EXERCISE 5.14. Strengthen Mertens' theorem, showing that $\prod_{p \leq x}(1 - 1/p) \sim B_1/(\log x)$ for some constant B_1. Hint: use the result from the previous exercise. (Note: $B_1 \approx 0.561459483566885$.)

EXERCISE 5.15. Strengthen the result of Exercise 5.11, showing that

$$\prod_{2 < p \leq x} (1 - 2/p) \sim B_2/(\log x)^2$$

for some constant B_2. (Note: $B_2 \approx 0.832429065662$.)

5.4 The sieve of Eratosthenes

As an application of Theorem 5.10, consider the **sieve of Eratosthenes**. This is an algorithm for generating all the primes up to a given bound k. It uses an array $A[2 \ldots k]$, and runs as follows.

> for $n \leftarrow 2$ to k do $A[n] \leftarrow 1$
> for $n \leftarrow 2$ to $\lfloor \sqrt{k} \rfloor$ do
>   if $A[n] = 1$ then
> $i \leftarrow 2n$; while $i \leq k$ do $\{ A[i] \leftarrow 0; i \leftarrow i + n \}$

When the algorithm finishes, we have $A[n] = 1$ if and only if n is prime, for $n = 2, \ldots, k$. This can easily be proven using the fact (see Exercise 1.1) that a composite number n between 2 and k must be divisible by a prime that is at most $\sqrt{k}$, and by proving by induction on n that at the beginning of the nth iteration of the main loop, $A[i] = 0$ iff i is divisible by a prime less than n, for $i = n, \ldots, k$. We leave the details of this to the reader.

We are more interested in the running time of the algorithm. To analyze the running time, we assume that all arithmetic operations take constant time; this is reasonable, since all the quantities computed in the algorithm are bounded by k, and we need to at least be able to index all entries of the array A, which has size k.

Every time we execute the inner loop of the algorithm, we perform $O(k/n)$ steps to clear the entries of A indexed by multiples of n. Naively, we could bound the running time by a constant times

$$\sum_{n \leq \sqrt{k}} k/n,$$

which is $O(k \operatorname{len}(k))$, where we have used a little calculus (see §A2) to derive that

$$\sum_{n=1}^{\ell} 1/n = \int_1^{\ell} \frac{dy}{y} + O(1) \sim \log \ell.$$

However, the inner loop is executed only for prime values of n; thus, the running time is proportional to

$$\sum_{p \le \sqrt{k}} k/p,$$

and so by Theorem 5.10 is $\Theta(k \operatorname{len}(\operatorname{len}(k)))$.

EXERCISE 5.16. Give a detailed proof of the correctness of the above algorithm.

EXERCISE 5.17. One drawback of the above algorithm is its use of space: it requires an array of size k. Show how to modify the algorithm, without substantially increasing its running time, so that one can enumerate all the primes up to k, using an auxiliary array of size just $O(\sqrt{k})$.

EXERCISE 5.18. Design and analyze an algorithm that on input k outputs the table of values $\tau(n)$ for $n = 1, \ldots, k$, where $\tau(n)$ is the number of positive divisors of n. Your algorithm should run in time $O(k \operatorname{len}(k))$.

5.5 The prime number theorem ... and beyond

In this section, we survey a number of theorems and conjectures related to the distribution of primes. This is a vast area of mathematical research, with a number of very deep results. We shall be stating a number of theorems from the literature in this section without proof; while our intent is to keep the text as self contained as possible, and to avoid degenerating into "mathematical tourism," it nevertheless is a good idea to occasionally have a somewhat broader perspective. In the following chapters, we shall not make any critical use of the theorems in this section.

5.5.1 The prime number theorem

The main theorem in the theory of the density of primes is the following.

Theorem 5.14 (Prime number theorem). *We have*

$$\pi(x) \sim x/\log x.$$

Proof. Literature—see §5.6. □

As we saw in Exercise 5.12, if $\pi(x)/(x/\log x)$ tends to a limit as $x \to \infty$, then the limit must be 1, so in fact the hard part of proving the prime number theorem is to show that $\pi(x)/(x/\log x)$ does indeed tend to some limit.

One simple consequence of the prime number theorem, together with Theorem 5.4, is the following:

Theorem 5.15. *We have*

$$\vartheta(x) \sim x.$$

EXERCISE 5.19. Using the prime number theorem, show that $p_n \sim n \log n$, where p_n denotes the nth prime.

EXERCISE 5.20. Using the prime number theorem, show that Bertrand's postulate can be strengthened (asymptotically) as follows: for all $\epsilon > 0$, there exist positive constants c and x_0, such that for all $x \geq x_0$, we have

$$\pi((1 + \epsilon)x) - \pi(x) \geq c \frac{x}{\log x}.$$

5.5.2 The error term in the prime number theorem

The prime number theorem says that

$$|\pi(x) - x/\log x| \leq \delta(x),$$

where $\delta(x) = o(x/\log x)$. A natural question is: how small is the "error term" $\delta(x)$? It turns out that:

Theorem 5.16. *We have*

$$\pi(x) = x/\log x + O(x/(\log x)^2).$$

This bound on the error term is not very impressive. The reason is that $x/\log x$ is not really the best "simple" function that approximates $\pi(x)$. It turns out that a better approximation to $\pi(x)$ is the **logarithmic integral**, defined for real $x \geq 2$ by

$$\mathrm{li}(x) := \int_2^x \frac{dt}{\log t}.$$

It is not hard to show (see Exercise 5.8) that

$$\mathrm{li}(x) = x/\log x + O(x/(\log x)^2).$$

Table 5.2. *Values of* $\pi(x)$, $\mathrm{li}(x)$, *and* $x/\log x$

x	$\pi(x)$	$\mathrm{li}(x)$	$x/\log x$
10^3	168	176.6	144.8
10^6	78498	78626.5	72382.4
10^9	50847534	50849233.9	48254942.4
10^{12}	37607912018	37607950279.8	36191206825.3
10^{15}	29844570422669	29844571475286.5	28952965460216.8
10^{18}	24739954287740860	24739954309690414.0	24127471216847323.8

Thus, $\mathrm{li}(x) \sim x/\log x \sim \pi(x)$. However, the error term in the approximation of $\pi(x)$ by $\mathrm{li}(x)$ is much better. This is illustrated numerically in Table 5.2; for example, at $x = 10^{18}$, $\mathrm{li}(x)$ approximates $\pi(x)$ with a relative error just under 10^{-9}, while $x/\log x$ approximates $\pi(x)$ with a relative error of about 0.025.

The sharpest proven result is the following:

Theorem 5.17. *Let* $\kappa(x) := (\log x)^{3/5}(\log \log x)^{-1/5}$. *Then for some* $c > 0$, *we have*

$$\pi(x) = \mathrm{li}(x) + O(xe^{-c\kappa(x)}).$$

Proof. Literature—see §5.6. $\square$

Note that the error term $xe^{-c\kappa(x)}$ is $o(x/(\log x)^k)$ for every fixed $k \geq 0$. Also note that Theorem 5.16 follows directly from the above theorem and Exercise 5.8.

Although the above estimate on the error term in the approximation of $\pi(x)$ by $\mathrm{li}(x)$ is pretty good, it is conjectured that the actual error term is much smaller:

Conjecture 5.18. *For all* $x \geq 2.01$, *we have*

$$|\pi(x) - \mathrm{li}(x)| < x^{1/2} \log x.$$

Conjecture 5.18 is equivalent to a famous conjecture called the **Riemann hypothesis**, which is an assumption about the location of the zeros of a certain function, called **Riemann's zeta function**. We give a *very* brief, high-level account of this conjecture, and its connection to the theory of the distribution of primes.

For real $s > 1$, the zeta function is defined as

$$\zeta(s) := \sum_{n=1}^{\infty} \frac{1}{n^s}. \tag{5.11}$$

Note that because $s > 1$, the infinite series defining $\zeta(s)$ converges. A simple, but important, connection between the zeta function and the theory of prime numbers is the following:

Theorem 5.19 (Euler's identity). *For real $s > 1$, we have*

$$\zeta(s) = \prod_p (1 - p^{-s})^{-1}, \tag{5.12}$$

where the product is over all primes p.

Proof. The rigorous interpretation of the infinite product on the right-hand side of (5.12) is as a limit of finite products. Thus, if $p_1, p_2, \ldots$ is the list of primes, we are really proving that

$$\zeta(s) = \lim_{r \to \infty} \prod_{i=1}^{r} (1 - p_i^{-s})^{-1}.$$

Now, from the identity

$$(1 - p_i^{-s})^{-1} = \sum_{e=0}^{\infty} p_i^{-es},$$

we have

$$\prod_{i=1}^{r} (1 - p_i^{-s})^{-1} = \left(1 + p_1^{-s} + p_1^{-2s} + \cdots \right) \cdots \left(1 + p_r^{-s} + p_r^{-2s} + \cdots \right)$$

$$= \sum_{e_1=0}^{\infty} \cdots \sum_{e_r=0}^{\infty} (p_1^{e_1} \cdots p_r^{e_r})^s$$

$$= \sum_{n=1}^{\infty} \frac{g_r(n)}{n^s},$$

where

$$g_r(n) := \begin{cases} 1 & \text{if } n \text{ is divisible only by the primes } p_1, \ldots, p_r; \\ 0 & \text{otherwise.} \end{cases}$$

Here, we have made use of the fact (see §A5) that we can multiply term-wise infinite series with non-negative terms.

Now, for any $\epsilon > 0$, there exists n_0 such that $\sum_{n=n_0}^{\infty} n^{-s} < \epsilon$ (because the series defining $\zeta(s)$ converges). Moreover, there exists an r_0 such that $g_r(n) = 1$ for all $n < n_0$ and $r \geq r_0$. Therefore, for $r \geq r_0$, we have

$$\left| \sum_{n=1}^{\infty} \frac{g_r(n)}{n^s} - \zeta(s) \right| \leq \sum_{n=n_0}^{\infty} n^{-s} < \epsilon.$$

It follows that

$$\lim_{r \to \infty} \sum_{n=1}^{\infty} \frac{g_r(n)}{n^s} = \zeta(s),$$

which proves the theorem. □

While Theorem 5.19 is nice, things become much more interesting if one extends the domain of definition of the zeta function to the complex plane. For the reader who is familiar with just a little complex analysis, it is easy to see that the infinite series defining the zeta function in (5.11) converges absolutely for complex numbers s whose real part is greater than 1, and that (5.12) holds as well for such s. However, it is possible to extend the domain of definition of ζ even further—in fact, one can extend the definition of ζ in a "nice way " (in the language of complex analysis, *analytically continue*) to the entire complex plane (except the point $s = 1$, where there is a simple pole). Exactly how this is done is beyond the scope of this text, but assuming this extended definition of ζ, we can now state the Riemann hypothesis:

Conjecture 5.20 (Riemann hypothesis). *For any complex number $s = x + yi$, where x and y are real numbers with $0 < x < 1$ and $x \neq 1/2$, we have $\zeta(s) \neq 0$.*

A lot is known about the zeros of the zeta function in the "critical strip," consisting of those points s whose real part is greater than 0 and less than 1: it is known that there are infinitely many of them, and there are even good estimates about their density. It turns out that one can apply standard tools in complex analysis, like contour integration, to the zeta function (and functions derived from it) to answer various questions about the distribution of primes. Indeed, such techniques may be used to prove the prime number theorem. However, if one assumes the Riemann hypothesis, then these techniques yield much sharper results, such as the bound in Conjecture 5.18.

EXERCISE 5.21. For any arithmetic function a, we can form the **Dirichlet series**

$$F_a(s) := \sum_{n=1}^{\infty} \frac{a(n)}{n^s}.$$

For simplicity we assume that s takes only real values, even though such series are usually studied for complex values of s.

(a) Show that if the Dirichlet series $F_a(s)$ converges absolutely for some real s, then it converges absolutely for all real $s' \geq s$.

(b) From part (a), conclude that for any given arithmetic function a, there is an **interval of absolute convergence** of the form (s_0, ∞), where we allow $s_0 = -\infty$ and $s_0 = \infty$, such that $F_a(s)$ converges absolutely for $s > s_0$, and does not converge absolutely for $s < s_0$.

(c) Let a and b be arithmetic functions such that $F_a(s)$ has an interval of absolute convergence (s_0, ∞) and $F_b(s)$ has an interval of absolute convergence (s_0', ∞), and assume that $s_0 < \infty$ and $s_0' < \infty$. Let $c := a \star b$ be the Dirichlet product of a and b, as defined in §2.6. Show that for all $s \in (\max(s_0, s_0'), \infty)$, the series $F_c(s)$ converges absolutely and, moreover, that $F_a(s)F_b(s) = F_c(s)$.

5.5.3 Explicit estimates

Sometimes, it is useful to have explicit estimates for $\pi(x)$, as well as related functions, like $\vartheta(x)$ and the nth prime function p_n. The following theorem presents a number of bounds that have been proved without relying on any unproved conjectures.

Theorem 5.21. *We have:*

(i) $\dfrac{x}{\log x}\left(1 + \dfrac{1}{2\log x}\right) < \pi(x) < \dfrac{x}{\log x}\left(1 + \dfrac{3}{2\log x}\right), \quad$ *for $x \geq 59$;*

(ii) $n(\log n + \log\log n - 3/2) < p_n < n(\log n + \log\log n - 1/2)$, *for $n \geq 20$;*

(iii) $x(1 - 1/(2\log x)) < \vartheta(x) < x(1 + 1/(2\log x)), \quad$ *for $x \geq 563$;*

(iv) $\log\log x + A - \dfrac{1}{2(\log x)^2} < \displaystyle\sum_{p \leq x} 1/p < \log\log x + A + \dfrac{1}{2(\log x)^2},$

for $x \geq 286$, where $A \approx 0.261497212847643$;

(v) $\dfrac{B_1}{\log x}\left(1 - \dfrac{1}{2(\log x)^2}\right) < \displaystyle\prod_{p \leq x}\left(1 - \dfrac{1}{p}\right) < \dfrac{B_1}{\log x}\left(1 + \dfrac{1}{2(\log x)^2}\right),$

for $x \geq 285$, where $B_1 \approx 0.561459483566885$.

Proof. Literature—see §5.6. $\square$

5.5.4 Primes in arithmetic progressions

The arithmetic progression of odd numbers $1, 3, 5, \ldots$ contains infinitely many primes, and it is natural to ask if other arithmetic progressions do as well. An arithmetic progression with first term a and common difference d consists of all integers of the form

$$md + a, \quad m = 0, 1, 2, \ldots.$$

If d and a have a common factor $c > 1$, then every term in the progression is divisible by c, and so there can be no more than one prime in the progression. So a necessary condition for the existence of infinitely many primes p with $p \equiv a \pmod{d}$ is that $\gcd(d, a) = 1$. A famous theorem due to Dirichlet states that this is a sufficient condition as well.

Theorem 5.22 (Dirichlet's theorem). *For any positive integer d and any integer a relatively prime to d, there are infinitely many primes p with $p \equiv a \pmod{d}$.*

Proof. Literature—see §5.6. □

We can also ask about the density of primes in arithmetic progressions. One might expect that for a fixed value of d, the primes are distributed in roughly equal measure among the $\phi(d)$ different residue classes $[a]_d$ with $\gcd(a, d) = 1$. This is in fact the case. To formulate such assertions, we define $\pi(x; d, a)$ to be the number of primes p up to x with $p \equiv a \pmod{d}$.

Theorem 5.23. *Let $d > 0$ be a fixed integer, and let $a \in \mathbb{Z}$ be relatively prime to d. Then*

$$\pi(x; d, a) \sim \frac{x}{\phi(d) \log x}.$$

Proof. Literature—see §5.6. □

The above theorem is only applicable in the case where d is fixed and $x \to \infty$. But what if we want an estimate on the number of primes p up to x with $p \equiv a \pmod{d}$, where x is, say, a fixed power of d? Theorem 5.23 does not help us here. The following conjecture does, however:

Conjecture 5.24. *For any real $x \geq 2$, integer $d \geq 2$, and $a \in \mathbb{Z}$ relatively prime to d, we have*

$$\left| \pi(x; d, a) - \frac{\operatorname{li}(x)}{\phi(d)} \right| \leq x^{1/2}(\log x + 2 \log d).$$

The above conjecture is in fact a consequence of a generalization of the Riemann hypothesis—see §5.6.

EXERCISE 5.22. Assuming Conjecture 5.24, show that for all α, ϵ, with $0 < \alpha < 1/2$ and $0 < \epsilon < 1$, there exists an x_0, such that for all $x > x_0$, for all $d \in \mathbb{Z}$ with $2 \leq d \leq x^\alpha$, and for all $a \in \mathbb{Z}$ relatively prime to d, the number of primes $p \leq x$ such that $p \equiv a \pmod{d}$ is at least $(1 - \epsilon) \operatorname{li}(x)/\phi(d)$ and at most $(1 + \epsilon) \operatorname{li}(x)/\phi(d)$.

It is an open problem to prove an unconditional density result analogous to Exercise 5.22 for any positive exponent α. The following, however, is known:

Theorem 5.25. *There exists a constant c such that for all integer $d \geq 2$ and $a \in \mathbb{Z}$ relatively prime to d, the least prime p with $p \equiv a \pmod{d}$ is at most $cd^{11/2}$.*

Proof. Literature—see §5.6. $\square$

5.5.5 Sophie Germain primes

A **Sophie Germain prime** is a prime p such that $2p + 1$ is also prime. Such primes are actually useful in a number of practical applications, and so we discuss them briefly here.

It is an open problem to prove (or disprove) that there are infinitely many Sophie Germain primes. However, numerical evidence, and heuristic arguments, strongly suggest not only that there are infinitely many such primes, but also a fairly precise estimate on the density of such primes.

Let $\pi^*(x)$ denote the number of Sophie Germain primes up to x.

Conjecture 5.26. *We have*

$$\pi^*(x) \sim C \frac{x}{(\log x)^2},$$

where C is the constant

$$C := 2 \prod_{q>2} \frac{q(q-2)}{(q-1)^2} \approx 1.32032,$$

and the product is over all primes $q > 2$.

The above conjecture is a special case of a more general conjecture, known as **Hypothesis H**. We can formulate a special case of Hypothesis H (which includes Conjecture 5.26), as follows:

Conjecture 5.27. *Let $(a_1, b_1), \ldots, (a_k, b_k)$ be distinct pairs of integers such that $a_i > 0$, and for all primes p, there exists an integer m such that*

$$\prod_{i=1}^{k} (ma_i + b_i) \not\equiv 0 \pmod{p}.$$

Let $P(x)$ be the number of integers m up to x such that $ma_i + b_i$ are simultaneously prime for $i = 1, \ldots, k$. Then

$$P(x) \sim D \frac{x}{(\log x)^k},$$

where

$$D := \prod_p \left\{ \left(1 - \frac{1}{p}\right)^{-k} \left(1 - \frac{\omega(p)}{p}\right) \right\},$$

the product being over all primes p, and $\omega(p)$ being the number of distinct solutions m modulo p to the congruence

$$\prod_{i=1}^{k} (ma_i + b_i) \equiv 0 \pmod{p}.$$

The above conjecture also includes (a strong version of) the famous **twin primes conjecture** as a special case: the number of primes p up to x such that $p + 2$ is also prime is $\sim Cx/(\log x)^2$, where C is the same constant as in Conjecture 5.26.

EXERCISE 5.23. Show that the constant C appearing in Conjecture 5.26 satisfies

$$2C = B_2/B_1^2,$$

where B_1 and B_2 are the constants from Exercises 5.14 and 5.15.

EXERCISE 5.24. Show that the quantity D appearing in Conjecture 5.27 is well defined, and satisfies $0 < D < \infty$.

5.6 Notes

The prime number theorem was conjectured by Gauss in 1791. It was proven independently in 1896 by Hadamard and de la Vallée Poussin. A proof of the prime number theorem may be found, for example, in the book by Hardy and Wright [44].

Theorem 5.21, as well as the estimates for the constants A, B_1, and B_2 mentioned in that theorem and Exercises 5.13, 5.14, and 5.15, are from Rosser and Schoenfeld [79].

Theorem 5.17 is from Walfisz [96].

Theorem 5.19, which made the first connection between the theory of prime numbers and the zeta function, was discovered in the 18th century by Euler. The Riemann hypothesis was made by Riemann in 1859, and to this day, remains one of the most vexing conjectures in mathematics. Riemann in fact showed that his conjecture about the zeros of the zeta function is equivalent to the conjecture that for each fixed $\epsilon > 0$, $\pi(x) = \text{li}(x) + O(x^{1/2+\epsilon})$. This was strengthened by von Koch in 1901, who showed that the Riemann hypothesis is true if and only if $\pi(x) = \mathrm{li}(x) + O(x^{1/2} \log x)$. See Chapter 1 of the book by Crandall and Pomerance [30] for more on the connection between the Riemann hypothesis and the theory of prime numbers; in particular, see Exercise 1.36 in that book for an outline of a proof that Conjecture 5.18 follows from the Riemann hypothesis.

A warning: some authors (and software packages) define the logarithmic integral using the interval of integration $(0, x)$, rather than $(2, x)$, which increases its value by a constant $c \approx 1.0452$.

Theorem 5.22 was proved by Dirichlet in 1837, while Theorem 5.23 was proved by de la Vallée Poussin in 1896. A result of Oesterlé [69] implies that Conjecture 5.24 for $d \geq 3$ is a consequence of an assumption about the location of the zeros of certain generalizations of Riemann's zeta function; the case $d = 2$ follows from the bound in Conjecture 5.18 under the ordinary Riemann hypothesis. Theorem 5.25 is from Heath-Brown [45].

Hypothesis H is from Hardy and Littlewood [43].

For the reader who is interested in learning more on the topics discussed in this chapter, we recommend the books by Apostol [8] and Hardy and Wright [44]; indeed, many of the proofs presented in this chapter are minor variations on proofs from these two books. Our proof of Bertrand's postulate is based on the presentation in Section 9.2 of Redmond [76]. See also Bach and Shallit [12] (especially Chapter 8), Crandall and Pomerance [30] (especially Chapter 1) for a more detailed overview of these topics.

The data in Tables 5.1 and 5.2 was obtained using the computer program *Maple*.

6

Finite and discrete probability distributions

This chapter introduces concepts from discrete probability theory. We begin with a discussion of finite probability distributions, and then towards the end of the chapter we discuss the more general notion of a discrete probability distribution.

6.1 Finite probability distributions: basic definitions

A **finite probability distribution** $\mathbf{D} = (\mathcal{U}, \mathsf{P})$ is a *finite*, non-empty set $\mathcal{U}$, together with a function P that maps $u \in \mathcal{U}$ to $\mathsf{P}[u] \in [0, 1]$, such that

$$\sum_{u \in \mathcal{U}} \mathsf{P}[u] = 1. \tag{6.1}$$

The set $\mathcal{U}$ is called the **sample space** and the function P is called the **probability function**.

Intuitively, the elements of $\mathcal{U}$ represent the possible outcomes of a random experiment, where the probability of outcome $u \in \mathcal{U}$ is $\mathsf{P}[u]$.

Up until §6.10, we shall use the phrase "probability distribution" to mean "finite probability distribution."

Example 6.1. If we think of rolling a fair die, then $\mathcal{U} := \{1, 2, 3, 4, 5, 6\}$, and $\mathsf{P}[u] := 1/6$ for all $u \in \mathcal{U}$ gives a probability distribution describing the possible outcomes of the experiment. $\square$

Example 6.2. More generally, if $\mathcal{U}$ is a finite set, and $\mathsf{P}[u] = 1/|\mathcal{U}|$ for all $u \in \mathcal{U}$, then $\mathbf{D}$ is called the **uniform distribution on** $\mathcal{U}$. $\square$

Example 6.3. A coin flip is an example of a **Bernoulli trial**, which is in general an experiment with only two possible outcomes: *success*, which occurs with probability p, and *failure*, which occurs with probability $q := 1 - p$. $\square$

An **event** is a subset $\mathcal{A}$ of $\mathcal{U}$, and the **probability of** $\mathcal{A}$ is defined to be

$$P[\mathcal{A}] := \sum_{u \in \mathcal{A}} P[u]. \tag{6.2}$$

Thus, we extend the domain of definition of P from outcomes $u \in \mathcal{U}$ to events $\mathcal{A} \subseteq \mathcal{U}$.

For an event $\mathcal{A} \subseteq \mathcal{U}$, let $\overline{\mathcal{A}}$ denote the complement of $\mathcal{A}$ in $\mathcal{U}$. We have $P[\emptyset] = 0$, $P[\mathcal{U}] = 1$, $P[\overline{\mathcal{A}}] = 1 - P[\mathcal{A}]$.

For any events $\mathcal{A}, \mathcal{B} \subseteq \mathcal{U}$, if $\mathcal{A} \subseteq \mathcal{B}$, then $P[\mathcal{A}] \leq P[\mathcal{B}]$. Also, for any events $\mathcal{A}, \mathcal{B} \subseteq \mathcal{U}$, we have

$$P[\mathcal{A} \cup \mathcal{B}] = P[\mathcal{A}] + P[\mathcal{B}] - P[\mathcal{A} \cap \mathcal{B}] \leq P[\mathcal{A}] + P[\mathcal{B}]; \tag{6.3}$$

in particular, if $\mathcal{A}$ and $\mathcal{B}$ are disjoint, then

$$P[\mathcal{A} \cup \mathcal{B}] = P[\mathcal{A}] + P[\mathcal{B}]. \tag{6.4}$$

More generally, for any events $\mathcal{A}_1, \ldots, \mathcal{A}_n \subseteq \mathcal{U}$ we have

$$P[\mathcal{A}_1 \cup \cdots \cup \mathcal{A}_n] \leq P[\mathcal{A}_1] + \cdots + P[\mathcal{A}_n], \tag{6.5}$$

and if the $\mathcal{A}_i$ are pairwise disjoint, then

$$P[\mathcal{A}_1 \cup \cdots \cup \mathcal{A}_n] = P[\mathcal{A}_1] + \cdots + P[\mathcal{A}_n]. \tag{6.6}$$

In working with events, one makes frequent use of the usual rules of Boolean logic. DeMorgan's law says that for events $\mathcal{A}$ and $\mathcal{B}$, we have

$$\overline{\mathcal{A} \cup \mathcal{B}} = \overline{\mathcal{A}} \cap \overline{\mathcal{B}} \quad \text{and} \quad \overline{\mathcal{A} \cap \mathcal{B}} = \overline{\mathcal{A}} \cup \overline{\mathcal{B}}.$$

We also have the distributive law: for events $\mathcal{A}, \mathcal{B}, \mathcal{C}$, we have

$$\mathcal{A} \cap (\mathcal{B} \cup \mathcal{C}) = (\mathcal{A} \cap \mathcal{B}) \cup (\mathcal{A} \cap \mathcal{C}) \quad \text{and} \quad \mathcal{A} \cup (\mathcal{B} \cap \mathcal{C}) = (\mathcal{A} \cup \mathcal{B}) \cap (\mathcal{A} \cup \mathcal{C}).$$

In some applications and examples, it is more natural to use the logical "or" connective "$\vee$" in place of "$\cup$," and the logical "and" connective "$\wedge$" in place of "$\cap$."

Example 6.4. Continuing with Example 6.1, the probability of an "odd roll" $\mathcal{A} = \{1, 3, 5\}$ is $1/2$. $\square$

Example 6.5. More generally, if $\mathbf{D}$ is the uniform distribution on a set $\mathcal{U}$ of cardinality n, and $\mathcal{A}$ is a subset of $\mathcal{U}$ of cardinality k, then $P[\mathcal{A}] = k/n$. $\square$

Example 6.6. Alice rolls two dice, and asks Bob to guess a value that appears on either of the two dice (without looking). Let us model this situation by considering the uniform distribution on $\{(x, y) : x, y = 1, \ldots, 6\}$, where x represents the value of the first die, and y the value of the second.

For $x = 1, \ldots, 6$, let $\mathcal{A}_x$ be the event that the first die is x, and $\mathcal{B}_x$ the event that the second die is x, Let $\mathcal{C}_x = \mathcal{A}_x \cup \mathcal{B}_x$ be the event that x appears on either of the two dice. No matter what value x Bob chooses, the probability that this choice is correct is

$$\mathsf{P}[\mathcal{C}_x] = \mathsf{P}[\mathcal{A}_x \cup \mathcal{B}_x] = \mathsf{P}[\mathcal{A}_x] + \mathsf{P}[\mathcal{B}_x] - \mathsf{P}[\mathcal{A}_x \cap \mathcal{B}_x]$$
$$= 1/6 + 1/6 - 1/36 = 11/36. \quad \square$$

If $\mathbf{D}_1 = (\mathcal{U}_1, \mathsf{P}_1)$ and $\mathbf{D}_2 = (\mathcal{U}_2, \mathsf{P}_2)$ are probability distributions, we can form the **product distribution** $\mathbf{D} = (\mathcal{U}, \mathsf{P})$, where $\mathcal{U} := \mathcal{U}_1 \times \mathcal{U}_2$, and $\mathsf{P}[(u_1, u_2)] := \mathsf{P}_1[u_1]\mathsf{P}_2[u_2]$. It is easy to verify that the product distribution is also a probability distribution. Intuitively, the elements (u_1, u_2) of $\mathcal{U}_1 \times \mathcal{U}_2$ denote the possible outcomes of two separate and independent experiments.

More generally, if $\mathbf{D}_i = (\mathcal{U}_i, \mathsf{P}_i)$ for $i = 1, \ldots, n$, we can define the product distribution $\mathbf{D} = (\mathcal{U}, \mathsf{P})$, where $\mathcal{U} := \mathcal{U}_1 \times \cdots \times \mathcal{U}_n$, and $\mathsf{P}[(u_1, \ldots, u_n)] := \mathsf{P}[u_1] \ldots \mathsf{P}[u_n]$.

***Example* 6.7.** We can view the probability distribution in Example 6.6 as the product of two copies of the uniform distribution on $\{1, \ldots, 6\}$. $\square$

***Example* 6.8.** Consider the product distribution of n copies of a Bernoulli trial (see Example 6.3), with associated success probability p and failure probability $q := 1 - p$. An element of the sample space is an n-tuple of success/failure values. Any such tuple that contains, say, k successes and $n - k$ failures, occurs with probability $p^k q^{n-k}$, regardless of the particular positions of the successes and failures. $\square$

EXERCISE 6.1. This exercise asks you to recast previously established results in terms of probability theory.

(a) Let $k \geq 2$ be an integer, and suppose an integer n is chosen at random from among all k-bit integers. Show that the probability that n is prime is $\Theta(1/k)$.

(b) Let n be a positive integer, and suppose that a and b are chosen at random from the set $\{1, \ldots, n\}$. Show that the probability that $\gcd(a, b) = 1$ is at least $1/4$.

(c) Let n be a positive integer, and suppose that a is chosen at random from the set $\{1, \ldots, n\}$. Show that the probability that $\gcd(a, n) = 1$ is $\Omega(1/\log\log n)$.

EXERCISE 6.2. Suppose $\mathcal{A}, \mathcal{B}, \mathcal{C}$ are events such that $\mathcal{A} \cap \overline{\mathcal{C}} = \mathcal{B} \cap \overline{\mathcal{C}}$. Show that $|P[\mathcal{A}] - P[\mathcal{B}]| \leq P[\mathcal{C}]$.

EXERCISE 6.3. Generalize equation (6.3) by proving the **inclusion/exclusion principle**: for events $\mathcal{A}_1, \ldots, \mathcal{A}_n$, we have

$$P[\mathcal{A}_1 \cup \cdots \cup \mathcal{A}_n] = \sum_i P[\mathcal{A}_i] - \sum_{i<j} P[\mathcal{A}_i \cap \mathcal{A}_j] +$$

$$\sum_{i<j<k} P[\mathcal{A}_i \cap \mathcal{A}_j \cap \mathcal{A}_k] - \cdots + (-1)^{n-1} P[\mathcal{A}_1 \cap \cdots \cap \mathcal{A}_n]$$

$$= \sum_{\ell=1}^{n} (-1)^{\ell-1} \sum_{i_1 < \cdots < i_\ell} P[\mathcal{A}_{i_1} \cap \cdots \cap \mathcal{A}_{i_\ell}].$$

EXERCISE 6.4. Show that for events $\mathcal{A}_1, \ldots, \mathcal{A}_n$, we have

$$P[\mathcal{A}_1 \cup \cdots \cup \mathcal{A}_n] \geq \sum_i P[\mathcal{A}_i] - \sum_{i<j} P[\mathcal{A}_i \cap \mathcal{A}_j].$$

EXERCISE 6.5. Generalize inequality (6.5) and the previous exercise by proving **Bonferroni's inequalities**: for events $\mathcal{A}_1, \ldots, \mathcal{A}_n$, and defining

$$e_m := P[\mathcal{A}_1 \cup \cdots \cup \mathcal{A}_n] - \sum_{\ell=1}^{m} (-1)^{\ell-1} \sum_{i_1 < \cdots < i_\ell} P[\mathcal{A}_{i_1} \cap \cdots \cap \mathcal{A}_{i_\ell}]$$

for $m = 1, \ldots, n$, we have $e_m \leq 0$ for odd m, and $e_m \geq 0$ for even m.

6.2 Conditional probability and independence

Let $\mathbf{D} = (\mathcal{U}, P)$ be a probability distribution.

For any event $\mathcal{B} \subseteq \mathcal{U}$ with $P[\mathcal{B}] \neq 0$ and any $u \in \mathcal{U}$, let us define

$$P[u \mid \mathcal{B}] := \begin{cases} P[u]/P[\mathcal{B}] & \text{if } u \in \mathcal{B}, \\ 0 & \text{otherwise.} \end{cases}$$

Viewing $\mathcal{B}$ as fixed, we may view the function $P[\cdot \mid \mathcal{B}]$ as a new probability function on the sample space $\mathcal{U}$, and this gives rise a new probability distribution $\mathbf{D}_{\mathcal{B}} := (P[\cdot \mid \mathcal{B}], \mathcal{U})$, called the **conditional distribution given** $\mathcal{B}$.

Intuitively, $\mathbf{D}_{\mathcal{B}}$ has the following interpretation: if a random experiment produces an outcome according to the distribution $\mathbf{D}$, and we learn that the event $\mathcal{B}$ has occurred, then the distribution $\mathbf{D}_{\mathcal{B}}$ assigns new probabilities to all possible outcomes, reflecting the partial knowledge that the event $\mathcal{B}$ has occurred.

As usual, we extend the domain of definition of $P[\cdot \mid \mathcal{B}]$ from outcomes to events. For any event $\mathcal{A} \subseteq \mathcal{U}$, we have

$$P[\mathcal{A} \mid \mathcal{B}] = \sum_{u \in \mathcal{A}} P[u \mid \mathcal{B}] = \frac{P[\mathcal{A} \cap \mathcal{B}]}{P[\mathcal{B}]}.$$

The value $P[\mathcal{A} \mid \mathcal{B}]$ is called the **conditional probability of $\mathcal{A}$ given $\mathcal{B}$**. Again, the intuition is that this is the probability that the event $\mathcal{A}$ occurs, given the partial knowledge that the event $\mathcal{B}$ has occurred.

For events $\mathcal{A}$ and $\mathcal{B}$, if $P[\mathcal{A} \cap \mathcal{B}] = P[\mathcal{A}] \cdot P[\mathcal{B}]$, then $\mathcal{A}$ and $\mathcal{B}$ are called **independent** events. If $P[\mathcal{B}] \neq 0$, a simple calculation shows that $\mathcal{A}$ and $\mathcal{B}$ are independent if and only if $P[\mathcal{A} \mid \mathcal{B}] = P[\mathcal{A}]$.

A collection $\mathcal{A}_1, \ldots, \mathcal{A}_n$ of events is called **pairwise independent** if $P[\mathcal{A}_i \cap \mathcal{A}_j] = P[\mathcal{A}_i]P[\mathcal{A}_j]$ for all $i \neq j$, and is called **mutually independent** if every subset $\mathcal{A}_{i_1}, \ldots, \mathcal{A}_{i_k}$ of the collection satisfies

$$P[\mathcal{A}_{i_1} \cap \cdots \cap \mathcal{A}_{i_k}] = P[\mathcal{A}_{i_1}] \cdots P[\mathcal{A}_{i_k}].$$

Example 6.9. In Example 6.6, suppose that Alice tells Bob the sum of the two dice before Bob makes his guess. For example, suppose Alice tells Bob the sum is 4. Then what is Bob's best strategy in this case? Let $\mathcal{S}_z$ be the event that the sum is z, for $z = 2, \ldots, 12$, and consider the conditional probability distribution given $\mathcal{S}_4$. This is the uniform distribution on the three pairs $(1,3), (2,2), (3,1)$. The numbers 1 and 3 both appear in two pairs, while the number 2 appears in just one pair. Therefore,

$$P[\mathcal{C}_1 \mid \mathcal{S}_4] = P[\mathcal{C}_3 \mid \mathcal{S}_4] = 2/3,$$

while

$$P[\mathcal{C}_2 \mid \mathcal{S}_4] = 1/3$$

and

$$P[\mathcal{C}_4 \mid \mathcal{S}_4] = P[\mathcal{C}_5 \mid \mathcal{S}_4] = P[\mathcal{C}_6 \mid \mathcal{S}_4] = 0.$$

Thus, if the sum is 4, Bob's best strategy is to guess either 1 or 3.

Note that the events $\mathcal{A}_1$ and $\mathcal{B}_2$ are independent, while the events $\mathcal{A}_1$ and $\mathcal{S}_4$ are not. $\square$

Example 6.10. Suppose we toss three fair coins. Let $\mathcal{A}_1$ be the event that the first coin is "heads," let $\mathcal{A}_2$ be the event that the second coin is "heads," and let $\mathcal{A}_3$ be the event that the third coin is "heads." Then the collection of events $\{\mathcal{A}_1, \mathcal{A}_2, \mathcal{A}_3\}$ is mutually independent.

Now let $\mathcal{B}_{12}$ be the event that the first and second coins agree (i.e., both "heads" or both "tails"), let $\mathcal{B}_{13}$ be the event that the first and third coins agree, and let $\mathcal{B}_{23}$ be the event that the second and third coins agree. Then the collection of events $\{\mathcal{B}_{12}, \mathcal{B}_{13}, \mathcal{B}_{23}\}$ is pairwise independent, but not mutually independent. Indeed, the probability that any one of the events occurs is $1/2$, and the probability that any two of the three events occurs is $1/4$; however, the probability that all three occurs is also $1/4$, since if any two events occur, then so does the third. $\square$

Suppose we have a collection $\mathcal{B}_1, \ldots, \mathcal{B}_n$ of events that partitions $\mathcal{U}$, such that each event $\mathcal{B}_i$ occurs with non-zero probability. Then it is easy to see that for any event $\mathcal{A}$,

$$\mathsf{P}[\mathcal{A}] = \sum_{i=1}^{n} \mathsf{P}[\mathcal{A} \cap \mathcal{B}_i] = \sum_{i=1}^{n} \mathsf{P}[\mathcal{A} \mid \mathcal{B}_i] \cdot \mathsf{P}[\mathcal{B}_i]. \tag{6.7}$$

Furthermore, if $\mathsf{P}[\mathcal{A}] \neq 0$, then for any $j = 1, \ldots, n$, we have

$$\mathsf{P}[\mathcal{B}_j \mid \mathcal{A}] = \frac{\mathsf{P}[\mathcal{A} \cap \mathcal{B}_j]}{\mathsf{P}[\mathcal{A}]} = \frac{\mathsf{P}[\mathcal{A} \mid \mathcal{B}_j]\mathsf{P}[\mathcal{B}_j]}{\sum_{i=1}^{n} \mathsf{P}[\mathcal{A} \mid \mathcal{B}_i]\mathsf{P}[\mathcal{B}_i]}. \tag{6.8}$$

This equality, known as **Bayes' theorem**, lets us compute the conditional probability $\mathsf{P}[\mathcal{B}_j \mid \mathcal{A}]$ in terms of the conditional probabilities $\mathsf{P}[\mathcal{A} \mid \mathcal{B}_i]$.

The equation (6.7) is useful for computing or estimating probabilities by conditioning on specific events $\mathcal{B}_i$ (i.e., by considering the conditional probability distribution given $\mathcal{B}_i$) in such a way that the conditional probabilities $\mathsf{P}[\mathcal{A} \mid \mathcal{B}_i]$ are easy to compute or estimate. Also, if we want to compute a conditional probability $\mathsf{P}[\mathcal{A} \mid \mathcal{C}]$, we can do so by partitioning $\mathcal{C}$ into events $\mathcal{B}_1, \ldots, \mathcal{B}_n$, where each $\mathcal{B}_i$ occurs with non-zero probability, and use the following simple fact:

$$\mathsf{P}[\mathcal{A} \mid \mathcal{C}] = \sum_{i=1}^{n} \mathsf{P}[\mathcal{A} \mid \mathcal{B}_i]\mathsf{P}[\mathcal{B}_i]/\mathsf{P}[\mathcal{C}]. \tag{6.9}$$

***Example* 6.11.** This example is based on the TV game show "Let's make a deal," which was popular in the 1970's. In this game, a contestant chooses one of three doors. Behind two doors is a "zonk," that is, something amusing but of little or no value, such as a goat, and behind one of the doors is a "grand prize," such as a car or vacation package. We may assume that the door behind which the grand prize is placed is chosen at random from among the three doors, with equal probability. After the contestant chooses a door, the host of the show, Monty Hall, always reveals a zonk behind one of the two doors not chosen by the contestant. The contestant is then given a choice: either stay with his initial choice of door, or switch to the other unopened door. After the contestant finalizes his decision on which door to choose, that door is opened and he wins whatever is behind the chosen door. The question is, which strategy is better for the contestant: to stay or to switch?

Let us evaluate the two strategies. If the contestant always stays with his initial selection, then it is clear that his probability of success is exactly $1/3$.

Now consider the strategy of always switching. Let $\mathcal{B}$ be the event that the contestant's initial choice was correct, and let $\mathcal{A}$ be the event that the contestant wins the grand prize. On the one hand, if the contestant's initial choice was correct, then switching will certainly lead to failure. That is, $\mathsf{P}[\mathcal{A} \mid \mathcal{B}] = 0$. On the other hand, suppose that the contestant's initial choice was incorrect, so that one of the zonks is behind the initially chosen door. Since Monty reveals the other zonk, switching will lead with certainty to success. That is, $\mathsf{P}[\mathcal{A} \mid \overline{\mathcal{B}}] = 1$. Furthermore, it is clear that $\mathsf{P}[\mathcal{B}] = 1/3$. So we compute

$$\mathsf{P}[\mathcal{A}] = \mathsf{P}[\mathcal{A} \mid \mathcal{B}]\mathsf{P}[\mathcal{B}] + \mathsf{P}[\mathcal{A} \mid \overline{\mathcal{B}}]\mathsf{P}[\overline{\mathcal{B}}] = 0 \cdot (1/3) + 1 \cdot (2/3) = 2/3.$$

Thus, the "stay" strategy has a success probability of $1/3$, while the "switch" strategy has a success probability of $2/3$. So it is better to switch than to stay.

Of course, real life is a bit more complicated. Monty did not always reveal a zonk and offer a choice to switch. Indeed, if Monty *only* revealed a zonk when the contestant had chosen the correct door, then switching would certainly be the wrong strategy. However, if Monty's choice itself was a random decision made independent of the contestant's initial choice, then switching is again the preferred strategy. □

***Example* 6.12.** Suppose that the rate of incidence of disease X in the overall population is 1%. Also suppose that there is a test for disease X; however, the test is not perfect: it has a 5% false positive rate (i.e., 5% of healthy patients test positive for the disease), and a 2% false negative rate (i.e., 2% of sick patients test negative for the disease). A doctor gives the test to a patient and it comes out positive. How should the doctor advise his patient? In particular, what is the probability that the patient actually has disease X, given a positive test result?

Amazingly, many trained doctors will say the probability is 95%, since the test has a false positive rate of 5%. However, this conclusion is completely wrong.

Let $\mathcal{A}$ be the event that the test is positive and let $\mathcal{B}$ be the event that the patient has disease X. The relevant quantity that we need to estimate is $\mathsf{P}[\mathcal{B} \mid \mathcal{A}]$; that is, the probability that the patient has disease X, given a positive test result. We use Bayes' theorem to do this:

$$P[\mathcal{B} \mid \mathcal{A}] = \frac{P[\mathcal{A} \mid \mathcal{B}]P[\mathcal{B}]}{P[\mathcal{A} \mid \mathcal{B}]P[\mathcal{B}] + P[\mathcal{A} \mid \overline{\mathcal{B}}]P[\overline{\mathcal{B}}]} = \frac{0.98 \cdot 0.01}{0.98 \cdot 0.01 + 0.05 \cdot 0.99} \approx 0.17.$$

Thus, the chances that the patient has disease X given a positive test result is just 17%. The correct intuition here is that it is much more likely to get a false positive than it is to actually have the disease.

Of course, the real world is a bit more complicated than this example suggests: the doctor may be giving the patient the test because other risk factors or symptoms may suggest that the patient is more likely to have the disease than a random member of the population, in which case the above analysis does not apply. □

EXERCISE 6.6. Consider again the situation in Example 6.12, but now suppose that the patient is visiting the doctor because he has symptom Y. Furthermore, it is known that everyone who has disease X exhibits symptom Y, while 10% of the population overall exhibits symptom Y. Assuming that the accuracy of the test is not affected by the presence of symptom Y, how should the doctor advise his patient should the test come out positive?

EXERCISE 6.7. Suppose we roll two dice, and let (x, y) denote the outcome (as in Example 6.6). For each of the following pairs of events $\mathcal{A}$ and $\mathcal{B}$, determine if they are independent or not:

   (a) $\mathcal{A}$: $x = y$; $\mathcal{B}$: $y = 1$.
   (b) $\mathcal{A}$: $x \geq y$; $\mathcal{B}$: $y = 1$.
   (c) $\mathcal{A}$: $x \geq y$; $\mathcal{B}$: $y^2 = 7y - 6$.
   (d) $\mathcal{A}$: $xy = 6$; $\mathcal{B}$: $y = 3$.

EXERCISE 6.8. Let $\mathcal{C}$ be an event that occurs with non-zero probability, and let $\mathcal{B}_1, \ldots, \mathcal{B}_n$ be a partition of $\mathcal{C}$, such that each event $\mathcal{B}_i$ occurs with non-zero probability. Let $\mathcal{A}$ be an event and let p be a real number with $0 \leq p \leq 1$. Suppose that for each $i = 1, \ldots, n$, the conditional probability of $\mathcal{A}$ given $\mathcal{B}_i$ is $\leq p$ (resp., $<, =, >, \geq p$). Show that the conditional probability of $\mathcal{A}$ given $\mathcal{C}$ is also $\leq p$ (resp., $<, =, >, \geq p$).

EXERCISE 6.9. Show that if two events $\mathcal{A}$ and $\mathcal{B}$ are independent, then so are $\mathcal{A}$ and $\overline{\mathcal{B}}$. More generally, show that if $\mathcal{A}_1, \ldots, \mathcal{A}_n$ are mutually independent, then so are $\mathcal{A}'_1, \ldots, \mathcal{A}'_n$, where each $\mathcal{A}'_i$ denotes either $\mathcal{A}_i$ or $\overline{\mathcal{A}}_i$.

EXERCISE 6.10. This exercise develops an alternative proof, based on probability theory, of Theorem 2.14. Let $n > 1$ be an integer and consider an experiment in which a number a is chosen at random from $\{0, \ldots, n-1\}$. If $n = p_1^{e_1} \cdots p_r^{e_r}$ is the prime factorization of n, let $\mathcal{A}_i$ be the event that a is divisible by p_i, for $i = 1, \ldots, r$.

(a) Show that
$$\phi(n)/n = \mathsf{P}[\overline{\mathcal{A}}_1 \cap \cdots \cap \overline{\mathcal{A}}_r],$$

where ϕ is Euler's phi function.

(b) Show that if $i_1, \ldots, i_\ell$ are distinct indices between 1 and r, then
$$\mathsf{P}[\mathcal{A}_{i_1} \cap \cdots \cap \mathcal{A}_{i_\ell}] = \frac{1}{p_{i_1} \cdots p_{i_\ell}}.$$

Conclude that the events $\mathcal{A}_i$ are mutually independent, and $\mathsf{P}[\mathcal{A}_i] = 1/p_i$.

(c) Using part (b) and the result of the previous exercise, show that
$$\mathsf{P}[\overline{\mathcal{A}}_1 \cap \cdots \cap \overline{\mathcal{A}}_r] = \prod_{i=1}^{r}(1 - 1/p_i).$$

(d) Combine parts (a) and (c) to derive the result of Theorem 2.14 that
$$\phi(n) = n \prod_{i=1}^{r}(1 - 1/p_i).$$

6.3 Random variables

Let $\mathbf{D} = (\mathcal{U}, \mathsf{P})$ be a probability distribution.

It is sometimes convenient to associate a real number, or other mathematical object, with each outcome $u \in \mathcal{U}$. Such an association is called a **random variable**; more formally, a random variable X is a function from $\mathcal{U}$ into a set $\mathcal{X}$. If $\mathcal{X}$ is a subset of the real numbers, then X is called a **real random variable**. When we speak of the **image** of X, we simply mean its image in the usual function-theoretic sense, that is, the set $X(\mathcal{U}) = \{X(u) : u \in \mathcal{U}\}$.

One may define any number of random variables on a given probability distribution. If $X : \mathcal{U} \to \mathcal{X}$ is a random variable, and $f : \mathcal{X} \to \mathcal{Y}$ is a function, then $f(X) := f \circ X$ is also a random variable.

Example **6.13.** Suppose we flip n fair coins. Then we may define a random variable X that maps each outcome to a bit string of length n, where a "head" is encoded as a 1-bit, and a "tail" is encoded as a 0-bit. We may define another random variable Y that is the number of "heads." The variable Y is a real random variable. $\square$

***Example* 6.14.** If $\mathcal{A}$ is an event, we may define a random variable X as follows: $X := 1$ if the event $\mathcal{A}$ occurs, and $X := 0$ otherwise. The variable X is called the **indicator variable for** $\mathcal{A}$. Conversely, if Y is any $0/1$-valued random variable, we can define the event $\mathcal{B}$ to be the subset of all possible outcomes that lead to $Y = 1$, and Y is the indicator variable for the event $\mathcal{B}$. Thus, we can work with either events or indicator variables, whichever is more natural and convenient. $\square$

Let $X : \mathcal{U} \to \mathcal{X}$ be a random variable. For $x \in \mathcal{X}$, we write "$X = x$" as shorthand for the event $\{u \in \mathcal{U} : X(u) = x\}$. More generally, for any predicate ϕ, we may write "$\phi(X)$" as shorthand for the event $\{u \in \mathcal{U} : \phi(X(u))\}$.

A random variable X defines a probability distribution on its image $\mathcal{X}$, where the probability associated with $x \in \mathcal{X}$ is $\mathsf{P}[X = x]$. We call this the **distribution of** X. For two random variables X, Y defined on a probability distribution, $Z := (X, Y)$ is also a random variable whose distribution is called the **joint distribution of** X **and** Y.

If X is a random variable, and $\mathcal{A}$ is an event with non-zero probability, then the **conditional distribution of** X **given** $\mathcal{A}$ is a probability distribution on the image $\mathcal{X}$ of X, where the probability associated with $x \in \mathcal{X}$ is $\mathsf{P}[X = x \mid \mathcal{A}]$.

We say two random variables X, Y are **independent** if for all x in the image of X and all y in the image of Y, the events $X = x$ and $Y = y$ are independent, which is to say,

$$\mathsf{P}[X = x \wedge Y = y] = \mathsf{P}[X = x]\mathsf{P}[Y = y].$$

Equivalently, X and Y are independent if and only if their joint distribution is equal to the product of their individual distributions. Alternatively, X and Y are independent if and only if for all values x taken by X with non-zero probability, the conditional distribution of Y given the event $X = x$ is the same as the distribution of Y.

Let $X_1, \ldots, X_n$ be a collection of random variables, and let $\mathcal{X}_i$ be the image of X_i for $i = 1, \ldots, n$. We say $X_1, \ldots, X_n$ are **pairwise independent** if for all $i, j = 1, \ldots, n$ with $i \neq j$, the variables X_i and X_j are independent. We say that $X_1, \ldots, X_n$ are **mutually independent** if for all $x_1 \in \mathcal{X}_1, \ldots, x_n \in \mathcal{X}_n$, we have

$$\mathsf{P}[X_1 = x_1 \wedge \cdots \wedge X_n = x_n] = \mathsf{P}[X_1 = x_1] \cdots \mathsf{P}[X_n = x_n].$$

More generally, for $k = 2, \ldots, n$, we say that $X_1, \ldots, X_n$ are **k-wise independent** if any k of them are mutually independent.

***Example* 6.15.** We toss three coins, and set $X_i := 0$ if the ith coin is "tails," and $X_i := 1$ otherwise. The variables X_1, X_2, X_3 are mutually independent. Let us set $Y_{12} := X_1 \oplus X_2$, $Y_{13} := X_1 \oplus X_3$, and $Y_{23} := X_2 \oplus X_3$, where "$\oplus$" denotes "exclusive or," that is, addition modulo 2. Then the variables Y_{12}, Y_{13}, Y_{23} are pairwise independent, but not mutually independent—observe that $Y_{12} \oplus Y_{13} = Y_{23}$. $\square$

The following is a simple but useful fact:

Theorem 6.1. *Let $X_i : \mathcal{U} \to \mathcal{X}_i$ be random variables, for $i = 1, \ldots, n$, and suppose that there exist functions $f_i : \mathcal{X}_i \to [0, 1]$, for $i = 1, \ldots, n$, such that*

$$\sum_{x_i \in \mathcal{X}_i} f_i(x_i) = 1 \quad (i = 1 \ldots n),$$

and

$$\mathsf{P}[X_1 = x_1 \wedge \cdots \wedge X_n = x_n] = f_1(x_1) \cdots f_n(x_n)$$

for all $x_1 \in \mathcal{X}_1, \ldots, x_n \in \mathcal{X}_n$. Then for any subset of distinct indices $i_1, \ldots, i_\ell \in \{1, \ldots, n\}$, we have

$$\mathsf{P}[X_{i_1} = x_{i_1} \wedge \cdots \wedge X_{i_\ell} = x_{i_\ell}] = f_{i_1}(x_{i_1}) \cdots f_{i_\ell}(x_{i_\ell})$$

for all $x_{i_1} \in \mathcal{X}_{i_1}, \ldots, x_{i_\ell} \in \mathcal{X}_{i_\ell}$.

Proof. To prove the theorem, it will suffice to show that we can "eliminate" a single variable, say X_n, meaning that for all $x_1, \ldots, x_{n-1}$, we have

$$\mathsf{P}[X_1 = x_1 \wedge \cdots \wedge X_{n-1} = x_{n-1}] = f_1(x_1) \cdots f_{n-1}(x_{n-1}).$$

Having established this, we may then proceed to eliminate any number of variables (the ordering of the variables is clearly irrelevant).

We have

$$\mathsf{P}[X_1 = x_1 \wedge \cdots \wedge X_{n-1} = x_{n-1}]$$

$$= \sum_{x_n \in \mathcal{X}_n} \mathsf{P}[X_1 = x_1 \wedge \cdots \wedge X_{n-1} = x_{n-1} \wedge X_n = x_n]$$

$$= \sum_{x_n \in \mathcal{X}_n} f_1(x_1) \cdots f_{n-1}(x_{n-1}) f_n(x_n)$$

$$= f_1(x_2) \cdots f_{n-1}(x_{n-1}) \sum_{x_n \in \mathcal{X}_n} f_n(x_n)$$

$$= f_1(x_1) \cdots f_{n-1}(x_{n-1}). \quad \square$$

The following three theorems are immediate consequences of the above theorem:

Theorem 6.2. *Let $X_i : \mathcal{U} \to \mathcal{X}_i$ be random variables, for $i = 1, \ldots, n$, such that*

$$\mathsf{P}[X_1 = x_1 \wedge \cdots \wedge X_n = x_n] = \frac{1}{|\mathcal{X}_1|} \cdots \frac{1}{|\mathcal{X}_n|} \quad (for\ all\ x_1 \in \mathcal{X}_1, \ldots, x_n \in \mathcal{X}_n).$$

Then the variables X_i are mutually independent with each X_i uniformly distributed over $\mathcal{X}_i$.

Theorem 6.3. *If $X_1, \ldots, X_n$ are mutually independent random variables, then they are k-wise independent for all $k = 2, \ldots, n$.*

Theorem 6.4. *If $\mathbf{D}_i = (\mathcal{U}_i, \mathsf{P}_i)$ are probability distributions for $i = 1, \ldots, n$, then the projection functions $\pi_i : \mathcal{U}_1 \times \cdots \times \mathcal{U}_n \to \mathcal{U}_i$, where $\pi_i(u_1, \ldots, u_n) = u_i$, are mutually independent random variables on the product distribution $\mathbf{D}_1 \times \cdots \times \mathbf{D}_n$.*

We also have:

Theorem 6.5. *If $X_1, \ldots, X_n$ are mutually independent random variables, and $g_1, \ldots, g_n$ are functions, then $g_1(X_1), \ldots, g_n(X_n)$ are also mutually independent random variables.*

Proof. The proof is a straightforward, if somewhat tedious, calculation. For $i = 1, \ldots, n$, let y_i be some value in the image of $g_i(X_i)$, and let $\mathcal{X}_i := g_i^{-1}(\{y_i\})$. We have

$$\mathsf{P}[g_1(X_1) = y_1 \wedge \cdots \wedge g_n(X_n) = y_n]$$

$$= \mathsf{P}\left[\left(\bigvee_{x_1 \in \mathcal{X}_1} X_1 = x_1 \right) \wedge \cdots \wedge \left(\bigvee_{x_n \in \mathcal{X}_n} X_n = x_n \right) \right]$$

$$= \mathsf{P}\left[\bigvee_{x_1 \in \mathcal{X}_1} \cdots \bigvee_{x_n \in \mathcal{X}_n} (X_1 = x_1 \wedge \cdots \wedge X_n = x_n) \right]$$

$$= \sum_{x_1 \in \mathcal{X}_1} \cdots \sum_{x_n \in \mathcal{X}_n} \mathsf{P}[X_1 = x_1 \wedge \cdots \wedge X_n = x_n]$$

$$= \sum_{x_1 \in \mathcal{X}_1} \cdots \sum_{x_n \in \mathcal{X}_n} \mathsf{P}[X_1 = x_1] \cdots \mathsf{P}[X_n = x_n]$$

$$= \left(\sum_{x_1 \in \mathcal{X}_1} \mathsf{P}[X_1 = x_1] \right) \cdots \left(\sum_{x_n \in \mathcal{X}_n} \mathsf{P}[X_n = x_n] \right)$$

$$= P\left[\bigvee_{x_1 \in \mathcal{X}_1} X_1 = x_1\right] \cdots P\left[\bigvee_{x_n \in \mathcal{X}_n} X_n = x_n\right]$$

$$= P[g_1(X_1) = y_1] \cdots P[g_n(X_n) = y_n]. \quad \Box$$

Example 6.16. If we toss n dice, and let X_i denote the value of the ith die for $i = 1, \ldots, n$, then the X_i are mutually independent random variables. If we set $Y_i := X_i^2$ for $i = 1, \ldots, n$, then the Y_i are also mutually independent random variables. $\Box$

Example 6.17. This example again illustrates the notion of pairwise independence. Let X and Y be independent and uniformly distributed over $\mathbb{Z}_p$, where p is a prime. For $a \in \mathbb{Z}_p$, let $Z_a := aX + Y$. Then we claim that each Z_a is uniformly distributed over $\mathbb{Z}_p$, and that the collection of random variables $\{Z_a : a \in \mathbb{Z}_p\}$ is pairwise independent.

To prove this claim, let $a, b \in \mathbb{Z}_p$ with $a \neq b$, and consider the map $f_{a,b} : \mathbb{Z}_p \times \mathbb{Z}_p \to \mathbb{Z}_p \times \mathbb{Z}_p$ that sends (x, y) to $(ax + y, bx + y)$. It is easy to see that $f_{a,b}$ is injective; indeed, if $ax + y = ax' + y'$ and $bx + y = bx' + y'$, then subtracting these two equations, we obtain $(a - b)x = (a - b)x'$, and since $a - b \neq [0]_p$, it follows that $x = x'$, which also implies $y = y'$. Since $f_{a,b}$ is injective, it must be a bijection from $\mathbb{Z}_p \times \mathbb{Z}_p$ onto itself. Thus, since (X, Y) is uniformly distributed over $\mathbb{Z}_p \times \mathbb{Z}_p$, so is $(Z_a, Z_b) = (aX + Y, bX + Y)$. So for all $z, z' \in \mathbb{Z}_p$, we have

$$P[Z_a = z \wedge Z_b = z'] = 1/p^2,$$

and so the claim follows from Theorem 6.2.

Note that the variables Z_a are not 3-wise independent, since the value of any two determines the value of all the rest (verify). $\Box$

Example 6.18. We can generalize the previous example as follows. Let $X_1, \ldots, X_t, Y$ be mutually independent and uniformly distributed over $\mathbb{Z}_p$, where p is prime, and for $a_1, \ldots, a_t \in \mathbb{Z}_p$, let $Z_{a_1,\ldots,a_t} := a_1 X_1 + \cdots + a_t X_t + Y$. We claim that each $Z_{a_1,\ldots,a_t}$ is uniformly distributed over $\mathbb{Z}_p$, and that the collection of all such $Z_{a_1,\ldots,a_t}$ is pairwise independent.

To prove this claim, it will suffice (by Theorem 6.2) to prove that for all

$$a_1, \ldots, a_t, \ b_1, \ldots, b_t, \ z, z' \in \mathbb{Z}_p,$$

subject to $(a_1, \ldots, a_t) \neq (b_1, \ldots, b_t)$, we have

$$P[Z_{a_1,\ldots,a_t} = z \wedge Z_{b_1,\ldots,b_t} = z'] = 1/p^2. \tag{6.10}$$

Since $(a_1, \ldots, a_t) \neq (b_1, \ldots, b_t)$, we know that $a_j \neq b_j$ for some $j = 1, \ldots, t$. Let us assume that $a_1 \neq b_1$ (the argument for $j > 1$ is analogous).

We first show that for all $x_2, \ldots, x_t \in \mathbb{Z}_p$, we have

$$\mathsf{P}[Z_{a_1,\ldots,a_t} = z \wedge Z_{b_1,\ldots,b_t} = z' \mid X_2 = x_2 \wedge \cdots \wedge X_t = x_t] = 1/p^2. \quad (6.11)$$

To prove (6.11), consider the conditional probability distribution given $X_2 = x_2 \wedge \cdots \wedge X_t = x_t$. In this conditional distribution, we have

$$Z_{a_1,\ldots,a_t} = a_1 X_1 + Y + c \quad \text{and} \quad Z_{b_1,\ldots,b_t} = b_1 X_1 + Y + d,$$

where

$$c := a_2 x_2 + \cdots + a_t x_t \quad \text{and} \quad d := b_2 x_2 + \cdots + b_t x_t,$$

and X_1 and Y are independent and uniformly distributed over $\mathbb{Z}_p$ (this follows from the mutual independence of $X_1, \ldots, X_t, Y$ before conditioning). By the result of the previous example, $(a_1 X_1 + Y, b_1 X_1 + Y)$ is uniformly distributed over $\mathbb{Z}_p \times \mathbb{Z}_p$, and since the function sending $(x, y) \in \mathbb{Z}_p \times \mathbb{Z}_p$ to $(x+c, y+d) \in \mathbb{Z}_p \times \mathbb{Z}_p$ is a bijection, it follows that $(a_1 X_1 + Y + c, b_1 X_1 + Y + d)$ is uniformly distributed over $\mathbb{Z}_p \times \mathbb{Z}_p$. That proves (6.11).

(6.10) now follows easily from (6.11), as follows:

$$
\begin{aligned}
&\mathsf{P}[Z_{a_1,\ldots,a_t} = z \wedge Z_{b_1,\ldots,b_t} = z'] \\
&\quad = \sum_{x_2,\ldots,x_t} \mathsf{P}[Z_{a_1,\ldots,a_t} = z \wedge Z_{b_1,\ldots,b_t} = z' \mid X_2 = x_2 \wedge \cdots \wedge X_t = x_t] \cdot \\
&\qquad\qquad \mathsf{P}[X_2 = x_2 \wedge \cdots \wedge X_t = x_t] \\
&\quad = \sum_{x_2,\ldots,x_t} \frac{1}{p^2} \cdot \mathsf{P}[X_2 = x_2 \wedge \cdots \wedge X_t = x_t] \\
&\quad = \frac{1}{p^2} \cdot \sum_{x_2,\ldots,x_t} \mathsf{P}[X_2 = x_2 \wedge \cdots \wedge X_t = x_t] \\
&\quad = \frac{1}{p^2} \cdot 1. \quad \square
\end{aligned}
$$

Using other algebraic techniques, there are many ways to construct pairwise and k-wise independent families of random variables. Such families play an important role in many areas of computer science.

Example 6.19. Suppose we perform an experiment by executing n Bernoulli trials (see Example 6.3), where each trial succeeds with the same probability p, and fails with probability $q := 1 - p$, independently of the outcomes of all the other trials. Let X denote the total number of successes. For $k = 0, \ldots, n$, let us calculate the probability that $X = k$.

To do this, let us introduce indicator variables $X_1, \ldots, X_n$, where for

$i = 1, \ldots, n$, we have $X_i = 1$ if the ith trial succeeds, and $X_i = 0$, otherwise. By assumption, the X_i are mutually independent. Then we see that $X = X_1 + \cdots + X_n$. Now, consider a fixed value $k = 0, \ldots, n$. Let $\mathcal{C}_k$ denote the collection of all subsets of $\{1, \ldots, n\}$ of size k. For $I \in \mathcal{C}_k$, let $\mathcal{A}_I$ be the event that $X_i = 1$ for all $i \in I$ and $X_i = 0$ for all $i \notin I$. Since the X_i are mutually independent, we see that $\mathsf{P}[\mathcal{A}_I] = p^k q^{n-k}$ (as in Example 6.8). Evidently, the collection of events $\{\mathcal{A}_I\}_{I \in \mathcal{C}_k}$ is a partition of the event that $X = k$. Therefore,

$$\mathsf{P}[X = k] = \sum_{I \in \mathcal{C}_k} \mathsf{P}[\mathcal{A}_I] = \sum_{I \in \mathcal{C}_k} p^k q^{n-k} = |\mathcal{C}_k| p^k q^{n-k}.$$

Finally, since

$$|\mathcal{C}_k| = \binom{n}{k},$$

we conclude that

$$\mathsf{P}[X = k] = \binom{n}{k} p^k q^{n-k}.$$

The distribution of the random variable X is called a **binomial distribution**. $\square$

EXERCISE 6.11. Let $X_1, \ldots, X_n$ be random variables, and let $\mathcal{X}_i$ be the image of X_i for $i = 1, \ldots, n$. Show that $X_1, \ldots, X_n$ are mutually independent if and only if for all $i = 2, \ldots, n$, and all $x_1 \in \mathcal{X}_1, \ldots, x_i \in \mathcal{X}_i$, we have

$$\mathsf{P}[X_i = x_i \mid X_{i-1} = x_{i-1} \wedge \cdots \wedge X_1 = x_1] = \mathsf{P}[X_i = x_i].$$

EXERCISE 6.12. Let $\mathcal{A}_1, \ldots, \mathcal{A}_n$ be events with corresponding indicator variables $X_1, \ldots, X_n$. Show that the events $\mathcal{A}_1, \ldots, \mathcal{A}_n$ are mutually independent if and only if the random variables $X_1, \ldots, X_n$ are mutually independent. Note: there is actually something non-trivial to prove here, since our definitions for independent events and independent random variables superficially look quite different.

EXERCISE 6.13. Let $\mathcal{C}$ be an event that occurs with non-zero probability, and let $\mathcal{B}_1, \ldots, \mathcal{B}_n$ be a partition of $\mathcal{C}$, such that each event $\mathcal{B}_i$ occurs with non-zero probability. Let X be a random variable whose image is $\mathcal{X}$, and let $\mathbf{D}'$ be a probability distribution on $\mathcal{X}$. Suppose that for each $i = 1, \ldots, n$, the conditional distribution of X given $\mathcal{B}_i$ is equal to $\mathbf{D}'$. Show that the conditional distribution of X given $\mathcal{C}$ is also equal to $\mathbf{D}'$.

EXERCISE 6.14. Let n be a positive integer, and let X be a random variable whose distribution is uniform over $\{0, \ldots, n-1\}$. For each positive divisor d of n, let use define the random variable $X_d := X \bmod d$. Show that for any positive divisors $d_1, \ldots, d_k$ of n, the random variables $X_{d_1}, \ldots, X_{d_k}$ are mutually independent if and only if $d_1, \ldots, d_k$ are pairwise relatively prime.

EXERCISE 6.15. With notation as in the previous exercise, let $n := 30$, and describe the conditional distribution of X_{15} given that $X_6 = 1$.

EXERCISE 6.16. Let W, X, Y be mutually independent and uniformly distributed over $\mathbb{Z}_p$, where p is prime. For any $a \in \mathbb{Z}_p$, let $Z_a := a^2 W + aX + Y$. Show that each Z_a is uniformly distributed over $\mathbb{Z}_p$, and that the collection of all Z_a is 3-wise independent.

EXERCISE 6.17. Let X_{ib}, for $i = 1, \ldots, k$ and $b \in \{0, 1\}$, be mutually independent random variables, each with a uniform distribution on $\{0, 1\}$. For $b_1, \ldots, b_k \in \{0, 1\}$, let us define the random variable

$$Y_{b_1 \cdots b_k} := X_{1b_1} \oplus \cdots \oplus X_{kb_k},$$

where "$\oplus$" denotes "exclusive or." Show that the 2^k variables $Y_{b_1 \cdots b_k}$ are pairwise independent, each with a uniform distribution over $\{0, 1\}$.

6.4 Expectation and variance

Let $\mathbf{D} = (\mathcal{U}, \mathsf{P})$ be a probability distribution. If X is a real random variable, then its **expected value** is

$$\mathsf{E}[X] := \sum_{u \in \mathcal{U}} X(u) \cdot \mathsf{P}[u]. \tag{6.12}$$

If $\mathcal{X}$ is the image of X, we have

$$\mathsf{E}[X] = \sum_{x \in \mathcal{X}} \sum_{u \in X^{-1}(\{x\})} x\mathsf{P}[u] = \sum_{x \in \mathcal{X}} x \cdot \mathsf{P}[X = x]. \tag{6.13}$$

From (6.13), it is clear that $\mathsf{E}[X]$ depends only on the distribution of X (and not on any other properties of the underlying distribution $\mathbf{D}$). More generally, by a similar calculation, one sees that if X is any random variable with image $\mathcal{X}$, and f is a real-valued function on $\mathcal{X}$, then

$$\mathsf{E}[f(X)] = \sum_{x \in \mathcal{X}} f(x)\mathsf{P}[X = x]. \tag{6.14}$$

We make a few trivial observations about expectation, which the reader may easily verify. First, if X is equal to a constant c (i.e., $X(u) = c$ for all

$u \in \mathcal{U}$), then $\mathsf{E}[X] = \mathsf{E}[c] = c$. Second, if X takes only non-negative values (i.e., $X(u) \geq 0$ all $u \in \mathcal{U}$), then $\mathsf{E}[X] \geq 0$. Similarly, if X takes only positive values, then $\mathsf{E}[X] > 0$.

A crucial property about expectation is the following:

Theorem 6.6 (Linearity of expectation). *For real random variables X and Y, and real number a, we have*

$$\mathsf{E}[X + Y] = \mathsf{E}[X] + \mathsf{E}[Y]$$

and

$$\mathsf{E}[aX] = a\mathsf{E}[X].$$

Proof. It is easiest to prove this using the defining equation (6.12) for expectation. For $u \in \mathcal{U}$, the value of the random variable $X + Y$ at u is by definition $X(u) + Y(u)$, and so we have

$$\mathsf{E}[X + Y] = \sum_{u \in \mathcal{U}} (X(u) + Y(u))\mathsf{P}[u]$$

$$= \sum_{u \in \mathcal{U}} X(u)\mathsf{P}[u] + \sum_{u \in \mathcal{U}} Y(u)\mathsf{P}[u]$$

$$= \mathsf{E}[X] + \mathsf{E}[Y].$$

For the second part of the theorem, by a similar calculation, we have

$$\mathsf{E}[aX] = \sum_{u} (aX(u))\mathsf{P}[u] = a\sum_{u} X(u)\mathsf{P}[u] = a\mathsf{E}[X]. \quad \square$$

More generally, the above theorem implies (using a simple induction argument) that for any real random variables $X_1, \dots, X_n$, we have

$$\mathsf{E}[X_1 + \cdots + X_n] = \mathsf{E}[X_1] + \cdots + \mathsf{E}[X_n].$$

So we see that expectation is linear; however, expectation is not in general multiplicative, except in the case of independent random variables:

Theorem 6.7. *If X and Y are independent real random variables, then $\mathsf{E}[XY] = \mathsf{E}[X]\mathsf{E}[Y]$.*

Proof. It is easiest to prove this using (6.14). We have

$$\mathsf{E}[XY] = \sum_{x,y} xy\mathsf{P}[X = x \wedge Y = y]$$

$$= \sum_{x,y} xy\mathsf{P}[X = x]\mathsf{P}[Y = y]$$

$$= \left(\sum_x x\mathsf{P}[X = x] \right) \left(\sum_y y\mathsf{P}[Y = y] \right)$$

$$= \mathsf{E}[X] \cdot \mathsf{E}[Y]. \quad \square$$

More generally, the above theorem implies (using a simple induction argument) that if $X_1, \ldots, X_n$ are mutually independent real random variables, then

$$\mathsf{E}[X_1 \cdots X_n] = \mathsf{E}[X_1] \cdots \mathsf{E}[X_n].$$

The following fact is sometimes quite useful:

Theorem 6.8. *If X is a random variable that takes values in the set $\{0, 1, \ldots, n\}$, then*

$$\mathsf{E}[X] = \sum_{i=1}^{n} \mathsf{P}[X \geq i].$$

Proof. For $i = 1, \ldots, n$, define the random variable X_i so that $X_i = 1$ if $X \geq i$ and $X_i = 0$ if $X < i$. Note that $\mathsf{E}[X_i] = 1 \cdot \mathsf{P}[X \geq i] + 0 \cdot \mathsf{P}[X < i] = \mathsf{P}[X \geq i]$. Moreover, $X = X_1 + \cdots + X_n$, and hence

$$\mathsf{E}[X] = \sum_{i=1}^{n} \mathsf{E}[X_i] = \sum_{i=1}^{n} \mathsf{P}[X \geq i]. \quad \square$$

The **variance** of a real random variable X is $\mathsf{Var}[X] := \mathsf{E}[(X - \mathsf{E}[X])^2]$. The variance provides a measure of the spread or dispersion of the distribution of X around its expected value $\mathsf{E}[X]$. Note that since $(X - \mathsf{E}[X])^2$ takes only non-negative values, variance is always non-negative.

Theorem 6.9. *Let X be a real random variable, and let a and b be real numbers. Then we have*

(i) $\mathsf{Var}[X] = \mathsf{E}[X^2] - (\mathsf{E}[X])^2$,

(ii) $\mathsf{Var}[aX] = a^2\mathsf{Var}[X]$, *and*

(iii) $\mathsf{Var}[X + b] = \mathsf{Var}[X]$.

Proof. Let $\mu := \mathsf{E}[X]$. For part (i), observe that

$$\mathsf{Var}[X] = \mathsf{E}[(X - \mu)^2] = \mathsf{E}[X^2 - 2\mu X + \mu^2]$$
$$= \mathsf{E}[X^2] - 2\mu\mathsf{E}[X] + \mathsf{E}[\mu^2] = \mathsf{E}[X^2] - 2\mu^2 + \mu^2$$
$$= \mathsf{E}[X^2] - \mu^2,$$

where in the third equality, we used the fact that expectation is linear, and in the fourth equality, we used the fact that $E[c] = c$ for constant c (in this case, $c = \mu^2$).

For part (ii), observe that

$$\mathsf{Var}[aX] = E[a^2 X^2] - (E[aX])^2 = a^2 E[X^2] - (a\mu)^2$$
$$= a^2 (E[X^2] - \mu^2) = a^2 \mathsf{Var}[X],$$

where we used part (i) in the first and fourth equality, and the linearity of expectation in the second.

Part (iii) follows by a similar calculation (verify):

$$\mathsf{Var}[X + b] = E[(X + b)^2] - (\mu + b)^2$$
$$= (E[X^2] + 2b\mu + b^2) - (\mu^2 + 2b\mu + b^2)$$
$$= E[X^2] - \mu^2 = \mathsf{Var}[X]. \quad \square$$

A simple consequence of part (i) of Theorem 6.9 is that $E[X^2] \geq (E[X])^2$.

Unlike expectation, the variance of a sum of random variables is not equal to the sum of the variances, unless the variables are *pairwise independent*:

Theorem 6.10. *If $X_1, \ldots, X_n$ is a collection of pairwise independent real random variables, then*

$$\mathsf{Var}\left[\sum_{i=1}^{n} X_i\right] = \sum_{i=1}^{n} \mathsf{Var}[X_i].$$

Proof. We have

$$\mathsf{Var}\left[\sum_i X_i\right] = E\left[\left(\sum_i X_i\right)^2\right] - \left(E[\sum_i X_i]\right)^2$$
$$= \sum_i E[X_i^2] + 2\sum_{\substack{i,j \\ j<i}} (E[X_i X_j] - E[X_i]E[X_j]) - \sum_i E[X_i]^2$$

(by Theorem 6.6 and rearranging terms)

$$= \sum_i E[X_i^2] - \sum_i E[X_i]^2$$

(by pairwise independence and Theorem 6.7)

$$= \sum_i \mathsf{Var}[X_i]. \quad \square$$

For any random variable X and event $\mathcal{B}$, with $P[\mathcal{B}] \neq 0$, we can define the **conditional expectation of X given $\mathcal{B}$**, denoted $E[X \mid \mathcal{B}]$, to be the expected value of X in the conditional probability distribution given $\mathcal{B}$. We have

$$\mathsf{E}[X \mid \mathcal{B}] = \sum_{u \in \mathcal{U}} X(u) \cdot \mathsf{P}[u \mid \mathcal{B}] = \sum_{x \in \mathcal{X}} x \mathsf{P}[X = x \mid \mathcal{B}], \qquad (6.15)$$

where $\mathcal{X}$ is the image of X.

If $\mathcal{B}_1, \ldots, \mathcal{B}_n$ is a collection of events that partitions $\mathcal{U}$, where each $\mathcal{B}_i$ occurs with non-zero probability, then it follows from the definitions that

$$\mathsf{E}[X] = \sum_{i=1}^{n} \mathsf{E}[X \mid \mathcal{B}_i] \mathsf{P}[\mathcal{B}_i]. \qquad (6.16)$$

Example 6.20. Let X be uniformly distributed over $\{1, \ldots, n\}$. Let us compute $\mathsf{E}[X]$ and $\mathsf{Var}[X]$. We have

$$\mathsf{E}[X] = \sum_{x=1}^{n} x \cdot \frac{1}{n} = \frac{n(n+1)}{2} \cdot \frac{1}{n} = \frac{n+1}{2}.$$

We also have

$$\mathsf{E}[X^2] = \sum_{x=1}^{n} x^2 \cdot \frac{1}{n} = \frac{n(n+1)(2n+1)}{6} \cdot \frac{1}{n} = \frac{(n+1)(2n+1)}{6}.$$

Therefore,

$$\mathsf{Var}[X] = \mathsf{E}[X^2] - (\mathsf{E}[X])^2 = \frac{n^2 - 1}{12}. \quad \square$$

Example 6.21. Let X denote the value of a die toss. Let $\mathcal{A}$ be the event that X is even. Then in the conditional probability space given $\mathcal{A}$, we see that X is uniformly distributed over $\{2, 4, 6\}$, and hence

$$\mathsf{E}[X \mid \mathcal{A}] = \frac{2 + 4 + 6}{3} = 4.$$

Similarly, in the conditional probability space given $\overline{\mathcal{A}}$, we see that X is uniformly distributed over $\{1, 3, 5\}$, and hence

$$\mathsf{E}[X \mid \overline{\mathcal{A}}] = \frac{1 + 3 + 5}{3} = 3.$$

We can compute the expected value of X using these conditional expectations; indeed, we have

$$\mathsf{E}[X] = \mathsf{E}[X \mid \mathcal{A}] \mathsf{P}[\mathcal{A}] + \mathsf{E}[X \mid \overline{\mathcal{A}}] \mathsf{P}[\overline{\mathcal{A}}] = 4 \cdot \frac{1}{2} + 3 \cdot \frac{1}{2} = \frac{7}{2},$$

which agrees with the calculation in previous example. $\square$

Example 6.22. Suppose that a random variable X takes the value 1 with probability p, and 0 with probability $q := 1 - p$. The distribution of X is that of a Bernoulli trial, as discussed in Example 6.3. Let us compute $\mathsf{E}[X]$ and $\mathsf{Var}[X]$. We have

$$\mathsf{E}[X] = 1 \cdot p + 0 \cdot q = p.$$

We also have

$$\mathsf{E}[X^2] = 1^2 \cdot p + 0^2 \cdot q = p.$$

Therefore,

$$\mathsf{Var}[X] = \mathsf{E}[X^2] - (\mathsf{E}[X])^2 = p - p^2 = pq. \;\; \square$$

Example 6.23. Suppose that $X_1, \ldots, X_n$ are mutually independent random variables such that each X_i takes the value 1 with probability p and 0 with probability $q := 1 - p$. Let us set $X := X_1 + \cdots + X_n$. Note that the distribution of each X_i is that of a Bernoulli trial, as in Example 6.3, and the distribution of X is a binomial distribution, as in Example 6.19. By the previous example, we have $\mathsf{E}[X_i] = p$ and $\mathsf{Var}[X_i] = pq$ for $i = 1, \ldots, n$. Let us compute $\mathsf{E}[X]$ and $\mathsf{Var}[X]$. By Theorem 6.6, we have

$$\mathsf{E}[X] = \sum_{i=1}^{n} \mathsf{E}[X_i] = np,$$

and by Theorem 6.10, and the fact that the X_i are mutually independent, we have

$$\mathsf{Var}[X] = \sum_{i=1}^{n} \mathsf{Var}[X_i] = npq. \;\; \square$$

EXERCISE 6.18. A casino offers you the following four dice games. In each game, you pay 15 dollars to play, and two dice are rolled. In the first game, the house pays out four times the value of the first die (in dollars). In the second, the house pays out twice the sum of the two dice. In the third, the house pays the square of the first. In the fourth, the house pays the product of the two dice. Which game should you play? That is, which game maximizes your expected winnings?

EXERCISE 6.19. Suppose X and Y are independent real random variables such that $\mathsf{E}[X] = \mathsf{E}[Y]$. Show that

$$\mathsf{E}[(X - Y)^2] = \mathsf{Var}[X] + \mathsf{Var}[Y].$$

EXERCISE 6.20. Show that the variance of any 0/1-valued random variable is at most 1/4.

EXERCISE 6.21. A die is tossed repeatedly until it comes up "1," or until it is tossed n times (whichever comes first). What is the expected number of tosses of the die?

EXERCISE 6.22. Suppose that 20 percent of the students who took a certain test were from school A and the average of their scores on the test was 65. Also, suppose that 30 percent of the students were from school B and the average of their scores was 85. Finally, suppose that the remaining 50 percent of the students were from school C and the average of their scores was 72. If a student is selected at random from the entire group that took the test, what is the expected value of his score?

EXERCISE 6.23. An urn contains $r \geq 0$ red balls and $b \geq 1$ black balls. Consider the following experiment. At each step in the experiment, a single ball is removed from the urn, randomly chosen from among all balls that remain in the urn: if a black ball is removed, the experiment halts, and if a red ball is removed, the experiment continues (without returning the red ball to the urn). Show that the expected number of steps performed is $(r + b + 1)/(b + 1)$.

6.5 Some useful bounds

In this section, we present several theorems that can be used to bound the probability that a random variable deviates from its expected value by some specified amount.

Theorem 6.11 (Markov's inequality). *Let X be a random variable that takes only non-negative real values. Then for any $t > 0$, we have*

$$P[X \geq t] \leq E[X]/t.$$

Proof. We have

$$E[X] = \sum_x x P[X = x] = \sum_{x<t} x P[X = x] + \sum_{x \geq t} x P[X = x].$$

Since X takes only non-negative values, all of the terms in the summation are non-negative. Therefore,

$$E[X] \geq \sum_{x \geq t} x P[X = x] \geq \sum_{x \geq t} t P[X = x] = t P[X \geq t]. \quad \square$$

Markov's inequality may be the only game in town when nothing more about the distribution of X is known besides its expected value. However, if the variance of X is also known, then one can get a better bound.

Theorem 6.12 (Chebyshev's inequality). *Let X be a real random variable. Then for any $t > 0$, we have*

$$P[|X - E[X]| \geq t] \leq \mathsf{Var}[X]/t^2.$$

Proof. Let $Y := (X - E[X])^2$. Then Y is always non-negative, and $E[Y] = \mathsf{Var}[X]$. Applying Markov's inequality to Y, we have

$$P[|X - E[X]| \geq t] = P[Y \geq t^2] \leq \mathsf{Var}[X]/t^2. \quad \square$$

An important special case of Chebyshev's inequality is the following. Suppose that $X_1, \ldots, X_n$ are *pairwise independent* real random variables, each with the same distribution. Let μ be the common value of $E[X_i]$ and ν the common value of $\mathsf{Var}[X_i]$. Set

$$\overline{X} := \frac{1}{n}(X_1 + \cdots + X_n).$$

The variable $\overline{X}$ is called the **sample mean** of $X_1, \ldots, X_n$. By the linearity of expectation, we have $E[\overline{X}] = \mu$, and since the X_i are pairwise independent, it follows from Theorem 6.10 (along with part (ii) of Theorem 6.9) that $\mathsf{Var}[\overline{X}] = \nu/n$. Applying Chebyshev's inequality, for any $\epsilon > 0$, we have

$$P[|\overline{X} - \mu| \geq \epsilon] \leq \frac{\nu}{n\epsilon^2}. \qquad (6.17)$$

The inequality (6.17) says that for all $\epsilon > 0$, and for all $\delta > 0$, there exists n_0 (depending on ϵ and δ, as well as the variance ν) such that $n \geq n_0$ implies

$$P[|\overline{X} - \mu| \geq \epsilon] \leq \delta. \qquad (6.18)$$

In words:

> *As n gets large, the sample mean closely approximates the expected value μ with high probability.*

This fact, known as the **law of large numbers**, justifies the usual intuitive interpretation given to expectation.

Let us now examine an even more specialized case of the above situation. Suppose that $X_1, \ldots, X_n$ are pairwise independent random variables, each of which takes the value 1 with probability p, and 0 with probability $q := 1 - p$. As before, let $\overline{X}$ be the sample mean of $X_1, \ldots, X_n$. As we calculated in

Example 6.22, the X_i have a common expected value p and variance pq. Therefore, by (6.17), for any $\epsilon > 0$, we have

$$P[|\overline{X} - p| \geq \epsilon] \leq \frac{pq}{n\epsilon^2}. \tag{6.19}$$

The bound on the right-hand side of (6.19) decreases linearly in n. If one makes the stronger assumption that the X_i are *mutually independent* (so that $X := X_1 + \cdots + X_n$ has a binomial distribution), one can obtain a much better bound that decreases *exponentially* in n:

Theorem 6.13 (Chernoff bound). *Let $X_1, \ldots, X_n$ be mutually independent random variables, such that each X_i is 1 with probability p and 0 with probability $q := 1 - p$. Assume that $0 < p < 1$. Also, let $\overline{X}$ be the sample mean of $X_1, \ldots, X_n$. Then for any $\epsilon > 0$, we have:*

(i) $P[\overline{X} - p \geq \epsilon] \leq e^{-n\epsilon^2/2q}$;

(ii) $P[\overline{X} - p \leq -\epsilon] \leq e^{-n\epsilon^2/2p}$;

(iii) $P[|\overline{X} - p| \geq \epsilon] \leq 2 \cdot e^{-n\epsilon^2/2}$.

Proof. First, we observe that (ii) follows directly from (i) by replacing X_i by $1 - X_i$ and exchanging the roles of p and q. Second, we observe that (iii) follows directly from (i) and (ii). Thus, it suffices to prove (i).

Let $\alpha > 0$ be a parameter, whose value will be determined later. Define the random variable $Z := e^{\alpha n(\overline{X} - p)}$. Since the function $x \mapsto e^{\alpha n x}$ is strictly increasing, we have $\overline{X} - p \geq \epsilon$ if and only if $Z \geq e^{\alpha n \epsilon}$. By Markov's inequality, it follows that

$$P[\overline{X} - p \geq \epsilon] = P[Z \geq e^{\alpha n \epsilon}] \leq E[Z]e^{-\alpha n \epsilon}. \tag{6.20}$$

So our goal is to bound $E[Z]$ from above.

For $i = 1, \ldots, n$, define the random variable $Z_i := e^{\alpha(X_i - p)}$. Note that $Z = \prod_{i=1}^{n} Z_i$, that the Z_i are mutually independent random variables (see Theorem 6.5), and that

$$E[Z_i] = e^{\alpha(1-p)}p + e^{\alpha(0-p)}q = pe^{\alpha q} + qe^{-\alpha p}.$$

It follows that

$$E[Z] = E[\prod_i Z_i] = \prod_i E[Z_i] = (pe^{\alpha q} + qe^{-\alpha p})^n.$$

We will prove below that

$$pe^{\alpha q} + qe^{-\alpha p} \leq e^{\alpha^2 q/2}. \tag{6.21}$$

From this, it follows that

$$\mathsf{E}[Z] \le e^{\alpha^2 qn/2}. \tag{6.22}$$

Combining (6.22) with (6.20), we obtain

$$\mathsf{P}[\overline{X} - p \ge \epsilon] \le e^{\alpha^2 qn/2 - \alpha n\epsilon}. \tag{6.23}$$

Now we choose the parameter α so as to minimize the quantity $\alpha^2 qn/2 - \alpha n\epsilon$. The optimal value of α is easily seen to be $\alpha = \epsilon/q$, and substituting this value of α into (6.23) yields (i).

To finish the proof of the theorem, it remains to prove the inequality (6.21). Let

$$\beta := pe^{\alpha q} + qe^{-\alpha p}.$$

We want to show that $\beta \le e^{\alpha^2 q/2}$, or equivalently, that $\log \beta \le \alpha^2 q/2$. We have

$$\beta = e^{\alpha q}(p + qe^{-\alpha}) = e^{\alpha q}(1 - q(1 - e^{-\alpha})),$$

and taking logarithms and applying parts (i) and (ii) of §A1, we obtain

$$\log \beta = \alpha q + \log(1 - q(1 - e^{-\alpha})) \le \alpha q - q(1 - e^{-\alpha}) = q(e^{-\alpha} + \alpha - 1) \le q\alpha^2/2.$$

This establishes (6.21) and completes the proof of the theorem. $\square$

Thus, the Chernoff bound is a quantitatively superior version of the law of large numbers, although its range of application is clearly more limited.

***Example* 6.24.** Suppose we toss 10,000 coins. The expected number of heads is 5,000. What is an upper bound on the probability α that we get 6,000 or more heads? Using Markov's inequality, we get $\alpha \le 5/6$. Using Chebyshev's inequality, and in particular, the inequality (6.19), we get

$$\alpha \le \frac{1/4}{10^4 10^{-2}} = \frac{1}{400}.$$

Finally, using the Chernoff bound, we obtain

$$\alpha \le e^{-10^4 10^{-2}/2(0.5)} = e^{-100} \approx 10^{-43.4}. \quad \square$$

EXERCISE 6.24. You are given a biased coin. You know that if tossed, it will come up heads with probability at least 51%, or it will come up tails with probability at least 51%. Design an experiment that attempts to determine the direction of the bias (towards heads or towards tails). The experiment should work by flipping the coin some number t times, and it should correctly determine the direction of the bias with probability at least 99%. Try to make t as small as possible.

6.6 The birthday paradox

This section discusses a number of problems related to the following question: how many people must be in a room before there is a good chance that two of them were born on the same day of the year? The answer is surprisingly few, whence the "paradox."

To answer this question, we index the people in the room with integers $1, \dots, k$, where k is the number of people in the room. We abstract the problem a bit, and assume that all years have the same number of days, say n — setting $n = 365$ corresponds to the original problem, except that leap years are not handled correctly, but we shall ignore this detail. For $i = 1, \dots, k$, let X_i denote the day of the year on which i's birthday falls. Let us assume that birthdays are uniformly distributed over $\{0, \dots, n-1\}$; this assumption is actually not entirely realistic, as it is well known that people are somewhat more likely to be born in some months than in others.

So for any $i = 1, \dots, k$ and $x = 0, \dots, n-1$, we have $\mathsf{P}[X_i = x] = 1/n$.

Let α be the probability that no two persons share the same birthday, so that $1 - \alpha$ is the probability that there is a pair of matching birthdays. We would like to know how big k must be relative to n so that α is not too large, say, at most $1/2$.

We can compute α as follows, assuming the X_i are *mutually independent*.

There are a total of n^k sequences of integers $(x_1, \dots, x_k)$, with each $x_i \in \{0, \dots, n-1\}$. Among these, there are a total of $n(n-1) \cdots (n-k+1)$ that contain no repetitions: there are n choices for x_1, and for any fixed value of x_1, there are $n-1$ choices for x_2, and so on. Therefore

$$\alpha = n(n-1) \cdots (n-k+1)/n^k = \left(1 - \frac{1}{n}\right)\left(1 - \frac{2}{n}\right) \cdots \left(1 - \frac{k-1}{n}\right). \quad (6.24)$$

Using the part (i) of §A1, we obtain

$$\alpha \le e^{-\sum_{i=1}^{k-1} i/n} = e^{-k(k-1)/2n}.$$

So if $k(k-1) \ge (2 \log 2)n$, we have $\alpha \le 1/2$. Thus, when k is at least a small constant times $n^{1/2}$, we have $\alpha \le 1/2$, so the probability that two people share the same birthday is at least $1/2$. For $n = 365$, $k \ge 23$ suffices. Indeed, one can simply calculate α in this case numerically from equation (6.24), obtaining $\alpha \approx 0.493$. Thus, if there are 23 people in the room, there is about a 50-50 chance that two people have the same birthday.

The above analysis assumed the X_i are mutually independent. However, we can still obtain useful upper bounds for α under much weaker independence assumptions.

For $i = 1, \ldots, k$ and $j = i + 1, \ldots, k$, let us define the indicator variable

$$W_{ij} := \begin{cases} 1 & \text{if } X_i = X_j, \\ 0 & \text{if } X_i \neq X_j. \end{cases}$$

If we assume that the X_i are pairwise independent, then

$$\mathsf{P}[W_{ij} = 1] = \mathsf{P}[X_i = X_j] = \sum_{x=0}^{n-1} \mathsf{P}[X_i = x \wedge X_j = x]$$

$$= \sum_{x=0}^{n-1} \mathsf{P}[X_i = x]\mathsf{P}[X_j = x] = \sum_{x=0}^{n-1} 1/n^2 = 1/n.$$

We can compute the expectation and variance (see Example 6.22):

$$\mathsf{E}[W_{ij}] = \frac{1}{n}, \qquad \mathsf{Var}[W_{ij}] = \frac{1}{n}\left(1 - \frac{1}{n}\right).$$

Now consider the random variable

$$W := \sum_{i=1}^{k} \sum_{j=i+1}^{k} W_{ij},$$

which represents the number of distinct pairs of people with the same birthday. There are $k(k-1)/2$ terms in this sum, so by the linearity of expectation, we have

$$\mathsf{E}[W] = \frac{k(k-1)}{2n}.$$

Thus, for $k(k-1) \geq 2n$, we "expect" there to be at least one pair of matching birthdays. However, this does not guarantee that the probability of a matching pair of birthdays is very high, assuming just pairwise independence of the X_i. For example, suppose that n is prime and the X_i are a subset of the family of pairwise independent random variables defined in Example 6.17. That is, each X_i is of the form $a_i X + Y$, where X and Y are uniformly and independently distributed modulo n. Then in fact, either all the X_i are distinct, or they are all equal, where the latter event occurs exactly when $X = [0]_n$, and so with probability $1/n$ — "when it rains, it pours."

To get a useful upper bound on the probability α that there are no matching birthdays, it suffices to assume that the X_i are *4-wise independent*. In this case, it is easy to verify that the variables W_{ij} are *pairwise* independent, since any two of the W_{ij} are determined by at most four of the X_i. Therefore, in this case, the variance of the sum is equal to the sum of the variances, and so

$$\text{Var}[W] = \frac{k(k-1)}{2n}\left(1 - \frac{1}{n}\right) \le \mathsf{E}[W].$$

Furthermore, by Chebyshev's inequality,

$$\alpha = \mathsf{P}[W = 0] \le \mathsf{P}[|W - \mathsf{E}[W]| \ge \mathsf{E}[W]]$$

$$\le \text{Var}[W]/\mathsf{E}[W]^2 \le 1/\mathsf{E}[W] = \frac{2n}{k(k-1)}.$$

Thus, if $k(k-1) \ge 4n$, then $\alpha \le 1/2$.

In many practical applications, it is more important to bound α from *below*, rather than from above; that is, to bound from above the probability $1 - \alpha$ that there are any collisions. For this, pairwise independence of the X_i suffices, since than we have $\mathsf{P}[W_{ij} = 1] = 1/n$, and by (6.5), we have

$$1 - \alpha \le \sum_{i=1}^{k} \sum_{j=i+1}^{k} \mathsf{P}[W_{ij} = 1] = \frac{k(k-1)}{2n},$$

which is at most $1/2$ provided $k(k-1) \le n$.

EXERCISE 6.25. Let $\alpha_1, \ldots, \alpha_n$ be real numbers with $\sum_{i=1}^{n} \alpha_i = 1$. Show that

$$0 \le \sum_{i=1}^{n} (\alpha_i - 1/n)^2 = \sum_{i=1}^{n} \alpha_i^2 - 1/n,$$

and in particular,

$$\sum_{i=1}^{n} \alpha_i^2 \ge 1/n.$$

EXERCISE 6.26. Let $\mathcal{X}$ be a set of size $n \ge 1$, and let X and X' be independent random variables, taking values in $\mathcal{X}$, and with the same distribution. Show that

$$\mathsf{P}[X = X'] = \sum_{x \in \mathcal{X}} \mathsf{P}[X = x]^2 \ge \frac{1}{n}.$$

EXERCISE 6.27. Let $\mathcal{X}$ be a set of size $n \ge 1$, and let x_0 be an arbitrary, fixed element of $\mathcal{X}$. Consider a random experiment in which a function F is chosen uniformly from among all n^n functions from $\mathcal{X}$ into $\mathcal{X}$. Let us define random variables X_i, for $i = 0, 1, 2, \ldots$, as follows:

$$X_0 := x_0, \quad X_{i+1} := F(X_i) \quad (i = 0, 1, 2, \ldots).$$

Thus, the value of X_i is obtained by applying the function F a total of i times to the starting value x_0. Since $\mathcal{X}$ has size n, the sequence $\{X_i\}$ must repeat at some point; that is, there exists a positive integer k (with $k \leq n$) such that $X_k = X_i$ for some $i = 0, \ldots, k-1$. Define the random variable K to be the smallest such value k.

(a) Show that for any $i \geq 0$ and any fixed values of $x_1, \ldots, x_i \in \mathcal{X}$ such that $x_0, x_1, \ldots, x_i$ are distinct, the conditional distribution of X_{i+1} given that $X_1 = x_1, \ldots, X_i = x_i$ is uniform over $\mathcal{X}$.

(b) Show that for any integer $k \geq 1$, we have $K \geq k$ if and only if $X_0, X_1, \ldots, X_{k-1}$ take on distinct values.

(c) From parts (a) and (b), show that for any $k = 1, \ldots, n$, we have

$$\mathsf{P}[K \geq k \mid K \geq k-1] = 1 - (k-1)/n,$$

and conclude that

$$\mathsf{P}[K \geq k] = \prod_{i=1}^{k-1}(1 - i/n) \leq e^{-k(k-1)/2n}.$$

(d) Show that

$$\sum_{k=1}^{\infty} e^{-k(k-1)/2n} = O(n^{1/2})$$

and then conclude from part (c) that

$$\mathsf{E}[K] = \sum_{k=1}^{n}\mathsf{P}[K \geq k] \leq \sum_{k=1}^{\infty} e^{-k(k-1)/2n} = O(n^{1/2}).$$

(e) Modify the above argument to show that $\mathsf{E}[K] = \Omega(n^{1/2})$.

EXERCISE 6.28. The setup for this exercise is identical to that of the previous exercise, except that now, the function F is chosen uniformly from among all $n!$ *permutations* of $\mathcal{X}$.

(a) Show that if $K = k$, then $X_k = X_0$.

(b) Show that for any $i \geq 0$ and any fixed values of $x_1, \ldots, x_i \in \mathcal{X}$ such that $x_0, x_1, \ldots, x_i$ are distinct, the conditional distribution of X_{i+1} given that $X_1 = x_1, \ldots, X_i = x_i$ is uniform over $\mathcal{X} \setminus \{x_1, \ldots, x_i\}$.

(c) Show that for any $k = 2, \ldots, n$, we have

$$\mathsf{P}[K \geq k \mid K \geq k-1] = 1 - \frac{1}{n-k+2},$$

and conclude that for all $k = 1, \ldots, n$, we have

$$P[K \geq k] = \prod_{i=0}^{k-2} \left(1 - \frac{1}{n-i}\right) = 1 - \frac{k-1}{n}.$$

(d) From part (c), show that K is uniformly distributed over $\{1, \ldots, n\}$, and in particular,

$$E[K] = \frac{n+1}{2}.$$

6.7 Hash functions

In this section, we apply the tools we have developed thus far to a particularly important area of computer science: the theory and practice of hashing.

The scenario is as follows. We have finite, non-empty sets $\mathcal{A}$ and $\mathcal{Z}$, with $|\mathcal{A}| = k$ and $|\mathcal{Z}| = n$, and a finite, non-empty set $\mathcal{H}$ of **hash functions**, each of which map elements of $\mathcal{A}$ into $\mathcal{Z}$. More precisely, each element $h \in \mathcal{H}$ defines a function that maps $a \in \mathcal{A}$ to an element $z \in \mathcal{Z}$, and we write $z = h(a)$; the value z is called the **hash code of a (under h)**, and we say that a **hashes to z (under h)**. Note that two distinct elements of $\mathcal{H}$ may happen to define the same function. We call $\mathcal{H}$ a **family of hash functions (from $\mathcal{A}$ to $\mathcal{Z}$)**.

Let H be a random variable whose distribution is uniform on $\mathcal{H}$. For any $a \in \mathcal{A}$, $H(a)$ denotes the random variable whose value is $z = h(a)$ when $H = h$. For any $\ell = 1, \ldots, k$, we say that $\mathcal{H}$ is an **ℓ-wise independent** family of hash functions if each $H(a)$ is uniformly distributed over $\mathcal{Z}$, and the collection of all $H(a)$ is ℓ-wise independent; in case $\ell = 2$, we say that $\mathcal{H}$ is a **pairwise independent** family of hash functions. Pairwise independence is equivalent to saying that for all $a, a' \in \mathcal{A}$, with $a \neq a'$, and all $z, z' \in \mathcal{Z}$,

$$P[H(a) = z \wedge H(a') = z'] = \frac{1}{n^2}.$$

Example **6.25.** Examples 6.17 and 6.18 provide explicit constructions for pairwise independent families of hash functions. In particular, from the discussion in Example 6.17, if n is prime, and we take $\mathcal{A} := \mathbb{Z}_n$, $\mathcal{Z} := \mathbb{Z}_n$, and $\mathcal{H} := \{h_{x,y} : x, y \in \mathbb{Z}_n\}$, where for $h_{x,y} \in \mathcal{H}$ and $a \in \mathcal{A}$ we define $h_{x,y}(a) := ax + y$, then $\mathcal{H}$ is a pairwise independent family of hash functions from $\mathcal{A}$ to $\mathcal{Z}$.

Similarly, Example 6.18 yields a pairwise independent family of hash functions from $\mathcal{A} := \mathbb{Z}_n^{\times t}$ to $\mathcal{Z} := \mathbb{Z}_n$, with $\mathcal{H} := \{h_{x_1, \ldots, x_t, y} : x_1, \ldots, x_t, y \in \mathbb{Z}_n\}$, where for $h_{x_1,\dots,x_t,y} \in \mathcal{H}$ and $(a_1,\dots,a_t) \in \mathcal{A}$, we define

$$h_{x_1,\dots,x_t,y}(a_1,\dots,a_t) := a_1 x_1 + \cdots + a_t x_t + y.$$

In practice, the inputs to such a hash function may be long bit strings, which we chop into small pieces so that each piece can be viewed as an element of $\mathbb{Z}_n$. $\square$

6.7.1 Hash tables

Pairwise independent families of hash functions may be used to implement a data structure known as a **hash table**, which in turn may be used to implement a **dictionary**.

Assume that $\mathcal{H}$ is a family of hash functions from $\mathcal{A}$ to $\mathcal{Z}$, where $|\mathcal{A}| = k$ and $|\mathcal{Z}| = n$. A hash function is chosen at random from $\mathcal{H}$; an element $a \in \mathcal{A}$ is inserted into the hash table by storing the value of a into a **bin** indexed by the hash code of a; likewise, to see if a particular value $a \in \mathcal{A}$ is stored in the hash table, one must search in the bin indexed by the hash code of a.

So as to facilitate fast storage and retrieval, one typically wants the elements stored in the hash table to be distributed in roughly equal proportions among all the bins.

Assuming that $\mathcal{H}$ is a pairwise independent family of hash functions, one can easily derive some useful results, such as the following:

- If the hash table holds q values, then for any value $a \in \mathcal{A}$, the expected number of other values that are in the bin indexed by a's hash code is at most q/n. This result bounds the expected amount of "work" we have to do to search for a value in its corresponding bin, which is essentially equal to the size of the bin. In particular, if $q = O(n)$, then the expected amount of work is constant. See Exercise 6.32 below.

- If the table holds q values, with $q(q-1) \le n$, then with probability at least $1/2$, each value lies in a distinct bin. This result is useful if one wants to find a "perfect" hash function that hashes q fixed values to distinct bins: if n is sufficiently large, we can just choose hash functions at random until we find one that works. See Exercise 6.33 below.

- If the table holds n values, then the expected value of the maximum number of values in any bin is $O(n^{1/2})$. See Exercise 6.34 below.

Results such as these, and others, can be obtained using a broader notion of hashing called **universal hashing**. We call $\mathcal{H}$ a **universal** family of hash functions if for all $a, a' \in \mathcal{A}$, with $a \neq a'$, we have

$$\mathsf{P}[H(a) = H(a')] \leq \frac{1}{n}.$$

Note that the pairwise independence property implies the universal property (see Exercise 6.29 below). There are even weaker notions that are relevant in practice; for example, in some applications, it is sufficient to require that $\mathsf{P}[H(a) = H(a')] \leq c/n$ for some constant c.

EXERCISE 6.29. Show that any pairwise independent family of hash functions is also a universal family of hash functions.

EXERCISE 6.30. Let $\mathcal{A} := \mathbb{Z}_n^{\times(t+1)}$ and $\mathcal{Z} := \mathbb{Z}_n$, where n is prime. Let $\mathcal{H} := \{h_{x_1,\ldots,x_t} : x_1, \ldots, x_t \in \mathbb{Z}_n\}$ be a family of hash functions from $\mathcal{A}$ to $\mathcal{Z}$, where for $h_{x_1,\ldots,x_t} \in \mathcal{H}$, and for $(a_0, a_1, \ldots, a_t) \in \mathcal{A}$, we define

$$h_{x_1,\ldots,x_t}(a_0, a_1, \ldots, a_t) := a_0 + a_1 x_1 + \cdots + a_t x_t.$$

Show that $\mathcal{H}$ is universal, but not pairwise independent.

EXERCISE 6.31. Let k be a prime and let n be any positive integer. Let $\mathcal{A} := \{0, \ldots, k - 1\}$ and $\mathcal{Z} := \{0, \ldots, n - 1\}$. Let

$$\mathcal{H} := \{h_{x,y} : x = 1, \ldots, k - 1, \ y = 0, \ldots, k - 1\},$$

be a family of hash functions from $\mathcal{A}$ to $\mathcal{Z}$, where for $h_{x,y} \in \mathcal{H}$ and for $a \in \mathcal{A}$, we define

$$h_{x,y}(a) := ((ax + y) \bmod k) \bmod n.$$

Show that $\mathcal{H}$ is universal. Hint: first show that for any $a, a' \in \mathcal{A}$ with $a \neq a'$, the number of $h \in \mathcal{H}$ such that $h(a) = h(a')$ is equal to the number of pairs of integers (r, s) such that

$$0 \leq r < k, \ 0 \leq s < k, \ r \neq s, \ \text{and} \ r \equiv s \ (\bmod \ n).$$

In the following three exercises, assume that $\mathcal{H}$ is a universal family of hash functions from $\mathcal{A}$ to $\mathcal{Z}$, where $|\mathcal{A}| = k$ and $|\mathcal{Z}| = n$, and that H is a random variable uniformly distributed over $\mathcal{H}$.

EXERCISE 6.32. Let $a_1, \ldots, a_q$ be distinct elements of $\mathcal{A}$, and let $a \in \mathcal{A}$. Define L to be the number of indices $i = 1, \ldots, q$ such that $H(a_i) = H(a)$. Show that

$$\mathsf{E}[L] \leq \begin{cases} 1 + (q - 1)/n & \text{if } a \in \{a_1, \ldots, a_q\}; \\ q/n & \text{otherwise.} \end{cases}$$

EXERCISE 6.33. Let $a_1, \ldots, a_q$ be distinct elements of $\mathcal{A}$, and assume that $q(q-1) \le n$. Show that the probability that $H(a_i) = H(a_j)$ for some i, j with $i \ne j$, is at most $1/2$.

EXERCISE 6.34. Assume $k \ge n$, and let $a_1, \ldots, a_n$ be distinct elements of $\mathcal{A}$. For $z \in \mathcal{Z}$, define the random variable $B_z := \{a_i : H(a_i) = z\}$. Define the random variable $M := \max\{|B_z| : z \in \mathcal{Z}\}$. Show that $\mathsf{E}[M] = O(n^{1/2})$.

EXERCISE 6.35. A family $\mathcal{H}$ of hash functions from $\mathcal{A}$ to $\mathcal{Z}$ is called ϵ-**universal** if for H uniformly distributed over $\mathcal{H}$, and for all $a, a' \in \mathcal{A}$ with $a \ne a'$, we have $\mathsf{P}[H(a) = H(a')] \le \epsilon$. Show that if $\mathcal{H}$ is ϵ-universal, then we must have

$$\epsilon \ge \frac{1}{|\mathcal{Z}|} - \frac{1}{|\mathcal{A}|}.$$

Hint: using Exercise 6.26, first show that if H, A, A' are mutually independent random variables, with H uniformly distributed over $\mathcal{H}$, and A and A' uniformly distributed over $\mathcal{A}$, then $\mathsf{P}[A \ne A' \wedge H(A) = H(A')] \ge 1/|\mathcal{Z}| - 1/|\mathcal{A}|$.

6.7.2 Message authentication

Pairwise independent families of hash functions may be used to implement a **message authentication scheme**, which is a mechanism to detect if a message has been tampered with in transit between two parties. Unlike an error correcting code (such as the one discussed in §4.5.1), a message authentication scheme should be effective against *arbitrary* tampering.

As above, assume that $\mathcal{H}$ is a family of hash functions from $\mathcal{A}$ to $\mathcal{Z}$, where $|\mathcal{A}| = k$ and $|\mathcal{Z}| = n$. Suppose that Alice and Bob somehow agree upon a hash function chosen at random from $\mathcal{H}$. At some later time, Alice transmits a message $a \in \mathcal{A}$ to Bob over an insecure network. In addition to sending a, Alice also sends the hash code z of a. Upon receiving a pair (a, z), Bob checks that the hash code of a is indeed equal to z: if so, he accepts the message as authentic (i.e., originating from Alice); otherwise, he rejects the message.

Now suppose that an adversary is trying to trick Bob into accepting an inauthentic message (i.e., one not originating from Alice). Assuming that $\mathcal{H}$ is a pairwise independent family of hash functions, it is not too hard to see that the adversary can succeed with probability no better than $1/n$, regardless of the strategy or computing power of the adversary. Indeed, on the one hand, suppose the adversary gives Bob a pair (a', z') at some time before Alice sends her message. In this case, the adversary knows nothing about the hash function, and so the correct value of the hash code of a' is completely unpredictable: it is equally likely to be any element of $\mathcal{Z}$. Therefore, no matter how clever the adversary is in choosing a' and z', Bob will accept (a', z') as authentic with probability only $1/n$. On the other hand, suppose the adversary waits until Alice sends her message, intercepting the message/hash code pair (a, z) sent by Alice, and gives Bob a pair (a', z'), where $a' \neq a$, instead of the pair (a, z). Again, since the adversary does not know anything about the hash function other than the fact that the hash code of a is equal to z, the correct hash code of a' is completely unpredictable, and again, Bob will accept (a', z') as authentic with probability only $1/n$.

One can easily make n large enough so that the probability that an adversary succeeds is so small that for all practical purposes it is impossible to trick Bob (e.g., $n \approx 2^{100}$).

More formally, and more generally, one can define an ϵ**-forgeable message authentication scheme** to be a family $\mathcal{H}$ of hash functions from $\mathcal{A}$ to $\mathcal{Z}$ with the following property: if H is uniformly distributed over $\mathcal{H}$, then

(i) for all $a \in \mathcal{A}$ and $z \in \mathcal{Z}$, we have $\mathsf{P}[H(a) = z] \leq \epsilon$, and

(ii) for all $a \in \mathcal{A}$ and all functions $f : \mathcal{Z} \to \mathcal{A}$ and $g : \mathcal{Z} \to \mathcal{Z}$, we have

$$\mathsf{P}[A' \neq a \wedge H(A') = Z'] \leq \epsilon,$$

where $Z := H(a)$, $A' := f(Z)$, and $Z' := g(Z)$.

Intuitively, part (i) of this definition says that it is impossible to guess the hash code of any message with probability better than ϵ; further, part (ii) of this definition says that even after seeing the hash code of one message, it is impossible to guess the hash code of a different message with probability better than ϵ, regardless the choice of the first message (i.e., the value a) and regardless of the strategy used to pick the second message and its putative hash code, given the hash code of the first message (i.e., the functions f and g).

EXERCISE 6.36. Suppose that a family $\mathcal{H}$ of hash functions from $\mathcal{A}$ to $\mathcal{Z}$ is an ϵ-forgeable message authentication scheme. Show that $\epsilon \geq 1/|\mathcal{Z}|$.

EXERCISE 6.37. Suppose that $\mathcal{H}$ is a family of hash functions from $\mathcal{A}$ to $\mathcal{Z}$ and that $|\mathcal{A}| > 1$. Show that if $\mathcal{H}$ satisfies part (ii) of the definition of an ϵ-forgeable message authentication scheme, then it also satisfies part (i) of the definition.

EXERCISE 6.38. Let $\mathcal{H}$ be a family of hash functions from $\mathcal{A}$ to $\mathcal{Z}$. For $\epsilon \geq 0$, we call $\mathcal{H}$ **pairwise ϵ-predictable** if the following holds: for H uniformly distributed over $\mathcal{H}$, for all $a, a' \in \mathcal{A}$, and for all $z, z' \in \mathcal{Z}$, we have $\mathsf{P}[H(a) = z] \leq \epsilon$ and

$$\mathsf{P}[H(a) = z] > 0 \text{ and } a' \neq a \text{ implies } \mathsf{P}[H(a') = z' \mid H(a) = z] \leq \epsilon.$$

(a) Show that if $\mathcal{H}$ is pairwise ϵ-predictable, then it is an ϵ-forgeable message authentication scheme.

(b) Show that if $\mathcal{H}$ is pairwise independent, then it is pairwise $1/|\mathcal{Z}|$-predictable. Combining this with part (a), we see that if $\mathcal{H}$ is pairwise independent, then it is a $1/|\mathcal{Z}|$-forgeable message authentication scheme (which makes rigorous the intuitive argument given above).

(c) Give an example of a family of hash functions that is an ϵ-forgeable message authentication scheme for some $\epsilon < 1$, but is *not* pairwise ϵ-predictable for any $\epsilon < 1$.

EXERCISE 6.39. Give an example of an ϵ-forgeable message authentication scheme, where ϵ is very small, but where if Alice authenticates *two* distinct messages using the same hash function, an adversary can easily forge the hash code of any message he likes (after seeing Alice's two messages and their hash codes). This shows that, as we have defined a message authentication scheme, Alice should only authenticate a *single* message per hash function (t messages may be authenticated using t hash functions).

EXERCISE 6.40. Let $\mathcal{H}$ be an ϵ-universal family of hash functions from $\mathcal{A}$ to $\mathcal{Y}$ (see Exercise 6.35), and let $\mathcal{H}'$ be a pairwise independent family of hash functions from $\mathcal{Y}$ to $\mathcal{Z}$. Define the composed family $\mathcal{H}' \circ \mathcal{H}$ of hash functions from $\mathcal{A}$ to $\mathcal{Z}$ as $\mathcal{H}' \circ \mathcal{H} := \{\phi_{h',h} : h' \in \mathcal{H}', h \in \mathcal{H}\}$, where $\phi_{h',h}(a) := h'(h(a))$ for $\phi_{h',h} \in \mathcal{H}' \circ \mathcal{H}$ and for $a \in \mathcal{A}$. Show that $\mathcal{H}' \circ \mathcal{H}$ is an $(\epsilon + 1/|\mathcal{Z}|)$-forgeable message authentication scheme.

6.8 Statistical distance

This section discusses a useful measure "distance" between two random variables. Although important in many applications, the results of this section (and the next) will play only a very minor role in the remainder of the text.

Let X and Y be random variables which both take values on a finite set

$\mathcal{V}$. We define the **statistical distance between** X **and** Y as

$$\Delta[X;Y] := \frac{1}{2} \sum_{v \in \mathcal{V}} |P[X = v] - P[Y = v]|.$$

Theorem 6.14. *For random variables* X, Y, Z, *we have*

(i) $0 \le \Delta[X;Y] \le 1$,

(ii) $\Delta[X;X] = 0$,

(iii) $\Delta[X;Y] = \Delta[Y;X]$, *and*

(iv) $\Delta[X;Z] \le \Delta[X;Y] + \Delta[Y;Z]$.

Proof. Exercise. $\square$

Note that $\Delta[X;Y]$ depends only on the individual distributions of X and Y, and not on the joint distribution of X and Y. As such, one may speak of the statistical distance between two distributions, rather than between two random variables.

***Example* 6.26.** Suppose X has the uniform distribution on $\{1, \ldots, n\}$, and Y has the uniform distribution on $\{1, \ldots, n-k\}$, where $0 \le k \le n-1$. Let us compute $\Delta[X;Y]$. We could apply the definition directly; however, consider the following graph of the distributions of X and Y:

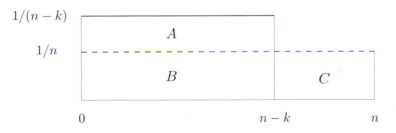

The statistical distance between X and Y is just $1/2$ times the area of regions A and C in the diagram. Moreover, because probability distributions sum to 1, we must have

$$\text{area of } B + \text{area of } A = 1 = \text{area of } B + \text{area of } C,$$

and hence, the areas of region A and region C are the same. Therefore,

$$\Delta[X;Y] = \text{area of } A = \text{area of } C = k/n. \quad \square$$

The following characterization of statistical distance is quite useful:

Theorem 6.15. *Let* X *and* Y *be random variables taking values on a set*

$\mathcal{V}$. *For any $\mathcal{W} \subseteq \mathcal{V}$, we have*

$$\Delta[X;Y] \geq |P[X \in \mathcal{W}] - P[Y \in \mathcal{W}]|,$$

and equality holds if $\mathcal{W}$ is either the set of all $v \in \mathcal{V}$ such that $P[X = v] < P[Y = v]$, or the complement of this set.

Proof. Suppose we partition the set $\mathcal{V}$ into two sets: the set $\mathcal{V}_0$ consisting of those $v \in \mathcal{V}$ such that $P[X = v] < P[Y = v]$, and the set $\mathcal{V}_1$ consisting of those $v \in \mathcal{V}$ such that $P[X = v] \geq P[Y = v]$. Consider the following rough graph of the distributions of X and Y, where the elements of $\mathcal{V}_0$ are placed to the left of the elements of $\mathcal{V}_1$:

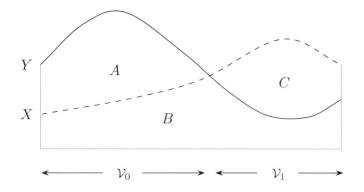

Now, as in Example 6.26,

$$\Delta[X;Y] = \text{area of } A = \text{area of } C.$$

Further, consider any subset $\mathcal{W}$ of $\mathcal{V}$. The quantity $|P[X \in \mathcal{W}] - P[Y \in \mathcal{W}]|$ is equal to the absolute value of the difference of the area of the subregion of A that lies above $\mathcal{W}$ and the area of the subregion of C that lies above $\mathcal{W}$. This quantity is maximized when $\mathcal{W} = \mathcal{V}_0$ or $\mathcal{W} = \mathcal{V}_1$, in which case it is equal to $\Delta[X;Y]$. $\square$

We can restate Theorem 6.15 as follows:

$$\Delta[X;Y] = \max\{|P[\phi(X)] - P[\phi(Y)]| : \phi \text{ is a predicate on } \mathcal{V}\}.$$

This implies that when $\Delta[X;Y]$ is very small, then for *any* predicate ϕ, the events $\phi(X)$ and $\phi(Y)$ occur with almost the same probability. Put another way, there is no "statistical test" that can effectively distinguish between the distributions of X and Y. For many applications, this means that the distribution of X is "for all practical purposes" equivalent to that of Y, and hence in analyzing the behavior of X, we can instead analyze the behavior of Y, if that is more convenient.

Theorem 6.16. *Let X, Y be random variables taking values on a set $\mathcal{V}$, and let f be a function from $\mathcal{V}$ into a set $\mathcal{W}$. Then $\Delta[f(X); f(Y)] \leq \Delta[X; Y]$.*

Proof. By Theorem 6.15, for any subset $\mathcal{W}'$ of $\mathcal{W}$, we have

$$|\mathsf{P}[f(X) \in \mathcal{W}'] - \mathsf{P}[f(Y) \in \mathcal{W}']| =$$
$$|\mathsf{P}[X \in f^{-1}(\mathcal{W}')] - \mathsf{P}[Y \in f^{-1}(\mathcal{W}')]| \leq \Delta[X; Y].$$

In particular, again by Theorem 6.15,

$$\Delta[f(X); f(Y)] = |\mathsf{P}[f(X) \in \mathcal{W}'] - \mathsf{P}[f(Y) \in \mathcal{W}']|$$

for some $\mathcal{W}'$. $\square$

***Example* 6.27.** Let X be uniformly distributed on the set $\{0, \ldots, n-1\}$, and let Y be uniformly distributed on the set $\{0, \ldots, m-1\}$, for $m \geq n$. Let $f(y) := y \bmod n$. We want to compute an upper bound on the statistical distance between X and $f(Y)$. We can do this as follows. Let $m = qn - r$, where $0 \leq r < n$, so that $q = \lceil m/n \rceil$. Also, let Z be uniformly distributed over $\{0, \ldots, qn-1\}$. Then $f(Z)$ is uniformly distributed over $\{0, \ldots, n-1\}$, since every element of $\{0, \ldots, n-1\}$ has the same number (namely, q) of pre-images under f which lie in the set $\{0, \ldots, qn-1\}$. Therefore, by the previous theorem,

$$\Delta[X; f(Y)] = \Delta[f(Z); f(Y)] \leq \Delta[Z; Y],$$

and as we saw in Example 6.26,

$$\Delta[Z; Y] = r/qn < 1/q \leq n/m.$$

Therefore,

$$\Delta[X; f(Y)] < n/m. \quad \square$$

We close this section with two useful theorems.

Theorem 6.17. *Let X and Y be random variables taking values on a set $\mathcal{V}$, and let W be a random variable taking values on a set $\mathcal{W}$. Further, suppose that X and W are independent, and that Y and W are independent. Then the statistical distance between (X, W) and (Y, W) is equal to the statistical distance between X and Y; that is,*

$$\Delta[X, W; Y, W] = \Delta[X, Y].$$

Proof. From the definition of statistical distance,

$$2\Delta[X, W; Y, W] = \sum_{v,w} |P[X = v \wedge W = w] - P[Y = v \wedge W = w]|$$

$$= \sum_{v,w} |P[X = v]P[W = w] - P[Y = v]P[W = w]|$$

(by independence)

$$= \sum_{v,w} P[W = w]|P[X = v] - P[Y = v]|$$

$$= (\sum_{w} P[W = w])(\sum_{v} |P[X = v] - P[Y = v]|)$$

$$= 1 \cdot 2\Delta[X; Y]. \quad \Box$$

Theorem 6.18. *Let* $U_1, \ldots, U_\ell, V_1, \ldots, V_\ell$ *be mutually independent random variables. We have*

$$\Delta[U_1, \ldots, U_\ell; V_1, \ldots, V_\ell] \leq \sum_{i=1}^{\ell} \Delta[U_i; V_i].$$

Proof. We introduce random variables $W_0, \ldots, W_\ell$, defined as follows:

$$W_0 := (U_1, \ldots, U_\ell),$$
$$W_i := (V_1, \ldots, V_i, U_{i+1}, \ldots, U_\ell) \quad \text{for } i = 1, \ldots, \ell - 1, \text{ and}$$
$$W_\ell := (V_1, \ldots, V_\ell).$$

By definition,

$$\Delta[U_1, \ldots, U_\ell; V_1, \ldots, V_\ell] = \Delta[W_0; W_\ell].$$

Moreover, by part (iv) of Theorem 6.14, we have

$$\Delta[W_0; W_\ell] \leq \sum_{i=1}^{\ell} \Delta[W_{i-1}; W_i].$$

Now consider any fixed index $i = 1, \ldots, \ell$. By Theorem 6.17, we have

$$\Delta[W_{i-1}; W_i] = \Delta[\, U_i, (V_1, \ldots, V_{i-1}, U_{i+1}, \ldots, U_\ell);$$
$$V_i, (V_1, \ldots, V_{i-1}, U_{i+1}, \ldots, U_\ell)]$$
$$= \Delta[U_i; V_i].$$

The theorem now follows immediately. $\Box$

The technique used in the proof of the previous theorem is sometimes called a **hybrid argument**, as one considers the sequence of "hybrid" variables $W_0, W_1, \ldots, W_\ell$, and shows that the distance between each consecutive pair of variables is small.

EXERCISE 6.41. Let X and Y be independent random variables, each uniformly distributed over $\mathbb{Z}_p$, where p is prime. Calculate $\Delta[X, Y; X, XY]$.

EXERCISE 6.42. Let n be a large integer that is the product of two distinct primes of roughly the same bit length. Let X be uniformly distributed over $\mathbb{Z}_n$, and let Y be uniformly distributed over $\mathbb{Z}_n^*$. Show that $\Delta[X; Y] = O(n^{-1/2})$.

EXERCISE 6.43. Let $\mathcal{V}$ be a finite set, and consider any function $\phi : \mathcal{V} \to \{0, 1\}$. Let B be a random variable uniformly distributed over $\{0, 1\}$, and for $b = 0, 1$, let X_b be a random variable taking values in $\mathcal{V}$, and assume that X_b and B are independent. Show that

$$|\mathsf{P}[\phi(X_B) = B] - \tfrac{1}{2}| = \tfrac{1}{2}|\mathsf{P}[\phi(X_0) = 1] - \mathsf{P}[\phi(X_1) = 1]| \leq \tfrac{1}{2}\Delta[X_0; X_1].$$

EXERCISE 6.44. Let X, Y be random variables on a probability distribution, and let $\mathcal{B}_1, \ldots, \mathcal{B}_n$ be events that partition of the underlying sample space, where each $\mathcal{B}_i$ occurs with non-zero probability. For $i = 1, \ldots, n$, let X_i and Y_i denote the random variables X and Y in the conditional probability distribution given $\mathcal{B}_i$; that is, $\mathsf{P}[X_i = v] = \mathsf{P}[X = v \mid \mathcal{B}_i]$, and $\mathsf{P}[Y_i = v] = \mathsf{P}[Y = v \mid \mathcal{B}_i]$. Show that

$$\Delta[X; Y] \leq \sum_{i=1}^{n} \Delta[X_i; Y_i]\mathsf{P}[\mathcal{B}_i].$$

EXERCISE 6.45. Let X and Y be random variables that take the same value unless a certain event $\mathcal{F}$ occurs. Show that $\Delta[X; Y] \leq \mathsf{P}[\mathcal{F}]$.

EXERCISE 6.46. Let M be a large integer. Consider three random experiments. In the first, we generate a random integer n between 1 and M, and then a random integer w between 1 and n. In the second, we generate a random integer n between 2 and M, and then generate a random integer w between 1 and n. In the third, we generate a random integer n between 2 and M, and then a random integer w between 2 and n. For $i = 1, 2, 3$, let X_i denote the outcome (n, w) of the ith experiment. Show that $\Delta[X_1; X_2] = O(1/M)$ and $\Delta[X_2; X_3] = O(\log M/M)$, and conclude that $\Delta[X_1; X_3] = O(\log M/M)$.

EXERCISE 6.47. Show that Theorem 6.17 is not true if we drop the independence assumptions.

EXERCISE 6.48. Show that the hypothesis of Theorem 6.18 can be weakened: all one needs to assume is that $X_1, \ldots, X_\ell$ are mutually independent, and that $Y_1, \ldots, Y_\ell$ are mutually independent.

EXERCISE 6.49. Let $Y_1, \ldots, Y_\ell$ be mutually independent random variables, where each Y_i is uniformly distributed on $\{0, \ldots, m-1\}$. For $i = 1, \ldots, \ell$, define $Z_i := \sum_{j=1}^{i} jY_j$. Let n be a prime greater than ℓ. Let $\mathcal{S}$ be any finite subset of $\mathbb{Z}^{\times \ell}$. Let $\mathcal{A}$ be the event that for some $(a_1, \ldots, a_\ell) \in \mathcal{S}$, we have $Z_i \equiv a_i \pmod{n}$ for $i = 1, \ldots, \ell$. Show that

$$\mathsf{P}[\mathcal{A}] \leq |\mathcal{S}|/n^\ell + \ell n/m.$$

EXERCISE 6.50. Let $\mathcal{X}$ be a set of size $n \geq 1$. Let F be a random function from $\mathcal{X}$ into $\mathcal{X}$. Let G be a random permutation of $\mathcal{X}$. Let $x_1, \ldots, x_\ell$ be distinct, fixed elements of $\mathcal{X}$. Show that

$$\Delta[F(x_1), \ldots, F(x_\ell); G(x_1), \ldots, G(x_\ell)] \leq \frac{\ell(\ell-1)}{2n}.$$

EXERCISE 6.51. Let $\mathcal{H}$ be a family hash functions from $\mathcal{A}$ to $\mathcal{Z}$ such that (i) each $h \in \mathcal{H}$ maps $\mathcal{A}$ injectively into $\mathcal{Z}$, and (ii) there exists ϵ, with $0 \leq \epsilon \leq 1$, such that $\Delta[H(a); H(a')] \leq \epsilon$ for all $a, a' \in \mathcal{A}$, where H is uniformly distributed over $\mathcal{H}$. Show that $|\mathcal{H}| \geq (1-\epsilon)|\mathcal{A}|$.

6.9 Measures of randomness and the leftover hash lemma (∗)

In this section, we discuss different ways to measure "how random" a probability distribution is, and relations among them. Consider a distribution defined on a finite sample space $\mathcal{V}$. In some sense, the "most random" distribution on $\mathcal{V}$ is the uniform distribution, while the least random would be a "point mass" distribution, that is, a distribution where one point $v \in \mathcal{V}$ in the sample space has probability 1, and all other points have probability 0.

We define three measures of randomness. Let X be a random variable taking values on a set $\mathcal{V}$ of size N.

1. We say X is δ-**uniform on** $\mathcal{V}$ if the statistical distance between X and the uniform distribution on $\mathcal{V}$ is equal to δ; that is,

$$\delta = \frac{1}{2} \sum_{v \in \mathcal{V}} |\mathsf{P}[X = v] - 1/N|.$$

2. The **guessing probability** $\gamma(X)$ of X is defined to be

$$\gamma(X) := \max\{\mathsf{P}[X = v] : v \in \mathcal{V}\}.$$

3. The **collision probability** $\kappa(X)$ of X is defined to be

$$\kappa(X) := \sum_{v \in \mathcal{V}} \mathsf{P}[X = v]^2.$$

Observe that if X is uniformly distributed on $\mathcal{V}$, then it is 0-uniform on $\mathcal{V}$, and $\gamma(X) = \kappa(X) = 1/N$. Also, if X has a point mass distribution, then it is $(1 - 1/N)$-uniform on $\mathcal{V}$, and $\gamma(X) = \kappa(X) = 1$. The quantity $\log_2(1/\gamma(X))$ is sometimes called the **min entropy** of X, and the quantity $\log_2(1/\kappa(X))$ is sometimes called the **Renyi entropy** of X. The collision probability $\kappa(X)$ has the following interpretation: if X and X' are identically distributed independent random variables, then $\kappa(X) = \mathsf{P}[X = X']$ (see Exercise 6.26).

We first state some easy inequalities:

Theorem 6.19. *Let X be a random variable taking values on a set $\mathcal{V}$ of size N, such that X is δ-uniform on $\mathcal{V}$, $\gamma := \gamma(X)$, and $\kappa := \kappa(X)$. Then we have:*

(i) $\kappa \geq 1/N$;
(ii) $\gamma^2 \leq \kappa \leq \gamma \leq 1/N + \delta$.

Proof. Part (i) is immediate from Exercise 6.26. The other inequalities are left as easy exercises. □

This theorem implies that the collision and guessing probabilities are minimal for the uniform distribution, which perhaps agrees with ones intuition.

While the above theorem implies that γ and κ are close to $1/N$ when δ is small, the following theorem provides a converse of sorts:

Theorem 6.20. *If X is δ-uniform on $\mathcal{V}$, $\kappa := \kappa(X)$, and $N := |\mathcal{V}|$, then*

$$\kappa \geq \frac{1 + 4\delta^2}{N}.$$

Proof. We may assume that $\delta > 0$, since otherwise the theorem is already true, simply from the fact that $\kappa \geq 1/N$.

For $v \in \mathcal{V}$, let $p_v := \mathsf{P}[X = v]$. We have $\delta = \frac{1}{2} \sum_v |p_v - 1/N|$, and hence

$1 = \sum_v q_v$, where $q_v := |p_v - 1/N|/(2\delta)$. So we have

$$\frac{1}{N} \le \sum_v q_v^2 \quad \text{(by Exercise 6.25)}$$

$$= \frac{1}{4\delta^2} \sum_v (p_v - 1/N)^2$$

$$= \frac{1}{4\delta^2} \left(\sum_v p_v^2 - 1/N\right) \quad \text{(again by Exercise 6.25)}$$

$$= \frac{1}{4\delta^2} (\kappa - 1/N),$$

from which the theorem follows immediately. $\square$

We are now in a position to state and prove a very useful result which, intuitively, allows us to convert a "low quality" source of randomness into a "high quality" source of randomness, making use of a universal family of hash functions (see §6.7.1).

Theorem 6.21 (Leftover hash lemma). *Let $\mathcal{H}$ be a universal family of hash functions from $\mathcal{A}$ to $\mathcal{Z}$, where $\mathcal{Z}$ is of size n. Let H denote a random variable with the uniform distribution on $\mathcal{H}$, and let A denote a random variable taking values in $\mathcal{A}$, and with H, A independent. Let $\kappa := \kappa(A)$. Then $(H, H(A))$ is δ-uniform on $\mathcal{H} \times \mathcal{Z}$, where*

$$\delta \le \sqrt{n\kappa}/2.$$

Proof. Let Z denote a random variable uniformly distributed on $\mathcal{Z}$, with H, A, Z mutually independent. Let $m := |\mathcal{H}|$ and $\delta := \Delta[H, H(A); H, Z]$.

Let us compute the collision probability $\kappa(H, H(A))$. Let H' have the same distribution as H and A' have the same distribution as A, with H, H', A, A' mutually independent. Then

$$\kappa(H, H(A)) = \mathsf{P}[H = H' \wedge H(A) = H'(A')]$$

$$= \mathsf{P}[H = H']\mathsf{P}[H(A) = H(A')]$$

$$= \frac{1}{m}\left(\mathsf{P}[H(A) = H(A') \mid A = A']\mathsf{P}[A = A'] + \right.$$

$$\left. \mathsf{P}[H(A) = H(A') \mid A \ne A']\mathsf{P}[A \ne A']\right)$$

$$\le \frac{1}{m}(\mathsf{P}[A = A'] + \mathsf{P}[H(A) = H(A') \mid A \ne A'])$$

$$\leq \frac{1}{m}(\kappa + 1/n)$$

$$= \frac{1}{mn}(n\kappa + 1).$$

Applying Theorem 6.20 to the random variable $(H, H(A))$, which takes values on the set $\mathcal{H} \times \mathcal{Z}$ of size $N := mn$, we see that $4\delta^2 \leq n\kappa$, from which the theorem immediately follows. $\square$

***Example* 6.28.** Suppose A is uniformly distributed over a subset $\mathcal{A}'$ of $\mathcal{A}$, where $|\mathcal{A}'| \geq 2^{160}$, so that $\kappa(A) \leq 2^{-160}$. Suppose that $\mathcal{H}$ is a universal family of hash functions from $\mathcal{A}$ to $\mathcal{Z}$, where $|\mathcal{Z}| \leq 2^{64}$. If H is uniformly distributed over $\mathcal{H}$, independently of A, then the leftover hash lemma says that $(H, H(A))$ is δ-uniform on $\mathcal{H} \times \mathcal{Z}$, with

$$\delta \leq \sqrt{2^{64}2^{-160}}/2 = 2^{-49}. \quad \square$$

The leftover hash lemma allows one to convert "low quality" sources of randomness into "high quality" sources of randomness. Suppose that to conduct an experiment, we need to sample a random variable Z whose distribution is uniform on a set $\mathcal{Z}$ of size n, or at least δ-uniform for a small value of δ. However, we may not have direct access to a source of "real" randomness whose distribution looks anything like that of the desired uniform distribution, but rather, only to a "low quality" source of randomness. For example, one could model various characteristics of a person's typing at the keyboard, or perhaps various characteristics of the internal state of a computer (both its software and hardware) as a random process. We cannot say very much about the probability distributions associated with such processes, but perhaps we can conservatively estimate the collision or guessing probability associated with these distributions. Using the leftover hash lemma, we can hash the output of this random process, using a suitably generated random hash function. The hash function acts like a "magnifying glass": it "focuses" the randomness inherent in the "low quality" source distribution onto the set $\mathcal{Z}$, obtaining a "high quality," nearly uniform, distribution on $\mathcal{Z}$.

Of course, this approach requires a random hash function, which may be just as difficult to generate as a random element of $\mathcal{Z}$. The following theorem shows, however, that we can at least use the same "magnifying glass" many times over, with the statistical distance from uniform of the output distribution increasing linearly in the number of applications of the hash function.

Theorem 6.22. *Let $\mathcal{H}$ be a universal family of hash functions from $\mathcal{A}$ to $\mathcal{Z}$, where $\mathcal{Z}$ is of size n. Let H denote a random variable with the uniform distribution on $\mathcal{H}$, and let $A_1, \ldots, A_\ell$ denote random variables taking values in $\mathcal{A}$, with $H, A_1, \ldots, A_\ell$ mutually independent. Let $\kappa := \max\{\kappa(\mathcal{A}_1), \ldots, \kappa(\mathcal{A}_\ell)\}$. Then $(H, H(A_1), \ldots, H(A_\ell))$ is δ'-uniform on $\mathcal{H} \times \mathcal{Z}^{\times \ell}$, where*

$$\delta' \leq \ell \sqrt{n\kappa}/2.$$

Proof. Let $Z_1, \ldots, Z_\ell$ denote random variables with the uniform distribution on $\mathcal{Z}$, with $H, A_1, \ldots, A_\ell, Z_1, \ldots, Z_\ell$ mutually independent. We shall make a hybrid argument (as in the proof of Theorem 6.18). Define random variables $W_0, W_1, \ldots, W_\ell$ as follows:

$$W_0 := (H, H(A_1), \ldots, H(A_\ell)),$$
$$W_i := (H, Z_1, \ldots, Z_i, H(A_{i+1}), \ldots, H(A_\ell)) \quad \text{for } i = 1, \ldots, \ell-1, \text{ and}$$
$$W_\ell := (H, Z_1, \ldots, Z_\ell).$$

We have

$$\delta' = \Delta[W_0; W_\ell]$$

$$\leq \sum_{i=1}^{\ell} \Delta[W_{i-1}; W_i] \quad \text{(by part (iv) of Theorem 6.14)}$$

$$\leq \sum_{i=1}^{\ell} \Delta[H, Z_1, \ldots, Z_{i-1}, H(A_i), A_{i+1}, \ldots, A_\ell;$$
$$\qquad H, Z_1, \ldots, Z_{i-1}, \quad Z_i, \quad A_{i+1}, \ldots, A_\ell]$$
$$\text{(by Theorem 6.16)}$$

$$= \sum_{i=1}^{\ell} \Delta[H, H(A_i); H, Z_i] \quad \text{(by Theorem 6.17)}$$

$$\leq \ell \sqrt{n\kappa}/2 \quad \text{(by Theorem 6.21).} \quad \square$$

Another source of "low quality" randomness arises in certain cryptographic applications, where we have a "secret" random variable A that is distributed uniformly over a large subset of some set $\mathcal{A}$, but we want to derive from A a "secret key" whose distribution is close to that of the uniform distribution on a specified "key space" $\mathcal{Z}$ (typically, $\mathcal{Z}$ is the set of all bit strings of some specified length). The leftover hash lemma, combined with Theorem 6.22, allows us to do this using a "public" hash function — generated at random once and for all, published for all to see, and used over and over to derive secret keys as needed.

EXERCISE 6.52. Consider again the situation in Theorem 6.21. Suppose that $\mathcal{Z} = \{0, \ldots, n-1\}$, but that we would rather have an almost-uniform distribution over $\mathcal{Z}' = \{0, \ldots, t-1\}$, for some $t < n$. While it may be possible to work with a different family of hash functions, we do not have to if n is large enough with respect to t, in which case we can just use the value $H(A) \bmod t$. If Z' is uniformly distributed over $\mathcal{Z}'$, show that

$$\Delta[H, H(A) \bmod t; H, Z'] \leq \sqrt{n\kappa}/2 + t/n.$$

EXERCISE 6.53. Suppose X and Y are random variables with images $\mathcal{X}$ and $\mathcal{Y}$, respectively, and suppose that for some ϵ, we have $\mathsf{P}[X = x \mid Y = y] \leq \epsilon$ for all $x \in \mathcal{X}$ and $y \in \mathcal{Y}$. Let $\mathcal{H}$ be a universal family of hash functions from $\mathcal{X}$ to $\mathcal{Z}$, where $\mathcal{Z}$ is of size n. Let H denote a random variable with the uniform distribution on $\mathcal{H}$, and Z denote a random variable with the uniform distribution on $\mathcal{Z}$, where the three variables H, Z, and (X, Y) are mutually independent. Show that the statistical distance between $(Y, H, H(X))$ and (Y, H, Z) is at most $\sqrt{n\epsilon}/2$.

6.10 Discrete probability distributions

In addition to working with probability distributions over finite sample spaces, one can also work with distributions over infinite sample spaces. If the sample space is countable, that is, either finite or *countably* infinite, then the distribution is called a **discrete probability distribution**. We shall not consider any other types of probability distributions in this text. The theory developed in §§6.1–6.5 extends fairly easily to the countably infinite setting, and in this section, we discuss how this is done.

6.10.1 Basic definitions

To say that the sample space $\mathcal{U}$ is countably infinite simply means that there is a bijection f from the set of positive integers onto $\mathcal{U}$; thus, we can enumerate the elements of $\mathcal{U}$ as $u_1, u_2, u_3, \ldots$, where $u_i = f(i)$.

As in the finite case, the probability function assigns to each $u \in \mathcal{U}$ a value $\mathsf{P}[u] \in [0, 1]$. The basic requirement that the probabilities sum to one (equation (6.1)) is the requirement that the infinite series $\sum_{i=1}^{\infty} \mathsf{P}[u_i]$ converges to one. Luckily, the convergence properties of an infinite series whose terms are all non-negative is invariant under a re-ordering of terms (see §A4), so it does not matter how we enumerate the elements of $\mathcal{U}$.

***Example* 6.29.** Suppose we flip a fair coin repeatedly until it comes up "heads," and let the outcome u of the experiment denote the number of coins flipped. We can model this experiment as a discrete probability distribution $\mathbf{D} = (\mathcal{U}, \mathsf{P})$, where $\mathcal{U}$ consists of the set of all positive integers, and where for $u \in \mathcal{U}$, we set $\mathsf{P}[u] = 2^{-u}$. We can check that indeed $\sum_{u=1}^{\infty} 2^{-u} = 1$, as required.

One may be tempted to model this experiment by setting up a probability distribution on the sample space of all infinite sequences of coin tosses; however, this sample space is not countably infinite, and so we cannot construct a discrete probability distribution on this space. While it is possible to extend the notion of a probability distribution to such spaces, this would take us too far afield. $\square$

***Example* 6.30.** More generally, suppose we repeatedly execute a Bernoulli trial until it succeeds, where each execution succeeds with probability $p > 0$ independently of the previous trials, and let the outcome u of the experiment denote the number of trials executed. Then we associate the probability $\mathsf{P}[u] = q^{u-1}p$ with each positive integer u, where $q := 1 - p$, since we have $u - 1$ failures before the one success. One can easily check that these probabilities sum to 1. Such a distribution is called a **geometric distribution**. $\square$

***Example* 6.31.** The series $\sum_{i=1}^{\infty} 1/i^3$ converges to some positive number c. Therefore, we can define a probability distribution on the set of positive integers, where we associate with each $i \geq 1$ the probability $1/ci^3$. $\square$

***Example* 6.32.** More generally, if $x_i, i = 1, 2, \ldots$, are non-negative numbers, and $0 < c := \sum_{i=1}^{\infty} x_i < \infty$, then we can define a probability distribution on the set of positive integers, assigning the probability x_i/c to i. $\square$

As in the finite case, an event is an arbitrary subset $\mathcal{A}$ of $\mathcal{U}$. The probability $\mathsf{P}[\mathcal{A}]$ of $\mathcal{A}$ is defined as the sum of the probabilities associated with the elements of $\mathcal{A}$—in the definition (6.2), the sum is treated as an infinite series when $\mathcal{A}$ is infinite. This series is guaranteed to converge, and its value does not depend on the particular enumeration of the elements of $\mathcal{A}$.

***Example* 6.33.** Consider the geometric distribution discussed in Example 6.30, where p is the success probability of each Bernoulli trial, and $q := 1 - p$. For integer $i \geq 1$, consider the event $\mathcal{A}$ that the number of trials executed is at least i. Formally, $\mathcal{A}$ is the set of all integers greater than or equal to i. Intuitively, $\mathsf{P}[\mathcal{A}]$ should be q^{i-1}, since we perform at least i trials if and only if the first $i - 1$ trials fail. Just to be sure, we can compute

$$P[\mathcal{A}] = \sum_{u \geq i} P[u] = \sum_{u \geq i} q^{u-1}p = q^{i-1}p \sum_{u \geq 0} q^u = q^{i-1}p \cdot \frac{1}{1-q} = q^{i-1}. \quad \square$$

It is an easy matter to check that all the statements made in §6.1 carry over *verbatim* to the case of countably infinite sample spaces. Moreover, it also makes sense in the countably infinite case to consider events that are a union or intersection of a countably infinite number of events:

Theorem 6.23. *Let $\mathcal{A}_1, \mathcal{A}_2, \ldots$ be an infinite sequence of events.*

(i) *If $\mathcal{A}_i \subseteq \mathcal{A}_{i+1}$ for all $i \geq 1$, then $P[\bigcup_{i \geq 1} \mathcal{A}_i] = \lim_{i \to \infty} P[\mathcal{A}_i]$.*

(ii) *In general, we have $P[\bigcup_{i \geq 1} \mathcal{A}_i] \leq \sum_{i \geq 1} P[\mathcal{A}_i]$.*

(iii) *If the $\mathcal{A}_i$ are pairwise disjoint, then $P[\bigcup_{i \geq 1} \mathcal{A}_i] = \sum_{i \geq 1} P[\mathcal{A}_i]$.*

(iv) *If $\mathcal{A}_i \supseteq \mathcal{A}_{i+1}$ for all $i \geq 1$, then $P[\bigcap_{i \geq 1} \mathcal{A}_i] = \lim_{i \to \infty} P[\mathcal{A}_i]$.*

Proof. For (i), let $\mathcal{A} := \bigcup_{i \geq 1} \mathcal{A}_i$, and let $a_1, a_2, \ldots$ be an enumeration of the elements of $\mathcal{A}$. For any $\epsilon > 0$, there exists a value k_0 such that $\sum_{i=1}^{k_0} a_i > P[\mathcal{A}] - \epsilon$. Also, there is some k_1 such that $\{a_1, \ldots, a_{k_0}\} \subseteq \mathcal{A}_{k_1}$. Therefore, for any $k \geq k_1$, we have $P[\mathcal{A}] - \epsilon < P[\mathcal{A}_k] \leq P[\mathcal{A}]$.

(ii) and (iii) follow by applying (i) to the sequence $\{\bigcup_{j=1}^i \mathcal{A}_j\}_i$, and making use of (6.5) and (6.6), respectively.

(iv) follows by applying (i) to the sequence $\{\overline{\mathcal{A}_i}\}$, using (the infinite version of) DeMorgan's law. $\square$

6.10.2 Conditional probability and independence

All of the definitions and results in §6.2 carry over *verbatim* to the countably infinite case. Equation (6.7) as well as Bayes' theorem (equation 6.8) and equation (6.9) extend *mutatis mutandus* to the case of an infinite partition $\mathcal{B}_1, \mathcal{B}_2, \ldots$.

6.10.3 Random variables

All of the definitions and results in §6.3 carry over *verbatim* to the countably infinite case (except Theorem 6.2, which of course only makes sense in the finite setting).

6.10.4 Expectation and variance

We define the expected value of a real random variable X exactly as before:

$$\mathsf{E}[X] := \sum_{u \in \mathcal{U}} X(u) \cdot \mathsf{P}[u],$$

where, of course, the sum is an infinite series. However, if X may take negative values, then we require that the series converges *absolutely*; that is, we require that $\sum_{u \in \mathcal{U}} |X(u)| \cdot \mathsf{P}[u] < \infty$ (see §A4). Otherwise, we say the expected value of X **does not exist**. Recall from calculus that a series that converges absolutely will itself converge, and will converge to the same value under a re-ordering of terms. Thus, if the expectation exists at all, its value is independent of the ordering on $\mathcal{U}$. For a non-negative random variable X, if its expectation does not exist, one may express this as "$\mathsf{E}[X] = \infty$."

All of the results in §6.4 carry over essentially unchanged, except that one must pay some attention to "convergence issues."

Equations (6.13) and (6.14) hold, but with the following caveats (verify):

- If X is a real random variable with image $\mathcal{X}$, then its expected value $\mathsf{E}[X]$ exists if and only if the series $\sum_{x \in \mathcal{X}} x\mathsf{P}[X = x]$ converges absolutely, in which case $\mathsf{E}[X]$ is equal to the value of the latter series.

- If X is a random variable with image $\mathcal{X}$ and f a real-valued function on $\mathcal{X}$, then $\mathsf{E}[f(X)]$ exists if and only if the series $\sum_{x \in \mathcal{X}} f(x)\mathsf{P}[X = x]$ converges absolutely, in which case $\mathsf{E}[f(X)]$ is equal to the value of the latter series.

Example **6.34.** Let X be a random variable whose distribution is as in Example 6.31. Since the series $\sum 1/n^2$ converges and the series $\sum 1/n$ diverges, the expectation $\mathsf{E}[X]$ exists, while $\mathsf{E}[X^2]$ does not. $\square$

Theorems 6.6 and 6.7 hold under the additional hypothesis that $\mathsf{E}[X]$ and $\mathsf{E}[Y]$ exist.

If $X_1, X_2, \ldots$ is an infinite sequence of real random variables, then the random variable $X := \sum_{i=1}^{\infty} X_i$ is well defined provided the series $\sum_{i=1}^{\infty} X_i(u)$ converges for all $u \in \mathcal{U}$. One might hope that $\mathsf{E}[X] = \sum_{i=1}^{\infty} \mathsf{E}[X_i]$; however, this is not in general true, even if the individual expectations $\mathsf{E}[X_i]$ are non-negative, and even if the series defining X converges absolutely for all u; nevertheless, it is true when the X_i are non-negative:

Theorem 6.24. *Let $X := \sum_{i \geq 1} X_i$, where each X_i takes non-negative values only. Then we have*

$$\mathsf{E}[X] = \sum_{i \geq 1} \mathsf{E}[X_i].$$

Proof. We have

$$\sum_{i \geq 1} \mathsf{E}[X_i] = \sum_{i \geq 1} \sum_{u \in \mathcal{U}} X_i(u)\mathsf{P}[u] = \sum_{u \in \mathcal{U}} \sum_{i \geq 1} X_i(u)\mathsf{P}[u]$$

$$= \sum_{u \in \mathcal{U}} \mathsf{P}[u] \sum_{i \geq 1} X_i(u) = \mathsf{E}[X],$$

where we use the fact that we may reverse the order of summation in an infinite double summation of non-negative terms (see §A5). $\square$

Using this theorem, one can prove the analog of Theorem 6.8 for countably infinite sample spaces, using exactly the same argument.

Theorem 6.25. *If X is a random variable that takes non-negative integer values, then*

$$\mathsf{E}[X] = \sum_{i=1}^{\infty} \mathsf{P}[X \geq i].$$

A nice picture to keep in mind with regards to Theorem 6.25 is the following. Let $p_i := \mathsf{P}[X = i]$ for $i = 0, 1, \ldots,$ and let us arrange the probabilities p_i in a table as follows:

$$\begin{array}{ccc} p_1 & & \\ p_2 & p_2 & \\ p_3 & p_3 & p_3 \\ \vdots & & \ddots \end{array}$$

Summing the ith row of this table, we get $i\mathsf{P}[X = i]$, and so $\mathsf{E}[X]$ is equal to the sum of all the entries in the table. However, we may compute the same sum column by column, and the sum of the entries in the ith column is $\mathsf{P}[X \geq i]$.

***Example* 6.35.** Suppose X is a random variable with a geometric distribution, as in Example 6.30, with an associated success probability p and failure probability $q := 1 - p$. As we saw in Example 6.33, for all integer $i \geq 1$, we have $\mathsf{P}[X \geq i] = q^{i-1}$. We may therefore apply Theorem 6.25 to easily compute the expected value of X:

$$\mathsf{E}[X] = \sum_{i=1}^{\infty} \mathsf{P}[X \geq i] = \sum_{i=1}^{\infty} q^{i-1} = \frac{1}{1-q} = \frac{1}{p}. \quad \square$$

***Example* 6.36.** To illustrate that Theorem 6.24 does not hold in general, consider the geometric distribution on the positive integers, where $\mathsf{P}[j] = 2^{-j}$ for $j \geq 1$. For $i \geq 1$, define the random variable X_i so that $X_i(i) = 2^i$,

$X_i(i+1) = -2^{i+1}$, and $X_i(j) = 0$ for all $j \notin \{i, i+1\}$. Then $\mathsf{E}[X_i] = 0$ for all $i \geq 1$, and so $\sum_{i \geq 1} \mathsf{E}[X_i] = 0$. Now define $X := \sum_{i \geq 1} X_i$. This is well defined, and in fact $X(1) = 2$, while $X(j) = 0$ for all $j > 1$. Hence $\mathsf{E}[X] = 1$. $\square$

The variance $\mathsf{Var}[X]$ of X exists if and only if $\mathsf{E}[X]$ and $\mathsf{E}[(X - \mathsf{E}[X])^2]$ exist, which holds if and only if $\mathsf{E}[X]$ and $\mathsf{E}[X^2]$ exist.

Theorem 6.9 holds under the additional hypothesis that $\mathsf{E}[X]$ and $\mathsf{E}[X^2]$ exist. Similarly, Theorem 6.10 holds under the additional hypothesis that $\mathsf{E}[X_i]$ and $\mathsf{E}[X_i^2]$ exist for each i.

The definition of conditional expectation carries over verbatim, as do equations (6.15) and (6.16). The analog of (6.16) for infinite partitions $\mathcal{B}_1, \mathcal{B}_2, \ldots$ does not hold in general, but does hold if X is always non-negative.

6.10.5 Some useful bounds

Both Theorems 6.11 and 6.12 (Markov's and Chebyshev's inequalities) hold, under the additional hypothesis that the relevant expectations and variances exist.

EXERCISE 6.54. Suppose X is a random variable taking positive integer values, and that for some real number q, with $0 \leq q \leq 1$, and for all integers $i \geq 1$, we have $\mathsf{P}[X \geq i] = q^{i-1}$. Show that X has a geometric distribution with associated success probability $p := 1 - q$.

EXERCISE 6.55. A gambler plays a simple game in a casino: with each play of the game, the gambler may bet any number m of dollars; a coin is flipped, and if it comes up "heads," the casino pays m dollars to the gambler, and otherwise, the gambler pays m dollars to the casino. The gambler plays the game repeatedly, using the following strategy: he initially bets a dollar; each time he plays, if he wins, he pockets his winnings and goes home, and otherwise, he doubles his bet and plays again.

(a) Show that if the gambler has an infinite amount of money (so he can keep playing no matter how many times he looses), then his expected winnings are one dollar. Hint: model the gambler's winnings as a random variable on a geometric distribution, and compute its expected value.

(b) Show that if the gambler has a finite amount of money (so that he can only afford to loose a certain number of times), then his expected winnings are zero (regardless of how much money he starts with).

Hint: in this case, you can model the gambler's winnings as a random variable on a finite probability distribution.

6.11 Notes

Our Chernoff bound (Theorem 6.13) is one of a number of different types of bounds that appear in the literature under the rubric of "Chernoff bound."

Universal and pairwise independent hash functions, with applications to hash tables and message authentication codes, were introduced by Carter and Wegman [25, 99].

The leftover hash lemma (Theorem 6.21) was originally stated and proved by Impagliazzo, Levin, and Luby [46], who use it to obtain an important result in the theory of cryptography. Our proof of the leftover hash lemma is loosely based on one by Impagliazzo and Zuckermann [47], who also present further applications.

7

Probabilistic algorithms

It is sometimes useful to endow our algorithms with the ability to generate random numbers. To simplify matters, we only consider algorithms that generate random bits. Where such random bits actually come from will not be of great concern to us here. In a practical implementation, one would use a pseudo-random bit generator, which should produce bits that "for all practical purposes" are "as good as random." While there is a well-developed theory of pseudo-random bit generation (some of which builds on the ideas in §6.9), we will not delve into this here. Moreover, the pseudo-random bit generators used in practice are not based on this general theory, and are much more ad hoc in design. So, although we will present a rigorous formal theory of probabilistic algorithms, the application of this theory to practice is ultimately a bit heuristic.

7.1 Basic definitions

Formally speaking, we will add a new type of instruction to our random access machine (described in §3.2):

random bit This type of instruction is of the form $\alpha \leftarrow \text{RANDOM}$, where α takes the same form as in arithmetic instructions. Execution of this type of instruction assigns to α a value sampled from the uniform distribution on $\{0, 1\}$, independently from the execution of all other random-bit instructions.

In describing algorithms at a high level, we shall write "$b \leftarrow_R \{0, 1\}$" to denote the assignment of a random bit to the variable b, and "$s \leftarrow_R \{0, 1\}^{\times \ell}$" to denote the assignment of a random bit string of length ℓ to the variable s.

In describing the behavior of such a **probabilistic** or **randomized algorithm** A, for any input x, we view its running time and output as random

148

variables, denoted $T_A(x)$ and $A(x)$, respectively. The **expected running time** of A on input x is defined as the expected value $\mathsf{E}[T_A(x)]$ of the random variable $T_A(x)$. Note that in defining expected running time, we are not considering the *input* to be drawn from some probability distribution. One could, of course, define such a notion; however, it is not always easy to come up with a distribution on the input space that reasonably models a particular real-world situation. We do not pursue this issue any more here.

We say that a probabilistic algorithm A runs in **expected polynomial time** if there exist constants c, d such that for all $n \geq 0$ and all inputs x of length n, we have $\mathsf{E}[T_A(x)] \leq n^c + d$. We say that A runs in **strict polynomial time** if there exist constants c, d such that for all n and all inputs x of length n, A *always* halts on input x within $n^c + d$, regardless of its random choices.

Defining the distributions of $T_A(x)$ and $A(x)$ is a bit tricky. Things are quite straightforward if A *always* halts on input x after a finite number of steps, regardless of the outcomes of its random choices: in this case, we can naturally view $T_A(x)$ and $A(x)$ as random variables on a uniform distribution over bit strings of some particular length—such a random bit string may be used as the source of random bits for the algorithm. However, if there is no a priori bound on the number of steps, things become more complicated: think of an algorithm that generates random bits one at a time until it generates, say, a 1 bit—just as in Example 6.29, we do not attempt to model this as a probability distribution on the uncountable set of infinite bit strings, but rather, we directly define an appropriate discrete probability distribution that models the execution of A on input x.

7.1.1 Defining the probability distribution

A warning to the reader: *the remainder of this section is a bit technical, and you might want to skip ahead to §7.2 on first reading, if you are willing to trust your intuition regarding probabilistic algorithms.*

To motivate our definition, which may at first seem a bit strange, consider again Example 6.29. We could view the sample space in that example to be the set of all bit strings consisting of zero or more 0 bits, followed by a single 1 bit, and to each such bit string σ of this special form, we assign the probability $2^{-|\sigma|}$, where $|\sigma|$ denotes the length of σ. The "random experiment" we have in mind is to generate random bits one at a time until one of these special "halting" strings is generated. In developing the definition of the probability distribution for a probabilistic algorithm, we simply consider more general sets of "halting" strings, determined by the algorithm and its input.

To simplify matters, we assume that the machine produces a stream of random bits, one with every instruction executed, and if the instruction happens to be a random-bit instruction, then this is the bit it uses. For any bit string σ, we can run A on input x for up to $|\sigma|$ steps, using σ for the stream of random bits, and observe the behavior of the algorithm. The reader may wish to visualize σ as a finite path in an infinite binary tree, where we start at the root, branching to the left if the next bit in σ is a 0 bit, and branching to the right if the next bit in σ is a 1 bit. In this context, we call σ an **execution path**. Some further terminology will be helpful:

- If A halts in at most $|\sigma|$ steps, then we call σ a **complete execution path**;

- if A halts in exactly $|\sigma|$ steps, then we call σ an **exact execution path**;

- if A does not halt in fewer than $|\sigma|$ steps, then we call σ a **partial execution path**.

The sample space $\mathcal{S}$ of the probability distribution associated with A on input x consists of all *exact* execution paths. Clearly, $\mathcal{S}$ is **prefix free**; that is, no string in $\mathcal{S}$ is a proper prefix of another.

Theorem 7.1. *If $\mathcal{S}$ is a prefix-free set of bit strings, then $\sum_{\sigma \in \mathcal{S}} 2^{-|\sigma|} \leq 1$.*

Proof. We first claim that the theorem holds for any finite prefix-free set $\mathcal{S}$. We may assume that $\mathcal{S}$ is non-empty, since otherwise, the claim is trivial. We prove the claim by induction on the sum of the lengths of the elements of $\mathcal{S}$. The base case is when $\mathcal{S}$ contains just the empty string, in which case the claim is clear. If $\mathcal{S}$ contains non-empty strings, let τ be a string in $\mathcal{S}$ of maximal length, and let τ' be the prefix of length $|\tau| - 1$ of τ. Now remove from $\mathcal{S}$ all strings which have τ' as a prefix (there are either one or two such strings), and add to $\mathcal{S}$ the string τ'. It is easy to see (verify) that the resulting set $\mathcal{S}'$ is also prefix-free, and that

$$\sum_{\sigma \in \mathcal{S}} 2^{-|\sigma|} \leq \sum_{\sigma \in \mathcal{S}'} 2^{-|\sigma|}.$$

The claim now follows by induction.

For the general case, let $\sigma_1, \sigma_2, \ldots$ be a particular enumeration of $\mathcal{S}$, and consider the partial sums $S_i = \sum_{j=1}^{i} 2^{-|\sigma_j|}$ for $i = 1, 2, \ldots$. From the above claim, each of these partial sums is at most 1, from which it follows that $\lim_{i \to \infty} S_i \leq 1$. $\square$

From the above theorem, if $\mathcal{S}$ is the sample space associated with algorithm A on input x, we have

$$S := \sum_{\sigma \in \mathcal{S}} 2^{-|\sigma|} \leq 1.$$

Assume that $S = 1$. Then we say that A **halts with probability 1 on input** x, and we define the distribution $\mathbf{D}_{A,x}$ associated with A on input x to be the distribution on $\mathcal{S}$ that assigns the probability $2^{-|\sigma|}$ to each bit string $\sigma \in \mathcal{S}$. We also define $T_A(x)$ and $A(x)$ as random variables on the distribution $\mathbf{D}_{A,x}$ in the natural way: for each $\sigma \in \mathcal{S}$, we define $T_A(x)$ to be $|\sigma|$ and $A(x)$ to be the output produced by A on input x using σ to drive its execution.

All of the above definitions assumed that A halts with probability 1 on input x, and indeed, we shall only be interested in algorithms that halt with probability 1 on all inputs. However, to analyze a given algorithm, we still have to prove that it halts with probability 1 on all inputs before we can use these definitions and bring to bear all the tools of discrete probability theory. To this end, it is helpful to study various finite probability distributions associated with the execution of A on input x. For every integer $k \geq 0$, let us consider the uniform distribution on bit strings of length k, and for each $j = 0, \ldots, k$, define $\mathcal{H}_j^{(k)}$ to be the event that such a random k-bit string causes A on input x to halt within j steps.

A couple of observations are in order. First, if $\mathcal{S}$ is the set of all exact execution paths for A on input x, then we have (verify)

$$\mathsf{P}[\mathcal{H}_j^{(k)}] = \sum_{\substack{\sigma \in \mathcal{S} \\ |\sigma| \leq j}} 2^{-|\sigma|}.$$

From this it follows that for all non-negative integers j, k, k' with $j \leq \min\{k, k'\}$, we have

$$\mathsf{P}[\mathcal{H}_j^{(k)}] = \mathsf{P}[\mathcal{H}_j^{(k')}].$$

Defining $H_k := \mathsf{P}[\mathcal{H}_k^{(k)}]$, it also follows that the sequence $\{H_k\}_{k \geq 0}$ is non-decreasing and bounded above by 1, and that A halts with probability 1 on input x if and only if

$$\lim_{k \to \infty} H_k = 1.$$

A simple necessary condition for halting with probability 1 on a given input is that for all partial execution paths, there exists some extension that is a complete execution path. Intuitively, if this does not hold, then with some non-zero probability, the algorithm falls into an infinite loop. More formally, if there exists a partial execution path of length j that cannot be extended to a complete execution path, then for all $k \geq j$ we have

$$H_k \leq 1 - 2^{-j}.$$

This does not, however, guarantee halting with probability 1. A simple sufficient condition is the following:

> *There exists a bound ℓ (possibly depending on the input) such that for every partial execution path σ, there exists a complete execution path that extends σ and whose length at most $|\sigma| + \ell$.*

To see why this condition implies that A halts with probability 1, observe that if A runs for $k\ell$ steps without halting, then the probability that it does not halt within $(k+1)\ell$ steps is at most $1 - 2^{-\ell}$. More formally, let us define $\overline{H}_k := 1 - H_k$, and note that for all $k \geq 0$, we have

$$\begin{aligned} \overline{H}_{(k+1)\ell} &= \mathsf{P}[\overline{\mathcal{H}}_{(k+1)\ell}^{((k+1)\ell)} \mid \overline{\mathcal{H}}_{k\ell}^{((k+1)\ell)}] \cdot \mathsf{P}[\overline{\mathcal{H}}_{k\ell}^{((k+1)\ell)}] \\ &\leq (1 - 2^{-\ell})\mathsf{P}[\overline{\mathcal{H}}_{k\ell}^{((k+1)\ell)}] \\ &= (1 - 2^{-\ell})\overline{H}_{k\ell}, \end{aligned}$$

and hence (by an induction argument on k), we have

$$\overline{H}_{k\ell} \leq (1 - 2^{-\ell})^k,$$

from which it follows that

$$\lim_{k \to \infty} H_k = 1.$$

It is usually fairly straightforward to verify this property for a particular algorithm "by inspection."

***Example* 7.1.** Consider the following algorithm:

    repeat
        $b \leftarrow_R \{0, 1\}$
    until $b = 1$

Since every loop is only a constant number of instructions, and since there is one chance to terminate with every loop iteration, the algorithm halts with probability 1. $\square$

***Example* 7.2.** Consider the following algorithm:

$$i \leftarrow 0$$

repeat

$$\quad i \leftarrow i + 1$$
$$\quad s \leftarrow_R \{0, 1\}^{\times i}$$

until $s = 0^{\times i}$

For positive integer n, consider the probability p_n of executing at least n loop iterations (each p_n is defined using an appropriate finite probability distribution). We have

$$p_n = \prod_{i=1}^{n-1}(1 - 2^{-i}) \geq \prod_{i=1}^{n-1} e^{-2^{-i+1}} = e^{-\sum_{i=0}^{n-2} 2^{-i}} \geq e^{-2},$$

where we have made use of the estimate (iii) in §A1. As p_n does not tend to zero as $n \to \infty$, we may conclude that the algorithm does not halt with probability 1.

Note that every partial execution path can be extended to a complete execution path, but the length of the extension is not bounded. $\square$

The following three exercises develop tools which simplify the analysis of probabilistic algorithms.

EXERCISE 7.1. Consider a probabilistic algorithm A that halts with probability 1 on input x, and consider the probability distribution $\mathbf{D}_{A,x}$ on the set S of exact execution paths. Let τ be a fixed, partial execution path, and let $\mathcal{B} \subseteq S$ be the event that consists of all exact execution paths that extend τ. Show that $\mathsf{P}[\mathcal{B}] = 2^{-|\tau|}$.

EXERCISE 7.2. Consider a probabilistic algorithm A that halts with probability 1 on input x, and consider the probability distribution $\mathbf{D}_{A,x}$ on the set S of exact execution paths. For a bit string σ and an integer $k \geq 0$, let $\{\sigma\}_k$ denote the value of σ truncated to the first k bits. Suppose that $\mathcal{B} \subseteq S$ is an event of the form

$$\mathcal{B} = \{\sigma \in S : \phi(\{\sigma\}_k)\}$$

for some predicate ϕ and some integer $k \geq 0$. Intuitively, this means that $\mathcal{B}$ is completely determined by the first k bits of the execution path. Now consider the uniform distribution on $\{0, 1\}^{\times k}$. Let us define an event $\mathcal{B}'$ in this distribution as follows. For $\sigma \in \{0, 1\}^{\times k}$, let us run A on input x using the execution path σ for k steps or until A halts (whichever comes first). If the number of steps executed was t (where $t \leq k$), then we put σ in $\mathcal{B}'$ if and only if $\phi(\{\sigma\}_t)$. Show that the probability that the event $\mathcal{B}$ occurs (with respect to the distribution $\mathbf{D}_{A,x}$) is the same as the probability that $\mathcal{B}'$ occurs (with respect to the uniform distribution on $\{0,1\}^{\times k}$). Hint: use Exercise 7.1.

The above exercise is very useful in simplifying the analysis of probabilistic algorithms. One can typically reduce the analysis of some event of interest into the analysis of a collection of events, each of which is determined by the first k bits of the execution path for some fixed k. The probability of an event that is determined by the first k bits of the execution path may then be calculated by analyzing the behavior of the algorithm on a random k-bit execution path.

EXERCISE 7.3. Suppose algorithm A calls algorithm B as a subroutine. In the probability distribution $\mathbf{D}_{A,x}$, consider a particular partial execution path τ that drives A to a point where A invokes algorithm B with a particular input y (determined by x and τ). Consider the conditional probability distribution given that τ is a prefix of A's actual execution path. We can define a random variable X on this conditional distribution whose value is the subpath traced out by the invocation of subroutine B. Show that the distribution of X is the same as $\mathbf{D}_{B,y}$. Hint: use Exercise 7.1.

The above exercise is also very useful in simplifying the analysis of probabilistic algorithms, in that it allows us to analyze a subroutine in isolation, and use the results in the analysis of an algorithm that calls that subroutine.

EXERCISE 7.4. Let A be a probabilistic algorithm, and for an input x and integer $k \geq 0$, consider the experiment in which we choose a random execution path of length k, and run A on input x for up to k steps using the selected execution path. If A halts within k steps, we define $A_k(x)$ to be the output produced by A, and $T_{A_k}(x)$ to be the actual number of steps executed by A; otherwise, we define $A_k(x)$ to be the distinguished value "$\perp$" and $T_{A_k}(x)$ to be k.

(a) Show that if A halts with probability 1 on input x, then for all possible outputs y,

$$\mathsf{P}[A(x) = y] = \lim_{k \to \infty} \mathsf{P}[A_k(x) = y].$$

(b) Show that if A halts with probability 1 on input x, then

$$\mathsf{E}[T_A(x)] = \lim_{k \to \infty} \mathsf{E}[T_{A_k}(x)].$$

EXERCISE 7.5. One can generalize the notion of a discrete, probabilistic process, as follows. Let Γ be a finite or countably infinite set. Let f be a function mapping sequences of one or more elements of Γ to $[0, 1]$, such that the following property holds:

for all finite sequences $(\gamma_1, \ldots, \gamma_{i-1})$, where $i \geq 1$, $f(\gamma_1, \ldots, \gamma_{i-1}, \gamma)$ is non-zero for at most a finite number of $\gamma \in \Gamma$, and

$$\sum_{\gamma \in \Gamma} f(\gamma_1, \ldots, \gamma_{i-1}, \gamma) = 1.$$

Now consider any prefix-free set $\mathcal{S}$ of finite sequences of elements of Γ. For $\sigma = (\gamma_1, \ldots, \gamma_n) \in \mathcal{S}$, define

$$\mathsf{P}[\sigma] := \prod_{i=1}^{n} f(\gamma_1, \ldots, \gamma_i).$$

Show that $\sum_{\sigma \in \mathcal{S}} \mathsf{P}[\sigma] \leq 1$, and hence we may define a probability distribution on $\mathcal{S}$ using the probability function $\mathsf{P}[\cdot]$ if this sum is 1. The intuition is that we are modeling a process in which we start out in the "empty" configuration; at each step, if we are in configuration $(\gamma_1, \ldots, \gamma_{i-1})$, we halt if this is a "halting" configuration, that is, an element of $\mathcal{S}$, and otherwise, we move to configuration $(\gamma_1, \ldots, \gamma_{i-1}, \gamma)$ with probability $f(\gamma_1, \ldots, \gamma_{i-1}, \gamma)$.

7.2 Approximation of functions

Suppose f is a function mapping bit strings to bit strings. We may have an algorithm A that **approximately computes** f in the following sense: there exists a constant ϵ, with $0 \leq \epsilon < 1/2$, such that for all inputs x, $\mathsf{P}[A(x) = f(x)] \geq 1 - \epsilon$. The value ϵ is a bound on the **error probability**, which is defined as $\mathsf{P}[A(x) \neq f(x)]$.

7.2.1 Reducing the error probability

There is a standard "trick" by which one can make the error probability very small; namely, run A on input x some number, say t, times, and take the majority output as the answer. Using the Chernoff bound (Theorem 6.13), the error probability for the iterated version of A is bounded by $\exp[-(1/2 - \epsilon)^2 t/2]$, and so the error probability decreases exponentially with the number of iterations. This bound is derived as follows. For $i = 1, \ldots, t$, let X_i be a random variable representing the outcome of the ith iteration of A; more precisely, $X_i = 1$ if $A(x) \neq f(x)$ on the ith iteration, and $X_i = 0$ otherwise. Let ϵ_x be the probability that $A(x) \neq f(x)$. The probability that the majority output is wrong is equal to the probability that the sample mean of $X_1, \ldots, X_t$ exceeds the mean ϵ_x by at least $1/2 - \epsilon_x$. Part (i) of Theorem 6.13 says that this occurs with probability at most

$$\exp\left[\frac{-(1/2 - \epsilon_x)^2 t}{2(1 - \epsilon_x)}\right] \leq \exp\left[\frac{-(1/2 - \epsilon)^2 t}{2}\right].$$

7.2.2 Strict polynomial time

If we have an algorithm A that runs in expected polynomial time, and which approximately computes a function f, then we can easily turn it into a new algorithm A' that runs in *strict* polynomial time, and also approximates f, as follows. Suppose that $\epsilon < 1/2$ is a bound on the error probability, and $T(n)$ is a polynomial bound on the expected running time for inputs of length n. Then A' simply runs A for at most $tT(n)$ steps, where t is any constant chosen so that $\epsilon + 1/t < 1/2$—if A does not halt within this time bound, then A' simply halts with an arbitrary output. The probability that A' errs is at most the probability that A errs plus the probability that A runs for more than $tT(n)$ steps. By Markov's inequality (Theorem 6.11), the latter probability is at most $1/t$, and hence A' approximates f as well, but with an error probability bounded by $\epsilon + 1/t$.

7.2.3 Language recognition

An important special case of approximately computing a function is when the output of the function f is either 0 or 1 (or equivalently, *false* or *true*). In this case, f may be viewed as the characteristic function of the language $L := \{x : f(x) = 1\}$. (It is the tradition of computational complexity theory to call sets of bit strings "languages.") There are several "flavors" of probabilistic algorithms for approximately computing the characteristic function f of a language L that are traditionally considered—for the purposes of these definitions, we may restrict ourselves to algorithms that output either 0 or 1:

- We call a probabilistic, expected polynomial-time algorithm an **Atlantic City algorithm** for recognizing L if it approximately computes f with error probability bounded by a constant $\epsilon < 1/2$.

- We call a probabilistic, expected polynomial-time algorithm A a **Monte Carlo algorithm** for recognizing L if for some constant $\delta > 0$, we have:

  - for any $x \in L$, we have $\mathsf{P}[A(x) = 1] \geq \delta$, and
  - for any $x \notin L$, we have $\mathsf{P}[A(x) = 1] = 0$.

- We call a probabilistic, expected polynomial-time algorithm a **Las Vegas algorithm** for recognizing L if it computes f correctly on all inputs x.

One also says an Atlantic City algorithm has **two-sided error**, a Monte Carlo algorithm has **one-sided error**, and a Las Vegas algorithm has **zero-sided error**.

EXERCISE 7.6. Show that any language recognized by a Las Vegas algorithm is also recognized by a Monte Carlo algorithm, and that any language recognized by a Monte Carlo algorithm is also recognized by an Atlantic City algorithm.

EXERCISE 7.7. Show that if L is recognized by an Atlantic City algorithm that runs in expected polynomial time, then it is recognized by an Atlantic City algorithm that runs in strict polynomial time, and whose error probability is at most 2^{-n} on inputs of length n.

EXERCISE 7.8. Show that if L is recognized by a Monte Carlo algorithm that runs in expected polynomial time, then it is recognized by a Monte Carlo algorithm that runs in strict polynomial time, and whose error probability is at most 2^{-n} on inputs of length n.

EXERCISE 7.9. Show that a language is recognized by a Las Vegas algorithm iff the language and its complement are recognized by Monte Carlo algorithms.

EXERCISE 7.10. Show that if L is recognized by a Las Vegas algorithm that runs in strict polynomial time, then L may be recognized in deterministic polynomial time.

EXERCISE 7.11. Suppose that for a given language L, there exists a probabilistic algorithm A that runs in expected polynomial time, and always outputs either 0 or 1. Further suppose that for some constants α and c, where

- α is a rational number with $0 \leq \alpha < 1$, and
- c is a positive integer,

and for all sufficiently large n, and all inputs x of length n, we have

- if $x \notin L$, then $\mathsf{P}[A(x) = 1] \leq \alpha$, and
- if $x \in L$, then $\mathsf{P}[A(x) = 1] \geq \alpha + 1/n^c$.

(a) Show that there exists an Atlantic City algorithm for L.

(b) Show that if $\alpha = 0$, then there exists a Monte Carlo algorithm for L.

7.3 Flipping a coin until a head appears

In this and subsequent sections of this chapter, we discuss a number of specific probabilistic algorithms.

Let us begin with the following simple algorithm (which was already presented in Example 7.1) that essentially flips a coin until a head appears:

repeat
$$b \leftarrow_R \{0, 1\}$$
until $b = 1$

Let X be a random variable that represents the number of loop iterations made by the algorithm. It should be fairly clear that X has a geometric distribution, where the associated probability of success is $1/2$ (see Example 6.30). However, let us derive this fact from more basic principles. Define random variables $B_1, B_2, \ldots$, where B_i represents the value of the bit assigned to b in the ith loop iteration, if $X \geq i$, and $\star$ otherwise. Clearly, exactly one B_i will take the value 1, in which case X takes the value i.

Evidently, for each $i \geq 1$, if the algorithm actually enters the ith loop iteration, then B_i is uniformly distributed over $\{0, 1\}$, and otherwise, $B_i = \star$. That is:

$$\mathsf{P}[B_i = 0 \mid X \geq i] = 1/2, \quad \mathsf{P}[B_i = 1 \mid X \geq i] = 1/2,$$
$$\mathsf{P}[B_i = \star \mid X < i] = 1.$$

From this, we see that

$$\mathsf{P}[X \geq 1] = 1, \quad \mathsf{P}[X \geq 2] = \mathsf{P}[B_1 = 0 \mid X \geq 1]\mathsf{P}[X \geq 1] = 1/2,$$
$$\mathsf{P}[X \geq 3] = \mathsf{P}[B_2 = 0 \mid X \geq 2]\mathsf{P}[X \geq 2] = (1/2)(1/2) = 1/4,$$

and by induction on i, we see that

$$\mathsf{P}[X \geq i] = \mathsf{P}[B_{i-1} = 0 \mid X \geq i - 1]\mathsf{P}[X \geq i - 1] = (1/2)(1/2^{i-2}) = 1/2^{i-1},$$

from which it follows (see Exercise 6.54) that X has a geometric distribution with associated success probability $1/2$.

Now consider the expected value $\mathsf{E}[X]$. By the discussion in Example 6.35, we have $\mathsf{E}[X] = 2$. If Y denotes the total running time of the algorithm, then $Y \leq cX$ for some constant c, and hence

$$\mathsf{E}[Y] \leq c\mathsf{E}[X] = 2c,$$

and we conclude that the expected running time of the algorithm is a constant, the exact value of which depends on the details of the implementation.

[Readers who skipped §7.1.1 may also want to skip this paragraph.]
As was argued in Example 7.1, the above algorithm halts with probability 1. To make the above argument completely rigorous, we should formally justify that claim that the conditional distribution of B_i, given that $X \geq i$, is uniform over $\{0,1\}$. We do not wish to assume that the values of the B_i are located at pre-determined positions of the execution path; rather, we shall employ a more generally applicable technique. For any $i \geq 1$, we shall condition on a particular partial execution path τ that drives the algorithm to the point where it is just about to sample the bit B_i, and show that in this conditional probability distribution, B_i is uniformly distributed over $\{0,1\}$. To do this rigorously in our formal framework, let us define the event $\mathcal{A}_\tau$ to be the event that τ is a prefix of the execution path. If $|\tau| = \ell$, then the events $\mathcal{A}_\tau$, $\mathcal{A}_\tau \wedge (B_i = 0)$, and $\mathcal{A}_\tau \wedge (B_i = 1)$ are determined by the first $\ell+1$ bits of the execution path. We can then consider corresponding events in a probabilistic experiment wherein we observe the behavior of the algorithm on a random $(\ell+1)$-bit execution path (see Exercise 7.2). In the latter experiment, it is clear that the conditional probability distribution of B_i, given that the first ℓ bits of the actual execution path σ agree with τ, is uniform over $\{0,1\}$, and thus, the same holds in the original probability distribution. Since this holds for all relevant τ, it follows (by a discrete version of Exercise 6.13) that it holds conditioned on $X \geq i$.

We have analyzed the above algorithm in excruciating detail. As we proceed, many of these details will be suppressed, as they can all be handled by very similar (and completely routine) arguments.

7.4 Generating a random number from a given interval

Suppose we want to generate a number n uniformly at random from the interval $\{0, \ldots, M-1\}$, for a given integer $M \geq 1$.

If M is a power of 2, say $M = 2^k$, then we can do this directly as follows: generate a random k-bit string s, and convert s to the integer $I(s)$ whose base-2 representation is s; that is, if $s = b_{k-1}b_{k-2} \cdots b_0$, where the b_i are bits, then

$$I(s) := \sum_{i=0}^{k-1} b_i 2^i.$$

In the general case, we do not have a direct way to do this, since we can only directly generate random bits. However, suppose that M is a k-bit number, so that $2^{k-1} \leq M < 2^k$. Then the following algorithm does the job:

Algorithm RN:

repeat
$\qquad s \leftarrow_R \{0,1\}^{\times k}$
$\qquad n \leftarrow I(s)$
until $n < M$
output n

Let X denote the number of loop iterations of this algorithm, Y its running time, and N its output.

In every loop iteration, n is uniformly distributed over $\{0, \ldots, 2^k - 1\}$, and the event $n < M$ occurs with probability $M/2^k$; moreover, conditioning on the latter event, n is uniformly distributed over $\{0, \ldots, M - 1\}$. It follows that X has a geometric distribution with an associated success probability $p := M/2^k \geq 1/2$, and that N is uniformly distributed over $\{0, \ldots, M - 1\}$. We have $\mathsf{E}[X] = 1/p \leq 2$ (see Example 6.35) and $Y \leq ckX$ for some implementation-dependent constant c, from which it follows that

$$\mathsf{E}[Y] \leq ck\mathsf{E}[X] \leq 2ck.$$

Thus, the expected running time of Algorithm RN is $O(k)$.

Hopefully, the above argument is clear and convincing. However, as in the previous section, we can derive these results from more basic principles. Define random variables $N_1, N_2, \ldots$, where N_i represents the value of n in the ith loop iteration, if $X \geq i$, and $\star$ otherwise.

Evidently, for each $i \geq 1$, if the algorithm actually enters the ith loop iteration, then N_i is uniformly distributed over $\{0, \ldots, 2^k - 1\}$, and otherwise, $N_i = \star$. That is:

$$\mathsf{P}[N_i = j \mid X \geq i] = 1/2^k \quad (j = 0, \ldots, 2^k - 1),$$
$$\mathsf{P}[N_i = \star \mid X < i] = 1.$$

From this fact, we can derive all of the above results.

As for the distribution of X, it follows from a simple induction argument that $\mathsf{P}[X \geq i] = q^{i-1}$, where $q := 1 - p$; indeed, $\mathsf{P}[X \geq 1] = 1$, and for $i \geq 2$, we have

$$\mathsf{P}[X \geq i] = \mathsf{P}[N_{i-1} \geq M \mid X \geq i - 1]\mathsf{P}[X \geq i - 1] = q \cdot q^{i-2} = q^{i-1}.$$

It follows that X has a geometric distribution with associated success probability p (see Exercise 6.54).

As for the distribution of N, by (a discrete version of) Exercise 6.13, it suffices to show that for all $i \geq 1$, the conditional distribution of N given that

$X = i$ is uniform on $\{0, \dots, M - 1\}$. Observe that for any $j = 0, \dots, M - 1$, we have

$$\mathsf{P}[N = j \mid X = i] = \frac{\mathsf{P}[N = j \wedge X = i]}{\mathsf{P}[X = i]} = \frac{\mathsf{P}[N_i = j \wedge X \geq i]}{\mathsf{P}[N_i < M \wedge X \geq i]}$$

$$= \frac{\mathsf{P}[N_i = j \mid X \geq i]\mathsf{P}[X \geq i]}{\mathsf{P}[N_i < M \mid X \geq i]\mathsf{P}[X \geq i]} = \frac{1/2^k}{M/2^k}$$

$$= 1/M.$$

[Readers who skipped §7.1.1 may also want to skip this paragraph.] To make the above argument completely rigorous, we should first show that the algorithm halts with probability 1, and then show that the conditional distribution of N_i, given that $X \geq i$, is indeed uniform on $\{0, \dots, 2^k - 1\}$, as claimed above. That the algorithm halts with probability 1 follows from the fact that in every loop iteration, there is at least one choice of s that will cause the algorithm to halt. To analyze the conditional distribution on N_i, one considers various conditional distributions, conditioning on particular partial execution paths τ that bring the computation just to the beginning of the ith loop iteration; for any particular such τ, the ith loop iteration will terminate in at most $\ell := |\tau| + ck$ steps, for some constant c. Therefore, the conditional distribution of N_i, given the partial execution path τ, can be analyzed by considering the execution of the algorithm on a random ℓ-bit execution path (see Exercise 7.2). It is then clear that the conditional distribution of N_i given the partial execution path τ is uniform over $\{0, \dots, 2^k - 1\}$, and since this holds for all relevant τ, it follows (by a discrete version of Exercise 6.13) that the conditional distribution of N_i, given that the ith loop is entered, is uniform over $\{0, \dots, 2^k - 1\}$.

Of course, by adding an appropriate value to the output of Algorithm RN, we can generate random numbers uniformly in an interval $\{A, \dots, B\}$, for given A and B. In what follows, we shall denote the execution of this algorithm as

$$n \leftarrow_R \{A, \dots, B\}.$$

We also mention the following alternative approach to generating a random number from an interval. Given a positive k-bit integer M, and a parameter $t > 0$, we do the following:

Algorithm RN′:

$s \leftarrow_R \{0, 1\}^{\times(k+t)}$
$n \leftarrow I(s) \bmod M$
output n

Compared with Algorithm RN, Algorithm RN′ has the advantage that there are no loops — it halts in a bounded number of steps; however, it has the disadvantage that its output is *not* uniformly distributed over the interval $\{0, \ldots, M-1\}$. Nevertheless, the statistical distance between its output distribution and the uniform distribution on $\{0, \ldots, M-1\}$ is at most 2^{-t} (see Example 6.27 in §6.8). Thus, by choosing t suitably large, we can make the output distribution "as good as uniform" for most practical purposes.

EXERCISE 7.12. Prove that no probabilistic algorithm that always halts in a bounded number of steps can have an output distribution that is uniform on $\{0, \ldots, M-1\}$, unless M is a power of 2.

EXERCISE 7.13. Let A_1 and A_2 be probabilistic algorithms such that, for any input x, the random variables $A_1(x)$ and $A_2(x)$ take on one of a finite number of values, and let δ_x be the statistical distance between $A_1(x)$ and $A_2(x)$. Let B be any probabilistic algorithm that always outputs 0 or 1. For for $i = 1, 2$, let C_i be the algorithm that given an input x, first runs A_i on that input, obtaining a value y, then it runs B on input y, obtaining a value z, which it then outputs. Show that $|P[C_1(x) = 1] - P[C_2(x) = 1]| \leq \delta_x$.

7.5 Generating a random prime

Suppose we are given an integer $M \geq 2$, and want to generate a random prime between 2 and M. One way to proceed is simply to generate random numbers until we get a prime. This idea will work, assuming the existence of an efficient algorithm *IsPrime* that determines whether or not a given integer $n > 1$ is prime.

Now, the most naive method of testing if n is prime is to see if any of the numbers between 2 and $n-1$ divide n. Of course, one can be slightly more clever, and only perform this divisibility check for prime numbers between 2 and $\sqrt{n}$ (see Exercise 1.1). Nevertheless, such an approach does not give rise to a polynomial-time algorithm. Indeed, the design and analysis of efficient primality tests has been an active research area for many years. There is, in fact, a deterministic, polynomial-time algorithm for testing primality, which we shall discuss later, in Chapter 22. For the moment, we shall just assume we have such an algorithm, and use it as a "black box."

Our algorithm to generate a random prime between 2 and M runs as follows:

Algorithm RP:

repeat
$$n \leftarrow_R \{2, \ldots, M\}$$
until *IsPrime*(n)
output n

We now wish to analyze the running time and output distribution of Algorithm RP on input M. Let $k := \text{len}(M)$.

First, consider a single iteration of the main loop of Algorithm RP, viewed as a stand-alone probabilistic experiment. For any fixed prime p between 2 and M, the probability that the variable n takes the value p is precisely $1/(M-1)$. Thus, every prime is equally likely, and the probability that n is a prime is precisely $\pi(M)/(M-1)$.

Let us also consider the expected running time μ of a single loop iteration. To this end, define W_n to be the running time of algorithm *IsPrime* on input n. Also, define

$$W'_M := \frac{1}{M-1} \sum_{n=2}^{M} W_n.$$

That is, W'_M is the average value of W_n, for a random choice of $n \in \{2, \ldots, M\}$. Thus, μ is equal to W'_M, plus the expected running time of Algorithm RN, which is $O(k)$, plus any other small overhead, which is also $O(k)$. So we have $\mu \le W'_M + O(k)$, and assuming that $W'_M = \Omega(k)$, which is perfectly reasonable, we have $\mu = O(W'_M)$.

Next, let us consider the behavior of Algorithm RP as a whole. From the above discussion, it follows that when this algorithm terminates, its output will be uniformly distributed over the set of all primes between 2 and M. If T denotes the number of loop iterations performed by the algorithm, then $\mathsf{E}[T] = (M-1)/\pi(M)$, which by Chebyshev's theorem (Theorem 5.1) is $\Theta(k)$.

So we have bounded the expected number of loop iterations. We now want to bound the expected overall running time. For $i \ge 1$, let X_i denote the amount of time (possibly zero) spent during the ith loop iteration of the algorithm, so that $X := \sum_{i \ge 1} X_i$ is the total running time of Algorithm RP. Note that

$$\begin{aligned}
\mathsf{E}[X_i] &= \mathsf{E}[X_i \mid T \ge i]\mathsf{P}[T \ge i] + \mathsf{E}[X_i \mid T < i]\mathsf{P}[T < i] \\
&= \mathsf{E}[X_i \mid T \ge i]\mathsf{P}[T \ge i] \\
&= \mu\mathsf{P}[T \ge i],
\end{aligned}$$

because $X_i = 0$ when $T < i$ and $\mathsf{E}[X_i \mid T \geq i]$ is by definition equal to μ. Then we have

$$\mathsf{E}[X] = \sum_{i \geq 1} \mathsf{E}[X_i] = \mu \sum_{i \geq 1} \mathsf{P}[T \geq i] = \mu\mathsf{E}[T] = O(kW'_M).$$

7.5.1 Using a probabilistic primality test

In the above analysis, we assumed that *IsPrime* was a deterministic, polynomial-time algorithm. While such an algorithm exists, there are in fact simpler and more efficient algorithms that are probabilistic. We shall discuss such an algorithm in greater depth later, in Chapter 10. This algorithm (like several other algorithms for primality testing) has one-sided error in the following sense: if the input n is prime, then the algorithm always outputs *true*; otherwise, if n is composite, the output may be *true* or *false*, but the probability that the output is *true* is at most c, where $c < 1$ is a constant. In the terminology of §7.2, such an algorithm is essentially a Monte Carlo algorithm for the language of *composite* numbers. If we want to reduce the error probability for composite inputs to some very small value ϵ, we can iterate the algorithm t times, with t chosen so that $c^t \leq \epsilon$, outputting *true* if all iterations output *true*, and outputting *false* otherwise. This yields an algorithm for primality testing that makes errors only on composite inputs, and then only with probability at most ϵ.

Let us analyze the behavior of Algorithm RP under the assumption that *IsPrime* is implemented by a probabilistic algorithm (such as described in the previous paragraph) with an error probability for composite inputs bounded by ϵ. Let us define W_n to be the expected running time of *IsPrime* on input n, and as before, we define

$$W'_M := \frac{1}{M-1} \sum_{n=2}^{M} W_n.$$

Thus, W'_M is the expected running time of algorithm *IsPrime*, where the average is taken with respect to randomly chosen n *and* the random choices of the algorithm itself.

Consider a single loop iteration of Algorithm RP. For any fixed prime p between 2 and M, the probability that n takes the value p is $1/(M-1)$. Thus, if the algorithm halts with a prime, every prime is equally likely. Now, the algorithm will halt if n is prime, or if n is composite and the primality test makes a mistake; therefore, the the probability that it halts at all is at least $\pi(M)/(M-1)$. So we see that the expected number of loop iterations should be no more than in the case where we use a deterministic primality test. Using the same argument as was used before to estimate the expected total running time of Algorithm RP, we find that this is $O(kW'_M)$.

As for the probability that Algorithm RP mistakenly outputs a composite, one might be tempted to say that this probability is at most ϵ, the probability that *IsPrime* makes a mistake. However, in drawing such a conclusion, we would be committing the fallacy of Example 6.12—to correctly analyze the probability that Algorithm RP mistakenly outputs a composite, one must take into account the rate of incidence of the "primality disease," as well as the error rate of the test for this disease.

Let us be a bit more precise. Again, consider the probability distribution defined by a single loop iteration, and let $\mathcal{A}$ be the event that *IsPrime* outputs *true*, and $\mathcal{B}$ the event that n is composite. Let $\beta := \mathsf{P}[\mathcal{B}]$ and $\alpha := \mathsf{P}[\mathcal{A} \mid \mathcal{B}]$. First, observe that, by definition, $\alpha \leq \epsilon$. Now, the probability δ that the algorithm halts and outputs a composite in this loop iteration is

$$\delta = \mathsf{P}[\mathcal{A} \wedge \mathcal{B}] = \alpha\beta.$$

The probability δ' that the algorithm halts and outputs either a prime or composite is

$$\delta' = \mathsf{P}[\mathcal{A}] = \mathsf{P}[\mathcal{A} \wedge \mathcal{B}] + \mathsf{P}[\mathcal{A} \wedge \overline{\mathcal{B}}] = \mathsf{P}[\mathcal{A} \wedge \mathcal{B}] + \mathsf{P}[\overline{\mathcal{B}}] = \alpha\beta + (1 - \beta).$$

Now consider the behavior of Algorithm RP as a whole. With T being the number of loop iterations as before, we have

$$\mathsf{E}[T] = \frac{1}{\delta'} = \frac{1}{\alpha\beta + (1 - \beta)}, \tag{7.1}$$

and hence

$$\mathsf{E}[T] \leq \frac{1}{(1 - \beta)} = \frac{M - 1}{\pi(M)} = O(k).$$

Let us now consider the probability γ that the output of Algorithm RP is composite. For $i \geq 1$, let $\mathcal{C}_i$ be the event that the algorithm halts and outputs a composite number in the ith loop iteration. The events $\mathcal{C}_i$ are pairwise disjoint, and moreover,

$$\mathsf{P}[\mathcal{C}_i] = \mathsf{P}[\mathcal{C}_i \wedge T \geq i] = \mathsf{P}[\mathcal{C}_i \mid T \geq i]\mathsf{P}[T \geq i] = \delta\mathsf{P}[T \geq i].$$

So we have

$$\gamma = \sum_{i\geq 1} \mathsf{P}[\mathcal{C}_i] = \sum_{i\geq 1} \delta\mathsf{P}[T \geq i] = \delta\mathsf{E}[T] = \frac{\alpha\beta}{\alpha\beta + (1 - \beta)}, \tag{7.2}$$

and hence

$$\gamma \leq \frac{\alpha}{(1-\beta)} \leq \frac{\epsilon}{(1-\beta)} = \epsilon \frac{M-1}{\pi(M)} = O(k\epsilon).$$

Another way of analyzing the output distribution of Algorithm RP is to consider its statistical distance Δ from the uniform distribution on the set of primes between 2 and M. As we have already argued, every prime between 2 and M is equally likely to be output, and in particular, any fixed prime p is output with probability at most $1/\pi(M)$. It follows from Theorem 6.15 that $\Delta = \gamma$.

7.5.2 Generating a random k-bit prime

Instead of generating a random prime between 2 and M, we may instead want to generate a random k-bit prime, that is, a prime between 2^{k-1} and $2^k - 1$. Bertrand's postulate (Theorem 5.7) tells us that there exist such primes for every $k \geq 2$, and that in fact, there are $\Omega(2^k/k)$ such primes. Because of this, we can modify Algorithm RP, so that each candidate n is chosen at random from the interval $\{2^{k-1}, \ldots, 2^k - 1\}$, and all of the results of this section carry over essentially without change. In particular, the expected number of trials until the algorithm halts is $O(k)$, and if a probabilistic primality test as in §7.5.1 is used, with an error probability of ϵ, the probability that the output is not prime is $O(k\epsilon)$.

EXERCISE 7.14. Design and analyze an efficient probabilistic algorithm that takes as input an integer $M \geq 2$, and outputs a random element of $\mathbb{Z}_M^*$.

EXERCISE 7.15. Suppose Algorithm RP is implemented using an imperfect random number generator, so that the statistical distance between the output distribution of the random number generator and the uniform distribution on $\{2, \ldots, M\}$ is equal to δ (e.g., Algorithm RN' in §7.4). Assume that $2\delta < \pi(M)/(M-1)$. Also, let λ denote the expected number of iterations of the main loop of Algorithm RP, let Δ denote the statistical distance between its output distribution and the uniform distribution on the primes up to M, and let $k := \text{len}(M)$.

    (a) Assuming the primality test is deterministic, show that $\lambda = O(k)$ and $\Delta = O(\delta k)$.

    (b) Assuming the primality test is probabilistic, with one-sided error ϵ, as in §7.5.1, show that $\lambda = O(k)$ and $\Delta = O((\delta + \epsilon)k)$.

EXERCISE 7.16. Analyze Algorithm RP assuming that the primality test is implemented by an "Atlantic City" algorithm with error probability at most ϵ.

EXERCISE 7.17. Consider the following probabilistic algorithm that takes as input a positive integer M:

$S \leftarrow \emptyset$
repeat
$\qquad n \leftarrow_R \{1, \ldots, M\}$
$\qquad S \leftarrow S \cup \{n\}$
until $|S| = M$

Show that the expected number of iterations of the main loop is $\sim M \log M$.

The following exercises assume the reader has studied §7.1.1.

EXERCISE 7.18. Consider the following algorithm (which takes no input):

$j \leftarrow 1$
repeat
$\qquad j \leftarrow j + 1$
$\qquad n \leftarrow_R \{0, \ldots, j-1\}$
until $n = 0$

Show that this algorithm halts with probability 1, but that its expected running time does not exist. (Compare this algorithm with the one in Example 7.2, which does not even halt with probability 1.)

EXERCISE 7.19. Now consider the following modification to the algorithm in the previous exercise:

$j \leftarrow 2$
repeat
$\qquad j \leftarrow j + 1$
$\qquad n \leftarrow_R \{0, \ldots, j-1\}$
until $n = 0$ or $n = 1$

Show that this algorithm halts with probability 1, and that its expected running time exists (and is equal to some implementation-dependent constant).

7.6 Generating a random non-increasing sequence

The following algorithm, Algorithm RS, will be used in the next section as a fundamental subroutine in a beautiful algorithm (Algorithm RFN) that generates random numbers in *factored form*. Algorithm RS takes as input an integer $M \geq 2$, and runs as follows:

Algorithm RS:

$n_0 \leftarrow M$
$i \leftarrow 0$
repeat
    $i \leftarrow i + 1$
    $n_i \leftarrow_R \{1, \ldots, n_{i-1}\}$
until $n_i = 1$
$t \leftarrow i$
Output $(n_1, \ldots, n_t)$

We analyze first the output distribution, and then the running time.

7.6.1 Analysis of the output distribution

Let $N_1, N_2, \ldots$ be random variables denoting the choices of $n_1, n_2, \ldots$ (for completeness, define $N_i := 1$ if loop i is never entered).

A particular output of the algorithm is a non-increasing chain $(n_1, \ldots, n_t)$, where $n_1 \geq n_2 \geq \cdots \geq n_{t-1} > n_t = 1$. For any such chain, we have

$$P[N_1 = n_1 \wedge \cdots \wedge N_t = n_t] = P[N_1 = n_1]P[N_2 = n_2 \mid N_1 = n_1] \cdots$$
$$P[N_t = n_t \mid N_1 = n_1 \wedge \cdots \wedge N_{t-1} = n_{t-1}]$$
$$= \frac{1}{M} \cdot \frac{1}{n_1} \cdot \cdots \cdot \frac{1}{n_{t-1}}. \tag{7.3}$$

This completely describes the output distribution, in the sense that we have determined the probability with which each non-increasing chain appears as an output. However, there is another way to characterize the output distribution that is significantly more useful. For $j = 2, \ldots, M$, define the random variable E_j to be the number of occurrences of j among the N_i. The E_j determine the N_i, and *vice versa*. Indeed, $E_M = e_M, \ldots, E_2 = e_2$ iff the output of the algorithm is the non-increasing chain

$$(\underbrace{M, \ldots, M}_{e_M \text{ times}}, \underbrace{M-1, \ldots, M-1}_{e_{M-1} \text{ times}}, \ldots, \underbrace{2, \ldots, 2}_{e_2 \text{ times}}, 1).$$

From (7.3), we can therefore directly compute

$$P[E_M = e_M \wedge \ldots \wedge E_2 = e_2] = \frac{1}{M} \prod_{j=2}^{M} \frac{1}{j^{e_j}}. \tag{7.4}$$

Notice that we can write $1/M$ as a telescoping product:

$$\frac{1}{M} = \frac{M-1}{M} \cdot \frac{M-2}{M-1} \cdot \ldots \cdot \frac{2}{3} \cdot \frac{1}{2} = \prod_{j=2}^{M} (1 - 1/j),$$

so we can re-write (7.4) as

$$\mathsf{P}[E_M = e_M \wedge \cdots \wedge E_2 = e_2] = \prod_{j=2}^{M} j^{-e_j} (1 - 1/j). \qquad (7.5)$$

Notice that for $j = 2, \ldots, M$,

$$\sum_{e_j \geq 0} j^{-e_j} (1 - 1/j) = 1,$$

and so by (a discrete version of) Theorem 6.1, the variables E_j are mutually independent, and for all $j = 2, \ldots, M$ and integers $e_j \geq 0$, we have

$$\mathsf{P}[E_j = e_j] = j^{-e_j} (1 - 1/j). \qquad (7.6)$$

In summary, we have shown that the variables E_j are mutually independent, where for $j = 2, \ldots, M$, the variable $E_j + 1$ has a geometric distribution with an associated success probability of $1 - 1/j$.

Another, perhaps more intuitive, analysis of the joint distribution of the E_j runs as follows. Conditioning on the event $E_M = e_M, \ldots, E_{j+1} = e_{j+1}$, one sees that the value of E_j is the number of times the value j appears in the sequence $N_i, N_{i+1}, \ldots$, where $i = e_M + \cdots + e_{j+1} + 1$; moreover, in this conditional probability distribution, it is not too hard to convince oneself that N_i is uniformly distributed over $\{1, \ldots, j\}$. Hence the probability that $E_j = e_j$ in this conditional probability distribution is the probability of getting a run of exactly e_j copies of the value j in an experiment in which we successively choose numbers between 1 and j at random, and this latter probability is clearly $j^{-e_j} (1 - 1/j)$.

7.6.2 Analysis of the running time

Let T be the random variable that takes the value t when the output is $(n_1, \ldots, n_t)$. Clearly, it is the value of T that essentially determines the running time of the algorithm.

With the random variables E_j defined as above, we see that $T = 1 + \sum_{j=2}^{M} E_j$. Moreover, for each j, $E_j + 1$ has a geometric distribution with associated success probability $1 - 1/j$, and hence

$$\mathsf{E}[E_j] = \frac{1}{1 - 1/j} - 1 = \frac{1}{j - 1}.$$

Thus,

$$\mathsf{E}[T] = 1 + \sum_{j=2}^{M} \mathsf{E}[E_j] = 1 + \sum_{j=1}^{M-1} \frac{1}{j} = \int_1^M \frac{dy}{y} + O(1) \sim \log M.$$

Intuitively, this is roughly as we would expect, since with probability $1/2$, each successive n_i is at most one half as large as its predecessor, and so after $O(\operatorname{len}(M))$ steps, we expect to reach 1.

To complete the running time analysis, let us consider the total number of times X that the main loop of Algorithm RN in §7.4 is executed. For $i = 1, 2, \ldots$, let X_i denote the number of times that loop is executed in the ith loop of Algorithm RS, defining this to be zero if the ith loop is never reached. So $X = \sum_{i=1}^{\infty} X_i$. Arguing just as in §7.5, we have

$$\mathsf{E}[X] = \sum_{i \geq 1} \mathsf{E}[X_i] \leq 2 \sum_{i \geq 1} \mathsf{P}[T \geq i] = 2\mathsf{E}[T] \sim 2\log M.$$

To finish, if Y denotes the running time of Algorithm RS on input M, then we have $Y \leq c\operatorname{len}(M)(X + 1)$ for some constant c, and hence $\mathsf{E}[Y] = O(\operatorname{len}(M)^2)$.

EXERCISE 7.20. Show that when Algorithm RS runs on input M, the expected number of (not necessarily distinct) primes in the output sequence is $\sim \log\log M$.

EXERCISE 7.21. For $j = 2, \ldots, M$, let $F_j := 1$ if j appears in the output of Algorithm RS on input M, and let $F_j := 0$ otherwise. Determine the joint distribution of the F_j. Using this, show that the expected number of distinct primes appearing in the output sequence is $\sim \log\log M$.

7.7 Generating a random factored number

We now present an efficient algorithm that generates a random factored number. That is, on input $M \geq 2$, the algorithm generates a number r uniformly distributed over the interval $\{1, \ldots, M\}$, but instead of the usual output format for such a number r, the output consists of the prime factorization of r.

As far as anyone knows, there are no efficient algorithms for factoring large numbers, despite years of active research in search of such an algorithm. So our algorithm to generate a random factored number will *not* work by generating a random number and then factoring it.

Our algorithm will use Algorithm RS in §7.6 as a subroutine. In addition, as we did in §7.5, we shall assume the existence of a deterministic, polynomial-time primality test *IsPrime*. We denote its running time on input n by W_n, and set $W_M^* := \max\{W_n : n = 2, \ldots, M\}$.

In the analysis of the algorithm, we shall make use of Mertens' theorem, which we proved in Chapter 5 (Theorem 5.13).

On input $M \geq 2$, the algorithm to generate a random factored number $r \in \{1, \ldots, M\}$ runs as follows:

Algorithm RFN:

    repeat
        Run Algorithm RS on input M, obtaining $(n_1, \ldots, n_t)$
(∗)   Let $n_{i_1}, \ldots, n_{i_\ell}$ be the primes among $n_1, \ldots, n_t$, including duplicates
(∗∗)   Set $r \leftarrow \prod_{j=1}^{\ell} n_{i_j}$
        If $r \leq M$ then
                $s \leftarrow_R \{1, \ldots, M\}$
                if $s \leq r$ then output $n_{i_1}, \ldots, n_{i_\ell}$ and halt
    forever

Notes:

(∗) For $i = 1, \ldots, t-1$, the number n_i is tested for primality algorithm *IsPrime*.

(∗∗) We assume that the product is computed by a simple iterative procedure that halts as soon as the partial product exceeds M. This ensures that the time spent forming the product is always $O(\mathrm{len}(M)^2)$, which simplifies the analysis.

Let us now analyze the running time and output distribution of Algorithm RFN on input M. Let $k := \mathrm{len}(M)$.

To analyze this algorithm, let us first consider a single iteration of the main loop as a random experiment in isolation. Let $n = 1, \ldots, M$ be a fixed integer, and let us calculate the probability that the variable r takes the particular value n in this loop iteration. Let $n = \prod_{p \leq M} p^{e_p}$ be the prime factorization of n. Then r takes the value n iff $E_p = e_p$ for all primes $p \leq M$, which by the analysis in §7.6, happens with probability precisely

$$\prod_{p \leq M} p^{-e_p}(1 - 1/p) = \frac{U(M)}{n},$$

where

$$U(M) := \prod_{p \leq M} (1 - 1/p).$$

Now, the probability that this loop iteration produces n as output is equal to the probability that r takes the value n *and* $s \leq n$, which is

$$\frac{U(M)}{n} \cdot \frac{n}{M} = \frac{U(M)}{M}.$$

Thus, every n is equally likely, and summing over all $n = 1, \ldots, M$, we see that the probability that this loop iteration succeeds in producing *some* output is $U(M)$.

Now consider the expected running time of this loop iteration. From the analysis in §7.6, it is easy to see that this is $O(kW_M^*)$. That completes the analysis of a single loop iteration.

Finally, consider the behavior of Algorithm RFN as a whole. From our analysis of an individual loop iteration, it is clear that the output distribution of Algorithm RFN is as required, and if H denotes the number of loop iterations of the algorithm, then $\mathsf{E}[H] = U(M)^{-1}$, which by Mertens' theorem is $O(k)$. Since the expected running time of each individual loop iteration is $O(kW_M^*)$, it follows that the expected total running time is $O(k^2 W_M^*)$.

7.7.1 *Using a probabilistic primality test* (∗)

Analogous to the discussion in §7.5.1, we can analyze the behavior of Algorithm RFN under the assumption that *IsPrime* is a probabilistic algorithm which may erroneously indicate that a composite number is prime with probability bounded by ϵ. Here, we assume that W_n denotes the expected running time of the primality test on input n, and set $W_M^* := \max\{W_n : n = 2, \ldots, M\}$.

The situation here is a bit more complicated than in the case of Algorithm RP, since an erroneous output of the primality test in Algorithm RFN could lead either to the algorithm halting prematurely (with a wrong output), or to the algorithm being delayed (because an opportunity to halt may be missed).

Let us first analyze in detail the behavior of a single iteration of the main loop of Algorithm RFN. Let $\mathcal{A}$ denote the event that the primality test makes a mistake in this loop iteration, and let $\delta := \mathsf{P}[\mathcal{A}]$. If T is the number of loop iterations in a given run of Algorithm RS, it is easy to see that

$$\delta \leq \epsilon\,\mathsf{E}[T] = \epsilon\,\ell(M),$$

where

$$\ell(M) := 1 + \sum_{j=1}^{M-1} \frac{1}{j} \leq 2 + \log M.$$

Now, let $n = 1, \ldots, M$ be a fixed integer, and let us calculate the probability α_n that the correct prime factorization of n is output in this loop iteration. Let $\mathcal{B}_n$ be the event that the primes among the output of Algorithm RS multiply out to n. Then $\alpha_n = \mathsf{P}[\mathcal{B}_n \wedge \overline{\mathcal{A}}](n/M)$. Moreover, because of the mutual independence of the E_j, not only does it follow that $\mathsf{P}[\mathcal{B}_n] = U(M)/n$, but it also follows that $\mathcal{B}_n$ and $\mathcal{A}$ are independent events: to see this, note that $\mathcal{B}_n$ is determined by the variables $\{E_j : j \text{ prime}\}$, and $\mathcal{A}$ is determined by the variables $\{E_j : j \text{ composite}\}$ and the random choices of the primality test. Hence,

$$\alpha_n = \frac{U(M)}{M}(1 - \delta).$$

Thus, every n is equally likely to be output. If $\mathcal{C}$ is the event that the algorithm halts with *some* output (correct or not) in this loop iteration, then

$$\mathsf{P}[\mathcal{C}] \geq U(M)(1 - \delta), \tag{7.7}$$

and

$$\mathsf{P}[\mathcal{C} \vee \mathcal{A}] = U(M)(1 - \delta) + \delta = U(M) - \delta U(M) + \delta \geq U(M). \tag{7.8}$$

The expected running time of a single loop iteration of Algorithm RFN is also easily seen to be $O(kW_M^*)$. That completes the analysis of a single loop iteration.

We next analyze the total running time of Algorithm RFN. If H is the number of loop iterations of Algorithm RFN, it follows from (7.7) that

$$\mathsf{E}[H] \leq \frac{1}{U(M)(1 - \delta)},$$

and assuming that $\epsilon\ell(M) \leq 1/2$, it follows that the expected running time of Algorithm RFN is $O(k^2 W_M^*)$.

Finally, we analyze the statistical distance Δ between the output distribution of Algorithm RFN and the uniform distribution on the numbers 1 to M, in correct factored form. Let H' denote the first loop iteration i for which the event $\mathcal{C} \vee \mathcal{A}$ occurs, meaning that the algorithm either halts or the primality test makes a mistake. Then, by (7.8), H' has a geometric distribution with an associated success probability of at least $U(M)$. Let $\mathcal{A}_i$ be the event that the primality makes a mistake *for the first time* in loop iteration i, and let $\mathcal{A}^*$ is the event that the primality test makes a mistake in any loop iteration. Observe that $\mathsf{P}[\mathcal{A}_i \mid H' \geq i] = \delta$ and $\mathsf{P}[\mathcal{A}_i \mid H' < i] = 0$, and so

$$\mathsf{P}[\mathcal{A}_i] = \mathsf{P}[\mathcal{A}_i \mid H' \geq i]\mathsf{P}[H' \geq i] = \delta\mathsf{P}[H' \geq i],$$

from which it follows that

$$\mathsf{P}[\mathcal{A}^*] = \sum_{i \geq 1} \mathsf{P}[\mathcal{A}_i] = \sum_{i \geq 1} \delta\mathsf{P}[H' \geq i] = \delta\mathsf{E}[H'] \leq \delta U(M)^{-1}.$$

Now, if γ is the probability that the output of Algorithm RFN is not in correct factored form, then

$$\gamma \leq \mathsf{P}[\mathcal{A}^*] = \delta U(M)^{-1} = O(k^2\epsilon).$$

We have already argued that each value n between 1 and M, in correct factored form, is equally likely to be output, and in particular, each such value occurs with probability at most $1/M$. It follows from Theorem 6.15 that $\Delta = \gamma$ (verify).

EXERCISE 7.22. To simplify the analysis, we analyzed Algorithm RFN using the worst-case estimate W_M^* on the expected running time of the primality test. Define

$$W_M^+ := \sum_{j=2}^{M} \frac{W_j}{j - 1},$$

where W_n denotes the expected running time of a probabilistic implementation of *IsPrime* on input n. Show that the expected running time of Algorithm RFN is $O(kW_M^+)$, assuming $\epsilon\ell(M) \leq 1/2$.

EXERCISE 7.23. Analyze Algorithm RFN assuming that the primality test is implemented by an "Atlantic City" algorithm with error probability at most ϵ.

7.8 The RSA cryptosystem

Algorithms for generating large primes, such as Algorithm RP in §7.5, have numerous applications in cryptography. One of the most well known and important such applications is the RSA cryptosystem, named after its inventors Rivest, Shamir, and Adleman. We give a brief overview of this system here.

Suppose that Alice wants to send a secret message to Bob over an insecure network. An adversary may be able to eavesdrop on the network, and so sending the message "in the clear" is not an option. Using older, more traditional cryptographic techniques would require that Alice and Bob share a secret key between them; however, this creates the problem of securely generating such a shared secret. The RSA cryptosystem is an example of a "public key" cryptosystem. To use the system, Bob simply places a "public key" in the equivalent of an electronic telephone book, while keeping a corresponding "private key" secret. To send a secret message to Bob, Alice obtains Bob's public key from the telephone book, and uses this to encrypt her message. Upon receipt of the encrypted message, Bob uses his secret key to decrypt it, obtaining the original message.

Here is how the RSA cryptosystem works. To generate a public key/private key pair, Bob generates two very large random primes p and q. To be secure, p and q should be quite large—typically, they are chosen to be around 512 bits in length. We require that $p \neq q$, but the probability that two random 512-bit primes are equal is negligible, so this is hardly an issue. Next, Bob computes $n := pq$. Bob also selects an integer $e > 1$ such that $\gcd(e, \phi(n)) = 1$. Here, $\phi(n) = (p-1)(q-1)$. Finally, Bob computes $d := e^{-1} \bmod \phi(n)$. The public key is the pair (n, e), and the private key is the pair (n, d). The integer e is called the "encryption exponent" and d is called the "decryption exponent."

After Bob publishes his public key (n, e), Alice may send a secret message to Bob as follows. Suppose that a message is encoded in some canonical way as a number between 0 and $n-1$—we can always interpret a bit string of length less than $\text{len}(n)$ as such a number. Thus, we may assume that a message is an element α of $\mathbb{Z}_n$. To encrypt the message α, Alice simply computes $\beta := \alpha^e$. The encrypted message is β. When Bob receives β, he computes $\gamma := \beta^d$, and interprets γ as a message. (Note that if Bob stores the factorization of n, then he may speed up the decryption process using the algorithm in Exercise 7.28 below.)

The most basic requirement of any encryption scheme is that decryption should "undo" encryption. In this case, this means that for all $\alpha \in \mathbb{Z}_n$, we should have

$$(\alpha^e)^d = \alpha. \tag{7.9}$$

If $\alpha \in \mathbb{Z}_n^*$, then this is clearly the case, since we have $ed = 1 + \phi(n)k$ for some positive integer k, and hence by Euler's theorem (Theorem 2.15), we have

$$(\alpha^e)^d = \alpha^{ed} = \alpha^{1+\phi(n)k} = \alpha \cdot \alpha^{\phi(n)k} = \alpha.$$

Even if $\alpha \notin \mathbb{Z}_n^*$, equation (7.9) still holds. To see this, let $\alpha = [a]_n$, with $\gcd(a, n) \neq 1$. There are three possible cases. First, if $a \equiv 0 \pmod{n}$, then trivially, $a^{ed} \equiv 0 \pmod{n}$. Second, if $a \equiv 0 \pmod{p}$ but $a \not\equiv 0 \pmod{q}$, then trivially $a^{ed} \equiv 0 \pmod{p}$, and

$$a^{ed} \equiv a^{1+\phi(n)k} \equiv a \cdot a^{\phi(n)k} \equiv a \pmod{q},$$

where the last congruence follows from the fact that $\phi(n)k$ is a multiple of $q - 1$, which is a multiple of the multiplicative order of a modulo q (again by Euler's theorem). Thus, we have shown that $a^{ed} \equiv a \pmod{p}$ and $a^{ed} \equiv a \pmod{q}$, from which it follows that $a^{ed} \equiv a \pmod{n}$. The third case, where $a \not\equiv 0 \pmod{p}$ and $a \equiv 0 \pmod{q}$, is treated in the same way as the second. Thus, we have shown that equation (7.9) holds for all $\alpha \in \mathbb{Z}_n$.

Of course, the interesting question about the RSA cryptosystem is whether or not it really is secure. Now, if an adversary, given only the public key (n, e), were able to factor n, then he could easily compute the decryption exponent d. It is widely believed that factoring n is computationally infeasible, for sufficiently large n, and so this line of attack is ineffective, barring a breakthrough in factorization algorithms. However, there may be other possible lines of attack. For example, it is natural to ask whether one can compute the decryption exponent without having to go to the trouble of factoring n. It turns out that the answer to this question is no: if one could compute the decryption exponent d, then $ed - 1$ would be a multiple of $\phi(n)$, and as we shall see later in §10.6, given any multiple of $\phi(n)$, we can easily factor n.

Thus, computing the encryption exponent is equivalent to factoring n, and so this line of attack is also ineffective. But there still could be other lines of attack. For example, even if we assume that factoring large numbers is infeasible, this is not enough to guarantee that for a given encrypted message β, the adversary is unable to compute β^d (although nobody actually knows how to do this without first factoring n).

The reader should be warned that the proper notion of security for an encryption scheme is quite subtle, and a detailed discussion of this is well beyond the scope of this text. Indeed, the simple version of RSA presented here suffers from a number of security problems (because of this, actual implementations of public-key encryption schemes based on RSA are somewhat more complicated). We mention one such problem here (others are examined in some of the exercises below). Suppose an eavesdropping adversary knows that Alice will send one of a few, known, candidate messages. For example, an adversary may know that Alice's message is either "let's meet today" or "let's meet tomorrow." In this case, the adversary can encrypt for himself all of the candidate messages, intercept Alice's actual encrypted message, and then by simply comparing encryptions, the adversary can determine which particular message Alice encrypted. This type of attack works simply because the encryption algorithm is deterministic, and in fact, any deterministic encryption algorithm will be vulnerable to this type of attack. To avoid this type of attack, one must use a *probabilistic* encryption algorithm. In the case of the RSA cryptosystem, this is often achieved by padding the message with some random bits before encrypting it.

EXERCISE 7.24. Alice submits a bid to an auction, and so that other bidders cannot see her bid, she encrypts it under the public key of the auction service. Suppose that the auction service provides a public key for an RSA encryption scheme, with a modulus n. Assume that bids are encoded simply as integers between 0 and $n - 1$ prior to encryption. Also, assume that Alice submits a bid that is a "round number," which in this case means that her bid is a number that is divisible by 10. Show how an eavesdropper can submit an encryption of a bid that exceeds Alice's bid by 10%, without even knowing what Alice's bid is. In particular, your attack should work even if the space of possible bids is very large.

EXERCISE 7.25. To speed up RSA encryption, one may choose a very small encryption exponent. This exercise develops a "small encryption exponent attack" on RSA. Suppose Bob, Bill, and Betty have RSA public keys with moduli n_1, n_2, and n_3, and all three use encryption exponent 3. Assume that n_1, n_2, n_3 are pairwise relatively prime. Suppose that Alice sends an encryption of the same message to Bob, Bill, and Betty — that is, Alice encodes her message as an integer a, with $0 \le a < \min\{n_1, n_2, n_3\}$, and computes the three encrypted messages $\beta_i := [a^3]_{n_i}$, for $i = 1, \ldots, 3$. Show how to recover Alice's message from these three encrypted messages.

EXERCISE 7.26. To speed up RSA decryption, one might choose a small decryption exponent, and then derive the encryption exponent from this. This exercise develops a "small decryption exponent attack" on RSA. Suppose $n = pq$, where p and q are distinct primes with $\text{len}(p) = \text{len}(q)$. Let d and e be integers such that $1 < d < \phi(n)$, $1 < e < \phi(n)$, and $de \equiv 1 \pmod{\phi(n)}$.

Further, assume that

$$4d < n^{1/4}.$$

Show how to efficiently compute d, given n and e. Hint: since $de \equiv 1 \pmod{\phi(n)}$, it follows that $de = 1 + k\phi(n)$ for an integer k with $0 < k < d$; let $r := kn - de$, and show that $|r| < n^{3/4}$; next, show how to recover d (along with r and k) using Theorem 4.6.

EXERCISE 7.27. Suppose there is a probabilistic algorithm A that takes as input an integer n of the form $n = pq$, where p and q are distinct primes. The algorithm also takes as input an integer $e > 1$, with $\gcd(e, \phi(n)) = 1$, and an element $\beta \in \mathbb{Z}_n^*$. It outputs either "failure," or $\alpha \in \mathbb{Z}_n^*$ such that $\alpha^e = \beta$. Furthermore, assume that A runs in strict polynomial time, and that for all n and e of the above form, and for randomly chosen $\beta \in \mathbb{Z}_n^*$, A succeeds in finding α as above with probability $\epsilon(n, e)$. Here, the probability is taken over the random choice of β, as well as the random choices made during the execution of A. Show how to use A to construct another probabilistic algorithm A' that takes as input n and e as above, as well as $\beta \in \mathbb{Z}_n^*$, runs in expected polynomial time, and that satisfies the following property:

if $\epsilon(n, e) \geq 0.001$, then *for all* $\beta \in \mathbb{Z}_n^*$, A' finds $\alpha \in \mathbb{Z}_n^*$ with $\alpha^e = \beta$ with probability at least 0.999.

The algorithm A' in the above exercise is an example of what is called a **random self-reduction**, that is, an algorithm that reduces the task of solving an arbitrary instance of a given problem to that of solving a random instance of the problem. Intuitively, the fact that a problem is random self-reducible in this sense means that the problem is no harder in "the worst case" than in "the average case."

EXERCISE 7.28. This exercise develops an algorithm for speeding up RSA decryption. Suppose that we are given two distinct ℓ-bit primes, p and q, an element $\beta \in \mathbb{Z}_n$, where $n := pq$, and an integer d, where $1 < d < \phi(n)$. Using the algorithm from Exercise 3.26, we can compute β^d at a cost of essentially 2ℓ squarings in $\mathbb{Z}_n$. Show how this can be improved, making use of the factorization of n, so that the total cost is essentially that of ℓ squarings in $\mathbb{Z}_p$ and ℓ squarings in $\mathbb{Z}_q$, leading to a roughly four-fold speed-up in the running time.

7.9 Notes

See Luby [59] for an exposition of the theory of pseudo-random bit generation.

Our approach in §7.1 to defining the probability distribution associated with the execution of a probabilistic algorithm is a bit unusual (indeed, it is a bit unusual among papers and textbooks on the subject to even bother to formally define much of anything). There are alternative approaches. One approach is to define the output distribution and expected running time of an algorithm on a given input directly, using the identities in Exercise 7.4, and avoid the construction of an underlying probability distribution. However, without such a probability distribution, we would have very few tools at our disposal to analyze the output distribution and running time of particular algorithms. Another approach (which we dismissed with little justification early on in §7.1) is to attempt to define a distribution that models an infinite random bit string. One way to do this is to identify an infinite bit string with the real number in the unit interval $[0, 1]$ obtained by interpreting the bit string as a number written in base 2, and then use continuous probability theory (which we have not developed here, but which is covered in a standard undergraduate course on probability theory), applied to the uniform distribution on $[0, 1]$. There are a couple of problems with this approach. First, the above identification of bit strings with numbers is not quite one-to-one. Second, when one tries to define the notion of expected running time, numerous technical problems arise; in particular, the usual definition of an expected value in terms of an integral would require us to integrate functions that are not Riemann integrable. To properly deal with all of these issues, one would have to develop a good deal of measure theory (σ-algebras, Lesbegue integration, and so on), at the level normally covered in a graduate-level course on probability or measure theory.

The algorithm presented here for generating a random factored number is due to Kalai [50], although the analysis presented here is a bit different, and our analysis using a probabilistic primality test is new. Kalai's algorithm is significantly simpler, though less efficient than, an earlier algorithm due to Bach [9], which uses an expected number of $O(k)$ primality tests, as opposed to the $O(k^2)$ primality tests used by Kalai's algorithm.

The RSA cryptosystem was invented by Rivest, Shamir, and Adleman [78]. There is a vast literature on cryptography. One starting point is the book by Menezes, van Oorschot, and Vanstone [62]. The attack in Exercise 7.26 is due to Wiener [104]; this attack was recently strengthened by Boneh and Durfee [19].

8

Abelian groups

This chapter introduces the notion of an abelian group. This is an abstraction that models many different algebraic structures, and yet despite the level of generality, a number of very useful results can be easily obtained.

8.1 Definitions, basic properties, and examples

Definition 8.1. *An **abelian group** is a set G together with a binary operation $\star$ on G such that*

(i) *for all $a, b, c \in G$, $a \star (b \star c) = (a \star b) \star c$ (i.e., $\star$ is associative),*

(ii) *there exists $e \in G$ (called the **identity element**) such that for all $a \in G$, $a \star e = a = e \star a$,*

(iii) *for all $a \in G$ there exists $a' \in G$ (called the **inverse of** a) such that $a \star a' = e = a' \star a$,*

(iv) *for all $a, b \in G$, $a \star b = b \star a$ (i.e., $\star$ is commutative).*

While there is a more general notion of a **group**, which may be defined simply by dropping property (iv) in Definition 8.1, we shall not need this notion in this text. The restriction to abelian groups helps to simplify the discussion significantly. Because we will only be dealing with abelian groups, we may occasionally simply say "group" instead of "abelian group."

Before looking at examples, let us state some very basic properties of abelian groups that follow directly from the definition:

Theorem 8.2. *Let G be an abelian group with binary operation $\star$. Then we have:*

(i) *G contains only one identity element;*

(ii) *every element of G has only one inverse.*

Proof. Suppose e, e' are both identities. Then we have

$$e = e \star e' = e',$$

where we have used part (ii) of Definition 8.1, once with e' as the identity, and once with e as the identity. That proves part (i) of the theorem.

To prove part (ii) of the theorem, let $a \in G$, and suppose that a has two inverses, a' and a''. Then using parts (i)–(iii) of Definition 8.1, we have

$$
\begin{aligned}
a' &= a' \star e \quad \text{(by part (ii))} \\
&= a' \star (a \star a'') \quad \text{(by part (iii) with inverse } a'' \text{ of } a) \\
&= (a' \star a) \star a'' \quad \text{(by part (i))} \\
&= e \star a'' \quad \text{(by part (iii) with inverse } a' \text{ of } a) \\
&= a'' \quad \text{(by part (ii))}. \quad \square
\end{aligned}
$$

These uniqueness properties justify use of the definite article in Definition 8.1 in conjunction with the terms "identity element" and "inverse." Note that we never used part (iv) of the definition in the proof of the above theorem.

Abelian groups are lurking everywhere, as the following examples illustrate.

Example 8.1. The set of integers $\mathbb{Z}$ under addition forms an abelian group, with 0 being the identity, and $-a$ being the inverse of $a \in \mathbb{Z}$. $\square$

Example 8.2. For integer n, the set $n\mathbb{Z} = \{nz : z \in \mathbb{Z}\}$ under addition forms an abelian group, again, with 0 being the identity, and $n(-z)$ being the inverse of nz. $\square$

Example 8.3. The set of non-negative integers under addition does not form an abelian group, since additive inverses do not exist for positive integers. $\square$

Example 8.4. The set of integers under multiplication does not form an abelian group, since inverses do not exist for integers other than ± 1. $\square$

Example 8.5. The set of integers $\{\pm 1\}$ under multiplication forms an abelian group, with 1 being the identity, and -1 its own inverse. $\square$

Example 8.6. The set of rational numbers $\mathbb{Q} = \{a/b : a, b \in \mathbb{Z}, \ b \neq 0\}$ under addition forms an abelian group, with 0 being the identity, and $(-a)/b$ being the inverse of a/b. $\square$

***Example* 8.7.** The set of non-zero rational numbers $\mathbb{Q}^*$ under multiplication forms an abelian group, with 1 being the identity, and b/a being the inverse of a/b. □

***Example* 8.8.** The set $\mathbb{Z}_n$ under addition forms an abelian group, where $[0]_n$ is the identity, and where $[-a]_n$ is the inverse of $[a]_n$. □

***Example* 8.9.** The set $\mathbb{Z}_n^*$ of residue classes $[a]_n$ with $\gcd(a, n) = 1$ under multiplication forms an abelian group, where $[1]_n$ is the identity, and if b is a multiplicative inverse of a modulo n, then $[b]_n$ is the inverse of $[a]_n$. □

***Example* 8.10.** Continuing the previous example, let us set $n = 15$, and enumerate the elements of $\mathbb{Z}_{15}^*$. They are

$$[1], [2], [4], [7], [8], [11], [13], [14].$$

An alternative enumeration is

$$[\pm 1], [\pm 2], [\pm 4], [\pm 7]. \quad \square$$

***Example* 8.11.** As another special case, consider $\mathbb{Z}_5^*$. We can enumerate the elements of this groups as

$$[1], [2], [3], [4]$$

or alternatively as

$$[\pm 1], [\pm 2]. \quad \square$$

***Example* 8.12.** For any positive integer n, the set of n-bit strings under the "exclusive or" operation forms an abelian group, where the "all zero" bit string is the identity, and every bit string is its own inverse. □

***Example* 8.13.** The set of all arithmetic functions f, such that $f(1) \neq 0$, with multiplication defined by the Dirichlet product (see §2.6) forms an abelian group, where the special arithmetic function I is the identity, and inverses are provided by the result of Exercise 2.27. □

***Example* 8.14.** The set of all finite bit strings under concatenation does not form an abelian group. Although concatenation is associative and the empty string acts as an identity element, inverses do not exist (except for the empty string), nor is concatenation commutative. □

***Example* 8.15.** The set of 2×2 integer matrices with determinant ± 1, together with the binary operation of matrix multiplication, is an example of a *non-abelian* group; that is, it satisfies properties (i)–(iii) of Definition 8.1, but not property (iv). □

***Example* 8.16.** The set of all permutations on a given set of size $n \geq 3$, together with the binary operation of function composition, is another example of a non-abelian group (for $n = 1, 2$, it is an abelian group). $\square$

Note that in specifying a group, one must specify both the underlying set G as well as the binary operation; however, in practice, the binary operation is often implicit from context, and by abuse of notation, one often refers to G itself as the group. For example, when talking about the abelian groups $\mathbb{Z}$ and $\mathbb{Z}_n$, it is understood that the group operation is addition, while when talking about the abelian group $\mathbb{Z}_n^*$, it is understood that the group operation is multiplication.

Typically, instead of using a special symbol like "$\star$" for the group operation, one uses the usual addition ("$+$") or multiplication ("$\cdot$") operations. For any particular, concrete abelian group, the most natural choice of notation is clear (e.g., addition for $\mathbb{Z}$ and $\mathbb{Z}_n$, multiplication for $\mathbb{Z}_n^*$); however, for a "generic" group, the choice is largely a matter of taste. By convention, whenever we consider a "generic" abelian group, we shall use *additive* notation for the group operation, unless otherwise specified.

If an abelian group G is written additively, then the identity element is denoted by 0_G (or just 0 if G is clear from context), and the inverse of an element $a \in G$ is denoted by $-a$. For $a, b \in G$, $a - b$ denotes $a + (-b)$. If n is a positive integer, then $n \cdot a$ denotes $a + a + \cdots + a$, where there are n terms in the sum—note that $1 \cdot a = a$. Moreover, $0 \cdot a$ denotes 0_G, and if n is a negative integer, then $n \cdot a$ denotes $(-n)(-a)$.

If an abelian group G is written multiplicatively, then the identity element is denoted by 1_G (or just 1 if G is clear from context), and the inverse of an element $a \in G$ is denoted by a^{-1} or $1/a$. As usual, one may write ab in place of $a \cdot b$. For $a, b \in G$, a/b denotes $a \cdot b^{-1}$. If n is a positive integer, then a^n denotes $a \cdot a \cdots \cdot a$, where there are n terms in the product—note that $a^1 = a$. Moreover, a^0 denotes 1_G, and if n is a negative integer, then a^n denotes $(a^{-1})^{-n}$.

An abelian group G may be infinite or finite. If the group is finite, we define its **order** to be the number of elements in the underlying set G; otherwise, we say that the group has **infinite order**.

***Example* 8.17.** The order of the additive group $\mathbb{Z}_n$ is n. $\square$

***Example* 8.18.** The order of the multiplicative group $\mathbb{Z}_n^*$ is $\phi(n)$, where ϕ is Euler's phi function, defined in §2.4. $\square$

***Example* 8.19.** The additive group $\mathbb{Z}$ has infinite order. $\square$

We now record a few more simple but useful properties of abelian groups.

Theorem 8.3. *Let G be an abelian group. Then for all $a, b, c \in G$ and $n, m \in \mathbb{Z}$, we have:*

   (i) if $a + b = a + c$, then $b = c$;

   (ii) the equation $a + x = b$ has a unique solution $x \in G$;

  (iii) $-(a + b) = (-a) + (-b)$;

  (iv) $-(-a) = a$;

   (v) $(-n)a = -(na) = n(-a)$;

  (vi) $(n + m)a = na + ma$;

 (vii) $n(ma) = (nm)a = m(na)$;

(viii) $n(a + b) = na + nb$.

Proof. Exercise. $\square$

If $G_1, \ldots, G_k$ are abelian groups, we can form the **direct product** $G := G_1 \times \cdots \times G_k$, which consists of all k-tuples $(a_1, \ldots, a_k)$ with $a_1 \in G_1, \ldots, a_k \in G_k$. We can view G in a natural way as an abelian group if we define the group operation component-wise:

$$(a_1, \ldots, a_k) + (b_1, \ldots, b_k) := (a_1 + b_1, \ldots, a_k + b_k).$$

Of course, the groups $G_1, \ldots, G_k$ may be different, and the group operation applied in the ith component corresponds to the group operation associated with G_i. We leave it to the reader to verify that G is in fact an abelian group.

EXERCISE 8.1. In this exercise, you are to generalize the Möbius inversion formula, discussed in §2.6, to arbitrary abelian groups. Let $\mathcal{F}$ be the set of all functions mapping positive integers to integers. Let G be an abelian group, and let $\mathcal{G}$ be the set of all functions mapping positive integers to elements of G. For $f \in \mathcal{F}$ and $g \in \mathcal{G}$, we can define the Dirichlet product $f \star g \in \mathcal{G}$ as follows:

$$(f \star g)(n) := \sum_{d \mid n} f(d)g(n/d),$$

the sum being over all positive divisors d of n. Let $I, J, \mu \in \mathcal{F}$ be as defined in §2.6.

  (a) Show that for all $f, g \in \mathcal{F}$ and all $h \in \mathcal{G}$, we have $(f \star g) \star h = f \star (g \star h)$.

  (b) Show that for all $f \in \mathcal{G}$, we have $I \star f = f$.

  (c) Show that for all $f, F \in \mathcal{G}$, we have $F = J \star f$ if and only if $f = \mu \star F$.

8.2 Subgroups

We next introduce the notion of a subgroup.

Definition 8.4. *Let G be an abelian group, and let H be a non-empty subset of G such that*

> *(i) $a + b \in H$ for all $a, b \in H$, and*

> *(ii) $-a \in H$ for all $a \in H$.*

*Then H is called a **subgroup of** G.*

In words: H is a subgroup of G if it is closed under the group operation and taking inverses.

Multiplicative notation: if the abelian group G in the above definition is written using multiplicative notation, then H is a subgroup if $ab \in H$ and $a^{-1} \in H$ for all $a, b \in H$.

Theorem 8.5. *If G is an abelian group, and H is a subgroup of G, then H contains 0_G; moreover, the binary operation of G, when restricted to H, yields a binary operation that makes H into an abelian group whose identity is 0_G.*

Proof. First, to see that $0_G \in H$, just pick any $a \in H$, and using both properties of the definition of a subgroup, we see that $0_G = a + (-a) \in H$.

Next, note that by property (i) of Definition 8.4, H is closed under addition, which means that the restriction of the binary operation "+" on G to H induces a well defined binary operation on H. So now it suffices to show that H, together with this operation, satisfy the defining properties of an abelian group. Associativity and commutativity follow directly from the corresponding properties for G. Since 0_G acts as the identity on G, it does so on H as well. Finally, property (ii) of Definition 8.4 guarantees that every element $a \in H$ has an inverse in H, namely, $-a$. $\square$

Clearly, for an abelian group G, the subsets G and $\{0_G\}$ are subgroups. These are not very interesting subgroups. An easy way to sometimes find other, more interesting, subgroups within an abelian group is by using the following two theorems.

Theorem 8.6. *Let G be an abelian group, and let m be an integer. Then $mG := \{ma : a \in G\}$ is a subgroup of G.*

Proof. For $ma, mb \in mG$, we have $ma + mb = m(a+b) \in mG$, and $-(ma) = m(-a) \in mG$. $\square$

Theorem 8.7. *Let G be an abelian group, and let m be an integer. Then $G\{m\} := \{a \in G : ma = 0_G\}$ is a subgroup of G.*

Proof. If $ma = 0_G$ and $mb = 0_G$, then $m(a+b) = ma + mb = 0_G + 0_G = 0_G$ and $m(-a) = -(ma) = -0_G = 0_G$. $\square$

Multiplicative notation: if the abelian group G in the above two theorems is written using multiplicative notation, then we write the subgroup of the first theorem as $G^m := \{a^m : a \in G\}$. The subgroup in the second theorem is denoted in the same way: $G\{m\} := \{a \in G : a^m = 1_G\}$.

Example 8.20. For every integer m, the set $m\mathbb{Z}$ is the subgroup of the additive group $\mathbb{Z}$ consisting of all integer multiples of m. Two such subgroups $m\mathbb{Z}$ and $m'\mathbb{Z}$ are equal if and only if $m = \pm m'$. The subgroup $\mathbb{Z}\{m\}$ is equal to $\mathbb{Z}$ if $m = 0$, and is equal to $\{0\}$ otherwise. $\square$

Example 8.21. Let n be a positive integer, let $m \in \mathbb{Z}$, and consider the subgroup $m\mathbb{Z}_n$ of the additive group $\mathbb{Z}_n$. Now, $[b]_n \in m\mathbb{Z}_n$ if and only if there exists $x \in \mathbb{Z}$ such that $mx \equiv b \pmod{n}$. By Theorem 2.7, such an x exists if and only if $d \mid b$, where $d := \gcd(m, n)$. Thus, $m\mathbb{Z}_n$ consists precisely of the n/d distinct residue classes

$$[i \cdot d]_n \quad (i = 0, \ldots, n/d - 1),$$

and in particular, $m\mathbb{Z}_n = d\mathbb{Z}_n$.

Now consider the subgroup $\mathbb{Z}_n\{m\}$ of $\mathbb{Z}_n$. The residue class $[x]_n$ is in $\mathbb{Z}_n\{m\}$ if and only if $mx \equiv 0 \pmod{n}$. By Theorem 2.7, this happens if and only if $x \equiv 0 \pmod{n/d}$, where $d = \gcd(m, n)$ as above. Thus, $\mathbb{Z}_n\{m\}$ consists precisely of the d residue classes

$$[i \cdot n/d]_n \quad (i = 0, \ldots, d - 1),$$

and in particular, $\mathbb{Z}_n\{m\} = \mathbb{Z}_n\{d\} = (n/d)\mathbb{Z}_n$. $\square$

Example 8.22. For $n = 15$, consider again the table in Example 2.3. For $m = 1, 2, 3, 4, 5, 6$, the elements appearing in the mth row of that table form the subgroup $m\mathbb{Z}_n$ of $\mathbb{Z}_n$, and also the subgroup $\mathbb{Z}_n\{n/d\}$, where $d := \gcd(m, n)$. $\square$

Because the abelian groups $\mathbb{Z}$ and $\mathbb{Z}_n$ are of such importance, it is a good idea to completely characterize all subgroups of these abelian groups. As the following two theorems show, the subgroups in the above examples are the *only* subgroups of these groups.

Theorem 8.8. *If G is a subgroup of $\mathbb{Z}$, then there exists a unique non-negative integer m such that $G = m\mathbb{Z}$. Moreover, for two non-negative integers m_1 and m_2, we have $m_1\mathbb{Z} \subseteq m_2\mathbb{Z}$ if and only if $m_2 \mid m_1$.*

Proof. Actually, we have already proven this. One only needs to observe that a subset G of $\mathbb{Z}$ is a subgroup if and only if it is an ideal of $\mathbb{Z}$, as defined in §1.2 (see Exercise 1.7). The first statement of the theorem then follows from Theorem 1.5. The second statement follows easily from the definitions, as was observed in §1.2. $\square$

Theorem 8.9. *If G is a subgroup of $\mathbb{Z}_n$, then there exists a unique positive integer d dividing n such that $G = d\mathbb{Z}_n$. Also, for positive divisors d_1, d_2 of n, we have $d_1\mathbb{Z}_n \subseteq d_2\mathbb{Z}_n$ if and only if $d_2 \mid d_1$.*

Proof. Let $\rho : \mathbb{Z} \to \mathbb{Z}_n$ be the map that sends $a \in \mathbb{Z}$ to $[a]_n \in \mathbb{Z}_n$. Clearly, ρ is surjective. Consider the pre-image $\rho^{-1}(G) \subseteq \mathbb{Z}$ of G.

We claim that $\rho^{-1}(G)$ is a subgroup of $\mathbb{Z}$. To see this, observe that for $a, b \in \mathbb{Z}$, if $[a]_n$ and $[b]_n$ belong to G, then so do $[a + b]_n = [a]_n + [b]_n$ and $-[a]_n = [-a]_n$, and thus $a + b$ and $-a$ belong to the pre-image.

Since $\rho^{-1}(G)$ is a subgroup of $\mathbb{Z}$, by the previous theorem, we have $\rho^{-1}(G) = d\mathbb{Z}$ for some non-negative integer d. Moreover, it is clear that $n \in \rho^{-1}(G)$, and hence $d \mid n$. That proves the existence part of the theorem.

Next, we claim that for any divisor d of n, we have $\rho^{-1}(d\mathbb{Z}_n) = d\mathbb{Z}$. To see this, note that $\rho^{-1}(d\mathbb{Z}_n)$ consists of all integers b such that $dx \equiv b \pmod{n}$ has an integer solution x, and by Theorem 2.7, this congruence admits a solution if and only if $d \mid b$. That proves the claim.

Now consider any two positive divisors d_1, d_2 of n. Since $d_1\mathbb{Z}_n \subseteq d_2\mathbb{Z}_n$ if and only if $\rho^{-1}(d_1\mathbb{Z}_n) \subseteq \rho^{-1}(d_2\mathbb{Z}_n)$, the remaining statements of the theorem follow from the corresponding statements of Theorem 8.8 and the above claim. $\square$

Of course, not all abelian groups have such a simple subgroup structure.

Example 8.23. Consider the group $G = \mathbb{Z}_2 \times \mathbb{Z}_2$. For any non-zero $\alpha \in G$, $\alpha + \alpha = 0_G$. From this, it is easy to see that the set $H = \{0_G, \alpha\}$ is a subgroup of G. However, for any integer m, $mG = G$ if m is odd, and $mG = \{0_G\}$ if m is even. Thus, the subgroup H is not of the form mG for any m. $\square$

Example 8.24. Consider again the group $\mathbb{Z}_n^*$, for $n = 15$, discussed in Example 8.10. As discussed there, we have $\mathbb{Z}_{15}^* = \{[\pm 1], [\pm 2], [\pm 4], [\pm 7]\}$.

Therefore, the elements of $(\mathbb{Z}_{15}^*)^2$ are

$$[1]^2 = [1], \ [2]^2 = [4], \ [4]^2 = [16] = [1], \ [7]^2 = [49] = [4];$$

thus, $(\mathbb{Z}_{15}^*)^2$ has order 2, consisting as it does of the two distinct elements $[1]$ and $[4]$.

Going further, one sees that $(\mathbb{Z}_{15}^*)^4 = \{[1]\}$. Thus, $\alpha^4 = [1]$ for all $\alpha \in \mathbb{Z}_{15}^*$.

By direct calculation, one can determine that $(\mathbb{Z}_{15}^*)^3 = \mathbb{Z}_{15}^*$; that is, cubing simply permutes $\mathbb{Z}_{15}^*$.

For any integer m, write $m = 4q + r$, where $0 \le r < 4$. Then for any $\alpha \in \mathbb{Z}_{15}^*$, we have $\alpha^m = \alpha^{4q+r} = \alpha^{4q} \alpha^r = \alpha^r$. Thus, $(\mathbb{Z}_{15}^*)^m$ is either $\mathbb{Z}_{15}^*$, $(\mathbb{Z}_{15}^*)^2$, or $\{[1]\}$.

However, there are certainly other subgroups of $\mathbb{Z}_{15}^*$ — for example, the subgroup $\{[\pm 1]\}$. □

Example 8.25. Consider again the group $\mathbb{Z}_5^*$ from Example 8.11. As discussed there, $\mathbb{Z}_5^* = \{[\pm 1], [\pm 2]\}$. Therefore, the elements of $(\mathbb{Z}_5^*)^2$ are

$$[1]^2 = [1], \ [2]^2 = [4] = [-1];$$

thus, $(\mathbb{Z}_5^*)^2 = \{[\pm 1]\}$ and has order 2.

There are in fact no other subgroups of $\mathbb{Z}_5^*$ besides $\mathbb{Z}_5^*$, $\{[\pm 1]\}$, and $\{[1]\}$. Indeed, if H is a subgroup containing $[2]$, then we must have $H = \mathbb{Z}_5^*$: $[2] \in H$ implies $[2]^2 = [4] = [-1] \in H$, which implies $[-2] \in H$ as well. The same holds if H is a subgroup containing $[-2]$. □

Example 8.26. Consider again the group of arithmetic functions f, such that $f(1) \ne 0$, with multiplication defined by the Dirichlet product, discussed in Example 8.13. By the results of Exercises 2.21 and 2.28, we see that the subset of all multiplicative arithmetic functions is a subgroup of this group. □

The following two theorems may be used to simplify verifying that a subset is a subgroup.

Theorem 8.10. *If G is an abelian group, and H is a non-empty subset of G such that $a - b \in H$ for all $a, b \in H$, then H is a subgroup of G.*

Proof. Since H is non-empty, let c be an arbitrary element of H. Then $0_G = c - c \in H$. It follows that for all $a \in H$, we have $-a = 0_G - a \in H$, and for all $a, b \in H$, we have $a + b = a - (-b) \in H$. □

Theorem 8.11. *If G is an abelian group, and H is a non-empty, finite subset of G such that $a + b \in H$ for all $a, b \in H$, then H is a subgroup of G.*

Proof. We only need to show that $-a \in H$ for all $a \in H$. Let $a \in H$ be given. If $a = 0_G$, then clearly $-a = 0_G \in H$, so assume that $a \neq 0_G$, and consider the set S of all elements of G of the form ma, for $m = 1, 2, \ldots$. Since H is closed under addition, it follows that $S \subseteq H$. Moreover, since H is finite, S must be finite, and hence there must exist integers m_1, m_2 such that $m_1 > m_2 > 0$ and $m_1 a = m_2 a$; that is, $ra = 0_G$, where $r := m_1 - m_2 > 0$. We may further assume that $r > 1$, since otherwise $a = 0_G$, and we are assuming that $a \neq 0_G$. It follows that $a + (r-1)a = 0_G$, and so $-a = (r-1)a \in S$. $\square$

We close this section with two theorems that provide useful ways to build new subgroups out of old subgroups.

Theorem 8.12. *If H_1 and H_2 are subgroups of an abelian group G, then so is*

$$H_1 + H_2 := \{h_1 + h_2 : h_1 \in H_1, h_2 \in H_2\}.$$

Proof. Consider two elements in $H_1 + H_2$, which we can write as $h_1 + h_2$ and $h_1' + h_2'$, where $h_1, h_1' \in H_1$ and $h_2, h_2' \in H_2$. Then by the closure properties of subgroups, $h_1 + h_1' \in H_1$ and $h_2 + h_2' \in H_2$, and hence $(h_1 + h_2) + (h_1' + h_2') = (h_1 + h_1') + (h_2 + h_2') \in H_1 + H_2$. Similarly, $-(h_1 + h_2) = (-h_1) + (-h_2) \in H_1 + H_2$. $\square$

Multiplicative notation: if the abelian group G in the above theorem is written multiplicatively, then the subgroup defined in the theorem is written $H_1 \cdot H_2 := \{h_1 h_2 : h_1 \in H_1, h_2 \in H_2\}$.

Theorem 8.13. *If H_1 and H_2 are subgroups of an abelian group G, then so is $H_1 \cap H_2$.*

Proof. If $h \in H_1 \cap H_2$ and $h' \in H_1 \cap H_2$, then since $h, h' \in H_1$, we have $h + h' \in H_1$, and since $h, h' \in H_2$, we have $h + h' \in H_2$; therefore, $h + h' \in H_1 \cap H_2$. Similarly, $-h \in H_2$ and $-h \in H_2$, and therefore, $-h \in H_1 \cap H_2$. $\square$

EXERCISE 8.2. Show that if H' is a subgroup of an abelian group G, then a set $H \subseteq H'$ is a subgroup of G if and only if H is a subgroup of H'.

EXERCISE 8.3. Let G be an abelian group with subgroups H_1 and H_2. Show that any subgroup H of G that contains $H_1 \cup H_2$ contains $H_1 + H_2$, and $H_1 \subseteq H_2$ if and only if $H_1 + H_2 = H_2$.

EXERCISE 8.4. Let H_1 be a subgroup of an abelian group G_1 and H_2 a subgroup of an abelian group G_2. Show that $H_1 \times H_2$ is a subgroup of $G_1 \times G_2$.

EXERCISE 8.5. Let G_1 and G_2 be abelian groups, and let H be a subgroup of $G_1 \times G_2$. Define

$$H_1 := \{h_1 \in G_1 : (h_1, h_2) \in H \text{ for some } h_2 \in G_2\}.$$

Show that H_1 is a subgroup of G_1.

EXERCISE 8.6. Give an example of specific abelian groups G_1 and G_2, along with a subgroup H of $G_1 \times G_2$, such that H cannot be written as $H_1 \times H_2$, where H_1 is a subgroup of G_1 and H_2 is a subgroup of G_2.

8.3 Cosets and quotient groups

We now generalize the notion of a congruence relation.

Let G be an abelian group, and let H be a subgroup of G. For $a, b \in G$, we write $a \equiv b \pmod{H}$ if $a - b \in H$. In other words, $a \equiv b \pmod{H}$ if and only if $a = b + h$ for some $h \in H$.

Analogously to Theorem 2.2, if we view the subgroup H as fixed, then the following theorem says that the binary relation "$\cdot \equiv \cdot \pmod{H}$" is an equivalence relation on the set G:

Theorem 8.14. *Let G be an abelian group and H a subgroup of G. For all $a, b, c \in G$, we have:*

  (i) $a \equiv a \pmod{H}$;

  (ii) $a \equiv b \pmod{H}$ *implies* $b \equiv a \pmod{H}$;

  (iii) $a \equiv b \pmod{H}$ *and* $b \equiv c \pmod{H}$ *implies* $a \equiv c \pmod{H}$.

Proof. For (i), observe that H contains $0_G = a - a$. For (ii), observe that if H contains $a - b$, then it also contains $-(a - b) = b - a$. For (iii), observe that if H contains $a - b$ and $b - c$, then it also contains $(a - b) + (b - c) = a - c$. $\square$

Since the binary relation "$\cdot \equiv \cdot \pmod{H}$" is an equivalence relation, it partitions G into equivalence classes. It is easy to see (verify) that for any $a \in G$, the equivalence class containing a is precisely the set $a + H := \{a + h : h \in H\}$, and this set is called the **coset of H in G containing** a, and an element of such a coset is called a **representative** of the coset.

Multiplicative notation: if G is written multiplicatively, then $a \equiv b \pmod{H}$ means $a/b \in H$, and the coset of H in G containing a is $aH := \{ah : h \in H\}$.

Example 8.27. Let $G := \mathbb{Z}$ and $H := n\mathbb{Z}$ for some positive integer n. Then

$a \equiv b \pmod{H}$ if and only if $a \equiv b \pmod{n}$. The coset $a + H$ is exactly the same thing as the residue class $[a]_n$. $\square$

***Example* 8.28.** Let $G := \mathbb{Z}_4$ and let H be the subgroup $2G = \{[0], [2]\}$ of G. The coset of H containing $[1]$ is $\{[1], [3]\}$. These are all the cosets of H in G. $\square$

Theorem 8.15. *Any two cosets of a subgroup H in an abelian group G have equal cardinality; that is, there is a bijective map from one coset to the other.*

Proof. It suffices to exhibit a bijection between H and $a + H$ for any $a \in G$. The map $f_a : H \to a + H$ that sends $h \in H$ to $a + h$ is easily seen to be just such a bijection. $\square$

An incredibly useful consequence of the above theorem is:

Theorem 8.16 (Lagrange's theorem). *If G is a finite abelian group, and H is a subgroup of G, then the order of H divides the order of G.*

Proof. This is an immediate consequence of the previous theorem, and the fact that the cosets of H in G partition G. $\square$

Analogous to Theorem 2.3, we have:

Theorem 8.17. *Let G be an abelian group and H a subgroup. For $a, a', b, b' \in G$, if $a \equiv a' \pmod{H}$ and $b \equiv b' \pmod{H}$, then $a + b \equiv a' + b' \pmod{H}$.*

Proof. Now, $a \equiv a' \pmod{H}$ and $b \equiv b' \pmod{H}$ means that $a' = a + h_1$ and $b' = b + h_2$ for $h_1, h_2 \in H$. Therefore, $a' + b' = (a + h_1) + (b + h_2) = (a + b) + (h_1 + h_2)$, and since $h_1 + h_2 \in H$, this means that $a + b \equiv a' + b' \pmod{H}$. $\square$

Let G be an abelian group and H a subgroup. Theorem 8.17 allows us to define a binary operation on the collection of cosets of H in G in the following natural way: for $a, b \in G$, define

$$(a + H) + (b + H) := (a + b) + H.$$

The fact that this definition is unambiguous follows immediately from Theorem 8.17. Also, one can easily verify that this operation defines an abelian group, where H acts as the identity element, and the inverse of a coset $a + H$ is $(-a) + H$. The resulting group is called the **quotient group of G modulo H**, and is denoted G/H. The order of the group G/H is sometimes denoted $[G : H]$ and is called the **index of H in G**.

Multiplicative notation: if G is written multiplicatively, then the definition of the group operation of G/H is expressed

$$(aH) \cdot (bH) := (ab)H.$$

Theorem 8.18. *Let G be a finite abelian group and H a subgroup. Then $[G : H] = |G|/|H|$. Moreover, if H' is another subgroup of G with $H \subseteq H'$, then*

$$[G : H] = [G : H'][H' : G].$$

Proof. The fact that $[G : H] = |G|/|H|$ follows directly from Theorem 8.15. The fact that $[G : H] = [G : H'][H' : G]$ follows from a simple calculation:

$$[G : H'] = \frac{|G|}{|H'|} = \frac{|G|/|H|}{|H'|/|H|} = \frac{[G : H]}{[H' : H]}. \quad \square$$

Example 8.29. For the additive group of integers $\mathbb{Z}$ and the subgroup $n\mathbb{Z}$ for $n > 0$, the quotient group $\mathbb{Z}/n\mathbb{Z}$ is precisely the same as the additive group $\mathbb{Z}_n$ that we have already defined. For $n = 0$, $\mathbb{Z}/n\mathbb{Z}$ is essentially just a "renaming" of $\mathbb{Z}$. $\square$

Example 8.30. Let $G := \mathbb{Z}_6$ and $H = 3G$ be the subgroup of G consisting of the two elements $\{[0], [3]\}$. The cosets of H in G are $\alpha := H = \{[0], [3]\}$, $\beta := [1] + H = \{[1], [4]\}$, and $\gamma := [2] + H = \{[2], [5]\}$. If we write out an addition table for G, grouping together elements in cosets of H in G, then we also get an addition table for the quotient group G/H:

$+$	$[0]$	$[3]$	$[1]$	$[4]$	$[2]$	$[5]$
$[0]$	$[0]$	$[3]$	$[1]$	$[4]$	$[2]$	$[5]$
$[3]$	$[3]$	$[0]$	$[4]$	$[1]$	$[5]$	$[2]$
$[1]$	$[1]$	$[4]$	$[2]$	$[5]$	$[3]$	$[0]$
$[4]$	$[4]$	$[1]$	$[5]$	$[2]$	$[0]$	$[3]$
$[2]$	$[2]$	$[5]$	$[3]$	$[0]$	$[4]$	$[1]$
$[5]$	$[5]$	$[2]$	$[0]$	$[3]$	$[1]$	$[4]$

This table illustrates quite graphically the point of Theorem 8.17: for any two cosets, if we take any element from the first and add it to any element of the second, we always end up in the same coset.

We can also write down just the addition table for G/H:

$+$	α	β	γ
α	α	β	γ
β	β	γ	α
γ	γ	α	β

Note that by replacing α with $[0]_3$, β with $[1]_3$, and γ with $[2]_3$, the addition table for G/H becomes the addition table for $\mathbb{Z}_3$. In this sense, we can view G/H as essentially just a "renaming" of $\mathbb{Z}_3$. $\square$

***Example* 8.31.** Let us return to Example 8.24. The group $\mathbb{Z}_{15}^*$, as we saw, is of order 8. The subgroup $(\mathbb{Z}_{15}^*)^2$ of $\mathbb{Z}_{15}^*$ has order 2. Therefore, the quotient group $\mathbb{Z}_{15}^*/(\mathbb{Z}_{15}^*)^2$ has order 4. Indeed, the cosets are $\alpha_{00} = \{[1], [4]\}$, $\alpha_{01} = \{[-1], [-4]\}$, $\alpha_{10} = \{[2], [-7]\}$, and $\alpha_{11} = \{[7], [-2]\}$. In the quotient group, α_{00} is the identity; moreover, we have

$$\alpha_{01}^2 = \alpha_{10}^2 = \alpha_{11}^2 = \alpha_{00}$$

and

$$\alpha_{01}\alpha_{10} = \alpha_{11}, \ \ \alpha_{10}\alpha_{11} = \alpha_{01}, \ \ \alpha_{01}\alpha_{11} = \alpha_{10}.$$

This completely describes the behavior of the group operation of the quotient group. Note that this group is essentially just a "renaming" of the group $\mathbb{Z}_2 \times \mathbb{Z}_2$. $\square$

***Example* 8.32.** As we saw in Example 8.25, $(\mathbb{Z}_5^*)^2 = \{[\pm 1]\}$. Therefore, the quotient group $\mathbb{Z}_5^*/(\mathbb{Z}_5^*)^2$ has order 2. The cosets of $(\mathbb{Z}_5^*)^2$ in $\mathbb{Z}_5^*$ are $\alpha_0 = \{[\pm 1]\}$ and $\alpha_1 = \{[\pm 2]\}$. In the group $\mathbb{Z}_5^*/(\mathbb{Z}_5^*)^2$, α_0 is the identity, and α_1 is its own inverse, and we see that this group is essentially just a "renaming" of $\mathbb{Z}_2$. $\square$

EXERCISE 8.7. Let H be a subgroup of an abelian group G, and let a and a' be elements of G, with $a \equiv a' \pmod{H}$.

(a) Show that $-a \equiv -a' \pmod{H}$.

(b) Show that $na \equiv na' \pmod{H}$ for all $n \in \mathbb{Z}$.

EXERCISE 8.8. Let G be an abelian group, and let $\sim$ be an equivalence relation on G. Further, suppose that for all $a, a', b \in G$, if $a \sim a'$, then $a + b \sim a' + b$. Let $H := \{a \in G : a \sim 0_G\}$. Show that H is a subgroup of G, and that for all $a, b \in G$, we have $a \sim b$ if and only if $a \equiv b \pmod{H}$.

EXERCISE 8.9. Let H be a subgroup of an abelian group G.

(a) Show that if H' is a subgroup of G containing H, then H'/H is a subgroup of G/H.

(b) Show that if K is a subgroup of G/H, then the set $H' := \{a \in G : a + H \in K\}$ is a subgroup of G containing H.

8.4 Group homomorphisms and isomorphisms

Definition 8.19. *A **group homomorphism** is a function ρ from an abelian group G to an abelian group G' such that $\rho(a + b) = \rho(a) + \rho(b)$ for all $a, b \in G$.*

Note that in the equality $\rho(a + b) = \rho(a) + \rho(b)$ in the above definition, the addition on the left-hand side is taking place in the group G while the addition on the right-hand side is taking place in the group G'.

Two sets play a critical role in understanding a group homomorphism $\rho : G \to G'$. The first set is the image of ρ, that is, the set $\rho(G) = \{\rho(a) : a \in G\}$. The second set is the **kernel** of ρ, defined as the set of all elements of G that are mapped to $0_{G'}$ by ρ, that is, the set $\rho^{-1}(\{0_{G'}\}) = \{a \in G : \rho(a) = 0_{G'}\}$. We introduce the following notation for these sets: $\mathrm{img}(\rho)$ denotes the image of ρ, and $\ker(\rho)$ denotes the kernel of ρ.

Example 8.33. For any abelian group G and any integer m, the map that sends $a \in G$ to $ma \in G$ is clearly a group homomorphism from G into G, since for $a, b \in G$, we have $m(a + b) = ma + mb$. The image of this homomorphism is mG and the kernel is $G\{m\}$. We call this map the m-**multiplication map on** G. If G is written multiplicatively, we call this the m-**power map on** G, and its image is G^m. $\square$

Example 8.34. Consider the m-multiplication map on $\mathbb{Z}_n$. As we saw in Example 8.21, if $d := \gcd(n, m)$, the image $m\mathbb{Z}_n$ of this map is a subgroup of $\mathbb{Z}_n$ of order n/d, while its kernel $\mathbb{Z}_n\{m\}$ is a subgroup of order d. $\square$

Example 8.35. Let G be an abelian group and let a be a fixed element of G. Let $\rho : \mathbb{Z} \to G$ be the map that sends $z \in \mathbb{Z}$ to $za \in G$. It is easy to see that this is group homomorphism, since

$$\rho(z + z') = (z + z')a = za + z'a = \rho(z) + \rho(z'). \quad \square$$

Example 8.36. As a special case of the previous example, let n be a positive integer and let α be an element of $\mathbb{Z}_n^*$. Let $\rho : \mathbb{Z} \to \mathbb{Z}_n^*$ be the group homomorphism that sends $z \in \mathbb{Z}$ to $\alpha^z \in \mathbb{Z}_n^*$. If the multiplicative order of α is equal to k, then as discussed in §2.5, the image of ρ consists of the k distinct group elements $\alpha^0, \alpha^1, \ldots, \alpha^{k-1}$. The kernel of ρ consists of those integers a such that $\alpha^a = [1]_n$. Again by the discussion in §2.5, the kernel of ρ is equal to $k\mathbb{Z}$. $\square$

Example 8.37. We may generalize Example 8.35 as follows. Let G be an abelian group, and let $a_1, \ldots, a_k$ be fixed elements of G. Let $\rho : \mathbb{Z}^{\times k} \to G$

be the map that sends $(z_1, \ldots, z_k) \in \mathbb{Z}^{\times k}$ to $z_1 a_1 + \cdots + z_k a_k \in G$. The reader may easily verify that ρ is a group homomorphism. $\square$

***Example* 8.38.** As a special case of the previous example, let $p_1, \ldots, p_k$ be distinct primes, and let $\rho : \mathbb{Z}^{\times k} \to \mathbb{Q}^*$ be the group homomorphism that sends $(z_1, \ldots, z_k) \in \mathbb{Z}^{\times k}$ to $p_1^{z_1} \cdots p_k^{z_k} \in \mathbb{Q}^*$. The image of ρ is the set of all non-zero fractions whose numerator and denominator are divisible only by the primes $p_1, \ldots, p_k$. The kernel of ρ contains only the all-zero tuple $0^{\times k}$. $\square$

The following theorem summarizes some of the most important properties of group homomorphisms.

Theorem 8.20. *Let ρ be a group homomorphism from G to G'.*

(i) $\rho(0_G) = 0_{G'}$.

(ii) $\rho(-a) = -\rho(a)$ *for all $a \in G$.*

(iii) $\rho(na) = n\rho(a)$ *for all $n \in \mathbb{Z}$ and $a \in G$.*

(iv) *For any subgroup H of G, $\rho(H)$ is a subgroup of G'.*

(v) $\ker(\rho)$ *is a subgroup of G.*

(vi) *For all $a, b \in G$, $\rho(a) = \rho(b)$ if and only if $a \equiv b \pmod{\ker(\rho)}$.*

(vii) ρ *is injective if and only if $\ker(\rho) = \{0_G\}$.*

(viii) *For any subgroup H' of G', $\rho^{-1}(H')$ is a subgroup of G containing $\ker(\rho)$.*

Proof.

(i) We have
$$0_{G'} + \rho(0_G) = \rho(0_G) = \rho(0_G + 0_G) = \rho(0_G) + \rho(0_G).$$

Now cancel $\rho(0_G)$ from both sides (using part (i) of Theorem 8.3).

(ii) We have
$$0_{G'} = \rho(0_G) = \rho(a + (-a)) = \rho(a) + \rho(-a),$$

and hence $\rho(-a)$ is the inverse of $\rho(a)$.

(iii) For $n = 0$, this follows from part (i). For $n > 0$, this follows from the definitions by induction on n. For $n < 0$, this follows from the positive case and part (v) of Theorem 8.3.

(iv) For any $a, b \in H$, we have $a + b \in H$ and $-a \in H$; hence, $\rho(H)$ contains $\rho(a + b) = \rho(a) + \rho(b)$ and $\rho(-a) = -\rho(a)$.

(v) If $\rho(a) = 0_{G'}$ and $\rho(b) = 0_{G'}$, then $\rho(a+b) = \rho(a)+\rho(b) = 0_{G'}+0_{G'} = 0_{G'}$, and $\rho(-a) = -\rho(a) = -0_{G'} = 0_{G'}$.

(vi) $\rho(a) = \rho(b)$ iff $\rho(a) - \rho(b) = 0_{G'}$ iff $\rho(a - b) = 0_{G'}$ iff $a - b \in \ker(\rho)$ iff $a \equiv b \pmod{\ker(\rho)}$.

(vii) If ρ is injective, then in particular, $\rho^{-1}(\{0_{G'}\})$ cannot contain any other element besides 0_G. If ρ is not injective, then there exist two distinct elements $a, b \in G$ with $\rho(a) = \rho(b)$, and by part (vi), $\ker(\rho)$ contains the element $a - b$, which is non-zero.

(viii) This is very similar to part (v). If $\rho(a) \in H'$ and $\rho(b) \in H'$, then $\rho(a + b) = \rho(a) + \rho(b) \in H'$, and $\rho(-a) = -\rho(a) \in H'$. Moreover, since H' contains $0_{G'}$, we must have $\rho^{-1}(H') \supseteq \rho^{-1}(\{0_{G'}\}) = \ker(\rho)$.

$\square$

Part (vii) of the above theorem is particular useful: to check that a group homomorphism is injective, it suffices to determine if $\ker(\rho) = \{0_G\}$. Thus, the injectivity and surjectivity of a given group homomorphism $\rho : G \to G'$ may be characterized in terms of its kernel and image:

- ρ is injective if and only if $\ker(\rho) = \{0_G\}$;

- ρ is surjective if and only if $\operatorname{img}(\rho) = G'$.

The next three theorems establish some further convenient facts about group homomorphisms.

Theorem 8.21. *If $\rho : G \to G'$ and $\rho' : G' \to G''$ are group homomorphisms, then so is their composition $\rho' \circ \rho : G \to G''$.*

Proof. For $a, b \in G$, we have $\rho'(\rho(a + b)) = \rho'(\rho(a) + \rho(b)) = \rho'(\rho(a)) + \rho'(\rho(b))$. $\square$

Theorem 8.22. *Let $\rho_i : G \to G_i$, for $i = 1, \ldots, n$, be group homomorphisms. Then the map $\rho : G \to G_1 \times \cdots \times G_n$ that sends $a \in G$ to $(\rho_1(a), \ldots, \rho_n(a))$ is a group homomorphism with kernel $\ker(\rho_1) \cap \cdots \cap \ker(\rho_n)$.*

Proof. Exercise. $\square$

Theorem 8.23. *Let $\rho_i : G_i \to G$, for $i = 1, \ldots, n$, be group homomorphisms. Then the map $\rho : G_1 \times \cdots \times G_n \to G$ that sends $(a_1, \ldots, a_n)$ to $\rho_1(a_1) + \cdots + \rho_n(a_n)$ is a group homomorphism.*

Proof. Exercise. $\square$

Consider a group homomorphism $\rho : G \to G'$. If ρ is bijective, then ρ is called a **group isomorphism** of G with G'. If such a group isomorphism ρ exists, we say that G **is isomorphic to** G', and write $G \cong G'$. Moreover, if $G = G'$, then ρ is called a **group automorphism** on G.

Theorem 8.24. *If ρ is a group isomorphism of G with G', then the inverse function ρ^{-1} is a group isomorphism of G' with G.*

Proof. For $a', b' \in G'$, we have

$$\rho(\rho^{-1}(a') + \rho^{-1}(b')) = \rho(\rho^{-1}(a')) + \rho(\rho^{-1}(b')) = a' + b',$$

and hence $\rho^{-1}(a') + \rho^{-1}(b') = \rho^{-1}(a' + b')$. $\square$

Because of this theorem, if G is isomorphic to G', we may simply say that "G and G' are isomorphic."

We stress that a group isomorphism of G with G' is essentially just a "renaming" of the group elements — all structural properties of the group are preserved, even though the two groups might look quite different superficially.

Example 8.39. As was shown in Example 8.30, the quotient group G/H discussed in that example is isomorphic to $\mathbb{Z}_3$. As was shown in Example 8.31, the quotient group $\mathbb{Z}_{15}^*/(\mathbb{Z}_{15}^*)^2$ is isomorphic to $\mathbb{Z}_2 \times \mathbb{Z}_2$. As was shown in Example 8.32, the quotient group $\mathbb{Z}_5^*/(\mathbb{Z}_5^*)^2$ is isomorphic to $\mathbb{Z}_2$. $\square$

Example 8.40. If $\gcd(n, m) = 1$, then the m-multiplication map on $\mathbb{Z}_n$ is a group automorphism. $\square$

The following four theorems provide important constructions of group homomorphisms.

Theorem 8.25. *If H is a subgroup of an abelian group G, then the map $\rho : G \to G/H$ given by $\rho(a) = a + H$ is a surjective group homomorphism whose kernel is H.*

Proof. This really just follows from the definition of the quotient group. To verify that ρ is a group homomorphism, note that

$$\rho(a + b) = (a + b) + H = (a + H) + (b + H) = \rho(a) + \rho(b).$$

Surjectivity follows from the fact that every coset is of the form $a + H$ for some $a \in G$. The fact that $\ker(\rho) = H$ follows from the fact that $a + H$ is the coset of H in G containing a, and so this is equal to H if and only if $a \in H$. $\square$

The homomorphism of the above theorem is called the **natural map** from G to G/H.

Theorem 8.26. *Let ρ be a group homomorphism from G into G'. Then the map $\bar{\rho} : G/\ker(\rho) \to \operatorname{img}(\rho)$ that sends the coset $a + \ker(\rho)$ for $a \in G$ to $\rho(a)$ is unambiguously defined and is a group isomorphism of $G/\ker(\rho)$ with $\operatorname{img}(\rho)$.*

Proof. Let $K := \ker(\rho)$. To see that the definition $\bar{\rho}$ is unambiguous, note that if $a \equiv a' \pmod{K}$, then by part (vi) of Theorem 8.20, $\rho(a) = \rho(a')$. To see that $\bar{\rho}$ is a group homomorphism, note that

$$\bar{\rho}((a + K) + (b + K)) = \bar{\rho}((a + b) + K) = \rho(a + b) = \rho(a) + \rho(b)$$
$$= \bar{\rho}(a + K) + \bar{\rho}(b + K).$$

It is clear that $\bar{\rho}$ maps onto $\operatorname{img}(\rho)$, since any element of $\operatorname{img}(\rho)$ is of the form $\rho(a)$ for some $a \in G$, and the map $\bar{\rho}$ sends $a + K$ to $\rho(a)$. Finally, to see that $\bar{\rho}$ is injective, suppose that $\bar{\rho}(a + K) = 0_{G'}$; then we have $\rho(a) = 0_{G'}$, and hence $a \in K$; from this, it follows that $a + K$ is equal to K, which is the zero element of G/K. Injectivity then follows from part (vii) of Theorem 8.20, applied to $\bar{\rho}$. $\square$

The following theorem is an easy generalization of the previous one.

Theorem 8.27. *Let ρ be a group homomorphism from G into G'. Then for any subgroup H contained in $\ker(\rho)$, the map $\bar{\rho} : G/H \to \operatorname{img}(\rho)$ that sends the coset $a + H$ for $a \in G$ to $\rho(a)$ is unambiguously defined and is a group homomorphism from G/H onto $\operatorname{img}(\rho)$ with kernel $\ker(\rho)/H$.*

Proof. Exercise—just mimic the proof of the previous theorem. $\square$

Theorem 8.28. *Let G be an abelian group with subgroups H_1, H_2. Then the map $\rho : H_1 \times H_2 \to H_1 + H_2$ that sends (h_1, h_2) to $h_1 + h_2$ is a surjective group homomorphism. Moreover, if $H_1 \cap H_2 = \{0_G\}$, then ρ is a group isomorphism of $H_1 \times H_2$ with $H_1 + H_2$.*

Proof. The fact that ρ is a group homomorphism is just a special case of Theorem 8.23, applied to the inclusion maps $\rho_1 : H_1 \to H_1 + H_2$ and $\rho_2 : H_2 \to H_1 + H_2$. One can also simply verify this by direct calculation: for $h_1, h_1' \in H_1$ and $h_2, h_2' \in H_2$, we have

$$\rho(h_1 + h_1', h_2 + h_2') = (h_1 + h_1') + (h_2 + h_2')$$
$$= (h_1 + h_2) + (h_1' + h_2')$$
$$= \rho(h_1, h_2) + \rho(h_1', \rho_2').$$

Moreover, from the definition of $H_1 + H_2$, we see that ρ is in fact surjective.

Now assume that $H_1 \cap H_2 = \{0_G\}$. To see that ρ is injective, it suffices to show that $\ker(\rho)$ is trivial; that is, it suffices to show that for all $h_1 \in H_1$ and $h_2 \in H_2$, $h_1 + h_2 = 0_G$ implies $h_1 = 0_G$ and $h_2 = 0_G$. But $h_1 + h_2 = 0_G$ implies $h_1 = -h_2 \in H_2$, and hence $h_1 \in H_1 \cap H_2 = \{0_G\}$, and so $h_1 = 0_G$. Similarly, one shows that $h_2 = 0_G$, and that finishes the proof. $\square$

Example 8.41. For $n \geq 1$, the natural map ρ from $\mathbb{Z}$ to $\mathbb{Z}_n$ sends $a \in \mathbb{Z}$ to the residue class $[a]_n$. This map is a surjective group homomorphism with kernel $n\mathbb{Z}$. $\square$

Example 8.42. We may restate the Chinese remainder theorem (Theorem 2.8) in more algebraic terms. Let $n_1, \ldots, n_k$ be pairwise relatively prime, positive integers. Consider the map from the group $\mathbb{Z}$ to the group $\mathbb{Z}_{n_1} \times \cdots \times \mathbb{Z}_{n_k}$ that sends $x \in \mathbb{Z}$ to $([x]_{n_1}, \ldots, [x]_{n_k})$. It is easy to see that this map is a group homomorphism (this follows from Example 8.41 and Theorem 8.22). In our new language, the Chinese remainder theorem says that this group homomorphism is surjective and that the kernel is $n\mathbb{Z}$, where $n = \prod_{i=1}^{k} n_i$. Therefore, by Theorem 8.26, the map that sends $[x]_n \in \mathbb{Z}_n$ to $([x]_{n_1}, \ldots, [x]_{n_k})$ is a group isomorphism of the group $\mathbb{Z}_n$ with the group $\mathbb{Z}_{n_1} \times \cdots \times \mathbb{Z}_{n_k}$. $\square$

Example 8.43. Let n_1, n_2 be positive integers with $n_1 > 1$ and $n_1 \mid n_2$. Then the map $\bar{\rho} : \mathbb{Z}_{n_2} \to \mathbb{Z}_{n_1}$ that sends $[a]_{n_2}$ to $[a]_{n_1}$ is a surjective group homomorphism, and $[a]_{n_2} \in \ker(\bar{\rho})$ if and only if $n_1 \mid a$; that is, $\ker(\bar{\rho}) = n_1 \mathbb{Z}_{n_2}$. The map $\bar{\rho}$ can also be viewed as the map obtained by applying Theorem 8.27 with the natural map ρ from $\mathbb{Z}$ to $\mathbb{Z}_{n_1}$ and the subgroup $n_2\mathbb{Z}$ of $\mathbb{Z}$, which is contained in $\ker(\rho) = n_1\mathbb{Z}$. $\square$

Example 8.44. Let us reconsider Example 8.21. Let n be a positive integer, let $m \in \mathbb{Z}$, and consider the subgroup $m\mathbb{Z}_n$ of the additive group $\mathbb{Z}_n$. Let $\rho_1 : \mathbb{Z} \to \mathbb{Z}_n$ be the natural map, and let $\rho_2 : \mathbb{Z}_n \to \mathbb{Z}_n$ be the m-multiplication map. The composed map $\rho = \rho_2 \circ \rho_1$ from $\mathbb{Z}$ to $\mathbb{Z}_n$ is also a group homomorphism. The kernel of ρ consists of those integers a such that $am \equiv 0 \pmod{n}$, and so Theorem 2.7 implies that $\ker(\rho) = (n/d)\mathbb{Z}$, where $d := \gcd(m, n)$. The image of ρ is $m\mathbb{Z}_n$. Theorem 8.26 therefore implies that the map $\bar{\rho} : \mathbb{Z}_{n/d} \to m\mathbb{Z}_n$ that sends $[a]_{n/d}$ to $[ma]_n$ is a group isomorphism. $\square$

EXERCISE 8.10. Verify that the "is isomorphic to" relation on abelian groups is an equivalence relation; that is, for all abelian groups G_1, G_2, G_3, we have:

(a) $G_1 \cong G_1$;

(b) $G_1 \cong G_2$ implies $G_2 \cong G_1$;

(c) $G_1 \cong G_2$ and $G_2 \cong G_3$ implies $G_1 \cong G_3$.

EXERCISE 8.11. Let G_1, G_2 be abelian groups, and let $\rho : G_1 \times G_2 \to G_1$ be the map that sends $(a_1, a_2) \in G_1 \times G_2$ to $a_1 \in G_1$. Show that ρ is a surjective group homomorphism whose kernel is $\{0_{G_1}\} \times G_2$.

EXERCISE 8.12. Suppose that G, G_1, and G_2 are abelian groups, and that $\rho : G_1 \times G_2 \to G$ is a group isomorphism. Let $H_1 := \rho(G_1 \times \{0_{G_2}\})$ and $H_2 := \rho(\{0_{G_1}\} \times G_2)$. Show that

(a) H_1 and H_2 are subgroups of G,

(b) $H_1 + H_2 = G$, and

(c) $H_1 \cap H_2 = \{0_G\}$.

EXERCISE 8.13. Let ρ be a group homomorphism from G into G'. Show that for any subgroup H of G, we have $\rho^{-1}(\rho(H)) = H + \ker(\rho)$.

EXERCISE 8.14. Let ρ be a group homomorphism from G into G'. Show that the subgroups of G containing $\ker(\rho)$ are in one-to-one correspondence with the subgroups of $\text{img}(\rho)$, where the subgroup H of G containing $\ker(\rho)$ corresponds to the subgroup $\rho(H)$ of $\text{img}(\rho)$.

EXERCISE 8.15. Let G be an abelian group with subgroups $H \subseteq H'$.

(a) Show that we have a group isomorphism

$$G/H' \cong \frac{G/H}{H'/H}.$$

(b) Show that if $[G : H]$ is finite (even though G itself may have infinite order), then $[G : H] = [G : H'] \cdot [H' : H]$.

EXERCISE 8.16. Show that if $G = G_1 \times G_2$ for abelian groups G_1 and G_2, and H_1 is a subgroup of G_1 and H_2 is a subgroup of G_2, then $G/(H_1 \times H_2) \cong G_1/H_1 \times G_2/H_2$.

EXERCISE 8.17. Let ρ_1 and ρ_2 be group homomorphisms from G into G'. Show that the map $\rho : G \to G'$ that sends $a \in G$ to $\rho_1(a) + \rho_2(a) \in G'$ is also a group homomorphism.

EXERCISE 8.18. Let G and G' be abelian groups. Consider the set H of all group homomorphisms $\rho : G \to G'$. This set is non-empty, since the map that sends everything in G to $0_{G'}$ is trivially an element of H. We may define an addition operation on H as follows: for $\rho_1, \rho_2 \in H$, let $\rho_1 + \rho_2$ be the map $\rho : G \to G'$ that sends $a \in G$ to $\rho_1(a) + \rho_2(a)$. By the previous exercise, ρ is also in H, and so this addition operation is a well-defined binary operation on H. Show that H, together with this addition operation, forms an abelian group.

EXERCISE 8.19. This exercise develops an alternative, "quick and dirty" proof of the Chinese remainder theorem, based on group theory and a counting argument. Let $n_1, \ldots, n_k$ be pairwise relatively prime, positive integers, and let $n := n_1 \cdots n_k$. Consider the map $\rho : \mathbb{Z} \to \mathbb{Z}_{n_1} \times \cdots \times \mathbb{Z}_{n_k}$ that sends $x \in \mathbb{Z}$ to $([x]_{n_1}, \ldots, [x]_{n_k})$.

   (a) Using the results of Example 8.41 and Theorem 8.22, show (directly) that ρ is a group homomorphism with kernel $n\mathbb{Z}$.

   (b) Using Theorem 8.26, conclude that the map $\bar\rho$ given by that theorem, which sends $[x]_n$ to $([x]_{n_1}, \ldots, [x]_{n_k})$, is an injective group homomorphism from $\mathbb{Z}_n$ into $\mathbb{Z}_{n_1} \times \cdots \times \mathbb{Z}_{n_k}$.

   (c) Since $|\mathbb{Z}_n| = n = |\mathbb{Z}_{n_1} \times \cdots \times \mathbb{Z}_{n_k}|$, conclude that the map $\bar\rho$ is surjective, and so is an isomorphism between $\mathbb{Z}_n$ and $\mathbb{Z}_{n_1} \times \cdots \times \mathbb{Z}_{n_k}$.

Although simple, this proof does not give us an explicit formula for computing $\bar\rho^{-1}$.

EXERCISE 8.20. Let p be an odd prime; consider the squaring map on $\mathbb{Z}_p^*$.

   (a) Using Exercise 2.5, show that the kernel of the squaring map on $\mathbb{Z}_p^*$ consists of the two elements $[\pm 1]_p$.

   (b) Using the results of this section, conclude that there are $(p-1)/2$ squares in $\mathbb{Z}_p^*$, each of which has precisely two square roots in $\mathbb{Z}_p^*$.

EXERCISE 8.21. Consider the group homomorphism $\rho : \mathbb{Z} \times \mathbb{Z} \times \mathbb{Z} \to \mathbb{Q}^*$ that sends (a, b, c) to $2^a 3^b 12^c$. Describe the image and kernel of ρ.

EXERCISE 8.22. This exercise develops some simple — but extremely useful — connections between group theory and probability theory. Let $\rho : G \to G'$ be a group homomorphism, where G and G' are finite abelian groups.

   (a) Show that if g is a random variable with the uniform distribution on G, then $\rho(g)$ is a random variable with the uniform distribution on $\mathrm{img}(\rho)$.

   (b) Show that if g is a random variable with the uniform distribution on G, and g' is a fixed element in $\mathrm{img}(\rho)$, then the conditional distribution of g, given that $\rho(g) = g'$, is the uniform distribution on $\rho^{-1}(\{g'\})$.

   (c) Show that if g_1' is a fixed element of G', g_1 is uniformly distributed over $\rho^{-1}(\{g_1'\})$, g_2' is a fixed element of G', and g_2 is a fixed element of $\rho^{-1}(\{g_2'\})$, then $g_1 + g_2$ is uniformly distributed over $\rho^{-1}(\{g_1' + g_2'\})$.

(d) Show that if g_1' is a fixed element of G', g_1 is uniformly distributed over $\rho^{-1}(\{g_1'\})$, g_2' is a fixed element of G', g_2 is uniformly distributed over $\rho^{-1}(\{g_2'\})$, and g_1 and g_2 are independent, then $g_1 + g_2$ is uniformly distributed over $\rho^{-1}(\{g_1' + g_2'\})$.

8.5 Cyclic groups

Let G be an abelian group. For $a \in G$, define $\langle a \rangle := \{za : z \in \mathbb{Z}\}$. It is easy to see that $\langle a \rangle$ is a subgroup of G—indeed, it is the image of the group homomorphism discussed in Example 8.35. Moreover, $\langle a \rangle$ is the smallest subgroup of G containing a; that is, $\langle a \rangle$ contains a, and any subgroup H of G that contains a must also contain $\langle a \rangle$. The subgroup $\langle a \rangle$ is called **the subgroup (of G) generated by** a. Also, one defines the **order** of a to be the order of the subgroup $\langle a \rangle$.

More generally, for $a_1, \ldots, a_k \in G$, we define $\langle a_1, \ldots, a_k \rangle := \{z_1 a_1 + \cdots + z_k a_k : z_1, \ldots, z_k \in \mathbb{Z}\}$. One also verifies that $\langle a_1, \ldots, a_k \rangle$ is a subgroup of G, and indeed, is the smallest subgroup of G that contains $a_1, \ldots, a_k$. The subgroup $\langle a_1, \ldots, a_k \rangle$ is called the **subgroup (of G) generated by** $a_1, \ldots, a_k$.

An abelian group G is said to be **cyclic** if $G = \langle a \rangle$ for some $a \in G$, in which case, a is called a **generator for** G. An abelian group G is said to be **finitely generated** if $G = \langle a_1, \ldots, a_k \rangle$ for some $a_1, \ldots, a_k \in G$.

Multiplicative notation: if G is written multiplicatively, then $\langle a \rangle := \{a^z : z \in \mathbb{Z}\}$, and $\langle a_1, \ldots, a_k \rangle := \{a_1^{z_1} \cdots a_k^{z_k} : z_1, \ldots, z_k \in \mathbb{Z}\}$; also, for emphasis and clarity, we use the term **multiplicative order of** a.

Classification of cyclic groups. We can very easily classify all cyclic groups. Suppose that G is a cyclic group with generator a. Consider the map $\rho : \mathbb{Z} \to G$ that sends $z \in \mathbb{Z}$ to $za \in G$. As discussed in Example 8.35, this map is a group homomorphism, and since a is a generator for G, it must be surjective.

Case 1: $\ker(\rho) = \{0\}$. In this case, ρ is an isomorphism of $\mathbb{Z}$ with G.

Case 2: $\ker(\rho) \neq \{0\}$. In this case, since $\ker(\rho)$ is a subgroup of $\mathbb{Z}$ different from $\{0\}$, by Theorem 8.8, it must be of the form $n\mathbb{Z}$ for some $n > 0$. Hence, by Theorem 8.26, the map $\bar{\rho} : \mathbb{Z}_n \to G$ that sends $[z]_n$ to za is an isomorphism of $\mathbb{Z}_n$ with G.

So we see that a cyclic group is isomorphic either to the additive group $\mathbb{Z}$

or the additive group $\mathbb{Z}_n$, for some positive integer n. We have thus classified all cyclic groups "up to isomorphism." From this classification, we obtain:

Theorem 8.29. *Let G be an abelian group and let $a \in G$.*

   (i) If there exists a positive integer m such that $ma = 0_G$, then the least such positive integer n is the order of a; in this case, we have:

        – *for any integer z, $za = 0_G$ if and only if $n \mid z$, and more generally, for integers z_1, z_2, $z_1 a = z_2 a$ if and only if $z_1 \equiv z_2 \pmod{n}$;*

        – *the subgroup $\langle a \rangle$ consists of the n distinct elements*

$$0 \cdot a, 1 \cdot a, \ldots, (n-1) \cdot a.$$

  (ii) If G has finite order, then $|G| \cdot a = 0_G$ and the order of a divides $|G|$.

Proof. Part (i) follows immediately from the above classification, along with part (vi) of Theorem 8.20. Part (ii) follows from part (i), along with Lagrange's theorem (Theorem 8.16), since $\langle a \rangle$ is a subgroup of G. $\square$

***Example* 8.45.** The additive group $\mathbb{Z}$ is a cyclic group generated by 1. The only other generator is -1. More generally, the subgroup of $\mathbb{Z}$ generated by $m \in \mathbb{Z}$ is $m\mathbb{Z}$. $\square$

***Example* 8.46.** The additive group $\mathbb{Z}_n$ is a cyclic group generated by $[1]_n$. More generally, for $m \in \mathbb{Z}$, the subgroup of $\mathbb{Z}_n$ generated by $[m]_n$ is equal to $m\mathbb{Z}_n$, which by Example 8.21 has order $n/\gcd(m, n)$. In particular, $[m]_n$ generates $\mathbb{Z}_n$ if and only if m is relatively prime to n, and hence, the number of generators of $\mathbb{Z}_n$ is $\phi(n)$. $\square$

***Example* 8.47.** Consider the additive group $G := \mathbb{Z}_{n_1} \times \mathbb{Z}_{n_2}$, and let $\alpha := ([1]_{n_1}, [1]_{n_2}) \in \mathbb{Z}_{n_1} \times \mathbb{Z}_{n_2}$. For $m \in \mathbb{Z}$, we have $m\alpha = 0_G$ if and only if $n_1 \mid m$ and $n_2 \mid m$. This implies that α generates a subgroup of G of order $\mathrm{lcm}(n_1, n_2)$.

    Suppose that $\gcd(n_1, n_2) = 1$. From the above discussion, it follows that G is cyclic of order $n_1 n_2$. One could also see this directly using the Chinese remainder theorem: as we saw in Example 8.42, the Chinese remainder theorem gives us an isomorphism of G with the cyclic group $\mathbb{Z}_{n_1 n_2}$.

    Conversely, if $d := \gcd(n_1, n_2) > 1$, then all elements of $\mathbb{Z}_{n_1} \times \mathbb{Z}_{n_2}$ have order dividing $n_1 n_2/d$, and so $\mathbb{Z}_{n_1} \times \mathbb{Z}_{n_2}$ cannot be cyclic. $\square$

***Example* 8.48.** For $a, n \in \mathbb{Z}$ with $n > 0$ and $\gcd(a, n) = 1$, the definition in this section of the multiplicative order of $\alpha := [a]_n \in \mathbb{Z}_n^*$ is consistent with that given in §2.5, and is also the same as the multiplicative order of a modulo n. Indeed, Euler's theorem (Theorem 2.15) is just a special case of part (ii) of Theorem 8.29. Also, α is a generator for $\mathbb{Z}_n^*$ if and only if a is a primitive root modulo n. $\square$

Example 8.49. As we saw in Example 8.24, all elements of $\mathbb{Z}_{15}^*$ have multiplicative order dividing 4, and since $\mathbb{Z}_{15}^*$ has order 8, we conclude that $\mathbb{Z}_{15}^*$ is not cyclic. $\square$

Example 8.50. The group $\mathbb{Z}_5^*$ is cyclic, with $[2]$ being a generator:

$$[2]^2 = [4] = [-1], \quad [2]^3 = [-2], \quad [2]^4 = [1]. \quad \square$$

Example 8.51. Based on the calculations in Example 2.6, we may conclude that $\mathbb{Z}_7^*$ is cyclic, with both $[3]$ and $[5]$ being generators. $\square$

The following two theorems completely characterize the subgroup structure of cyclic groups. Actually, we have already proven the results in these two theorems, but nevertheless, these results deserve special emphasis.

Theorem 8.30. *Let G be a cyclic group of infinite order.*

   (i) *G is isomorphic to $\mathbb{Z}$.*

   (ii) *The subgroups of G are in one-to-one correspondence with the non-negative integers, where each such integer m corresponds to the cyclic group mG.*

   (iii) *For any two non-negative integers m, m', $mG \subseteq m'G$ if and only if $m' \mid m$.*

Proof. That $G \cong \mathbb{Z}$ was established in our classification of cyclic groups, it suffices to prove the other statements of the theorem for $G = \mathbb{Z}$. It is clear that for any integer m, the subgroup $m\mathbb{Z}$ is cyclic, as m is a generator. This fact, together with Theorem 8.8, establish all the other statements. $\square$

Theorem 8.31. *Let G be a cyclic group of finite order n.*

   (i) *G is isomorphic to $\mathbb{Z}_n$.*

   (ii) *The subgroups of G are in one-to-one correspondence with the positive divisors of n, where each such divisor d corresponds to the subgroup dG; moreover, dG is a cyclic group of order n/d.*

   (iii) *For each positive divisor d of n, we have $dG = G\{n/d\}$; that is, the kernel of the (n/d)-multiplication map is equal to the image of the d-multiplication map; in particular, $G\{n/d\}$ has order n/d.*

(iv) *For any two positive divisors d, d' of n, we have $dG \subseteq d'G$ if and only if $d' \mid d$.*

(v) *For any positive divisor d of n, the number of elements of order d in G is $\phi(d)$.*

(vi) *For any integer m, we have $mG = dG$ and $G\{m\} = G\{d\}$, where $d := \gcd(m, n)$.*

Proof. That $G \cong \mathbb{Z}_n$ was established in our classification of cyclic groups, and so it suffices to prove the other statements of the theorem for $G = \mathbb{Z}_n$.

The one-to-one correspondence in part (ii) was established in Theorem 8.9. The fact that $d\mathbb{Z}_n$ is cyclic of order n/d can be seen in a number of ways; indeed, in Example 8.44 we constructed an isomorphism of $\mathbb{Z}_{n/d}$ with $d\mathbb{Z}_n$.

Part (iii) was established in Example 8.21.

Part (iv) was established in Theorem 8.9.

For part (v), the elements of order d in $\mathbb{Z}_n$ are all contained in $\mathbb{Z}_n\{d\}$, and so the number of such elements is equal to the number of generators of $\mathbb{Z}_n\{d\}$. The group $\mathbb{Z}_n\{d\}$ is cyclic of order d, and so is isomorphic to $\mathbb{Z}_d$, and as we saw in Example 8.46, this group has $\phi(d)$ generators.

Part (vi) was established in Example 8.21. $\square$

Since cyclic groups are in some sense the simplest kind of abelian group, it is nice to have some sufficient conditions under which a group must be cyclic. The following theorems provide such conditions.

Theorem 8.32. *If G is an abelian group of prime order, then G is cyclic.*

Proof. Let $|G| = p$. Let $a \in G$ with $a \neq 0_G$, and let k be the order of a. As the order of an element divides the order of the group, we have $k \mid p$, and so $k = 1$ or $k = p$. Since $a \neq 0_G$, we must have $k \neq 1$, and so $k = p$, which implies that a generates G. $\square$

Theorem 8.33. *If G_1 and G_2 are finite cyclic groups of relatively prime order, then $G_1 \times G_2$ is also cyclic.*

Proof. This follows from Example 8.47, together with our classification of cyclic groups. $\square$

Theorem 8.34. *Any subgroup of a cyclic group is cyclic.*

Proof. This is just a restatement of part (ii) of Theorem 8.30 and part (ii) of Theorem 8.31 $\square$

Theorem 8.35. *If $\rho : G \to G'$ is a group homomorphism, and G is cyclic, then $\mathrm{img}(G)$ is cyclic.*

Proof. If G is generated by a, then it is easy to see that the image of ρ is generated by $\rho(a)$. $\square$

The next three theorems are often useful in calculating the order of a group element.

Theorem 8.36. *Let G be an abelian group, let $a \in G$ be of finite order n, and let m be an arbitrary integer. Then the order of ma is $n/\gcd(m, n)$.*

Proof. By our classification of cyclic groups, we know that the subgroup $\langle a \rangle$ is isomorphic to $\mathbb{Z}_n$, where under this isomorphism, a corresponds to $[1]_n$ and ma corresponds to $[m]_n$. The theorem then follows from the observations in Example 8.46. $\square$

Theorem 8.37. *Suppose that a is an element of an abelian group, and for some prime p and integer $e \geq 1$, we have $p^e a = 0_G$ and $p^{e-1} a \neq 0_G$. Then a has order p^e.*

Proof. If m is the order of a, then since $p^e a = 0_G$, we have $m \mid p^e$. So $m = p^f$ for some $f = 0, \ldots, e$. If $f < e$, then $p^{e-1} a = 0_G$, contradicting the assumption that $p^{e-1} a \neq 0_G$. $\square$

Theorem 8.38. *Suppose G is an abelian group with $a_1, a_2 \in G$ such that a_1 is of finite order n_1, a_2 is of finite order n_2, and $\gcd(n_1, n_2) = 1$. Then the order of $a_1 + a_2$ is $n_1 n_2$.*

Proof. Let m be the order of $a_1 + a_2$. It is clear that $n_1 n_2 (a_1 + a_2) = 0_G$, and hence m divides $n_1 n_2$.

We claim that $\langle a_1 \rangle \cap \langle a_2 \rangle = \{0_G\}$. To see this, suppose $a \in \langle a_1 \rangle \cap \langle a_2 \rangle$. Then since $a \in \langle a_1 \rangle$, the order of a must divide n_1. Likewise, since $a \in \langle a_2 \rangle$, the order of a must divide n_2. From the assumption that $\gcd(n_1, n_2) = 1$, it follows that the order of a must be 1, meaning that $a = 0_G$.

Since $m(a_1 + a_2) = 0_G$, it follows that $ma_1 = -ma_2$. This implies that ma_1 belongs to $\langle a_2 \rangle$, and since ma_1 trivially belongs to $\langle a_1 \rangle$, we see that ma_1 belongs to $\langle a_1 \rangle \cap \langle a_2 \rangle$. From the above claim, it follows that $ma_1 = 0_G$, and hence n_1 divides m. By a symmetric argument, we see that n_2 divides m. Again, since $\gcd(n_1, n_2) = 1$, we see that $n_1 n_2$ divides m. $\square$

For an abelian group G, we say that an integer k **kills** G if $kG = \{0_G\}$. Consider the set $\mathcal{K}_G$ of integers that kill G. Evidently, $\mathcal{K}_G$ is a subgroup of $\mathbb{Z}$, and hence of the form $m\mathbb{Z}$ for a uniquely determined non-negative integer m. This integer m is called the **exponent** of G. If $m \neq 0$, then we see that m is the least positive integer that kills G.

We first state some basic properties.

Theorem 8.39. *Let G be an abelian group of exponent m.*

   (i) For any integer k such that $kG = \{0_G\}$, we have $m \mid k$.

   (ii) If G has finite order, then m divides $|G|$.

   (iii) If $m \neq 0$, then for any $a \in G$, the order of a is finite, and the order of a divides m.

   (iv) If G is cyclic, then the exponent of G is 0 if G is infinite, and is $|G|$ is G is finite.

Proof. Exercise. $\square$

The next two theorems develop some crucial properties about the structure of finite abelian groups.

Theorem 8.40. *If a finite abelian group G has exponent m, then G contains an element of order m. In particular, a finite abelian group is cyclic if and only if its order equals its exponent.*

Proof. The second statement follows immediately from the first. For the first statement, assume that $m > 1$, and let $m = \prod_{i=1}^{r} p_i^{e_i}$ be the prime factorization of m.

First, we claim that for each $i = 1, \ldots, r$, there exists $a_i \in G$ such that $(m/p_i)a_i \neq 0_G$. Suppose the claim were false: then for some i, $(m/p_i)a = 0_G$ for all $a \in G$; however, this contradicts the minimality property in the definition of the exponent m. That proves the claim.

Let $a_1, \ldots, a_r$ be as in the above claim. Then by Theorem 8.37, $(m/p_i^{e_i})a_i$ has order $p_i^{e_i}$ for each $i = 1, \ldots, r$. Finally, by Theorem 8.38, the group element

$$(m/p_1^{e_1})a_1 + \cdots + (m/p_r^{e_r})a_r$$

has order m. $\square$

Theorem 8.41. *Let G be a finite abelian group of order n. If p is a prime dividing n, then G contains an element of order p.*

Proof. We can prove this by induction on n.

If $n = 1$, then the theorem is vacuously true.

Now assume $n > 1$ and that the theorem holds for all groups of order strictly less than n. Let a be any non-zero element of G, and let m be the order of a. Since a is non-zero, we must have $m > 1$. If $p \mid m$, then $(m/p)a$ is an element of order p, and we are done. So assume that $p \nmid m$ and consider the quotient group G/H, where H is the subgroup of G generated by a. Since H has order m, G/H has order n/m, which is strictly less than n, and since $p \nmid m$, we must have $p \mid (n/m)$. So we can apply the induction hypothesis to the group G/H and the prime p, which says that there is an element $b \in G$ such that $b + H \in G/H$ has order p. If ℓ is the order of b, then $\ell b = 0_G$, and so $\ell b \equiv 0_G \pmod{H}$, which implies that the order of $b + H$ divides ℓ. Thus, $p \mid \ell$, and so $(\ell/p)b$ is an element of G of order p. $\square$

As a corollary, we have:

Theorem 8.42. *Let G be a finite abelian group. Then the primes dividing the exponent of G are the same as the primes dividing its order.*

Proof. Since the exponent divides the order, any prime dividing the exponent must divide the order. Conversely, if a prime p divides the order, then since there is an element of order p in the group, the exponent must be divisible by p. $\square$

EXERCISE 8.23. Let G be an abelian group of order n, and let m be an integer. Show that $mG = G$ if and only if $\gcd(m, n) = 1$.

EXERCISE 8.24. Let G be an abelian group of order mm', where $\gcd(m, m') = 1$. Consider the map $\rho : mG \times m'G$ to G that sends (a, b) to $a + b$. Show that ρ is a group isomorphism.

EXERCISE 8.25. Let G be an abelian group, $a \in G$, and $m \in \mathbb{Z}$, such that $m > 0$ and $ma = 0_G$. Let $m = p_1^{e_1} \cdots p_r^{e_r}$ be the prime factorization of m. For $i = 1, \ldots, r$, let f_i be the largest non-negative integer such that $f_i \le e_i$ and $m/p_i^{f_i} \cdot a = 0_G$. Show that the order of a is equal to $p_1^{e_1 - f_1} \cdots p_r^{e_r - f_r}$.

EXERCISE 8.26. Show that for finite abelian groups G_1, G_2 whose exponents are m_1 and m_2, the exponent of $G_1 \times G_2$ is $\mathrm{lcm}(m_1, m_2)$.

EXERCISE 8.27. Give an example of an abelian group G whose exponent is zero, but where every element of G has finite order.

EXERCISE 8.28. Show how Theorem 2.11 easily follows from Theorem 8.31.

8.6 The structure of finite abelian groups (∗)

We next state a theorem that classifies all finite abelian groups up to isomorphism.

Theorem 8.43 (Fundamental theorem of finite abelian groups). *A finite abelian group (with more than one element) is isomorphic to a direct* *product of cyclic groups*

$$\mathbb{Z}_{p_1^{e_1}} \times \cdots \times \mathbb{Z}_{p_r^{e_r}},$$

where the p_i are primes (not necessarily distinct) and the e_i are positive integers. This direct product of cyclic groups is unique up to the order of the factors.

An alternative statement of this theorem is the following:

Theorem 8.44. *A finite abelian group (with more than one element) is isomorphic to a direct product of cyclic groups*

$$\mathbb{Z}_{m_1} \times \cdots \times \mathbb{Z}_{m_t},$$

where each $m_i > 1$, and where for $i = 1, \ldots, t-1$, we have $m_i \mid m_{i+1}$. Moreover, the integers $m_1, \ldots, m_t$ are uniquely determined, and m_t is the exponent of the group.

EXERCISE 8.29. Show that Theorems 8.43 and 8.44 are equivalent; that is, show that each one implies the other. To do this, give a natural one-to-one correspondence between sequences of prime powers (as in Theorem 8.43) and sequences of integers $m_1, \ldots, m_t$ (as in Theorem 8.44), and also make use of Example 8.47.

EXERCISE 8.30. Using the fundamental theorem of finite abelian groups (either form), give short and simple proofs of Theorems 8.40 and 8.41.

We now prove Theorem 8.44, which we break into two lemmas, the first of which proves the existence part of the theorem, and the second of which proves the uniqueness part.

Lemma 8.45. *A finite abelian group (with more than one element) is isomorphic to a direct product of cyclic groups*

$$\mathbb{Z}_{m_1} \times \cdots \times \mathbb{Z}_{m_t},$$

where each $m_i > 1$, and where for $i = 1, \ldots, t-1$, we have $m_i \mid m_{i+1}$; moreover, m_t is the exponent of the group.

Proof. Let G be a finite abelian group with more than one element, and let m be the exponent of G. By Theorem 8.40, there exists an element $a \in G$ of order m. Let $A = \langle a \rangle$. Then $A \cong \mathbb{Z}_m$. Now, if $A = G$, the lemma is proved. So assume that $A \subsetneq G$.

We will show that there exists a subgroup B of G such that $G = A + B$ and $A \cap B = \{0\}$. From this, Theorem 8.28 gives us an isomorphism of G

with $A \times B$. Moreover, the exponent of B is clearly a divisor of m, and so the lemma will follow by induction (on the order of the group).

So it suffices to show the existence of a subgroup B as above. We prove this by contradiction. Suppose that there is no such subgroup, and among all subgroups B such that $A \cap B = \{0\}$, assume that B is maximal, meaning that there is no subgroup B' of G such that $B \subsetneq B'$ and $A \cap B' = \{0\}$. By assumption $C := A + B \subsetneq G$.

Let d be any element of G that lies outside of C. Consider the quotient group G/C, and let r be the order of $d + C$ in G/C. Note that $r > 1$ and $r \mid m$. We shall define a group element d' with slightly nicer properties than d, as follows. Since $rd \in C$, we have $rd = sa + b$ for some $s \in \mathbb{Z}$ and $b \in B$. We claim that $r \mid s$. To see this, note that $0 = md = (m/r)rd = (m/r)sa + (m/r)b$, and since $A \cap B = \{0\}$, we have $(m/r)sa = 0$, which can only happen if $r \mid s$. That proves the claim. This allows us to define $d' := d - (s/r)a$. Since $d \equiv d' \pmod{C}$, we see that $d' + C$ also has order r in G/C, but also that $rd' \in B$.

We next show that $A \cap (B + \langle d' \rangle) = \{0\}$, which will yield the contradiction we seek, and thus prove the lemma. Because $A \cap B = \{0\}$, it will suffice to show that $A \cap (B + \langle d' \rangle) \subseteq B$. Now, suppose we have a group element $b' + xd' \in A$, with $b' \in B$ and $x \in \mathbb{Z}$. Then in particular, $xd' \in C$, and so $r \mid x$, since $d' + C$ has order r in G/C. Further, since $rd' \in B$, we have $xd' \in B$, whence $b' + xd' \in B$. $\square$

Lemma 8.46. *Suppose that $G := \mathbb{Z}_{m_1} \times \cdots \times \mathbb{Z}_{m_t}$ and $H := \mathbb{Z}_{n_1} \times \cdots \times \mathbb{Z}_{n_t}$ are isomorphic, where the m_i and n_i are positive integers (possibly 1) such that $m_i \mid m_{i+1}$ for $i = 1, \ldots, t-1$. Then $m_i = n_i$ for $i = 1, \ldots, t$.*

Proof. Clearly, $\prod_i m_i = |G| = |H| = \prod_i n_i$. We prove the lemma by induction on the order of the group. If the group order is 1, then clearly all m_i and n_i must be 1, and we are done. Otherwise, let p be a prime dividing the group order. Now, suppose that p divides $m_r, \ldots, m_t$ but not $m_1, \ldots, m_{r-1}$, and that p divides $n_s, \ldots, n_t$ but not $n_1, \ldots, n_{s-1}$, where $r \leq t$ and $s \leq t$. Evidently, the groups pG and pH are isomorphic. Moreover,

$$pG \cong \mathbb{Z}_{m_1} \times \cdots \times \mathbb{Z}_{m_{r-1}} \times \mathbb{Z}_{m_r/p} \times \cdots \times \mathbb{Z}_{m_t/p},$$

and

$$pH \cong \mathbb{Z}_{n_1} \times \cdots \times \mathbb{Z}_{n_{s-1}} \times \mathbb{Z}_{n_s/p} \times \cdots \times \mathbb{Z}_{n_t/p}.$$

Thus, we see that $|pG| = |G|/p^{t-r+1}$ and $|pH| = |H|/p^{t-s+1}$, from which it follows that $r = s$, and the lemma then follows by induction. $\square$

9
Rings

This chapter introduces the notion of a ring, more specifically, a commutative ring with unity. The theory of rings provides a useful conceptual framework for reasoning about a wide class of interesting algebraic structures. Intuitively speaking, a ring is an algebraic structure with addition and multiplication operations that behave like we expect addition and multiplication should. While there is a lot of terminology associated with rings, the basic ideas are fairly simple.

9.1 Definitions, basic properties, and examples

Definition 9.1. *A **commutative ring with unity** is a set R together with addition and multiplication operations on R, such that:*

  (i) *the set R under addition forms an abelian group, and we denote the additive identity by 0_R;*

 (ii) *multiplication is associative; that is, for all $a, b, c \in R$, we have $a(bc) = (ab)c$;*

(iii) *multiplication distributes over addition; that is, for all $a, b, c \in R$, we have $a(b + c) = ab + ac$ and $(b + c)a = ba + ca$;*

 (iv) *there exists a multiplicative identity; that is, there exists an element $1_R \in R$, such that $1_R \cdot a = a = a \cdot 1_R$ for all $a \in R$;*

  (v) *multiplication is commutative; that is, for all $a, b \in R$, we have $ab = ba$.*

There are other, more general (and less convenient) types of rings—one can drop properties (iv) and (v), and still have what is called a **ring**. We shall not, however, be working with such general rings in this text. Therefore, to simplify terminology, **from now on, by a "ring," we shall always mean a commutative ring with unity**.

Let R be a ring. Notice that because of the distributive law, for any fixed $a \in R$, the map from R to R that sends $b \in R$ to $ab \in R$ is a group homomorphism with respect to the underlying additive group of R. We call this the a-**multiplication map**.

We first state some simple facts:

Theorem 9.2. *Let R be a ring. Then:*

  (i) *the multiplicative identity 1_R is unique;*

  (ii) $0_R \cdot a = 0_R$ *for all $a \in R$;*

  (iii) $(-a)b = a(-b) = -(ab)$ *for all $a, b \in R$;*

  (iv) $(-a)(-b) = ab$ *for all $a, b \in R$;*

  (v) $(na)b = a(nb) = n(ab)$ *for all $n \in \mathbb{Z}$ and $a, b \in R$.*

Proof. Part (i) may be proved using the same argument as was used to prove part (i) of Theorem 8.2. Parts (ii), (iii), and (v) follow directly from parts (i), (ii), and (iii) of Theorem 8.20, using appropriate multiplication maps, discussed above. Part (iv) follows from parts (iii) and (iv) of Theorem 8.3. $\square$

Example 9.1. The set $\mathbb{Z}$ under the usual rules of multiplication and addition forms a ring. $\square$

Example 9.2. For $n \geq 1$, the set $\mathbb{Z}_n$ under the rules of multiplication and addition defined in §2.3 forms a ring. $\square$

Example 9.3. The set $\mathbb{Q}$ of rational numbers under the usual rules of multiplication and addition forms a ring. $\square$

Example 9.4. The set $\mathbb{R}$ of real numbers under the usual rules of multiplication and addition forms a ring. $\square$

Example 9.5. The set $\mathbb{C}$ of complex numbers under the usual rules of multiplication and addition forms a ring. Any $\alpha \in \mathbb{C}$ can be written (uniquely) as $\alpha = a + bi$, with $a, b \in \mathbb{R}$, and $i = \sqrt{-1}$. If $\alpha' = a' + b'i$ is another complex number, with $a', b' \in \mathbb{R}$, then

$$\alpha + \alpha' = (a + a') + (b + b')i \quad \text{and} \quad \alpha\alpha' = (aa' - bb') + (ab' + a'b)i.$$

The fact that $\mathbb{C}$ is a ring can be verified by direct calculation; however, we shall see later that this follows easily from more general considerations.

Recall the **complex conjugation** operation, which sends α to $\bar{\alpha} := a - bi$. One can verify by direct calculation that complex conjugation is both additive and multiplicative; that is, $\overline{\alpha + \alpha'} = \bar{\alpha} + \bar{\alpha}'$ and $\overline{\alpha \cdot \alpha'} = \bar{\alpha} \cdot \bar{\alpha}'$.

The **norm** of α is $N(\alpha) := \alpha\bar{\alpha} = a^2 + b^2$. So we see that $N(\alpha)$ is a non-negative real number, and is zero iff $\alpha = 0$. Moreover, from the multiplicativity of complex conjugation, it is easy to see that the norm is multiplicative as well: $N(\alpha\alpha') = \alpha\alpha'\overline{\alpha\alpha'} = \alpha\alpha'\bar{\alpha}\bar{\alpha}' = N(\alpha)N(\alpha')$. $\square$

***Example* 9.6.** Consider the set $\mathcal{F}$ of all arithmetic functions, that is, functions mapping positive integers to real numbers. We can define addition and multiplication operations on $\mathcal{F}$ in a natural, point-wise fashion: for $f, g \in \mathcal{F}$, let $f + g$ be the function that sends n to $f(n) + g(n)$, and let $f \cdot g$ be the function that sends n to $f(n)g(n)$. These operations of addition and multiplication make $\mathcal{F}$ into a ring: the additive identity is the function that is everywhere 0, and the multiplicative identity is the function that is everywhere 1.

Another way to make $\mathcal{F}$ into a ring is to use the addition operation as above, together with the Dirichlet product, which we defined in §2.6, for the multiplication operation. In this case, the multiplicative identity is the function I that we defined in §2.6, which takes the value 1 at 1 and the value 0 everywhere else. The reader should verify that the distributive law holds. $\square$

Note that in a ring R, if $1_R = 0_R$, then for all $a \in R$, we have $a = 1_R \cdot a = 0_R \cdot a = 0_R$, and hence the ring R is **trivial**, in the sense that it consists of the single element 0_R, with $0_R + 0_R = 0_R$ and $0_R \cdot 0_R = 0_R$. If $1_R \neq 0_R$, we say that R is **non-trivial**. We shall rarely be concerned with trivial rings for their own sake; however, they do sometimes arise in certain constructions.

If $R_1, \dots, R_k$ are rings, then the set of all k-tuples $(a_1, \dots, a_k)$ with $a_i \in R_i$ for $i = 1, \dots, k$, with addition and multiplication defined component-wise, forms a ring. The ring is denoted by $R_1 \times \cdots \times R_k$, and is called the **direct product** of $R_1, \dots, R_k$.

The **characteristic** of a ring R is defined as the exponent of the underlying additive group (see §8.5). Note that for $m \in \mathbb{Z}$ and $a \in R$, we have

$$ma = m(1_R \cdot a) = (m \cdot 1_R)a,$$

so that if $m \cdot 1_R = 0_R$, then $ma = 0_R$ for all $a \in R$. Thus, if the additive order of 1_R is infinite, the characteristic of R is zero, and otherwise, the characteristic of R is equal to the additive order of 1_R.

***Example* 9.7.** The ring $\mathbb{Z}$ has characteristic zero, $\mathbb{Z}_n$ has characteristic n, and $\mathbb{Z}_{n_1} \times \mathbb{Z}_{n_2}$ has characteristic $\text{lcm}(n_1, n_2)$. $\square$

For elements a, b in a ring R, we say that b **divides** a, or alternatively, that a is **divisible by** b, if there exists $c \in R$ such that $a = bc$. If b divides a, then b is called a **divisor** of a, and we write $b \mid a$. Note Theorem 1.1 holds for an arbitrary ring.

When there is no possibility for confusion, one may write "0" instead of "0_R" and "1" instead of "1_R." Also, one may also write, for example, 2_R to denote $2 \cdot 1_R$, 3_R to denote $3 \cdot 1_R$, and so on; moreover, where the context is clear, one may use an implicit "type cast," so that $m \in \mathbb{Z}$ really means $m \cdot 1_R$.

For $a \in R$ and positive integer n, the expression a^n denotes the product $a \cdot a \cdots a$, where there are n terms in the product. One may extend this definition to $n = 0$, defining a^0 to be the multiplicative identity 1_R.

EXERCISE 9.1. Verify the usual "rules of exponent arithmetic" for a ring R. That is, show that for $a \in R$, and non-negative integers n_1, n_2, we have

$$(a^{n_1})^{n_2} = a^{n_1 n_2} \quad \text{and} \quad a^{n_1} a^{n_2} = a^{n_1 + n_2}.$$

EXERCISE 9.2. Show that the familiar **binomial theorem** holds in an arbitrary ring R; that is, for $a, b \in R$ and positive integer n, we have

$$(a + b)^n = \sum_{i=0}^{n} \binom{n}{i} a^{n-i} b^i.$$

EXERCISE 9.3. Show that

$$\left(\sum_{i=1}^{n} a_i \right) \left(\sum_{j=1}^{m} b_j \right) = \sum_{i=1}^{n} \sum_{j=1}^{m} a_i b_j,$$

where the a_i and b_j are elements of a ring R.

9.1.1 Units and fields

Let R be a ring. We call $u \in R$ a **unit** if it divides 1_R, that is, if $uu' = 1_R$ for some $u' \in R$. In this case, it is easy to see that u' is uniquely determined, and it is called the **multiplicative inverse** of u, and we denote it by u^{-1}. Also, for $a \in R$, we may write a/u to denote au^{-1}. It is clear that a unit u divides every $a \in R$.

We denote the set of units by R^*. It is easy to verify that the set R^* is closed under multiplication, from which it follows that R^* is an abelian group, called the **multiplicative group of units** of R. If $u \in R^*$, then of course $u^n \in R^*$ for all non-negative integers n, and the multiplicative inverse of u^n is $(u^{-1})^n$, which we may also write as u^{-n} (which is consistent with our notation for abelian groups).

If R is non-trivial and every non-zero element of R has a multiplicative inverse, then R is called a **field**.

Example 9.8. The only units in the ring $\mathbb{Z}$ are ± 1. Hence, $\mathbb{Z}$ is not a field. $\square$

Example 9.9. For positive integer n, the units in $\mathbb{Z}_n$ are the residue classes $[a]_n$ with $\gcd(a, n) = 1$. In particular, if n is prime, all non-zero residue classes are units, and if n is composite, some non-zero residue classes are not units. Hence, $\mathbb{Z}_n$ is a field if and only if n is prime. Of course, the notation $\mathbb{Z}_n^*$ introduced in this section for the group of units of the ring $\mathbb{Z}_n$ is consistent with the notation introduced in §2.3. $\square$

Example 9.10. Every non-zero element of $\mathbb{Q}$ is a unit. Hence, $\mathbb{Q}$ is a field. $\square$

Example 9.11. Every non-zero element of $\mathbb{R}$ is a unit. Hence, $\mathbb{R}$ is a field. $\square$

Example 9.12. For non-zero $\alpha = a + bi \in \mathbb{C}$, with $a, b \in \mathbb{R}$, we have $c :=$ $N(\alpha) = a^2 + b^2 > 0$. It follows that the complex number $\bar{\alpha}c^{-1} = (ac^{-1}) + (-bc^{-1})i$ is the multiplicative inverse of α, since $\alpha \cdot \bar{\alpha}c^{-1} = (\alpha\bar{\alpha})c^{-1} = 1$. Hence, every non-zero element of $\mathbb{C}$ is a unit, and so $\mathbb{C}$ is a field. $\square$

Example 9.13. For rings $R_1, \ldots, R_k$, it is easy to see that the multiplicative group of units of the direct product $R_1 \times \cdots \times R_k$ is equal to $R_1^* \times \cdots \times R_k^*$. Indeed, by definition, $(a_1, \ldots, a_k)$ has a multiplicative inverse if and only if each individual a_i does. $\square$

Example 9.14. Consider the rings of arithmetic functions defined in Example 9.6. If multiplication is defined point-wise, then an arithmetic function f is a unit if and only if $f(n) \neq 0$ for all n. If multiplication is defined in terms of the Dirichlet product, then by the result of Exercise 2.27, an arithmetic function f is a unit if and only if $f(1) \neq 0$. $\square$

9.1.2 Zero divisors and integral domains

Let R be a ring. An element $a \in R$ is called a **zero divisor** if $a \neq 0_R$ and there exists non-zero $b \in R$ such that $ab = 0_R$.

If R is non-trivial and has no zero divisors, then it is called an **integral domain**. Put another way, a non-trivial ring R is an integral domain if and only if the following holds: for all $a, b \in R$, $ab = 0_R$ implies $a = 0_R$ or $b = 0_R$.

Note that if u is a unit in R, it cannot be a zero divisor (if $ub = 0_R$, then multiplying both sides of this equation by u^{-1} yields $b = 0_R$). In particular, it follows that any field is an integral domain.

***Example* 9.15.** $\mathbb{Z}$ is an integral domain. $\square$

***Example* 9.16.** For $n > 1$, $\mathbb{Z}_n$ is an integral domain if and only if n is prime. In particular, if n is composite, so $n = n_1 n_2$ with $1 < n_1 < n$ and $1 < n_2 < n$, then $[n_1]_n$ and $[n_2]_n$ are zero divisors: $[n_1]_n [n_2]_n = [0]_n$, but $[n_1]_n \neq [0]_n$ and $[n_2]_n \neq [0]_n$. $\square$

***Example* 9.17.** $\mathbb{Q}$, $\mathbb{R}$, and $\mathbb{C}$ are fields, and hence are also integral domains. $\square$

***Example* 9.18.** For two non-trivial rings R_1, R_2, an element $(a_1, a_2) \in R_1 \times R_2$ is a zero divisor if and only if a_1 is a zero divisor, a_2 is a zero divisor, or exactly one of a_1 or a_2 is zero. In particular, $R_1 \times R_2$ is not an integral domain. $\square$

We have the following "cancellation law":

Theorem 9.3. *If R is a ring, and $a, b, c \in R$ such that $a \neq 0_R$ and a is not a zero divisor, then $ab = ac$ implies $b = c$.*

Proof. $ab = bc$ implies $a(b - c) = 0_R$. The fact that $a \neq 0$ and a is not a zero divisor implies that we must have $b - c = 0_R$, and so $b = c$. $\square$

Theorem 9.4. *If D is an integral domain, then:*
  (i) *for all $a, b, c \in D$, $a \neq 0_D$ and $ab = ac$ implies $b = c$;*
  (ii) *for all $a, b \in D$, $a \mid b$ and $b \mid a$ if and only if $a = bc$ for some $c \in D^*$.*
  (iii) *for all $a, b \in D$ with $b \neq 0_D$ and $b \mid a$, there is a unique $c \in D$ such that $a = bc$, which we may denote as a/b.*

Proof. The first statement follows immediately from the previous theorem and the definition of an integral domain.

For the second statement, if $a = bc$ for $c \in D^*$, then we also have $b = ac^{-1}$; thus, $b \mid a$ and $a \mid b$. Conversely, $a \mid b$ implies $b = ax$ for $x \in D$, and $b \mid a$ implies $a = by$ for $y \in D$, and hence $b = bxy$. If $b = 0_R$, then the equation $a = by$ implies $a = 0_R$, and so the statement holds for any c; otherwise, cancel b, we have $1_D = xy$, and so x and y are units.

For the third statement, if $a = bc$ and $a = bc'$, then $bc = bc'$, and cancel b. $\square$

Theorem 9.5. *The characteristic of an integral domain is either zero or a prime.*

Proof. By way of contradiction, suppose that D is an integral domain with characteristic m that is neither zero nor prime. Since, by definition, D is not a trivial ring, we cannot have $m = 1$, and so m must be composite. Say $m = st$, where $1 < s < m$ and $1 < t < m$. Since m is the additive order of 1_D, it follows that $(s \cdot 1_D) \neq 0_D$ and $(t \cdot 1_D) \neq 0_D$; moreover, since D is an integral domain, it follows that $(s \cdot 1_D)(t \cdot 1_D) \neq 0_D$. So we have

$$0_D = m \cdot 1_D = (st) \cdot 1_D = (s \cdot 1_D)(t \cdot 1_D) \neq 0_D,$$

a contradiction. $\square$

Theorem 9.6. *Any finite integral domain is a field.*

Proof. Let D be a finite integral domain, and let a be any non-zero element of D. Consider the a-multiplication map that sends $b \in D$ to ab, which is a group homomorphism on the additive group of D. Since a is not a zero-divisor, it follows that the kernel of the a-multiplication map is $\{0_D\}$, hence the map is injective, and by finiteness, it must be surjective as well. In particular, there must be an element $b \in D$ such that $ab = 1_D$. $\square$

Theorem 9.7. *Any finite field F must be of cardinality p^w, where p is prime, w is a positive integer, and p is the characteristic of F.*

Proof. By Theorem 9.5, the characteristic of F is either zero or a prime, and since F is finite, it must be prime. Let p denote the characteristic. By definition, p is the exponent of the additive group of F, and by Theorem 8.42, the primes dividing the exponent are the same as the primes dividing the order, and hence F must have cardinality p^w for some positive integer w. $\square$

Of course, for every prime p, $\mathbb{Z}_p$ is a finite field of cardinality p. As we shall see later (in Chapter 20), for every prime p and positive integer w, there exists a field of cardinality p^w. Later in this chapter, we shall see some specific examples of finite fields whose cardinality is not prime (Examples 9.35 and 9.47).

EXERCISE 9.4. Let R be a ring of characteristic $m > 0$, and let n be any integer. Show that:

(a) if $\gcd(n, m) = 1$, then $n \cdot 1_R$ is a unit;

(b) if $1 < \gcd(n, m) < m$, then $n \cdot 1_R$ is a zero divisor;

(c) otherwise, $n \cdot 1_R = 0_R$.

EXERCISE 9.5. Let D be an integral domain, $m \in \mathbb{Z}$, and $a \in D$. Show that $ma = 0_D$ if and only if m is a multiple of the characteristic of D or $a = 0_D$.

EXERCISE 9.6. For $n \geq 1$, and for all $a, b \in \mathbb{Z}_n$, show that if $a \mid b$ and $b \mid a$, then $a = bc$ for some $c \in \mathbb{Z}_n^*$. Thus, part (ii) of Theorem 9.4 may hold for some rings that are not integral domains.

EXERCISE 9.7. This exercise depends on results in §8.6. Using the fundamental theorem of finite abelian groups, show that the additive group of a finite field of characteristic p and cardinality p^w is isomorphic to $\mathbb{Z}_p^{\times w}$.

9.1.3 Subrings

Definition 9.8. *A subset S of a ring R is called a **subring** if*

(i) S is a subgroup of the additive group R,

(ii) S is closed under multiplication, and

(iii) $1_R \in S$.

It is clear that the operations of addition and multiplication on a ring R make a subring S of R into a ring, where 0_R is the additive identity of S and 1_R is the multiplicative identity of S. One may also call R an **extension ring** of S.

Some texts do not require that 1_R belongs to a subring S, and instead require only that S contains a multiplicative identity, which may be different than that of R. This is perfectly reasonable, but for simplicity, we restrict ourselves to the case when $1_R \in S$.

Expanding the above definition, we see that a subset S of R is a subring if and only if $1_R \in S$ and for all $a, b \in S$, we have

$$a + b \in S, \quad -a \in S, \quad \text{and} \quad ab \in S.$$

If fact, to verify that S is a subring, it suffices to show that $-1_R \in S$ and that S is closed under addition and multiplication; indeed, if $-1_R \in S$ and S is closed under multiplication, then S is closed under negation, and further, $1_R = -(-1_R) \in S$.

***Example* 9.19.** $\mathbb{Z}$ is a subring of $\mathbb{Q}$. $\square$

***Example* 9.20.** $\mathbb{Q}$ is a subring of $\mathbb{R}$. $\square$

***Example* 9.21.** $\mathbb{R}$ is a subring of $\mathbb{C}$.

Note that for $\alpha := a + bi \in \mathbb{C}$, with $a, b \in \mathbb{R}$, we have $\bar{\alpha} = \alpha$ iff $a + bi = a - bi$ iff $b = 0$. That is, $\bar{\alpha} = \alpha$ iff $\alpha \in \mathbb{R}$. $\square$

***Example* 9.22.** The set $\mathbb{Z}[i]$ of complex numbers of the form $a + bi$, with $a, b \in \mathbb{Z}$, is a subring of $\mathbb{C}$. It is called the ring of **Gaussian integers**. Since $\mathbb{C}$ is a field, it contains no zero divisors, and hence $\mathbb{Z}[i]$ contains no zero divisors. Hence, $\mathbb{Z}[i]$ is an integral domain.

Let us determine the units of $\mathbb{Z}[i]$. If $\alpha \in \mathbb{Z}[i]$ is a unit, then there exists $\alpha' \in \mathbb{Z}[i]$ such that $\alpha\alpha' = 1$. Taking norms, we obtain

$$1 = N(1) = N(\alpha\alpha') = N(\alpha)N(\alpha').$$

Clearly, the norm of a Gaussian integer is a non-negative integer, and so $N(\alpha)N(\alpha') = 1$ implies $N(\alpha) = 1$. Now, if $\alpha = a + bi$, with $a, b \in \mathbb{Z}$, then $N(\alpha) = a^2 + b^2$, and so $N(\alpha) = 1$ implies $\alpha = \pm 1$ or $\alpha = \pm i$. Conversely, it is clear that ± 1 and $\pm i$ are indeed units, and so these are the only units in $\mathbb{Z}[i]$. $\square$

***Example* 9.23.** Let m be a positive integer, and let $\mathbb{Q}^{(m)}$ be the set of rational numbers of the form a/b, where a and b are integers, and b is relatively prime to m. Then $\mathbb{Q}^{(m)}$ is a subring of $\mathbb{Q}$, since for any $a, b, c, d \in \mathbb{Z}$ with $\gcd(b, m) = 1$ and $\gcd(d, m) = 1$, we have

$$\frac{a}{b} + \frac{c}{d} = \frac{ad + bc}{bd} \quad \text{and} \quad \frac{a}{b} \cdot \frac{c}{d} = \frac{ac}{bd},$$

and since $\gcd(bd, m) = 1$, it follows that the sum and product of any two element of $\mathbb{Q}^{(m)}$ is again in $\mathbb{Q}^{(m)}$. Clearly, $\mathbb{Q}^{(m)}$ contains -1, and so it follows that $\mathbb{Q}^{(m)}$ is a subring of $\mathbb{Q}$. The units of $\mathbb{Q}^{(m)}$ are precisely those rational numbers of the form a/b, where $\gcd(a, m) = \gcd(b, m) = 1$. $\square$

***Example* 9.24.** If R and S are non-trivial rings, then $R' := R \times \{0_S\}$ is not a subring of $R \times S$: although it satisfies the first two requirements of the definition of a subring, it does not satisfy the third. However, R' does contain an element that acts as a multiplicative identity of R', namely $(1_R, 0_S)$, and hence could be viewed as a subring of $R \times S$ under a more liberal definition. $\square$

Theorem 9.9. *Any subring of an integral domain is also an integral domain.*

Proof. If D' is a subring of the integral domain D, then any zero divisor in D' would itself be a zero divisor in D. $\square$

Note that it is not the case that a subring of a field is always a field: the subring $\mathbb{Z}$ of $\mathbb{Q}$ is a counter-example. If F' is a subring of a field F, and F' is itself a field, then we say that F' is a **subfield** of F, and that F is an **extension field** of F'.

Example 9.25. $\mathbb{Q}$ is a subfield of $\mathbb{R}$, which in turn is a subfield of $\mathbb{C}$. $\square$

EXERCISE 9.8. Show that the set $\mathbb{Q}[i]$ of complex numbers of the form $a+bi$, with $a, b \in \mathbb{Q}$, is a subfield of $\mathbb{C}$.

EXERCISE 9.9. Show that if S and S' are subrings of R, then so is $S \cap S'$.

EXERCISE 9.10. Let $\mathcal{F}$ be the set of all functions $f : \mathbb{R} \to \mathbb{R}$, and let $\mathcal{C}$ be the subset of $\mathcal{F}$ of continuous functions.

  (a) Show that with addition and multiplication of functions defined in the natural, point-wise fashion, $\mathcal{F}$ is a ring, but not an integral domain.
  (b) Let $a, b \in \mathcal{F}$. Show that if $a \mid b$ and $b \mid a$, then there is a $c \in \mathcal{F}^*$ such that $a = bc$.
  (c) Show that $\mathcal{C}$ is a subring of $\mathcal{F}$, and show that all functions in $\mathcal{C}^*$ are either everywhere positive or everywhere negative.
  (d) Define $a, b \in \mathcal{C}$ by $a(t) = b(t) = t$ for $t < 0$, $a(t) = b(t) = 0$ for $0 \le t \le 1$, and $a(t) = -b(t) = t - 1$ for $t > 1$. Show that in the ring $\mathcal{C}$, we have $a \mid b$ and $b \mid a$, yet there is no $c \in \mathcal{C}^*$ such that $a = bc$. Thus, part (ii) of Theorem 9.4 does not hold in a general ring.

9.2 Polynomial rings

If R is a ring, then we can form the **ring of polynomials** $R[\mathtt{X}]$, consisting of all polynomials $a_0 + a_1 \mathtt{X} + \cdots + a_k \mathtt{X}^k$ in the indeterminate, or "formal" variable, $\mathtt{X}$, with coefficients in R, and with addition and multiplication being defined in the usual way.

Example 9.26. Let us define a few polynomials over the ring $\mathbb{Z}$:

$$a := 3 + \mathtt{X}^2, \ b := 1 + 2\mathtt{X} - \mathtt{X}^3, \ c := 5, \ d := 1 + \mathtt{X}, \ e := \mathtt{X}, \ f := 4\mathtt{X}^3.$$

We have

$$a + b = 4 + 2\mathtt{X} + \mathtt{X}^2 - \mathtt{X}^3, \ a \cdot b = 3 + 6\mathtt{X} + \mathtt{X}^2 - \mathtt{X}^3 - \mathtt{X}^5, \ cd + ef = 5 + 5\mathtt{X} + 4\mathtt{X}^4. \ \square$$

As illustrated in the previous example, elements of R are also polynomials. Such polynomials are called **constant polynomials**; all other polynomials are called **non-constant polynomials**. The set R of constant polynomials clearly forms a subring of $R[\mathtt{X}]$. In particular, 0_R is the additive identity in $R[\mathtt{X}]$ and 1_R is the multiplicative identity in $R[\mathtt{X}]$.

For completeness, we present a more formal definition of the ring $R[X]$. The reader should bear in mind that this formalism is rather tedious, and may be more distracting than it is enlightening. It is technically convenient to view a polynomial as having an *infinite* sequence of coefficients $a_0, a_1, a_2, \ldots$, where each coefficient belongs to R, but where only a finite number of the coefficients are non-zero. We may write such a polynomial as an infinite sum $\sum_{i=0}^{\infty} a_i X^i$; however, this notation is best thought of "syntactic sugar": there is really nothing more to the polynomial than this sequence of coefficients. With this notation, if

$$a = \sum_{i=0}^{\infty} a_i X^i \quad \text{and} \quad b = \sum_{i=0}^{\infty} b_i X^i,$$

then

$$a + b := \sum_{i=0}^{\infty} (a_i + b_i) X^i, \tag{9.1}$$

and

$$a \cdot b := \sum_{i=0}^{\infty} \left(\sum_{k=0}^{i} a_k b_{i-k} \right) X^i. \tag{9.2}$$

We should first verify that these addition and multiplication operations actually produce coefficient sequences with only a finite number of non-zero terms. Suppose that for non-negative integers k and ℓ, we have $a_i = 0_R$ for all $i > k$ and $b_i = 0_R$ for all $i > \ell$. Then it is clear that the coefficient of X^i in $a + b$ is zero for all $i > \max\{k, \ell\}$, and it is also not too hard to see that the coefficient of X^i in $a \cdot b$ is zero for all $i > k + \ell$.

We leave it to the reader to verify that $R[X]$, with addition and multiplication defined as above, actually satisfies the definition of a ring — this is entirely straightforward, but tedious.

For $c \in R$, we may identify c with the polynomial $\sum_{i=0}^{\infty} c_i X^i$, where $c_0 = c$ and $c_i = 0_R$ for $i > 0$. Strictly speaking, c and $\sum_{i=0}^{\infty} c_i X^i$ are not the same mathematical object, but there will certainly be no possible confusion in treating them as such. Thus, from a narrow, legalistic point of view, R is not a subring of $R[X]$, but we shall not let such let such annoying details prevent us from continuing to speak of it as such. As one last matter of notation, we may naturally write X to denote the polynomial $\sum_{i=0}^{\infty} a_i X^i$, where $a_1 = 1_R$ and $a_i = 0_R$ for all $i \neq 1$.

With all of these conventions and definitions, we can return to the practice of writing polynomials as we did in Example 9.26, without any loss of precision. Note that by definition, if R is the trivial ring, then so is $R[X]$.

9.2.1 *Polynomials versus polynomial functions*

Of course, a polynomial $a = \sum_{i=0}^{k} a_i \mathsf{X}^i$ defines a polynomial function on R that sends $\alpha \in R$ to $\sum_{i=0}^{k} a_i \alpha^i$, and we denote the value of this function as $a(\alpha)$. However, it is important to regard polynomials over R as formal expressions, and not to identify them with their corresponding functions. In particular, two polynomials are equal if and only if their coefficients are equal. This distinction is important, since there are rings R over which two different polynomials define the same function. One can of course define the ring of polynomial functions on R, but in general, that ring has a different structure from the ring of polynomials over R.

Example 9.27. In the ring $\mathbb{Z}_p$, for prime p, by Fermat's little theorem (Theorem 2.16), we have $\alpha^p - \alpha = [0]_p$ for all $\alpha \in \mathbb{Z}_p$. But consider the polynomial $a := \mathsf{X}^p - \mathsf{X} \in \mathbb{Z}_p[\mathsf{X}]$. We have $a(\alpha) = [0]_p$ for all $\alpha \in \mathbb{Z}_p$, and hence the function defined by a is the zero function, yet a is definitely *not* the zero polynomial. $\square$

More generally, if R is a subring of a ring E, a polynomial $a = \sum_{i=0}^{k} a_i \mathsf{X}^i \in R[\mathsf{X}]$ defines a polynomial function from E to E that sends $\alpha \in E$ to $\sum_{i=0}^{k} a_i \alpha^i \in E$, and the value of this function is denoted $a(\alpha)$.

If $E = R[\mathsf{X}]$, then evaluating a polynomial $a \in R[\mathsf{X}]$ at a point $\alpha \in E$ amounts to polynomial composition. For example, if $a = \mathsf{X}^2 + \mathsf{X}$ then

$$a[\ \mathsf{X} + 1\ ] = (\mathsf{X} + 1)^2 + (\mathsf{X} + 1) = \mathsf{X}^2 + 3\mathsf{X} + 2.$$

A simple, but important, fact is the following:

Theorem 9.10. *Let R be a subring of a ring E. For $a, b \in R[\mathsf{X}]$ and $\alpha \in E$, if $p := ab \in R[\mathsf{X}]$ and $s := a + b \in R[\mathsf{X}]$, then we have*

$$p(\alpha) = a(\alpha)b(\alpha) \quad and \quad s(\alpha) = a(\alpha) + b(\alpha).$$

Also, if $c \in R[\mathsf{X}]$ is a constant polynomial, then $c(\alpha) = c$ for all $\alpha \in E$.

Proof. Exercise. $\square$

> Note that the syntax for polynomial evaluation creates some potential ambiguities: if a is a polynomial, one could interpret $a(b + c)$ as either a times $b + c$, or a evaluated at $b + c$; usually, the meaning will be clear from context, but to avoid such ambiguities, if the intended meaning is the former, we shall generally write this as, say, $a \cdot (b + c)$ or $(b + c)a$, and if the intended meaning is the latter, we shall generally write this as $a[\ b + c\ ]$.
>
> So as to keep the distinction between ring elements and indeterminates clear, we shall use the symbol "X" only to denote the latter. Also, for a polynomial $a \in R[\mathsf{X}]$, we shall in general write this simply

as "a," and not as "$a(\mathtt{X})$." Of course, the choice of the symbol "$\mathtt{X}$" is arbitrary; occasionally, we may use other symbols, such as "$\mathtt{Y}$," as alternatives.

9.2.2 Basic properties of polynomial rings

Let R be a ring. For non-zero $a \in R[\mathtt{X}]$, if $a = \sum_{i=0}^{k} a_i \mathtt{X}^i$ with $a_k \neq 0_R$, then we call k the **degree** of a, denoted $\deg(a)$, we call a_k the **leading coefficient** of a, denoted $\mathrm{lc}(a)$, and we call a_0 the **constant term** of a. If $\mathrm{lc}(a) = 1_R$, then a is called **monic**.

Suppose $a = \sum_{i=0}^{k} a_i \mathtt{X}^i$ and $b = \sum_{i=0}^{\ell} b_i \mathtt{X}^i$ are polynomials such that $a_k \neq 0_R$ and $b_\ell \neq 0_R$, so that $\deg(a) = k$ and $\mathrm{lc}(a) = a_k$, and $\deg(b) = \ell$ and $\mathrm{lc}(b) = b_\ell$. When we multiply these two polynomials, we get

$$ab = a_0 b_0 + (a_0 b_1 + a_1 b_0)\mathtt{X} + \cdots + a_k b_\ell \mathtt{X}^{k+\ell}.$$

In particular, $\deg(ab) \leq \deg(a) + \deg(b)$. If either of a_k or b_ℓ are not zero divisors, then $a_k b_\ell$ is not zero, and hence $\deg(ab) = \deg(a) + \deg(b)$. However, if both a_k and b_ℓ are zero divisors, then we may have $a_k b_\ell = 0_R$, in which case, the product ab may be zero, or perhaps $ab \neq 0_R$ but $\deg(ab) < \deg(a) + \deg(b)$.

***Example* 9.28.** Over the ring $\mathbb{Z}_6$, consider the polynomials $a := [1] + [2]\mathtt{X}$ and $b = [1] + [3]\mathtt{X}$. We have $ab = [1] + [5]\mathtt{X} + [6]\mathtt{X}^2 = [1] + [5]\mathtt{X}$. Thus, $\deg(ab) = 1 < 2 = \deg(a) + \deg(b)$. $\square$

For the zero polynomial, we establish the following conventions: its leading coefficient and constant term are defined to be 0_R, and its degree is defined to be $-\infty$. With these conventions, we may succinctly state that

> *for all $a, b \in R[\mathtt{X}]$, we have $\deg(ab) \leq \deg(a) + \deg(b)$, with equality guaranteed to hold unless the leading coefficients of both a and b are zero divisors.*

In the case where the ring of coefficients is as integral domain, we can say significantly more:

Theorem 9.11. *Let D be an integral domain. Then:*

(i) *for all $a, b \in D[\mathtt{X}]$, we have $\deg(ab) = \deg(a) + \deg(b)$;*

(ii) *$D[\mathtt{X}]$ is an integral domain;*

(iii) *$(D[\mathtt{X}])^* = D^*$.*

Proof. Exercise. $\square$

9.2.3 Division with remainder

An extremely important property of polynomials is a division with remainder property, analogous to that for the integers:

Theorem 9.12 (Division with remainder property). *Let R be a ring. For $a, b \in R[X]$ with $b \neq 0_R$ and $\mathrm{lc}(b) \in R^*$, there exist unique $q, r \in R[X]$ such that $a = bq + r$ and $\deg(r) < \deg(b)$.*

Proof. Consider the set S of polynomials of the form $a - zb$ with $z \in R[X]$. Let $r = a - qb$ be an element of S of minimum degree. We must have $\deg(r) < \deg(b)$, since otherwise, we would have $r' := r - (\mathrm{lc}(r)\,\mathrm{lc}(b)^{-1}X^{\deg(r)-\deg(b)}) \cdot b \in S$, and $\deg(r') < \deg(r)$, contradicting the minimality of $\deg(r)$.

That proves the existence of r and q. For uniqueness, suppose that $a = bq + r$ and $a = bq' + r'$, where $\deg(r) < \deg(b)$ and $\deg(r') < \deg(b)$. This implies $r' - r = b \cdot (q - q')$. However, if $q \neq q'$, then

$$\deg(b) > \deg(r' - r) = \deg(b \cdot (q - q')) = \deg(b) + \deg(q - q') \geq \deg(b),$$

which is impossible. Therefore, we must have $q = q'$, and hence $r = r'$. $\square$

If $a = bq + r$ as in the above theorem, we define $a \bmod b := r$. Clearly, $b \mid a$ if and only if $a \bmod b = 0_R$. Moreover, note that if $\deg(a) < \deg(b)$, then $q = 0$ and $r = a$; otherwise, if $\deg(a) \geq \deg(b)$, then $q \neq 0$ and $\deg(a) = \deg(b) + \deg(q)$.

As a consequence of the above theorem, we have:

Theorem 9.13. *For a ring R and $a \in R[X]$ and $\alpha \in R$, $a(\alpha) = 0_R$ if and only if $(X - \alpha)$ divides a.*

Proof. If R is the trivial ring, there is nothing to prove, so assume that R is non-trivial. Let us write $a = (X - \alpha)q + r$, with $q, r \in R[X]$ and $\deg(r) < 1$, which means that $r \in R$. Then we have $a(\alpha) = (\alpha - \alpha)q(\alpha) + r = r$. Thus, $a(\alpha) = 0_R$ if and only if $a \bmod (X - \alpha) = 0_R$, which holds if and only if $X - \alpha$ divides a. $\square$

With R, a, α as in the above theorem, we say that α is a **root** of a if $a(\alpha) = 0_R$.

Theorem 9.14. *Let D be an integral domain, and let $a \in D[X]$, with $\deg(a) = k \geq 0$. Then a has at most k roots.*

Proof. We can prove this by induction. If $k = 0$, this means that a is a non-zero element of D, and so it clearly has no roots.

Now suppose that $k > 0$. If a has no roots, we are done, so suppose that

a has a root α. Then we can write $a = (\mathsf{X} - \alpha)q$, where $\deg(q) = k - 1$. Now, for any root β of a with $\beta \neq \alpha$, we have $0_D = a(\beta) = (\beta - \alpha)q(\beta)$, and using the fact that D is an integral domain, we must have $q(\beta) = 0_D$. Thus, the only roots of a are α and the roots of q. By induction, q has at most $k - 1$ roots, and hence a has at most k roots. $\square$

Theorem 9.14 has many applications, among which is the following beautiful theorem that establishes an important property of the multiplicative structure of an integral domain:

Theorem 9.15. *Let D be an integral domain and G a subgroup of D^* of finite order. Then G is cyclic.*

Proof. Let n be the order of G, and suppose G is not cyclic. Then by Theorem 8.40, we have that the exponent m of G is strictly less than n. It follows that $\alpha^m = 1_D$ for all $\alpha \in G$. That is, all the elements of G are roots of the polynomial $\mathsf{X}^m - 1_D \in D[\mathsf{X}]$. But since a polynomial of degree m over D has at most m roots, this contradicts the fact that $m < n$. $\square$

As a special case of Theorem 9.15, we have:

Theorem 9.16. *For any finite field F, the group F^* is cyclic. In particular, if p is prime, then $\mathbb{Z}_p^*$ is cyclic; that is, there is a primitive root modulo p.*

EXERCISE 9.11. Let D be an infinite integral domain, and let $a \in D[\mathsf{X}]$. Show that if $a(\alpha) = 0_D$ for all $\alpha \in D$, then $a = 0_D$. Thus, for an infinite integral domain D, there is a one-to-one correspondence between polynomials over D and polynomial functions on D.

EXERCISE 9.12. This exercise develops a message authentication scheme (see §6.7.2) that allows one to hash long messages using a relatively small set of hash functions. Let F be a finite field of cardinality q and let t be a positive integer. Let $\mathcal{A} := F^{\times t}$ and $\mathcal{Z} := F$. Define a family $\mathcal{H}$ of hash functions from $\mathcal{A}$ to $\mathcal{Z}$ as follows: let $\mathcal{H} := \{h_{\alpha,\beta} : \alpha, \beta \in F\}$, where for all $h_{\alpha,\beta} \in \mathcal{H}$ and all $(a_1, \ldots, a_t) \in \mathcal{A}$, we define

$$h_{\alpha,\beta}(a_1, \ldots, a_t) := \beta + \sum_{i=1}^{t} a_i \alpha^i \in \mathcal{Z}.$$

Show that $\mathcal{H}$ is a t/q-forgeable message authentication scheme. (Compare this with the second pairwise independent family of hash functions discussed in Example 6.25, which is much larger, but which is only $1/q$-forgeable; in practice, using the smaller family of hash functions with a somewhat higher forging probability may be a good trade-off.)

EXERCISE 9.13. This exercise develops an alternative proof of Theorem 9.15. Let n be the order of the group. Using Theorem 9.14, show that for all $d \mid n$, there are at most d elements in the group whose multiplicative order divides d. From this, deduce that for all $d \mid n$, the number of elements of multiplicative order d is either 0 or $\phi(d)$. Now use Theorem 2.11 to deduce that for all $d \mid n$ (and in particular, for $d = n$), the number of elements of multiplicative order d is equal to $\phi(d)$.

EXERCISE 9.14. Let F be a field of characteristic other than 2, so that the $2_F \neq 0_F$. Show that the familiar **quadratic formula** holds for F. That is, for $a, b, c \in F$ with $a \neq 0_F$, the polynomial $f := aX^2 + bX + c \in F[X]$ has a root if and only if there exists $z \in F$ such that $z^2 = d$, where d is the **discriminant** of f, defined as $d := b^2 - 4ac$, and in this case the roots of f are

$$\frac{-b \pm z}{2a}.$$

EXERCISE 9.15. Let R be a ring, let $a \in R[X]$, with $\deg(a) = k \geq 0$, and let α be an element of R.

(a) Show that there exists an integer m, with $0 \leq m \leq k$, and a polynomial $q \in R[X]$, such that

$$a = (X - \alpha)^m q \text{ and } q(\alpha) \neq 0_R.$$

(b) Show that the values m and q in part (a) are uniquely determined (by a and α).

(c) Show that $m > 0$ if and only if α is a root of a.

Let $m_\alpha(a)$ denote the value m in the previous exercise; for completeness, one can define $m_\alpha(a) := \infty$ if a is the zero polynomial. If $m_\alpha(a) > 0$, then α is called a root of a of **multiplicity** $m_\alpha(a)$; if $m_\alpha(a) = 1$, then α is called a **simple root** of a, and if $m_\alpha(a) > 1$, then α is called a **multiple root** of a.

The following exercise refines Theorem 9.14, taking into account multiplicities.

EXERCISE 9.16. Let D be an integral domain, and let $a \in D[X]$, with $\deg(a) = k \geq 0$. Show that

$$\sum_{\alpha \in D} m_\alpha(a) \leq k.$$

EXERCISE 9.17. Let D be an integral domain, let $a, b \in D[X]$, and let $\alpha \in D$. Show that $m_\alpha(ab) = m_\alpha(a) + m_\alpha(b)$.

EXERCISE 9.18. Let R be a ring, let $a \in R[X]$, with $\deg(a) = k \geq 0$, let $\alpha \in R$, and let $m := m_\alpha(a)$. Show that if we evaluate a at $X + \alpha$, we have

$$a[\ X + \alpha\ ] = \sum_{i=m}^{k} b_i X^i,$$

where $b_m, \ldots, b_k \in R$ and $b_m \neq 0_R$.

9.2.4 Formal derivatives

Let R be any ring, and let $a \in R[X]$ be a polynomial. If $a = \sum_{i=0}^{\ell} a_i X^i$, we define the **formal derivative** of a as

$$\mathbf{D}(a) := \sum_{i=1}^{\ell} i a_i X^{i-1}.$$

We stress that unlike the "analytical" notion of derivative from calculus, which is defined in terms of limits, this definition is purely "symbolic." Nevertheless, some of the usual rules for derivatives still hold:

Theorem 9.17. *Let R be a ring. For all $a, b \in R[X]$ and $c \in R$, we have*

(i) $\mathbf{D}(a + b) = \mathbf{D}(a) + \mathbf{D}(b)$;

(ii) $\mathbf{D}(ca) = c\mathbf{D}(a)$;

(iii) $\mathbf{D}(ab) = \mathbf{D}(a)b + a\mathbf{D}(b)$.

Proof. Parts (i) and (ii) follow immediately by inspection, but part (iii) requires some proof. First, note that part (iii) holds trivially if either a or b are zero, so let us assume that neither are zero.

We first prove part (iii) for **monomials**, that is, polynomials of the form cX^i for non-zero $c \in R$ and $i \geq 0$. Suppose $a = cX^i$ and $b = dX^j$. If $i = 0$, so $a = c$, then the result follows from part (ii) and the fact that $\mathbf{D}(c) = 0$; when $j = 0$, the result holds by a symmetric argument. So assume that $i > 0$ and $j > 0$. Now, $\mathbf{D}(a) = icX^{i-1}$ and $\mathbf{D}(b) = jdX^{j-1}$, and $\mathbf{D}(ab) = \mathbf{D}(cdX^{i+j}) = (i+j)cdX^{i+j-1}$. The result follows from a simple calculation.

Having proved part (iii) for monomials, we now prove it in general on induction on the total number of monomials appearing in a and b. If the total number is 2, then both a and b are monomials, and we are in the base case; otherwise, one of a and b must consist of at least two monomials, and for concreteness, say it is b that has this property. So we can write $b = b_1 + b_2$, where both b_1 and b_2 have fewer monomials than does b. Applying part (i) and the induction hypothesis for part (iii), we have

$$\begin{aligned}
\mathbf{D}(ab) &= \mathbf{D}(ab_1 + ab_2) \\
&= \mathbf{D}(ab_1) + \mathbf{D}(ab_2) \\
&= \mathbf{D}(a)b_1 + a\mathbf{D}(b_1) + \mathbf{D}(a)b_2 + a\mathbf{D}(b_2) \\
&= \mathbf{D}(a) \cdot (b_1 + b_2) + a \cdot (\mathbf{D}(b_1) + \mathbf{D}(b_2)) \\
&= \mathbf{D}(a) \cdot (b_1 + b_2) + a \cdot \mathbf{D}(b_1 + b_2) \\
&= \mathbf{D}(a)b + a\mathbf{D}(b). \quad \square
\end{aligned}$$

EXERCISE 9.19. Let R be a ring, let $a \in R[\mathtt{X}]$, and let $\alpha \in R$ be a root of a. Show that α is a multiple root of a if and only if α is a root of $\mathbf{D}(a)$ (see Exercise 9.15).

EXERCISE 9.20. Let R be a ring, let $a \in R[\mathtt{X}]$ with $\deg(a) = k \geq 0$, and let $\alpha \in R$. Show that if we evaluate a at $\mathtt{X} + \alpha$, writing

$$a\big[\ \mathtt{X} + \alpha\ \big] = \sum_{i=0}^{k} b_i \mathtt{X}^i,$$

with $b_0, \ldots, b_k \in R$, then we have

$$i! \cdot b_i = (\mathbf{D}^i(a))(\alpha) \quad \text{for } i = 0, \ldots, k.$$

EXERCISE 9.21. Let F be a field such that every non-constant polynomial $a \in F[\mathtt{X}]$ has a root $\alpha \in F$. (The field $\mathbb{C}$ is an example of such a field, an important fact which we shall not be proving in this text.) Show that for every positive integer r that is not a multiple of the characteristic of F, there exists an element $\zeta \in F^*$ of multiplicative order r, and that every element in F^* whose order divides r is a power of ζ.

9.2.5 Multi-variate polynomials

One can naturally generalize the notion of a polynomial in a single variable to that of a polynomial in several variables. We discuss these ideas briefly here—they will play only a minor role in the remainder of the text.

Consider the ring $R[\mathtt{X}]$ of polynomials over a ring R. If $\mathtt{Y}$ is another indeterminate, we can form the ring $R[\mathtt{X}][\mathtt{Y}]$ of polynomials in $\mathtt{Y}$ whose coefficients are themselves polynomials in $\mathtt{X}$ over the ring R. One may write $R[\mathtt{X}, \mathtt{Y}]$ instead of $R[\mathtt{X}][\mathtt{Y}]$. An element of $R[\mathtt{X}, \mathtt{Y}]$ is called a **bivariate polynomial**.

Consider a typical element $a \in R[X, Y]$, which may be written

$$a = \sum_{j=0}^{\ell} \left(\sum_{i=0}^{k} a_{ij} X^i \right) Y_j. \tag{9.3}$$

Rearranging terms, this may also be written as

$$a = \sum_{\substack{0 \le i \le k \\ 0 \le j \le \ell}} a_{ij} X^i Y^j, \tag{9.4}$$

or as

$$a = \sum_{i=0}^{k} \left(\sum_{j=0}^{\ell} a_{ij} Y^j \right) X^j. \tag{9.5}$$

If a is written as in (9.4), the terms $a_{ij} X^i Y^j$ with $a_{ij} \ne 0_R$ are called **monomials**. The **total degree** of such a monomial $a_{ij} X^i Y^j$ is defined to be $i + j$, and if a is non-zero, then the **total degree** of a, denoted $\mathrm{Deg}(a)$, is defined to be the maximum total degree of any monomial appearing in (9.4). We define the total degree of the zero polynomial to be $-\infty$. The reader may verify that for any $a, b \in R[X, Y]$, we have $\mathrm{Deg}(ab) \le \mathrm{Deg}(a) + \mathrm{Deg}(b)$, while equality holds if R is an integral domain.

When a is written as in (9.5), one sees that we can naturally view a as an element of $R[Y][X]$, that is, as a polynomial in X whose coefficients are polynomials in Y. From a strict, syntactic point of view, the rings $R[Y][X]$ and $R[X][Y]$ are not the same, but there is no harm done in blurring this distinction when convenient. We denote by $\deg_X(a)$ the degree of a, viewed as a polynomial in X, and by $\deg_Y(a)$ the degree of a, viewed as a polynomial in Y. Analogously, one can formally differentiate a with respect to either X or Y, obtaining the "partial" derivatives $D_X(a)$ and $D_Y(a)$.

Example **9.29.** Let us illustrate, with a particular example, the three different forms—as in (9.3), (9.4), and (9.5)—of expressing a bivariate polynomial. In the ring $\mathbb{Z}[X, Y]$ we have

$$\begin{aligned} a &= (5X^2 - 3X + 4)Y + (2X^2 + 1) \\ &= 5X^2 Y + 2X^2 - 3XY + 4Y + 1 \\ &= (5Y + 2)X^2 + (-3Y)X + (4Y + 1). \end{aligned}$$

We have $\mathrm{Deg}(a) = 3$, $\deg_X(a) = 2$, and $\deg_Y(a) = 1$. $\square$

More generally, if $X_1, \ldots, X_n$ are indeterminates, we can form the ring

$R[\mathsf{X}_1, \ldots, \mathsf{X}_n]$ of **multi-variate polynomials** in n variables over R. Formally, we can think of this ring as $R[\mathsf{X}_1][\mathsf{X}_2] \cdots [\mathsf{X}_n]$. Any multi-variate polynomial can be expressed uniquely as the sum of monomials of the form $c\mathsf{X}_1^{e_1} \cdots \mathsf{X}_n^{e_n}$ for non-zero $c \in R$ and non-negative integers $e_1, \ldots, e_n$; the total degree of such a monomial is defined to be $\sum_i e_i$, and the total degree of a multi-variate polynomial a, denoted $\mathrm{Deg}(a)$, is defined to be the maximum degree of its monomials. As above, for $a, b \in R[\mathsf{X}_1, \ldots, \mathsf{X}_n]$, we have $\mathrm{Deg}(ab) \leq \mathrm{Deg}(a) + \mathrm{Deg}(b)$, while equality always holds if R is an integral domain.

Just as for bivariate polynomials, the order of the indeterminates is not important, and for any $i = 1, \ldots, n$, one can naturally view any $a \in R[\mathsf{X}_1, \ldots, \mathsf{X}_n]$ as a polynomial in X_i over the ring $R[\mathsf{X}_1, \ldots, \mathsf{X}_{i-1}, \mathsf{X}_{i+1}, \ldots, \mathsf{X}_n]$, and define $\deg_{\mathsf{X}_i}(a)$ to be the degree of a when viewed in this way. Analogously, one can formally differentiate a with respect to any variable X_i, obtaining the "partial" derivative $\mathbf{D}_{\mathsf{X}_i}(a)$.

Just as polynomials in a single variable define polynomial functions, so do polynomials in several variables. If R is a subring of E, $a \in R[\mathsf{X}_1, \ldots, \mathsf{X}_n]$, and $\alpha = (\alpha_1, \ldots, \alpha_n) \in E^{\times n}$, we define $a(\alpha)$ to be the element of E obtained by evaluating the expression obtained by substituting α_i for X_i in a. Theorem 9.10 carries over directly to the multi-variate case.

EXERCISE 9.22. Let R be a ring, and let $\alpha_1, \ldots, \alpha_n$ be elements of R. Show that any polynomial $a \in R[\mathsf{X}_1, \ldots, \mathsf{X}_n]$ can be expressed as

$$a = (\mathsf{X}_1 - \alpha_1)q_1 + \cdots + (\mathsf{X}_n - \alpha_n)q_n + r,$$

where $q_1, \ldots, q_n \in R[\mathsf{X}_1, \ldots, \mathsf{X}_n]$ and $r \in R$. Moreover, show that the value of r appearing in such an expression is uniquely determined (by a and $\alpha_1, \ldots, \alpha_n$).

EXERCISE 9.23. This exercise generalizes Theorem 9.14. Let D be an integral domain, and let $a \in D[\mathsf{X}_1, \ldots, \mathsf{X}_n]$, with $\mathrm{Deg}(a) = k \geq 0$. Let T be a finite subset of D. Show that the number of elements $\alpha \in T^{\times n}$ such that $a(\alpha) = 0$ is at most $k|T|^{n-1}$.

EXERCISE 9.24. Let F be a finite field of cardinality q, and let t be a positive integer. Let $\mathcal{A} := F^{\times t}$ and $\mathcal{Z} := F$. Use the result of the previous exercise to construct a family $\mathcal{H}$ of hash functions from $\mathcal{A}$ to $\mathcal{Z}$ that is an $O(\mathrm{len}(t)/q)$-forgeable message authentication scheme, where $\log_q |\mathcal{H}| = \mathrm{len}(t) + O(1)$. (See §6.7.2 and also Exercise 9.12.)

9.3 Ideals and quotient rings

Definition 9.18. *Let R be a ring. An **ideal of** R is a subgroup I of the additive group of R that is closed under multiplication by elements of R, that is, for all $a \in I$ and $r \in R$, we have $ar \in I$.*

Expanding the above definition, we see that a non-empty subset I of R is an ideal of R if and only if for all $a, b \in I$ and $r \in R$, we have

$$a + b \in I, \quad -a \in I, \quad \text{and} \quad ar \in I.$$

Observe that the condition $-a \in I$ is redundant, as it is implied by the condition $ar \in I$ with $r = -1_R$. Note that in the case when R is the ring $\mathbb{Z}$, this definition of an ideal is consistent with that given in §1.2.

Clearly, $\{0_R\}$ and R are ideals of R. From the fact that an ideal I is closed under multiplication by elements of R, it is easy to see that $I = R$ if and only if $1_R \in I$.

Example 9.30. For $m \in \mathbb{Z}$, the set $m\mathbb{Z}$ is not only a subgroup of the additive group $\mathbb{Z}$, it is also an ideal of the ring $\mathbb{Z}$. □

Example 9.31. For $m \in \mathbb{Z}$, the set $m\mathbb{Z}_n$ is not only a subgroup of the additive group $\mathbb{Z}_n$, it is also an ideal of the ring $\mathbb{Z}_n$. □

Example 9.32. In the previous two examples, we saw that for some rings, the notion of an additive subgroup coincides with that of an ideal. Of course, that is the exception, not the rule. Consider the ring of polynomial $R[\mathtt{X}]$. Suppose a is a non-zero polynomial in $R[\mathtt{X}]$. The additive subgroup generated by a consists of polynomials whose degrees are at most that of a. However, this subgroup is not an ideal, since any ideal containing a must also contain $a \cdot \mathtt{X}^i$ for all $i \geq 0$, and must therefore contain polynomials of arbitrarily high degree. □

Let $a_1, \ldots, a_k$ be elements of a ring R. Then it is easy to see that the set

$$a_1 R + \cdots + a_k R := \{a_1 r_1 + \cdots + a_k r_k : r_1, \ldots, r_k \in R\}$$

is an ideal of R, and contains $a_1, \ldots, a_k$. It is called the **ideal of R generated by** $a_1, \ldots, a_k$. Clearly, any ideal I of R that contains $a_1, \ldots, a_k$ must contain $a_1 R + \cdots + a_k R$, and in this sense, $a_1 R + \cdots + a_k R$ is the smallest ideal of R containing $a_1, \ldots, a_k$. An alternative notation that is often used is to write $(a_1, \ldots, a_k)$ to denote the ideal generated by $a_1, \ldots, a_k$, when the ring R is clear from context. If an ideal I is of the form $aR = \{ar : r \in R\}$ for some $a \in R$, then we say that I is a **principal ideal**.

Note that if I and J are ideals of a ring R, then so are $I + J := \{x + y : x \in I, y \in J\}$ and $I \cap J$ (verify).

Since an ideal I of a ring R is a subgroup of the additive group R, we may adopt the congruence notation in §8.3, writing $a \equiv b \pmod{I}$ if and only if $a - b \in I$.

Note that if $I = dR$, then $a \equiv b \pmod{I}$ if and only if $d \mid (a - b)$, and as a matter of notation, one may simply write this congruence as $a \equiv b \pmod{d}$.

Just considering R as an additive group, then as we saw in §8.3, we can form the additive group R/I of cosets, where $(a + I) + (b + I) := (a + b) + I$. By also considering the multiplicative structure of R, we can view R/I as a ring. To do this, we need the following fact:

Theorem 9.19. *Let I be an ideal of a ring R, and let $a, a', b, b' \in R$. If $a \equiv a' \pmod{I}$ and $b \equiv b' \pmod{I}$, then $ab \equiv a'b' \pmod{I}$.*

Proof. If $a' = a + x$ for $x \in I$ and $b' = b + y$ for $y \in I$, then $a'b' = ab + ay + bx + xy$. Since I is closed under multiplication by elements of R, we see that $ay, bx, xy \in I$, and since it is closed under addition, $ay + bx + xy \in I$. Hence, $a'b' - ab \in I$. $\square$

This theorem is perhaps one of the main motivations for the definition of an ideal. It allows us to define multiplication on R/I as follows: for $a, b \in R$,

$$(a + I) \cdot (b + I) := ab + I.$$

The above theorem is required to show that this definition is unambiguous. Once that is done, it is straightforward to show that all the properties that make R a ring are inherited by R/I — we leave the details of this to the reader. In particular, the multiplicative identity of R/I is the coset $1_R + I$. The ring R/I is called the **quotient ring** or **residue class ring of R modulo I**.

Elements of R/I may be called **residue classes**. As a matter of notation, for $a \in R$, we define $[a]_I := a + I$, and if $I = dR$, we may write this simply as $[a]_d$. If I is clear from context, we may also just write $[a]$.

***Example* 9.33.** For $n \geq 1$, the ring $\mathbb{Z}_n$ is precisely the quotient ring $\mathbb{Z}/n\mathbb{Z}$. $\square$

***Example* 9.34.** Let f be a monic polynomial over a ring R with $\deg(f) = \ell \geq 0$, and consider the quotient ring $E := R[X]/fR[X]$. By the division with remainder property for polynomials (Theorem 9.12), for every $a \in R[X]$, there exists a unique polynomial $b \in R[X]$ such that $a \equiv b \pmod{f}$ and

$\deg(b) < \ell$. From this, it follows that every element of E can be written uniquely as $[b]_f$, where $b \in R[X]$ is a polynomial of degree less than ℓ.

The assumption that f is monic may be relaxed a bit: all that really matters in this example is that the leading coefficient of f is a unit, so that the division with remainder property applies. Also, note that in this situation, we will generally prefer the more compact notation $R[X]/(f)$, instead of $R[X]/fR[X]$. $\square$

Example 9.35. Consider the polynomial $f := X^2 + X + 1 \in \mathbb{Z}_2[X]$ and the quotient ring $E := \mathbb{Z}_2[X]/(f)$. Let us name the elements of E as follows:

$$00 := [0]_f, \quad 01 := [1]_f, \quad 10 := [X]_f, \quad 11 := [X+1]_f.$$

With this naming convention, addition of two elements in E corresponds to just computing the bit-wise exclusive-or of their names. More precisely, the addition table for E is the following:

+	00	01	10	11
00	00	01	10	11
01	01	00	11	10
10	10	11	00	01
11	11	10	01	00

Note that 00 acts as the additive identity for E, and that as an additive group, E is isomorphic to the additive group $\mathbb{Z}_2 \times \mathbb{Z}_2$.

As for multiplication in E, one has to compute the product of two polynomials, and then reduce modulo f. For example, to compute $10 \cdot 11$, using the identity $X^2 \equiv X + 1 \pmod{f}$, one sees that

$$X \cdot (X + 1) \equiv X^2 + X \equiv (X + 1) + X \equiv 1 \pmod{f};$$

thus, $10 \cdot 11 = 01$. The reader may verify the following multiplication table for E:

·	00	01	10	11
00	00	00	00	00
01	00	01	10	11
10	00	10	11	01
11	00	11	01	10

Observe that 01 acts as the multiplicative identity for E. Notice that every non-zero element of E has a multiplicative inverse, and so E is in fact a field. By Theorem 9.16, we know that E^* must be cyclic (this fact also follows from Theorem 8.32, and the fact that $|E^*| = 3$.) Indeed, the reader may verify that both 10 and 11 have multiplicative order 3.

This is the first example we have seen of a finite field whose cardinality is not prime. □

EXERCISE 9.25. Let I be an ideal of a ring R, and let x and y be elements of R with $x \equiv y \pmod{I}$. Let $f \in R[X]$. Show that $f(x) \equiv f(y) \pmod{I}$.

EXERCISE 9.26. Let p be a prime, and consider the ring $\mathbb{Q}^{(p)}$ (see Example 9.23). Show that any non-zero ideal of $\mathbb{Q}^{(p)}$ is of the form (p^i), for some uniquely determined integer $i \geq 0$.

EXERCISE 9.27. Let R be a ring. Show that if I is a non-empty subset of $R[X]$ that is closed under addition, multiplication by elements of R, and multiplication by X, then I is an ideal of $R[X]$.

For the following three exercises, we need some definitions. An ideal I of a ring R is called **prime** if $I \subsetneq R$ and if for all $a, b \in R$, $ab \in I$ implies $a \in I$ or $b \in I$. An ideal I of a ring R is called **maximal** if $I \subsetneq R$ and there are no ideals J of R such that $I \subsetneq J \subsetneq R$.

EXERCISE 9.28. Let R be a ring. Show that:

(a) an ideal I of R is prime if and only if R/I is an integral domain;

(b) an ideal I of R is maximal if and only if R/I is a field;

(c) all maximal ideals of R are also prime ideals.

EXERCISE 9.29. This exercise explores some examples of prime and maximal ideals.

(a) Show that in the ring $\mathbb{Z}$, the ideal $\{0\}$ is prime but not maximal, and that the maximal ideals are precisely those of the form $p\mathbb{Z}$, where p is prime.

(b) More generally, show that in an integral domain D, the ideal $\{0\}$ is prime, and this ideal is maximal if and only if D is a field.

(c) Show that in the ring $F[X, Y]$, where F is a field, the ideal (X, Y) is maximal, while the ideals (X) and (Y) are prime, but not maximal.

EXERCISE 9.30. It is a fact that all non-trivial rings R contain at least one maximal ideal. Showing this in general requires some fancy set-theoretic notions. This exercise develops a proof in the case where R is countable (i.e., finite or countably infinite).

(a) Show that if R is non-trivial but finite, then it contains a maximal ideal.

(b) Assume that R is countably infinite, and let $a_1, a_2, a_3, \ldots$ be an enumeration of the elements of R. Define a sequence of ideals $I_0, I_1, I_2, \ldots$, as follows. Set $I_0 := \{0_R\}$, and for $i \geq 0$, define

$$I_{i+1} := \begin{cases} I_i + a_i R & \text{if } I_i + a_i R \subsetneq R; \\ I_i & \text{otherwise.} \end{cases}$$

Finally, set

$$I := \bigcup_{i=0}^{\infty} I_i.$$

Show that I is a maximal ideal of R. Hint: first show that I is an ideal; then show that $I \subsetneq R$ by assuming that $1_R \in I$ and deriving a contradiction; finally, show that I is maximal by assuming that for some $i = 1, 2, \ldots$, we have $I \subsetneq I + a_i R \subsetneq R$, and deriving a contradiction.

For the following three exercises, we need the following definition: for subsets X, Y of a ring R, let $X \cdot Y$ denote the set of all finite sums of the form

$$x_1 y_1 + \cdots + x_\ell y_\ell \quad \text{(with } x_k \in X, \ y_k \in Y \text{ for } k = 1, \ldots, \ell, \text{ for some } \ell \geq 0).$$

Note that $X \cdot Y$ contains 0_R (the "empty" sum, with $\ell = 0$).

EXERCISE 9.31. Let R be a ring, and S a subset of R. Show that $S \cdot R$ is an ideal of R, and is the smallest ideal of R containing S.

EXERCISE 9.32. Let I and J be two ideals of a ring R. Show that:

(a) $I \cdot J$ is an ideal;

(b) if I and J are principal ideals, with $I = aR$ and $J = bR$, then $I \cdot J = abR$, and so is also a principal ideal;

(c) $I \cdot J \subseteq I \cap J$;

(d) if $I + J = R$, then $I \cdot J = I \cap J$.

EXERCISE 9.33. Let S be a subring of a ring R. Let I be an ideal of R, and J an ideal of S. Show that:

(a) $I \cap S$ is an ideal of S, and that $(I \cap S) \cdot R$ is an ideal of R contained in I;

(b) $(J \cdot R) \cap S$ is an ideal of S containing J.

9.4 Ring homomorphisms and isomorphisms

Definition 9.20. *A function ρ from a ring R to a ring R' is called a **ring homomorphism** if it is a group homomorphism with respect to the underlying additive groups of R and R', and if in addition,*

(i) $\rho(ab) = \rho(a)\rho(b)$ *for all* $a, b \in R$, *and*

(ii) $\rho(1_R) = 1_{R'}$.

Expanding the definition, we see that the requirements that ρ must satisfy in order to be a ring homomorphism are that for all $a, b \in R$, we have $\rho(a + b) = \rho(a) + \rho(b)$ and $\rho(ab) = \rho(a)\rho(b)$, and that $\rho(1_R) = 1_{R'}$. Note that some texts do not require that $\rho(1_R) = 1_{R'}$.

Since a ring homomorphism ρ from R to R' is also an additive group homomorphism, we may also adopt the notation and terminology for image and kernel, and note that all the results of Theorem 8.20 apply as well here. In particular, $\rho(0_R) = 0_{R'}$, $\rho(a) = \rho(b)$ if and only if $a \equiv b \pmod{\ker(\rho)}$, and ρ is injective if and only if $\ker(\rho) = \{0_R\}$. However, we may strengthen Theorem 8.20 as follows:

Theorem 9.21. *Let $\rho : R \to R'$ be a ring homomorphism.*

(i) *For any subring S of R, $\rho(S)$ is a subring of R'.*

(ii) *For any ideal I of R, $\rho(I)$ is an ideal of* $\mathrm{img}(\rho)$.

(iii) $\ker(\rho)$ *is an ideal of R.*

(iv) *For any ideal I' of R', $\rho^{-1}(I')$ is an ideal of R.*

Proof. Exercise. $\square$

Theorems 8.21 and 8.22 have natural ring analogs—one only has to show that the corresponding group homomorphisms are also ring homomorphisms:

Theorem 9.22. *If $\rho : R \to R'$ and $\rho' : R' \to R''$ are ring homomorphisms, then so is their composition $\rho' \circ \rho : R \to R''$.*

Proof. Exercise. $\square$

Theorem 9.23. *Let $\rho_i : R \to R_i$, for $i = 1, \ldots, n$, be ring homomorphisms. Then the map $\rho : R \to R_1 \times \cdots \times R_n$ that sends $a \in R$ to $(\rho_1(a), \ldots, \rho_n(a))$ is a ring homomorphism.*

Proof. Exercise. $\square$

If a ring homomorphism $\rho : R \to R'$ is a bijection, then it is called a **ring isomorphism** of R with R'. If such a ring isomorphism ρ exists, we say that R **is isomorphic to** R', and write $R \cong R'$. Moreover, if $R = R'$, then ρ is called a **ring automorphism** on R.

Analogous to Theorem 8.24, we have:

Theorem 9.24. *If ρ is a ring isomorphism of R with R', then the inverse function ρ^{-1} is a ring isomorphism of R' with R.*

Proof. Exercise. $\square$

Because of this theorem, if R is isomorphic to R', we may simply say that "R and R' are isomorphic."

We stress that a ring isomorphism ρ of R with R' is essentially just a "renaming" of elements; in particular, ρ maps units to units and zero divisors to zero divisors (verify); moreover, the restriction of the map ρ to R^* yields a *group* isomorphism of R^* with $(R')^*$ (verify).

An injective ring homomorphism $\rho : R \to E$ is called an **embedding** of R in E. In this case, $\operatorname{img}(\rho)$ is a subring of E and $R \cong \operatorname{img}(\rho)$. If the embedding is a natural one that is clear from context, we may simply identify elements of R with their images in E under the embedding, and as a slight abuse of terminology, we shall say that R as a subring of E.

We have already seen an example of this, namely, when we formally defined the ring of polynomials $R[\mathtt{X}]$ over R, we defined the map $\rho : R \to R[\mathtt{X}]$ that sends $c \in R$ to the polynomial whose constant term is c, and all other coefficients zero. This map ρ is clearly an embedding, and it was via this embedding that we identified elements of R with elements of $R[\mathtt{X}]$, and so viewed R as a subring of $R[\mathtt{X}]$.

This practice of identifying elements of a ring with their images in another ring under a natural embedding is very common. We shall see more examples of this later (in particular, Example 9.43 below).

Theorems 8.25, 8.26, and 8.27 also have natural ring analogs—again, one only has to show that the corresponding group homomorphisms are also ring homomorphisms:

Theorem 9.25. *If I is an ideal of a ring R, then the natural map $\rho : R \to R/I$ given by $\rho(a) = a + I$ is a surjective ring homomorphism whose kernel is I.*

Proof. Exercise. $\square$

Theorem 9.26. *Let ρ be a ring homomorphism from R into R'. Then the map $\bar{\rho} : R/\ker(\rho) \to \operatorname{img}(\rho)$ that sends the coset $a + \ker(\rho)$ for $a \in R$ to $\rho(a)$ is unambiguously defined and is a ring isomorphism of $R/\ker(\rho)$ with $\operatorname{img}(\rho)$.*

Proof. Exercise. □

Theorem 9.27. *Let ρ be a ring homomorphism from R into R'. Then for any ideal I contained in $\ker(\rho)$, the map $\bar{\rho} : R/I \to \mathrm{img}(\rho)$ that sends the coset $a + I$ for $a \in R$ to $\rho(a)$ is unambiguously defined and is a ring homomorphism from R/I onto $\mathrm{img}(\rho)$ with kernel $\ker(\rho)/I$.*

Proof. Exercise. □

***Example* 9.36.** For $n \geq 1$, the natural map ρ from $\mathbb{Z}$ to $\mathbb{Z}_n$ sends $a \in \mathbb{Z}$ to the residue class $[a]_n$. In Example 8.41, we noted that this is a surjective group homomorphism on the underlying additive groups, with kernel $n\mathbb{Z}$; however, this map is also a ring homomorphism. □

***Example* 9.37.** As we saw in Example 8.42, if $n_1, \ldots, n_k$ are pairwise relatively prime, positive integers, then the map from $\mathbb{Z}$ to $\mathbb{Z}_{n_1} \times \cdots \times \mathbb{Z}_{n_k}$ that sends $x \in \mathbb{Z}$ to $([x]_{n_1}, \ldots, [x]_{n_k})$ is a surjective group homomorphism on the underlying additive groups, with kernel $n\mathbb{Z}$, where $n = \prod_{i=1}^{k} n_i$. However, this map is also a ring homomorphism (this follows from Example 9.36 and Theorem 9.23). Therefore, by Theorem 9.26, the map that sends $[x]_n \in \mathbb{Z}_n$ to $([x]_{n_1}, \ldots, [x]_{n_k})$ is a ring isomorphism of the ring $\mathbb{Z}_n$ with the ring $\mathbb{Z}_{n_1} \times \cdots \times \mathbb{Z}_{n_k}$. It follows that the restriction of this map to $\mathbb{Z}_n^*$ yields a *group* isomorphism of the *multiplicative* groups $\mathbb{Z}_n^*$ and $\mathbb{Z}_{n_1}^* \times \cdots \times \mathbb{Z}_{n_k}^*$ (see Example 9.13). □

***Example* 9.38.** As we saw in Example 8.43, if n_1, n_2 are positive integers with $n_1 > 1$ and $n_1 \mid n_2$, then the map $\bar{\rho} : \mathbb{Z}_{n_2} \to \mathbb{Z}_{n_1}$ that sends $[a]_{n_2}$ to $[a]_{n_1}$ is a surjective group homomorphism on the underlying additive groups with kernel $n_1\mathbb{Z}_{n_2}$. This map is also a ring homomorphism. The map $\bar{\rho}$ can also be viewed as the map obtained by applying Theorem 9.27 with the natural map ρ from $\mathbb{Z}$ to $\mathbb{Z}_{n_1}$ and the ideal $n_2\mathbb{Z}$ of $\mathbb{Z}$, which is contained in $\ker(\rho) = n_1\mathbb{Z}$. □

***Example* 9.39.** Let R be a subring of a ring E, and fix $\alpha \in E$. The **polynomial evaluation map** $\rho : R[\mathsf{X}] \to E$ that sends $a \in R[\mathsf{X}]$ to $a(\alpha) \in E$ is a ring homomorphism from $R[\mathsf{X}]$ into E (see Theorem 9.10). The image of ρ consists of all polynomial expressions in α with coefficients in R, and is denoted $R[\alpha]$. Note that $R[\alpha]$ is a subring of E containing $R \cup \{\alpha\}$, and is the smallest such subring of E. □

***Example* 9.40.** We can generalize the previous example to multi-variate polynomials. If R is a subring of a ring E and $\alpha_1, \ldots, \alpha_n \in E$, then the map $\rho : R[\mathsf{X}_1, \ldots, \mathsf{X}_n] \to E$ that sends $a \in R[\mathsf{X}_1, \ldots, \mathsf{X}_n]$ to $a(\alpha_1, \ldots, \alpha_n)$ is a ring homomorphism. Its image consists of all polynomial expressions in $\alpha_1, \ldots, \alpha_n$ with coefficients in R, and is denoted $R[\alpha_1, \ldots, \alpha_n]$. Moreover, this image is a subring of E containing $R \cup \{\alpha_1, \ldots, \alpha_n\}$, and is the smallest such subring of E. $\square$

Example 9.41. For any ring R, consider the map $\rho : \mathbb{Z} \to R$ that sends $m \in \mathbb{Z}$ to $m \cdot 1_R$ in R. This is clearly a ring homomorphism (verify). If $\ker(\rho) = \{0\}$, then $\text{img}(\rho) \cong \mathbb{Z}$, and so the ring $\mathbb{Z}$ is embedded in R, and R has characteristic zero. If $\ker(\rho) = n\mathbb{Z}$ for $n > 0$, then $\text{img}(\rho) \cong \mathbb{Z}_n$, and so the ring $\mathbb{Z}_n$ is embedded in R, and R has characteristic n. Note that we have $n = 1$ if and only if R is trivial.

Note that $\text{img}(\rho)$ is the smallest subring of R; indeed, since any subring of R must contain 1_R and be closed under addition and subtraction, it must contain $\text{img}(\rho)$. $\square$

Example 9.42. Let R be a ring of prime characteristic p. For any $a, b \in R$, we have (see Exercise 9.2)

$$(a + b)^p = \sum_{k=0}^{p} \binom{p}{k} a^{p-k} b^k.$$

However, by Exercise 1.12, all of the binomial coefficients are multiples of p, except for $k = 0$ and $k = p$, and hence in the ring R, all of these terms vanish, leaving us with

$$(a + b)^p = a^p + b^p.$$

This result is often jokingly referred to as the "freshman's dream," for somewhat obvious reasons.

Of course, as always, we have

$$(ab)^p = a^p b^p \quad \text{and} \quad 1_R^p = 1_R,$$

and so it follows that the map $\rho : R \to R$ that sends $a \in R$ to a^p is a ring homomorphism. It also immediately follows that for any integer $e \geq 1$, the e-fold composition $\rho^e : R \to R$ that sends $a \in R$ to a^{p^e} is also a ring homomorphism. $\square$

Example 9.43. As in Example 9.34, let f be a monic polynomial over a ring R with $\deg(f) = \ell$, but now assume that $\ell > 0$. Consider the natural map ρ from $R[X]$ to the quotient ring $E := R[X]/(f)$ that sends $a \in R[X]$ to $[a]_f$. If we restrict ρ to the subring R of $R[X]$, we obtain an embedding of R into E. Since this is a very natural embedding, one usually simply identifies elements of R with their images in E under ρ, and regards R as a subring of E. Taking this point of view, we see that if $a = \sum_i a_i \mathsf{X}^i$, then

$$[a]_f = \left[\sum_i a_i \mathsf{X}^i\right]_f = \sum_i a_i ([\mathsf{X}]_f)^i = a(\eta),$$

where $\eta := [\mathsf{X}]_f \in E$. Therefore, the map ρ may be viewed as the polynomial evaluation map, as in Example 9.39, that sends $a \in R[\mathsf{X}]$ to $a(\eta) \in E$. Note that we have $E = R[\eta]$; moreover, every element of E can be expressed uniquely as $b(\eta)$ for some $b \in R[\mathsf{X}]$ of degree less than ℓ, and more generally, for arbitrary $a, b \in R[\mathsf{X}]$, we have $a(\eta) = b(\eta)$ if and only if $a \equiv b \pmod{f}$. $\square$

Example 9.44. As a special case of Example 9.43, let $f := \mathsf{X}^2 + 1 \in \mathbb{R}[\mathsf{X}]$, and consider the quotient ring $\mathbb{R}[\mathsf{X}]/(f)$. If we set $i := [\mathsf{X}]_f \in \mathbb{R}[\mathsf{X}]/(f)$, then every element of $\mathbb{R}[\mathsf{X}]/(f)$ can be expressed uniquely as $a + bi$, where $a, b \in \mathbb{R}$. Moreover, we have $i^2 = -1$, and more generally, for $a, b, a', b' \in \mathbb{R}$, we have

$$(a + bi) + (a' + b'i) = (a + a') + (b + b')i$$

and

$$(a + bi) \cdot (a' + b'i) = (aa' - bb') + (ab' + a'b)i.$$

Thus, the rules for arithmetic in $\mathbb{R}[\mathsf{X}]/(f)$ are precisely the familiar rules of complex arithmetic, and so $\mathbb{C}$ and $\mathbb{R}[\mathsf{X}]/(f)$ are essentially the same, as rings. Indeed, the "algebraically correct" way of defining the complex numbers $\mathbb{C}$ is simply to define them to be the quotient ring $\mathbb{R}[\mathsf{X}]/(f)$ in the first place. This will be our point of view from now on. $\square$

Example 9.45. Consider the polynomial evaluation map $\rho : \mathbb{R}[\mathsf{X}] \to \mathbb{C} = R[\mathsf{X}]/(\mathsf{X}^2 + 1)$ that sends $g \in \mathbb{R}[\mathsf{X}]$ to $g(-i)$. For any $g \in \mathbb{R}[\mathsf{X}]$, we may write $g = (\mathsf{X}^2 + 1)q + a + b\mathsf{X}$, where $q \in \mathbb{R}[\mathsf{X}]$ and $a, b \in \mathbb{R}$. Since $(-i)^2 + 1 = i^2 + 1 = 0$, we have $g(-i) = ((-i)^2 + 1)q(-i) + a - bi = a - bi$. Clearly, then, ρ is surjective and the kernel of ρ is the ideal of $\mathbb{R}[\mathsf{X}]$ generated by the polynomial $\mathsf{X}^2 + 1$. By Theorem 9.26, we therefore get a ring automorphism $\bar{\rho}$ on $\mathbb{C}$ that sends $a + bi \in \mathbb{C}$ to $a - bi$. In fact, $\bar{\rho}$ it is none other than the complex conjugation map. Indeed, this is the "algebraically correct" way of defining complex conjugation in the first place. $\square$

Example 9.46. We defined the ring $\mathbb{Z}[i]$ of Gaussian integers in Example 9.22 as a subring of $\mathbb{C}$. Let us verify that the notation $\mathbb{Z}[i]$ introduced in Example 9.22 is consistent with that introduced in Example 9.39. Consider the polynomial evaluation map $\rho : \mathbb{Z}[\mathsf{X}] \to \mathbb{C}$ that sends $g \in \mathbb{Z}[\mathsf{X}]$ to $g(i) \in \mathbb{C}$.

For any $g \in \mathbb{Z}[X]$, we may write $g = (X^2 + 1)q + a + bX$, where $q \in \mathbb{Z}[X]$ and $a, b \in \mathbb{Z}$. Since $i^2 + 1 = 0$, we have $g(i) = (i^2 + 1)q(i) + a + bi = a + bi$. Clearly, then, the image of ρ is the set $\{a + bi : a, b \in \mathbb{Z}\}$, and the kernel of ρ is the ideal of $\mathbb{Z}[X]$ generated by the polynomial $X^2 + 1$. This shows that $\mathbb{Z}[i]$ in Example 9.22 is the same as $\mathbb{Z}[i]$ in Example 9.39, and moreover, Theorem 9.26 implies that $\mathbb{Z}[i]$ is isomorphic to $\mathbb{Z}[X]/(X^2 + 1)$.

Thus, we can directly construct the Gaussian integers as the quotient ring $\mathbb{Z}[X]/(X^2 + 1)$. Likewise the field $\mathbb{Q}[i]$ (see Exercise 9.8) can be constructed directly as $\mathbb{Q}[X]/(X^2 + 1)$. Such direct constructions are appealing in that they are purely "elementary," as they do not appeal to anything so "sophisticated" as the real numbers. $\square$

***Example* 9.47.** Let p be a prime, and consider the quotient ring $E := \mathbb{Z}_p[X]/(X^2 + 1)$. If we set $i := [X]_{X^2+1} \in E$, then $E = \mathbb{Z}_p[i] = \{a + bi : a, b \in \mathbb{Z}_p\}$. In particular, E is a ring of cardinality p^2. Moreover, the rules for addition and multiplication in E look exactly the same as they do in $\mathbb{C}$: for $a, b, a', b' \in \mathbb{Z}_p$, we have

$$(a + bi) + (a' + b'i) = (a + a') + (b + b')i$$

and

$$(a + bi) \cdot (a' + b'i) = (aa' - bb') + (ab' + a'b)i.$$

Note that E may or may not be a field.

On the one hand, suppose that $c^2 = -1$ for some $c \in \mathbb{Z}_p$ (for example, $p = 2$, $p = 5$, $p = 13$). Then $(c + i)(c - i) = c^2 + 1 = 0$, and so E is not an integral domain.

On the other hand, suppose there is no $c \in \mathbb{Z}_p$ such that $c^2 = -1$ (for example, $p = 3$, $p = 7$). Then for any $a, b \in \mathbb{Z}_p$, not both zero, we must have $a^2 + b^2 \neq 0$; indeed, suppose that $a^2 + b^2 = 0$, and that, say, $b \neq 0$; then we would have $(a/b)^2 = -1$, contradicting the assumption that -1 has no square root in $\mathbb{Z}_p$. Since $\mathbb{Z}_p$ is a field, it follows that the same formula for multiplicative inverses in $\mathbb{C}$ applies in E, namely,

$$(a + bi)^{-1} = \frac{a - bi}{a^2 + b^2}.$$

This construction provides us with more examples of finite fields whose cardinality is not prime. $\square$

***Example* 9.48.** If $\rho : R \to R'$ is a ring homomorphism, then we can extend ρ in a natural way to a ring homomorphism from $R[X]$ to $R'[X]$, by defining $\rho(\sum_i a_i X^i) := \sum_i \rho(a_i) X^i$. We leave it to the reader to verify that this indeed is a ring homomorphism. $\square$

EXERCISE 9.34. Verify that the "is isomorphic to" relation on rings is an equivalence relation; that is, for all rings R_1, R_2, R_3, we have:

(a) $R_1 \cong R_1$;

(b) $R_1 \cong R_2$ implies $R_2 \cong R_1$;

(c) $R_1 \cong R_2$ and $R_2 \cong R_3$ implies $R_1 \cong R_3$.

EXERCISE 9.35. Let R_1, R_2 be rings, and let $\rho : R_1 \times R_2 \to R_1$ be the map that sends $(a_1, a_2) \in R_1 \times R_2$ to $a_1 \in R_1$. Show that ρ is a surjective ring homomorphism whose kernel is $\{0_{R_1}\} \times R_2$.

EXERCISE 9.36. Let ρ be a ring homomorphism from R into R'. Show that the ideals of R containing $\ker(\rho)$ are in one-to-one correspondence with the ideals of $\mathrm{img}(\rho)$, where the ideal I of R containing $\ker(\rho)$ corresponds to the ideal $\rho(I)$ of $\mathrm{img}(\rho)$.

EXERCISE 9.37. Let $\rho : R \to S$ be a ring homomorphism. Show that $\rho(R^*) \subseteq S^*$, and that the restriction of ρ to R^* yields a group homomorphism $\rho^* : R^* \to S^*$ whose kernel is $(1_R + \ker(\rho)) \cap R^*$.

EXERCISE 9.38. Show that if F is a field, then the only ideals of F are $\{0_F\}$ and F. From this, conclude the following: if $\rho : F \to R$ is a ring homomorphism from F into a non-trivial ring R, then ρ must be an embedding.

EXERCISE 9.39. Let n be a positive integer.

(a) Show that the rings $\mathbb{Z}[\mathsf{X}]/(n)$ and $\mathbb{Z}_n[\mathsf{X}]$ are isomorphic.

(b) Assuming that $n = pq$, where p and q are distinct primes, show that the rings $\mathbb{Z}_n[\mathsf{X}]$ and $\mathbb{Z}_p[\mathsf{X}] \times \mathbb{Z}_q[\mathsf{X}]$ are isomorphic.

EXERCISE 9.40. Let n be a positive integer, let $f \in \mathbb{Z}[\mathsf{X}]$ be a monic polynomial, and let $\bar{f}$ be the image of f in $\mathbb{Z}_n[\mathsf{X}]$ (i.e., $\bar{f}$ is obtained by applying the natural map from $\mathbb{Z}$ to $\mathbb{Z}_n$ coefficient-wise to f). Show that the rings $\mathbb{Z}[\mathsf{X}]/(n, f)$ and $\mathbb{Z}_n[\mathsf{X}]/(\bar{f})$ are isomorphic.

EXERCISE 9.41. Let R be a ring, and let $\alpha_1, \ldots, \alpha_n$ be elements of R. Show that the rings R and $R[\mathsf{X}_1, \ldots, \mathsf{X}_n]/(\mathsf{X}_1 - \alpha_1, \ldots, \mathsf{X}_n - \alpha_n)$ are isomorphic.

EXERCISE 9.42. Let $\rho : R \to R'$ be a ring homomorphism, and suppose that we extend ρ, as in Example 9.48, to a ring homomorphism from $R[\mathsf{X}]$ to $R'[\mathsf{X}]$. Show that for any $a \in R[\mathsf{X}]$, we have $\mathbf{D}(\rho(a)) = \rho(\mathbf{D}(a))$, where $\mathbf{D}(\cdot)$ denotes the formal derivative.

EXERCISE 9.43. This exercise and the next generalize the Chinese remainder theorem to arbitrary rings. Suppose I and J are two ideals of a ring R such that $I + J = R$. Show that the map $\rho : R \to R/I \times R/J$ that sends $a \in R$ to $([a]_I, [a]_J)$ is a surjective ring homomorphism with kernel $I \cdot J$. Conclude that $R/(I \cdot J)$ is isomorphic to $R/I \times R/J$.

EXERCISE 9.44. Generalize the previous exercise, showing that $R/(I_1 \cdots I_k)$ is isomorphic to $R/I_1 \times \cdots \times R/I_k$, where R is a ring, and $I_1, \ldots, I_k$ are ideals of R, provided $I_i + I_j = R$ for all i, j such that $i \neq j$.

EXERCISE 9.45. Let F be a field and let d be an element of F that is not a perfect square (i.e., there does not exist $e \in F$ such that $e^2 = d$). Let $E := F[\mathsf{X}]/(\mathsf{X}^2 - d)$, and let $\eta := [\mathsf{X}]_{\mathsf{X}^2 - d}$, so that $E = F[\eta] = \{a + b\eta : a, b \in F\}$.

    (a) Show that the quotient ring E is a field, and write down the formula for the inverse of $a + b\eta \in E$.

    (b) Show that the map that sends $a + b\eta \in E$ to $a - b\eta$ is a ring automorphism on E.

EXERCISE 9.46. Let $\mathbb{Q}^{(m)}$ be the subring of $\mathbb{Q}$ defined in Example 9.23. Let us define the map $\rho : \mathbb{Q}^{(m)} \to \mathbb{Z}_m$ as follows. For $a/b \in \mathbb{Q}$ with b relatively prime to m, $\rho(a/b) := [a]_m([b]_m)^{-1}$. Show that ρ is unambiguously defined, and is a surjective ring homomorphism. Also, describe the kernel of ρ.

EXERCISE 9.47. Let $\rho : R \to R'$ be a map from a ring R to a ring R' that satisfies all the requirements of a ring homomorphism, except that we do not require that $\rho(1_R) = 1_{R'}$.

    (a) Give a concrete example of such a map ρ, such that $\rho(1_R) \neq 1_{R'}$ and $\rho(1_R) \neq 0_{R'}$.

    (b) Show that $\mathrm{img}(\rho)$ is a ring in which $\rho(1_R)$ plays the role of the multiplicative identity.

    (c) Show that if R' is an integral domain, and $\rho(1_R) \neq 0_{R'}$, then $\rho(1_R) = 1_{R'}$, and hence ρ satisfies our definition of a ring homomorphism.

    (d) Show that if ρ is surjective, then $\rho(1_R) = 1_{R'}$, and hence ρ satisfies our definition of a ring homomorphism.

10

Probabilistic primality testing

In this chapter, we discuss some simple and efficient probabilistic tests for primality.

10.1 Trial division

Suppose we are given an integer $n > 1$, and we want to determine whether n is prime or composite. The simplest algorithm to describe and to program is **trial division**. We simply divide n by 2, 3, and so on, testing if any of these numbers evenly divide n. Of course, we don't need to go any further than $\sqrt{n}$, since if n has any non-trivial factors, it must have one that is no greater than $\sqrt{n}$ (see Exercise 1.1). Not only does this algorithm determine whether n is prime or composite, it also produces a non-trivial factor of n in case n is composite.

Of course, the drawback of this algorithm is that it is terribly inefficient: it requires $\Theta(\sqrt{n})$ arithmetic operations, which is exponential in the binary length of n. Thus, for practical purposes, this algorithm is limited to quite small n. Suppose, for example, that n has 100 decimal digits, and that a computer can perform 1 billion divisions per second (this is much faster than any computer existing today). Then it would take on the order of 10^{33} *years* to perform $\sqrt{n}$ divisions.

In this chapter, we discuss a much faster primality test that allows 100 decimal digit numbers to be tested for primality in less than a second. Unlike the above test, however, this test does not find a factor of n when n is composite. Moreover, the algorithm is probabilistic, and may in fact make a mistake. However, the probability that it makes a mistake can be made so small as to be irrelevant for all practical purposes. Indeed, we can easily make the probability of error as small as 2^{-100} — should one really care about an event that happens with such a miniscule probability?

10.2 The structure of $\mathbb{Z}_n^*$

Before going any further, we have to have a firm understanding of the group $\mathbb{Z}_n^*$, for integer $n > 1$. As we know, $\mathbb{Z}_n^*$ consists of those elements $[a]_n \in \mathbb{Z}_n$ such that a is an integer relatively prime to n. Suppose $n = p_1^{e_1} \cdots p_r^{e_r}$ is the factorization of n into primes. By the Chinese remainder theorem, we have the ring isomorphism

$$\mathbb{Z}_n \cong \mathbb{Z}_{p_1^{e_1}} \times \cdots \times \mathbb{Z}_{p_r^{e_r}}$$

which induces a group isomorphism

$$\mathbb{Z}_n^* \cong \mathbb{Z}_{p_1^{e_1}}^* \times \cdots \times \mathbb{Z}_{p_r^{e_r}}^*.$$

Thus, to determine the structure of the group $\mathbb{Z}_n^*$ for general n, it suffices to determine the structure for $n = p^e$, where p is prime. By Theorem 2.13, we already know the order of the group $\mathbb{Z}_{p^e}^*$, namely, $\phi(p^e) = p^{e-1}(p-1)$.

The main result of this section is the following:

Theorem 10.1. *If p is an odd prime, then for any positive integer e, the group $\mathbb{Z}_{p^e}^*$ is cyclic. The group $\mathbb{Z}_{2^e}^*$ is cyclic for $e = 1$ or 2, but not for $e \geq 3$. For $e \geq 3$, $\mathbb{Z}_{2^e}^*$ is isomorphic to the additive group $\mathbb{Z}_2 \times \mathbb{Z}_{2^{e-2}}$.*

In the case where $e = 1$, this theorem is a special case of Theorem 9.16, which we proved in §9.2.3. Note that for $e > 1$, the ring $\mathbb{Z}_{p^e}$ is *not* a field, and so Theorem 9.16 cannot be used directly. To deal with the case $e > 1$, we need a few simple facts.

Theorem 10.2. *Let p be a prime. For integer $e \geq 1$, if $a \equiv b \pmod{p^e}$, then $a^p \equiv b^p \pmod{p^{e+1}}$.*

Proof. We have $a = b + cp^e$ for some $c \in \mathbb{Z}$. Thus, $a^p = b^p + pb^{p-1}cp^e + dp^{2e}$ for an integer d. It follows that $a^p \equiv b^p \pmod{p^{e+1}}$. $\square$

Theorem 10.3. *Let p be a prime. Let $e \geq 1$ be an integer and assume $p^e > 2$. If $a \equiv 1 + p^e \pmod{p^{e+1}}$, then $a^p \equiv 1 + p^{e+1} \pmod{p^{e+2}}$.*

Proof. By Theorem 10.2, $a^p \equiv (1 + p^e)^p \pmod{p^{e+2}}$. Expanding $(1 + p^e)^p$, we have

$$(1 + p^e)^p = 1 + p \cdot p^e + \sum_{k=2}^{p-1} \binom{p}{k} p^{ek} + p^{ep}.$$

By Exercise 1.12, all of the terms in the sum on k are divisible by p^{1+2e}, and $1 + 2e \geq e + 2$ for all $e \geq 1$. For the term p^{ep}, the assumption that $p^e > 2$ means that either $p \geq 3$ or $e \geq 2$, which implies $ep \geq e + 2$. $\square$

Now consider Theorem 10.1 in the case where p is odd. As we already know that $\mathbb{Z}_p^*$ is cyclic, assume $e > 1$. Let $x \in \mathbb{Z}$ be chosen so that $[x]_p$ generates $\mathbb{Z}_p^*$. Suppose the multiplicative order of $[x]_{p^e} \in \mathbb{Z}_{p^e}^*$ is m. Then as $x^m \equiv 1 \pmod{p^e}$ implies $x^m \equiv 1 \pmod{p}$, it must be the case that $p - 1$ divides m, and so $[x^{m/(p-1)}]_{p^e}$ has multiplicative order exactly $p - 1$. By Theorem 8.38, if we find an integer y such that $[y]_{p^e}$ has multiplicative order p^{e-1}, then $[x^{m/(p-1)}y]_{p^e}$ has multiplicative order $(p - 1)p^{e-1}$, and we are done. We claim that $y := 1 + p$ does the job. Any integer between 0 and $p^e - 1$ can be expressed as an e-digit number in base p; for example, $y = (0 \cdots 0\,1\,1)_p$. If we compute successive pth powers of y modulo p^e, then by Theorem 10.3 we have

$$
\begin{aligned}
y \bmod p^e &= (0 \quad \cdots \quad 0\,1\,1)_p, \\
y^p \bmod p^e &= (* \quad \cdots \quad *\,1\,0\,1)_p, \\
y^{p^2} \bmod p^e &= (* \quad \cdots \quad *\,1\,0\,0\,1)_p, \\
&\vdots \\
y^{p^{e-2}} \bmod p^e &= (1\,0 \quad \cdots \quad 0\,1)_p, \\
y^{p^{e-1}} \bmod p^e &= (0 \quad \cdots \quad 0\,1)_p.
\end{aligned}
$$

Here, "$*$" indicates an arbitrary digit. From this table of values, it is clear (see Theorem 8.37) that $[y]_{p^e}$ has multiplicative order p^{e-1}. That proves Theorem 10.1 for odd p.

We now prove Theorem 10.1 in the case $p = 2$. For $e = 1$ and $e = 2$, the theorem is easily verified. Suppose $e \geq 3$. Consider the subgroup $G \subseteq \mathbb{Z}_{2^e}^*$ generated by $[5]_{2^e}$. Expressing integers between 0 and $2^e - 1$ as e-digit binary numbers, and applying Theorem 10.3, we have

$$
\begin{aligned}
5 \bmod 2^e &= (0 \quad \cdots \quad 0\,1\,0\,1)_2, \\
5^2 \bmod 2^e &= (* \quad \cdots \quad *\,1\,0\,0\,1)_2, \\
&\vdots \\
5^{2^{e-3}} \bmod 2^e &= (1\,0 \quad \cdots \quad 0\,1)_2, \\
5^{2^{e-2}} \bmod 2^e &= (0 \quad \cdots \quad 0\,1)_2.
\end{aligned}
$$

So it is clear (see Theorem 8.37) that $[5]_{2^e}$ has multiplicative order 2^{e-2}. We claim that $[-1]_{2^e} \notin G$. If it were, then since it has multiplicative order 2, and since any cyclic group of even order has precisely one element of order 2 (see Theorem 8.31), it must be equal to $[5^{2^{e-3}}]_{2^e}$; however, it is clear from the above calculation that $5^{2^{e-3}} \not\equiv -1 \pmod{2^e}$. Let $H \subseteq \mathbb{Z}_{2^e}^*$ be the subgroup generated by $[-1]_{2^e}$. Then from the above, $G \cap H = \{[1]_{2^e}\}$, and hence by Theorem 8.28, $G \times H$ is isomorphic to the subgroup $G \cdot H$ of $\mathbb{Z}_{2^e}^*$.

But since the orders of $G \times H$ and $\mathbb{Z}_{2^e}^*$ are equal, we must have $G \cdot H = \mathbb{Z}_{2^e}^*$. That proves the theorem.

EXERCISE 10.1. Show that if n is a positive integer, the group $\mathbb{Z}_n^*$ is cyclic if and only if

$$n = 1, 2, 4, p^e, \text{ or } 2p^e,$$

where p is an odd prime and e is a positive integer.

EXERCISE 10.2. Let $n = pq$, where p and q are distinct primes such that $p = 2p' + 1$ and $q = 2q' + 1$, where p' and q' are themselves prime. Show that the subgroup $(\mathbb{Z}_n^*)^2$ of squares is a cyclic group of order $p'q'$.

EXERCISE 10.3. Let $n = pq$, where p and q are distinct primes such that $p \nmid (q - 1)$ and $q \nmid (p - 1)$.

(a) Show that the map that sends $[a]_n \in \mathbb{Z}_n^*$ to $[a^n]_{n^2} \in (\mathbb{Z}_{n^2}^*)^n$ is a group isomorphism.

(b) Consider the element $\alpha := [1 + n]_{n^2} \in \mathbb{Z}_{n^2}^*$; show that for any non-negative integer k, $\alpha^k = [1 + kn]_{n^2}$, and conclude that α has multiplicative order n.

(c) Show that the map from $\mathbb{Z}_n \times \mathbb{Z}_n^*$ to $\mathbb{Z}_{n^2}^*$ that sends $([k]_n, [a]_n)$ to $[(1 + kn)a^n]_{n^2}$ is a group isomorphism.

10.3 The Miller–Rabin test

We describe in this section a fast (polynomial time) test for primality, known as the **Miller–Rabin test**. The algorithm, however, is probabilistic, and may (with small probability) make a mistake.

We assume for the remainder of this section that the number n we are testing for primality is an odd integer greater than 1.

Several probabilistic primality tests, including the Miller–Rabin test, have the following general structure. Define $\mathbb{Z}_n^+$ to be the set of non-zero elements of $\mathbb{Z}_n$; thus, $|\mathbb{Z}_n^+| = n - 1$, and if n is prime, $\mathbb{Z}_n^+ = \mathbb{Z}_n^*$. Suppose also that we define a set $L_n \subseteq \mathbb{Z}_n^+$ such that:

- there is an efficient algorithm that on input n and $\alpha \in \mathbb{Z}_n^+$, determines if $\alpha \in L_n$;

- if n is prime, then $L_n = \mathbb{Z}_n^*$;

- if n is composite, $|L_n| \leq c(n - 1)$ for some constant $c < 1$.

To test n for primality, we set an "error parameter" t, and choose random elements $\alpha_1, \ldots, \alpha_t \in \mathbb{Z}_n^+$. If $\alpha_i \in L_n$ for all $i = 1, \ldots, t$, then we output *true*; otherwise, we output *false*.

It is easy to see that if n is prime, this algorithm always outputs *true*, and if n is composite this algorithm outputs *true* with probability at most c^t. If $c = 1/2$ and t is chosen large enough, say $t = 100$, then the probability that the output is wrong is so small that for all practical purposes, it is "just as good as zero."

We now make a first attempt at defining a suitable set L_n. Let us define

$$L_n := \{\alpha \in \mathbb{Z}_n^+ : \alpha^{n-1} = 1\}.$$

Note that $L_n \subseteq \mathbb{Z}_n^*$, since if $\alpha^{n-1} = 1$, then α has a multiplicative inverse, namely, α^{n-2}. Using a repeated-squaring algorithm, we can test if $\alpha \in L_n$ in time $O(\mathrm{len}(n)^3)$.

Theorem 10.4. *If n is prime, then $L_n = \mathbb{Z}_n^*$. If n is composite and $L_n \subsetneq \mathbb{Z}_n^*$, then $|L_n| \leq (n-1)/2$.*

Proof. Note that L_n is the kernel of the $(n-1)$-power map on $\mathbb{Z}_n^*$, and hence is a subgroup of $\mathbb{Z}_n^*$.

If n is prime, then we know that $\mathbb{Z}_n^*$ is a group of order $n-1$. Since the order of a group element divides the order of the group, we have $\alpha^{n-1} = 1$ for all $\alpha \in \mathbb{Z}_n^*$. That is, $L_n = \mathbb{Z}_n^*$.

Suppose that n is composite and $L_n \subsetneq \mathbb{Z}_n^*$. Since the order of a subgroup divides the order of the group, we have $|\mathbb{Z}_n^*| = m|L_n|$ for some integer $m > 1$. From this, we conclude that

$$|L_n| = \frac{1}{m}|\mathbb{Z}_n^*| \leq \frac{1}{2}|\mathbb{Z}_n^*| \leq \frac{n-1}{2}. \quad \square$$

Unfortunately, there are odd composite numbers n such that $L_n = \mathbb{Z}_n^*$. Such numbers are called **Carmichael numbers**. The smallest Carmichael number is

$$561 = 3 \cdot 11 \cdot 17.$$

Carmichael numbers are extremely rare, but it is known that there are infinitely many of them, so we can not ignore them. The following theorem puts some constraints on Carmichael numbers.

Theorem 10.5. *A Carmichael number n is of the form $n = p_1 \cdots p_r$, where the p_i are distinct primes, $r \geq 3$, and $(p_i - 1) \mid (n-1)$ for $i = 1, \ldots, r$.*

Proof. Let $n = p_1^{e_1} \cdots p_r^{e_r}$ be a Carmichael number. By the Chinese remainder theorem, we have an isomorphism of $\mathbb{Z}_n^*$ with the group

$$\mathbb{Z}_{p_1^{e_1}}^* \times \cdots \times \mathbb{Z}_{p_r^{e_r}}^*,$$

and we know that each group $\mathbb{Z}_{p_i^{e_i}}^*$ is cyclic of order $p_i^{e_i-1}(p_i - 1)$. Thus, the power $n - 1$ kills the group $\mathbb{Z}_n^*$ if and only if it kills all the groups $\mathbb{Z}_{p_i^{e_i}}^*$, which happens if and only if $p_i^{e_i-1}(p_i - 1) \mid (n - 1)$. Now, on the one hand, $n \equiv 0 \pmod{p_i}$. On the other hand, if $e_i > 1$, we would have $n \equiv 1 \pmod{p_i}$, which is clearly impossible. Thus, we must have $e_i = 1$.

It remains to show that $r \geq 3$. Suppose $r = 2$, so that $n = p_1 p_2$. We have

$$n - 1 = p_1 p_2 - 1 = (p_1 - 1)p_2 + (p_2 - 1).$$

Since $(p_1 - 1) \mid (n - 1)$, we must have $(p_1 - 1) \mid (p_2 - 1)$. By a symmetric argument, $(p_2 - 1) \mid (p_1 - 1)$. Hence, $p_1 = p_2$, a contradiction. $\square$

To obtain a good primality test, we need to define a different set L_n', which we do as follows. Let $n - 1 = 2^h m$, where m is odd (and $h \geq 1$ since n is assumed odd), and define

$$L_n' := \{\alpha \in \mathbb{Z}_n^+ : \quad \alpha^{m2^h} = 1 \quad \text{and}$$
$$\text{for } j = 0, \ldots, h - 1, \ \alpha^{m2^{j+1}} = 1 \text{ implies } \alpha^{m2^j} = \pm 1\}.$$

The Miller–Rabin test uses this set L_n', in place of the set L_n defined above. It is clear from the definition that $L_n' \subseteq L_n$.

Testing whether a given $\alpha \in \mathbb{Z}_n^+$ belongs to L_n' can be done using the following procedure:

> $\beta \leftarrow \alpha^m$
> if $\beta = 1$ then return *true*
> for $j \leftarrow 0$ to $h - 1$ do
> > if $\beta = -1$ then return *true*
> > if $\beta = +1$ then return *false*
> > $\beta \leftarrow \beta^2$
>
> return *false*

It is clear that using a repeated-squaring algorithm, this procedure runs in time $O(\text{len}(n)^3)$. We leave it to the reader to verify that this procedure correctly determines membership in L_n'.

Theorem 10.6. *If n is prime, then $L_n' = \mathbb{Z}_n^*$. If n is composite, then $|L_n'| \leq (n - 1)/4$.*

The rest of this section is devoted to a proof of this theorem. Let $n - 1 = m2^h$, where m is odd.

Case 1: n is prime. Let $\alpha \in \mathbb{Z}_n^*$. Since $\mathbb{Z}_n^*$ is a group of order $n - 1$, and the order of a group element divides the order of the group, we know that $\alpha^{m2^h} = \alpha^{n-1} = 1$. Now consider any index $j = 0, \ldots, h - 1$ such that $\alpha^{m2^{j+1}} = 1$, and consider the value $\beta := \alpha^{m2^j}$. Then since $\beta^2 = \alpha^{m2^{j+1}} = 1$, the only possible choices for β are ± 1—this is because $\mathbb{Z}_n^*$ is cyclic of even order and so there are exactly two elements of $\mathbb{Z}_n^*$ whose multiplicative order divides 2, namely ± 1. So we have shown that $\alpha \in L_n'$.

Case 2: $n = p^e$, where p is prime and $e > 1$. Certainly, L_n' is contained in the kernel K of the $(n-1)$-power map on $\mathbb{Z}_n^*$. By Theorem 8.31, $|K| = \gcd(\phi(n), n-1)$. Since $n = p^e$, we have $\phi(n) = p^{e-1}(p-1)$, and so

$$|L_n'| \leq |K| = \gcd(p^{e-1}(p-1), p^e - 1) = p - 1 = \frac{p^e - 1}{p^{e-1} + \cdots + 1} \leq \frac{n-1}{4}.$$

Case 3: $n = p_1^{e_1} \cdots p_r^{e_r}$ is the prime factorization of n, and $r > 1$. For $i = 1, \ldots, r$, let R_i denote the ring $\mathbb{Z}_{p_i^{e_i}}$, and let

$$\theta : R_1 \times \cdots \times R_r \to \mathbb{Z}_n$$

be the ring isomorphism provided by the Chinese remainder theorem. Also, let $\phi(p_i^{e_i}) = m_i 2^{h_i}$, with m_i odd, for $i = 1, \ldots, r$, and let $\ell := \min\{h, h_1, \ldots, h_r\}$. Note that $\ell \geq 1$, and that each R_i^* is a cyclic group of order $m_i 2^{h_i}$.

We first claim that for any $\alpha \in L_n'$, we have $\alpha^{m2^\ell} = 1$. To prove this, first note that if $\ell = h$, then by definition, $\alpha^{m2^\ell} = 1$, so suppose that $\ell < h$. By way of contradiction, suppose that $\alpha^{m2^\ell} \neq 1$, and let j be the largest index in the range $\ell, \ldots, h - 1$ such that $\alpha^{m2^{j+1}} = 1$. By the definition of L_n', we must have $\alpha^{m2^j} = -1$. Since $\ell < h$, we must have $\ell = h_i$ for some particular index $i = 1, \ldots, r$. Writing $\alpha = \theta(\alpha_1, \ldots, \alpha_r)$, we have $\alpha_i^{m2^j} = -1$. This implies that the multiplicative order of α_i^m is equal to 2^{j+1} (see Theorem 8.37). However, since $j \geq \ell = h_i$, this contradicts the fact that the order of a group element (in this case, α_i^m) must divide the order of the group (in this case, R_i^*).

From the claim in the previous paragraph, and the definition of L_n', it follows that $\alpha \in L_n'$ implies $\alpha^{m2^{\ell-1}} = \pm 1$. We now consider an experiment in which α is chosen at random from $\mathbb{Z}_n^*$ (that is, with a uniform distribution), and show that $\mathsf{P}[\alpha^{m2^{\ell-1}} = \pm 1] \leq 1/4$, from which the theorem will follow.

Write $\alpha = \theta(\alpha_1, \ldots, \alpha_r)$. As α is uniformly distributed over $\mathbb{Z}_n^*$, each α_i is uniformly distributed over R_i^*, and the collection of all the α_i is a mutually independent collection of random variables.

For $i = 1, \ldots, r$ and $j = 0, \ldots, h$, let $G_i(j)$ denote the image of the $(m2^j)$-power map on R_i^*. By Theorem 8.31, we have

$$|G_i(j)| = \frac{m_i 2^{h_i}}{\gcd(m_i 2^{h_i}, m2^j)}.$$

Because $\ell \le h$ and $\ell \le h_i$, a simple calculation shows that

$$|G_i(h)| \text{ divides } |G_i(\ell)| \quad \text{and} \quad 2|G_i(\ell)| = |G_i(\ell - 1)|.$$

In particular, $|G_i(\ell - 1)|$ is even and is no smaller than $2|G_i(h)|$. The fact that $|G_i(\ell - 1)|$ is even implies that $-1 \in G_i(\ell - 1)$.

The event $\alpha^{m2^{\ell-1}} = \pm 1$ occurs if and only if either

(E_1) $\alpha_i^{m2^{\ell-1}} = 1$ for $i = 1, \ldots, r$, or

(E_2) $\alpha_i^{m2^{\ell-1}} = -1$ for $i = 1, \ldots, r$.

Since the events E_1 and E_2 are disjoint, and since the values $\alpha_i^{m2^{\ell-1}}$ are mutually independent, with each value $\alpha_i^{m2^{\ell-1}}$ uniformly distributed over $G_i(\ell - 1)$ (see part (a) of Exercise 8.22), and since $G_i(\ell - 1)$ contains ± 1, we have

$$\mathsf{P}[\alpha^{m2^{\ell-1}} = \pm 1] = \mathsf{P}[E_1] + \mathsf{P}[E_2] = 2 \prod_{i=1}^{r} \frac{1}{|G_i(\ell - 1)|},$$

and since $|G_i(\ell - 1)| \ge 2|G_i(h)|$, we have

$$\mathsf{P}[\alpha^{m2^{\ell-1}} = \pm 1] \le 2^{-r+1} \prod_{i=1}^{r} \frac{1}{|G_i(h)|}. \tag{10.1}$$

If $r \ge 3$, then (10.1) directly implies that $\mathsf{P}[\alpha^{m2^{\ell-1}} = \pm 1] \le 1/4$, and we are done. So suppose that $r = 2$. In this case, Theorem 10.5 implies that n is not a Carmichael number, which implies that for some $i = 1, \ldots, r$, we must have $G_i(h) \ne \{1\}$, and so $|G_i(h)| \ge 2$, and (10.1) again implies that $\mathsf{P}[\alpha^{m2^{\ell-1}} = \pm 1] \le 1/4$.

That completes the proof of Theorem 10.6.

EXERCISE 10.4. Show that an integer $n > 1$ is prime if and only if there exists an element in $\mathbb{Z}_n^*$ of multiplicative order $n - 1$.

EXERCISE 10.5. Let p be a prime. Show that $n := 2p + 1$ is a prime if and only if $2^{n-1} \equiv 1 \pmod{n}$.

EXERCISE 10.6. Here is another primality test that takes as input an odd integer $n > 1$, and a positive integer parameter t. The algorithm chooses $\alpha_1, \ldots, \alpha_t \in \mathbb{Z}_n^+$ at random, and computes

$$\beta_i := \alpha_i^{(n-1)/2} \quad (i = 1, \ldots, t).$$

If $(\beta_1, \ldots, \beta_t)$ is of the form $(\pm 1, \pm 1, \ldots, \pm 1)$, but is not equal to $(1, 1, \ldots, 1)$, the algorithm outputs *true*; otherwise, the algorithm outputs *false*. Show that if n is prime, then the algorithm outputs *false* with probability at most 2^{-t}, and if n is composite, the algorithm outputs *true* with probability at most 2^{-t}.

In the terminology of §7.2, the algorithm in the above exercise is an example of an "Atlantic City" algorithm for the language of prime numbers (or equivalently, the language of composite numbers), while the Miller–Rabin test is an example of a "Monte Carlo" algorithm for the language of *composite* numbers.

10.4 Generating random primes using the Miller–Rabin test

The Miller–Rabin test is the most practical algorithm known for testing primality, and because of this, it is widely used in many applications, especially cryptographic applications where one needs to generate large, random primes (as we saw in §7.8). In this section, we discuss how one uses the Miller–Rabin test in several practically relevant scenarios where one must generate large primes.

10.4.1 Generating a random prime between 2 and M

Suppose one is given an integer $M \geq 2$, and wants to generate a random prime between 2 and M. We can do this by simply picking numbers at random until one of them passes a primality test. We discussed this problem in some detail in §7.5, where we assumed that we had a primality test *IsPrime*. The reader should review §7.5, and §7.5.1 in particular. In this section, we discuss aspects of this problem that are specific to the situation where the Miller–Rabin test is used to implement *IsPrime*.

To be more precise, let us define the following algorithm $MR(n, t)$, which takes as input integers n and t, with $n > 1$ and $t \geq 1$, and runs as follows:

Algorithm $MR(n, t)$:

if $n = 2$ then return *true*

if n is even then return *false*

repeat t times

$\qquad \alpha \leftarrow_R \{1, \ldots, n-1\}$

$\qquad$ if $\alpha \notin L'_n$ return *false*

return *true*

So we shall implement *IsPrime*$(\cdot)$ as $MR(\cdot, t)$, where t is an auxiliary parameter. By Theorem 10.6, if n is prime, the output of $MR(n, t)$ is always *true*, while if n is composite, the output is *true* with probability at most 4^{-t}. Thus, this implementation of *IsPrime* satisfies the assumptions in §7.5.1, with $\epsilon = 4^{-t}$.

Let $\gamma(M, t)$ be the probability that the output of Algorithm RP in §7.5— using this implementation of *IsPrime*—is composite. Then as we discussed in §7.5.1,

$$\gamma(M, t) \leq 4^{-t} \frac{M-1}{\pi(M)} = O(4^{-t}k), \qquad (10.2)$$

where $k = \text{len}(M)$. Furthermore, if the output of Algorithm RP is prime, then every prime is equally likely; that is, conditioning on the event that the output is prime, the conditional output distribution is uniform over all primes.

Let us now consider the expected running time of Algorithm RP. As was shown in §7.5.1, this is $O(kW'_M)$, where W'_M is the expected running time of *IsPrime* where the average is taken with respect to the random choice of input $n \in \{2, \ldots, M\}$ and the random choices of the primality test itself. Clearly, we have $W'_M = O(tk^3)$, since $MR(n, t)$ executes at most t iterations of the Miller–Rabin test, and each such test takes time $O(k^3)$. This leads to an expected total running time bound of $O(tk^4)$. However, this estimate for W'_M is overly pessimistic. Intuitively, this is because when n is composite, we expect to perform very few Miller–Rabin tests—only when n is prime do we actually perform all t of them. To make a rigorous argument, consider the experiment in which n is chosen at random from $\{2, \ldots, M\}$, and $MR(n, t)$ is executed. Let Y be the number of times the basic Miller–Rabin test is actually executed. Conditioned on any fixed, odd, prime value of n, the value of Y is always t. Conditioned on any fixed, odd, composite value of n, the distribution of Y is geometric with an associated success probability of at least 3/4; thus, the conditional expectation of Y is at most 4/3 in this case. Thus, we have

$$\mathsf{E}[Y] = \mathsf{E}[Y \mid n \text{ prime}]\mathsf{P}[n \text{ prime}] + \mathsf{E}[Y \mid n \text{ composite}]\mathsf{P}[n \text{ composite}]$$
$$\leq t\pi(M)/(M-1) + 4/3.$$

Thus, $\mathsf{E}[Y] \leq 4/3 + O(t/k)$, from which it follows that $W'_M = O(k^3 + tk^2)$, and hence the expected total running time of Algorithm RP is actually $O(k^4 + tk^3)$.

Note that the above estimate (10.2) for $\gamma(M,t)$ is actually quite pessimistic. This is because the error probability 4^{-t} is a worst-case estimate; in fact, for "most" composite integers n, the probability that $MR(n,t)$ outputs *true* is much smaller than this. In fact, $\gamma(M,1)$ is *very* small for large M. For example, the following is known:

Theorem 10.7. *We have*

$$\gamma(M,1) \leq \exp[-(1+o(1))\log(M)\log(\log(\log(M)))/\log(\log(M))].$$

Proof. Literature—see §10.7. $\square$

The bound in the above theorem goes to zero quite quickly—faster than $(\log M)^{-c}$ for any positive constant c. While the above theorem is asymptotically very good, in practice, one needs explicit bounds. For example, the following *lower* bounds for $-\log_2(\gamma(2^k, 1))$ are known:

k	200	300	400	500	600
	3	19	37	55	74

Given an upper bound on $\gamma(M,1)$, we can bound $\gamma(M,t)$ for $t \geq 2$ using the following inequality:

$$\gamma(M,t) \leq \frac{\gamma(M,1)}{1 - \gamma(M,1)} 4^{-t+1}. \tag{10.3}$$

To prove (10.3), it is not hard to see that on input M, the output distribution of Algorithm RP is the same as that of the following algorithm:

```
repeat
    repeat
        n ←_R {2, ..., M}
    until MR(n, 1)
    n₁ ← n
until MR(n₁, t − 1)
output n₁
```

Consider for a moment a single execution of the outer loop of the above algorithm. Let β be the probability that n_1 is composite, and let α be the conditional probability that $MR(n_1, t-1)$ outputs *true*, given that n_1 is composite. Evidently, $\beta = \gamma(M, 1)$ and $\alpha \leq 4^{-t+1}$.

Now, using *exactly* the same reasoning as was used to derive equation (7.2) in §7.5.1, we find that

$$\gamma(M, t) = \frac{\alpha\beta}{\alpha\beta + (1 - \beta)} \leq \frac{\alpha\beta}{1 - \beta} \leq \frac{4^{-t+1}\gamma(M, 1)}{1 - \gamma(M, 1)},$$

which proves (10.3).

Given that $\gamma(M, 1)$ is so small, for large M, Algorithm RP actually exhibits the following behavior in practice: it generates a random value $n \in \{2, \ldots, M\}$; if n is odd and composite, then the very *first* iteration of the Miller–Rabin test will detect this with overwhelming probability, and no more iterations of the test are performed on this n; otherwise, if n is prime, the algorithm will perform $t - 1$ more iterations of the Miller–Rabin test, "just to make sure."

EXERCISE 10.7. Consider the problem of generating a random Sophie Germain prime between 2 and M (see §5.5.5). One algorithm to do this is as follows:

> repeat
> > $n \leftarrow_R \{2, \ldots, M\}$
> > if $MR(n, t)$ then
> > > if $MR(2n + 1, t)$ then
> > > > output n and halt
>
> forever

Assuming Conjecture 5.26, show that this algorithm runs in expected time $O(k^5 + tk^4)$, and outputs a number that is not a Sophie Germain prime with probability $O(4^{-t}k^2)$. As usual, $k := \mathrm{len}(M)$.

EXERCISE 10.8. Improve the algorithm in the previous exercise, so that under the same assumptions, it runs in expected time $O(k^5 + tk^3)$, and outputs a number that is not a Sophie Germain prime with probability $O(4^{-t}k^2)$, or even better, show that this probability is at most $\gamma(M, t)\pi^*(M)/\pi(M) = O(\gamma(M, t)k)$, where $\pi^*(M)$ is defined as in §5.5.5.

EXERCISE 10.9. Suppose in Algorithm RFN in §7.7 we implement algorithm *IsPrime*$(\cdot)$ as $MR(\cdot, t)$, where t is a parameter satisfying $4^{-t}(2 + \log M) \leq$

$1/2$, if M is the input to RFN. Show that the expected running time of Algorithm RFN in this case is $O(k^5 + tk^4 \operatorname{len}(k))$. Hint: use Exercise 7.20.

10.4.2 Trial division up to a small bound

In generating a random prime, most candidates n will in fact be composite, and so it makes sense to cast these out as quickly as possible. Significant efficiency gains can be achieved by testing if a given candidate n is divisible by any small primes up to a given bound s, before we subject n to a Miller–Rabin test. This strategy makes sense, since for a small, "single precision" prime p, we can test if $p \mid n$ essentially in time $O(\operatorname{len}(n))$, while a single iteration of the Miller–Rabin test takes time $O(\operatorname{len}(n)^3)$ steps.

To be more precise, let us define the following algorithm $MRS(n, t, s)$, which takes as input integers n, t, and s, with $n > 1$, $t \geq 1$, and $s > 1$:

Algorithm $MRS(n, t, s)$:

for each prime $p \leq s$ do
    if $p \mid n$ then
        if $p = n$ then return *true* else return *false*

repeat t times
    $\alpha \leftarrow_R \{1, \dots, n-1\}$
    if $\alpha \notin L'_n$ return *false*

return *true*

In an implementation of the above algorithm, one would most likely use the sieve of Eratosthenes (see §5.4) to generate the small primes.

Note that $MRS(n, t, 2)$ is equivalent to $MR(n, t)$. Also, it is clear that the probability that $MRS(n, t, s)$ makes a mistake is no more than the probability that $MR(n, t)$ makes a mistake. Therefore, using MRS in place of MR will not increase the probability that the output of Algorithm RP is a composite—indeed, it is likely that this probability decreases significantly.

Let us now analyze the impact on the running time. To do this, we need to estimate the probability $\tau(M, s)$ that a randomly chosen number between 2 and M is not divisible by any primes up to s. If M is sufficiently large with respect to s, the following heuristic argument can be made rigorous, as we will discuss below. The probability that a random number is divisible by a prime p is about $1/p$, so the probability that it is not divisible by p is about $1 - 1/p$. Assuming that these events are essentially independent for different values of p (this is the heuristic part), we estimate

$$\tau(M, s) \approx \prod_{p \leq s}(1 - 1/p) \sim B_1/\log s,$$

where $B_1 \approx 0.56146$ is the constant from Exercise 5.14 (see also Theorem 5.21).

Of course, performing the trial division takes some time, so let us also estimate the expected number $\kappa(M, s)$ of trial divisions performed. If $p_1, p_2, \ldots, p_r$ are the primes up to s, then for $i = 1, \ldots, r$, the probability that we perform at least i trial divisions is precisely $\tau(M, p_i - 1)$. From this, it follows (see Theorem 6.8) that

$$\kappa(M, s) = \sum_{p \leq s}\tau(M, p - 1) \approx \sum_{p \leq s}B_1/\log p.$$

Using Exercise 5.9 and the Prime number theorem, we obtain

$$\kappa(M, s) \approx \sum_{p \leq s}B_1/\log p \sim B_1\pi(s)/\log s \sim B_1 s/(\log s)^2.$$

If $k = \operatorname{len}(M)$, for a random $n \in \{2, \ldots, M\}$, the expected amount of time spent within $MRS(n, t, s)$ performing the Miller–Rabin test is now easily seen to be $O(k^3/\operatorname{len}(s) + tk^2)$. Further, assuming that each individual trial division step takes time $O(\operatorname{len}(n))$, the expected running time of trial division up to s is $O(ks/\operatorname{len}(s)^2)$. This estimate does not take into account the time to generate the small primes using the sieve of Eratosthenes. These values might be pre-computed, in which case this time is zero, but even if we compute them on the fly, this takes time $O(s\operatorname{len}(\operatorname{len}(s)))$, which is dominated by $O(ks/\operatorname{len}(s)^2))$ for any reasonable value of s (in particular, for $s \leq k^{O(1)}$).

So provided $s = o(k^2\operatorname{len}(k))$, the running time of MRS will be dominated by the Miller–Rabin test, which is what we want, of course—if we spend as much time on trial division as the time it would take to perform a single Miller–Rabin test, we might as well just perform the Miller–Rabin test. In practice, one should use a very conservative bound for s, probably no more than k^2, since getting s arbitrarily close to optimal does not really provide that much benefit, while if we choose s too large, it can actually do significant harm.

From the above estimates, we can conclude that with $k \leq s \leq k^2$, the expected running time W'_M of $MRS(n, t, s)$, with respect to a randomly chosen n between 2 and M, is

$$W'_M = O(k^3/\operatorname{len}(k) + tk^2). \tag{10.4}$$

From this, it follows that the expected running time of Algorithm RP on input M is $O(k^4/\operatorname{len}(k) + tk^3)$. Thus, we effectively reduce the running time by a factor proportional to $\operatorname{len}(k)$, which is a very real and noticeable improvement in practice.

> The reader may have noticed that in our analysis of *MRS*, we assumed that computing $n \bmod p$ for a "small" prime p takes time $O(\operatorname{len}(n))$. However, if we strictly followed the rules established in Theorem 3.3, we should charge time $O(\operatorname{len}(n)\operatorname{len}(p))$ for this division step. To answer this charge that we have somehow "cheated," we offer the following remarks.
>
> First, in practice the primes p are so small that they surely will fit into a single digit in the underlying representation of integers as vectors of digits, and so estimating the cost as $O(\operatorname{len}(n))$ rather than $O(\operatorname{len}(n)\operatorname{len}(p))$ seems more realistic.
>
> Second, even if one uses the bound $O(\operatorname{len}(n)\operatorname{len}(p))$, one can carry out a similar analysis, obtaining the same result (namely, a speedup by a factor proportional to $\operatorname{len}(k)$) except that one should choose s from a slightly smaller range (namely, $s = o(k^2)$).

As we already mentioned, the above analysis is heuristic, but the results are correct. We shall now discuss how this analysis can be made rigorous; however, we should remark that any such rigorous analysis is mainly of theoretical interest only—in any practical implementation, the optimal choice of the parameter s is best determined by experiment, with the analysis being used only as a rough guide. Now, to make the analysis rigorous, we need prove that the estimate $\tau(M, s) \approx \prod_{p \leq s}(1 - 1/p)$ is sufficiently accurate. Proving such estimates takes us into the realm of "sieve theory." The larger M is with respect to s, the easier it is to prove such estimates. We shall prove only the simplest and most naive such estimate, but it is still good enough for our purposes, if we do not care too much about hidden big-O constants.

Before stating any results, let us restate the problem slightly. For real $y \geq 0$, let us call a positive integer "y-rough" if it is not divisible by any prime p up to y. For real $x \geq 0$, let us define $R(x, y)$ to be the number of y-rough integers up to x. Thus, since $\tau(M, s)$ is the probability that a random integer between 2 and M is s-rough, and 1 is by definition s-rough, we have $\tau(M, s) = (R(M, s) - 1)/(M - 1)$.

Theorem 10.8. *For any real $x \geq 0$ and $y \geq 0$, we have*

$$\left| R(x, y) - x \prod_{p \leq y}(1 - 1/p) \right| \leq 2^{\pi(y)}.$$

Proof. To simplify the notation, we shall use the Möbius function μ (see

§2.6). Also, for a real number u, let us write $u = \lfloor u \rfloor + \{u\}$, where $0 \le \{u\} < 1$. Let P be the product of the primes up to the bound y.

Now, there are $\lfloor x \rfloor$ positive integers up to x, and of these, for each prime p dividing P, precisely $\lfloor x/p \rfloor$ are divisible by p, for each pair p, p' of distinct primes dividing P, precisely $\lfloor x/pp' \rfloor$ are divisible by pp', and so on. By inclusion/exclusion (see Exercise 6.3), we have

$$R(x, y) = \sum_{d|P} \mu(d) \lfloor x/d \rfloor = \sum_{d|P} \mu(d)(x/d) - \sum_{d|P} \mu(d)\{x/d\}.$$

Moreover,

$$\sum_{d|P} \mu(d)(x/d) = x \sum_{d|P} \mu(d)/d = x \prod_{p \le y} (1 - 1/p),$$

and

$$\left| \sum_{d|P} \mu(d)\{x/d\} \right| \le \sum_{d|P} 1 = 2^{\pi(y)}.$$

That proves the theorem. $\square$

This theorem only says something non-trivial when y is quite small. Nevertheless, using Chebyshev's theorem on the density of primes, along with Mertens' theorem, it is not hard to see that this theorem implies that $\tau(M, s) = O(1/\log s)$ when $s = O(\log M \log \log M)$, which implies the estimate (10.4) above. We leave the details as an exercise for the reader.

EXERCISE 10.10. Prove the claim made above that $\tau(M, s) = O(1/\log s)$ when $s = O(\log M \log \log M)$. More precisely, show that there exist constants c, d, and s_0, such that for all M and d satisfying $s_0 \le s \le c \log M \log \log M$, we have $\tau(M, s) \le d/\log s$. From this, derive the estimate (10.4) above.

EXERCISE 10.11. Let f be a polynomial with integer coefficients. For real $x \ge 0$ and $y \ge 0$, define $R_f(x, y)$ to be the number of integers m up to x such that $f(m)$ is y-rough. For positive integer M, define $\omega_f(M)$ to be the number of integers $m \in \{0, \dots, M-1\}$ such that $f(m) \equiv 0 \pmod{M}$. Show that

$$\left| R_f(x, y) - x \prod_{p \le y} (1 - \omega_f(p)/p) \right| \le \prod_{p \le y} (1 + \omega_f(p)).$$

EXERCISE 10.12. Consider again the problem of generating a random Sophie Germain prime, as discussed in Exercises 10.7 and 10.8. A useful idea is to first test if *either* n *or* $2n + 1$ are divisible by any small primes up to some bound s, before performing any more expensive tests. Using this idea, design and analyze an algorithm that improves the running time of the algorithm in Exercise 10.8 to $O(k^5 / \operatorname{len}(k)^2 + tk^3)$ — under the same assumptions, and achieving the same error probability bound as in that exercise. Hint: first show that the previous exercise implies that the number of positive integers m up to x such that both m and $2m + 1$ are y-rough is at most

$$x \cdot \frac{1}{2} \prod_{2 < p \leq y} (1 - 2/p) + 3^{\pi(y)}.$$

EXERCISE 10.13. Design an algorithm that takes as input a prime q and a bound M, and outputs a random prime p between 2 and M such that $p \equiv 1 \pmod{q}$. Clearly, we need to assume that M is sufficiently large with respect to q. Analyze your algorithm assuming Conjecture 5.24 (and using the result of Exercise 5.22). State how large M must be with respect to q, and under these assumptions, show that your algorithm runs in time $O(k^4 / \operatorname{len}(k) + tk^3)$, and that its output is incorrect with probability $O(4^{-t}k)$. As usual, $k := \operatorname{len}(M)$.

10.4.3 Generating a random k-bit prime

In some applications, we want to generate a random prime of fixed size — a random 1024-bit prime, for example. More generally, let us consider the following problem: given integer $k \geq 2$, generate a random k-bit prime, that is, a prime in the interval $[2^{k-1}, 2^k)$.

Bertrand's postulate (Theorem 5.7) implies that there exists a constant $c > 0$ such that $\pi(2^k) - \pi(2^{k-1}) \geq c2^{k-1}/k$ for all $k \geq 2$.

Now let us modify Algorithm RP so that it takes as input integer $k \geq 2$, and repeatedly generates a random n in the interval $\{2^{k-1}, \dots, 2^k - 1\}$ until *IsPrime*(n) returns *true*. Let us call this variant Algorithm RP′. Further, let us implement *IsPrime*$(\cdot)$ as $MR(\cdot, t)$, for some auxiliary parameter t, and define $\gamma'(k, t)$ to be the probability that the output of Algorithm RP′ — with this implementation of *IsPrime* — is composite.

Then using exactly the same reasoning as above,

$$\gamma'(k, t) \leq 4^{-t} \frac{2^{k-1}}{\pi(2^k) - \pi(2^{k-1})} = O(4^{-t}k).$$

As before, if the output of Algorithm RP′ is prime, then every k-bit prime is equally likely, and the expected running time is $O(k^4 + tk^3)$. By doing some trial division as above, this can be reduced to $O(k^4 / \operatorname{len}(k) + tk^3)$.

The function $\gamma'(k,t)$ has been studied a good deal; for example, the following is known:

Theorem 10.9. *For all $k \geq 2$, we have*

$$\gamma'(k,1) \leq k^2 4^{2-\sqrt{k}}.$$

Proof. Literature—see §10.7. □

Upper bounds for $\gamma'(k,t)$ for specific values of k and t have been computed. The following table lists some known *lower* bounds for $-\log_2(\gamma'(k,t))$ for various values of k and t:

$t \backslash k$	200	300	400	500	600
1	11	19	37	56	75
2	25	33	46	63	82
3	34	44	55	70	88
4	41	53	63	78	95
5	47	60	72	85	102

Using exactly the same reasoning as the derivation of (10.3), one sees that

$$\gamma'(k,t) \leq \frac{\gamma'(k,1)}{1 - \gamma'(k,1)} 4^{-t+1}.$$

10.5 Perfect power testing and prime power factoring

Consider the following problem: we are given a integer $n > 1$, and want to determine if n is a **perfect power**, which means that $n = d^e$ for integers d and e, both greater than 1. Certainly, if such d and e exist, then it must be the case that $2^e \leq n$, so we can try all possible candidate values of e, running from 2 to $\lfloor \log_2 n \rfloor$. For each such candidate value of e, we can test if $n = d^e$ for some d as follows. Suppose n is a k-bit number, that is, $2^{k-1} \leq n < 2^k$. Then $2^{(k-1)/e} \leq n^{1/e} < 2^{k/e}$. So any integer eth root of n must lie in the set $\{u, \ldots, v-1\}$, where $u := 2^{\lfloor (k-1)/e \rfloor}$ and $v := 2^{\lceil k/e \rceil}$. Using u and v as starting values, we can perform a binary search:

repeat
  $w \leftarrow \lfloor (u+v)/2 \rfloor$
  $z \leftarrow w^e$
  if $z = n$ then
    declare than $n = w^e$ is an a perfect eth power, and stop
  else if $z < n$ then
    $u \leftarrow w + 1$
  else
    $v \leftarrow w$
until $u \geq v$
declare that n is not a perfect eth power

If $n = d^e$ for some integer d, then the following invariant holds (verify): at the beginning of each loop iteration, we have $u \leq d < v$. Thus, if n is a perfect eth power, this will be discovered. That proves the correctness of the algorithm.

As to its running time, note that with each loop iteration, the length $v - u$ of the search interval decreases by a factor of at least 2 (verify). Therefore, after t iterations the interval will be of length at most $2^{k/e+1}/2^t$, so after at most $k/e + 2$ iterations, the interval will be of length less than 1, and hence of length zero, and the algorithm will halt. So the number of loop iterations is $O(k/e)$. The power w^e computed in each iteration is no more than $2^{(k/e+1)e} = 2^{k+e} \leq 2^{2k}$, and hence can be computed in time $O(k^2)$ (see Exercise 3.22). Hence the overall cost of testing if n is an eth power using this algorithm is $O(k^3/e)$.

Trying all candidate values of e from 1 to $\lfloor \log_2 n \rfloor$ yields an overall running time for perfect power testing of $O(\sum_e k^3/e)$, which is $O(k^3 \operatorname{len}(k))$. To find the largest possible value of e for which n is an eth power, we should examine the candidates from highest to lowest.

Using the above algorithm for perfect power testing and an efficient primality test, we can determine if an integer n is a prime power p^e, and if so, compute p and e: we find the largest positive integer e (possibly 1) such that $n = d^e$ for integer d, and test if d is a prime using an efficient primality test.

10.6 Factoring and computing Euler's phi function

In this section, we use some of the ideas developed to analyze the Miller–Rabin test to prove that the problem of factoring n and the problem of computing $\phi(n)$ are equivalent. By equivalent, we mean that given an efficient algorithm to solve one problem, we can efficiently solve the other, and *vice versa.*

Clearly, one direction is easy: if we can factor n into primes, so

$$n = p_1^{e_1} \cdots p_r^{e_r}, \tag{10.5}$$

then we can simply compute $\phi(n)$ using the formula

$$\phi(n) = p_1^{e_1-1}(p_1 - 1) \cdots p_r^{e_r-1}(p_r - 1).$$

For the other direction, first consider the special case where $n = pq$, for distinct primes p and q. Suppose we are given n and $\phi(n)$, so that we have two equations in the unknowns p and q:

$$n = pq \quad \text{and} \quad \phi(n) = (p-1)(q-1).$$

Substituting n/p for q in the second equation, and simplifying, we obtain

$$p^2 + (\phi(n) - n - 1)p + n,$$

which can be solved using the quadratic formula.

For the general case, it is just as easy to prove a stronger result: given any non-zero multiple of the *exponent* of $\mathbb{Z}_n^*$, we can efficiently factor n. In particular, this will show that we can efficiently factor Carmichael numbers.

Before stating the algorithm in its full generality, we can convey the main idea by considering the special case where $n = pq$, where p and q are distinct primes, with $p \equiv q \equiv 3 \pmod 4$. Suppose we are given such an n, along with $f \neq 0$ that is a common multiple of $p - 1$ and $q - 1$. The algorithm works as follows: let $f = 2^h m$, where m is odd; choose a random, non-zero element α of $\mathbb{Z}_n$; test if either $\gcd(\text{rep}(\alpha), n)$ or $\gcd(\text{rep}(\alpha^m) + 1, n)$ splits n (recall that $\text{rep}(\alpha)$ denotes the canonical representative of α).

The assumption that $p \equiv 3 \pmod 4$ means that $(p-1)/2$ is an odd integer, and since f is a multiple of $p - 1$, it follows that $\gcd(m, p - 1) = (p - 1)/2$, and hence the image of $\mathbb{Z}_p^*$ under the m-power map is the subgroup of $\mathbb{Z}_p^*$ of order 2, which is $\{\pm 1\}$. Likewise, the image of $\mathbb{Z}_q^*$ under the m-power map is $\{\pm 1\}$. Let $\theta : \mathbb{Z}_p \times \mathbb{Z}_q \to \mathbb{Z}_n$ be the ring isomorphism from the Chinese remainder theorem. Now, if α in the above algorithm does not lie in $\mathbb{Z}_n^*$, then certainly $\gcd(\text{rep}(\alpha), n)$ splits n. Otherwise, condition on the event that $\alpha \in \mathbb{Z}_n^*$. In this conditional probability distribution, α is uniformly distributed over $\mathbb{Z}_n^*$, and $\beta := \alpha^m$ is uniformly distributed over $\theta(\pm 1, \pm 1)$. Let us consider each of these four possibilities:

- $\beta = \theta(1, 1)$ implies $\beta + 1 = \theta(2, 2)$, and so $\gcd(\text{rep}(\beta) + 1, n) = 1$;
- $\beta = \theta(-1, -1)$ implies $\beta + 1 = \theta(0, 0)$, and so $\gcd(\text{rep}(\beta) + 1, n) = n$;

- $\beta = \theta(-1, 1)$ implies $\beta + 1 = \theta(0, 2)$, and so $\gcd(\operatorname{rep}(\beta) + 1, n) = p$;
- $\beta = \theta(1, -1)$ implies $\beta + 1 = \theta(2, 0)$, and so $\gcd(\operatorname{rep}(\beta) + 1, n) = q$.

Thus, if $\beta = \theta(-1, 1)$ or $\beta = \theta(1, -1)$, which happens with probability $1/2$, then $\gcd(\operatorname{rep}(\beta) + 1, n)$ splits n. Therefore, the overall probability that we split n is at least $1/2$.

We now present the algorithm in its full generality. We first introduce some notation; namely, let $\lambda(n)$ denote the exponent of $\mathbb{Z}_n^*$. If the prime factorization of n is as in (10.5), then by the Chinese remainder theorem, we have

$$\lambda(n) = \operatorname{lcm}(\lambda(p_1^{e_1}), \dots, \lambda(p_r^{e_r})).$$

Moreover, for any prime power p^e, by Theorem 10.1, we have

$$\lambda(p^e) = \begin{cases} p^{e-1}(p-1) & \text{if } p \neq 2 \text{ or } e \leq 2, \\ 2^{e-2} & \text{if } p = 2 \text{ and } e \geq 3. \end{cases}$$

In particular, if $m \mid n$, then $\lambda(m) \mid \lambda(n)$.

Now, returning to our factorization problem, we are given n and a non-zero multiple f of $\lambda(n)$, and want to factor n. We may as well assume that n is odd; otherwise, we can pull out all the factors of 2, obtaining n' such that $n = 2^e n'$, where n' is odd and f is a multiple of $\lambda(n')$, thus, reducing to the odd case.

So now, assume n is odd and f is a multiple of $\lambda(n)$. Assume that f is of the form $f = 2^h m$, where m is odd. Our factoring algorithm, which we describe recursively, runs as follows.

> if n is a prime power p^e then
>   output e copies of p and return
> generate a random, non-zero element α of $\mathbb{Z}_n$
> $d_1 \leftarrow \gcd(\operatorname{rep}(\alpha), n)$
> if $d_1 \neq 1$, then recursively factor d_1 and n/d_1 (using the same f),
>   and return
> $\alpha \leftarrow \alpha^m$
> for $j \leftarrow 0$ to $h - 1$ do
> $d_2 \leftarrow \gcd(\operatorname{rep}(\alpha) + 1, n)$
>   if $d_2 \notin \{1, n\}$, then recursively factor d_2 and n/d_2
>   (using the same f), and return
> $\alpha \leftarrow \alpha^2$
> recursively factor n (using the same f)

It is clear that when the algorithm terminates, its output consists of the list of all primes (including duplicates) dividing n, assuming the primality test does not make a mistake.

To analyze the running time of the algorithm, assume that the prime factorization of n is as in (10.5). By the Chinese remainder theorem, we have a ring isomorphism

$$\theta : \mathbb{Z}_{p_1^{e_1}} \times \cdots \times \mathbb{Z}_{p_r^{e_r}} \to \mathbb{Z}_n.$$

Let $\lambda(p_i^{e_i}) = m_i 2^{h_i}$, where m_i is odd, for $i = 1, \ldots, r$, and let $\ell :=$ $\max\{h_1, \ldots, h_r\}$. Note that since $\lambda(n) \mid f$, we have $\ell \le h$.

Consider one execution of the body of the recursive algorithm. If n is a prime power, this will be detected immediately, and the algorithm will return. Here, even if we are using probabilistic primality test, such as the Miller–Rabin test, that always says that a prime is a prime, the algorithm will certainly halt. So assume that n is not a prime power, which means that $r \ge 2$. If the chosen value of α is not in $\mathbb{Z}_n^*$, then d_1 will be a non-trivial divisor of n. Otherwise, conditioning on the event that $\alpha \in \mathbb{Z}_n^*$, the distribution of α is uniform over $\mathbb{Z}_n^*$. Consider the value $\beta := \alpha^{m 2^{\ell-1}}$.

We claim that with probability at least $1/2$, $\gcd(\mathrm{rep}(\beta) + 1, n)$ is a non-trivial divisor of n. To prove this claim, let us write

$$\beta = \theta(\beta_1, \ldots, \beta_r),$$

where $\beta_i \in \mathbb{Z}_{p_i^{e_i}}^*$ for $i = 1, \ldots, r$. Note that for those i with $h_i < \ell$, the $m 2^{\ell-1}$-power map kills the group $\mathbb{Z}_{p_i^{e_i}}^*$, while for those i with $h_i = \ell$, the image of $\mathbb{Z}_{p_i^{e_i}}^*$ under the $m 2^{\ell-1}$-power map is $\{\pm 1\}$. Without loss of generality, assume that the indices i such that $h_i = \ell$ are numbered $1, \ldots, r'$, where $1 \le r' \le r$. The values β_i for $i = 1, \ldots, r'$ are uniformly and independently distributed over $\{\pm 1\}$, while for all $i > r'$, $\beta_i = 1$. Thus, the value of $\gcd(\mathrm{rep}(\beta) + 1, n)$ is the product of all prime powers $p_i^{e_i}$, with $\beta_i = -1$, which will be non-trivial unless either (1) all the β_i are 1, or (2) $r' = r$ and all the β_i are -1. Consider two cases. First, if $r' < r$, then only event (1) is possible, and this occurs with probability $2^{-r'} \le 1/2$. Second, if $r' = r$, then each of events (1) and (2) occurs with probability 2^{-r}, and so the probability that either occurs is $2^{-r+1} \le 1/2$. That proves the claim.

From the claim, it follows that with probability at least $1/2$, we will obtain a non-trivial divisor d_2 of n when $j = \ell - 1$ (if not before).

So we have shown that with probability at least $1/2$, one execution of the body will succeed in splitting n into non-trivial factors. After at most $\log_2 n$ such successes, we will have completely factored n. Therefore, the expected number of recursive invocations of the algorithm is $O(\mathrm{len}(n))$.

EXERCISE 10.14. Suppose you are given an integer n of the form $n = pq$, where p and q are distinct, ℓ-bit primes, with $p = 2p' + 1$ and $q = 2q' + 1$, where p' and q' are themselves prime. Suppose that you are also given an integer m such that $\gcd(m, p'q') \neq 1$. Show how to efficiently factor n.

EXERCISE 10.15. Suppose there is a probabilistic algorithm A that takes as input an integer n of the form $n = pq$, where p and q are distinct, ℓ-bit primes, with $p = 2p' + 1$ and $q = 2q' + 1$, where p' and q' are prime. The algorithm also takes as input $\alpha, \beta \in (\mathbb{Z}_n^*)^2$. It outputs either "failure," or integers x, y, not both zero, such that $\alpha^x \beta^y = 1$. Furthermore, assume that A runs in strict polynomial time, and that for all n of the above form, and for randomly chosen $\alpha, \beta \in (\mathbb{Z}_n^*)^2$, A succeeds in finding x, y as above with probability $\epsilon(n)$. Here, the probability is taken over the random choice of α and β, as well as the random choices made during the execution of A. Show how to use A to construct another probabilistic algorithm A' that takes as input n as above, runs in expected polynomial time, and that satisfies the following property:

> if $\epsilon(n) \geq 0.001$, then A' factors n with probability at least 0.999.

10.7 Notes

The Miller–Rabin test is due to Miller [63] and Rabin [75]. The paper by Miller defined the set L_n', but did not give a probabilistic analysis. Rather, Miller showed that under a generalization of the Riemann hypothesis, for composite n, the least positive integer a such that $[a]_n \in \mathbb{Z}_n \setminus L_n'$ is at most $O((\log n)^2)$, thus giving rise to a deterministic primality test whose correctness depends on the above unproved hypothesis. The later paper by Rabin re-interprets Miller's result in the context of probabilistic algorithms.

Bach [10] gives an explicit version of Miller's result, showing that under the same assumptions, the least positive integer a such that $[a]_n \in \mathbb{Z}_n \setminus L_n'$ is at most $2(\log n)^2$; more generally, Bach shows the following holds under a generalization of the Riemann hypothesis:

> For any positive integer n, and any proper subgroup $G \subsetneq \mathbb{Z}_n^*$, the least positive integer a such that $[a]_n \in \mathbb{Z}_n \setminus G$ is at most $2(\log n)^2$, and the least positive integer b such that $[b]_n \in \mathbb{Z}_n^* \setminus G$ is at most $3(\log n)^2$.

The first efficient probabilistic primality test was invented by Solovay and Strassen [94] (their paper was actually submitted for publication in 1974).

Later, in Chapter 22, we shall discuss a recently discovered, deterministic, polynomial-time (though not very practical) primality test, whose analysis does not rely on any unproved hypothesis.

Carmichael numbers are named after R. D. Carmichael, who was the first to discuss them, in work published in the early 20th century. Alford, Granville, and Pomerance [7] proved that there are infinitely many Carmichael numbers.

Exercise 10.6 is based on Lehmann [55].

Theorem 10.7, as well as the table of values just below it, are from Kim and Pomerance [53]. In fact, these bounds hold for the weaker test based on L_n.

Our analysis in §10.4.2 is loosely based on a similar analysis in §4.1 of Maurer [61]. Theorem 10.8 and its generalization in Exercise 10.11 are certainly not the best results possible in this area. The general goal of "sieve theory" is to prove useful upper and lower bounds for quantities like $R_f(x, y)$ that hold when y is as large as possible with respect to x. For example, using a technique known as Brun's pure sieve, one can show that for $\log y < \sqrt{\log x}$, there exist β and β', both of absolute value at most 1, such that

$$R_f(x, y) = (1 + \beta e^{-\sqrt{\log x}})x \prod_{p \leq y}(1 - \omega_f(p)/p) + \beta'\sqrt{x}.$$

Thus, this gives us very sharp estimates for $R_f(x, y)$ when x tends to infinity, and y is bounded by any fixed polynomial in $\log x$. For a proof of this result, see §2.2 of Halberstam and Richert [42] (the result itself is stated as equation 2.16). Brun's pure sieve is really just the first non-trivial sieve result, developed in the early 20th century; even stronger results, extending the useful range of y (but with larger error terms), have subsequently been proved.

Theorem 10.9, as well as the table of values immediately below it, are from Damgård, Landrock, and Pomerance [32].

The algorithm presented in §10.6 for factoring an integer given a multiple of $\phi(n)$ (or, for that matter, $\lambda(n)$) is essentially due to Miller [63]. However, just as for his primality test, Miller presents his algorithm as a deterministic algorithm, which he analyzes under a generalization of the Riemann hypothesis. The probabilistic version of Miller's factoring algorithm appears to be "folklore."

11

Finding generators and discrete logarithms in $\mathbb{Z}_p^*$

As we have seen in Theorem 9.16, for a prime p, $\mathbb{Z}_p^*$ is a cyclic group of order $p - 1$. This means that there exists a generator $\gamma \in \mathbb{Z}_p^*$, such that for all $\alpha \in \mathbb{Z}_p^*$, α can be written uniquely as $\alpha = \gamma^x$, where x is an integer with $0 \le x < p - 1$; the integer x is called the **discrete logarithm** of α to the base γ, and is denoted $\log_\gamma \alpha$.

This chapter discusses some computational problems in this setting; namely, how to efficiently find a generator γ, and given γ and α, how to compute $\log_\gamma \alpha$.

More generally, if γ generates a subgroup G of $\mathbb{Z}_p^*$ of order q, where $q \mid (p - 1)$, and $\alpha \in G$, then $\log_\gamma \alpha$ is defined to be the unique integer x with $0 \le x < q$ and $\alpha = \gamma^x$. In some situations it is more convenient to view $\log_\gamma \alpha$ as an element of $\mathbb{Z}_q$. Also for $x \in \mathbb{Z}_q$, with $x = [a]_q$, one may write γ^x to denote γ^a. There can be no confusion, since if $x = [a']_q$, then $\gamma^{a'} = \gamma^a$. However, in this chapter, we shall view $\log_\gamma \alpha$ as an integer.

Although we work in the group $\mathbb{Z}_p^*$, all of the algorithms discussed in this chapter trivially generalize to any finite cyclic group that has a suitably compact representation of group elements and an efficient algorithm for performing the group operation on these representations.

11.1 Finding a generator for $\mathbb{Z}_p^*$

There is no efficient algorithm known for this problem, unless the prime factorization of $p - 1$ is given, and even then, we must resort to the use of a probabilistic algorithm. Of course, factoring in general is believed to be a very difficult problem, so it may not be easy to get the prime factorization of $p - 1$. However, if our goal is to construct a large prime p, together with a generator for $\mathbb{Z}_p^*$, then we may use Algorithm RFN in §7.7 to generate a random factored number n in some range, test $n + 1$ for primality, and then repeat until we get a factored number n such that $p = n + 1$ is prime. In this way, we can generate a random prime p in a given range along with the factorization of $p - 1$.

We now present an efficient probabilistic algorithm that takes as input an odd prime p, along with the prime factorization

$$p - 1 = \prod_{i=1}^{r} q_i^{e_i},$$

and outputs a generator for $\mathbb{Z}_p^*$. It runs as follows:

> for $i \leftarrow 1$ to r do
> > repeat
> > > choose $\alpha \in \mathbb{Z}_p^*$ at random
> > > compute $\beta \leftarrow \alpha^{(p-1)/q_i}$
> >
> > until $\beta \neq 1$
> > $\gamma_i \leftarrow \alpha^{(p-1)/q_i^{e_i}}$
>
> $\gamma \leftarrow \prod_{i=1}^{r} \gamma_i$
> output γ

First, let us analyze the correctness of this algorithm. When the ith loop iteration terminates, by construction, we have

$$\gamma_i^{q_i^{e_i}} = 1 \quad \text{but} \quad \gamma_i^{q_i^{e_i-1}} \neq 1.$$

It follows (see Theorem 8.37) that γ_i has multiplicative order $q_i^{e_i}$. From this, it follows (see Theorem 8.38) that γ has multiplicative order $p - 1$.

Thus, we have shown that if the algorithm terminates, its output is always correct.

Let us now analyze the running time of this algorithm. Consider the repeat/until loop in the ith iteration of the outer loop, for $i = 1, \dots, r$, and let X_i be the random variable whose value is the number of iterations of this repeat/until loop. Since α is chosen at random from $\mathbb{Z}_p^*$, the value of β is uniformly distributed over the image of the $(p - 1)/q_i$-power map (see Exercise 8.22), and since the latter is a subgroup of $\mathbb{Z}_p^*$ of order q_i, we see that $\beta = 1$ with probability $1/q_i$. Thus, X_i has a geometric distribution with associated success probability $1 - 1/q_i$, and therefore, $\mathsf{E}[X_i] = 1/(1 - 1/q_i) \leq 2$. Set $X := X_1 + \cdots + X_r$. Note that $\mathsf{E}[X] = \mathsf{E}[X_1] + \cdots + \mathsf{E}[X_r] \leq 2r$. The running time T of the entire algorithm is $O(X \cdot \operatorname{len}(p)^3)$, and hence the expected running is $\mathsf{E}[T] = O(r \operatorname{len}(p)^3)$, and since $r \leq \log_2 p$, we have $\mathsf{E}[T] = O(\operatorname{len}(p)^4)$.

Although this algorithm is quite practical, there are asymptotically faster algorithms for this problem (see Exercise 11.2).

EXERCISE 11.1. Suppose we are not given the prime factorization of $p - 1$, but rather, just a prime q dividing $p - 1$, and we want to find an element of multiplicative order q in $\mathbb{Z}_p^*$. Design and analyze an efficient algorithm to do this.

EXERCISE 11.2. Suppose we are given a prime p, along with the prime factorization $p - 1 = \prod_{i=1}^{r} q_i^{e_i}$.

  (a) If, in addition, we are given $\alpha \in \mathbb{Z}_p^*$, show how to compute the multiplicative order of α in time $O(r \operatorname{len}(p)^3)$. Hint: use Exercise 8.25.

  (b) Improve the running time bound to $O(\operatorname{len}(r) \operatorname{len}(p)^3)$. Hint: use Exercise 3.30.

  (c) Modifying the algorithm you developed for part (b), show how to construct a generator for $\mathbb{Z}_p^*$ in expected time $O(\operatorname{len}(r) \operatorname{len}(p)^3)$.

EXERCISE 11.3. Suppose we are given a positive integer n, along with its prime factorization $n = p_1^{e_1} \cdots p_r^{e_r}$, and that for each $i = 1, \ldots, r$, we are also given the prime factorization of $p_i - 1$. Show how to efficiently compute the multiplicative order of any element $\alpha \in \mathbb{Z}_n^*$.

EXERCISE 11.4. Suppose there is an efficient algorithm that takes as input a positive integer n and an element $\alpha \in \mathbb{Z}_n^*$, and computes the multiplicative order of α. Show how to use this algorithm to be build an efficient integer factoring algorithm.

11.2 Computing discrete logarithms $\mathbb{Z}_p^*$

In this section, we consider algorithms for computing the discrete logarithm of $\alpha \in \mathbb{Z}_p^*$ to a given base γ. The algorithms we present here are, in the worst case, exponential-time algorithms, and are by no means the best possible; however, in some special cases, these algorithms are not so bad.

11.2.1 Brute-force search

Suppose that $\gamma \in \mathbb{Z}_p^*$ generates a subgroup G of $\mathbb{Z}_p^*$ of order $q > 1$ (not necessarily prime), and we are given $p, q, \gamma,$ and $\alpha \in G$, and wish to compute $\log_\gamma \alpha$.

The simplest algorithm to solve the problem is **brute-force search**:

$$\beta \leftarrow 1$$
$$i \leftarrow 0$$
while $\beta \neq \alpha$ do
    $\beta \leftarrow \beta \cdot \gamma$
    $i \leftarrow i + 1$
output i

This algorithm is clearly correct, and the main loop will always halt after at most q iterations (assuming, as we are, that $\alpha \in G$). So the total running time is $O(q \operatorname{len}(p)^2)$.

11.2.2 Baby step/giant step method

As above, suppose that $\gamma \in \mathbb{Z}_p^*$ generates a subgroup G of $\mathbb{Z}_p^*$ of order $q > 1$ (not necessarily prime), and we are given p, q, γ, and $\alpha \in G$, and wish to compute $\log_\gamma \alpha$.

A faster algorithm than brute-force search is the **baby step/giant step method**. It works as follows.

Let us choose an approximation m to $q^{1/2}$. It does not have to be a very good approximation—we just need $m = \Theta(q^{1/2})$. Also, let $m' = \lfloor q/m \rfloor$, so that $m' = \Theta(q^{1/2})$ as well.

The idea is to compute all the values γ^i for $i = 0, \ldots, m-1$ (the "baby steps") and to build a "lookup table" L that contains all the pairs (γ^i, i), and that supports fast lookups on the first component of these pairs. That is, given $\beta \in \mathbb{Z}_p^*$, we should be able to quickly determine if $\beta = \gamma^i$ for some $i = 0, \ldots, m-1$, and if so, determine the value of i. Let us define $L(\beta) := i$ if $\beta = \gamma^i$ for some $i = 0, \ldots, m-1$; otherwise, define $L(\beta) := -1$.

Using an appropriate data structure, we can build the table L in time $O(q^{1/2} \operatorname{len}(p)^2)$ (just compute successive powers of γ, and insert them in the table), and we can perform a lookup in time $O(\operatorname{len}(p))$. One such data structure is a *radix tree* (also called a *search trie*); other data structures may be used (for example, a *hash table* or a *binary search tree*), but these may yield slightly different running times for building the table and/or for table lookup.

After building the lookup table, we execute the following procedure (the "giant steps"):

$$\gamma' \leftarrow \gamma^{-m}$$
$$\beta \leftarrow \alpha, \quad j \leftarrow 0, \quad i \leftarrow L(\beta)$$
while $i = -1$ do
$$\beta \leftarrow \beta \cdot \gamma', \quad j \leftarrow j+1, \quad i \leftarrow L(\beta)$$
$$x \leftarrow jm + i$$
output x

To analyze this procedure, suppose that $\alpha = \gamma^x$ with $0 \le x < q$. Now, x can be written in a unique way as $x = vm + u$, where u and v are integers with $0 \le u < m$ and $0 \le v \le m'$. In the jth loop iteration, for $j = 0, 1, \ldots,$ we have

$$\beta = \alpha\gamma^{-mj} = \gamma^{(v-j)m+u}.$$

So we will detect $i \ne -1$ precisely when $j = v$, in which case $i = u$. Thus, the output will be correct, and the total running time of the algorithm (for both the "baby steps" and "giant steps" parts) is easily seen to be $O(q^{1/2}\operatorname{len}(p)^2)$.

While this algorithm is much faster than brute-force search, it has the drawback that it requires a table $\Theta(q^{1/2})$ elements of $\mathbb{Z}_p$. Of course, there is a "time/space trade-off" here: by choosing m smaller, we get a table of size $O(m)$, but the running time will be proportional to $O(q/m)$. In §11.2.5 below, we discuss an algorithm that runs (at least heuristically) in time $O(q^{1/2}\operatorname{len}(q)\operatorname{len}(p)^2)$, but which requires space for only a constant number of elements of $\mathbb{Z}_p$.

11.2.3 Groups of order q^e

Suppose that $\gamma \in \mathbb{Z}_p^*$ generates a subgroup G of $\mathbb{Z}_p^*$ of order q^e, where $q > 1$ and $e \ge 1$, and we are given p, q, e, γ, and $\alpha \in G$, and wish to compute $\log_\gamma \alpha$.

There is a simple algorithm that allows one to reduce this problem to the problem of computing discrete logarithms in the subgroup of $\mathbb{Z}_p^*$ of order q.

It is perhaps easiest to describe the algorithm recursively. The base case is when $e = 1$, in which case, we use an algorithm for the subgroup of $\mathbb{Z}_p^*$ of order q. For this, we might employ the algorithm in §11.2.2, or if q is *very* small, the algorithm in §11.2.1.

Suppose now that $e > 1$. We choose an integer f with $0 < f < e$. Different strategies for choosing f yield different algorithms—we discuss this below. Suppose $\alpha = \gamma^x$, where $0 \le x < q^e$. Then we can write $x = q^f v + u$, where

u and v are integers with $0 \le u < q^f$ and $0 \le v < q^{e-f}$. Therefore,

$$\alpha^{q^{e-f}} = \gamma^{q^{e-f}u}.$$

Note that $\gamma^{q^{e-f}}$ has multiplicative order q^f, and so if we recursively compute the discrete logarithm of $\alpha^{q^{e-f}}$ to the base $\gamma^{q^{e-f}}$, we obtain u.

Having obtained u, observe that

$$\alpha/\gamma^u = \gamma^{q^f v}.$$

Note also that γ^{q^f} has multiplicative order q^{e-f}, and so if we recursively compute the discrete logarithm of α/γ^u to the base γ^{q^f}, we obtain v, from which we then compute $x = q^f v + u$.

Let us put together the above ideas succinctly in a recursive procedure $RDL(p, q, e, \gamma, \alpha)$ that runs as follows:

> if $e = 1$ then
>> return $\log_\gamma \alpha$ // *base case: use a different algorithm*
>
> else
>> select $f \in \{1, \ldots, e-1\}$
>> $u \leftarrow RDL(p, q, f, \gamma^{q^{e-f}}, \alpha^{q^{e-f}})$ // $0 \le u < q^f$
>> $v \leftarrow RDL(p, q, e-f, \gamma^{q^f}, \alpha/\gamma^u)$ // $0 \le v < q^{e-f}$
>> return $q^f v + u$

To analyze the running time of this recursive algorithm, note that the running time of the body of one recursive invocation (not counting the running time of the recursive calls it makes) is $O(e \operatorname{len}(q) \operatorname{len}(p)^2)$. To calculate the total running time, we have to sum up the running times of all the recursive calls plus the running times of all the base cases.

Regardless of the strategy for choosing f, the total number of base case invocations is e. Note that all the base cases compute discrete logarithms to the base $\gamma^{q^{e-1}}$. Assuming we implement the base case using the baby step/giant step algorithm in §11.2.2, the total running time for all the base cases is therefore $O(eq^{1/2} \operatorname{len}(p)^2)$.

The total running time for the recursion (not including the base case computations) depends on the strategy used to choose the split f.

- If we always choose $f = 1$ or $f = e - 1$, then the total running time for the recursion is $O(e^2 \operatorname{len}(q) \operatorname{len}(p)^2)$. Note that if $f = 1$, then the algorithm is essentially tail recursive, and so may be easily converted to an iterative algorithm without the need for a stack.

- If we use a "balanced" divide-and-conquer strategy, choosing $f \approx e/2$, then the total running time of the recursion is

$O(e \operatorname{len}(e) \operatorname{len}(q) \operatorname{len}(p)^2)$. To see this, note that the depth of the "recursion tree" is $O(\operatorname{len}(e))$, while the running time per level of the recursion tree is $O(e \operatorname{len}(q) \operatorname{len}(p)^2)$.

Assuming we use the faster, balanced recursion strategy, the total running time, including both the recursion and base cases, is:

$$O((eq^{1/2} + e \operatorname{len}(e) \operatorname{len}(q)) \cdot \operatorname{len}(p)^2).$$

11.2.4 Discrete logarithms in $\mathbb{Z}_p^*$

Suppose that we are given a prime p, along with the prime factorization

$$p - 1 = \prod_{i=1}^{r} q_i^{e_i},$$

a generator γ for $\mathbb{Z}_p^*$, and $\alpha \in \mathbb{Z}_p^*$. We wish to compute $\log_\gamma \alpha$.

Suppose that $\alpha = \gamma^x$, where $0 \le x < p - 1$. Then for $i = 1, \ldots, r$, we have

$$\alpha^{(p-1)/q_i^{e_i}} = \gamma^{(p-1)/q_i^{e_i} x}.$$

Note that $\gamma^{(p-1)/q_i^{e_i}}$ has multiplicative order $q_i^{e_i}$, and if x_i is the discrete logarithm of $\alpha^{(p-1)/q_i^{e_i}}$ to the base $\gamma^{(p-1)/q_i^{e_i}}$, then we have $0 \le x_i < q_i^{e_i}$ and $x \equiv x_i \pmod{q_i^{e_i}}$.

Thus, if we compute the values $x_1, \ldots, x_r$, using the algorithm in §11.2.3, we can obtain x using the algorithm of the Chinese remainder theorem (see Theorem 4.5). If we define $q := \max\{q_1, \ldots, q_r\}$, then the running time of this algorithm will be bounded by $q^{1/2} \operatorname{len}(p)^{O(1)}$.

We conclude that

> *the difficulty of computing discrete logarithms in $\mathbb{Z}_p^*$ is determined by the size of the largest prime dividing $p - 1$.*

11.2.5 A space-efficient square-root time algorithm

We present a more space-efficient alternative to the algorithm in §11.2.2, the analysis of which we leave as a series of exercises for the reader.

The algorithm makes a somewhat heuristic assumption that we have a function that "behaves" for all practical purposes like a random function. Such functions can indeed be constructed using cryptographic techniques under reasonable intractability assumptions; however, for the particular application here, one can get by in practice with much simpler constructions.

Let p be a prime, q a prime dividing $p - 1$, γ an element of $\mathbb{Z}_p^*$ that generates a subgroup G of $\mathbb{Z}_p^*$ of order q, and $\alpha \in G$. Let F be a function mapping elements of G to $\{0, \ldots, q - 1\}$. Define $H : G \to G$ to be the function that sends β to $\beta\alpha\gamma^{F(\beta)}$.

The algorithm runs as follows:

$i \leftarrow 1$
$x \leftarrow 0,\ \beta \leftarrow \alpha,$
$x' \leftarrow F(\beta),\ \beta' \leftarrow H(\beta)$
while $\beta \neq \beta'$ do
    $x \leftarrow (x + F(\beta)) \bmod q,\ \beta \leftarrow H(\beta)$
    $x' \leftarrow (x' + F(\beta')) \bmod q,\ \beta' \leftarrow H(\beta')$
    $x' \leftarrow (x' + F(\beta')) \bmod q,\ \beta' \leftarrow H(\beta')$
    $i \leftarrow i + 1$
if $i < q$ then
    output $(x - x')i^{-1} \bmod q$
else
    output "fail"

To analyze this algorithm, let us define $\beta_1, \beta_2, \ldots,$ as follows: $\beta_1 := \alpha$ and for $i > 1$, $\beta_i := H(\beta_{i-1})$.

EXERCISE 11.5. Show that each time the main loop of the algorithm is entered, we have $\beta = \beta_i = \gamma^x \alpha^i$, and $\beta' = \beta_{2i} = \gamma^{x'} \alpha^{2i}$.

EXERCISE 11.6. Show that if the loop terminates with $i < q$, the value output is equal to $\log_\gamma \alpha$.

EXERCISE 11.7. Let j be the smallest index such that $\beta_j = \beta_k$ for some index $k < j$. Show that $j \leq q + 1$ and that the loop terminates with $i < j$ (and in particular, $i \leq q$).

EXERCISE 11.8. Assume that F is a random function, meaning that it is chosen at random, uniformly from among all functions from G into $\{0, \ldots, q-1\}$. Show that this implies that H is a random function, meaning that it is uniformly distributed over all functions from G into G.

EXERCISE 11.9. Assuming that F is a random function as in the previous exercise, apply the result of Exercise 6.27 to conclude that the expected running time of the algorithm is $O(q^{1/2} \operatorname{len}(q) \operatorname{len}(p)^2)$, and that the probability that the algorithm fails is exponentially small in q.

11.3 The Diffie–Hellman key establishment protocol

One of the main motivations for studying algorithms for computing discrete logarithms is the relation between this problem and the problem of breaking a protocol called the **Diffie–Hellman key establishment protocol**, named after its inventors.

In this protocol, Alice and Bob need never to have talked to each other before, but nevertheless, can establish a shared secret key that nobody else can easily compute. To use this protocol, a third party must provide a "telephone book," which contains the following information:

- p, q, and γ, where p and q are primes with $q \mid (p-1)$, and γ is an element generating a subgroup G of $\mathbb{Z}_p^*$ of order q;

- an entry for each user, such as Alice or Bob, that contains the user's name, along with a "public key" for that user, which is an element of the group G.

To use this system, Alice posts her public key in the telephone book, which is of the form $\alpha = \gamma^x$, where $x \in \{0, \dots, q-1\}$ is chosen by Alice at random. The value of x is Alice's "secret key," which Alice never divulges to anybody. Likewise, Bob posts his public key, which is of the form $\beta = \gamma^y$, where $y \in \{0, \dots, q-1\}$ is chosen by Bob at random, and is his secret key.

To establish a shared key known only between them, Alice retrieves Bob's public key β from the telephone book, and computes $\kappa_A := \beta^x$. Likewise, Bob retrieves Alice's public key α, and computes $\kappa_B := \alpha^y$. It is easy to see that

$$\kappa_A = \beta^x = (\gamma^y)^x = \gamma^{xy} = (\gamma^x)^y = \alpha^y = \kappa_B,$$

and hence Alice and Bob share the same secret key $\kappa := \kappa_A = \kappa_B$.

Using this shared secret key, they can then use standard methods for encryption and message authentication to hold a secure conversation. We shall not go any further into how this is done; rather, we briefly (and only superficially) discuss some aspects of the security of the key establishment protocol itself. Clearly, if an attacker obtains α and β from the telephone book, and computes $x = \log_\gamma \alpha$, then he can compute Alice and Bob's shared key as $\kappa = \beta^x$ — in fact, given x, an attacker can efficiently compute *any* key shared between Alice and another user.

Thus, if this system is to be secure, it should be very difficult to compute discrete logarithms. However, the assumption that computing discrete logarithms is hard is not enough to guarantee security. Indeed, it is not entirely inconceivable that the discrete logarithm problem is hard, and yet the problem of computing κ from α and β is easy. The latter problem — computing κ from α and β — is called the **Diffie–Hellman problem**.

As in the discussion of the RSA cryptosystem in §7.8, the reader is warned that the above discussion about security is a bit of an oversimplification. A complete discussion of all the security issues related to the above protocol is beyond the scope of this text.

Note that in our presentation of the Diffie–Hellman protocol, we work with a generator of a subgroup G of $\mathbb{Z}_p^*$ of prime order, rather than a generator for $\mathbb{Z}_p^*$. There are several reasons for doing this: one is that there are no known discrete logarithm algorithms that are any more practical in G than in $\mathbb{Z}_p^*$, provided the order q of G is sufficiently large; another is that by working in G, the protocol becomes substantially more efficient. In typical implementations, p is 1024 bits long, so as to protect against subexponential-time algorithms such as those discussed later in §16.2, while q is 160 bits long, which is enough to protect against the square-root-time algorithms discussed in §11.2.2 and §11.2.5. The modular exponentiations in the protocol will run several times faster using "short," 160-bit exponents rather than "long," 1024-bit exponents.

For the following exercise, we need the following notions from complexity theory.

- We say problem A is **deterministic poly-time reducible** to problem B if there exists a deterministic algorithm R for solving problem A that makes calls to a subroutine for problem B, where the running time of R (not including the running time for the subroutine for B) is polynomial in the input length.

- We say that A and B are **deterministic poly-time equivalent** if A is deterministic poly-time reducible to B and B is deterministic poly-time reducible to A.

EXERCISE 11.10. Consider the following problems.

(a) Given a prime p, a prime q that divides $p - 1$, an element $\gamma \in \mathbb{Z}_p^*$ generating a subgroup G of $\mathbb{Z}_p^*$ of order q, and two elements $\alpha, \beta \in G$, compute γ^{xy}, where $x := \log_\gamma \alpha$ and $y := \log_\gamma \beta$. (This is just the Diffie–Hellman problem.)

(b) Given a prime p, a prime q that divides $p - 1$, an element $\gamma \in \mathbb{Z}_p^*$ generating a subgroup G of $\mathbb{Z}_p^*$ of order q, and an element $\alpha \in G$, compute γ^{x^2}, where $x := \log_\gamma \alpha$.

(c) Given a prime p, a prime q that divides $p - 1$, an element $\gamma \in \mathbb{Z}_p^*$ generating a subgroup G of $\mathbb{Z}_p^*$ of order q, and two elements $\alpha, \beta \in G$, with $\beta \neq 1$, compute $\gamma^{xy'}$, where $x := \log_\gamma \alpha$, $y' := y^{-1} \bmod q$, and $y := \log_\gamma \beta$.

(d) Given a prime p, a prime q that divides $p - 1$, an element $\gamma \in \mathbb{Z}_p^*$

generating a subgroup G of $\mathbb{Z}_p^*$ of order q, and an element $\alpha \in G$, with $\alpha \neq 1$, compute $\gamma^{x'}$, where $x' := x^{-1} \bmod q$ and $x := \log_\gamma \alpha$.

Show that these problems are deterministic poly-time equivalent. Moreover, your reductions should preserve the values of p, q, and γ; that is, if the algorithm that reduces one problem to another takes as input an instance of the former problem of the form $(p, q, \gamma, \ldots)$, it should invoke the subroutine for the latter problem with inputs of the form $(p, q, \gamma, \ldots)$.

EXERCISE 11.11. Suppose there is a probabilistic algorithm A that takes as input a prime p, a prime q that divides $p - 1$, and an element $\gamma \in \mathbb{Z}_p^*$ generating a subgroup G of $\mathbb{Z}_p^*$ of order q. The algorithm also takes as input $\alpha \in G$. It outputs either "failure," or $\log_\gamma \alpha$. Furthermore, assume that A runs in strict polynomial time, and that for all p, q, and γ of the above form, and for randomly chosen $\alpha \in G$, A succeeds in computing $\log_\gamma \alpha$ with probability $\epsilon(p, q, \gamma)$. Here, the probability is taken over the random choice of α, as well as the random choices made during the execution of A. Show how to use A to construct another probabilistic algorithm A' that takes as input p, q, and γ as above, as well as $\alpha \in G$, runs in expected polynomial time, and that satisfies the following property:

> if $\epsilon(p, q, \gamma) \geq 0.001$, then *for all* $\alpha \in G$, A' computes $\log_\gamma \alpha$ with probability at least 0.999.

The algorithm A' in the previous exercise is another example of a random self-reduction (see discussion following Exercise 7.27).

EXERCISE 11.12. Let p be a prime, q a prime that divides $p - 1$, $\gamma \in \mathbb{Z}_p^*$ an element that generates a subgroup G of $\mathbb{Z}_p^*$ of order q, and $\alpha \in G$. For $\delta \in G$, a **representation of δ with respect to γ and α** is a pair of integers (r, s), with $0 \leq r < q$ and $0 \leq s < q$, such that $\gamma^r \alpha^s = \delta$.

(a) Show that for any $\delta \in G$, there are precisely q representations (r, s) of δ with respect to γ and α, and among these, there is precisely one with $s = 0$.

(b) Show that given a representation (r, s) of 1 with respect to γ and α such that $s \neq 0$, we can efficiently compute $\log_\gamma \alpha$.

(c) Show that given any $\delta \in G$, along with any two distinct representations of δ with respect to γ and α, we can efficiently compute $\log_\gamma \alpha$.

(d) Suppose we are given access to an "oracle" that, when presented with any $\delta \in G$, tells us some representation of δ with respect to γ and α. Show how to use this oracle to efficiently compute $\log_\gamma \alpha$.

The following two exercises examine the danger of the use of "short" exponents in discrete logarithm based cryptographic schemes that *do not* work with a group of prime order.

EXERCISE 11.13. Let p be a prime and let $p - 1 = q_1^{e_1} \cdots q_r^{e_r}$ be the prime factorization of $p - 1$. Let γ be a generator for $\mathbb{Z}_p^*$. Let X, Y be positive numbers. Let Q be the product of all the prime powers $q_i^{e_i}$ with $q_i \leq Y$. Suppose you are given p, the primes q_i dividing $p - 1$ with $q_i \leq Y$, along with γ and an element α of $\mathbb{Z}_p^*$. Assuming that $x := \log_\gamma \alpha < X$, show how to compute x in time

$$(Y^{1/2} + (X/Q)^{1/2}) \cdot \operatorname{len}(p)^{O(1)}.$$

EXERCISE 11.14. Continuing with the previous exercise, let Q' be the product of all the primes q_i dividing $p - 1$ with $q_i \leq Y$. Note that $Q' \mid Q$. The goal of this exercise is to heuristically estimate the expected value of $\log Q'$, assuming p is a large, random prime. The heuristic part is this: we shall assume that for any prime $q \leq Y$, the probability that q divides $p - 1$ for a randomly chosen "large" prime p is $\sim 1/q$. Under this assumption, show that

$$\mathsf{E}[\log Q'] \sim \log Y.$$

The results of the previous two exercises caution against the use of "short" exponents in cryptographic schemes based on the discrete logarithm problem for $\mathbb{Z}_p^*$. Indeed, suppose that p is a random 1024-bit prime, and that for reasons of efficiency, one chooses $X \approx 2^{160}$, thinking that a method such as the baby step/giant step method would require $\approx 2^{80}$ steps to recover x. However, if we choose $Y \approx 2^{80}$, then we have reason to expect Q to be at least about 2^{80}, in which case X/Q is at most about 2^{80}, and so we can in fact recover x in roughly 2^{40} steps, which may be a feasible number of steps, whereas 2^{80} steps may not be. Of course, none of these issues arise if one works in a subgroup of $\mathbb{Z}_p^*$ of large prime order, which is the recommended practice.

An interesting fact about the Diffie–Hellman problem is that there is no known efficient algorithm to recognize a solution to the problem. Some cryptographic protocols actually rely on the apparent difficulty of this decision problem, which is called the **decisional Diffie–Hellman problem**. The following three exercises develop a random self-reducibility property for this decision problem.

EXERCISE 11.15. Let p be a prime, q a prime dividing $p - 1$, and γ an element of $\mathbb{Z}_p^*$ that generates a subgroup G of order q. Let $\alpha \in G$, and let H be the subgroup of $G \times G$ generated by (γ, α). Let $\tilde{\gamma}, \tilde{\alpha}$ be arbitrary elements of G, and define the map

$$\rho: \quad \mathbb{Z}_q \times \mathbb{Z}_q \to G \times G$$
$$([r]_q, [s]_q) \mapsto (\gamma^r \tilde{\gamma}^s, \alpha^r \tilde{\alpha}^s).$$

Show that the definition of ρ is unambiguous, that ρ is a group homomorphism, and that

- if $(\tilde{\gamma}, \tilde{\alpha}) \in H$, then $\text{img}(\rho) = H$, and
- if $(\tilde{\gamma}, \tilde{\alpha}) \notin H$, then $\text{img}(\rho) = G \times G$.

EXERCISE 11.16. For p, q, γ as in the previous exercise, let $\mathcal{D}_{p,q,\gamma}$ consist of all triples of the form $(\gamma^x, \gamma^y, \gamma^{xy})$, and let $\mathcal{R}_{p,q,\gamma}$ consist of all triples of the form $(\gamma^x, \gamma^y, \gamma^z)$. Using the result from the previous exercise, design a probabilistic algorithm that runs in expected polynomial time, and that on input p, q, γ, along with a triple $\Gamma \in \mathcal{R}_{p,q,\gamma}$, outputs a triple $\Gamma^* \in \mathcal{R}_{p,q,\gamma}$ such that

- if $\Gamma \in \mathcal{D}_{p,q,\gamma}$, then Γ^* is uniformly distributed over $\mathcal{D}_{p,q,\gamma}$, and
- if $\Gamma \notin \mathcal{D}_{p,q,\gamma}$, then Γ^* is uniformly distributed over $\mathcal{R}_{p,q,\gamma}$.

EXERCISE 11.17. Suppose that A is a probabilistic algorithm that takes as input p, q, γ as in the previous exercise, along a triple $\Gamma^* \in \mathcal{R}_{p,q,\gamma}$, and outputs either 0 or 1. Furthermore, assume that A runs in strict polynomial time. Define two random variables, $X_{p,q,\gamma}$ and $Y_{p,q,\gamma}$, as follows:

- $X_{p,q,\gamma}$ is defined to be the output of A on input p, q, γ, and Γ^*, where Γ^* is uniformly distributed over $\mathcal{D}_{p,q,\gamma}$, and
- $Y_{p,q,\gamma}$ is defined to be the output of A on input p, q, γ, and Γ^*, where Γ^* is uniformly distributed over $\mathcal{R}_{p,q,\gamma}$.

In both cases, the value of the random variable is determined by the random choice of Γ^*, as well as the random choices made by the algorithm. Define

$$\epsilon(p, q, \gamma) := \left| P[X_{p,q,\gamma} = 1] - P[Y_{p,q,\gamma} = 1] \right|.$$

Using the result of the previous exercise, show how to use A to design a probabilistic, expected polynomial-time algorithm that takes as input p, q, γ as above, along with $\Gamma \in \mathcal{R}_{p,q,\gamma}$, and outputs either "yes" or "no," so that

> if $\epsilon(p, q, \gamma) \geq 0.001$, then for *all* $\Gamma \in \mathcal{R}_{p,q,\gamma}$, the probability that A' correctly determines whether $\Gamma \in \mathcal{D}_{p,q,\gamma}$ is at least 0.999.

Hint: use the Chernoff bound.

The following exercise demonstrates that distinguishing "Diffie–Hellman triples" from "random triples" is hard only if the order of the underlying group is not divisible by any small primes, which is another reason we have chosen to work with groups of large prime order.

EXERCISE 11.18. Assume the notation of the previous exercise, but let us drop the restriction that q is prime. Design and analyze a deterministic algorithm A that takes inputs p, q, γ and $\Gamma^* \in \mathcal{R}_{p,q,\gamma}$, that outputs 0 or 1, and that satisfies the following property: if t is the *smallest* prime dividing q, then A runs in time $(t + \operatorname{len}(p))^{O(1)}$, and the "distinguishing advantage" $\epsilon(p, q, \gamma)$ for A on inputs p, q, γ is at least $1/t$.

11.4 Notes

The probabilistic algorithm in §11.1 for finding a generator for $\mathbb{Z}_p^*$ can be made deterministic under a generalization of the Riemann hypothesis. Indeed, as discussed in §10.7, under such a hypothesis, Bach's result [10] implies that for each prime $q \mid (p - 1)$, the least positive integer a such that $[a]_p \in \mathbb{Z}_p^* \setminus (\mathbb{Z}_p^*)^q$ is at most $2 \log p$.

Related to the problem of constructing a generator for $\mathbb{Z}_p^*$ is the question of how big is the smallest positive integer g such that $[g]_p$ is a generator for $\mathbb{Z}_p^*$; that is, how big is the smallest (positive) primitive root modulo p. The best bounds on the least primitive root are also obtained using the same generalization of the Riemann hypothesis mentioned above. Under this hypothesis, Wang [98] showed that the least primitive root modulo p is $O(r^6 \operatorname{len}(p)^2)$, where r is the number of distinct prime divisors of $p - 1$. Shoup [90] improved Wang's bound to $O(r^4 \operatorname{len}(r)^4 \operatorname{len}(p)^2)$ by adapting a result of Iwaniec [48, 49] and applying it to Wang's proof. The best unconditional bound on the smallest primitive root modulo p is $p^{1/4+o(1)}$ (this bound is also in Wang [98]). Of course, just because there exists a small primitive root, there is no known way to efficiently recognize a primitive root modulo p without knowing the prime factorization of $p - 1$.

As we already mentioned, all of the algorithms presented in this chapter are completely "generic," in the sense that they work in *any* finite cyclic group — we really did not exploit any properties about $\mathbb{Z}_p^*$ other than the fact that it is a cyclic group. In fact, as far as such "generic" algorithms go, the algorithms presented here for discrete logarithms are optimal [67, 93]. However, there are faster, "non-generic" algorithms (though still not polynomial time) for discrete logarithms in $\mathbb{Z}_p^*$. We shall examine one such algorithm later, in Chapter 16.

The "baby step/giant step" algorithm in §11.2.2 is due to Shanks [86]. See, for example, the book by Cormen, Leiserson, Rivest, and Stein [29] for appropriate data structures to implement the lookup table used in that algorithm. In particular, see Problem 12-2 in [29] for a brief introduction to radix trees, which is the data structure that yields the best running time (at least in principle) for our application.

The algorithms in §11.2.3 and §11.2.4 are variants of an algorithm published by Pohlig and Hellman [71]. See Chapter 4 of [29] for details on how one analyzes recursive algorithms, such as the one presented in §11.2.3; in particular, Section 4.2 in [29] discusses in detail the notion of a **recursion tree**.

The algorithm in §11.2.5 is a variant of an algorithm of Pollard [72]; in fact, Pollard's algorithm is a bit more efficient than the one presented here, but the analysis of its running time depends on stronger heuristics. Pollard's paper also describes an algorithm for computing discrete logarithms that lie in a restricted interval—if the interval has width w, this algorithm runs (heuristically) in time $w^{1/2} \operatorname{len}(p)^{O(1)}$, and requires space for $O(\operatorname{len}(w))$ elements of $\mathbb{Z}_p$. This algorithm is useful in reducing the space requirement for the algorithm of Exercise 11.13.

The key establishment protocol in §11.3 is from Diffie and Hellman [33]. That paper initiated the study of **public key cryptography**, which has proved to be a very rich field of research.

Exercises 11.13 and 11.14 are based on van Oorschot and Wiener [70].

For more on the decisional Diffie–Hellman assumption, see Boneh [18].

12

Quadratic residues and quadratic reciprocity

12.1 Quadratic residues

For positive integer n, an integer a is called a **quadratic residue modulo** n if $\gcd(a, n) = 1$ and $x^2 \equiv a \pmod{n}$ for some integer x; in this case, we say that x is a **square root of** a **modulo** n.

The quadratic residues modulo n correspond exactly to the subgroup of squares $(\mathbb{Z}_n^*)^2$ of $\mathbb{Z}_n^*$; that is, a is a quadratic residue modulo n if and only if $[a]_n \in (\mathbb{Z}_n^*)^2$.

Let us first consider the case where $n = p$, where p is an odd prime. In this case, we know that $\mathbb{Z}_p^*$ is cyclic of order $p-1$ (see Theorem 9.16). Recall that the subgroups any finite cyclic group are in one-to-one correspondence with the positive divisors of the order of the group (see Theorem 8.31). For any $d \mid (p-1)$, consider the d-power map on $\mathbb{Z}_p^*$ that sends $\alpha \in \mathbb{Z}_p^*$ to α^d. The image of this map is the unique subgroup of $\mathbb{Z}_p^*$ of order $(p-1)/d$, and the kernel of this map is the unique subgroup of order d. This means that the image of the 2-power map is of order $(p-1)/2$ and must be the same as the kernel of the $(p-1)/2$-power map. Since the image of the $(p-1)/2$-power map is of order 2, it must be equal to the subgroup $\{\pm 1\}$. The kernel of the 2-power map is of order 2, and so must also be equal to the subgroup $\{\pm 1\}$.

Translating from group-theoretic language to the language of congruences, we have shown:

Theorem 12.1. *For an odd prime p, the number of quadratic residues a modulo p, with $0 \le a < p$, is $(p-1)/2$. Moreover, if x is a square root of a modulo p, then so is $-x$, and any square root y of a modulo p satisfies $y \equiv \pm x \pmod{p}$. Also, for any integer $a \not\equiv 0 \pmod{p}$, we have $a^{(p-1)/2} \equiv \pm 1 \pmod{p}$, and moreover, a is a quadratic residue modulo p if and only if $a^{(p-1)/2} \equiv 1 \pmod{p}$.*

283

Now consider the case where $n = p^e$, where p is an odd prime and $e > 1$. We also know that $\mathbb{Z}_{p^e}^*$ is a cyclic group of order $p^{e-1}(p-1)$ (see Theorem 10.1), and so everything that we said in discussing the case $\mathbb{Z}_p^*$ applies here as well. In particular, for $a \not\equiv 0 \pmod{p}$, a is a quadratic residue modulo p^e if and only if $a^{p^{e-1}(p-1)/2} \equiv 1 \pmod{p^e}$. However, we can simplify this a bit. Note that $a^{p^{e-1}(p-1)/2} \equiv 1 \pmod{p^e}$ implies $a^{p^{e-1}(p-1)/2} \equiv 1 \pmod{p}$, and by Fermat's little theorem, this implies $a^{(p-1)/2} \equiv 1 \pmod{p}$. Conversely, by Theorem 10.2, $a^{(p-1)/2} \equiv 1 \pmod{p}$ implies $a^{p^{e-1}(p-1)/2} \equiv 1 \pmod{p^e}$. Thus, we have shown:

Theorem 12.2. *For an odd prime p and integer $e > 1$, the number of quadratic residues a modulo p^e, with $0 \le a < p^e$, is $p^{e-1}(p-1)/2$. Moreover, if x is a square root of a modulo p^e, then so is $-x$, and any square root y of a modulo p^e satisfies $y \equiv \pm x \pmod{p^e}$. Also, for any integer $a \not\equiv 0 \pmod{p}$, we have $a^{p^{e-1}(p-1)/2} \equiv \pm 1 \pmod{p}$, and moreover, a is a quadratic residue modulo p^e iff $a^{p^{e-1}(p-1)/2} \equiv 1 \pmod{p^e}$ iff $a^{(p-1)/2} \equiv 1 \pmod{p}$ iff a is a quadratic residue modulo p.*

Now consider an arbitrary odd integer $n > 1$, and let $n = \prod_{i=1}^{r} p_i^{e_i}$ be its prime factorization. Recall the group isomorphism implied by the Chinese remainder theorem:

$$\mathbb{Z}_n^* \cong \mathbb{Z}_{p_1^{e_1}}^* \times \cdots \times \mathbb{Z}_{p_r^{e_r}}^*.$$

Now,

$$(\alpha_1, \ldots, \alpha_r) \in \mathbb{Z}_{p_1^{e_1}}^* \times \cdots \times \mathbb{Z}_{p_r^{e_r}}^*$$

is a square if and only if there exist $\beta_1, \ldots, \beta_r$ with $\beta_i \in \mathbb{Z}_{p_i^{e_i}}^*$ and $\alpha_i = \beta_i^2$ for $i = 1, \ldots, r$, in which case, we see that the square roots of $(\alpha_1, \ldots, \alpha_r)$ comprise the 2^r elements $(\pm\beta_1, \ldots, \pm\beta_r)$. Thus we have:

Theorem 12.3. *Consider an odd, positive integer n with prime factorization $n = \prod_{i=1}^{r} p_i^{e_i}$. The number of quadratic residues a modulo n, with $0 \le a < n$, is $\phi(n)/2^r$. Moreover, if a is a quadratic residue modulo n, then there are precisely 2^r distinct integers x, with $0 \le x < n$, such that $x^2 \equiv a \pmod{n}$. Also, an integer a is a quadratic residue modulo n if and only if it is a quadratic residue modulo p_i for $i = 1, \ldots, r$.*

That completes our investigation of the case where n is odd. We shall not investigate the case where n is even, as it is a bit messy, and is not of particular importance.

12.2 The Legendre symbol

For an odd prime p and an integer a with $\gcd(a, p) = 1$, the **Legendre symbol** $(a \mid p)$ is defined to be 1 if a is a quadratic residue modulo p, and -1 otherwise. For completeness, one defines $(a \mid p) = 0$ if $p \mid a$. The following theorem summarizes the essential properties of the Legendre symbol.

Theorem 12.4. *Let p be an odd prime, and let $a, b \in \mathbb{Z}$. Then we have*

(i) $(a \mid p) \equiv a^{(p-1)/2} \pmod{p}$; *in particular,* $(-1 \mid p) = (-1)^{(p-1)/2}$;

(ii) $(a \mid p)(b \mid p) = (ab \mid p)$;

(iii) $a \equiv b \pmod{p}$ *implies* $(a \mid p) = (b \mid p)$;

(iv) $(2 \mid p) = (-1)^{(p^2-1)/8}$;

(v) *if q is an odd prime, then*

$$(p \mid q) = (-1)^{\frac{p-1}{2}\frac{q-1}{2}}(q \mid p).$$

Part (v) of this theorem is called the **law of quadratic reciprocity**. Note that when $p = q$, both $(p \mid q)$ and $(q \mid p)$ are zero, and so the statement of part (v) is trivially true—the interesting case is when $p \neq q$, and in this case, part (v) is equivalent to saying that

$$(p \mid q)(q \mid p) = (-1)^{\frac{p-1}{2}\frac{q-1}{2}}.$$

Part (i) of this theorem follows from Theorem 12.1. Part (ii) is an immediate consequence of part (i), and part (iii) is clear from the definition.

The rest of this section is devoted to a proof of parts (iv) and (v) of this theorem. The proof is completely elementary, although a bit technical.

Theorem 12.5 (Gauss' lemma). *Let p be an odd prime and let a be an integer not divisible by p. Define $\alpha_j := ja \bmod p$ for $j = 1, \ldots, (p-1)/2$, and let n be the number of indices j for which $\alpha_j > p/2$. Then $(a \mid p) = (-1)^n$.*

Proof. Let $r_1, \ldots, r_n$ denote the values α_j that exceed $p/2$, and let $s_1, \ldots, s_k$ denote the remaining values α_j. The r_i and s_i are all distinct and non-zero. We have $0 < p - r_i < p/2$ for $i = 1, \ldots, n$, and no $p - r_i$ is an s_j; indeed, if $p - r_i = s_j$, then $s_j \equiv -r_i \pmod{p}$, and writing $s_j = ua \bmod p$ and $r_i = va \bmod p$, for some $u, v = 1, \ldots, (p-1)/2$, we have $ua \equiv -va \pmod{p}$, which implies $u \equiv -v \pmod{p}$, which is impossible.

It follows that the sequence of numbers $s_1, \ldots, s_k, p - r_1, \ldots, p - r_n$ is just a re-ordering of $1, \ldots, (p-1)/2$. Then we have

$$((p-1)/2)! \equiv s_1 \cdots s_k(-r_1) \cdots (-r_n)$$
$$\equiv (-1)^n s_1 \cdots s_k r_1 \cdots r_n$$
$$\equiv (-1)^n((p-1)/2)!\, a^{(p-1)/2} \pmod{p},$$

and canceling the factor $((p-1)/2)!$, we obtain $a^{(p-1)/2} \equiv (-1)^n \pmod{p}$, and the result follows from the fact that $(a \mid p) \equiv a^{(p-1)/2} \pmod{p}$. $\square$

Theorem 12.6. *If p is an odd prime and $\gcd(a, 2p) = 1$, then $(a \mid p) = (-1)^t$ where $t = \sum_{j=1}^{(p-1)/2} \lfloor ja/p \rfloor$. Also, $(2 \mid p) = (-1)^{(p^2-1)/8}$.*

Proof. Let a be an integer not divisible by p, but which may be even, and let us adopt the same notation as in the statement and proof of Theorem 12.5; in particular, $\alpha_1, \ldots, \alpha_{(p-1)/2}$, $r_1, \ldots, r_n$, and $s_1, \ldots, s_k$ are as defined there. Note that $ja = p\lfloor ja/p \rfloor + \alpha_j$, for $j = 1, \ldots, (p-1)/2$, so we have

$$\sum_{j=1}^{(p-1)/2} ja = \sum_{j=1}^{(p-1)/2} p\lfloor ja/p \rfloor + \sum_{j=1}^{n} r_j + \sum_{j=1}^{k} s_j. \tag{12.1}$$

Also, we saw in the proof of Theorem 12.5 that the integers $s_1, \ldots, s_k, p - r_1, \ldots, p - r_n$ are a re-ordering of $1, \ldots, (p-1)/2$, and hence

$$\sum_{j=1}^{(p-1)/2} j = \sum_{j=1}^{n}(p - r_j) + \sum_{j=1}^{k} s_j = np - \sum_{j=1}^{n} r_j + \sum_{j=1}^{k} s_j. \tag{12.2}$$

Subtracting (12.2) from (12.1), we get

$$(a-1) \sum_{j=1}^{(p-1)/2} j = p\left(\sum_{j=1}^{(p-1)/2} \lfloor ja/p \rfloor - n\right) + 2\sum_{j=1}^{n} r_j. \tag{12.3}$$

Note that

$$\sum_{j=1}^{(p-1)/2} j = \frac{p^2 - 1}{8}, \tag{12.4}$$

which together with (12.3) implies

$$(a-1)\frac{p^2 - 1}{8} \equiv \sum_{j=1}^{(p-1)/2} \lfloor ja/p \rfloor - n \pmod{2}. \tag{12.5}$$

If a is odd, (12.5) implies

$$n \equiv \sum_{j=1}^{(p-1)/2} \lfloor ja/p \rfloor \pmod{2}. \tag{12.6}$$

If $a = 2$, then $\lfloor 2j/p \rfloor = 0$ for $j = 1, \ldots, (p-1)/2$, and (12.5) implies

$$n \equiv \frac{p^2 - 1}{8} \pmod{2}. \tag{12.7}$$

The theorem now follows from (12.6) and (12.7), together with Theorem 12.5. $\square$

Note that this last theorem proves part (iv) of Theorem 12.4. The next theorem proves part (v).

Theorem 12.7. *If p and q are distinct odd primes, then*

$$(p \mid q)(q \mid p) = (-1)^{\frac{p-1}{2}\frac{q-1}{2}}.$$

Proof. Let S be the set of pairs of integers (x, y) with $1 \le x \le (p-1)/2$ and $1 \le y \le (q-1)/2$. Note that S contains no pair (x, y) with $qx = py$, so let us partition S into two subsets: S_1 contains all pairs (x, y) with $qx > py$, and S_2 contains all pairs (x, y) with $qx < py$. Note that $(x, y) \in S_1$ if and only if $1 \le x \le (p-1)/2$ and $1 \le y \le \lfloor qx/p \rfloor$. So $|S_1| = \sum_{x=1}^{(p-1)/2} \lfloor qx/p \rfloor$. Similarly, $|S_2| = \sum_{y=1}^{(q-1)/2} \lfloor py/q \rfloor$. So we have

$$\frac{p-1}{2}\frac{q-1}{2} = |S| = |S_1| + |S_2| = \sum_{x=1}^{(p-1)/2} \lfloor qx/p \rfloor + \sum_{y=1}^{(q-1)/2} \lfloor py/q \rfloor,$$

and Theorem 12.6 implies

$$(p \mid q)(q \mid p) = (-1)^{\frac{p-1}{2}\frac{q-1}{2}}. \quad \square$$

12.3 The Jacobi symbol

Let a, n be integers, where n is positive and odd, so that $n = q_1 \cdots q_k$, where the q_i are odd primes, not necessarily distinct. Then the **Jacobi symbol** $(a \mid n)$ is defined as

$$(a \mid n) := (a \mid q_1) \cdots (a \mid q_k),$$

where $(a \mid q_j)$ is the Legendre symbol. Note that $(a \mid 1) = 1$ for all $a \in \mathbb{Z}$. Thus, the Jacobi symbol essentially extends the domain of definition of the Legendre symbol. Note that $(a \mid n) \in \{0, \pm 1\}$, and that $(a \mid n) = 0$

if and only if $\gcd(a, n) > 1$. Also, note that if a is a quadratic residue modulo n, then $(a \mid n) = 1$; however, $(a \mid n) = 1$ does not imply that a is a quadratic residue modulo n. The following theorem summarizes the essential properties of the Jacobi symbol.

Theorem 12.8. *Let m, n be odd, positive integers, an let a, b be integers. Then*

(i) $(ab \mid n) = (a \mid n)(b \mid n)$;

(ii) $(a \mid mn) = (a \mid m)(a \mid n)$;

(iii) $a \equiv b \pmod{n}$ *implies* $(a \mid n) = (b \mid n)$;

(iv) $(-1 \mid n) = (-1)^{(n-1)/2}$;

(v) $(2 \mid n) = (-1)^{(n^2-1)/8}$;

(vi) $(m \mid n) = (-1)^{\frac{m-1}{2} \frac{n-1}{2}} (n \mid m)$.

Proof. Parts (i)–(iii) follow directly from the definition (exercise).

For parts (iv) and (vi), one can easily verify (exercise) that for odd integers $n_1, \ldots, n_k$,

$$\sum_{i=1}^{k} (n_i - 1)/2 \equiv (n_1 \cdots n_k - 1)/2 \pmod{2}.$$

Part (iv) easily follows from this fact, along with part (ii) of this theorem and part (i) of Theorem 12.4 (exercise). Part (vi) easily follows from this fact, along with parts (i) and (ii) of this theorem, and part (v) of Theorem 12.4 (exercise).

For part (v), one can easily verify (exercise) that for odd integers $n_1, \ldots, n_k$,

$$\sum_{1 \le i \le k} (n_i^2 - 1)/8 \equiv (n_1^2 \cdots n_k^2 - 1)/8 \pmod{2}.$$

Part (v) easily follows from this fact, along with part (ii) of this theorem, and part (iv) of Theorem 12.4 (exercise). □

As we shall see later, this theorem is extremely useful from a computational point of view—with it, one can efficiently compute $(a \mid n)$, without having to know the prime factorization of either a or n. Also, in applying this theorem it is useful to observe that for odd integers m, n,

- $(-1)^{(n-1)/2} = 1$ iff $n \equiv 1 \pmod{4}$;
- $(-1)^{(n^2-1)/8} = 1$ iff $n \equiv \pm 1 \pmod{8}$;
- $(-1)^{((m-1)/2)((n-1)/2)} = 1$ iff $m \equiv 1 \pmod{4}$ or $n \equiv 1 \pmod{4}$.

It is sometimes useful to view the Jacobi symbol as a group homomorphism. Let n be an odd, positive integer. Define the **Jacobi map**

$$J_n : \quad \mathbb{Z}_n^* \to \{\pm 1\}$$
$$[a]_n \mapsto (a \mid n).$$

First, we note that by part (iii) of Theorem 12.8, this definition is unambiguous. Second, we note that since $\gcd(a, n) = 1$ implies $(a \mid n) = \pm 1$, the image of J_n is indeed contained in $\{\pm 1\}$. Third, we note that by part (i) of Theorem 12.8, J_n is a group homomorphism.

Since J_n is a group homomorphism, it follows that its kernel, $\ker(J_n)$, is a subgroup of $\mathbb{Z}_n^*$.

EXERCISE 12.1. Let n be an odd, positive integer. Show that $[\mathbb{Z}_n^* : (\mathbb{Z}_n^*)^2] = 2^r$, where r is the number of distinct prime divisors of n.

EXERCISE 12.2. Let n be an odd, positive integer, and consider the Jacobi map J_n.

(a) Show that $(\mathbb{Z}_n^*)^2 \subseteq \ker(J_n)$.

(b) Show that if n is the square of an integer, then $\ker(J_n) = \mathbb{Z}_n^*$.

(c) Show that if n is not the square of an integer, then $[\mathbb{Z}_n^* : \ker(J_n)] = 2$ and $[\ker(J_n) : (\mathbb{Z}_n^*)^2] = 2^{r-1}$, where r is the number of distinct prime divisors of n.

EXERCISE 12.3. Let p and q be distinct primes, with $p \equiv q \equiv 3 \pmod 4$, and let $n := pq$.

(a) Show that $[-1]_n \in \ker(J_n) \setminus (\mathbb{Z}_n^*)^2$, and from this, conclude that the cosets of $(\mathbb{Z}_n^*)^2$ in $\ker(J_n)$ are the two distinct cosets $(\mathbb{Z}_n^*)^2$ and $[-1]_n(\mathbb{Z}_n^*)^2$.

(b) Show that the squaring map on $(\mathbb{Z}_n^*)^2$ is a group automorphism.

(c) Let $\delta \in \mathbb{Z}_n^* \setminus \ker(J_n)$. Show that the map from $\{0, 1\} \times \{0, 1\} \times (\mathbb{Z}_n^*)^2 \to \mathbb{Z}_n^*$ that sends (a, b, γ) to $\delta^a (-1)^b \gamma$ is a bijection.

12.4 Notes

The proof we present here of Theorem 12.4 is essentially the one from Niven and Zuckerman [68]. Our proof of Theorem 12.8 is essentially the one found in Bach and Shallit [12].

13

Computational problems related to quadratic residues

13.1 Computing the Jacobi symbol

Suppose we are given an odd, positive integer n, along with an integer a, and we want to compute the Jacobi symbol $(a \mid n)$. Theorem 12.8 suggests the following algorithm:

$t \leftarrow 1$
repeat
    // *loop invariant: n is odd and positive*
    $a \leftarrow a \bmod n$
    if $a = 0$
        if $n = 1$ return t else return 0
    compute a', h such that $a = 2^h a'$ and a' is odd
    if $h \not\equiv 0 \pmod 2$ and $n \not\equiv \pm 1 \pmod 8$ then $t \leftarrow -t$
    if $a' \not\equiv 1 \pmod 4$ and $n \not\equiv 1 \pmod 4$ then $t \leftarrow -t$
    $(a, n) \leftarrow (n, a')$
forever

That this algorithm correctly computes the Jacobi symbol $(a \mid n)$ follows directly from Theorem 12.8. Using an analysis similar to that of Euclid's algorithm, one easily sees that the running time of this algorithm is $O(\mathrm{len}(a) \, \mathrm{len}(n))$.

EXERCISE 13.1. Develop a "binary" Jacobi symbol algorithm, that is, one that uses only addition, subtractions, and "shift" operations, analogous to the binary gcd algorithm in Exercise 4.1.

EXERCISE 13.2. This exercise develops a probabilistic primality test based on the Jacobi symbol. For odd integer $n > 1$, define

$$G_n := \{\alpha \in \mathbb{Z}_n^* : \alpha^{(n-1)/2} = [J_n(\alpha)]_n\},$$

where $J_n : \mathbb{Z}_n^* \to \{\pm 1\}$ is the Jacobi map.

(a) Show that G_n is a subgroup of $\mathbb{Z}_n^*$.

(b) Show that if n is prime, then $G_n = \mathbb{Z}_n^*$.

(c) Show that if n is composite, then $G_n \subsetneq \mathbb{Z}_n^*$.

(d) Based on parts (a)–(c), design and analyze an efficient probabilistic primality test that works by choosing a random, non-zero element $\alpha \in \mathbb{Z}_n$, and testing if $\alpha \in G_n$.

13.2 Testing quadratic residuosity

In this section, we consider the problem of testing whether a is a quadratic residue modulo n, for given integers a and n, from a computational perspective.

13.2.1 Prime modulus

For an odd prime p, we can test if an integer a is a quadratic residue modulo p by either performing the exponentiation $a^{(p-1)/2} \bmod p$ or by computing the Legendre symbol $(a \mid p)$. Assume that $0 \le a < p$. Using a standard repeated squaring algorithm, the former method takes time $O(\operatorname{len}(p)^3)$, while using the Euclidean-like algorithm of the previous section, the latter method takes time $O(\operatorname{len}(p)^2)$. So clearly, the latter method is to be preferred.

13.2.2 Prime-power modulus

For an odd prime p, we know that a is a quadratic residue modulo p^e if and only if a is a quadratic residue modulo p. So this case immediately reduces to the previous case.

13.2.3 Composite modulus

For odd, composite n, if we know the factorization of n, then we can also determine if a is a quadratic residue modulo n by determining if it is a quadratic residue modulo each prime divisor p of n. However, without knowledge of this factorization (which is in general believed to be hard to compute), there is no efficient algorithm known. We can compute the Jacobi symbol $(a \mid n)$;

if this is -1 or 0, we can conclude that a is not a quadratic residue; otherwise, we cannot conclude much of anything.

13.3 Computing modular square roots

In this section, we consider the problem of computing a square root of a modulo n, given integers a and n, where a is a quadratic residue modulo n.

13.3.1 *Prime modulus*

Let p be an odd prime, and let a be an integer such that $0 < a < p$ and $(a \mid p) = 1$. We would like to compute a square root of a modulo p. Let $\alpha := [a]_p \in \mathbb{Z}_p^*$, so that we can restate our problem of that of finding $\beta \in \mathbb{Z}_p^*$ such that $\beta^2 = \alpha$, given $\alpha \in (\mathbb{Z}_p^*)^2$.

We first consider the special case where $p \equiv 3 \pmod{4}$, in which it turns out that this problem can be solved very easily. Indeed, we claim that in this case

$$\beta := \alpha^{(p+1)/4}$$

is a square root of α—note that since $p \equiv 3 \pmod{4}$, the number $(p+1)/4$ is an integer. To show that $\beta^2 = \alpha$, suppose $\alpha = \tilde{\beta}^2$ for some $\tilde{\beta} \in \mathbb{Z}_p^*$. We know that there is such a $\tilde{\beta}$, since we are assuming that $\alpha \in (\mathbb{Z}_p^*)^2$. Then we have

$$\beta^2 = \alpha^{(p+1)/2} = \tilde{\beta}^{p+1} = \tilde{\beta}^2 = \alpha,$$

where we used Fermat's little theorem for the third equality. Using a repeated-squaring algorithm, we can compute β in time $O(\text{len}(p)^3)$.

Now we consider the general case, where we may have $p \not\equiv 3 \pmod{4}$. Here is one way to efficiently compute a square root of α, assuming we are given, in addition to α, an auxiliary input $\gamma \in \mathbb{Z}_p^* \setminus (\mathbb{Z}_p^*)^2$ (how one obtains such a γ is discussed below).

Let us write $p - 1 = 2^h m$, where m is odd. For any $\delta \in \mathbb{Z}_p^*$, δ^m has multiplicative order dividing 2^h. Since $\alpha^{2^{h-1}m} = 1$, α^m has multiplicative order dividing 2^{h-1}. Since $\gamma^{2^{h-1}m} = -1$, γ^m has multiplicative order precisely 2^h. Since there is only one subgroup of $\mathbb{Z}_p^*$ of order 2^h, it follows that γ^m generates this subgroup, and that $\alpha^m = \gamma^{mx}$ for $0 \le x < 2^h$ and x is even. We can find x by computing the discrete logarithm of α^m to the base γ^m, using the algorithm in §11.2.3. Setting $\kappa = \gamma^{mx/2}$, we have

$$\kappa^2 = \alpha^m.$$

We are not quite done, since we now have a square root of α^m, and not of α. Since m is odd, we may write $m = 2t + 1$ for some non-negative integer t. It then follows that

$$(\kappa\alpha^{-t})^2 = \kappa^2\alpha^{-2t} = \alpha^m\alpha^{-2t} = \alpha^{m-2t} = \alpha.$$

Thus, $\kappa\alpha^{-t}$ is a square root of α.

Let us summarize the above algorithm for computing a square root of $\alpha \in (\mathbb{Z}_p^*)^2$, assuming we are given $\gamma \in \mathbb{Z}_p^* \setminus (\mathbb{Z}_p^*)^2$, in addition to α:

Compute positive integers m, h such that $p - 1 = 2^h m$ with m odd
$\gamma' \leftarrow \gamma^m$, $\alpha' \leftarrow \alpha^m$
Compute $x \leftarrow \log_{\gamma'} \alpha'$ //   note that $0 \le x < 2^h$ and x is even
$\beta \leftarrow (\gamma')^{x/2}\alpha^{-\lfloor m/2 \rfloor}$
output β

The total amount of work done outside the discrete logarithm calculation amounts to just a handful of exponentiations modulo p, and so takes time $O(\text{len}(p)^3)$. The time to compute the discrete logarithm is $O(h\,\text{len}(h)\,\text{len}(p)^2)$. So the total running time of this procedure is

$$O(\text{len}(p)^3 + h\,\text{len}(h)\,\text{len}(p)^2).$$

The above procedure assumed we had at hand a non-square γ. If $h = 1$, which means that $p \equiv 3 \pmod 4$, then $(-1 \mid p) = -1$, and so we are done. However, we have already seen how to efficiently compute a square root in this case.

If $h > 1$, we can find a non-square γ using a probabilistic search algorithm. Simply choose γ at random, test if it is a square, and if so, repeat. The probability that a random element of $\mathbb{Z}_p^*$ is a square is $1/2$; thus, the expected number of trials until we find a non-square is 2, and hence the expected running time of this probabilistic search algorithm is $O(\text{len}(p)^2)$.

EXERCISE 13.3. Let p be an odd prime, and let $f \in \mathbb{Z}_p[X]$ be a polynomial with $0 \le \deg(f) \le 2$. Design and analyze an efficient, probabilistic algorithm that determines if f has any roots in $\mathbb{Z}_p$, and if so, finds all of the roots. Hint: see Exercise 9.14.

EXERCISE 13.4. Show that the following two problems are deterministic, poly-time equivalent (see discussion just above Exercise 11.10 in §11.3):

(a) Given an odd prime p and $\alpha \in (\mathbb{Z}_p^*)^2$, find $\beta \in \mathbb{Z}_p^*$ such that $\beta^2 = \alpha$.
(b) Given an odd prime p, find an element of $\mathbb{Z}_p^* \setminus (\mathbb{Z}_p^*)^2$.

EXERCISE 13.5. Design and analyze an efficient, deterministic algorithm that takes as input primes p and q, such that $q \mid (p-1)$, along with an element $\alpha \in \mathbb{Z}_p^*$, and determines whether or not $\alpha \in (\mathbb{Z}_p^*)^q$.

EXERCISE 13.6. Design and analyze an efficient, deterministic algorithm that takes as input primes p and q, such that $q \mid (p-1)$ but $q^2 \nmid (p-1)$, along with an element $\alpha \in (\mathbb{Z}_p^*)^q$, and computes a qth root of α, that is, an element $\beta \in \mathbb{Z}_p^*$ such that $\beta^q = \alpha$.

EXERCISE 13.7. We are given a positive integer n, two elements $\alpha, \beta \in \mathbb{Z}_n$, and integers e and f such that $\alpha^e = \beta^f$ and $\gcd(e, f) = 1$. Show how to efficiently compute $\gamma \in \mathbb{Z}_n$ such that $\gamma^e = \beta$. Hint: use the extended Euclidean algorithm.

EXERCISE 13.8. Design and analyze an algorithm that takes as input primes p and q, such that $q \mid (p-1)$, along with an element $\alpha \in (\mathbb{Z}_p^*)^q$, and computes a qth root of α. (Unlike Exercise 13.6, we now allow $q^2 \mid (p-1)$.) Your algorithm may be probabilistic, and should have an expected running time that is bounded by $q^{1/2}$ times a polynomial in $\mathrm{len}(p)$. Hint: the previous exercise may be useful.

EXERCISE 13.9. Let p be an odd prime, γ be a generator for $\mathbb{Z}_p^*$, and α be any element of $\mathbb{Z}_p^*$. Define

$$B(p, \gamma, \alpha) := \begin{cases} 1 & \text{if } \log_\gamma \alpha \geq (p-1)/2; \\ 0 & \text{if } \log_\gamma \alpha < (p-1)/2. \end{cases}$$

Suppose that there is an algorithm that efficiently computes $B(p, \gamma, \alpha)$ for all p, γ, α as above. Show how to use this algorithm as a subroutine in an efficient, probabilistic algorithm that computes $\log_\gamma \alpha$ for all p, γ, α as above. Hint: in addition to the algorithm that computes B, use algorithms for testing quadratic residuosity and computing square roots modulo p, and "read off" the bits of $\log_\gamma \alpha$ one at a time.

13.3.2 Prime-power modulus

Let p be an odd prime, let a be an integer relatively prime to p, and let $e > 1$ be an integer. We know that a is a quadratic residue modulo p^e if and only if a is a quadratic residue modulo p. Suppose that a is a quadratic residue modulo p, and that we have found an integer z such that $z^2 \equiv a \pmod{p}$, using, say, one of the procedures described in §13.3.1. From this, we can easily compute a square root of a modulo p^e using the following technique, which is known as **Hensel lifting**.

More generally, suppose we have computed an integer z such that $z^2 \equiv a \pmod{p^f}$, for some $f \geq 1$, and we want to find an integer $\hat{z}$ such that $\hat{z}^2 \equiv a \pmod{p^{f+1}}$. Clearly, if $\hat{z}^2 \equiv a \pmod{p^{f+1}}$, then $\hat{z}^2 \equiv a \pmod{p^f}$, and so $\hat{z} \equiv \pm z \pmod{p^f}$. So let us set $\hat{z} = z + p^f u$, and solve for u. We have

$$\hat{z}^2 \equiv (z + p^f u)^2 \equiv z^2 + 2zp^f u + p^{2f} u^2 \equiv z^2 + 2zp^f u \pmod{p^{f+1}}.$$

So we want to find integer u such that

$$2zp^f u \equiv a - z^2 \pmod{p^{f+1}}.$$

Since $p^f \mid (z^2 - a)$, by Theorem 2.5, the above congruence holds if and only if

$$2zu \equiv \frac{a - z^2}{p^f} \pmod{p}.$$

From this, we can easily compute the desired value u, since $\gcd(2z, p) = 1$.

By iterating the above procedure, starting with a square root of a modulo p, we can quickly find a square root of a modulo p^e. We leave a detailed analysis of the running time of this procedure to the reader.

EXERCISE 13.10. Suppose you are given a polynomial $f \in \mathbb{Z}[\mathsf{X}]$, along with a prime p and a root z of f modulo p, that is, an integer z such that $f(z) \equiv 0 \pmod{p}$. Further, assume that z is simple root of f modulo p, meaning that $\mathbf{D}(f)(z) \not\equiv 0 \pmod{p}$, where $\mathbf{D}(f)$ is the formal derivative of f. Show that for any integer $e \geq 1$, f has a root modulo p^e, and give an efficient procedure to find it. Also, show that the root modulo p^e is uniquely determined, in the following sense: if two such roots are congruent modulo p, then they are congruent modulo p^e.

13.3.3 Composite modulus

To find square roots modulo n, where n is an odd composite modulus, if we know the prime factorization of n, then we can use the above procedures for finding square roots modulo primes and prime powers, and then use the algorithm of the Chinese remainder theorem to get a square root modulo n.

However, if the factorization of n is not known, then there is no efficient algorithm known for computing square roots modulo n. In fact, one can show that the problem of finding square roots modulo n is at least as hard as the problem of factoring n, in the sense that if there is an efficient algorithm for computing square roots modulo n, then there is an efficient (probabilistic) algorithm for factoring n.

Here is an algorithm to factor n, using a modular square-root algorithm as a subroutine. For simplicity, we assume that n is of the form $n = pq$, where p and q are distinct, odd primes. Choose β to be a random, non-zero element of $\mathbb{Z}_n$. If $d := \gcd(\mathrm{rep}(\beta), n) > 1$, then output d (recall that $\mathrm{rep}(\beta)$ denotes the canonical representative of β). Otherwise, set $\alpha := \beta^2$, and feed n and α to the modular square-root algorithm, obtaining a square root $\beta' \in \mathbb{Z}_n^*$ of α. If the square-root algorithm returns $\beta' \in \mathbb{Z}_n^*$ such that $\beta' = \pm\beta$, then output "failure"; otherwise, output $\gcd(\mathrm{rep}(\beta - \beta'), n)$, which is a non-trivial divisor of n.

Let us analyze this algorithm. If $d > 1$, we split n, so assume that $d = 1$, which means that $\beta \in \mathbb{Z}_n^*$. In this case, β is uniformly distributed over $\mathbb{Z}_n^*$, and α is uniformly distributed over $(\mathbb{Z}_n^*)^2$. Let us condition on an a *fixed* value of α, and on fixed random choices made by the modular square-root algorithm (in general, this algorithm may be probabilistic). In this conditional probability distribution, the value β' returned by the algorithm is completely determined. If $\theta : \mathbb{Z}_p \times \mathbb{Z}_q \to \mathbb{Z}_n$ is the ring isomorphism of the Chinese remainder theorem, and $\beta' = \theta(\beta_1', \beta_2')$, then in this conditional probability distribution, β is uniformly distributed over the four square roots of α, which we may write as $\theta(\pm\beta_1', \pm\beta_2')$.

With probability $1/4$, we have $\beta = \theta(\beta_1', \beta_2') = \beta'$, and with probability $1/4$, we have $\beta = \theta(-\beta_1', -\beta_2') = -\beta'$, and so with probability $1/2$, we have $\beta = \pm\beta'$, in which case we fail to factor n. However, with probability $1/4$, we have $\beta = \theta(-\beta_1', \beta_2')$, in which case $\beta - \beta' = \theta(-2\beta_1', 0)$, and since $2\beta_1' \neq 0$, we have $p \nmid \mathrm{rep}(\beta - \beta')$ and $q \mid \mathrm{rep}(\beta - \beta')$, and so $\gcd(\mathrm{rep}(\beta - \beta'), n) = q$. Similarly, with probability $1/4$, we have $\beta = \theta(\beta_1', -\beta_2')$, in which case $\beta - \beta' = \theta(0, -2\beta_2')$, and since $2\beta_2' \neq 0$, we have $p \mid \mathrm{rep}(\beta - \beta')$ and $q \nmid \mathrm{rep}(\beta - \beta')$, and so $\gcd(\mathrm{rep}(\beta - \beta'), n) = p$. Thus, with probability $1/2$, we have $\beta \neq \pm\beta'$, and $\gcd(\mathrm{rep}(\beta - \beta'), n)$ splits n.

Since we split n with probability $1/2$ conditioned on any fixed choice $\alpha \in (\mathbb{Z}_n^*)^2$ and any fixed random choices of the modular square-root algorithm, it follows that we split n with probability $1/2$ conditioned simply on the event that $\beta \in \mathbb{Z}_n^*$. Also, conditioned on the event that $\beta \notin \mathbb{Z}_n^*$, we split n with certainty, and so we may conclude that the above algorithm splits n with probability at least $1/2$.

EXERCISE 13.11. Generalize the algorithm above to efficiently factor arbitrary integers, given a subroutine that computes arbitrary modular square roots.

13.4 The quadratic residuosity assumption

Loosely speaking, the **quadratic residuosity (QR)** assumption is the assumption that it is hard to distinguish squares from non-squares in $\mathbb{Z}_n^*$, where n is of the form $n = pq$, and p and q are distinct primes. This assumption plays an important role in cryptography. Of course, since the Jacobi symbol is easy to compute, for this assumption to make sense, we have to restrict our attention to elements of $\ker(J_n)$, where $J_n : \mathbb{Z}_n^* \to \{\pm 1\}$ is the Jacobi map. We know that $(\mathbb{Z}_n^*)^2 \subseteq \ker(J_n)$ (see Exercise 12.2). Somewhat more precisely, the QR assumption is the assumption that it is hard to distinguish a random element in $\ker(J_n) \setminus (\mathbb{Z}_n^*)^2$ from a random element in $(\mathbb{Z}_n^*)^2$, given n (but not its factorization!).

To give a rough idea as to how this assumption may be used in cryptography, assume that $p \equiv q \equiv 3 \pmod 4$, so that $[-1]_n \in \ker(J_n) \setminus (\mathbb{Z}_n^*)^2$, and moreover, $\ker(J_n) \setminus (\mathbb{Z}_n^*)^2 = [-1]_n (\mathbb{Z}_n^*)^2$ (see Exercise 12.3). The value n can be used as a public key in a public-key cryptosystem (see §7.8). Alice, knowing the public key, can encrypt a single bit $b \in \{0, 1\}$ as $\beta := (-1)^b \alpha^2$, where Alice chooses $\alpha \in \mathbb{Z}_n^*$ at random. The point is, if $b = 0$, then β is uniformly distributed over $(\mathbb{Z}_n^*)^2$, and if $b = 1$, then β is uniformly distributed over $\ker(J_n) \setminus (\mathbb{Z}_n^*)^2$. Now Bob, knowing the secret key, which is the factorization of n, can easily determine if $\beta \in (\mathbb{Z}_n^*)^2$ or not, and hence deduce the value of the encrypted bit b. However, under the QR assumption, an eavesdropper, seeing just n and β, cannot effectively figure out what b is.

Of course, the above scheme is much less efficient than the RSA cryptosystem presented in §7.8, but nevertheless, has attractive properties; in particular, its security is very closely tied to the QR assumption, whereas the security of RSA is a bit less well understood.

EXERCISE 13.12. Suppose that A is a probabilistic algorithm that takes as input n of the form $n = pq$, where p and q are distinct primes such that $p \equiv q \equiv 3 \pmod 4$. The algorithm also takes as input $\alpha \in \ker(J_n)$, and outputs either 0 or 1. Furthermore, assume that A runs in strict polynomial time. Define two random variables, X_n and Y_n, as follows: X_n is defined to be the output of A on input n and a value α chosen at random from $\ker(J_n) \setminus (\mathbb{Z}_n^*)^2$, and Y_n is defined to be the output of A on input n and a value α chosen at random from $(\mathbb{Z}_n^*)^2$. In both cases, the value of the random variable is determined by the random choice of α, as well as the random choices made by the algorithm. Define $\epsilon(n) := |\mathsf{P}[X_n = 1] - \mathsf{P}[Y_n = 1]|$. Show how to use A to design a probabilistic, expected polynomial time algorithm A' that takes as input n as above and $\alpha \in \ker(J_n)$, and outputs either "square" or "non-square," with the following property:

> if $\epsilon(n) \geq 0.001$, then *for all* $\alpha \in \ker(J_n)$, the probability that
> A' correctly identifies whether $\alpha \in (\mathbb{Z}_n^*)^2$ is at least 0.999.

Hint: use the Chernoff bound.

EXERCISE 13.13. Assume the same notation as in the previous exercise. Define the random variable X_n' to be the output of A on input n and a value α chosen at random from $\ker(J_n)$. Show that $|\mathsf{P}[X_n' = 1] - \mathsf{P}[Y_n = 1]| = \epsilon(n)/2$. Thus, the problem of distinguishing $\ker(J_n)$ from $(\mathbb{Z}_n^*)^2$ is essentially equivalent to the problem of distinguishing $\ker(J_n) \setminus (\mathbb{Z}_n^*)^2$ from $(\mathbb{Z}_n^*)^2$.

13.5 Notes

Exercise 13.2 is based on Solovay and Strassen [94].

The probabilistic algorithm in §13.3.1 for computing square roots modulo p can be made deterministic under a generalization of the Riemann hypothesis. Indeed, as discussed in §10.7, under such a hypothesis, Bach's result [10] implies that the least positive integer that is not a quadratic residue modulo p is at most $2 \log p$ (this follows by applying Bach's result with the subgroup $(\mathbb{Z}_p^*)^2$ of $\mathbb{Z}_p^*$). Thus, we may find the required element $\gamma \in \mathbb{Z}_p^* \setminus (\mathbb{Z}_n^*)^2$ in deterministic polynomial time, just by brute-force search. The best *unconditional* bound on the smallest positive integer that is not a quadratic residue modulo p is due to Burgess [22], who gives a bound of $p^{\alpha + o(1)}$, where $\alpha := 1/(4\sqrt{e}) \approx 0.15163$.

Goldwasser and Micali [39] introduced the quadratic residuosity assumption to cryptography (as discussed in §13.4). This assumption has subsequently been used as the basis for numerous cryptographic schemes.

14

Modules and vector spaces

In this chapter, we introduce the basic definitions and results concerning modules over a ring R and vector spaces over a field F. The reader may have seen some of these notions before, but perhaps only in the context of vector spaces over a specific field, such as the real or complex numbers, and not in the context of, say, finite fields like $\mathbb{Z}_p$.

14.1 Definitions, basic properties, and examples

Throughout this section, R denotes a ring.

Definition 14.1. *An R-**module** is an abelian group M, which we shall write using additive notation, together with a **scalar multiplication** operation that maps $a \in R$ and $\alpha \in M$ to an element $a\alpha \in M$, such that the following properties are satisfied for all $a, b \in R$ and $\alpha, \beta \in M$:*

(i) $a(b\alpha) = (ab)\alpha$,

(ii) $(a + b)\alpha = a\alpha + b\alpha$,

(iii) $a(\alpha + \beta) = a\alpha + a\beta$,

(iv) $1_R\alpha = \alpha$.

One may also call an R-module M a **module over** R. Elements of R are often referred to as **scalars**, and elements of M may be called **vectors**.

Note that for an R-module M, for fixed $a \in R$, the map that sends $\alpha \in M$ to $a\alpha \in M$ is a group homomorphism with respect to the additive group operation of M; likewise, for fixed $\alpha \in M$, the map that sends $a \in R$ to $a\alpha \in M$ is a group homomorphism from the additive group of R into the additive group of M.

The following theorem summarizes a few basic facts which follow directly from the observations in the previous paragraph, and basic facts about group homomorphisms (see Theorem 8.20):

Theorem 14.2. *If M is a module over R, then for all $a \in R$, $\alpha \in M$, and $m \in \mathbb{Z}$, we have:*

(i) $0_R \alpha = 0_M$,

(ii) $a0_M = 0_M$,

(iii) $(-a)\alpha = -(a\alpha) = a(-\alpha)$,

(iv) $(ma)\alpha = m(a\alpha) = a(m\alpha)$.

Proof. Exercise. $\Box$

The definition of a module includes the **trivial** module, consisting of just the zero element 0_M. If R is the trivial ring, then any R-module is trivial, since for all $\alpha \in M$, we have $\alpha = 1_R\alpha = 0_R\alpha = 0_M$.

Example 14.1. A simple but extremely important example of an R-module is the set $R^{\times n}$ of n-tuples of elements of R, where addition and scalar multiplication are defined component-wise—that is, for $\alpha = (a_1, \ldots, a_n) \in R^{\times n}$, $\beta = (b_1, \ldots, a_n) \in R^{\times n}$, and $a \in R$, we have

$$\alpha + \beta = (a_1 + b_1, \ldots, a_n + b_n) \quad \text{and} \quad a\alpha = (aa_1, \ldots, aa_n). \quad \Box$$

Example 14.2. The ring of polynomials $R[X]$ over R forms an R-module in the natural way, with addition and scalar multiplication defined in terms of the addition and multiplication operations of the polynomial ring. $\Box$

Example 14.3. As in Example 9.34, let f be a monic polynomial over R of degree $\ell \geq 0$, and consider the quotient ring $E := R[X]/(f)$. Then E is a module over R, with addition defined in terms of the addition operation of R, and scalar multiplication defined by $a[g]_f := [ag]_f$, for $a \in R$ and $g \in R[X]$. If $f = 1$, then E is trivial. $\Box$

Example 14.4. If E is any ring containing R as a subring (i.e., E is an extension ring of R), then E is a module over R, with addition and scalar multiplication defined in terms of the addition and multiplication operations of E. $\Box$

Example 14.5. If $M_1, \ldots, M_n$ are R-modules, then so is the direct product $M_1 \times \cdots \times M_n$, where addition and scalar product are defined component-wise. $\Box$

Example 14.6. Any abelian group G, written additively, can be viewed as a $\mathbb{Z}$-module, with scalar multiplication defined in terms of the usual integer multiplication map (see parts (vi)–(viii) of Theorem 8.3). $\square$

Example 14.7. Let G be any group, written additively, whose exponent divides n. Then we may define a scalar multiplication that maps $[m]_n \in \mathbb{Z}_n$ and $\alpha \in G$ to $m\alpha$. That this map is unambiguously defined follows from the fact that G has exponent dividing n, so that if $m \equiv m' \pmod{n}$, we have $m\alpha - m'\alpha = (m - m')\alpha = 0_G$, since $n \mid (m - m')$. It is easy to check that this scalar multiplication operation indeed makes G into a $\mathbb{Z}_n$-module. $\square$

Example 14.8. Of course, viewing a group as a module does not depend on whether or not we happen to use additive notation for the group operation. If we specialize the previous example to the group $G = \mathbb{Z}_p^*$, where p is prime, then we may view G as a $\mathbb{Z}_{p-1}$-module. However, since the group operation itself is written multiplicatively, the "scalar product" of $[m]_{p-1} \in \mathbb{Z}_{p-1}$ and $\alpha \in \mathbb{Z}_p^*$ is the power α^m. $\square$

14.2 Submodules and quotient modules

Again, throughout this section, R denotes a ring. The notions of subgroups and quotient groups extend in the obvious way to R-modules.

Definition 14.3. *Let M be an R-module. A subset N is a **submodule** of M if*

(i) *N is a subgroup of the additive group M, and*

(ii) *N is closed under scalar multiplication; that is, for all $a \in R$ and $\alpha \in N$, we have $a\alpha \in N$.*

It is easy to see that a submodule N of an R-module M is also an R-module in its own right, with addition and scalar multiplication operations inherited from M.

Expanding the above definition, we see that a subset N of M is a submodule if and only if for all $a \in R$ and all $\alpha, \beta \in N$, we have

$$\alpha + \beta \in N, \quad -\alpha \in N, \quad \text{and} \quad a\alpha \in N.$$

Observe that the condition $-\alpha \in N$ is redundant, as it is implied by the condition $a\alpha \in N$ with $a = -1_R$.

For $m \in \mathbb{Z}$, it is easy to see (verify) that not only are mM and $M\{m\}$ subgroups of M (see Theorems 8.6 and 8.7), they are also submodules of M. Moreover, for $a \in R$, $aM := \{a\alpha : \alpha \in M\}$ and $M\{a\} := \{\alpha \in M : a\alpha = 0_M\}$ are also submodules of M (verify).

Let $\alpha_1, \ldots, \alpha_n$ be elements of M. In general, the subgroup $\langle \alpha_1, \ldots, \alpha_n \rangle$ will not be a submodule of M. Instead, let us consider the set $\langle \alpha_1, \ldots, \alpha_n \rangle_R$, consisting of all R-**linear combinations** of $\alpha_1, \ldots, \alpha_n$, with coefficients taken from R:

$$\langle \alpha_1, \ldots, \alpha_n \rangle_R := \{ a_1 \alpha_1 + \cdots + a_n \alpha_n : a_1, \ldots, a_n \in R \}.$$

It is not hard to see (verify) that $\langle \alpha_1, \ldots, \alpha_n \rangle_R$ is a submodule of M containing $\alpha_1, \ldots, \alpha_n$; it is called the submodule **spanned** or **generated** by $\alpha_1, \ldots, \alpha_n$. Moreover, it is easy to see (verify) that any submodule containing $\alpha_1, \ldots, \alpha_n$ must contain $\langle \alpha_1, \ldots, \alpha_n \rangle_R$. As a matter of definition, we allow $n = 0$, in which case, the spanned submodule is $\{0_M\}$.

If N_1 and N_2 are submodules of M, then $N_1 + N_2$ and $N_1 \cap N_2$ are not only subgroups of M, they are also submodules of M (verify).

Example 14.9. For integer $\ell \geq 0$, define $R[\mathtt{X}]_{<\ell}$ to be the set of polynomials of degree less than ℓ. The reader may verify that $R[\mathtt{X}]_{<\ell}$ is a submodule of the R-module $R[\mathtt{X}]$. If $\ell = 0$, then this submodule is the trivial submodule $\{0_R\}$. □

Example 14.10. Let G be an abelian group. As in Example 14.6, we can view G as a $\mathbb{Z}$-module in a natural way. Subgroups of G are just the same thing as submodules of G, and for $a_1, \ldots, a_n \in G$, the subgroup $\langle a_1, \ldots, a_n \rangle$ is the same as the submodule $\langle a_1, \ldots, a_n \rangle_{\mathbb{Z}}$. □

Example 14.11. Any ring R can be viewed as an R-module in the obvious way, with addition and scalar multiplication defined in terms of the addition and multiplication operations of R. With respect to this module structure, ideals of R are just the same thing as submodules of R, and for $a_1, \ldots, a_n \in R$, the ideal $(a_1, \ldots, a_n)$ is the same as the submodule $\langle a_1, \ldots, a_n \rangle_R$. □

Example 14.12. Let $\alpha_1, \ldots, \alpha_n$ and $\beta_1, \ldots, \beta_m$ be elements of an R-module. Assume that each α_i can be expressed as an R-linear combination of $\beta_1, \ldots, \beta_m$. Then the submodule spanned by $\alpha_1, \ldots, \alpha_n$ is contained in the submodule spanned by $\beta_1, \ldots, \beta_m$.

One can see this in a couple of different ways. First, the assumption that each α_i can be expressed as an R-linear combination of $\beta_1, \ldots, \beta_m$ means that the submodule $\langle \beta_1, \ldots, \beta_m \rangle_R$ contains the elements $\alpha_1, \ldots, \alpha_n$, and so by the general properties sketched above, this submodule must contain $\langle \alpha_1, \ldots, \alpha_n \rangle_R$.

One can also see this via an explicit calculation. Suppose that

$$\alpha_i = \sum_{j=1}^{m} c_{ij}\beta_j \quad (i = 1, \ldots, n),$$

where the c_{ij} are elements of R. Then for any element γ in the submodule spanned by $\alpha_1, \ldots, \alpha_n$, there exist $a_1, \ldots, a_n \in R$ with

$$\gamma = \sum_{i=1}^{n} a_i\alpha_i = \sum_{i=1}^{n} a_i \sum_{j=1}^{m} c_{ij}\beta_j = \sum_{j=1}^{m} \left(\sum_{i=1}^{n} a_i c_{ij} \right) \beta_j,$$

and hence γ is contained in the submodule spanned by $\beta_1, \ldots, \beta_m$. $\square$

If N is a submodule of M, then in particular, it is also a subgroup of M, and we can form the quotient group M/N in the usual way (see §8.3). Moreover, because N is closed under scalar multiplication, we can also define a scalar multiplication on M/N in a natural way. Namely, for $a \in R$ and $\alpha \in M$, we define

$$a \cdot (\alpha + N) := (a\alpha) + N.$$

As usual, one must check that this definition is unambiguous, that is, if $\alpha \equiv \alpha' \pmod{N}$, then $a\alpha \equiv a\alpha' \pmod{N}$. But this follows from the fact that N is closed under scalar multiplication (verify). One can also easily check (verify) that with scalar multiplication defined in this way, M/N is an R-module; it is called the **quotient module of M modulo N**.

14.3 Module homomorphisms and isomorphisms

Again, throughout this section, R is a ring. The notion of a group homomorphism extends in the obvious way to R-modules.

Definition 14.4. *Let M and M' be modules over R. An R-module homomorphism from M to M' is a map $\rho : M \to M'$, such that*

(i) ρ is a group homomorphism from M to M', and

(ii) for all $a \in R$ and $\alpha \in M$, we have $\rho(a\alpha) = a\rho(\alpha)$.

An R-module homomorphism is also called an **R-linear map**. We shall use this terminology from now on. Expanding the definition, we see that a map $\rho : M \to M'$ is an R-linear map if and only if $\rho(\alpha + \beta) = \rho(\alpha) + \rho(\beta)$ and $\rho(a\alpha) = a\rho(\alpha)$ for all $\alpha, \beta \in M$ and all $a \in R$.

Since an R-module homomorphism is also a group homomorphism on the underlying additive groups, all of the statements in Theorem 8.20 apply. In particular, an R-linear map is injective if and only if the kernel is trivial (i.e., contains only the zero element). However, in the case of R-module homomorphisms, we can extend Theorem 8.20, as follows:

Theorem 14.5. *Let $\rho : M \to M'$ be an R-linear map.*

(i) For any submodule N of M, $\rho(N)$ is a submodule of M'.

(ii) $\ker(\rho)$ is a submodule of M.

(iii) For any submodule N' of M', $\rho^{-1}(N')$ is a submodule of M.

Proof. Exercise. □

Theorems 8.21, 8.22, and 8.23 have natural R-module analogs:

Theorem 14.6. *If $\rho : M \to M'$ and $\rho' : M' \to M''$ are R-linear maps, then so is their composition $\rho' \circ \rho : M \to M''$.*

Proof. Exercise. □

Theorem 14.7. *Let $\rho_i : M \to M_i$, for $i = 1, \ldots, n$, be R-linear maps. Then the map $\rho : M \to M_1 \times \cdots \times M_n$ that sends $\alpha \in M$ to $(\rho_1(\alpha), \ldots, \rho_n(\alpha))$ is an R-linear map.*

Proof. Exercise. □

Theorem 14.8. *Let $\rho_i : M_i \to M$, for $i = 1, \ldots, n$, be R-linear maps. Then the map $\rho : M_1 \times \cdots \times M_n \to M$ that sends $(\alpha_1, \ldots, \alpha_n)$ to $\rho_1(\alpha_1) + \cdots + \rho_n(\alpha_n)$ is an R-linear map.*

Proof. Exercise. □

If an R-linear map $\rho : M \to M'$ is bijective, then it is called an **R-module isomorphism** of M with M'. If such an R-module isomorphism ρ exists, we say that M **is isomorphic to** M', and write $M \cong M'$. Moreover, if $M = M'$, then ρ is called an **R-module automorphism** on M.

Analogous to Theorem 8.24, we have:

Theorem 14.9. *If ρ is a R-module isomorphism of M with M', then the inverse function ρ^{-1} is an R-module isomorphism of M' with M.*

Proof. Exercise. □

Theorems 8.25, 8.26, 8.27, and 8.28 generalize immediately to R-modules:

Theorem 14.10. *If N is a submodule of an R-module M, then the natural map $\rho : M \to M/N$ given by $\rho(\alpha) = \alpha + N$ is a surjective R-linear map whose kernel is N.*

Proof. Exercise. □

Theorem 14.11. *Let ρ be an R-linear map from M into M'. Then the map $\bar{\rho} : M/\ker(\rho) \to \text{img}(\rho)$ that sends the coset $\alpha + \ker(\rho)$ for $\alpha \in M$ to $\rho(\alpha)$ is unambiguously defined and is an R-module isomorphism of $M/\ker(\rho)$ with $\text{img}(\rho)$.*

Proof. Exercise. □

Theorem 14.12. *Let ρ be an R-linear map from M into M'. Then for any submodule N contained in $\ker(\rho)$, the map $\bar{\rho} : M/N \to \text{img}(\rho)$ that sends the coset $\alpha + N$ for $\alpha \in M$ to $\rho(\alpha)$ is unambiguously defined and is an R-linear map from M/N onto $\text{img}(\rho)$ with kernel $\ker(\rho)/N$.*

Proof. Exercise. □

Theorem 14.13. *Let M be an R-module with submodules N_1, N_2. Then the map $\rho : N_1 \times N_2 \to N_1 + N_2$ that sends (α_1, α_2) to $\alpha_1 + \alpha_2$ is a surjective R-linear map. Moreover, if $N_1 \cap N_2 = \{0_M\}$, then ρ is an R-module isomorphism of $N_1 \times N_2$ with $N_1 + N_2$.*

Proof. Exercise. □

***Example* 14.13.** Let M be an R-module, and let m be an integer. Then the m-multiplication on M is not only a group homomorphism, but it is an R-linear map. □

***Example* 14.14.** Let M be an R-module, and let a be an element of R. The a-**multiplication map on** M is the map that sends $\alpha \in M$ to $a\alpha \in M$. This is an R-linear map whose image is aM, and whose kernel is $M\{a\}$. The set of all $a \in R$ for which $aM = \{0_M\}$ is called the R-**exponent of** M, and is easily seen to be an ideal of R (verify). □

***Example* 14.15.** Let M be an R-module, and let α be an element of M. Then the map $\rho : R \to M$ given by $\rho(a) = a\alpha$ is an R-linear map. The image of this map is $\langle\alpha\rangle_R$. The kernel of this map is called the R-**order of** α, and is easily seen to be an ideal of R (verify). □

***Example* 14.16.** Consider again the R-module $R[\mathsf{X}]/(f)$ discussed in Example 14.3, where f is monic of degree ℓ. As an R-module, $R[\mathsf{X}]/(f)$ is isomorphic to $R[\mathsf{X}]_{<\ell}$ (see Example 14.9). Indeed, based on the observations in Example 9.34, the map $\rho : R[\mathsf{X}]_{<\ell} \to R[\mathsf{X}]/(f)$ that sends a polynomial $g \in R[\mathsf{X}]$ of degree less than ℓ to $[g]_f \in R[\mathsf{X}]/(f)$ is an isomorphism of $R[\mathsf{X}]_{<\ell}$ with $R[\mathsf{X}]/(f)$. Furthermore, $R[\mathsf{X}]_{<\ell}$ is isomorphic as an R-module to $R^{\times \ell}$.

Indeed, the map $\rho' : R[X]_{<\ell} \to R^{\times \ell}$ that sends $g = \sum_{i=0}^{\ell-1} g_i X^i \in R[X]_{<\ell}$ to $(g_0, \ldots, g_{\ell-1}) \in R^{\times \ell}$ is an isomorphism of $R[X]_{<\ell}$ with $R^{\times \ell}$. $\square$

Example 14.17. Let E and E' be ring extensions of the ring R. As we saw in Example 14.4, E and E' may be viewed as R-modules in a natural way. Suppose that $\rho : E \to E'$ is a ring homomorphism whose restriction to R is the identity map (i.e., $\rho(a) = a$ for all $a \in R$). Then ρ is an R-linear map. Indeed, for any $a \in R$ and $\alpha, \beta \in E$, we have $\rho(\alpha + \beta) = \rho(\alpha) + \rho(\beta)$ and $\rho(a\alpha) = \rho(a)\rho(\alpha) = a\rho(\alpha)$. $\square$

14.4 Linear independence and bases

Throughout this section, R denotes a ring.

Definition 14.14. *We say that an R-module M is **finitely generated (over R)** if it is spanned by a finite number of elements, which is to say that $M = \langle \alpha_1, \ldots, \alpha_n \rangle_R$ for some $\alpha_1, \ldots, \alpha_n \in M$.*

*We say that a collection of elements $\alpha_1, \ldots, \alpha_n$ in M is **linearly dependent (over R)** if there exist $a_1, \ldots, a_n \in R$, not all zero, such that $a_1\alpha_1 + \cdots a_n\alpha_n = 0_M$; otherwise, we say that $\alpha_1, \ldots, \alpha_n$ are **linearly independent (over R)**.*

*We say that a collection $\alpha_1, \ldots, \alpha_n$ of elements in M is a **basis for M (over R)** if it is linearly independent and spans M.*

Note that in the above definition, the collection of elements $\alpha_1, \ldots, \alpha_n$ may contain duplicates; the collection may also be empty (i.e., $n = 0$), in which case, by definition, it is a basis for the trivial submodule $\{0_M\}$. Note that the ordering of the elements $\alpha_1, \ldots, \alpha_n$ makes no difference in any aspect of the definition.

Example 14.18. Consider the R-module $R^{\times n}$. Define $\alpha_1, \ldots, \alpha_n \in R^{\times n}$ as follows:

$$\alpha_1 := (1, 0, \ldots, 0), \ \alpha_2 := (0, 1, 0, \ldots, 0), \ldots, \ \alpha_n := (0, \ldots, 0, 1);$$

that is, α_i has a 1 in position i and is zero everywhere else. It is easy to see that $\alpha_1, \ldots, \alpha_n$ form a basis for $R^{\times n}$. Indeed, for any $a_1, \ldots, a_n \in R$, we have $a_1\alpha_1 + \cdots + a_n\alpha_n = (a_1, \ldots, a_n)$, from which it is clear that the α_i span $R^{\times n}$ and are linearly independent. The vectors $\alpha_1, \ldots, \alpha_n$ form what is called the **standard basis** for $R^{\times n}$. $\square$

Example 14.19. Consider the $\mathbb{Z}$-module $\mathbb{Z}^{\times 3}$. In addition to the standard basis

$$(1,0,0), (0,1,0), (0,0,1),$$

the vectors

$$\alpha_1 := (1,1,1), \ \alpha_2 := (0,1,0), \ \alpha_3 := (2,0,1)$$

also form a basis. To see this, first observe that for $a_1, a_2, a_3, b_1, b_2, b_3 \in \mathbb{Z}$, we have

$$(b_1, b_2, b_3) = a_1\alpha_1 + a_2\alpha_2 + a_3\alpha_3$$

if and only if

$$b_1 = a_1 + 2a_3, \ b_2 = a_1 + a_2, \text{ and } b_3 = a_1 + a_3. \tag{14.1}$$

If (14.1) holds with $b_1 = b_2 = b_3 = 0$, then subtracting the equation $a_1 + a_3 = 0$ from $a_1 + 2a_3 = 0$, we see that $a_3 = 0$, from which it easily follows that $a_1 = a_2 = 0$. This shows that the vectors are linearly independent. To show that they span $\mathbb{Z}^{\times 3}$, the reader may verify that for any given $b_1, b_2, b_3 \in \mathbb{Z}$, the values

$$a_1 := -b_1 + 2b_3, \ a_2 := b_1 + b_2 - 2b_3, \ a_3 := b_1 - b_3$$

satisfy (14.1).

The vectors

$$(1,1,1), (0,1,0), (1,0,1)$$

do not form a basis, as they are linearly dependent: the third vector is equal to the first minus the second.

The vectors $(1,0,12), (0,1,30), (0,0,18)$ are linearly independent, but do not span $\mathbb{Z}^{\times 3}$ — the last component of any $\mathbb{Z}$-linear combination of these vectors must be divisible by $\gcd(12, 30, 18) = 6$. These vectors do, however, form a basis for the $\mathbb{Q}$-module $\mathbb{Q}^{\times 3}$. $\square$

***Example* 14.20.** If R is non-trivial, the ring of polynomials $R[\mathsf{X}]$ is not finitely generated as an R-module, since any finite set of polynomials spans only polynomials of some bounded degree. $\square$

***Example* 14.21.** Consider the submodule $R[\mathsf{X}]_{<\ell}$ of $R[\mathsf{X}]$, where $\ell \geq 0$. If $\ell = 0$, then $R[\mathsf{X}]_{<\ell}$ is trivial; otherwise, $1, \mathsf{X}, \ldots, \mathsf{X}^{\ell-1}$ form a basis. $\square$

***Example* 14.22.** Consider again the ring $E = R[\mathsf{X}]/(f)$, where $f \in R[\mathsf{X}]$ is monic of degree $\ell \geq 0$. If $f = 1$, then E is trivial; otherwise, $1, \eta, \eta^2, \ldots, \eta^{\ell-1}$, where $\eta := [\mathsf{X}]_f \in E$, form a basis for E over R. $\square$

The next theorem highlights a critical property of bases:

Theorem 14.15. *If $\alpha_1, \ldots, \alpha_n$ form a basis for M, then the map $\rho : R^{\times n} \to M$ that sends $(a_1, \ldots, a_n) \in R^{\times n}$ to $a_1\alpha_1 + \cdots + a_n\alpha_n \in M$ is an R-module isomorphism of $R^{\times n}$ with M. In particular, every element of M can be expressed in a unique way as $a_1\alpha_1 + \cdots + a_n\alpha_n$, for $a_1, \ldots, a_n \in R$.*

Proof. To show this, one has to show (1) that ρ is an R-linear map, which follows immediately from the definitions, (2) that ρ is injective, which follows immediately from the linear independence of $\alpha_1, \ldots, \alpha_n$, and (3) that ρ is surjective, which follows immediately from the fact that $\alpha_1, \ldots, \alpha_n$ span M. $\square$

The following theorems develop important connections among the notions of spanning, linear independence, and linear maps.

Theorem 14.16. *Suppose that $\alpha_1, \ldots, \alpha_n$ span an R-module M and that $\rho : M \to M'$ is an R-linear map.*

(i) ρ is surjective if and only if $\rho(\alpha_1), \ldots, \rho(\alpha_n)$ span M'.

(ii) If $\rho(\alpha_1), \ldots, \rho(\alpha_n)$ are linearly independent, then ρ is injective.

Proof. Since the α_i span M, every element of M can be expressed as $\sum_i a_i\alpha_i$, where the a_i are in R. It follows that the image of ρ consists of all elements of M' of the form $\rho(\sum_i a_i\alpha_i) = \sum_i a_i\rho(\alpha_i)$. That is, the image of ρ is the submodule of M' spanned by $\rho(\alpha_1), \ldots, \rho(\alpha_n)$, which implies (i).

For (ii), suppose that ρ is not injective. Then $\rho(\alpha) = 0_{M'}$ for some $\alpha \neq 0_M$, and since the α_i span M, we can write $\alpha = \sum_i a_i\alpha_i$, where the a_i are in R. Since α is non-zero, some of the a_i must be non-zero. So we have $0_{M'} = \rho(\sum_i a_i\alpha_i) = \sum_i a_i\rho(\alpha_i)$, and hence $\rho(\alpha_1), \ldots, \rho(\alpha_n)$ are linearly dependent. $\square$

Theorem 14.17. *Suppose $\rho : M \to M'$ is an injective R-linear map and that $\alpha_1, \ldots, \alpha_n \in M$ are linearly independent. Then $\rho(\alpha_1), \ldots, \rho(\alpha_n)$ are linearly independent.*

Proof. Suppose that $0_{M'} = \sum_i a_i\rho(\alpha_i) = \rho(\sum_i a_i\alpha_i)$. Then, as $\ker(\rho) = \{0_M\}$, we must have $\sum_i a_i\alpha_i = 0_M$, and as the α_i are linearly independent, all the a_i must be zero. $\square$

Theorem 14.18. *Let $\alpha_1, \ldots, \alpha_n$ be a basis for an R-module M, and let $\rho : M \to M'$ be an R-linear map.*

(i) ρ is surjective if and only if $\rho(\alpha_1), \ldots, \rho(\alpha_n)$ span M'.

(ii) ρ is injective if and only if $\rho(\alpha_1), \ldots, \rho(\alpha_n)$ are linearly independent.

(iii) ρ is an isomorphism if and only if $\rho(\alpha_1), \ldots, \rho(\alpha_n)$ form a basis for M'.

Proof. (i) follows immediately from part (i) of Theorem 14.16. (ii) follows from part (ii) of Theorem 14.16 and Theorem 14.17. (iii) follows from (i) and (ii). $\square$

EXERCISE 14.1. Show that if a finite collection of elements of an R-module is linearly independent, then any sub-collection is also linearly independent.

EXERCISE 14.2. Assume R is non-trivial. Show that if a finite collection of elements of an R-module contains the zero element, or contains two identical elements, then it is not linearly independent.

EXERCISE 14.3. Assume R is trivial and that M is an R-module (which must also be trivial). Show that any finite collection of zero or more copies of 0_M is a basis for M.

EXERCISE 14.4. Let $\rho : M \to M'$ be an R-linear map. Show that if $\alpha_1, \ldots, \alpha_n \in M$ are linearly dependent, then $\rho(\alpha_1), \ldots, \rho(\alpha_n) \in M'$ are also linearly dependent.

14.5 Vector spaces and dimension

Throughout this section, F denotes a field.

A module over a field is also called a **vector space**. In particular, an F-module is called an **F-vector space**, or a **vector space over F**.

For vector spaces over F, one typically uses the terms **subspace** and **quotient space**, instead of (respectively) submodule and quotient module; likewise, one usually uses the terms **F-vector space homomorphism**, **isomorphism** and **automorphism**, as appropriate.

Throughout the rest of this section, V denotes a vector space over F.

We now develop the basic theory of dimension for *finitely generated* vector spaces. The following two theorems provide the keys to this theory.

Theorem 14.19. *If V is finitely generated, then any finite set of vectors that spans V contains a subset that is a basis.*

Proof. We give an "algorithmic" proof. Let $\alpha_1, \ldots, \alpha_n$ be a given set of vectors that spans V. Let S_0 be the empty set, and for $i = 1, \ldots, n$, do the following: if α_i does not belong to the subspace spanned by S_{i-1}, set $S_i := S_{i-1} \cup \{\alpha_i\}$, and otherwise, set $S_i := S_{i-1}$. We claim that S_n is a basis for V.

First, we show that S_n spans V. To do this, first note that for $i = 1, \ldots, n$, if α_i is not in S_n, then by definition, α_i is a linear combination of vectors in

$S_{i-1} \subseteq S_n$. In any case, each α_i is a linear combination of the vectors in S_n. Since any element β of V is a linear combination of $\alpha_1, \ldots, \alpha_n$, and each α_i is a linear combination of elements of S_n, it follows (see Example 14.12) that β is a linear combination of elements of S_n.

Second, we show that S_n is linearly independent. Suppose it were not. Then we could express 0_V as a non-trivial linear combination of elements in S_n. Let us write this as

$$0_V = a_1\alpha_1 + a_2\alpha_2 + \cdots + a_n\alpha_n,$$

where the only non-zero coefficients a_i are those with $\alpha_i \in S_n$. If j is the highest index with $a_j \neq 0_F$, then by definition $\alpha_j \in S_n$. However, we see that α_j is in fact in the span of S_{j-1}; indeed,

$$\alpha_j = (-a_j^{-1}a_1)\alpha_1 + \cdots + (-a_j^{-1}a_{j-1})\alpha_{j-1},$$

and by definition, the only terms with non-zero coefficients are those corresponding to the vectors in S_{j-1}. This means that we would not have added α_j to S_j at step j, which means α_j is not in S_n, a contradiction. $\square$

Theorem 14.20. *If V has a basis of size n, then any collection of $n+1$ elements of V is linearly dependent.*

Proof. Let $\alpha_1, \ldots, \alpha_n$ be a basis, and let $\beta_1, \ldots, \beta_{n+1}$ be any collection of $n+1$ vectors. We wish to show that $\beta_1, \ldots, \beta_{n+1}$ are linearly dependent.

Since the α_i span V, we know that β_1 is a linear combination of the α_i, say, $\beta_1 = a_1\alpha_1 + \cdots a_n\alpha_n$. If all the a_i were zero, then we would have $\beta_1 = 0_V$, and so trivially, $\beta_1, \ldots, \beta_{n+1}$ would be linearly dependent (see Exercise 14.2). So assume that not all a_i are zero, and for convenience, let us say that $a_1 \neq 0_F$. It follows that α_1 is a linear combination of $\beta_1, \alpha_2, \ldots, \alpha_n$; indeed,

$$\alpha_1 = a_1^{-1}\beta_1 + (-a_1^{-1}a_2)\alpha_2 + \cdots + (-a_1^{-1}a_n)\alpha_n.$$

It follows that $\beta_1, \alpha_2, \ldots, \alpha_n$ span V (see Example 14.12).

Next, consider β_2. This is a linear combination of $\beta_1, \alpha_2, \ldots, \alpha_n$, and we may assume that in this linear combination, the coefficient of one of $\alpha_2, \ldots, \alpha_n$ is non-zero (otherwise, we find a linear dependence among the β_j), and for convenience, let us say that the coefficient of α_2 is non-zero. As in the previous paragraph, it follows that $\beta_1, \beta_2, \alpha_3, \ldots, \alpha_n$ span V.

Continuing in this way, we find that $\beta_1, \ldots, \beta_n$ are either linearly dependent or they span V. In the latter case, we find that β_{n+1} is a linear combination of $\beta_1, \ldots, \beta_n$, and hence, the vectors $\beta_1, \ldots, \beta_n, \beta_{n+1}$ are linearly dependent. $\square$

We stress that the proofs of Theorems 14.19 and 14.20 both made critical use of the assumption that F is a *field*. An important corollary of Theorem 14.20 is the following:

Theorem 14.21. *If V is finitely generated, then any two bases have the same size.*

Proof. If one basis had more elements than another, then Theorem 14.20 would imply that the first basis was linearly dependent, which contradicts the definition of a basis. $\square$

Theorem 14.21 allows us to make the following definition:

Definition 14.22. *If V is finitely generated, the common size of any basis is called the* **dimension** *of V, and is denoted $\dim_F(V)$.*

Note that from the definitions, we have $\dim_F(V) = 0$ if and only if V is the trivial vector space (i.e., $V = \{0_V\}$). We also note that one often refers to a finitely generated vector space as a **finite dimensional** vector space. We shall give preference to this terminology from now on.

To summarize the main results in this section up to this point: if V is finite dimensional, it has a basis, and any two bases have the same size, which is called the dimension of V. The next theorem is simple consequences of these results.

Theorem 14.23. *Suppose that V is of finite dimension n, and let $\alpha_1, \ldots, \alpha_n \in V$. The following are equivalent:*

(i) $\alpha_1, \ldots, \alpha_n$ are linearly independent.

(ii) $\alpha_1, \ldots, \alpha_n$ span V.

(iii) $\alpha_1, \ldots, \alpha_n$ form a basis for V.

Proof. Let W be the subspace spanned by $\alpha_1, \ldots, \alpha_n$.

First, let us show that (i) implies (ii). Suppose $\alpha_1, \ldots, \alpha_n$ are linearly independent. Also, by way of contradiction, suppose that $W \subsetneq V$. Choose $\beta \in V \setminus W$. Then it follows that $\alpha_1, \ldots, \alpha_n, \beta$ are linearly independent; indeed, if we had a relation $0_V = a_1\alpha_1 + \cdots + a_n\alpha_n + b\beta$, then we must have $b = 0_F$ (otherwise, $\beta \in W$), and by the linear independence of $\alpha_1, \ldots, \alpha_n$, all the a_i must be zero as well. But then we have a set of $n + 1$ linearly independent vectors in V, which is impossible by Theorem 14.20.

Second, let us prove that (ii) implies (i). Let us assume that $\alpha_1, \ldots, \alpha_n$ are linearly dependent, and prove that $W \subsetneq V$. By Theorem 14.19, we can find a basis for W among the α_i, and since the α_i are linearly dependent, this basis must contain strictly fewer than n elements. Hence, $\dim_F(W) < \dim_F(V)$, and therefore, $W \subsetneq V$.

The theorem now follows from the above arguments, and the fact that, by definition, (iii) holds if and only if both (i) and (ii) hold. $\square$

We next examine the dimension of subspaces of finite dimensional vector spaces.

Theorem 14.24. *If V is finite dimensional, and W is a subspace of V, then W is also finite dimensional, and $\dim_F(W) \le \dim_F(V)$. Moreover, $\dim_F(W) = \dim_F(V)$ if and only if $W = V$.*

Proof. To see this, suppose $\dim_F(V) = n$, and assume that W is non-trivial. We shall construct a basis $\alpha_1, \ldots, \alpha_m$ for W, where $m \le n$. We can take α_1 to be any non-zero vector in W, α_2 to be any vector in W not in the subspace spanned by α_1, and so on. More generally, at stage $i = 1, 2, \ldots$, we take α_i to be any element of W not in the subspace spanned by $\alpha_1, \ldots, \alpha_{i-1}$. It is easy to see that at each stage i, the vectors $\alpha_1, \ldots, \alpha_i$ are linearly independent: if we had a relation $a_1\alpha_1 + \cdots a_j\alpha_j = 0_V$, where $j \le i$ and $a_j \ne 0_F$, this would imply that α_j lies in the subspace generated by $\alpha_1, \ldots, \alpha_{j-1}$, which contradicts the definition of how α_j was selected. Because of Theorem 14.20, this process must halt at some stage $m \le n$, and since the process does halt, it must be the case that $\alpha_1, \ldots, \alpha_m$ span W.

That proves that W is finite dimensional with $\dim_F(W) \le \dim_F(V)$. It remains to show that these dimensions are equal if and only if $W = V$. Now, if $W = V$, then clearly $\dim_F(W) = \dim_F(V)$. Conversely, if $\dim_F(W) = \dim_F(V)$, then by Theorem 14.23, any basis for W must already span V. $\square$

Theorem 14.25. *If V is finite dimensional, and W is a subspace of V, then the quotient space V/W is also finite dimensional, and*

$$\dim_F(V/W) = \dim_F(V) - \dim_F(W).$$

Proof. Suppose that S is a finite set of vectors that spans V. Then $\{\alpha + W : \alpha \in S\}$ is a finite set of vectors that spans V/W. It follows from Theorem 14.19 that V/W has a basis, say, $\alpha_1 + W, \ldots, \alpha_\ell + W$. Suppose that $\beta_1, \ldots, \beta_m$ is a basis for W. The theorem will follow immediately from the following:

Claim. The vectors

$$\alpha_1, \ldots, \alpha_\ell, \ \beta_1, \ldots, \beta_m \tag{14.2}$$

form a basis for V.

To see that these vectors span V, consider any element γ of V. Then since $\alpha_1 + W, \ldots, \alpha_\ell + W$ span V/W, we have $\gamma \equiv \sum_i a_i \alpha_i \pmod{W}$ for some $a_1, \ldots, a_\ell \in F$. If we set $\beta := \gamma - \sum_i a_i \alpha_i \in W$, then since $\beta_1, \ldots, \beta_m$ span W, we have $\beta = \sum_j b_j \beta_j$ for some $b_1, \ldots, b_m \in F$, and hence $\gamma = \sum_i a_i \alpha_i + \sum_j b_j \beta_j$. That proves that the vectors (14.2) span V. To prove they are linearly independent, suppose we have a relation of the form $\sum_i a_i \alpha_i + \sum_j b_j \beta_j = 0_V$, where $a_1, \ldots, a_\ell \in F$ and $b_1, \ldots, b_m \in F$. If any of the a_i were non-zero, this would contradict the assumption that $\alpha_1 + W, \ldots, \alpha_\ell + W$ are linearly independent. So assume that all the a_i are zero. If any of the b_j were non-zero, this would contradict the assumption that $\beta_1, \ldots, \beta_m$ are linearly independent. Thus, all the a_i and all the b_j must be zero, which proves that the vectors (14.2) are linearly independent. That proves the claim. $\square$

Theorem 14.26. *If V is of finite dimension, then any linearly independent set of elements of V can be extended to form a basis for V.*

Proof. This is actually implicit in the proof of the previous theorem. Let $\beta_1, \ldots, \beta_m \in V$ be linearly independent. Let W be the subspace of V spanned by $\beta_1, \ldots, \beta_m$, so that $\beta_1, \ldots, \beta_m$ form a basis for W. As in the proof of the previous theorem, we can choose $\alpha_1, \ldots, \alpha_\ell \in V$ such that $\alpha_1 + W, \ldots, \alpha_\ell + W$ form a basis for the quotient space V/W, so that

$$\alpha_1, \ldots, \alpha_\ell, \; \beta_1, \ldots, \beta_m$$

form a basis for V. $\square$

***Example* 14.23.** Suppose that F is finite, say $|F| = q$, and that V is finite dimensional, say $\dim_F(V) = n$. Then clearly $|V| = q^n$. If W is a subspace with $\dim_F(W) = m$, then $|W| = q^m$, and by Theorem 14.25, $\dim_F(V/W) = n - m$, and hence $|V/W| = q^{n-m}$. Just viewing V and W as additive groups, we know that the index of W in V is $[V : W] = |V/W| = |V|/|W| = q^{n-m}$, which agrees with the above calculations. $\square$

We next consider the relation between the notion of dimension and linear maps.

Theorem 14.27. *If V is of finite dimension n, and V is isomorphic to V', then V' is also of finite dimension n.*

Proof. If $\alpha_1, \ldots, \alpha_n$ is a basis for V, then by Theorem 14.18, $\rho(\alpha_1), \ldots, \rho(\alpha_n)$ is a basis for V'. $\square$

Theorem 14.28. *If $\rho : V \to V'$ is an F-linear map, and if V and V' are finite dimensional with $\dim_F(V) = \dim_F(V')$, then we have:*

ρ is injective if and only if ρ is surjective.

Proof. Let $\alpha_1, \ldots, \alpha_n$ be a basis for V. By Theorem 14.18, we know that ρ is injective if and only if $\rho(\alpha_1), \ldots, \rho(\alpha_n)$ are linearly independent, and that ρ is surjective if and only if $\rho(\alpha_1), \ldots, \rho(\alpha_n)$ span V'. Moreover, by Theorem 14.23, we know that the vectors $\rho(\alpha_1), \ldots, \rho(\alpha_n)$ are linearly independent if and only if they span V'. The theorem now follows immediately. $\square$

This last theorem turns out to be extremely useful in a number of settings. Generally, of course, if we have a function $f : A \to B$, injectivity does not imply surjectivity, nor does surjectivity imply injectivity. If A and B are finite sets of equal size, then these implications do indeed hold. Theorem 14.28 gives us another important setting where these implications hold, with finite dimensionality playing the role corresponding to finiteness.

Theorem 14.28 may be generalized as follows:

Theorem 14.29. *If V is finite dimensional, and $\rho : V \to V'$ is an F-linear map, then $\mathrm{img}(\rho)$ is a finite dimensional vector space, and*

$$\dim_F(V) = \dim_F(\mathrm{img}(\rho)) + \dim_F(\ker(\rho)).$$

Proof. As the reader may verify, this follows immediately from Theorem 14.25, together with Theorems 14.27 and 14.11. $\square$

Intuitively, one way to think of Theorem 14.29 is as a "law of conservation" for dimension: any "dimensionality" going into ρ that is not "lost" to the kernel of ρ must show up in the image of ρ.

EXERCISE 14.5. Show that if $V_1, \ldots, V_n$ are finite dimensional vector spaces, then $V_1 \times \cdots \times V_n$ has dimension $\sum_{i=1}^{n} \dim_F(V_i)$.

EXERCISE 14.6. Show that if V is a finite dimensional vector space with subspaces W_1 and W_2, such that $W_1 + W_2 = V$ and $W_1 \cap W_2 = \{0_V\}$, then $\dim_F(V) = \dim_F(W_1) + \dim_F(W_2)$.

EXERCISE 14.7. The theory of dimension for finitely generated vector spaces is quite elegant and powerful. There is a theory of dimension (of sorts) for modules over an arbitrary, non-trivial ring R, but it is much more awkward and limited. This exercise develops a proof of one aspect of this theory: if an R-module M has a basis at all, then any two bases have the same size.

To prove this, we need the fact that any non-trivial ring has a maximal ideal (this was proved in Exercise 9.30 for countable rings). Let n, m be positive integers, let $\alpha_1, \ldots, \alpha_m$ be elements of $R^{\times n}$, and let I be an ideal of R.

(a) Show that if $\alpha_1, \ldots, \alpha_m$ span $R^{\times n}$, then every element of $I^{\times n}$ can be expressed as $a_1\alpha_1 + \cdots a_m\alpha_m$, where $a_1, \ldots, a_m$ belong to I.

(b) Show that if $m > n$ and I is a maximal ideal, then there exist $a_1, \ldots, a_m \in R$, not all in I, such that $a_1\alpha_1 + \cdots a_m\alpha_m \in I^{\times n}$.

(c) From (a) and (b), deduce that if $m > n$, then $\alpha_1, \ldots, \alpha_m$ cannot be a basis for $R^{\times n}$.

(d) From (c), conclude that any two bases for a given R-module M must have the same size.

15

Matrices

In this chapter, we discuss basic definitions and results concerning matrices. We shall start out with a very general point of view, discussing matrices whose entries lie in an arbitrary ring R. Then we shall specialize to the case where the entries lie in a field F, where much more can be said.

One of the main goals of this chapter is to discuss "Gaussian elimination," which is an algorithm that allows us to efficiently compute bases for the image and kernel of an F-linear map.

In discussing the complexity of algorithms for matrices over a ring R, we shall treat a ring R as an "abstract data type," so that the running times of algorithms will be stated in terms of the number of arithmetic operations in R. If R is a finite ring, such as $\mathbb{Z}_m$, we can immediately translate this into a running time on a RAM (in later chapters, we will discuss other finite rings and efficient algorithms for doing arithmetic in them).

If R is, say, the field of rational numbers, a complete running time analysis would require an additional analysis of the sizes of the numbers that appear in the execution of the algorithm. We shall not attempt such an analysis here—however, we note that all the algorithms discussed in this chapter do in fact run in polynomial time when $R = \mathbb{Q}$, assuming we represent rational numbers as fractions in lowest terms. Another possible approach for dealing with rational numbers is to use floating point approximations. While this approach eliminates the size problem, it creates many new problems because of round-off errors. We shall not address any of these issues here.

15.1 Basic definitions and properties

Throughout this section, R denotes a ring.

For positive integers m and n, an $m \times n$ **matrix** A over a ring R is a rectangular array

$$A = \begin{pmatrix} a_{11} & a_{12} & \cdots & a_{1n} \\ a_{21} & a_{22} & \cdots & a_{2n} \\ \vdots & \vdots & & \vdots \\ a_{m1} & a_{m2} & \cdots & a_{mn} \end{pmatrix},$$

where each entry a_{ij} in the array is an element of R; the element a_{ij} is called the (i, j) **entry** of A, which we may denote by $A(i, j)$. For $i = 1, \ldots, m$, the *i*th **row** of A is

$$(a_{i1}, \ldots, a_{in}),$$

which we may denote by $A(i)$, and for $j = 1, \ldots, n$, the *j*th **column** of A is

$$\begin{pmatrix} a_{1j} \\ a_{2j} \\ \vdots \\ a_{mj} \end{pmatrix},$$

which we may denote by $A(\cdot, j)$. We regard a row of A as a $1 \times n$ matrix, and a column of A as an $m \times 1$ matrix.

The set of all $m \times n$ matrices over R is denoted by $R^{m \times n}$. Elements of $R^{1 \times n}$ are called **row vectors (of dimension n)** and elements of $R^{m \times 1}$ are called **column vectors (of dimension m)**. Elements of $R^{n \times n}$ are called **square matrices (of dimension n)**. We do not make a distinction between $R^{1 \times n}$ and $R^{\times n}$; that is, we view standard n-tuples as row vectors. Also, where there can be no confusion, we may interpret an element of $R^{1 \times 1}$ simply as an element of R.

We can define the familiar operations of scalar multiplication, addition, and multiplication on matrices:

- If $A \in R^{m \times n}$ and $c \in R$, then cA is the $m \times n$ matrix whose (i, j) entry is $cA(i, j)$.
- If $A, B \in R^{m \times n}$, then $A + B$ is the $m \times n$ matrix whose (i, j) entry is $A(i, j) + B(i, j)$.
- If $A \in R^{m \times n}$ and $B \in R^{n \times p}$, then AB is the $m \times p$ matrix whose (i, k) entry is

$$\sum_{j=1}^{n} A(i, j) B(j, k).$$

We can also define the difference $A - B := A + (-1_R)B$ of matrices of the same dimension, which is the same as taking the difference of corresponding entries. These operations satisfy the usual properties:

Theorem 15.1. *If $A, B, C \in R^{m \times n}$, $U, V \in R^{n \times p}$, $Z \in R^{p \times q}$, and $c, d \in R$, then*

(i) $c(dA) = (cd)A = d(cA)$,

(ii) $(A + B) + C = A + (B + C)$,

(iii) $A + B = B + A$,

(iv) $c(A + B) = cA + cB$,

(v) $(c + d)A = cA + dA$,

(vi) $(A + B)U = AU + BU$,

(vii) $A(U + V) = AU + AV$,

$(viii)$ $c(AU) = (cA)U = A(cU)$,

(ix) $A(UZ) = (AU)Z$.

Proof. All of these are trivial, except the last one which requires just a bit of computation to show that the (i, ℓ) entry of both $A(UZ)$ and $(AU)Z$ is (verify)

$$\sum_{j=1}^{n} \sum_{k=1}^{p} A(i,j)U(j,k)Z(k,\ell). \quad \square$$

Note that while matrix addition is commutative, matrix multiplication in general is not.

Some simple but useful facts to keep in mind are the following:

- If $A \in R^{m \times n}$ and $B \in R^{n \times p}$, then the kth column of AB is equal to Av, where $v = B(\cdot, k)$; also, the ith row of AB is equal to wB, where $w = A(i)$.

- If $A \in R^{m \times n}$ and $u = (u_1, \ldots, u_m) \in R^{1 \times m}$, then

$$uA = \sum_{i=1}^{m} u_i A(i).$$

  In words: uA is a linear combination of the rows of A, with coefficients taken from the corresponding entries of u.

- If $A \in R^{m \times n}$ and

$$v = \begin{pmatrix} v_1 \\ \vdots \\ v_n \end{pmatrix} \in R^{n \times 1},$$

then

$$Av = \sum_{j=1}^{n} v_j A(\cdot, j).$$

In words: Av is a linear combination of the columns of A, with coefficients taken from the corresponding entries of v.

If $A \in R^{m \times n}$, the **transpose** of A, denoted by $A^\top$, is defined to be the $n \times m$ matrix whose (j, i) entry is $A(i, j)$.

Theorem 15.2. *If $A, B \in R^{m \times n}$, $C \in R^{n \times p}$, and $c \in R$, then*

(i) $(A + B)^\top = A^\top + B^\top$,

(ii) $(cA)^\top = cA^\top$,

(iii) $(A^\top)^\top = A$,

(iv) $(AC)^\top = C^\top A^\top$.

Proof. Exercise. $\square$

An $n \times n$ matrix A is called a **diagonal matrix** if $A(i, j) = 0_R$ for $i \neq j$, which is to say that the entries off the "main diagonal" of A are all zero. A **scalar matrix** is a diagonal matrix whose diagonal entries are all the same. The scalar matrix I, where all the entries on the main diagonal are 1_R, is called the $n \times n$ **identity matrix**. It is easy to see that if A is an $n \times n$ matrix, then $AI = IA = A$. More generally, if B is an $n \times m$ matrix, then $IB = B$, and if C is an $m \times n$ matrix, then $CI = C$.

If A_i is an $n_i \times n_{i+1}$ matrix, for $i = 1, \ldots, k$, then by associativity of matrix multiplication (part (ix) of Theorem 15.1), we may write the product matrix $A_1 \cdots A_k$, which is an $n_1 \times n_{k+1}$ matrix, without any ambiguity. For an $n \times n$ matrix A, and a positive integer k, we write A^k to denote the product $A \cdots A$, where there are k terms in the product. Note that $A^1 = A$. We may extend this notation to $k = 0$, defining A^0 to be the $n \times n$ identity matrix.

One may readily verify the usual rules of exponent arithmetic: for non-negative integers k_1, k_2, we have

$$(A^{k_1})^{k_2} = A^{k_1 k_2} \quad \text{and} \quad A^{k_1} A^{k_2} = A^{k_1 + k_2}.$$

It is easy also to see that part (iv) of Theorem 15.2 implies that for all non-negative integers k, we have

$$(A^k)^\top = (A^\top)^k.$$

Algorithmic issues

For computational purposes, matrices are represented in the obvious way as arrays of elements of R. As remarked at the beginning of this chapter, we shall treat R as an "abstract data type," and not worry about how elements of R are actually represented; in discussing the complexity of algorithms, we shall simply count "operations in R," by which we mean additions, subtractions, multiplications; we shall sometimes also include equality testing and computing multiplicative inverses as "operations in R." In any real implementation, there will be other costs, such as incrementing counters, and so on, which we may safely ignore, as long as their number is at most proportional to the number of operations in R.

The following statements are easy to verify:

- We can multiply an $m \times n$ matrix times a scalar using mn operations in R.

- We can add two $m \times n$ matrices using mn operations in R.

- We can multiply an $m \times n$ matrix and an $n \times p$ matrix using $O(mnp)$ operations in R.

It is also easy to see that given an $m \times m$ matrix A, and a non-negative integer e, we can adapt the repeated squaring algorithm discussed in §3.4 so as to compute A^e using $O(\text{len}(e))$ multiplications of $m \times m$ matrices, and hence $O(\text{len}(e)m^3)$ operations in R.

15.2 Matrices and linear maps

Let R be a ring.

For positive integers m and n, we may naturally view $R^{1 \times m}$ and $R^{1 \times n}$ as R-modules. If A is an $m \times n$ matrix over R, then the map σ that sends $v \in R^{1 \times m}$ to $vA \in R^{1 \times n}$ is easily seen to be an R-linear map. Evidently, σ is injective if and only if the rows of A are linearly independent, and σ is surjective if and only if the rows of A span $R^{1 \times n}$. Likewise, the map τ that sends $w \in R^{n \times 1}$ to $Aw \in R^{m \times 1}$ is also an R-linear map. Again, τ is injective if and only if the columns of A are linearly independent, and τ is surjective if and only if the columns of A span $R^{m \times 1}$.

Thus, the matrix A defines in a natural way two different linear maps, one defined in terms of multiplying a row vector on the right by A, and the other in terms multiplying a column vector on the left by A. With either of these interpretations as a linear map, matrix multiplication has a natural interpretation as function composition. Let $A \in R^{m \times n}$ and $B \in R^{n \times p}$, and consider the product matrix $C = AB$. Let $\sigma_A, \sigma_B, \sigma_C$ be the maps defined by multiplication on the right by A, B, C, and let τ_A, τ_B, τ_C be the maps defined by multiplication on the left by A, B, C. Then it easily follows from the associativity of matrix multiplication that $\sigma_C = \sigma_B \circ \sigma_A$ and $\tau_C = \tau_A \circ \tau_B$.

We have seen how matrix/vector multiplication defines a linear map. Conversely, we shall now see that the action of any R-linear map can be viewed as a matrix/vector multiplication, provided the R-modules involved have bases (which will always be the case for finite dimensional vector spaces).

Let M be an R-module, and suppose that $\mathcal{A} = (\alpha_1, \ldots, \alpha_m)$, with $m > 0$, is a basis for M. In this setting, the ordering of the basis elements is important, and so we refer to $\mathcal{A}$ as an **ordered basis**. Now, $\mathcal{A}$ defines a canonical R-module isomorphism ϵ that sends $(a_1, \ldots, a_m) \in R^{1 \times m}$ to $a_1 \alpha_1 + \cdots + a_m \alpha_m \in M$. Thus, elements of M can be represented concretely as elements of $R^{1 \times m}$; however, this representation depends on the choice $\mathcal{A}$ of the ordered basis. The vector $\epsilon^{-1}(\alpha)$ is called the **coordinate vector of** α **(with respect to $\mathcal{A}$)**.

Let N be an R-module, and suppose $\mathcal{B} = (\beta_1, \ldots, \beta_n)$, with $n > 0$, is an ordered basis for N. Just as in the previous paragraph, $\mathcal{B}$ defines a canonical R-module isomorphism $\delta : R^{1 \times n} \to N$.

Now let $\rho : M \to N$ be an arbitrary R-linear map. For any $\alpha \in M$, if $\alpha = \epsilon(a_1, \ldots, a_m)$, then because ρ is R-linear, we have

$$\rho(\alpha) = \sum_{i=1}^{m} \rho(a_i \alpha_i) = \sum_{i=1}^{m} a_i \rho(\alpha_i).$$

Thus, the action of ρ on M is completely determined by its action on the α_i.

Let us now define an $m \times n$ matrix T whose ith row, for $i = 1, \ldots, m$, is defined to be $\delta^{-1}(\rho(\alpha_i))$, that is, the coordinate vector of $\rho(\alpha_i)$ with respect to the ordered basis $\mathcal{B}$. With T defined in this way, then for any $\alpha \in M$ we have

$$\delta^{-1}(\rho(\alpha)) = \epsilon^{-1}(\alpha)T.$$

In words: if we multiply the coordinate vector of α on the right by T, we get the coordinate vector of $\rho(\alpha)$.

A special case of the above is when $M = R^{1 \times m}$ and $N = R^{1 \times n}$, and $\mathcal{A}$ and $\mathcal{B}$ are the standard bases for M and N (i.e., for $i = 1, \ldots, m$, the ith vector of $\mathcal{A}$ has a 1 in position i and is zero everywhere else, and similarly for $\mathcal{B}$). In this case, $\rho(v) = vT$ for all $v \in R^{1 \times m}$.

To summarize, we see that an R-linear map ρ from M to N, together with particular ordered bases for M and N, uniquely determine a matrix T such that the action of multiplication on the right by T implements the action of ρ with respect to the given ordered bases. There may be many ordered bases for M and N to choose from, and different choices will in general lead to different matrices. In any case, from a computational perspective, the matrix T gives us an efficient way to compute the map ρ, assuming elements of M and N are represented as coordinate vectors with respect to the given ordered bases.

Of course, if one prefers, by simply transposing everything, one can equally well represent the action of ρ in terms of the action of multiplication of a column vector on the left by a matrix.

Example 15.1. Consider again the ring $E = R[\mathsf{X}]/(f)$, where $f \in R[\mathsf{X}]$ is monic of degree ℓ, and suppose that $\ell > 0$ (see Examples 9.34, 9.43, 14.3, and 14.22). Let $f = f_0 + f_1\mathsf{X} + \cdots f_{\ell-1}\mathsf{X}^{\ell-1} + \mathsf{X}^\ell$, where $f_0, \ldots, f_{\ell-1} \in R$. Consider the element $\eta = [\mathsf{X}]_f \in E$. Let $\rho : E \to E$ be the η-multiplication map, that is, the map that sends $\alpha \in E$ to $\eta\alpha \in E$. This is an R-linear map, and the matrix $T \in R^{\ell \times \ell}$ that represents this map with respect to the ordered basis $1, \eta, \eta^2, \ldots, \eta^{\ell-1}$ for E over R is readily seen to be

$$
T = \begin{pmatrix}
0 & 1 & 0 & \cdots & 0 \\
0 & 0 & 1 & \cdots & 0 \\
 & & & \ddots & \\
0 & 0 & 0 & \cdots & 1 \\
-f_0 & -f_1 & -f_2 & \cdots & -f_{\ell-1}
\end{pmatrix},
$$

where for $i = 1, \ldots, \ell - 1$, the ith row of T contains a 1 in position $i + 1$, and is zero everywhere else. This matrix is called the **companion matrix of** f. $\square$

EXERCISE 15.1. Let F be a finite field, and let A be a non-zero $m \times n$ matrix over F. Suppose one chooses a vector $v \in F^{1 \times m}$ at random. Show that the probability that vA is the zero vector is at most $1/|F|$.

EXERCISE 15.2. Design and analyze a probabilistic algorithm that takes as input matrices $A, B, C \in \mathbb{Z}_p^{m \times m}$, where p is a prime. The algorithm should run in time $O(m^2 \operatorname{len}(p)^2)$ and should output either "yes" or "no" so that the following holds:

- if $C = AB$, then the algorithm should always output "yes";
- if $C \neq AB$, then the algorithm should output "no" with probability at least 0.999.

15.3 The inverse of a matrix

Let R be a ring.

For a square matrix $A \in R^{n \times n}$, we call a matrix $X \in R^{n \times n}$ an **inverse** of A if $XA = AX = I$, where I is the $n \times n$ identity matrix.

It is easy to see that if A has an inverse, then the inverse is unique: if X and Y were inverses, then multiplying the equation $I = AY$ on the left by X, we obtain $X = X(AY) = (XA)Y = IY = Y$.

Because the inverse of A is uniquely determined, we denote it by A^{-1}. If A has an inverse, we say that A is **invertible**, or **non-singular**. If A is not invertible, it is sometimes called **singular**. We will use the terms "invertible" and "not invertible." Observe that A is the inverse of A^{-1}; that is, $(A^{-1})^{-1} = A$.

If A and B are invertible $n \times n$ matrices, then so is their product: in fact, it is easy to see that $(AB)^{-1} = B^{-1}A^{-1}$ (verify). It follows that if A is an invertible matrix, and k is a non-negative integer, then A^k is invertible with inverse $(A^{-1})^k$, which we also denote by A^{-k}.

It is also easy to see that A is invertible if and only if the transposed matrix $A^{\top}$ is invertible, in which case $(A^{\top})^{-1} = (A^{-1})^{\top}$. Indeed, $AX = I = XA$ holds if and only if $X^{\top}A^{\top} = I = A^{\top}X^{\top}$

The following theorem connects invertibility to linear maps.

Theorem 15.3. *Let $A \in R^{n \times n}$, and let $\rho : R^{1 \times n} \to R^{1 \times n}$ be the R-linear map that sends $v \in R^{1 \times n}$ to vA. Then A is invertible if and only if ρ is bijective.*

Proof. Suppose A is invertible, and let $X \in R^{n \times n}$ be its inverse. The map ρ is surjective, since for any $w \in R^{1 \times n}$, $w = wI = wXA = \rho(wX)$. The map ρ is injective, since if $\rho(v) = 0^{1 \times n}$, then $v = vI = vAX = \rho(v)X = 0^{1 \times n}$.

Suppose ρ is bijective, so that it is an R-module isomorphism. The inverse map ρ^{-1} is also an R-module isomorphism. Let X be the matrix representing ρ^{-1} with respect to the standard basis for $R^{1 \times n}$, so that for $w \in R^{1 \times n}$, we have $wX = \rho^{-1}(w)$. Since $\rho \circ \rho^{-1} = \rho^{-1} \circ \rho =$ the identity map, it follows that $XA = AX = I$. $\square$

We also have:

Theorem 15.4. *Let $A \in R^{n \times n}$. The following are equivalent:*

(i) A is invertible;

(ii) the rows of A form a basis for $R^{1 \times n}$;

(iii) the columns of A form a basis for $R^{n \times 1}$.

Proof. The equivalence of (i) and (ii) follows from the previous theorem, and the fact that the map ρ in that theorem is bijective if and only if the rows of A form a basis for $R^{1 \times n}$. The equivalence of (i) and (iii) follows by considering the transpose of A. $\square$

EXERCISE 15.3. Let R be a ring, and let A be a square matrix over R. Let us call X a **left inverse** of A if $XA = I$, and let us call Y a **right inverse** of A if $AY = I$.

(a) Show that if A has both a left inverse X and a right inverse Y, then $X = Y$ and hence A is invertible.

(b) Assume that R is a field. Show that if A has either a left inverse or a right inverse, then A is invertible.

Note that part (b) of the previous exercise holds for arbitrary rings, but the proof of this is non-trivial, and requires the development of the theory of determinants, which we do not cover in this text.

EXERCISE 15.4. Show that if A and B are two square matrices over a field such that their product AB is invertible, then both A and B themselves must be invertible.

EXERCISE 15.5. Show that if A is a square matrix over an arbitrary ring, and A^k is invertible for some $k > 0$, then A is invertible.

15.4 Gaussian elimination

Throughout this section, F denotes a field.

A matrix $B \in F^{m \times n}$ is said to be in **reduced row echelon form** if there exists a sequence of integers $(p_1, \ldots, p_r)$, with $0 \le r \le m$ and $1 \le p_1 < p_2 < \cdots < p_r \le n$, such that the following holds:

- for $i = 1, \ldots, r$, all of the entries in row i of B to the left of entry (i, p_i) are zero (i.e., $B(i, j) = 0$ for $j = 1, \ldots, p_i - 1$);

- for $i = 1, \ldots, r$, all of the entries in column p_i of B above entry (i, p_i) are zero (i.e., $B(i', p_i) = 0$ for $i' = 1, \ldots, i - 1$);

- for $i = 1, \ldots, r$, we have $B(i, p_i) = 1$;

- all entries in rows $r + 1, \ldots, m$ of B are zero (i.e., $B(i, j) = 0$ for $i = r + 1, \ldots, m$ and $j = 1, \ldots, n$).

It is easy to see that if B is in reduced row echelon form, the sequence $(p_1, \ldots, p_r)$ above is uniquely determined, and we call it the **pivot sequence** of B. Several further remarks are in order:

- All of the entries of B are completely determined by the pivot sequence, except for the entries (i, j) with $1 \le i \le r$ and $j > i$ with $j \notin \{p_{i+1}, \ldots, p_r\}$, which may be arbitrary.

- If B is an $n \times n$ matrix in reduced row echelon form whose pivot sequence is of length n, then B must be the $n \times n$ identity matrix.

- We allow for an empty pivot sequence (i.e., $r = 0$), which will be the case precisely when $B = 0^{m \times n}$.

Example 15.2. The following 4×6 matrix B over the rational numbers is in reduced row echelon form:

$$B = \begin{pmatrix} 0 & 1 & -2 & 0 & 0 & 3 \\ 0 & 0 & 0 & 1 & 0 & 2 \\ 0 & 0 & 0 & 0 & 1 & -4 \\ 0 & 0 & 0 & 0 & 0 & 0 \end{pmatrix}.$$

The pivot sequence of B is $(2, 4, 5)$. Notice that the first three rows of B are linearly independent, that columns 2, 4, and 5 are linearly independent, and that all of other columns of B are linear combinations of columns 2, 4, and 5. Indeed, if we truncate the pivot columns to their first three rows, we get the 3×3 identity matrix. $\square$

Generalizing the previous example, if a matrix is in reduced row echelon form, it is easy to deduce the following properties, which turn out to be quite useful:

Theorem 15.5. *If B is a matrix in reduced row echelon form with pivot sequence $(p_1, \ldots, p_r)$, then*

(i) *rows $1, 2, \ldots, r$ of B are linearly independent;*

(ii) *columns $p_1, \ldots, p_r$ of B are linearly independent, and all other columns of B can be expressed as linear combinations of columns $p_1, \ldots, p_r$.*

Proof. Exercise—just look at the matrix! $\square$

Gaussian elimination is an algorithm that transforms an arbitrary $m \times n$ matrix A into a $m \times n$ matrix B, where B is a matrix in reduced row echelon form obtained from A by a sequence of **elementary row operations**. There are three types of elementary row operations:

Type I: swap two rows,

Type II: multiply a row by a non-zero scalar,

Type III: add a scalar multiple of one row to a different row.

The application of any specific elementary row operation to an $m \times n$ matrix C can be affected by multiplying C on the left by a suitable $m \times m$ matrix M. Indeed, the matrix M corresponding to a particular elementary row operation is simply the matrix obtained by applying the same elementary row operation to the $m \times m$ identity matrix. It is easy to see that for any elementary row operation, the corresponding matrix M is invertible.

We now describe the basic version of Gaussian elimination. The input is an $m \times n$ matrix A.

1. $B \leftarrow A,\, r \leftarrow 0$
2. for $j \leftarrow 1$ to n do
3. $\ell \leftarrow 0,\, i \leftarrow r$
4.   while $\ell = 0$ and $i \leq m$ do
5. $i \leftarrow i + 1$
6.   if $B(i, j) \neq 0$ then $\ell \leftarrow i$
7.   if $\ell \neq 0$ then
8. $r \leftarrow r + 1$
9.   swap rows $B(r)$ and $B(\ell)$
10. $B(r) \leftarrow B(r, j)^{-1} B(r)$
11.   for $i \leftarrow 1$ to m do
12.   if $i \neq r$ then
13. $B(i) \leftarrow B(i) - B(i, j)B(r)$
14. output B

The algorithm works as follows. First, it makes a copy B of A (this is not necessary if the original matrix A is not needed afterwards). The algorithm proceeds column by column, starting with the left-most column, so that after processing column j, the first j columns of B are in reduced row echelon form, and the current value of r represents the length of the pivot sequence. To process column j, in steps 3–6 the algorithm first searches for a non-zero element among $B(r + 1, j), \ldots, B(m, j)$; if none is found, then the first $j + 1$ columns of B are already in reduced row echelon form. Otherwise, one of these non-zero elements is selected as the **pivot element** (the choice is arbitrary), which is then used in steps 8–13 to bring column j into the required form. After incrementing r, the pivot element is brought into position (r, j), using a Type I operation in step 9. Then the entry (r, j) is set to 1, using a Type II operation in step 10. Finally, all the entries above and below entry (r, j) are set to 0, using Type III operations in steps 11–13. Note that because columns $1, \ldots, j - 1$ of B were already in reduced row echelon form, none of these operations changes any values in these columns.

As for the complexity of the algorithm, it is easy to see that it performs

$O(mn)$ elementary row operations, each of which takes $O(n)$ operations in F, so a total of $O(mn^2)$ operations in F.

Example 15.3. Consider the execution of the Gaussian elimination algorithm on input

$$A = \begin{pmatrix} [0] & [1] & [1] \\ [2] & [1] & [2] \\ [2] & [2] & [0] \end{pmatrix} \in \mathbb{Z}_3^{3\times 3}.$$

After copying A into B, the algorithm transforms B as follows:

$$\begin{pmatrix} [0] & [1] & [1] \\ [2] & [1] & [2] \\ [2] & [2] & [0] \end{pmatrix} \xrightarrow{B(1)\leftrightarrow B(2)} \begin{pmatrix} [2] & [1] & [2] \\ [0] & [1] & [1] \\ [2] & [2] & [0] \end{pmatrix} \xrightarrow{B(1)\leftarrow[2]B(1)} \begin{pmatrix} [1] & [2] & [1] \\ [0] & [1] & [1] \\ [2] & [2] & [0] \end{pmatrix}$$

$$\xrightarrow{B(3)\leftarrow B(3)-[2]B(1)} \begin{pmatrix} [1] & [2] & [1] \\ [0] & [1] & [1] \\ [0] & [1] & [1] \end{pmatrix} \xrightarrow{B(1)\leftarrow B(1)-[2]B(2)} \begin{pmatrix} [1] & [0] & [2] \\ [0] & [1] & [1] \\ [0] & [1] & [1] \end{pmatrix}$$

$$\xrightarrow{B(3)\leftarrow B(3)-B(2)} \begin{pmatrix} [1] & [0] & [2] \\ [0] & [1] & [1] \\ [0] & [0] & [0] \end{pmatrix}$$

□

Suppose the Gaussian elimination algorithm performs a total of t elementary row operations. Then as discussed above, the application of the eth elementary row operation, for $e = 1, \ldots, t$, amounts to multiplying the current value of the matrix B on the left by a particular invertible $m \times m$ matrix M_e. Therefore, the final, output value of B satisfies the equation

$$B = MA \quad \text{where} \quad M = M_t M_{t-1} \cdots M_1.$$

Since the product of invertible matrices is also invertible, we see that M itself is invertible.

Although the algorithm as presented does not compute the matrix M, it can be easily modified to do so. The resulting algorithm, which we call **extended Gaussian elimination**, is the same as plain Gaussian elimination, except that we initialize the matrix M to be the $m \times m$ identity matrix, and we add the following steps:

- Just before step 9, we add the step: swap rows $M(r)$ and $M(\ell)$.
- Just before step 10, we add the step: $M(r) \leftarrow B(r,j)^{-1}M(r)$.
- Just before step 13, we add the step: $M(i) \leftarrow M(i) - B(i,j)M(r)$.

At the end of the algorithm we output M in addition to B.

So we simply perform the same elementary row operations on M that we perform on B. The reader may verify that the above algorithm is correct, and that it uses $O(mn(m + n))$ operations in F.

Example 15.4. Continuing with Example 15.3, the execution of the extended Gaussian elimination algorithm initializes M to the identity matrix, and then transforms M as follows:

$$\begin{pmatrix} [1] & [0] & [0] \\ [0] & [1] & [0] \\ [0] & [0] & [1] \end{pmatrix} \xrightarrow{M(1)\leftrightarrow M(2)} \begin{pmatrix} [0] & [1] & [0] \\ [1] & [0] & [0] \\ [0] & [0] & [1] \end{pmatrix} \xrightarrow{M(1)\leftarrow[2]M(1)} \begin{pmatrix} [0] & [2] & [0] \\ [1] & [0] & [0] \\ [0] & [0] & [1] \end{pmatrix}$$

$$\xrightarrow{M(3)\leftarrow M(3)-[2]M(1)} \begin{pmatrix} [0] & [2] & [0] \\ [1] & [0] & [0] \\ [0] & [2] & [1] \end{pmatrix} \xrightarrow{M(1)\leftarrow M(1)-[2]M(2)} \begin{pmatrix} [1] & [2] & [0] \\ [1] & [0] & [0] \\ [0] & [2] & [1] \end{pmatrix}$$

$$\xrightarrow{M(3)\leftarrow M(3)-M(2)} \begin{pmatrix} [1] & [2] & [0] \\ [1] & [0] & [0] \\ [2] & [2] & [1] \end{pmatrix}$$

□

EXERCISE 15.6. For each type of elementary row operation, describe the matrix M which corresponds to it, as well as M^{-1}.

EXERCISE 15.7. Given a matrix $B \in F^{m \times n}$ in reduced row echelon form, show how to compute its pivot sequence using $O(n)$ operations in F.

EXERCISE 15.8. In §4.4, we saw how to speed up matrix multiplication over $\mathbb{Z}$ using the Chinese remainder theorem. In this exercise, you are to do the same, but for performing Gaussian elimination over $\mathbb{Z}_p$, where p is a large prime. Suppose you are given an $m \times m$ matrix A over $\mathbb{Z}_p$, where $\text{len}(p) = \Theta(m)$. Straightforward application of Gaussian elimination would require $O(m^3)$ operations in $\mathbb{Z}_p$, each of which takes time $O(m^2)$, leading to a total running time of $O(m^5)$. Show how to use the techniques of §4.4 to reduce the running time of Gaussian elimination to $O(m^4)$.

15.5 Applications of Gaussian elimination

Throughout this section, A is an arbitrary $m \times n$ matrix over a field F, and $MA = B$, where M is an invertible $m \times m$ matrix, and B is in reduced row echelon form with pivot sequence $(p_1, \ldots, p_r)$. This is precisely the information produced by the extended Gaussian elimination algorithm, given

A as input (the pivot sequence can easily be "read" directly from B—see Exercise 15.7).

Let $V := F^{1 \times m}$, $W := F^{1 \times n}$, and $\rho : V \to W$ be the F-linear map that sends $v \in V$ to $vA \in W$.

Computing the image and kernel

Consider first the **row space** of A, that is, the vector space spanned by the rows of A, or equivalently, the image of ρ.

We claim that the row space of A is the same as the row space of B. To see this, note that for any $v \in V$, since $B = MA$, we have $vB = v(MA) = (vM)A$, and so the row space of B is contained in the row space of A. For the other containment, note that since M is invertible, we can write $A = M^{-1}B$, and apply the same argument.

Further, note that row space of B, and hence that of A, clearly has dimension r. Indeed, as stated in Theorem 15.5, the first r rows of B form a basis for the row space of B.

Consider next the kernel of ρ, or what we might call the **row null space** of A. We claim that the last $m - r$ rows of M form a basis for $\ker(\rho)$. Clearly, just from the fact that $MA = B$ and the fact that the last $m - r$ rows of B are zero, it follows that the last $m - r$ rows of M are contained in $\ker(\rho)$. Furthermore, as M is invertible, its rows form a basis for V (see Theorem 15.4), and so in particular, they are linearly independent. It therefore suffices to show that the last $m - r$ rows of M span the entire kernel. Now, suppose there were a vector $v \in \ker(\rho)$ outside the subspace spanned by the last $m - r$ rows of M. As the rows of M span V, we may write $v = a_1 M(1) + \cdots + a_m M(m)$, where $a_i \neq 0$ for some $i = 1, \ldots, r$. Setting $\tilde{v} := (a_1, \ldots, a_m)$, we see that $v = \tilde{v}M$, and so

$$\rho(v) = vA = (\tilde{v}M)A = \tilde{v}(MA) = \tilde{v}B,$$

and from the fact that the first r rows of B are linearly independent and the last $m - r$ rows of B are zero, we see that $\tilde{v}B$ is not the zero vector (and because $\tilde{v}$ has a non-zero entry in one its first r positions). We have derived a contradiction, and hence may conclude that the last $m - r$ rows of M span $\ker(\rho)$.

Finally, note that if $m = n$, then A is invertible if and only if its row space has dimension m, which holds if and only if $r = m$, and in the latter case, B will be the identity matrix, and hence M is the inverse of A.

Let us summarize the above discussion:

- *The first r rows of B form a basis for the row space of A (i.e., the image of ρ).*

- *The last $m - r$ rows of M form a basis for the row null space of A (i.e., the kernel of ρ).*

- *If $m = n$, then A is invertible (i.e., ρ is an isomorphism) if and only if $r = m$, in which case M is the inverse of A (i.e., the matrix representing ρ^{-1}).*

So we see that from the output of the extended Gaussian elimination algorithm, we can simply "read off" bases for both the image and the kernel, as well as the inverse (if it exists), of a linear map represented as a matrix with respect to some ordered bases. Also note that this procedure provides a "constructive" version of Theorem 14.29.

Example 15.5. Continuing with Examples 15.3 and 15.4, we see that the vectors $([1], [0], [2])$ and $([0], [1], [1])$ form a basis for the row space of A, while the vector $([2], [2], [1])$ is a basis for the row null space of A. $\square$

Solving linear systems of equations

Suppose that in addition to the matrix A, we are given $w \in W$, and want to find a solution v (or perhaps describe all solutions v), to the equation

$$vA = w. \tag{15.1}$$

Equivalently, we can phrase the problem as finding an element (or describing all elements) of the set $\rho^{-1}(w)$.

Now, if there exists a solution at all, say $v \in V$, then since $\rho(v) = \rho(\tilde{v})$ if and only if $v \equiv \tilde{v} \pmod{\ker(\rho)}$, it follows that the set of all solutions to (15.1) is equal to the coset $v + \ker(\rho)$. Thus, given a basis for $\ker(\rho)$ and any solution v to (15.1), we have a complete and concise description of the set of solutions to (15.1).

As we have discussed above, the last $m - r$ rows of M give us a basis for $\ker(\rho)$, so it suffices to determine if $w \in \operatorname{img}(\rho)$, and if so, determine a single pre-image v of w.

Also as we discussed, $\operatorname{img}(\rho)$, that is, the row space of A, is equal to the row space of B, and because of the special form of B, we can quickly and easily determine if the given w is in the row space of B, as follows. By definition, w is in the row space of B iff there exists a vector $\bar{v} \in V$ such that $\bar{v}B = w$. We may as well assume that all but the first r entries of $\bar{v}$ are zero. Moreover, $\bar{v}B = w$ implies that for $i = 1, \ldots, r$, the ith entry if $\bar{v}$ is equal to the p_ith entry of w. Thus, the vector $\bar{v}$, if it exists, is completely determined by the entries of w at positions $p_1, \ldots, p_r$. We can construct $\bar{v}$ satisfying these conditions, and then test if $\bar{v}B = w$. If not, then we may conclude that (15.1) has no solutions; otherwise, setting $v := \bar{v}M$, we see that $vA = (\bar{v}M)A = \bar{v}(MA) = \bar{v}B = w$, and so v is a solution to (15.1).

One easily verifies that if we implement the above procedure as an algorithm, the work done in addition to running the extended Gaussian elimination algorithm amounts to $O(m(n+m))$ operations in F.

A special case of the above procedure is when $m = n$ and A is invertible, in which case (15.1) has a unique solution, namely, $v := wM$, since in this case, $M = A^{-1}$.

The rank of a matrix

Define the **row rank** of A to be the dimension of its row space, which is $\dim_F(\mathrm{img}(\rho))$, and define the **column rank** of A to be the dimension of its **column space**, that is, the space spanned by the columns of A.

Now, the column space A may not be the same as the column space of B, but from the relation $B = MA$, and the fact that M is invertible, it easily follows that these two subspaces are isomorphic (via the isomorphism that sends v to Mv), and hence have the same dimension. Moreover, by Theorem 15.5, the column rank of B is r, which is the same as the row rank of A.

So we may conclude: *The column rank and row rank of A are the same.*

Because of this, we define the **rank** of a matrix to be the common value of its row and column rank.

The orthogonal complement of a subspace

So as to give equal treatment to rows and columns, one can also define the **column null space** of A to be the kernel of the linear map defined by multiplication on the left by A. By applying the results above to the transpose of A, we see that the column null space of A has dimension $n - r$, where r is the rank of A.

Let $U \subseteq W$ denote the row space of A, and let $\bar{U} \subseteq W$ denote the set of all vectors $\bar{u} \in W$ whose transpose $\bar{u}^\top$ belong to the column null space of A. Now, U is a subspace of W of dimension r and $\bar{U}$ is a subspace of W of dimension $n - r$.

Moreover, if $U \cap \bar{U} = \{0_V\}$, then by Theorem 14.13 we have an isomorphism of $U \times \bar{U}$ with $U + \bar{U}$, and since $U \times \bar{U}$ has dimension n, it must be the case that $U + \bar{U} = W$. It follows that every element of W can be expressed uniquely as $u + \bar{u}$, where $u \in U$ and $\bar{u} \in \bar{U}$.

Now, all of the conclusions in the previous paragraph hinged on the assumption that $U \cap \bar{U} = \{0_V\}$. The space $\bar{U}$ consists precisely of all vectors $\bar{u} \in W$ which are "orthogonal" to all vectors $u \in U$, in the sense that the "inner product" $u\bar{u}^\top$ is zero. For this reason, $\bar{U}$ is sometimes called the "orthogonal complement of U." The condition $U \cap \bar{U} = \{0_V\}$ is equivalent to saying that U contains no non-zero "self-orthogonal vectors" u such that $uu^\top = 0_F$. If F is the field of real numbers, then of course there are no non-zero self-orthogonal vectors, since $uu^\top$ is the sum of the squares of the entries of u. However, for other fields, there may very well be non-zero self-orthogonal vectors. As an example, if $F = \mathbb{Z}_2$, then any vector u with an even number of 1-entries is self orthogonal.

So we see that while much of the theory of vector spaces and matrices carries over without change from familiar ground fields, like the real numbers, to arbitrary ground fields F, not everything does. In particular, the usual decomposition of a vector space into a subspace and its orthogonal complement breaks down, as does any other procedure that relies on properties specific to "inner product spaces."

For the following three exercises, as above, A is an arbitrary $m \times n$ matrix over a field F, and $MA = B$, where M is an invertible $m \times m$ matrix, and B is in reduced row echelon form.

EXERCISE 15.9. Show that the column null space of A is the same as the column null space of B.

EXERCISE 15.10. Show how to compute a basis for the column null space of A using $O(r(n - r))$ operations in F, given A and B.

EXERCISE 15.11. Show that the matrix B is uniquely determined by A; more precisely, show that if $M'A = B'$, where M' is an invertible $m \times m$ matrix, and B' is in reduced row echelon form, then $B' = B$.

In the following two exercises, the theory of determinants could be used; however, they can all be solved directly, without too much difficulty, using just the ideas developed so far in the text.

EXERCISE 15.12. Let p be a prime. A matrix $A \in \mathbb{Z}^{m \times m}$ is called *invertible modulo* p if and only if there exists a matrix $X \in \mathbb{Z}^{m \times m}$ such that $AX \equiv XA \equiv I \pmod{p}$, where I is the $m \times m$ integer identity matrix. Here, two matrices are considered congruent with respect to a given modulus if and only if their corresponding entries are congruent. Show that A is invertible modulo p if and only if

- A is invertible over $\mathbb{Q}$, and
- the entries of A^{-1} lie in $\mathbb{Q}^{(p)}$ (see Example 9.23).

EXERCISE 15.13. You are given a matrix $A \in \mathbb{Z}^{m \times m}$ and a prime p such that A is invertible modulo p. Suppose that you are also given $w \in \mathbb{Z}^{1 \times m}$.

(a) Show how to efficiently compute a vector $v \in \mathbb{Z}^{1 \times m}$ such that $vA = w \pmod{p}$, and that v is uniquely determined modulo p.

(b) Given a vector v as in part (a), along with an integer $e \geq 1$, show how to efficiently compute $\hat{v} \in \mathbb{Z}^{1 \times m}$ such that $\hat{v}A = w \pmod{p^e}$, and that $\hat{v}$ is uniquely determined modulo p^e. Hint: mimic the "lifting" procedure discussed in §13.3.2.

(c) Using parts (a) and (b), design and analyze an efficient algorithm that takes the matrix A and the prime p as input, together with a bound H on the absolute value of the numerator and denominator of the entries of the vector v' that is the unique (rational) solution to the equation $v'A = w$. Your algorithm should run in time polynomial in the length of H, the length of p, and the sum of the lengths of the entries of A and w. Hint: use rational reconstruction, but be sure to fully justify its application.

Note that in the previous exercise, one can use the theory of determinants to derive good bounds, in terms of the lengths of the entries of A and w, on the size of the least prime p such that A is invertible modulo p (assuming A is invertible over the rationals), and the length of the numerator and denominator of the entries of rational solution v' to the equation $v'A = w$. The interested reader who is familiar with the basic theory of determinants is encouraged to establish such bounds.

The next two exercises illustrate how Gaussian elimination can be adapted, in certain cases, to work in rings that are not necessarily fields. Let R be an arbitrary ring. A matrix $B \in R^{m \times n}$ is said to be in **row echelon form** if there exists a pivot sequence $(p_1, \ldots, p_r)$, with $0 \leq r \leq m$ and $1 \leq p_1 < p_2 < \cdots < p_r \leq n$, such that the following holds:

- for $i = 1, \ldots, r$, all of the entries in row i of B to the left of entry (i, p_i) are zero;
- for $i = 1, \ldots, r$, we have $B(i, p_i) \neq 0$;
- all entries in rows $r + 1, \ldots, m$ of B are zero.

EXERCISE 15.14. Let R be the ring $\mathbb{Z}_{p^e}$, where p is prime and $e > 1$. Let $\pi := [p] \in R$. The goal of this exercise is to develop an efficient algorithm for the following problem: given a matrix $A \in R^{m \times n}$, with $m > n$, find a vector $v \in R^{1 \times m}$ such that $vA = 0^{1 \times n}$ but $v \notin \pi R^{1 \times m}$.

(a) Show how to modify the extended Gaussian elimination algorithm to solve the following problem: given a matrix $A \in R^{m \times n}$, compute $M \in R^{m \times m}$ and $B \in R^{m \times n}$, such that $MA = B$, M is invertible, and B is in row echelon form. Your algorithm should run in time $O(mn(m+n)e^2 \operatorname{len}(p)^2)$. Assume that the input includes the values p and e. Hint: when choosing a pivot element, select one divisible by a minimal power of π; as in ordinary Gaussian elimination, your algorithm should only use elementary row operations to transform the input matrix.

(b) Using the fact that the matrix M computed in part (a) is invertible, argue that none of its rows belong to $\pi R^{1 \times m}$.

(c) Argue that if $m > n$ and the matrix B computed in part (a) has pivot sequence $(p_1, \ldots, p_r)$, then $m - r > 0$ and if v is any one of the last $m - r$ rows of M, then $vA = 0^{1 \times n}$.

(d) Give an example that shows that the first r rows of B need not be linearly independent and that the last $m - r$ rows of M need not span the kernel of the R-linear map that sends $w \in R^{1 \times m}$ to $wA \in R^{1 \times n}$.

EXERCISE 15.15. Let R be the ring $\mathbb{Z}_\ell$, where $\ell > 1$ is an integer. You are given a matrix $A \in R^{m \times n}$. Show how to efficiently compute $M \in R^{m \times m}$ and $B \in R^{m \times n}$ such that $MA = B$, M is invertible, and B is in row echelon form. Your algorithm should run in time $O(mn(m+n)\operatorname{len}(\ell)^2)$. Hint: to zero-out entries, you should use "rotations"—for integers a, b, d, s, t with

$$d = \gcd(a, b) \neq 0 \quad \text{and} \quad as + bt = d,$$

and for row indices r, i, a rotation simultaneously updates rows r and i of a matrix C as follows:

$$(C(r), C(i)) \leftarrow (sC(r) + tC(i), -\frac{b}{d}C(r) + \frac{a}{d}C(i));$$

observe that if $C(r, j) = [a]_\ell$ and $C(i, j) = [b]_\ell$ before applying the rotation, then $C(r, j) = [d]_\ell$ and $C(i, j) = [0]_\ell$ after the rotation.

15.6 Notes

While a trivial application of the defining formulas yields a simple algorithm for multiplying two $m \times m$ matrices over a ring R that uses $O(m^3)$ operations in R, this algorithm is not the best, asymptotically speaking. The currently fastest algorithm for this problem, due to Coppersmith and Winograd [28], uses $O(m^\omega)$ operations in R, where $\omega < 2.376$. We note, however, that the good old $O(m^3)$ algorithm is still the only one used in almost any practical setting.

16

Subexponential-time discrete logarithms and factoring

This chapter presents subexponential-time algorithms for computing discrete logarithms and for factoring. These algorithms are based on a common technique, which makes essential use of the notion of a **smooth number**.

16.1 Smooth numbers

If y is a non-negative real number, and m is a positive integer, then we say that m is y-**smooth** if all prime divisors of m are at most y.

For $0 \leq y \leq x$, let us define $\Psi(y, x)$ to be the number of y-smooth integers up to x. The following theorem gives us a lower bound on $\Psi(y, x)$, which will be crucial in the analysis of our discrete logarithm and factoring algorithms.

Theorem 16.1. *Let y be a function of x such that*

$$\frac{y}{\log x} \to \infty \quad and \quad u := \frac{\log x}{\log y} \to \infty$$

as $x \to \infty$. Then

$$\Psi(y, x) \geq x \cdot \exp[(-1 + o(1))u \log \log x].$$

Proof. Let us write $u = \lfloor u \rfloor + \delta$, where $0 \leq \delta < 1$. Let us split the primes up to y into two sets: the set V "very small" primes that are at most $y^\delta/2$, and the other primes W that are greater than $y^\delta/2$ but at most y. To simplify matters, let us also include the integer 1 in the set V.

By Bertrand's postulate (Theorem 5.7), there exists a constant $C > 0$ such that $|W| \geq Cy/\log y$ for sufficiently large y. By the assumption that $y/\log x \to \infty$ as $x \to \infty$, it follows that $|W| \geq 2\lfloor u \rfloor$ for sufficiently large x.

To derive the lower bound, we shall count those integers that can be built up by multiplying together $\lfloor u \rfloor$ distinct elements of W, together with one element of V. These products are clearly distinct, y-smooth numbers, and each is bounded by x, since each is at most $y^{\lfloor u \rfloor} y^\delta = y^u = x$.

If S denotes the set of all of these products, then for x sufficiently large, we have

$$
\begin{aligned}
|S| &= \binom{|W|}{\lfloor u \rfloor} \cdot |V| \\
&= \frac{|W|(|W|-1)\cdots(|W|-\lfloor u \rfloor + 1)}{\lfloor u \rfloor!} \cdot |V| \\
&\geq \left(\frac{|W|}{2u} \right)^{\lfloor u \rfloor} \cdot |V| \\
&\geq \left(\frac{Cy}{2u \log y} \right)^{\lfloor u \rfloor} \cdot |V| \\
&= \left(\frac{Cy}{2 \log x} \right)^{u-\delta} \cdot |V|.
\end{aligned}
$$

Taking logarithms, we have

$$
\begin{aligned}
\log |S| &\geq (u - \delta)(\log y - \log\log x + \log(C/2)) + \log |V| \\
&= \log x - u\log\log x + (\log |V| - \delta \log y) + \\
&\quad O(u + \log\log x). \tag{16.1}
\end{aligned}
$$

To prove the theorem, it suffices to show that

$$
\log |S| \geq \log x - (1 + o(1))u\log\log x.
$$

Under our assumption that $u \to \infty$, the term $O(u + \log\log x)$ in (16.1) is $o(u\log\log x)$, and so it will suffice to show that the term $\log |V| - \delta \log y$ is also $o(u\log\log x)$. But by Chebyshev's theorem (Theorem 5.1), for some positive constant D, we have

$$
Dy^\delta / \log y \leq |V| \leq y^\delta,
$$

and taking logarithms, and again using the fact that $u \to \infty$, we have

$$
\log |V| - \delta \log y = O(\log\log y) = o(u\log\log x). \quad \Box
$$

16.2 An algorithm for discrete logarithms

We now present a probabilistic, subexponential-time algorithm for computing discrete logarithms. The input to the algorithm is p, q, γ, α, where p and q are primes, with $q \mid (p-1)$, γ is an element of $\mathbb{Z}_p^*$ generating a subgroup G of $\mathbb{Z}_p^*$ of order q, and $\alpha \in G$.

We shall make the simplifying assumption that $q^2 \nmid (p-1)$, which is equivalent to saying that $q \nmid m := (p-1)/q$. Although not strictly necessary, this assumption simplifies the design and analysis of the algorithm, and moreover, for cryptographic applications, this assumption is almost always satisfied. (Exercises 16.1–16.3 below explore how this assumption may be lifted, as well as other generalizations.)

At a high level, the main goal of our discrete logarithm algorithm is to find a random representation of 1 with respect to γ and α—as discussed in Exercise 11.12, this allows us to compute $\log_\gamma \alpha$ (with high probability). More precisely, our main goal is to compute integers r and s in a probabilistic fashion, such that $\gamma^r \alpha^s = 1$ and $[s]_q$ is uniformly distributed over $\mathbb{Z}_q$. Having accomplished this, then with probability $1 - 1/q$, we shall have $s \not\equiv 0 \pmod{q}$, which allows us to compute $\log_\gamma \alpha$ as $-rs^{-1} \bmod q$.

Let G' be the subgroup of $\mathbb{Z}_p^*$ of order m. Our assumption that $q \nmid m$ implies that $G \cap G' = \{1\}$, since the multiplicative order of any element in the intersection must divide both q and m, and so the only possibility is that the multiplicative order is 1. Therefore, the map $\rho : G \times G' \to \mathbb{Z}_p^*$ that sends (β, δ) to $\beta\delta$ is injective (Theorem 8.28), and since $|\mathbb{Z}_p^*| = qm$, it must be surjective as well.

We shall use this fact in the following way: if β is chosen uniformly at random from G, and δ is chosen uniformly at random from G' (and independent of β), then $\beta\delta$ is uniformly distributed over $\mathbb{Z}_p^*$. Furthermore, since G' is the image of the q-power map on $\mathbb{Z}_p^*$, we may generate a random $\delta \in G'$ simply by choosing $\hat{\delta} \in \mathbb{Z}_p^*$ at random, and setting $\delta := \hat{\delta}^q$.

The discrete logarithm algorithm uses a "smoothness parameter" y, whose choice will be discussed below when we analyze the running time of the algorithm; for now, we only assume that $y < p$. Let $p_1, \ldots, p_k$ be an enumeration of the primes up to y. Let $\pi_i := [p_i]_p \in \mathbb{Z}_p^*$ for $i = 1, \ldots, k$.

The algorithm has two stages.

In the first stage, we find relations of the form

$$\gamma^{r_i} \alpha^{s_i} \delta_i = \pi_1^{e_{i1}} \cdots \pi_k^{e_{ik}}, \tag{16.2}$$

for integers $r_i, s_i, e_{i1}, \ldots, e_{ik}$, and $\delta_i \in G'$, and $i = 1, \ldots, k+1$.

We obtain one such relation by a randomized search, as follows: we choose $r_i, s_i \in \{0, \ldots, q-1\}$ at random, as well as $\hat{\delta}_i \in \mathbb{Z}_p^*$ at random; we then compute $\delta_i := \hat{\delta}_i^q$, $\beta_i := \gamma^{r_i} \alpha^{s_i}$, and $m_i := \mathrm{rep}(\beta_i \delta_i)$. Now, the value β_i is uniformly distributed over G, while δ_i is uniformly distributed over G'; therefore, the product $\beta_i \delta_i$ is uniformly distributed over $\mathbb{Z}_p^*$, and hence m_i

is uniformly distributed over $\{1, \ldots, p-1\}$. Next, we simply try to factor m_i by trial division, trying all the primes $p_1, \ldots, p_k$ up to y. If we are lucky, we completely factor m_i in this way, obtaining a factorization

$$m_i = p_1^{e_{i1}} \cdots p_k^{e_{ik}},$$

for some exponents $e_{i1}, \ldots, e_{ik}$, and we get the relation (16.2). If we are unlucky, then we simply try (and try again) until we are lucky.

For $i = 1, \ldots, k+1$, let $v_i := (e_{i1}, \ldots, e_{ik}) \in \mathbb{Z}^{\times k}$, and let $\bar{v}_i$ denote the image of v_i in $\mathbb{Z}_q^{\times k}$ (i.e., $\bar{v}_i := ([e_{i1}]_q, \ldots, [e_{ik}]_q)$). Since $\mathbb{Z}_q^{\times k}$ is a vector space over the field $\mathbb{Z}_q$ of dimension k, the vectors $\bar{v}_1, \ldots, \bar{v}_{k+1}$ must be linearly dependent. The second stage of the algorithm uses Gaussian elimination over $\mathbb{Z}_q$ (see §15.4) to find a linear dependence among the vectors $\bar{v}_1, \ldots, \bar{v}_{k+1}$, that is, to find integers $c_1, \ldots, c_{k+1} \in \{0, \ldots, q-1\}$, not all zero, such that

$$(e_1, \ldots, e_k) := c_1 v_1 + \cdots c_{k+1} v_{k+1} \in q\mathbb{Z}^{\times k}.$$

Raising each equation (16.2) to the power c_i, and multiplying them all together, we obtain

$$\gamma^r \alpha^s \delta = \pi_1^{e_1} \cdots \pi_k^{e_k},$$

where

$$r := \sum_{i=1}^{k+1} c_i r_i, \ s := \sum_{i=1}^{k+1} c_i s_i, \text{ and } \delta := \prod_{i=1}^{k+1} \delta_i^{c_i}.$$

Now, $\delta \in G'$, and since each e_i is a multiple of q, we also have $\pi_i^{e_i} \in G'$ for $i = 1, \ldots, k$. It follows that $\gamma^r \alpha^s \in G'$. But since $\gamma^r \alpha^s \in G$ as well, and $G \cap G' = \{1\}$, it follows that $\gamma^r \alpha^s = 1$. If we are lucky (and we will be with overwhelming probability, as we discuss below), we will have $s \not\equiv 0 \pmod{q}$, in which case, we can compute $s' := s^{-1} \bmod q$, obtaining

$$\alpha = \gamma^{-rs'},$$

and hence $-rs' \bmod q$ is the discrete logarithm of α to the base γ. If we are very unlucky, we will have $s \equiv 0 \pmod{q}$, at which point the algorithm simply quits, reporting "failure."

The entire algorithm, called Algorithm SEDL, is presented in Fig. 16.1.

As already argued above, if Algorithm SEDL does not output "failure," then its output is indeed the discrete logarithm of α to the base γ. There remain three questions to answer:

1. What is the expected running time of Algorithm SEDL?

$i \leftarrow 0$

repeat

    $i \leftarrow i + 1$

    repeat

        choose $r_i, s_i \in \{0, \ldots, q-1\}$ at random

        choose $\hat{\delta}_i \in \mathbb{Z}_p^*$ at random

        $\beta_i \leftarrow \gamma^{r_i} \alpha^{s_i}, \quad \delta_i \leftarrow \hat{\delta}_i^q, \quad m_i \leftarrow \mathrm{rep}(\beta_i \delta_i)$

        test if m_i is y-smooth (trial division)

    until $m_i = p_1^{e_{i1}} \cdots p_k^{e_{ik}}$ for some integers $e_{i1}, \ldots, e_{ik}$

until $i = k + 1$

set $v_i \leftarrow (e_{i1}, \ldots, e_{ik}) \in \mathbb{Z}^{\times k}$ for $i = 1, \ldots, k+1$

apply Gaussian elimination over $\mathbb{Z}_q$ to find integers $c_1, \ldots, c_{k+1} \in$
    $\{0, \ldots, q-1\}$, not all zero, such that
    $c_1 v_1 + \cdots + c_{k+1} v_{k+1} \in q\mathbb{Z}^{\times k}$.

$r \leftarrow \sum_{i=1}^{k+1} c_i r_i, \quad s \leftarrow \sum_{i=1}^{k+1} c_i s_i$

if $s \equiv 0 \pmod{q}$ then

    output "failure"

else

    output $-rs^{-1} \bmod q$

Fig. 16.1. Algorithm SEDL

2. How should the smoothness parameter y be chosen so as to minimize the expected running time?

3. What is the probability that Algorithm SEDL outputs "failure"?

Let us address these questions in turn. As for the expected running time, let σ be the probability that a random element of $\{1, \ldots, p-1\}$ is y-smooth. Then the expected number of attempts needed to produce a single relation is σ^{-1}, and so the expected number of attempts to produce $k+1$ relations is $(k+1)\sigma^{-1}$. In each attempt, we perform trial division using $p_1, \ldots, p_k$, along with a few other minor computations, leading to a total expected running time in stage 1 of $k^2 \sigma^{-1} \cdot \mathrm{len}(p)^{O(1)}$. The running time in stage 2 is dominated by that of the Gaussian elimination step, which takes time $k^3 \cdot \mathrm{len}(p)^{O(1)}$. Thus, if T is the total running time of the algorithm, then we have

$$\mathsf{E}[T] \leq (k^2 \sigma^{-1} + k^3) \cdot \mathrm{len}(p)^{O(1)}. \tag{16.3}$$

Let us assume for the moment that

$$y = \exp[(\log p)^{\lambda + o(1)}] \tag{16.4}$$

for some constant λ with $0 < \lambda < 1$. Our final choice of y will indeed satisfy this assumption. Consider the probability σ. We have

$$\sigma = \Psi(y, p-1)/(p-1) = \Psi(y, p)/(p-1) \geq \Psi(y, p)/p,$$

where for the second equality we use the assumption that $y < p$, so p is not y-smooth. With our assumption (16.4), we may apply Theorem 16.1 (with the given value of y and $x := p$), obtaining

$$\sigma \geq \exp[(-1 + o(1))(\log p/\log y) \log \log p].$$

By Chebyshev's theorem (Theorem 5.1), we know that $k = \Theta(y/\log y)$, and so $\log k = (1 + o(1)) \log y$. Moreover, assumption (16.4) implies that the factor $\mathrm{len}(p)^{O(1)}$ in (16.3) is of the form $\exp[o(\min(\log y, \log p/\log y))]$, and so we have

$$\mathsf{E}[T] \leq \exp[(1 + o(1)) \max\{(\log p/\log y) \log \log p + 2 \log y, \ 3 \log y\}]. \tag{16.5}$$

Let us find the value of y that minimizes the right-hand side of (16.5), ignoring the "o(1)" terms. Let $\mu := \log y$, $A := \log p \log \log p$, $S_1 := A/\mu + 2\mu$, and $S_2 := 3\mu$. We want to find μ that minimizes $\max\{S_1, S_2\}$. Using a little calculus, one sees that S_1 is minimized at $\mu = (A/2)^{1/2}$. With this choice of μ, we have $S_1 = (2\sqrt{2})A^{1/2}$ and $S_2 = (3/\sqrt{2})A^{1/2} < S_1$. Thus, choosing

$$y = \exp[(1/\sqrt{2})(\log p \log \log p)^{1/2}],$$

we obtain

$$\mathsf{E}[T] \leq \exp[(2\sqrt{2} + o(1))(\log p \log \log p)^{1/2}].$$

That takes care of the first two questions, although strictly speaking, we have only obtained an upper bound for the expected running time, and we have not shown that the choice of y is actually optimal, but we shall nevertheless content ourselves (for now) with these results. Finally, we deal with the third question, on the probability that the algorithm outputs "failure."

Lemma 16.2. *The probability that the algorithm outputs "failure" is $1/q$.*

Proof. Consider the values r_i, s_i, and β_i generated in the inner loop in stage 1. It is easy to see that, as random variables, the values s_i and β_i are independent, since conditioned on any fixed choice of s_i, the value r_i is uniformly distributed over $\{0, \ldots, q-1\}$, and hence β_i is uniformly distributed over

G. Turning this around, we see that conditioned on any fixed choice of β_i, the value s_i is uniformly distributed over $\{0, \ldots, q-1\}$.

So now let us condition on any fixed choice of values β_i and δ_i, for $i = 1, \ldots, k+1$, as determined at the end of stage 1 of the algorithm. By the remarks in the previous paragraph, we see that in this conditional probability distribution, the variables s_i are mutually independent and uniformly distributed over $\{0, \ldots, q-1\}$, and moreover, the behavior of the algorithm is completely determined, and in particular, the values $c_1, \ldots, c_{k+1}$ are fixed. Therefore, in this conditional probability distribution, the probability that the algorithm outputs failure is just the probability that $\sum_i s_i c_i \equiv 0 \pmod{q}$, which is $1/q$, since not all the c_i are zero modulo q. Since this equality holds for every choice of β_i and δ_i, the lemma follows. $\square$

Let us summarize the above discussion in the following theorem.

Theorem 16.3. *With the smoothness parameter set as*

$$y := \exp[(1/\sqrt{2})(\log p \log\log p)^{1/2}],$$

the expected running time of Algorithm SEDL is

$$\exp[(2\sqrt{2} + o(1))(\log p \log\log p)^{1/2}].$$

The probability that Algorithm SEDL outputs "failure" is $1/q$.

In the description and analysis of Algorithm SEDL, we have assumed that the primes $p_1, \ldots, p_k$ were pre-computed. Of course, we can construct this list of primes using, for example, the sieve of Eratosthenes (see §5.4), and the running time of this pre-computation will be dominated by the running time of Algorithm SEDL.

In the analysis of Algorithm SEDL, we relied crucially on the fact that in generating a relation, each candidate element $\gamma^{r_i} \alpha^{s_i} \delta_i$ was uniformly distributed over $\mathbb{Z}_p^*$. If we simply left out the δ_i, then the candidate element would be uniformly distributed over the subgroup G, and Theorem 16.1 simply would not apply. Although the algorithm might anyway work as expected, we would not be able to prove this.

EXERCISE 16.1. Using the result of Exercise 15.14, show how to modify Algorithm SEDL to work in the case where $p - 1 = q^e m$, $e > 1$, $q \nmid m$, γ generates the subgroup G of $\mathbb{Z}_p^*$ of order q^e, and $\alpha \in G$. Your algorithm should compute $\log_\gamma \alpha$ with roughly the same expected running time and success probability as Algorithm SEDL.

EXERCISE 16.2. Using the algorithm of the previous exercise as a subroutine, design and analyze an algorithm for the following problem. The input is p, q, γ, α, where p is a prime, q is a prime dividing $p - 1$, γ generates the subgroup G of $\mathbb{Z}_p^*$ of order q, and $\alpha \in G$; note that we may have $q^2 \mid (p-1)$. The output is $\log_\gamma \alpha$. Your algorithm should always succeed in computing this discrete logarithm, and its expected running time should be bounded by a constant times the expected running time of the algorithm of the previous exercise.

EXERCISE 16.3. Using the result of Exercise 15.15, show how to modify Algorithm SEDL to solve the following problem: given a prime p, a generator γ for $\mathbb{Z}_p^*$, and an element $\alpha \in \mathbb{Z}_p^*$, compute $\log_\gamma \alpha$. Your algorithm should work without knowledge of the factorization of $p - 1$; its expected running time should be roughly the same as that of Algorithm SEDL, but its success probability may be lower. In addition, explain how the success probability may be significantly increased at almost no cost by collecting a few extra relations.

EXERCISE 16.4. Let $n = pq$, where p and q are distinct, large primes. Let e be a prime, with $e < n$ and $e \nmid (p - 1)(q - 1)$. Let x be a positive integer, with $x < n$. Suppose you are given n (but not its factorization!) along with e and x. In addition, you are given access to two "oracles," which you may invoke as often as you like.

- The first oracle is a "challenge oracle": each invocation of the oracle produces a "challenge" $a \in \{1, \ldots, x\}$ — distributed uniformly and independently of all other challenges.

- The second oracle is a "solution oracle": you invoke this oracle with the index of a previous challenge oracle; if the corresponding challenge was a, the solution oracle returns the eth root of a modulo n; that is, the solution oracle returns $b \in \{1, \ldots, n - 1\}$ such that $b^e \equiv a \pmod{n}$ — note that b always exists and is uniquely determined.

Let us say that you "win" if you are able to compute the eth root modulo n of any challenge, but *without* invoking the solution oracle with the corresponding index of the challenge (otherwise, winning would be trivial, of course).

(a) Design a probabilistic algorithm that wins the above game, using an expected number of

$$\exp[(c + o(1))(\log x \log \log x)^{1/2}] \cdot \text{len}(n)^{O(1)}$$

steps, for some constant c, where a "step" is either a computation step or an oracle invocation (either challenge or solution). Hint: Gaussian elimination over the field $\mathbb{Z}_e$.

(b) Suppose invocations of the challenge oracle are "cheap," while invocations of the solution oracle are relatively "expensive." How would you modify your strategy in part (a)?

Exercise 16.4 has implications in cryptography. A popular way of implementing a public-key primitive known as a "digital signature" works as follows: to digitally sign a message M (which may be an arbitrarily long bit string), first apply a "hash function" or "message digest" H to M, obtaining an integer a in some fixed range $\{1, \ldots, x\}$, and then compute the signature of M as the eth root b of a modulo n. Anyone can verify that such a signature b is correct by checking that $b^e \equiv H(M) \pmod{n}$; however, it would appear to be difficult to "forge" a signature without knowing the factorization of n. Indeed, one can prove the security of this signature scheme by assuming that it is hard to compute the eth root of a random number modulo n, and by making the heuristic assumption that H is a random function (see §16.5). However, for this proof to work, the value of x must be close to n; otherwise, if x is significantly smaller than n, as the result of this exercise, one can break the signature scheme at a cost that is roughly the same as the cost of factoring numbers around the size of x, rather than the size of n.

16.3 An algorithm for factoring integers

We now present a probabilistic, subexponential-time algorithm for factoring integers. The algorithm uses techniques very similar to those used in Algorithm SEDL in §16.2.

Let $n > 1$ be the integer we want to factor. We make a few simplifying assumptions. First, we assume that n is odd — this is not a real restriction, since we can always pull out any factors of 2 in a pre-processing step. Second, we assume that n is not a perfect power, that is, not of the form a^b for integers $a > 1$ and $b > 1$ — this is also not a real restriction, since we can always partially factor n using the algorithm in §10.5 if n is a perfect power. Third, we assume that n is not prime — this may be efficiently checked using, say, the Miller–Rabin test (see §10.3). Fourth, we assume that n is not divisible by any primes up to a "smoothness parameter" y — we can ensure this using trial division, and it will be clear that the running time of this pre-computation is dominated by that of the algorithm itself.

With these assumptions, the prime factorization of n is of the form

$$n = q_1^{f_1} \cdots q_w^{f_w},$$

where the q_i are distinct, odd primes, all greater than y, the f_i are positive integers, and $w > 1$.

The main goal of our factoring algorithm is to find a random square root of 1 in $\mathbb{Z}_n$. Let

$$\theta : \mathbb{Z}_{q_1^{f_1}} \times \cdots \times \mathbb{Z}_{q_w^{f_w}} \to \mathbb{Z}_n$$

be the ring isomorphism of the Chinese remainder theorem. The square roots of 1 in $\mathbb{Z}_n$ are precisely those elements of the form $\theta(\pm 1, \dots, \pm 1)$, and if β is a random square root of 1, then with probability $1 - 2^{-w+1} \geq 1/2$, it will be of the form $\beta = \theta(\beta_1, \dots, \beta_w)$, where the β_i are neither all 1 nor all -1 (i.e., $\beta \neq \pm 1$). If this happens, then $\beta - 1 = \theta(\beta_1 - 1, \dots, \beta_w - 1)$, and so we see that some, but not all, of the values $\beta_i - 1$ will be zero. The value of $\gcd(\text{rep}(\beta - 1), n)$ is precisely the product of the prime powers $q_i^{f_i}$ such that $\beta_i - 1 = 0$, and hence this gcd will yield a non-trivial factorization of n, unless $\beta = \pm 1$.

Let $p_1, \dots, p_k$ be the primes up to the smoothness parameter y mentioned above. Let $\pi_i := [p_i]_n \in \mathbb{Z}_n^*$ for $i = 1, \dots, k$.

We first describe a simplified version of the algorithm, after which we modify the algorithm slightly to deal with a technical problem. Like Algorithm SEDL, this algorithm proceeds in two stages. In the first stage, we find relations of the form

$$\alpha_i^2 = \pi_1^{e_{i1}} \cdots \pi_k^{e_{ik}}, \tag{16.6}$$

for $\alpha_i \in \mathbb{Z}_n^*$, and $i = 1, \dots, k+1$.

We can obtain such a relation by randomized search, as follows: we select $\alpha_i \in \mathbb{Z}_n^*$ at random, square it, and try to factor $m_i := \text{rep}(\alpha_i^2)$ by trial division, trying all the primes $p_1, \dots, p_k$ up to y. If we are lucky, we obtain a factorization

$$m_i = p_1^{e_{i1}} \cdots p_k^{e_{ik}},$$

for some exponents $e_{i1}, \dots, e_{ik}$, yielding the relation (16.6); if not, we just keep trying.

For $i = 1, \dots, k+1$, let $v_i := (e_{i1}, \dots, e_{ik}) \in \mathbb{Z}^{\times k}$, and let $\bar{v}_i$ denote the image of v_i in $\mathbb{Z}_2^{\times k}$ (i.e., $\bar{v}_i := ([e_{i1}]_2, \dots, [e_{ik}]_2)$). Since $\mathbb{Z}_2^{\times k}$ is a vector space over the field $\mathbb{Z}_2$ of dimension k, the vectors $\bar{v}_1, \dots, \bar{v}_{k+1}$ must be linearly dependent. The second stage of the algorithm uses Gaussian elimination over $\mathbb{Z}_2$ to find a linear dependence among the vectors $\bar{v}_1, \ldots, \bar{v}_{k+1}$, that is, to find integers $c_1, \ldots, c_{k+1} \in \{0, 1\}$, not all zero, such that

$$(e_1, \ldots, e_k) := c_1 v_1 + \cdots c_{k+1} v_{k+1} \in 2\mathbb{Z}^{\times k}.$$

Raising each equation (16.6) to the power c_i, and multiplying them all together, we obtain

$$\alpha^2 = \pi_1^{e_1} \cdots \pi_k^{e_k},$$

where

$$\alpha := \prod_{i=1}^{k+1} \alpha_i^{c_i}.$$

Since each e_i is even, we can compute

$$\beta := \pi_1^{e_1/2} \cdots \pi_k^{e_k/2} \alpha^{-1},$$

and we see that β is a square root of 1 in $\mathbb{Z}_n$. A more careful analysis (see below) shows that in fact, β is uniformly distributed over all square roots of 1, and hence, with probability at least $1/2$, if we compute $\gcd(\mathrm{rep}(\beta - 1), n)$, we get a non-trivial factor of n.

That is the basic idea of the algorithm. There is, however, a technical problem. Namely, in the method outlined above for generating a relation, we attempt to factor $m_i := \mathrm{rep}(\alpha_i^2)$. Thus, the running time of the algorithm will depend in a crucial way on the probability that a random square modulo n is y-smooth. Unfortunately for us, Theorem 16.1 does not say anything about this situation — it only applies to the situation where a number is chosen at random from an interval $[1, x]$. There are (at least) three different ways to address this problem:

1. Ignore it, and just assume that the bounds in Theorem 16.1 apply to random squares modulo n (taking $x := n$ in the theorem).

2. Prove a version of Theorem 16.1 that applies to random squares modulo n.

3. Modify the factoring algorithm, so that Theorem 16.1 applies.

The first choice, while not completely unreasonable, is not very satisfying mathematically. It turns out that the second choice is a indeed a viable option (i.e., the theorem is true and is not so difficult to prove), but we opt for the third choice, as it is somewhat easier to carry out, and illustrates a probabilistic technique that is more generally useful.

So here is how we modify the basic algorithm. Instead of generating relations of the form (16.6), we generate relations of the form

$$\alpha_i^2 \delta = \pi_1^{e_{i1}} \cdots \pi_k^{e_{ik}}, \qquad (16.7)$$

for $\delta \in \mathbb{Z}_n^*$, $\alpha_i \in \mathbb{Z}_n^*$, and $i = 1, \ldots, k+2$. Note that the value δ is the same in all relations.

We generate these relations as follows. For the very first relation (i.e., $i = 1$), we repeatedly choose α_1 and δ in $\mathbb{Z}_n^*$ at random, until $\mathrm{rep}(\alpha_1^2 \delta)$ is y-smooth. Then, after having found the first relation, we find subsequent relations (i.e., for $i > 1$) by repeatedly choosing α_i in $\mathbb{Z}_n^*$ at random until $\mathrm{rep}(\alpha_i^2 \delta)$ is y-smooth, where δ is the same value that was used in the first relation. Now, Theorem 16.1 will apply directly to determine the success probability of each attempt to generate the first relation. Having found this relation, the value $\alpha_1^2 \delta$ will be uniformly distributed over all y-smooth elements of $\mathbb{Z}_n^*$ (i.e., elements whose integer representations are y-smooth). Consider the various cosets of $(\mathbb{Z}_n^*)^2$ in $\mathbb{Z}_n^*$. Intuitively, it is much more likely that a random y-smooth element of $\mathbb{Z}_n^*$ lies in a coset that contains many y-smooth elements, rather than a coset with very few, and indeed, it is reasonably likely that the fraction of y-smooth elements in the coset containing δ is not much less than the overall fraction of y-smooth elements in $\mathbb{Z}_n^*$. Therefore, for $i > 1$, each attempt to find a relation should succeed with reasonably high probability. This intuitive argument will be made rigorous in the analysis to follow.

The second stage is then modified as follows. For $i = 1, \ldots, k+2$, let $v_i := (e_{i1}, \ldots, e_{ik}, 1) \in \mathbb{Z}^{\times(k+1)}$, and let $\bar{v}_i$ denote the image of v_i in $\mathbb{Z}_2^{\times(k+1)}$. Since $\mathbb{Z}_2^{\times(k+1)}$ is a vector space over the field $\mathbb{Z}_2$ of dimension $k+1$, the vectors $\bar{v}_1, \ldots, \bar{v}_{k+2}$ must be linearly dependent. Therefore, we use Gaussian elimination over $\mathbb{Z}_2$ to find a linear dependence among the vectors $\bar{v}_1, \ldots, \bar{v}_{k+2}$, that is, to find integers $c_1, \ldots, c_{k+2} \in \{0, 1\}$, not all zero, such that

$$(e_1, \ldots, e_{k+1}) := c_1 v_1 + \cdots + c_{k+2} v_{k+2} \in 2\mathbb{Z}^{\times(k+1)}.$$

Raising each equation (16.7) to the power c_i, and multiplying them all together, we obtain

$$\alpha^2 \delta^{e_{k+1}} = \pi_1^{e_1} \cdots \pi_k^{e_k},$$

where

$$\alpha := \prod_{i=1}^{k+2} \alpha_i^{c_i}.$$

$i \leftarrow 0$

repeat

    $i \leftarrow i + 1$

    repeat

        choose $\alpha_i \in \mathbb{Z}_n^*$ at random

        if $i = 1$ then choose $\delta \in \mathbb{Z}_n^*$ at random

        $m_i \leftarrow \mathrm{rep}(\alpha_i^2 \delta)$

        test if m_i is y-smooth (trial division)

    until $m_i = p_1^{e_{i1}} \cdots p_k^{e_{ik}}$ for some integers $e_{i1}, \ldots, e_{ik}$

until $i = k + 2$

set $v_i \leftarrow (e_{i1}, \ldots, e_{ik}, 1) \in \mathbb{Z}^{\times(k+1)}$ for $i = 1, \ldots, k+2$

apply Gaussian elimination over $\mathbb{Z}_2$ to find integers $c_1, \ldots, c_{k+2} \in \{0, 1\}$, not all zero, such that
$(e_1, \ldots, e_{k+1}) := c_1 v_1 + \cdots + c_{k+2} v_{k+2} \in 2\mathbb{Z}^{\times(k+1)}$.

$\alpha \leftarrow \prod_{i=1}^{k+2} \alpha_i^{c_i}, \quad \beta \leftarrow \pi_1^{e_1/2} \cdots \pi_k^{e_k/2} \delta^{-e_{k+1}/2} \alpha^{-1}$

if $\beta = \pm 1$ then

    output "failure"

else

    output $\gcd(\mathrm{rep}(\beta - 1), n)$

Fig. 16.2. Algorithm SEF

Since each e_i is even, we can compute
$$\beta := \pi_1^{e_1/2} \cdots \pi_k^{e_k/2} \delta^{-e_{k+1}/2} \alpha^{-1},$$
which is a square root of 1 in $\mathbb{Z}_n$.

The entire algorithm, called Algorithm SEF, is presented in Fig. 16.2.

Now the analysis. From the discussion above, it is clear that Algorithm SEF either outputs "failure," or outputs a non-trivial factor of n. So we have the same three questions to answer as we did in the analysis of Algorithm SEDL:

1. What is the expected running time of Algorithm SEF?

2. How should the smoothness parameter y be chosen so as to minimize the expected running time?

3. What is the probability that Algorithm SEF outputs "failure"?

To answer the first question, let σ denote the probability that (the canonical representative of) a random element of $\mathbb{Z}_n^*$ is y-smooth. For $i = 1, \ldots, k + 2$, let X_i denote the number iterations of the inner loop of stage 1 in the ith iteration of the main loop; that is, X_i is the number of attempts made in finding the ith relation.

Lemma 16.4. *For $i = 1, \ldots, k + 2$, we have $\mathsf{E}[X_i] = \sigma^{-1}$.*

Proof. We first compute $\mathsf{E}[X_1]$. As δ is chosen uniformly from $\mathbb{Z}_n^*$ and independent of α_1, at each attempt to find a relation, $\alpha_1^2 \delta$ is uniformly distributed over $\mathbb{Z}_n^*$, and hence the probability that the attempt succeeds is precisely σ. This means $\mathsf{E}[X_1] = \sigma^{-1}$.

We next compute $\mathsf{E}[X_i]$ for $i > 1$. To this end, let us denote the cosets of $(\mathbb{Z}_n^*)^2$ by $\mathbb{Z}_n^*$ as $C_1, \ldots, C_t$. As it happens, $t = 2^w$, but this fact plays no role in the analysis. For $j = 1, \ldots, t$, let σ_j denote the probability that a random element of C_j is y-smooth, and let τ_j denote the probability that the final value of δ belongs to C_j.

We claim that for $j = 1, \ldots, t$, we have $\tau_j = \sigma_j \sigma^{-1} t^{-1}$. To see this, note that each coset C_j has the same number of elements, namely, $|\mathbb{Z}_n^*| t^{-1}$, and so the number of y-smooth elements in C_j is equal to $\sigma_j |\mathbb{Z}_n^*| t^{-1}$. Moreover, the final value of $\alpha_1^2 \delta$ is equally likely to be any one of the y-smooth numbers in $\mathbb{Z}_n^*$, of which there are $\sigma |\mathbb{Z}_n^*|$, and hence

$$\tau_j = \frac{\sigma_j |\mathbb{Z}_n^*| t^{-1}}{\sigma |\mathbb{Z}_n^*|} = \sigma_j \sigma^{-1} t^{-1},$$

which proves the claim.

Now, for a fixed value of δ and a random choice of $\alpha_i \in \mathbb{Z}_n^*$, one sees that $\alpha_i^2 \delta$ is uniformly distributed over the coset containing δ. Therefore, for $j = 1, \ldots, t$, we have

$$\mathsf{E}[X_i \mid \delta \in C_j] = \sigma_j^{-1}.$$

It follows that

$$\mathsf{E}[X_i] = \sum_{j=1}^{t} \mathsf{E}[X_i \mid \delta \in C_j] \cdot \mathsf{P}[\delta \in C_j]$$

$$= \sum_{j=1}^{t} \sigma_j^{-1} \cdot \tau_j = \sum_{j=1}^{t} \sigma_j^{-1} \cdot \sigma_j \sigma^{-1} t^{-1} = \sigma^{-1},$$

which proves the lemma. $\square$

So in stage 1, the expected number of attempts made in generating a single relation is σ^{-1}, each such attempt takes time $k \cdot \operatorname{len}(n)^{O(1)}$, and we have to generate $k + 2$ relations, leading to a total expected running time in stage 1 of $\sigma^{-1}k^2 \cdot \mathrm{len}(n)^{O(1)}$. Stage 2 is dominated by the cost of Gaussian elimination, which takes time $k^3 \cdot \mathrm{len}(n)^{O(1)}$. Thus, if T is the total running time of the algorithm, we have

$$\mathsf{E}[T] \le (\sigma^{-1}k^2 + k^3) \cdot \mathrm{len}(n)^{O(1)}.$$

By our assumption that n is not divisible by any primes up to y, all y-smooth integers up to $n-1$ are in fact relatively prime to n. Therefore, the number of y-smooth elements of $\mathbb{Z}_n^*$ is equal to $\Psi(y, n-1)$, and since n itself is not y-smooth, this is equal to $\Psi(y, n)$. From this, it follows that

$$\sigma = \Psi(y, n)/|\mathbb{Z}_n^*| \ge \Psi(y, n)/n.$$

The rest of the running time analysis is essentially the same as in the analysis of Algorithm SEDL; that is, assuming $y = \exp[(\log n)^{\lambda + o(1)}]$ for some constant $0 < \lambda < 1$, we obtain

$$\mathsf{E}[T] \le \exp[(1 + o(1)) \max\{(\log n/\log y) \log \log n + 2 \log y, \ 3 \log y\}]. \quad (16.8)$$

Setting $y = \exp[(1/\sqrt{2})(\log n \log \log n)^{1/2}]$, we obtain

$$\mathsf{E}[T] \le \exp[(2\sqrt{2} + o(1))(\log n \log \log n)^{1/2}].$$

That basically takes care of the first two questions. As for the third, we have:

Lemma 16.5. *The probability that the algorithm outputs "failure" is* $2^{-w+1} \le 1/2$.

Proof. Let ρ be the squaring map on $\mathbb{Z}_n^*$. By part (b) of Exercise 8.22, if we condition on any fixed values of $\delta, \alpha_1^2, \dots, \alpha_{k+2}^2$, as determined at the end of stage 1 of the algorithm, then in the resulting conditional probability distribution, the values $\alpha_1, \dots, \alpha_{k+2}$ are mutually independent, with each α_i uniformly distributed over $\rho^{-1}(\{\alpha_i^2\})$. Moreover, these fixed values of $\delta, \alpha_1^2, \dots, \alpha_{k+2}^2$ completely determine the behavior of the algorithm, and in particular, the values of $c_1, \dots, c_{k+2}$, α^2, and $e_1, \dots, e_{k+1}$. By part (d) of Exercise 8.22, it follows that α is uniformly distributed over $\rho^{-1}(\{\alpha^2\})$, and also that β is uniformly distributed over $\rho^{-1}(\{1\})$. Thus, in this conditional probability distribution, β is a random square root of 1, and so $\beta = \pm 1$ with probability 2^{-w+1}. Since this holds conditioned on all relevant choices of $\delta, \alpha_1^2, \dots, \alpha_{k+2}^2$, it also holds unconditionally. Finally, since we are assuming that $w > 1$, we have $2^{-w+1} \le 1/2$. $\square$

Let us summarize the above discussion in the following theorem.

Theorem 16.6. *With the smoothness parameter set as*

$$y := \exp[(1/\sqrt{2})(\log n \log \log n)^{1/2}],$$

the expected running time of Algorithm SEF is

$$\exp[(2\sqrt{2} + o(1))(\log n \log \log n)^{1/2}].$$

The probability that Algorithm SEF outputs "failure" is at most $1/2$.

EXERCISE 16.5. It is perhaps a bit depressing that after all that work, Algorithm SEF only succeeds (in the worst case) with probability $1/2$. Of course, to reduce the failure probability, we can simply repeat the entire computation—with ℓ repetitions, the failure probability drops to $2^{-\ell}$. However, there is a better way to reduce the failure probability. Suppose that in stage 1, instead of collecting $k + 2$ relations, we collect $k + 1 + \ell$ relations, where $\ell \geq 1$ is an integer parameter.

(a) Show that in stage 2, we can use Gaussian elimination over $\mathbb{Z}_2$ to find integer vectors

$$c^{(j)} = (c_1^{(j)}, \ldots, c_{k+1+\ell}^{(j)}) \in \{0, 1\}^{\times (k+1+\ell)} \quad (j = 1, \ldots, \ell)$$

such that

- over the field $\mathbb{Z}_2$, the images of the vectors $c^{(1)}, \ldots, c^{(\ell)}$ in $\mathbb{Z}_2^{\times (k+1+\ell)}$ are linearly independent, and
- for $j = 1, \ldots, \ell$, we have

$$c_1^{(j)} v_1 + \cdots + c_{k+1+\ell}^{(j)} v_{k+1+\ell} \in 2\mathbb{Z}^{\times (k+2)}.$$

(b) Show that given vectors $c^{(1)}, \ldots, c^{(\ell)}$ as in part (a), if for $j = 1, \ldots, \ell$, we set

$$(e_1^{(j)}, \ldots, e_{k+1}^{(j)}) \leftarrow c_1^{(j)} v_1 + \cdots + c_{k+1+\ell}^{(j)} v_{k+1+\ell},$$

$$\alpha^{(j)} \leftarrow \prod_{i=1}^{k+1+\ell} \alpha_i^{c_i^{(j)}},$$

and

$$\beta^{(j)} \leftarrow \pi_1^{e_1^{(j)}/2} \cdots \pi_k^{e_k^{(j)}/2} \delta^{-e_{k+1}^{(j)}/2} (\alpha^{(j)})^{-1},$$

then the values $\beta^{(1)}, \ldots, \beta^{(\ell)}$ are independent and uniformly distributed over the set of all square roots of 1 in $\mathbb{Z}_n$, and hence at least one of $\gcd(\mathrm{rep}(\beta^{(j)} - 1), n)$ splits n with probability at least $1 - 2^{-\ell}$.

So, for example, if we set $\ell = 20$, then the failure probability is reduced to less than one in a million, while the increase in running time over Algorithm SEF will hardly be noticeable.

16.4 Practical improvements

Our presentation and analysis of algorithms for discrete logarithms and factoring were geared towards simplicity and mathematical rigor. However, if one really wants to compute discrete logarithms or factor numbers, then a number of important practical improvements should be considered. In this section, we briefly sketch some of these improvements, focusing our attention on algorithms for factoring numbers (although some of the techniques apply to discrete logarithms as well).

16.4.1 Better smoothness density estimates

From an algorithmic point of view, the simplest way to improve the running times of both Algorithms SEDL and SEF is to use a more accurate smoothness density estimate, which dictates a different choice of the smoothness bound y in those algorithms, speeding them up significantly. While our Theorem 16.1 is a valid *lower bound* on the density of smooth numbers, it is not "tight," in the sense that the actual density of smooth numbers is somewhat higher. We quote from the literature the following result:

Theorem 16.7. *Let y be a function of x such that for some $\epsilon > 0$, we have*

$$y = \Omega((\log x)^{1+\epsilon}) \quad and \quad u := \frac{\log x}{\log y} \to \infty$$

as $x \to \infty$. Then

$$\Psi(y, x) = x \cdot \exp[(-1 + o(1))u \log u].$$

Proof. See §16.5. □

Let us apply this result to the analysis of Algorithm SEF. Assume that $y = \exp[(\log n)^{1/2 + o(1)}]$ —our choice of y will in fact be of this form. With this assumption, we have $\log \log y = (1/2 + o(1)) \log \log n$, and using Theorem 16.7, we can improve the inequality (16.8), obtaining instead (verify)

$$\mathsf{E}[T] \le \exp[(1 + o(1)) \max\{(1/2)(\log n / \log y) \log \log n + 2 \log y, 3 \log y\}].$$

From this, if we set

$$y := \exp[(1/2)(\log n \log \log n)^{1/2})],$$

we obtain

$$\mathsf{E}[T] \le \exp[(2 + o(1))(\log n \log \log n)^{1/2}].$$

An analogous improvement can be obtained for Algorithm SEDL.

Although this improvement reduces the constant $2\sqrt{2} \approx 2.828$ to 2, the constant is in the exponent, and so this improvement is not to be scoffed at!

16.4.2 The quadratic sieve algorithm

We now describe a practical improvement to Algorithm SEF. This algorithm, known as the **quadratic sieve**, is faster in practice than Algorithm SEF; however, its analysis is somewhat heuristic.

First, let us return to the simplified version of Algorithm SEF, where we collect relations of the form (16.6). Furthermore, instead of choosing the values α_i at random, we will choose them in a special way, as we now describe. Let

$$\tilde{n} := \lfloor \sqrt{n} \rfloor,$$

and define the polynomial

$$F := (\mathtt{X} + \tilde{n})^2 - n \in \mathbb{Z}[\mathtt{X}].$$

In addition to the usual "smoothness parameter" y, we need a "sieving parameter" z, whose choice will be discussed below. We shall assume that both y and z are of the form $\exp[(\log n)^{1/2+o(1)}]$, and our ultimate choices of y and z will indeed satisfy this assumption.

For all $s = 1, 2, \ldots, \lfloor z \rfloor$, we shall determine which values of s are "good," in the sense that the corresponding value $F(s)$ is y-smooth. For each good s, since we have $F(s) \equiv (s + \tilde{n})^2 \pmod{n}$, we obtain one relation of the form (16.6), with $\alpha_i := [s + \tilde{n}]_n$. If we find at least $k + 1$ good values of s, then we can apply Gaussian elimination as usual to find a square root β of 1 in $\mathbb{Z}_n$. Hopefully, we will have $\beta \ne \pm 1$, allowing us to split n.

Observe that for $1 \le s \le z$, we have

$$1 \le F(s) \le z^2 + 2zn^{1/2} \le n^{1/2+o(1)}.$$

Now, although the values $F(s)$ are not at all random, we might expect heuristically that the number of good s up to z is roughly equal to $\hat{\sigma}z$, where $\hat{\sigma}$ is the probability that a random integer in the interval $[1, n^{1/2}]$ is y-smooth, and by Theorem 16.7, we have

$$\hat{\sigma} = \exp[(-1/4 + o(1))(\log n / \log y) \log \log n].$$

If our heuristics are valid, this already gives us an improvement over Algorithm SEF, since now we are looking for y-smooth numbers near $n^{1/2}$, which are much more common than y-smooth numbers near n. But there is another improvement possible; namely, instead of testing each individual number $F(s)$ for smoothness using trial division, we can test them all at once using the following "sieving procedure":

> Create a vector $v[1 \ldots \lfloor z \rfloor]$, and initialize $v[s]$ to $F(s)$, for $1 \leq s \leq z$. For each prime p up to y, do the following:
>
> 1. Compute the roots of the polynomial F modulo p.
>
>   *This can be done quite efficiently, as follows. For $p = 2$, F has exactly one root modulo p, which is determined by the parity of $\tilde{n}$. For $p > 2$, we may use the familiar quadratic formula together with an algorithm for computing square roots modulo p, as discussed in Exercise 13.3. A quick calculation shows that the discriminant of F is n, and thus, F has a root modulo p if and only if n is a quadratic residue modulo p, in which case it will have two roots (under our usual assumptions, we cannot have $p \mid n$).*
>
> 2. Assume that the distinct roots of F modulo p lying in the interval $[1, p]$ are r_i, for $i = 1, \ldots, v_p$.
>
>   *Note that $v_p = 1$ for $p = 2$ and $v_p \in \{0, 2\}$ for $p > 2$. Also note that $F(s) \equiv 0 \pmod{p}$ if and only if $s \equiv r_i \pmod{p}$ for some $i = 1, \ldots, v_p$.*
>
>   For $i = 1, \ldots, v_p$, do the following:
>
> $$s \leftarrow r_i$$
> $$\text{while } s \leq z \text{ do}$$
> $$\quad \text{repeat} \quad v[s] \leftarrow v[s]/p \quad \text{until } p \nmid v[s]$$
> $$\quad s \leftarrow s + p$$

At the end of this sieving procedure, the good values of s may be identified as precisely those such that $v[s] = 1$. The running time of this sieving procedure is at most $\text{len}(n)^{O(1)}$ times

$$\sum_{p \leq y} \frac{z}{p} = z \sum_{p \leq y} \frac{1}{p} = O(z \log \log y) = z^{1+o(1)}.$$

Here, we have made use of Theorem 5.10, although this is not really necessary—for our purposes, the bound $\sum_{p \leq y}(1/p) = O(\log y)$ would suffice.

Note that this sieving procedure is a factor of $k^{1+o(1)}$ faster than the method for finding smooth numbers based on trial division. With just a little extra book-keeping, we can not only identify the good values of s, but we can also compute the factorization of $F(s)$ into primes.

Now, let us put together all the pieces. We have to choose z just large enough so as to find at least $k + 1$ good values of s up to z. So we should choose z so that $z \approx k/\hat{\sigma}$—in practice, we could choose an initial estimate for z, and if this choice of z does not yield enough relations, we could keep doubling z until we do get enough relations. Assuming that $z \approx k/\hat{\sigma}$, the cost of sieving is $(k/\hat{\sigma})^{1+o(1)}$, or

$$\exp[(1 + o(1))(1/4)(\log n / \log y) \log \log n + \log y].$$

The cost of Gaussian elimination is still $O(k^3)$, or

$$\exp[(3 + o(1)) \log y].$$

Thus, if T is the running time of the entire algorithm, we have

$$T \leq \exp[(1 + o(1)) \max\{(1/4)(\log n / \log y) \log \log n + \log y, \ 3 \log y\}].$$

Let $\mu := \log y$, $A := (1/4) \log n \log \log n$, $S_1 := A/\mu + \mu$ and $S_2 := 3\mu$, and let us find the value of μ that minimizes $\max\{S_1, S_2\}$. Using a little calculus, one finds that S_1 is minimized at $\mu = A^{1/2}$. For this value of μ, we have $S_1 = 2A^{1/2}$ and $S_2 = 3A^{1/2} > S_1$, and so this choice of μ is a bit larger than optimal. For $\mu < A^{1/2}$, S_1 is decreasing (as a function of μ), while S_2 is always increasing. It follows that the optimal value of μ is obtained by setting

$$A/\mu + \mu = 3\mu$$

and solving for μ. This yields $\mu = (A/2)^{1/2}$. So setting

$$y = \exp[(1/(2\sqrt{2}))(\log n \log \log n)^{1/2}],$$

we have

$$T \leq \exp[(3/(2\sqrt{2}) + o(1))(\log n \log \log n)^{1/2}].$$

Thus, we have reduced the constant in the exponent from 2, for Algorithm SEF (using the more accurate smoothness density estimates), to $3/(2\sqrt{2}) \approx 1.061$.

We mention one final improvement. The matrix to which we apply Gaussian elimination in stage 2 is "sparse"; indeed, since any integer less than n has $O(\log n)$ prime factors, the total number of non-zero entries in the matrix is $k^{1+o(1)}$. In this case, there are special algorithms for working with such sparse matrices, which allow us to perform stage 2 of the factoring algorithm in time $k^{2+o(1)}$, or

$$\exp[(2 + o(1)) \log y].$$

This gives us

$$T \leq \exp[(1 + o(1)) \max\{(1/4)(\log n/ \log y) \log \log n + \log y, \ 2 \log y\}],$$

and setting

$$y = \exp[(1/2)(\log n \log \log n)^{1/2}]$$

yields

$$T \leq \exp[(1 + o(1))(\log n \log \log n)^{1/2}].$$

Thus, this improvement reduces the constant in the exponent from $3/(2\sqrt{2}) \approx 1.061$ to 1. Moreover, the special algorithms designed to work with sparse matrices typically use much less space than ordinary Gaussian elimination—even if the input to Gaussian elimination is sparse, the intermediate matrices will not be. We shall discuss in detail later, in §19.4, one such algorithm for solving sparse systems of linear equations.

The quadratic sieve may fail to factor n, for one of two reasons: first, it may fail to find $k + 1$ relations; second, it may find these relations, but in stage 2, it only finds a trivial square root of 1. There is no rigorous theory to say why the algorithm should not fail for one of these two reasons, but experience shows that the algorithm does indeed work as expected.

16.5 Notes

Many of the algorithmic ideas in this chapter were first developed for the problem of factoring integers, and then later adapted to the discrete logarithm problem. The first (heuristic) subexponential-time algorithm for factoring integers, called the **continued fraction method** (not discussed here), was introduced by Lehmer and Powers [56], and later refined and implemented by Morrison and Brillhart [66]. The first rigorously analyzed subexponential-time algorithm for factoring integers was introduced by Dixon [34]. Algorithm SEF is a variation of Dixon's algorithm, which works the same way as Algorithm SEF, except that it generates relations of the form (16.6) directly (and indeed, it is possible to prove a variant of

Theorem 16.1, and for that matter, Theorem 16.7, for random squares modulo n). Algorithm SEF is based on an idea suggested by Rackoff (personal communication).

Theorem 16.7 was proved by Canfield, Erdős, and Pomerance [23]. The quadratic sieve was introduced by Pomerance [74]. Recall that the quadratic sieve has a heuristic running time of

$$\exp[(1 + o(1))(\log n \log \log n)^{1/2}].$$

This running time bound can also be achieved *rigorously* by a result of Lenstra and Pomerance [58], and to date, this is the best rigorous running time bound for factoring algorithms. We should stress, however, that most practitioners in this field are not so much interested in rigorous running time analyses as they are in actually factoring integers, and for such purposes, heuristic running time estimates are quite acceptable. Indeed, the quadratic sieve is much more practical than the algorithm in [58], which is mainly of theoretical interest.

There are two other factoring algorithms not discussed here, but that should anyway at least be mentioned. The first is the **elliptic curve method**, introduced by Lenstra [57]. Unlike all of the other known subexponential-time algorithms, the running time of this algorithm is sensitive to the sizes of the factors of n; in particular, if p is the smallest prime dividing n, the algorithm will find p (heuristically) in expected time

$$\exp[(\sqrt{2} + o(1))(\log p \log \log p)^{1/2}] \cdot \mathrm{len}(n)^{O(1)}.$$

This algorithm is quite practical, and is the method of choice when it is known (or suspected) that n has some small factors. It also has the advantage that it uses only polynomial space (unlike all of the other known subexponential-time factoring algorithms).

The second is the **number field sieve**, the basic idea of which was introduced by Pollard [73], and later generalized and refined by Buhler, Lenstra, and Pomerance [21], as well as by others. The number field sieve will split n (heuristically) in expected time

$$\exp[(c + o(1))(\log n)^{1/3}(\log \log n)^{2/3}],$$

where c is a constant (currently, the smallest value of c is 1.902, a result due to Coppersmith [27]). The number field sieve is currently the asymptotically fastest known factoring algorithm (at least, heuristically), and it is also practical, having been used to set the latest factoring record—the factorization of a 576-bit integer that is the product of two primes of about the

same size. See the web page `www.rsasecurity.com/rsalabs/challenges/`
`factoring/rsa576.html` for more details.

As for subexponential-time algorithms for discrete logarithms, Adleman [1] adapted the ideas used for factoring to the discrete logarithm problem, although it seems that some of the basic ideas were known much earlier. Algorithm SEDL is a variation on this algorithm, and the basic technique is usually referred to as the **index calculus method**. The basic idea of the number field sieve was adapted to the discrete logarithm problem by Gordon [40]; see also Adleman [2] and Schirokauer, Weber, and Denny [80].

For many more details and references for subexponential-time algorithms for factoring and discrete logarithms, see Chapter 6 of Crandall and Pomerance [30]. Also, see the web page `www.crypto-world.com/FactorWorld.`
`html` for links to research papers and implementation reports.

For more details regarding the security of signature schemes, as discussed following Exercise 16.4, see the paper by Bellare and Rogaway [13].

Last, but not least, we should mention the fact that there are in fact *polynomial-time* algorithms for factoring and discrete logarithms; however, these algorithms require special hardware, namely, a **quantum computer**. Shor [87, 88] showed that these problems could be solved in polynomial time on such a device; however, at the present time, it is unclear when and if such machines will ever be built. Much, indeed most, of modern-day cryptography will crumble if this happens, or if efficient "classical" algorithms for these problems are discovered (which is still a real possibility).

17

More rings

This chapter develops a number of other concepts concerning rings. These concepts will play important roles later in the text, and we prefer to discuss them now, so as to avoid too many interruptions of the flow of subsequent discussions.

17.1 Algebras

Let R be a ring. An R-**algebra** (or **algebra over** R) is a ring E, together with a ring homomorphism $\tau : R \to E$. Usually, the map τ will be clear from context, as in the following examples.

Example **17.1.** If E is a ring that contains R as a subring, then E is an R-algebra, where the associated map $\tau : R \to E$ is just the inclusion map. $\square$

Example **17.2.** Let $E_1, \ldots, E_n$ be R-algebras, with associated maps $\tau_i : R \to E_i$, for $i = 1, \ldots, n$. Then the direct product ring $E := E_1 \times \cdots \times E_n$ is naturally viewed as an R-algebra, via the map τ that sends $a \in R$ to $(\tau_1(a), \ldots, \tau_n(a)) \in E$. $\square$

Example **17.3.** Let E be an R-algebra, with associated map $\tau : R \to E$, and let I be an ideal of E. Consider the quotient ring E/I. If ρ is the natural map from E onto E/I, then the homomorphism $\rho \circ \tau$ makes E/I into an R-algebra, called the **quotient algebra of** E **modulo** I. $\square$

Example **17.4.** As a special case of the previous example, consider the ring $R[\mathrm{X}]$, viewed as an R-algebra via inclusion, and the ideal of R generated by f, where f is a monic polynomial. Then $R[\mathrm{X}]/(f)$ is naturally viewed as an R-algebra, via the map τ that sends $c \in R$ to $[c]_f \in R[\mathrm{X}]/(f)$. If $\deg(f) > 0$, then τ is an embedding of R in $R[X]/(f)$; if $\deg(f) = 0$, then $R[X]/(f)$ is the trivial ring, and τ maps everything to zero. $\square$

In some sense, an R-algebra is a generalization of the notion of an extension ring. When the map $\tau : R \to E$ is a canonical embedding, the language of R-algebras can be used if one wants to avoid the sloppiness involved in "identifying" elements of R with their image under τ in E, as we have done on occasion.

In this text, we will be particularly interested in the situation where E is an algebra over a field F. In this case, E either contains a copy of F, or is itself the trivial ring. To see this, let $\tau : F \to E$ be the associated map. Then since the kernel of τ is an ideal of F, it must either be $\{0_F\}$ or F. In the former case, τ is injective, and so E contains an isomorphic copy of F. In the latter case, our requirement that $\tau(1_F) = 1_E$ implies that $1_E = 0_E$, and so E is trivial.

Subalgebras

Let E be an R-algebra with associated map $\tau : R \to E$. A subset S of E is a **subalgebra** if S is a subring containing $\mathrm{img}(\tau)$. As an important special case, if τ is just the inclusion map, then a subring S of E is a subalgebra if and only if S contains R.

R-algebra homomorphisms

There is, of course, a natural notion of a homomorphism for R-algebras. Indeed, it is this notion that is our main motivation for introducing R-algebras in this text. If E and E' are R-algebras, with associated maps $\tau : R \to E$ and $\tau' : R \to E'$, then a map $\rho : E \to E'$ is called an R-**algebra homomorphism** if ρ is a ring homomorphism, and if for all $a \in R$, we have

$$\rho(\tau(a)) = \tau'(a).$$

As usual, if ρ is bijective, then it is called an R-**algebra isomorphism**, and if $R = R'$, it is called an R-**algebra automorphism**.

As an important special case, if τ and τ' are just inclusion maps, then a ring homomorphism $\rho : E \to E'$ is an R-algebra homomorphism if and only if the restriction of ρ to R is the identity map.

The reader should also verify the following facts. First, an R-algebra homomorphism maps subalgebras to subalgebras. Second, Theorems 9.22, 9.23, 9.24, 9.25, 9.26, and 9.27 carry over *mutatis mutandis* from rings to R-algebras.

Example 17.5. Since $\mathbb{C}$ contains $\mathbb{R}$ as a subring, we may naturally view $\mathbb{C}$ as an $\mathbb{R}$-algebra. The complex conjugation map on $\mathbb{C}$ that sends $a + bi$ to $a - bi$, for $a, b \in \mathbb{R}$, is an $\mathbb{R}$-algebra automorphism on $\mathbb{C}$ (see Example 9.5). $\square$

Example 17.6. Let p be a prime, and let F be the field $\mathbb{Z}_p$. If E is an F-algebra, with associated map $\tau : F \to E$, then the map $\rho : E \to E$ that sends $\alpha \in E$ to α^p is an F-algebra homomorphism. To see this, note that E is either trivial, or contains a copy of $\mathbb{Z}_p$. In the former case, there is nothing really to prove. In the latter case, E has characteristic p, and so the fact that ρ is a ring homomorphism follows from Example 9.42 (the "freshman's dream"); moreover, by Fermat's little theorem, for all $a \in F$, we have $\tau(a)^p = \tau(a^p) = \tau(a)$. $\square$

Polynomial evaluation

Let E be an R-algebra with associated map $\tau : R \to E$. Any polynomial $g \in R[\mathrm{X}]$ naturally defines a function on E: if $g = \sum_i g_i \mathrm{X}_i$, with each $g_i \in R$, and $\alpha \in E$, then

$$g(\alpha) := \sum_i \tau(g_i)\alpha^i.$$

For fixed $\alpha \in E$, the **polynomial evaluation map** $\rho : R[\mathrm{X}] \to E$ sends $g \in R[\mathrm{X}]$ to $g(\alpha) \in E$. It is easily verified that ρ is an R-algebra homomorphism (where we naturally view $R[\mathrm{X}]$ as an R-algebra via inclusion). The image of ρ is denoted $R[\alpha]$, and is a subalgebra of E. Indeed, $R[\alpha]$ is the smallest subalgebra of E containing α.

Note that if E contains R as a subring, then the notation $R[\alpha]$ has the same meaning as that introduced in Example 9.39.

We next state a very simple, but extremely useful, fact:

Theorem 17.1. *Let $\rho : E \to E'$ be an R-algebra homomorphism. Then for any $g \in R[\mathrm{X}]$ and $\alpha \in E$, we have*

$$\rho(g(\alpha)) = g(\rho(\alpha)).$$

Proof. Let $\tau : R \to E$ and $\tau' : R \to E'$ be the associated maps. Let

$g = \sum_i g_i \mathsf{X}^i \in R[\mathsf{X}]$. Then we have

$$\rho(g(\alpha)) = \rho(\sum_i \tau(g_i)\alpha^i) = \sum_i \rho(\tau(g_i)\alpha^i)$$

$$= \sum_i \rho(\tau(g_i))\rho(\alpha^i) = \sum_i \tau'(g_i)\rho(\alpha)^i$$

$$= g(\rho(\alpha)). \quad \square$$

As a special case of Theorem 17.1, if $E = R[\eta]$ for some $\eta \in E$, then every element of E can be expressed as $g(\eta)$ for some $g \in R[\mathsf{X}]$, and $\rho(g(\eta)) = g(\rho(\eta))$; hence, the action of ρ is completely determined by its action on η.

***Example* 17.7.** Let $E := R[\mathsf{X}]/(f)$ for some monic polynomial $f \in R[\mathsf{X}]$, so that $E = R[\eta]$, where $\eta := [\mathsf{X}]_f$, and let E' be any R-algebra.

Suppose that $\rho : E \to E'$ is an R-algebra homomorphism, and that $\eta' := \rho(\eta)$. The map ρ sends $g(\eta)$ to $g(\eta')$, for $g \in R[\mathsf{X}]$. Also, since $f(\eta) = 0_E$, we have $0_{E'} = \rho(f(\eta)) = f(\eta')$. Thus, η' must be a root of f.

Conversely, suppose that $\eta' \in E'$ is a root of f. Then the polynomial evaluation map from $R[\mathsf{X}]$ to E' that sends $g \in R[\mathsf{X}]$ to $g(\eta') \in E'$ is an R-algebra homomorphism whose kernel contains f, and this gives rise to the R-algebra homomorphism $\rho : E \to E'$ that sends $g(\eta)$ to $g(\eta')$, for $g \in R[\mathsf{X}]$. One sees that complex conjugation is just a special case of this construction (see Example 9.44). $\square$

R-algebras as R-modules

If E is an R-algebra, with associated map $\tau : R \to E$, we may naturally view E as an R-module, where we define a scalar multiplication operation as follows: for $a \in R$ and $\alpha \in E$, define

$$a \cdot \alpha := \tau(a)\alpha.$$

The reader may easily verify that with scalar multiplication so defined, E is an R-module.

Of course, if E is an algebra over a field F, then it is also a vector space over F.

EXERCISE 17.1. Show that any ring E may be viewed as a $\mathbb{Z}$-algebra.

EXERCISE 17.2. Show that the only $\mathbb{R}$-algebra homomorphisms from $\mathbb{C}$ into itself are the identity map and the complex conjugation map.

EXERCISE 17.3. Let E be an R-algebra, viewed as an R-module as discussed above.

(a) Show that for all $a \in R$ and $\alpha, \beta \in E$, we have $a \cdot (\alpha\beta) = (a \cdot \alpha)\beta$.

(b) Show that a subring S of E is a subalgebra if and only if it is also submodule.

(c) Show that if E' is another R-algebra, then a ring homomorphism $\rho : E \to E'$ is an R-algebra homomorphism if and only if it is an R-linear map.

EXERCISE 17.4. This exercise develops an alternative characterization of R-algebras. Let R be a ring, and let E be a ring, together with a scalar multiplication operation, that makes E into an R-module. Further suppose that for all $a \in R$ and $\alpha, \beta \in E$, we have $a(\alpha\beta) = (a\alpha)\beta$. Define the map $\tau : R \to E$ that sends $a \in R$ to $a \cdot 1_E \in E$. Show that τ is a ring homomorphism, so that E is an R-algebra, and also show that $\tau(a)\alpha = a\alpha$ for all $a \in R$ and $\alpha \in E$.

17.2 The field of fractions of an integral domain

Let D be any integral domain. Just as we can construct the field of rational numbers by forming fractions involving integers, we can construct a field consisting of fractions whose numerators and denominators are elements of D. This construction is quite straightforward, though a bit tedious.

To begin with, let S be the set of all pairs of the form (a, b), with $a, b \in D$ and $b \neq 0_D$. Intuitively, such a pair (a, b) is a "formal fraction," with numerator a and denominator b. We define a binary relation $\sim$ on S as follows: for $(a_1, b_1), (a_2, b_2) \in S$, we say $(a_1, b_1) \sim (a_2, b_2)$ if and only if $a_1 b_2 = a_2 b_1$. Our first task is to show that this is an equivalence relation:

Lemma 17.2. *For all $(a_1, b_1), (a_2, b_2), (a_3, b_3) \in S$, we have*

(i) $(a_1, b_1) \sim (a_1, b_1)$;

(ii) $(a_1, b_1) \sim (a_2, b_2)$ *implies* $(a_2, b_2) \sim (a_1, b_1)$;

(iii) $(a_1, b_1) \sim (a_2, b_2)$ *and* $(a_2, b_2) \sim (a_3, b_3)$ *implies* $(a_1, b_1) \sim (a_3, b_3)$.

Proof. (i) and (ii) are rather trivial, and we do not comment on these any further. As for (iii), assume that $a_1 b_2 = a_2 b_1$ and $a_2 b_3 = a_3 b_2$. Multiplying the first equation by b_3 we obtain $a_1 b_3 b_2 = a_2 b_3 b_1$ and substituting $a_3 b_2$ for $a_2 b_3$ on the right-hand side of this last equation, we obtain $a_1 b_3 b_2 = a_3 b_2 b_1$. Now, using the fact that b_2 is non-zero and that D is an integral domain, we may cancel b_2 from both sides, obtaining $a_1 b_3 = a_3 b_1$. $\square$

Since $\sim$ is an equivalence relation, it partitions S into equivalence classes, and for $(a, b) \in S$, we denote by $[a, b]$ the equivalence class containing (a, b), and we denote by K the collection of all such equivalence classes. Our next task is to define addition and multiplication operations on equivalence classes, mimicking the usual rules of arithmetic with fractions. We want to define the sum of $[a_1, b_1]$ and $[a_2, b_2]$ to be $[a_1 b_2 + a_2 b_1, b_1 b_2]$, and the product of $[a_1, b_1]$ and $[a_2, b_2]$ to be $[a_1 a_2, b_1 b_2]$. Note that since D is an integral domain, if b_1 and b_2 are non-zero, then so is the product $b_1 b_2$, and therefore $[a_1 b_2 + a_2 b_1, b_1 b_2]$ and $[a_1 a_2, b_1 b_2]$ are indeed equivalence classes. However, to ensure that this definition is unambiguous, and does not depend on the particular choice of representatives of the equivalence classes $[a_1, b_1]$ and $[a_2, b_2]$, we need the following lemma.

Lemma 17.3. *For* $(a_1, b_1), (a'_1, b'_1), (a_2, b_2), (a'_2, b'_2) \in S$ *with* $(a_1, b_1) \sim (a'_1, b'_1)$ *and* $(a_2, b_2) \sim (a'_2, b'_2)$, *we have*

$$(a_1 b_2 + a_2 b_1, b_1 b_2) \sim (a'_1 b'_2 + a'_2 b'_1, b'_1 b'_2)$$

and

$$(a_1 a_2, b_1 b_2) \sim (a'_1 a'_2, b'_1 b'_2).$$

Proof. This is a straightforward calculation. Assume that $a_1 b'_1 = a'_1 b_1$ and $a_2 b'_2 = a'_2 b_2$. Then we have

$$(a_1 b_2 + a_2 b_1) b'_1 b'_2 = a_1 b_2 b'_1 b'_2 + a_2 b_1 b'_1 b'_2 = a'_1 b_2 b_1 b'_2 + a'_2 b_1 b'_1 b_2$$
$$= (a'_1 b'_2 + a'_2 b'_1) b_1 b_2$$

and

$$a_1 a_2 b'_1 b'_2 = a'_1 a_2 b_1 b'_2 = a'_1 a'_2 b_1 b_2. \quad \square$$

In light of this lemma, we may unambiguously define addition and multiplication on K as follows: for $[a_1, b_1], [a_2, b_2] \in K$, we define

$$[a_1, b_1] + [a_2, b_2] := [a_1 b_2 + a_2 b_1, b_1 b_2]$$

and

$$[a_1, b_1] \cdot [a_2, b_2] := [a_1 a_2, b_1 b_2].$$

The next task is to show that K is a ring—we leave the details of this (which are quite straightforward) to the reader.

Lemma 17.4. *With addition and multiplication as defined above, K is a ring, with additive identity $[0_D, 1_D]$ and multiplicative identity $[1_D, 1_D]$.*

Proof. Exercise. □

Finally, we observe that K is in fact a field: it is clear that $[a, b]$ is a non-zero element of K if and only if $a \neq 0_D$, and hence any non-zero element $[a, b]$ of K has a multiplicative inverse, namely, $[b, a]$.

The field K is called the **field of fractions of** D. Consider the map $\tau : D \to K$ that sends $a \in D$ to $[a, 1_D] \in K$. It is easy to see that this map is a ring homomorphism, and one can also easily verify that it is injective. So, starting from D, we can synthesize "out of thin air" its field of fractions K, which essentially contains D as a subring, via the canonical embedding $\tau : D \to K$.

Now suppose that we are given a field L that contains D as a subring. Consider the set K' consisting of all elements in L of the form ab^{-1}, where $a, b \in D$ and $b \neq 0$—note that here, the arithmetic operations are performed using the rules for arithmetic in L. One may easily verify that K' is a subfield of L that contains D, and it is easy to see that this is the smallest subfield of L that contains D. The subfield K' of L may be referred to as the **field of fractions of** D **within** L. One may easily verify that the map $\rho : K \to L$ that sends $[a, b] \in K$ to $ab^{-1} \in L$ is an unambiguously defined ring homomorphism that maps K injectively onto K'; in particular, K is isomorphic as a ring to K'. It is in this sense that the field of fractions K is the smallest field containing D as a subring.

Somewhat more generally, suppose that L is a field, and that $\tau' : D \to L$ is an embedding. One may easily verify that the map $\rho : K \to L$ that sends $[a, b] \in K$ to $\tau'(a)\tau'(b)^{-1} \in L$ is an unambiguously defined, injective ring homomorphism. Moreover, we may view K and L as D-algebras, via the embeddings $\tau : D \to K$ and $\tau' : D \to L$, and the map ρ is seen to be a D-algebra homomorphism.

From now on, we shall simply write an element $[a, b]$ of K as a fraction, a/b. In this notation, the above rules for addition, multiplication, and testing equality in K now look quite familiar:

$$\frac{a_1}{b_1} + \frac{a_2}{b_2} = \frac{a_1 b_2 + a_2 b_1}{b_1 b_2}, \quad \frac{a_1}{b_1} \cdot \frac{a_2}{b_2} = \frac{a_1 a_2}{b_1 b_2}, \quad \text{and} \quad \frac{a_1}{b_1} = \frac{a_2}{b_2} \text{ iff } a_1 b_2 = a_2 b_1.$$

Observe that for $a, b \in D$, with $b \in 0_D$ and $b \mid a$, so that $a = bc$ for some $c \in D$, then the fraction $a/b \in K$ is equal to the fraction $c/1_D \in K$, and identifying the element $c \in D$ with its canonical image $c/1_D \in K$, we may simply write $c = a/b$. Note that this notation is consistent with that introduced in part (iii) of Theorem 9.4. A special case of this arises when $b \in D^*$, in which case $c = ab^{-1}$.

Function fields

An important special case of the above construction for the field of fractions of D is when $D = F[\mathbf{X}]$, where F is a field. In this case, the field of fractions is denoted $F(\mathbf{X})$, and is called the **field of rational functions (over F)**. This terminology is a bit unfortunate, since just as with polynomials, although the elements of $F(\mathbf{X})$ define functions, they are not (in general) in one-to-one correspondence with these functions.

Since $F[\mathbf{X}]$ is a subring of $F(\mathbf{X})$, and since F is a subring of $F[\mathbf{X}]$, we see that F is a subfield of $F(\mathbf{X})$.

More generally, we may apply the above construction to the ring $D = F[\mathbf{X}_1, \ldots, \mathbf{X}_n]$ of multi-variate polynomials over a field F, in which case the field of fractions is denoted $F(\mathbf{X}_1, \ldots, \mathbf{X}_n)$, and is also called the field of rational functions (over F, in the variables $\mathbf{X}_1, \ldots, \mathbf{X}_n$).

EXERCISE 17.5. Let F be a field of characteristic zero. Show that F contains an isomorphic copy of $\mathbb{Q}$.

EXERCISE 17.6. Show that the field of fractions of $\mathbb{Z}[i]$ within $\mathbb{C}$ is $\mathbb{Q}[i]$. (See Example 9.22 and Exercise 9.8.)

17.3 Unique factorization of polynomials

Throughout this section, F denotes a field.

Like the ring $\mathbb{Z}$, the ring $F[\mathbf{X}]$ of polynomials is an integral domain, and because of the division with remainder property for polynomials, $F[\mathbf{X}]$ has many other properties in common with $\mathbb{Z}$. Indeed, essentially all the ideas and results from Chapter 1 can be carried over almost verbatim from $\mathbb{Z}$ to $F[\mathbf{X}]$, and in this section, we shall do just that.

Recall that for $a, b \in F[\mathbf{X}]$, we write $b \mid a$ if $a = bc$ for some $c \in F[\mathbf{X}]$, and in this case, note that $\deg(a) = \deg(b) + \deg(c)$.

The units of $F[\mathbf{X}]$ are precisely the units F^* of F, that is, the non-zero constants. We call two polynomials $a, b \in F[\mathbf{X}]$ **associate** if $a = ub$ for $u \in F^*$. It is easy to see that a and b are associate if and only if $a \mid b$ and $b \mid a$—indeed, this follows as a special case of part (ii) of Theorem 9.4. Clearly, any non-zero polynomial a is associate to a unique monic polynomial (i.e., with leading coefficient 1), called the **monic associate** of a; indeed, the monic associate of a is $\mathrm{lc}(a)^{-1} \cdot a$.

We call a polynomial p **irreducible** if it is non-constant and all divisors of p are associate to 1 or p. Conversely, we call a polynomial n **reducible** if it is non-constant and is not irreducible. Equivalently, non-constant n is reducible if and only if there exist polynomials $a, b \in F[X]$ of degree strictly less that n such that $n = ab$.

Clearly, if a and b are associate polynomials, then a is irreducible if and only if b is irreducible.

The irreducible polynomials play a role similar to that of the prime numbers. Just as it is convenient to work with only positive prime numbers, it is also convenient to restrict attention to monic irreducible polynomials.

Corresponding to Theorem 1.3, every non-zero polynomial can be expressed as a unit times a product of monic irreducibles in an essentially unique way:

Theorem 17.5. *Every non-zero polynomial $n \in F[X]$ can be expressed as*

$$n = u \cdot p_1^{e_1} \cdots p_r^{e_r},$$

where $u \in F^*$, the p_i are distinct monic irreducible polynomials, and the e_i are positive integers. Moreover, this expression is unique, up to a reordering of the p_i.

To prove this theorem, we may assume that n is monic, since the non-monic case trivially reduces to the monic case.

The proof of the existence part of Theorem 17.5 is just as for Theorem 1.3. If n is 1 or a monic irreducible, we are done. Otherwise, there exist $a, b \in F[X]$ of degree strictly less than n such that $n = ab$, and again, we may assume that a and b are monic. By induction on degree, both a and b can be expressed as a product of monic irreducible polynomials, and hence, so can n.

The proof of the uniqueness part of Theorem 17.5 is almost identical to that of Theorem 1.3. As a special case of Theorem 9.12, we have the following division with remainder property, analogous to Theorem 1.4:

Theorem 17.6. *For $a, b \in F[X]$ with $b \neq 0$, there exist unique $q, r \in F[X]$ such that $a = bq + r$ and $\deg(r) < \deg(b)$.*

Analogous to Theorem 1.5, we have:

Theorem 17.7. *For any ideal $I \subseteq F[X]$, there exists a unique polynomial d such that $I = dF[X]$, where d is either zero or monic.*

Proof. We first prove the existence part of the theorem. If $I = \{0\}$, then $d = 0$ does the job, so let us assume that $I \neq \{0\}$. Let d be a monic polynomial of minimal degree in I. We want to show that $I = dF[X]$.

We first show that $I \subseteq dF[X]$. To this end, let c be any element in I. It suffices to show that $d \mid c$. Using Theorem 17.6, we may write $c = qd + r$, where $\deg(r) < \deg(d)$. Then by the closure properties of ideals, one sees that $r = c - qd$ is also an element of I, and by the minimality of the degree of d, we must have $r = 0$. Thus, $d \mid c$.

We next show that $dF[X] \subseteq I$. This follows immediately from the fact that $d \in I$ and the closure properties of ideals.

That proves the existence part of the theorem. As for uniqueness, note that if $dF[X] = d'F[X]$, we have $d \mid d'$ and $d' \mid d$, from which it follows that d and d' are associate, and so if d and d' are both either monic or zero, they must be equal. $\square$

For $a, b \in F[X]$, we call $d \in F[X]$ a **common divisor** of a and b if $d \mid a$ and $d \mid b$; moreover, we call such a d a **greatest common divisor** of a and b if d is monic or zero, and all other common divisors of a and b divide d. Analogous to Theorem 1.6, we have:

Theorem 17.8. *For any $a, b \in F[X]$, there exists a unique greatest common divisor d of a and b, and moreover, $aF[X] + bF[X] = dF[X]$.*

Proof. We apply the previous theorem to the ideal $I := aF[X] + bF[X]$. Let $d \in F[X]$ with $I = dF[X]$, as in that theorem. Note that $a, b, d \in I$ and d is monic or zero.

It is clear that d is a common divisor of a and b. Moreover, there exist $s, t \in F[X]$ such that $as + bt = d$. If $d' \mid a$ and $d' \mid b$, then clearly $d' \mid (as + bt)$, and hence $d' \mid d$.

Finally, for uniqueness, if d'' is a greatest common divisor of a and b, then $d \mid d''$ and $d'' \mid d$, and hence d'' is associate to d, and the requirement that d'' is monic or zero implies that $d'' = d$. $\square$

For $a, b \in F[X]$, we denote by $\gcd(a, b)$ the greatest common divisor of a and b. Note that as we have defined it, $\mathrm{lc}(a) \gcd(a, 0) = a$. Also note that when at least one of a or b are non-zero, $\gcd(a, b)$ is the unique monic polynomial of maximal degree that divides both a and b.

An immediate consequence of Theorem 17.8 is that for all $a, b \in F[X]$, there exist $s, t \in F[X]$ such that $as + bt = \gcd(a, b)$, and that when at least one of a or b are non-zero, $\gcd(a, b)$ is the unique monic polynomial of minimal degree that can be expressed as $as + bt$ for some $s, t \in F[X]$.

We say that $a, b \in F[X]$ are **relatively prime** if $\gcd(a, b) = 1$, which is the same as saying that the only common divisors of a and b are units. It is immediate from Theorem 17.8 that a and b are relatively prime if and only if $aF[X] + bF[X] = F[X]$, which holds if and only if there exist $s, t \in F[X]$ such that $as + bt = 1$.

Analogous to Theorem 1.7, we have:

Theorem 17.9. *For $a, b, c \in F[X]$ such that $c \mid ab$ and $\gcd(a, c) = 1$, we have $c \mid b$.*

Proof. Suppose that $c \mid ab$ and $\gcd(a, c) = 1$. Then since $\gcd(a, c) = 1$, by Theorem 17.8 we have $as + ct = 1$ for some $s, t \in F[X]$. Multiplying this equation by b, we obtain $abs + cbt = b$. Since c divides ab by hypothesis, it follows that $c \mid (abs + cbt)$, and hence $c \mid b$. $\square$

Analogous to Theorem 1.8, we have:

Theorem 17.10. *Let $p \in F[X]$ be irreducible, and let $a, b \in F[X]$. Then $p \mid ab$ implies that $p \mid a$ or $p \mid b$.*

Proof. Assume that $p \mid ab$. The only divisors of p are associate to 1 or p. Thus, $\gcd(p, a)$ is either 1 or the monic associate of p. If $p \mid a$, we are done; otherwise, if $p \nmid a$, we must have $\gcd(p, a) = 1$, and by the previous theorem, we conclude that $p \mid b$. $\square$

Now to prove the uniqueness part of Theorem 17.5. Suppose we have

$$p_1 \cdots p_r = p'_1 \cdots p'_s,$$

where $p_1, \ldots, p_r$ and $p'_1, \ldots, p'_s$ are monic irreducible polynomials (duplicates are allowed among the p_i and among the p'_j). If $r = 0$, we must have $s = 0$ and we are done. Otherwise, as p_1 divides the right-hand side, by inductively applying Theorem 17.10, one sees that p_1 is equal to p'_j for some j. We can cancel these terms and proceed inductively (on r).

That completes the proof of Theorem 17.5.

Analogous to Theorem 1.9, we have:

Theorem 17.11. *There are infinitely many monic irreducible polynomials in $F[X]$.*

If F is infinite, then this theorem is true simply because there are infinitely many monic, linear polynomials; in any case, one can also just prove this theorem by mimicking the proof of Theorem 1.9 (verify).

For a monic irreducible polynomial p, we may define the function ν_p, mapping non-zero polynomials to non-negative integers, as follows: for polynomial $n \neq 0$, if $n = p^e m$, where $p \nmid m$, then $\nu_p(n) := e$. We may then write the factorization of n into irreducibles as

$$n = u \prod_p p^{\nu_p(n)},$$

where the product is over all monic irreducible polynomials p, with all but finitely many of the terms in the product equal to 1.

Just as for integers, we may extend the domain of definition of ν_p to include 0, defining $\nu_p(0) := \infty$. For all polynomials a, b, we have

$$\nu_p(a \cdot b) = \nu_p(a) + \nu_p(b) \quad \text{for all } p. \tag{17.1}$$

From this, it follows that for all polynomials a, b, we have

$$b \mid a \quad \text{if and only if} \quad \nu_p(b) \leq \nu_p(a) \text{ for all } p, \tag{17.2}$$

and

$$\nu_p(\gcd(a, b)) = \min(\nu_p(a), \nu_p(b)) \quad \text{for all } p. \tag{17.3}$$

For $a, b \in F[X]$ a **common multiple** of a and b is a polynomial m such that $a \mid m$ and $b \mid m$; moreover, such an m is the **least common multiple** of a and b if m is monic or zero, and m divides all common multiples of a and b. In light of Theorem 17.5, it is clear that the least common multiple exists and is unique, and we denote the least common multiple of a and b by $\text{lcm}(a, b)$. Note that as we have defined it, $\text{lcm}(a, 0) = 0$, and that when both a and b are non-zero, $\text{lcm}(a, b)$ is the unique monic polynomial of minimal degree that is divisible by both a and b. Also, for all $a, b \in F[X]$, we have

$$\nu_p(\text{lcm}(a, b)) = \max(\nu_p(a), \nu_p(b)) \quad \text{for all } p, \tag{17.4}$$

and

$$\text{lc}(ab) \cdot \gcd(a, b) \cdot \text{lcm}(a, b) = ab. \tag{17.5}$$

Just as in §1.3, the notions of greatest common divisor and least common multiple generalize naturally from two to any number of polynomials. We also say that polynomials $a_1, \ldots, a_k \in F[X]$ are **pairwise relatively prime** if $\gcd(a_i, a_j) = 1$ for all i, j with $i \neq j$.

Also just as in §1.3, any rational function $a/b \in F(X)$ can be expressed as a fraction a'/b' in **lowest terms**, that is, $a/b = a'/b'$ and $\gcd(a', b') = 1$, and this representation is unique up to multiplication by units.

Many of the exercises in Chapter 1 carry over naturally to polynomials — the reader is encouraged to look over all of the exercises in that chapter, determining which have natural polynomial analogs, and work some of these out.

EXERCISE 17.7. Show that for $f \in F[X]$ of degree 2 or 3, we have f irreducible if and only if f has no roots in F.

17.4 Polynomial congruences

Throughout this section, F denotes a field.

Specializing the congruence notation introduced in §9.3 for arbitrary rings to the ring $F[X]$, for polynomials $a, b, n \in F[X]$, we write $a \equiv b \pmod{n}$ when $n \mid (a - b)$. Because of the division with remainder property for polynomials, we have the analog of Theorem 2.1:

Theorem 17.12. *Let* $n \in F[X]$ *be a non-zero polynomial. For every* $a \in F[X]$, *there exists a unique* $b \in F[X]$ *such that* $a \equiv b \pmod{n}$ *and* $\deg(b) < n$, *namely,* $b := a \bmod n$.

For a non-zero $n \in F[X]$, and $a \in F[X]$, we say that $a' \in F[X]$ is a **multiplicative inverse of** a **modulo** n if $aa' \equiv 1 \pmod{n}$.

All of the results we proved in §2.2 for solving linear congruences over the integers carry over almost identically to polynomials. As such, we do not give proofs of any of the results here. The reader may simply check that the proofs of the corresponding results translate almost directly.

Theorem 17.13. *Let* $a, n \in F[X]$ *with* $n \neq 0$. *Then* a *has a multiplicative inverse modulo* n *if and only if* a *and* n *are relatively prime.*

Theorem 17.14. *Let* $a, n, z, z' \in F[X]$ *with* $n \neq 0$. *If* a *is relatively prime to* n, *then* $az \equiv az' \pmod{n}$ *if and only if* $z \equiv z' \pmod{n}$. *More generally, if* $d := \gcd(a, n)$, *then* $az \equiv az' \pmod{n}$ *if and only if* $z \equiv z' \pmod{n/d}$.

Theorem 17.15. *Let* $a, b, n \in F[X]$ *with* $n \neq 0$. *If* a *is relatively prime to* n, *then the congruence* $az \equiv b \pmod{n}$ *has a solution* z; *moreover, any polynomial* z' *is a solution if and only if* $z \equiv z' \pmod{n}$.

As for integers, this theorem allows us to generalize the "mod" operation as follows: if $n \in F[X]$ is a non-zero polynomial, and $s \in F(X)$ is a rational function of the form b/a, where $a, b \in F[X]$, $a \neq 0$, and $\gcd(a, n) = 1$, then $s \bmod n$ denotes the unique polynomial z satisfying

$$az \equiv b \pmod{n} \quad \text{and} \quad \deg(z) < \deg(n).$$

With this notation, we can simply write $a^{-1} \bmod n$ to denote the unique multiplicative inverse of a modulo n with $\deg(a) < \deg(n)$.

Theorem 17.16. *Let* $a, b, n \in F[X]$ *with* $n \neq 0$, *and let* $d := \gcd(a, n)$. *If* $d \mid b$, *then the congruence* $az \equiv b \pmod{n}$ *has a solution* z, *and any polynomial* z' *is also a solution if and only if* $z \equiv z' \pmod{n/d}$. *If* $d \nmid b$, *then the congruence* $az \equiv b \pmod{n}$ *has no solution* z.

Theorem 17.17 (Chinese remainder theorem). *Let $n_1, \ldots, n_k \in F[X]$ be pairwise relatively prime, non-zero polynomials, and let $a_1, \ldots, a_k \in F[X]$ be arbitrary polynomials. Then there exists a polynomial $z \in F[X]$ such that*

$$z \equiv a_i \pmod{n_i} \quad (i = 1, \ldots, k).$$

Moreover, any other polynomial $z' \in F[X]$ is also a solution of these congruences if and only if $z \equiv z' \pmod{n}$, where $n := \prod_{i=1}^{k} n_i$.

Note that the Chinese remainder theorem (with Theorem 17.12) implies that there exists a unique solution $z \in F[X]$ to the given congruences with $\deg(z) < \deg(n)$.

The Chinese remainder theorem also has a more algebraic interpretation. Define quotient rings $E_i := F[X]/(n_i)$ for $i = 1, \ldots, k$, which we may naturally view as F-algebras (see Example 17.4), along with the product F-algebra $E := E_1 \times \cdots \times E_k$ (see Example 17.2). The map ρ from $F[X]$ to E that sends $z \in F[X]$ to $([z]_{n_1}, \ldots, [z]_{n_k}) \in E$ is an F-algebra homomorphism. The Chinese remainder theorem says that ρ is surjective, and that the kernel of ρ is the ideal of $F[X]$ generated by n, giving rise to an F-algebra isomorphism of $F[X]/(n)$ with E.

Let us recall the formula for the solution z (see proof of Theorem 2.8). We have

$$z := \sum_{i=1}^{k} w_i a_i,$$

where

$$w_i := n_i' m_i, \quad n_i' := n/n_i, \quad m_i := (n_i')^{-1} \bmod n_i \quad (i = 1, \ldots, k).$$

Now, let us consider the special case of the Chinese remainder theorem where $a_i \in F$ and $n_i = (X - b_i)$ with $b_i \in F$, for $i = 1, \ldots, k$. The condition that the n_i are pairwise relatively prime is equivalent to the condition that the b_i are all distinct. A polynomial z satisfies the system of congruences if and only if $z(b_i) = a_i$ for $i = 1, \ldots, k$. Moreover, we have $n_i' = \prod_{j \neq i}(X - b_j)$, and $m_i = 1/\prod_{j \neq i}(b_i - b_j) \in F$. So we get

$$z = \sum_{i=1}^{k} a_i \frac{\prod_{j \neq i}(X - b_j)}{\prod_{j \neq i}(b_i - b_j)}.$$

The reader will recognize this as the usual **Lagrange interpolation formula**. Thus, the Chinese remainder theorem for polynomials includes Lagrange interpolation as a special case.

Let us consider this situation from the point of view of vector spaces. Consider the map $\sigma : F[X]_{<k} \to F^{\times k}$ that sends $z \in F[X]$ of degree less than k to $(z(b_1), \ldots, z(b_k)) \in F^{\times k}$, where as above, $b_1, \ldots, b_k$ are distinct elements of F. We see that σ is an F-linear map, and by the Chinese remainder theorem, it is bijective. Thus, σ is an F-vector space isomorphism of $F[X]_{<k}$ with $F^{\times k}$.

We may encode elements of $F[X]_{<k}$ as row vectors in a natural way, encoding the polynomial $z = \sum_{i=0}^{k-1} z_i X^i$ as the row vector $(z_0, \ldots, z_{k-1}) \in F^{1 \times k}$. With this encoding, we have

$$\sigma(z) = (z_0, \ldots, z_{k-1})V,$$

where V is the $k \times k$ matrix

$$V := \begin{pmatrix} 1 & 1 & & 1 \\ b_1 & b_2 & & b_k \\ \vdots & \vdots & \cdots & \vdots \\ b_1^{k-1} & b_2^{k-1} & \cdots & b_k^{k-1} \end{pmatrix}.$$

The matrix V (well, actually its transpose) is known as a **Vandermonde matrix**. Because σ is an isomorphism, it follows that the matrix V is invertible.

More generally, consider any fixed elements $b_1, \ldots, b_\ell$ of F, where $\ell \leq k$, and consider the F-linear map $\sigma : F[X]_{<k} \to F^{\times \ell}$ that sends $z \in F[X]_{<k}$ to $(z(b_1), \ldots, z(b_\ell))$. If $z = \sum_{i=0}^{k-1} z_i X^i$, then

$$\sigma(z) = (z_0, \ldots, z_{k-1})W,$$

where W is the $k \times \ell$ matrix

$$W := \begin{pmatrix} 1 & 1 & & 1 \\ b_1 & b_2 & & b_\ell \\ \vdots & \vdots & \cdots & \vdots \\ b_1^{k-1} & b_2^{k-1} & \cdots & b_\ell^{k-1} \end{pmatrix}.$$

Now, if $b_i = b_j$ for some $i \neq j$, then the columns of W are linearly dependent, and hence the column rank of W is less than ℓ. Since the column rank of W is equal to its row rank, the dimension of the row space of W is less than ℓ, and hence, σ is not surjective. Conversely, if the b_i are all distinct, then since the submatrix of W consisting of its first ℓ rows is an invertible Vandermonde matrix, we see that the rank of W is equal to ℓ, and hence σ is surjective.

17.5 Polynomial quotient algebras

Throughout this section, F denotes a field.

Let $f \in F[X]$ be a monic polynomial, and consider the quotient ring $E := F[X]/(f)$. As discussed in Example 17.4, we may naturally view E as an F-algebra via the map τ that sends $c \in R$ to $[c]_f \in E$. Moreover, if $\deg(f) > 0$, then τ is an embedding of F in $F[X]/(f)$, and otherwise, if $f = 1$, then E is the trivial ring, and τ maps everything to zero.

Suppose that $\ell := \deg(f) > 0$. Let $\eta := [X]_f \in E$. Then $E = F[\eta]$, and as an F-vector space, E has dimension ℓ, with $1, \eta, \ldots, \eta^{\ell-1}$ being a basis (see Examples 9.34, 9.43, 14.3, and 14.22). That is, every element of E can be expressed uniquely as $g(\eta)$ for $g \in F[X]$ of degree less than ℓ.

Now, if f is irreducible, then every polynomial $a \not\equiv 0 \pmod{f}$ is relatively prime to f, and hence invertible modulo f; therefore, it follows that E is a field. Conversely, if f is not irreducible, then E cannot be a field—indeed, if g is a non-trivial factor of f, then $g(\eta)$ is a zero divisor.

If $F = \mathbb{Z}_p$ for a prime number p, and f is irreducible, then we see that E is a finite field of cardinality p^ℓ. In the next chapter, we shall see how one can perform arithmetic in such fields efficiently, and later, we shall also see how to efficiently construct irreducible polynomials of any given degree over a finite field.

Minimal polynomials. Now suppose that E is any F-algebra, and let α be an element of E. Consider the polynomial evaluation map $\rho : F[X] \to E$ that sends $g \in F[X]$ to $g(\alpha)$. The kernel of ρ is an ideal of $F[X]$, and since every ideal of $F[X]$ is principal, it follows that there exists a polynomial $\phi \in F[X]$ such that $\ker(\rho)$ is the ideal of $F[X]$ generated by ϕ; moreover, we can make the choice of ϕ unique by insisting that it is monic or zero. The polynomial ϕ is called the **minimal polynomial of** α **(over** F**)**. If $\phi = 0$, then ρ is injective, and hence the image $F[\alpha]$ of ρ is isomorphic (as an F-algebra) to $F[X]$. Otherwise, $F[\alpha]$ is isomorphic (as an F-algebra) to $F[X]/(\phi)$; moreover, since any polynomial that is zero at α is a polynomial multiple of ϕ, we see that ϕ is the unique monic polynomial of smallest degree that is zero at α.

If E has finite dimension, say n, as an F-vector space, then any element α of E has a non-zero minimal polynomial. Indeed, the elements $1_E, \alpha, \ldots, \alpha^n$ must be linearly dependent (as must be any $n + 1$ vectors in a vector space of dimension n), and hence there exist $c_0, \ldots, c_n \in F$, not all zero, such that

$$c_0 1_E + c_1 \alpha + \cdots + c_n \alpha^n = 0_E,$$

and therefore, the non-zero polynomial $g := \sum_i c_i X^i$ is zero at α.

***Example* 17.8.** The polynomial $X^2 + 1$ is irreducible over $\mathbb{R}$, since if it were not, it would have a root in $\mathbb{R}$ (see Exercise 17.7), which is clearly impossible, since -1 is not the square of any real number. It follows immediately that $\mathbb{C} = \mathbb{R}[X]/(X^2 + 1)$ is a field, without having to explicitly calculate a formula for the inverse of a non-zero complex number. $\square$

***Example* 17.9.** Consider the polynomial $f := X^4 + X^3 + 1$ over $\mathbb{Z}_2$. We claim that f is irreducible. It suffices to show that f has no irreducible factors of degree 1 or 2.

If f had a factor of degree 1, then it would have a root; however, $f(0) = 0 + 0 + 1 = 1$ and $f(1) = 1 + 1 + 1 = 1$. So f has no factors of degree 1.

Does f have a factor of degree 2? The polynomials of degree 2 are X^2, $X^2 + X$, $X^2 + 1$, and $X^2 + X + 1$. The first and second of these polynomials are divisible by X, and hence not irreducible, while the third has a 1 as a root, and hence is also not irreducible. The last polynomial, $X^2 + X + 1$, has no roots, and hence is the only irreducible polynomial of degree 2 over $\mathbb{Z}_2$. So now we may conclude that if f were not irreducible, it would have to be equal to

$$(X^2 + X + 1)^2 = X^4 + 2X^3 + 3X^2 + 2X + 1 = X^4 + X^2 + 1,$$

which it is not.

Thus, $E := \mathbb{Z}_2[X]/(f)$ is a field with $2^4 = 16$ elements. We may think of elements E as bit strings of length 4, where the rule for addition is bit-wise "exclusive-or." The rule for multiplication is more complicated: to multiply two given bit strings, we interpret the bits as coefficients of polynomials (with the left-most bit the coefficient of X^3), multiply the polynomials, reduce the product modulo f, and write down the bit string corresponding to the reduced product polynomial. For example, to multiply 1001 and 0011, we compute

$$(X^3 + 1)(X + 1) = X^4 + X^3 + X + 1,$$

and

$$(X^4 + X^3 + X + 1) \bmod (X^4 + X^3 + 1) = X.$$

Hence, the product of 1001 and 0011 is 0010.

Theorem 9.16 says that E^* is a cyclic group. Indeed, the element $\eta := 0010$ (i.e., $\eta = [X]_f$) is a generator for E^*, as the following table of powers shows:

i	η^i	i	η^i
1	0010	8	1110
2	0100	9	0101
3	1000	10	1010
4	1001	11	1101
5	1011	12	0011
6	1111	13	0110
7	0111	14	1100
		15	0001

Such a table of powers is sometimes useful for computations in small finite fields such as this one. Given $\alpha, \beta \in E^*$, we can compute $\alpha\beta$ by obtaining (by table lookup) i, j such that $\alpha = \eta^i$ and $\beta = \eta^j$, computing $k := (i + j) \bmod 15$, and then obtaining $\alpha\beta = \eta^k$ (again by table lookup). $\square$

EXERCISE 17.8. In the field E is Example 17.9, what is the minimal polynomial of 1011 over $\mathbb{Z}_2$?

EXERCISE 17.9. Show that if the factorization of f over $F[\text{X}]$ into irreducibles is as $f = f_1^{e_1} \cdots f_r^{e_r}$, and if $\alpha = [h]_f \in F[\text{X}]/(f)$, then the minimal polynomial ϕ of α over F is $\mathrm{lcm}(\phi_1, \ldots, \phi_r)$, where each ϕ_i is the minimal polynomial of $[h]_{f_i^{e_i}} \in F[\text{X}]/(f_i^{e_i})$ over F.

17.6 General properties of extension fields

We now discuss a few general notions related to extension fields. These are all quite simple applications of the theory developed so far. Recall that if F and E are fields, with F being a subring of E, then E is called an extension field of F. As usual, we shall blur the distinction between a subring and a canonical embedding; that is, if $\tau : F \to E$ is an canonical embedding, we shall simply identify elements of F with their images in E under τ, and in so doing, we may view E as an extension field of F. Usually, the map τ will be clear from context; for example, if $E = F[\text{X}]/(\phi)$ for some irreducible polynomial $\phi \in F[\text{X}]$, then we shall simply say that E is an extension field of F, although strictly speaking, F is embedded in E via the map that sends $a \in F$ to $[a]_\phi \in E$.

Let E be an extension field of a field F. Then E is an F-algebra, and in particular, an F-vector space. If E is a finite dimensional F-vector space, then we say that E is a **finite extension of** F, and $\dim_F(E)$ is called the

degree of the extension, and is denoted $(E : F)$; otherwise, we say that E is an **infinite extension of** F.

An element $\alpha \in E$ is called **algebraic over** F if there exists a non-zero polynomial $f \in F[X]$ such that $f(\alpha) = 0$; otherwise, α is called **transcendental over** F. If all elements of E are algebraic over F, then we call E an **algebraic extension of** F. From the discussion on minimal polynomials in §17.5, we may immediately state:

Theorem 17.18. *If E is a finite extension of F, then E is also an algebraic extension of F.*

Suppose $\alpha \in E$ is algebraic over F. Let ϕ be its minimal polynomial, so that $F[X]/(\phi)$ is isomorphic (as an F-algebra) to $F[\alpha]$. Since $F[\alpha]$ is a subring of a field, it must be an integral domain, which implies that ϕ is irreducible, which in turn implies that $F[\alpha]$ is a subfield of E. Moreover, the degree $(F[\alpha] : F)$ is equal to the degree of ϕ, and this number is called the **degree of** α **(over** F**)**. It is clear that if E is finite dimensional, then the degree of α is at most $(E : F)$.

Suppose that $\alpha \in E$ is transcendental over F. Consider the "rational function evaluation map" that sends $f/g \in F(X)$ to $f(\alpha)/g(\alpha) \in E$. Since no non-zero polynomial over F vanishes at α, it is easy to see that this map is well defined, and is in fact an injective F-algebra homomorphism from $F(X)$ into E. The image is denoted $F(\alpha)$, and this is clearly a subfield of E containing F and α, and it is plain to see that it is the smallest such subfield. It is also clear that $F(\alpha)$ has infinite dimension over F, since it contains an isomorphic copy of the infinite dimensional vector space $F[X]$.

More generally, for any $\alpha \in E$, algebraic or transcendental, we can define $F(\alpha)$ to be the set consisting of all elements of the form $f(\alpha)/g(\alpha) \in E$, where $f, g \in F[X]$ and $g(\alpha) \neq 0$. It is clear that $F(\alpha)$ is a field, and indeed, it is the smallest subfield of E containing F and α. If α is algebraic, then $F(\alpha) = F[\alpha]$, and is isomorphic (as an F-algebra) to $F[X]/(\phi)$, where ϕ is the minimal polynomial of α over F; otherwise, if α is transcendental, then $F(\alpha)$ is isomorphic (as an F-algebra) to the rational function field $F(X)$.

Example **17.10.** If $f \in F[X]$ is monic and irreducible, $E = F[X]/(f)$, and $\eta := [X]_f \in E$, then η is algebraic over F, its minimal polynomial over F is f, and its degree over F is equal to $\deg(f)$. Also, we have $E = F[\eta]$, and any element $\alpha \in E$ is algebraic of degree at most $\deg(f)$. $\square$

EXERCISE 17.10. In the field E is Example 17.9, find all the elements of degree 2 over $\mathbb{Z}_2$.

EXERCISE 17.11. Show that if E is a finite extension of F, with a basis $\alpha_1, \ldots, \alpha_n$ over F, and K is a finite extension of E, with a basis $\beta_1, \ldots, \beta_m$ over E, then

$$\alpha_i \beta_j \quad (i = 1, \ldots, n; \ j = 1, \ldots, m)$$

is a basis for K over F, and hence K is a finite extension of F and

$$(K : F) = (K : E)(E : F).$$

EXERCISE 17.12. Show that if E is an algebraic extension of F, and K is an algebraic extension of E, then K is an algebraic extension of F.

EXERCISE 17.13. Let E be an extension of F. Show that the set of all elements in E that are algebraic over F is a subfield of E containing F.

We close this section with a discussion of a **splitting field** — a finite extension of the coefficient field in which a given polynomial splits completely into linear factors. As the next theorem shows, splitting fields always exist.

Theorem 17.19. *Let F be a field, and $f \in F[X]$ a monic polynomial of degree ℓ. Then there exists a finite extension K of F in which f factors as*

$$f = (X - \alpha_1)(X - \alpha_2) \cdots (X - \alpha_\ell),$$

with $\alpha_1, \ldots, \alpha_\ell \in K$.

Proof. We prove the existence of K by induction on the degree ℓ of f. If $\ell = 0$, then the theorem is trivially true. Otherwise, let g be an irreducible factor of f, and set $E := F[X]/(g)$, so that $\alpha := [X]_g$ is a root of g, and hence of f, in E. So over the extension field E, f factors as

$$f = (X - \alpha)h,$$

where $h \in E[X]$ is a polynomial of degree $\ell - 1$. Applying the induction hypothesis, there exists a finite extension K of E such that h splits into linear factors over K. Thus, over K, f splits into linear factors, and by Exercise 17.11, K is a finite extension of F. $\square$

17.7 Formal power series and Laurent series

We discuss generalizations of polynomials that allow an infinite number of non-zero coefficients. Although we are mainly interested in the case where the coefficients come from a field F, we develop the basic theory for general rings R.

17.7.1 Formal power series

The ring $R[\![X]\!]$ of **formal power series over** R consists of all formal expressions of the form

$$a = a_0 + a_1X + a_2X^2 + \cdots,$$

where $a_0, a_1, a_2, \ldots \in R$. Unlike ordinary polynomials, we allow an infinite number of non-zero coefficients. We may write such a formal power series as

$$a = \sum_{i=0}^{\infty} a_iX^i.$$

The rules for addition and multiplication of formal power series are *exactly* the same as for polynomials. Indeed, the formulas (9.1) and (9.2) in §9.2 for addition and multiplication may be applied directly—all of the relevant sums are finite, and so everything is well defined.

We shall not attempt to interpret a formal power series as a function, and therefore, "convergence" issues shall simply not arise.

Clearly, $R[\![X]\!]$ contains $R[X]$ as a subring. Let us consider the group of units of $R[\![X]\!]$.

Theorem 17.20. *Let* $a = \sum_{i=0}^{\infty} a_iX^i \in R[\![X]\!]$. *Then* $a \in (R[\![X]\!])^*$ *if and only if* $a_0 \in R^*$.

Proof. If a_0 is not a unit, then it is clear that a is not a unit, since the constant term of a product formal power series is equal to the product of the constant terms.

Conversely, if a_0 is a unit, we show how to define the coefficients of the inverse $b = \sum_{i=0}^{\infty} b_iX^i$ of a. Let $ab = c = \sum_{i=0}^{\infty} c_iX^i$. We want $c = 1$, meaning that $c_0 = 1$ and $c_i = 0$ for all $i > 0$. Now, $c_0 = a_0b_0$, so we set $b_0 := a_0^{-1}$. Next, we have $c_1 = a_0b_1 + a_1b_0$, so we set $b_1 := -a_1b_0 \cdot a_0^{-1}$. Next, we have $c_2 = a_0b_2 + a_1b_1 + a_2b_0$, so we set $b_2 := -(a_1b_1 + a_2b_0) \cdot a_0^{-1}$. Continuing in this way, we see that if we define $b_i := -(a_1b_{i-1} + \cdots + a_ib_0) \cdot a_0^{-1}$ for $i \geq 1$, then $ab = 1$. $\square$

***Example* 17.11.** In the ring $R[\![X]\!]$, the multiplicative inverse of $1 - X$ is $\sum_{i=0}^{\infty} X^i$. $\square$

EXERCISE 17.14. For a field F, show that any non-zero ideal of $F[\![X]\!]$ is of the form (X^m) for some uniquely determined integer $m \geq 0$.

17.7.2 Formal Laurent series

One may generalize formal power series to allow a finite number of negative powers of X. The ring $R((X))$ of **formal Laurent series over** R consists of all formal expressions of the form

$$a = a_m X^m + a_{m+1} X^{m+1} + \cdots ,$$

where m is allowed to be any integer (possibly negative), and $a_m, a_{m+1}, \ldots \in R$. Thus, elements of $R((X))$ may have an infinite number of terms involving positive powers of X, but only a finite number of terms involving negative powers of X. We may write such a formal Laurent series as

$$a = \sum_{i=m}^{\infty} a_i X^i.$$

The rules for addition and multiplication of formal Laurent series are just as one would expect: if

$$a = \sum_{i=m}^{\infty} a_i X^i \quad \text{and} \quad b = \sum_{i=m}^{\infty} b_i X^i,$$

then

$$a + b := \sum_{i=m}^{\infty} (a_i + b_i) X^i, \tag{17.6}$$

and

$$a \cdot b := \sum_{i=2m}^{\infty} \left(\sum_{k=m}^{i-m} a_k b_{i-k} \right) X^i. \tag{17.7}$$

We leave it to the reader to verify that $R((X))$ is a ring containing $R[\![X]\!]$.

Theorem 17.21. *If D is an integral domain, then $D((X))$ is an integral domain.*

Proof. Let $a = \sum_{i=m}^{\infty} a_i X^i$ and $b = \sum_{i=n}^{\infty} b_i X^i$, where $a_m \neq 0$ and $b_n \neq 0$. Then $ab = \sum_{i=m+n}^{\infty} c_i$, where $c_{m+n} = a_m b_n \neq 0$. $\square$

Theorem 17.22. *Let $a \in R((X))$, and suppose that $a \neq 0$ and $a = \sum_{i=m}^{\infty} a_i X^i$ with $a_m \in R^*$. Then a has a multiplicative inverse in $R((X))$.*

Proof. We can write $a = X^m b$, where b is a formal power series whose constant term is a unit, and hence there is a formal power series c such that $bc = 1$. Thus, $X^{-m} c$ is the multiplicative inverse of a in $R((X))$. $\square$

As an immediate corollary, we have:

Theorem 17.23. *If F is a field, then $F((X))$ is a field.*

EXERCISE 17.15. Show that for a field F, $F((X))$ is the field of fractions of $F[[X]]$; that is, there is no proper subfield of $F((X))$ that contains $F[[X]]$.

17.7.3 Reversed formal Laurent series

While formal Laurent series are useful in some situations, in many others, it is more useful and natural to consider **reversed formal Laurent series over** R. These are formal expressions of the form

$$a = \sum_{i=-\infty}^{m} a_i X^i,$$

where $a_m, a_{m-1}, \ldots \in R$. Thus, in a reversed formal Laurent series, we allow an infinite number of terms involving negative powers of X, but only a finite number of terms involving positive powers of X.

The rules for addition and multiplication of reversed formal Laurent series are just as one would expect: if

$$a = \sum_{i=-\infty}^{m} a_i X^i \text{ and } b = \sum_{i=-\infty}^{m} b_i X^i,$$

then

$$a + b := \sum_{i=-\infty}^{m} (a_i + b_i) X^i, \tag{17.8}$$

and

$$a \cdot b := \sum_{i=-\infty}^{2m} \left(\sum_{k=i-m}^{m} a_k b_{i-k} \right) X^i. \tag{17.9}$$

The ring of all reversed formal Laurent series is denoted $R((X^{-1}))$, and as the notation suggests, the map that sends X to X^{-1} (and acts as the identity on R) is an isomorphism of $R((X))$ with $R((X^{-1}))$.

Now, for any $a = \sum_{i=-\infty}^{m} a_i X^i \in R((X^{-1}))$ with $a_m \neq 0$, let us define the **degree of** a, denoted $\deg(a)$, to be the value m, and the **leading coefficient of** a, denoted $\mathrm{lc}(a)$, to be the value a_m. As for ordinary polynomials, we define the degree of 0 to be $-\infty$, and the leading coefficient of 0 to be 0. Note that if a happens to be a polynomial, then these definitions of degree and leading coefficient agree with that for ordinary polynomials.

Theorem 17.24. *For $a, b \in R((\mathtt{X}^{-1}))$, we have $\deg(ab) \leq \deg(a) + \deg(b)$, where equality holds unless both $\mathrm{lc}(a)$ and $\mathrm{lc}(b)$ are zero divisors. Furthermore, if $b \neq 0$ and $\mathrm{lc}(b)$ is a unit, then b is a unit, and we have $\deg(ab^{-1}) = \deg(a) - \deg(b)$.*

Proof. Exercise. $\square$

It is also natural to define a **floor function** for reversed formal Laurent series: for $a \in R((\mathtt{X}^{-1}))$ with $a = \sum_{i=-\infty}^{m} a_i \mathtt{X}^i$, we define

$$\lfloor a \rfloor := \sum_{i=0}^{m} a_i \mathtt{X}^i \in R[\mathtt{X}];$$

that is, we compute the floor function by simply throwing away all terms involving negative powers of $\mathtt{X}$.

Now, let $a, b \in R[\mathtt{X}]$ with $b \neq 0$ and $\mathrm{lc}(b)$ a unit, and using the usual division with remainder property for polynomials, write $a = bq + r$, where $q, r \in R[\mathtt{X}]$ with $\deg(r) < \deg(b)$. Let b^{-1} denote the multiplicative inverse of b in $R((\mathtt{X}^{-1}))$. It is not too hard to see that $\lfloor ab^{-1} \rfloor = q$; indeed, multiplying the equation $a = bq + r$ by b^{-1}, we obtain $ab^{-1} = q + rb^{-1}$, and $\deg(rb^{-1}) < 0$, from which it follows that $\lfloor ab^{-1} \rfloor = q$.

Let F be a field. Since $F((\mathtt{X}^{-1}))$ is isomorphic to $F((\mathtt{X}))$, and the latter is a field, it follows that $F((\mathtt{X}^{-1}))$ is a field. Now, $F((\mathtt{X}^{-1}))$ contains $F[\mathtt{X}]$ as a subring, and hence contains (an isomorphic copy) of $F(\mathtt{X})$. Just as $F(\mathtt{X})$ corresponds to the field of rational numbers, $F((\mathtt{X}^{-1}))$ corresponds to the field real numbers. Indeed, we can think of real numbers as decimal numbers with a finite number of digits to the left of the decimal point and an infinite number to the right, and reversed formal Laurent series have a similar "syntactic" structure. In many ways, this syntactic similarity between the real numbers and reversed formal Laurent series is more than just superficial.

EXERCISE 17.16. Write down the rule for determining the multiplicative inverse of an element of $R((\mathtt{X}^{-1}))$ whose leading coefficient is a unit in R.

EXERCISE 17.17. Let F be a field of characteristic other than 2. Show that a non-zero $z \in F((\mathtt{X}^{-1}))$ has a square-root in $z \in F((\mathtt{X}^{-1}))$ if and only if $\deg(z)$ is even and $\mathrm{lc}(z)$ has a square-root in F.

EXERCISE 17.18. Let R be a ring, and let $\alpha \in R$. Show that the multiplicative inverse of $\mathtt{X} - \alpha$ in $R((\mathtt{X}^{-1}))$ is $\sum_{j=1}^{\infty} \alpha^{j-1} \mathtt{X}^{-j}$.

EXERCISE 17.19. Let R be an arbitrary ring, let $\alpha_1, \ldots, \alpha_\ell \in R$, and let

$$f := (\mathsf{X} - \alpha_1)(\mathsf{X} - \alpha_2) \cdots (\mathsf{X} - \alpha_\ell) \in R[\mathsf{X}].$$

For $j \geq 0$, define the "power sum"

$$s_j := \sum_{i=1}^{\ell} \alpha_i^j.$$

Show that in the ring $R((\mathsf{X}^{-1}))$, we have

$$\frac{\mathbf{D}(f)}{f} = \sum_{i=1}^{\ell} \frac{1}{(\mathsf{X} - \alpha_i)} = \sum_{j=1}^{\infty} s_{j-1} \mathsf{X}^{-j},$$

where $\mathbf{D}(f)$ is the formal derivative of f.

EXERCISE 17.20. Continuing with the previous exercise, derive **Newton's identities**, which state that if $f = \mathsf{X}^\ell + f_1 \mathsf{X}^{\ell-1} + \cdots + f_\ell$, with $f_1, \ldots, f_\ell \in R$, then

$$s_1 + f_1 = 0$$
$$s_2 + f_1 s_1 + 2f_2 = 0$$
$$s_3 + f_1 s_2 + f_2 s_1 + 3f_3 = 0$$
$$\vdots$$
$$s_\ell + f_1 s_{\ell-1} + \cdots + f_{\ell-1} s_1 + \ell f_\ell = 0$$
$$s_{j+\ell} + f_1 s_{j+\ell-1} + \cdots + f_{\ell-1} s_{j+1} + f_\ell s_j = 0 \quad (j \geq 1).$$

17.8 Unique factorization domains (∗)

As we have seen, both the integers and the ring $F[\mathsf{X}]$ of polynomials over a field enjoy a unique factorization property. These are special cases of a more general phenomenon, which we explore here.

Throughout this section, D denotes an integral domain.

We call $a, b \in D$ **associate** if $a = ub$ for some $u \in D^*$. Equivalently, a and b are associate if and only if $a \mid b$ and $b \mid a$. A non-zero element $p \in D$ is called **irreducible** if it is not a unit, and all divisors of p are associate to 1 or p. Equivalently, a non-zero, non-unit $p \in D$ is irreducible if and only if it cannot be expressed as $p = ab$ where neither a nor b are units.

Definition 17.25. *We call D a **unique factorization domain (UFD)** if*

(i) *every non-zero element of D that is not a unit can be written as a product of irreducibles in D, and*

(ii) *such a factorization into irreducibles is unique up to associates and the order in which the factors appear.*

Another way to state part (ii) of the above definition is that if $p_1 \cdots p_r$ and $p'_1 \cdots p'_s$ are two factorizations of some element as a product of irreducibles, then $r = s$, and there exists a permutation π on the indices $\{1, \ldots, r\}$ such that p_i and $p'_{\pi(i)}$ are associate.

As we have seen, both $\mathbb{Z}$ and $F[\mathsf{X}]$ are UFDs. In both of those cases, we chose to single out a distinguished irreducible element among all those associate to any given irreducible: for $\mathbb{Z}$, we always chose p to be positive, and for $F[\mathsf{X}]$, we chose p to be monic. For any specific unique factorization domain D, there may be such a natural choice, but in the general case, there will not be (see Exercise 17.21 below).

***Example* 17.12.** Having already seen two examples of UFDs, it is perhaps a good idea to look at an example of an integral domain that is not a UFD. Consider the subring $\mathbb{Z}[\sqrt{-3}]$ of the complex numbers, which consists of all complex numbers of the form $a + b\sqrt{-3}$, where $a, b \in \mathbb{Z}$. As this is a subring of the field $\mathbb{C}$, it is an integral domain (one may also view $\mathbb{Z}[\sqrt{-3}]$ as the quotient ring $\mathbb{Z}[\mathsf{X}]/(\mathsf{X}^2 + 3)$).

Let us first determine the units in $\mathbb{Z}[\sqrt{-3}]$. For $a, b \in \mathbb{Z}$, we have $N(a + b\sqrt{-3}) = a^2 + 3b^2$, where N is the usual norm map on $\mathbb{C}$ (see Example 9.5). If $\alpha \in \mathbb{Z}[\sqrt{-3}]$ is a unit, then there exists $\alpha' \in \mathbb{Z}[\sqrt{-3}]$ such that $\alpha\alpha' = 1$. Taking norms, we obtain

$$1 = N(1) = N(\alpha\alpha') = N(\alpha)N(\alpha').$$

Since the norm of an element of $\mathbb{Z}[\sqrt{-3}]$ is a non-negative integer, this implies that $N(\alpha) = 1$. If $\alpha = a + b\sqrt{-3}$, with $a, b \in \mathbb{Z}$, then $N(\alpha) = a^2 + 3b^2$, and it is clear that $N(\alpha) = 1$ if and only if $\alpha = \pm 1$. We conclude that the only units in $\mathbb{Z}[\sqrt{-3}]$ are ± 1.

Now consider the following two factorizations of 4 in $\mathbb{Z}[\sqrt{-3}]$:

$$4 = 2 \cdot 2 = (1 + \sqrt{-3})(1 - \sqrt{-3}). \tag{17.10}$$

We claim that 2 is irreducible. For suppose, say, that $2 = \alpha\alpha'$, for $\alpha, \alpha' \in \mathbb{Z}[\sqrt{-3}]$, with neither a unit. Taking norms, we have $4 = N(2) = N(\alpha)N(\alpha')$, and therefore, $N(\alpha) = N(\alpha') = 2$—but this is impossible, since there are no integers a and b such that $a^2 + 3b^2 = 2$. By the same reasoning, since $N(1 + \sqrt{-3}) = N(1 - \sqrt{-3}) = 4$, we see that $1 + \sqrt{-3}$ and $1 - \sqrt{-3}$ are both irreducible. Further, it is clear that 2 is not associate to either $1 + \sqrt{-3}$ or $1 - \sqrt{-3}$, and so the two factorizations of 4 in (17.10) are fundamentally different. □

For $a, b \in D$, we call $d \in D$ a **common divisor** of a and b if $d \mid a$ and $d \mid b$; moreover, we call such a d a **greatest common divisor** of a and b if all other common divisors of a and b divide d. We say that a and b are **relatively prime** if the only common divisors of a and b are units. It is immediate from the definition of a greatest common divisor that it is unique, up to multiplication by units, if it exists at all. Unlike in the case of $\mathbb{Z}$ and $F[\mathsf{X}]$, in the general setting, greatest common divisors need not exist; moreover, even when they do, we shall not attempt to "normalize" greatest common divisors, and we shall speak only of "a" greatest common divisor, rather than "the" greatest common divisor.

Just as for integers and polynomials, we can generalize the notion of a greatest common divisor in an arbitrary integral domain D from two to any number of elements of D, and we can also define a **least common multiple** of any number of elements as well.

Although these greatest common divisors and least common multiples need not exist in an arbitrary integral domain D, if D is a UFD, they will always exist. The existence question easily reduces to the question of the existence of a greatest common divisor and least common multiple of a and b, where a and b are non-zero elements of D. So assuming that D is a UFD, we may write

$$a = u \prod_{i=1}^{r} p_i^{e_i} \quad \text{and} \quad b = v \prod_{i=1}^{r} p_i^{f_i},$$

where u and v are units, $p_1, \ldots, p_r$ are non-associate irreducibles, and the e_i and f_i are non-negative integers, and it is easily seen that

$$\prod_{i=1}^{r} p^{\min(e_i, f_i)}$$

is a greatest common divisor of a and b, while

$$\prod_{i=1}^{r} p^{\max(e_i, f_i)}$$

is a least common multiple of a and b.

It is also evident that in a UFD D, if $c \mid ab$ and c and a are relatively prime, then $c \mid b$. In particular, if p is irreducible and $p \mid ab$, then $p \mid a$ or $p \mid b$. From this, we see that if p is irreducible, then the quotient ring D/pD is an integral domain, and so the ideal pD is a prime ideal (see discussion above Exercise 9.28).

In a general integral domain D, we say that an element $p \in D$ is **prime** if for all $a, b \in D$, $p \mid ab$ implies $p \mid a$ or $p \mid b$ (which is equivalent to saying that the ideal pD is prime). Thus, if D is a UFD, then all irreducibles are primes; however, in a general integral domain, this may not be the case. Here are a couple of simple but useful facts whose proofs we leave to the reader.

Theorem 17.26. *Any prime element in D is irreducible.*

Proof. Exercise. $\square$

Theorem 17.27. *Suppose D satisfies part (i) of Definition 17.25. Also, suppose that all irreducibles in D are prime. Then D is a UFD.*

Proof. Exercise. $\square$

EXERCISE 17.21.   (a) Show that the "is associate to" relation is an equivalence relation.

   (b) Consider an equivalence class C induced by the "is associate to" relation. Show that if C contains an irreducible element, then all elements of C are irreducible.

   (c) Suppose that for every equivalence class C that contains irreducibles, we choose one element of C, and call it a **distinguished irreducible**. Show that D is a UFD if and only if every non-zero element of D can be expressed as $u \cdot p_1^{e_1} \cdots p_r^{e_r}$, where u is a unit, $p_1, \ldots, p_r$ are distinguished irreducibles, and this expression is unique up to a reordering of the p_i.

EXERCISE 17.22. Show that the ring $\mathbb{Z}[\sqrt{-5}]$ is not a UFD.

EXERCISE 17.23. Let D be a UFD and F its field of fractions. Show that

   (a) every element $x \in F$ can be expressed as $x = a/b$, where $a, b \in D$ are relatively prime, and

   (b) that if $x = a/b$ for $a, b \in D$ relatively prime, then for any other $a', b' \in D$ with $x = a'/b'$, we have $a' = ca$ and $b' = cb$ for some $c \in D$.

EXERCISE 17.24. Let D be a UFD and let $p \in D$ be irreducible. Show that there is no prime ideal Q of D with $\{0_D\} \subsetneq Q \subsetneq pD$.

17.8.1 Unique factorization in Euclidean and principal ideal domains

Our proofs of the unique factorization property in both $\mathbb{Z}$ and $F[X]$ hinged on the division with remainder property for these rings. This notion can be generalized, as follows.

Definition 17.28. *D is said to be a **Euclidean domain** if there is a "size function" S mapping the non-zero elements of D to the set of non-negative integers, such that for $a, b \in D$ with $b \neq 0$, there exist $q, r \in D$, with the property that $a = bq + r$ and either $r = 0$ or $S(r) < S(b)$.*

***Example* 17.13.** Both $\mathbb{Z}$ and $F[X]$ are Euclidean domains. In $\mathbb{Z}$, we can take the ordinary absolute value function $|\cdot|$ as a size function, and for $F[X]$, the function $\deg(\cdot)$ will do. □

***Example* 17.14.** Recall again the ring

$$\mathbb{Z}[i] = \{a + bi : a, b \in \mathbb{Z}\}$$

of Gaussian integers from Example 9.22. Let us show that this is a Euclidean domain, using the usual norm map N on complex numbers (see Example 9.5) for the size function. Let $\alpha, \beta \in \mathbb{Z}[i]$, with $\beta \neq 0$. We want to show the existence of $\xi, \rho \in \mathbb{Z}[i]$ such that $\alpha = \beta\xi + \rho$, where $N(\rho) < N(\beta)$. Suppose that in the field $\mathbb{C}$, we compute $\alpha\beta^{-1} = r + si$, where $r, s \in \mathbb{Q}$. Let m, n be integers such that $|m - r| \leq 1/2$ and $|n - s| \leq 1/2$—such integers m and n always exist, but may not be uniquely determined. Set $\xi := m + ni \in \mathbb{Z}[i]$ and $\rho := \alpha - \beta\xi$. Then we have

$$\alpha\beta^{-1} = \xi + \delta,$$

where $\delta \in \mathbb{C}$ with $N(\delta) \leq 1/4 + 1/4 = 1/2$, and

$$\rho = \alpha - \beta\xi = \alpha - \beta(\alpha\beta^{-1} - \delta) = \delta\beta,$$

and hence

$$N(\rho) = N(\delta\beta) = N(\delta)N(\beta) \leq \frac{1}{2}N(\beta). \quad □$$

Theorem 17.29. *If D is a Euclidean domain and I is an ideal of D, then there exists $d \in D$ such that $I = dD$.*

Proof. If $I = \{0\}$, then $d = 0$ does the job, so let us assume that $I \neq \{0\}$. Let d be an non-zero element of I such that $S(d)$ is minimal, where S is a size function that makes D into a Euclidean domain. We claim that $I = dD$.

It will suffice to show that for all $c \in I$, we have $d \mid c$. Now, we know that there exists $q, r \in D$ such that $c = qd + r$, where either $r = 0$ or $S(r) < S(d)$. If $r = 0$, we are done; otherwise, r is a non-zero element of I with $S(r) < S(d)$, contradicting the minimality of $S(d)$. $\square$

Recall that an ideal of the form $I = dD$ is called a principal ideal. If all ideals of D are principal, then D is called a **principal ideal domain (PID)**. Theorem 17.29 says that any Euclidean domain is a PID.

PIDs enjoy many nice properties, including:

Theorem 17.30. *If D is a PID, then D is a UFD.*

For the rings $\mathbb{Z}$ and $F[X]$, the proof of part (i) of Definition 17.25 was a quite straightforward induction argument (as it also would be for any Euclidean domain). For a general PID, however, this requires a different sort of argument. We begin with the following fact:

Theorem 17.31. *If D is a PID, and $I_1 \subseteq I_2 \subseteq \cdots$ is an ascending chain of ideals of D, then there exists an integer k such that $I_k = I_{k+1} = \cdots$.*

Proof. Let $I := \bigcup_{i=1}^{\infty} I_i$. It is easy to see that I is an ideal. Thus, $I = dD$ for some $d \in D$. But $d \in \bigcup_{i=1}^{\infty} I_i$ implies that $d \in I_k$ for some k, which shows that $I = dD \subseteq I_k$. It follows that $I = I_k = I_{k+1} = \cdots$. $\square$

We can now prove the existence part of Theorem 17.30:

Theorem 17.32. *If D is a PID, then every non-zero, non-unit element of D can be expressed as a product of irreducibles in D.*

Proof. Let $n \in D$, $n \neq 0$, and n not a unit. If n is irreducible, we are done. Otherwise, we can write $n = ab$, where neither a nor b are units. As ideals, we have $nD \subsetneq aD$ and $nD \subsetneq bD$. If we continue this process recursively, building up a "factorization tree" where n is at the root, a and b are the children of n, and so on, then the recursion must stop, since any infinite path in the tree would give rise to a chain of ideals

$$nD = I_1 \subsetneq I_2 \subsetneq \cdots ,$$

contradicting Theorem 17.31. $\square$

The proof of the uniqueness part of Theorem 17.30 is essentially the same as for proofs we gave for $\mathbb{Z}$ and $F[X]$.

Analogous to Theorems 1.6 and 17.8, we have:

Theorem 17.33. *Let D be a PID. For any $a, b \in D$, there exists a greatest common divisor d of a and b, and moreover, $aD + bD = dD$.*

Proof. Exercise. □

As an immediate consequence of the previous theorem, we see that in a PID D, for all $a, b \in D$ with greatest common divisor d, there exist $s, t \in D$ such that $as + bt = d$; moreover, $a, b \in D$ are relatively prime if and only if there exist $s, t \in D$ such that $as + bt = 1$.

Analogous to Theorems 1.7 and 17.9, we have:

Theorem 17.34. *Let D be a PID. For $a, b, c \in D$ such that $c \mid ab$ and a and c are relatively prime, we have $c \mid b$.*

Proof. Exercise. □

Analogous to Theorems 1.8 and 17.10, we have:

Theorem 17.35. *Let D be a PID. Let $p \in D$ be irreducible, and let $a, b \in D$. Then $p \mid ab$ implies that $p \mid a$ or $p \mid b$. That is, all irreducibles in D are prime.*

Proof. Exercise. □

Theorem 17.30 now follows immediately from Theorems 17.32, 17.35, and 17.27.

EXERCISE 17.25. Show that $\mathbb{Z}[\sqrt{-2}]$ is a Euclidean domain.

EXERCISE 17.26. Consider the polynomial

$$X^3 - 1 = (X - 1)(X^2 + X + 1).$$

Over $\mathbb{C}$, the roots of $X^3 - 1$ are $1, (-1 \pm \sqrt{-3})/2$. Let $\omega := (-1 + \sqrt{-3})/2$, and note that $\omega^2 = -1 - \omega = (-1 - \sqrt{-3})/2$, and $\omega^3 = 1$.

(a) Show that the ring $\mathbb{Z}[\omega]$ consists of all elements of the form $a + b\omega$, where $a, b \in \mathbb{Z}$, and is an integral domain. This ring is called the ring of **Eisenstein integers**.

(b) Show that the only units in $\mathbb{Z}[\omega]$ are ± 1, $\pm\omega$, and $\pm\omega^2$.

(c) Show that $\mathbb{Z}[\omega]$ is a Euclidean domain.

EXERCISE 17.27. Show that in a PID, all non-zero prime ideals are maximal.

Recall that for a complex number $\alpha = a + bi$, with $a, b \in \mathbb{R}$, the norm of α was defined as $N(\alpha) = \alpha\bar{\alpha} = a^2 + b^2$ (see Example 9.5). There are other measures of the "size" of a complex number that are useful. The **absolute value** of α is defined as $|\alpha| := \sqrt{N(\alpha)} = \sqrt{a^2 + b^2}$. The **max norm** of α is defined as $M(\alpha) := \max\{|a|, |b|\}$.

EXERCISE 17.28. Let $\alpha, \beta \in \mathbb{C}$. Prove the following statements.

(a) $|\alpha\beta| = |\alpha||\beta|$.

(b) $|\alpha + \beta| \leq |\alpha| + |\beta|$.

(c) $N(\alpha + \beta) \leq 2(N(\alpha) + N(\beta))$.

(d) $M(\alpha) \leq |\alpha| \leq \sqrt{2}M(\alpha)$.

The following exercises develop algorithms for computing with Gaussian integers. We shall assume that for computational purposes, a Gaussian integer $\alpha = a + bi$, with $a, b \in \mathbb{Z}$, is represented as the pair of integers (a, b).

EXERCISE 17.29. Let $\alpha, \beta \in \mathbb{Z}[i]$.

(a) Show how to compute $M(\alpha)$ in time $O(\text{len}(M(\alpha)))$ and $N(\alpha)$ in time $O(\text{len}(M(\alpha))^2)$.

(b) Show how to compute $\alpha + \beta$ in time $O(\text{len}(M(\alpha)) + \text{len}(M(\beta)))$.

(c) Show how to compute $\alpha \cdot \beta$ in time $O(\text{len}(M(\alpha)) \cdot \text{len}(M(\beta)))$.

(d) Assuming $\beta \neq 0$, show how to compute $\xi, \rho \in \mathbb{Z}[i]$ such that $\alpha = \beta\xi + \rho$, $N(\rho) \leq \frac{1}{2}N(\beta)$, and $N(\xi) \leq 4N(\alpha)/N(\beta)$. Your algorithm should run in time $O(\text{len}(M(\alpha)) \cdot \text{len}(M(\beta)))$. Hint: see Example 17.14; also, to achieve the stated running time bound, your algorithm should first test if $M(\beta) \geq 2M(\alpha)$.

EXERCISE 17.30. Using the division with remainder algorithm from part (d) of the previous exercise, adapt the Euclidean algorithm for (ordinary) integers to work with Gaussian integers. On inputs $\alpha, \beta \in \mathbb{Z}[i]$, your algorithm should compute a greatest common divisor $\delta \in \mathbb{Z}[i]$ of α and β in time $O(\ell^3)$, where $\ell := \max\{\text{len}(M(\alpha)), \text{len}(M(\beta))\}$.

EXERCISE 17.31. Extend the algorithm of the previous exercise, so that it computes $\sigma, \tau \in \mathbb{Z}[i]$ such that $\alpha\sigma + \beta\tau = \delta$. Your algorithm should run in time $O(\ell^3)$, and it should also be the case that $\text{len}(M(\sigma))$ and $\text{len}(M(\tau))$ are $O(\ell)$.

The algorithms in the previous two exercises for computing greatest common divisors in $\mathbb{Z}[i]$ run in time cubic in the length of their input, whereas the corresponding algorithms for $\mathbb{Z}$ run in time quadratic in the length of their input. This is essentially because the running time of the algorithm for division with remainder discussed in Exercise 17.29 is insensitive to the size of the quotient.

To get a quadratic-time algorithm for computing greatest common divisors in $\mathbb{Z}[i]$, in the following exercises we shall develop an analog of the binary gcd algorithm for $\mathbb{Z}$.

EXERCISE 17.32. Let $\pi := 1 + i \in \mathbb{Z}[i]$.

(a) Show that $2 = \pi\bar{\pi} = -i\pi^2$, that $N(\pi) = 2$, and that π is irreducible in $\mathbb{Z}[i]$.

(b) Let $\alpha \in \mathbb{Z}[i]$, with $\alpha = a + bi$ for $a, b \in \mathbb{Z}$. Show that $\pi \mid \alpha$ if and only if $a - b$ is even, in which case
$$\frac{\alpha}{\pi} = \frac{a+b}{2} + \frac{b-a}{2}i.$$

(c) Show that for any $\alpha \in \mathbb{Z}[i]$, we have $\alpha \equiv 0 \pmod{\pi}$ or $\alpha \equiv 1 \pmod{\pi}$.

(d) Show that the quotient ring $\mathbb{Z}[i]/\pi\mathbb{Z}[i]$ is isomorphic to the ring $\mathbb{Z}_2$.

(e) Show that for any $\alpha \in \mathbb{Z}[i]$ with $\alpha \equiv 1 \pmod{\pi}$, there exists a unique $\epsilon \in \{\pm 1, \pm i\}$ such that $\alpha \equiv \epsilon \pmod{2\pi}$.

(f) Show that for any $\alpha, \beta \in \mathbb{Z}[i]$ with $\alpha \equiv \beta \equiv 1 \pmod{\pi}$, there exists a unique $\epsilon \in \{\pm 1, \pm i\}$ such that $\alpha \equiv \epsilon\beta \pmod{2\pi}$.

EXERCISE 17.33. We now present a "$(1+i)$-ary gcd algorithm" for Gaussian integers. Let $\pi := 1 + i \in \mathbb{Z}[i]$. The algorithm takes non-zero $\alpha, \beta \in \mathbb{Z}[i]$ as input, and runs as follows:

$$\rho \leftarrow \alpha, \ \rho' \leftarrow \beta, \ e \leftarrow 0$$
while $\pi \mid \rho$ and $\pi \mid \rho'$ do $\rho \leftarrow \rho/\pi, \ \rho' \leftarrow \rho'/\pi, \ e \leftarrow e+1$
repeat
        while $\pi \mid \rho$ do $\rho \leftarrow \rho/\pi$
        while $\pi \mid \rho'$ do $\rho' \leftarrow \rho'/\pi$
        if $M(\rho') < M(\rho)$ then $(\rho, \rho') \leftarrow (\rho', \rho)$
        determine $\epsilon \in \{\pm 1, \pm i\}$ such that $\rho' \equiv \epsilon\rho \pmod{2\pi}$
(∗) $\rho' \leftarrow \rho' - \epsilon\rho$
until $\rho' = 0$
$\delta \leftarrow \pi^e \cdot \rho$
output δ

Show that this algorithm correctly computes a greatest common divisor of α and β, and can be implemented so as to run in time $O(\ell^2)$, where $\ell := \max(\text{len}(M(\alpha)), \text{len}(M(\beta)))$. Hint: to analyze the running time, for $i = 1, 2, \ldots$, let v_i (respectively, v_i') denote the value of $|\rho\rho'|$ just before (respectively, after) the execution of the line marked (∗) in loop iteration i, and show that
$$v_i' \leq (1 + \sqrt{2})v_i \ \text{ and } \ v_{i+1} \leq v_i'/2\sqrt{2}.$$

EXERCISE 17.34. Extend the algorithm of the previous exercise, so that it computes $\sigma, \tau \in \mathbb{Z}[i]$ such that $\alpha\sigma + \beta\tau = \delta$. Your algorithm should run in time $O(\ell^2)$, and it should also be the case that $\mathrm{len}(M(\sigma))$ and $\mathrm{len}(M(\tau))$ are $O(\ell)$. Hint: adapt the algorithm in Exercise 4.2.

EXERCISE 17.35. In Exercise 17.32, we saw that 2 factors as $-i\pi^2$ in $\mathbb{Z}[i]$, where $\pi := 1 + i$ is irreducible. This exercise examines the factorization in $\mathbb{Z}[i]$ of prime numbers $p > 2$.

  (a) Suppose -1 is not congruent to the square of any integer modulo p. Show that p is irreducible in $\mathbb{Z}[i]$.
  (b) Suppose that $c^2 \equiv -1 \pmod{p}$ for some $c \in \mathbb{Z}$. Let $\gamma := c + i \in \mathbb{Z}[i]$ and let δ be a greatest common divisor in $\mathbb{Z}[i]$ of γ and p. Show that $p = \delta\bar{\delta}$, and that δ and $\bar{\delta}$ are non-associate, irreducible elements of $\mathbb{Z}[i]$.

17.8.2 Unique factorization in $D[X]$

In this section, we prove the following:

Theorem 17.36. *If D is a UFD, then so is $D[X]$.*

This theorem implies, for example, that $\mathbb{Z}[X]$ is a UFD. Applying the theorem inductively, one also sees that for any field F, the ring $F[X_1, \ldots, X_n]$ of multi-variate polynomials over F is also a UFD.

We begin with some simple observations. First, recall that for an integral domain D, $D[X]$ is an integral domain, and the units in $D[X]$ are precisely the units in D. Second, it is easy to see that an element of D is irreducible in D if and only if it is irreducible in $D[X]$. Third, for $c \in D$ and $f = \sum_i a_i X^i \in D[X]$, we have $c \mid f$ if and only if $c \mid a_i$ for all i.

We call a non-zero polynomial $f \in D[X]$ **primitive** if the only elements in D that divide f are units. If D is a UFD, then given any non-zero polynomial $f \in D[X]$, we can write it as $f = cf'$, where $c \in D$ and $f' \in D[X]$ is a primitive polynomial: just take c to be a greatest common divisor of all the coefficients of f.

It is easy to prove the existence part of Theorem 17.36:

Theorem 17.37. *Let D be a UFD. Any non-zero, non-unit element of $D[X]$ can be expressed as a product of irreducibles in $D[X]$.*

Proof. Let f be a non-zero, non-unit polynomial in $D[X]$. If f is a constant, then because D is a UFD, it factors into irreducibles in D. So assume f is not constant. If f is not primitive, we can write $f = cf'$, where c is a non-zero, non-unit in D, and f' is a primitive, non-constant polynomial in $D[X]$. Again, as D is a UFD, c factors into irreducibles in D.

From the above discussion, it suffices to prove the theorem for non-constant, primitive polynomials $f \in D[X]$. If f is itself irreducible, we are done. Otherwise, then we can write $f = gh$, where $g, h \in D[X]$ and neither g nor h are units. Further, by the assumption that f is a primitive, non-constant polynomial, both g and h must also be primitive, non-constant polynomials; in particular, both g and h have degree strictly less than $\deg(f)$, and the theorem follows by induction on degree. $\square$

The uniqueness part of Theorem 17.36 is (as usual) more difficult. We begin with the following fact:

Theorem 17.38. *Let D be a UFD, let p be an irreducible in D, and let $f, g \in D[X]$. Then $p \mid fg$ implies $p \mid f$ or $p \mid g$.*

Proof. Consider the quotient ring D/pD, which is an integral domain (because D is a UFD), and the corresponding ring of polynomials $(D/pD)[X]$, which is also an integral domain. Consider the natural map from $D[X]$ to $(D/pD)[X]$ that sends $a \in D[X]$ to the polynomial $\bar{a} \in (D/pD)[X]$ obtained by mapping each coefficient of a to its residue class modulo p. If $p \mid fg$, then we have

$$0 = \overline{fg} = \bar{f}\bar{g},$$

and since $(D/pD)[X]$ is an integral domain, it follows that $\bar{f} = 0$ or $\bar{g} = 0$, which means that $p \mid f$ or $p \mid g$. $\square$

Theorem 17.39. *Let D be a UFD. The product of two primitive polynomials in $D[X]$ is also primitive.*

Proof. Let $f, g \in D[X]$ be primitive polynomials, and let $h := fg$. If h is not primitive, then $m \mid h$ for some non-zero, non-unit $m \in D$, and as D is a UFD, there is some irreducible element $p \in D$ that divides m, and therefore, divides h as well. By Theorem 17.38, it follows that $p \mid f$ or $p \mid g$, which implies that either f is not primitive or g is not primitive. $\square$

Suppose that D is a UFD and that F is its field of fractions. Any non-zero polynomial $f \in F[X]$ can always be written as $f = (c/d)f'$, where $c, d \in D$, with $d \neq 0$, and $f' \in D[X]$ is primitive. To see this, clear the denominators of the coefficients of f, writing $df = f''$, where $0 \neq d \in D$ and $f'' \in D[X]$. Then take c to be a greatest common divisor of the coefficients of f'', so that $f'' = cf'$, where $f' \in D[X]$ is primitive. Then we have $f = (c/d)f'$, as required. Of course, we may assume that c and d are relatively prime—if not, we may divide c and d by a greatest common divisor.

As a consequence of the previous theorem, we have:

Theorem 17.40. *Let D be a UFD and let F be its field of fractions. Let $f, g \in D[X]$ and $h \in F[X]$ be non-zero polynomials such that $f = gh$ and g is primitive. Then $h \in D[X]$.*

Proof. Write $h = (c/d)h'$, where $c, d \in D$ and $h' \in D[X]$ is primitive. Let us assume that c and d are relatively prime. Then we have

$$d \cdot f = c \cdot gh'. \tag{17.11}$$

We claim that $d \in D^*$. To see this, note that (17.11) implies that $d \mid (c \cdot gh')$, and the assumption that c and d are relatively prime implies that $d \mid gh'$. But by Theorem 17.39, gh' is primitive, from which it follows that d is a unit. That proves the claim.

It follows that $c/d \in D$, and hence $h = (c/d)h' \in D[X]$. $\square$

Theorem 17.41. *Let D be a UFD and F its field of fractions. If $f \in D[X]$ with $\deg(f) > 0$ is irreducible, then f is also irreducible in $F[X]$.*

Proof. Suppose that f is not irreducible in $F[X]$, so that $f = gh$ for non-constant polynomials $g, h \in F[X]$, both of degree strictly less than that of f. We may write $g = (c/d)g'$, where $c, d \in D$ and $g' \in D[X]$ is primitive. Set $h' := (c/d)h$, so that $f = gh = g'h'$. By Theorem 17.40, we have $h' \in D[X]$, and this shows that f is not irreducible in $D[X]$. $\square$

Theorem 17.42. *Let D be a UFD. Let $f \in D[X]$ with $\deg(f) > 0$ be irreducible, and let $g, h \in D[X]$. If f divides gh in $D[X]$, then f divides either g or h in $D[X]$.*

Proof. Suppose that $f \in D[X]$ with $\deg(f) > 0$ is irreducible. This implies that f is a primitive polynomial. By Theorem 17.41, f is irreducible in $F[X]$, where F is the field of fractions of D. Suppose f divides gh in $D[X]$. Then because $F[X]$ is a UFD, f divides either g or h in $F[X]$. But Theorem 17.40 implies that f divides either g or h in $D[X]$. $\square$

Theorem 17.36 now follows immediately from Theorems 17.37, 17.38, and 17.42, together with Theorem 17.27.

In the proof of Theorem 17.36, there is a clear connection between factorization in $D[X]$ and $F[X]$, where F is the field of fractions of D. We should perhaps make this connection more explicit. Suppose $f \in D[X]$ factors into irreducibles in $D[X]$ as

$$f = c_1^{a_1} \cdots c_r^{a_r} h_1^{b_1} \cdots h_s^{b_s}.$$

where the c_i are non-associate, irreducible constants, and the h_i are non-associate, irreducible, non-constant polynomials (and in particular, primitive). By Theorem 17.41, the h_i are irreducible in $F[X]$. Moreover, by Theorem 17.40, the h_i are non-associate in $F[X]$. Therefore, in $F[X]$, f factors as

$$f = ch_1^{b_1} \cdots h_s^{b_s},$$

where $c := c_1^{a_1} \cdots c_r^{a_r}$ is a unit in F, and the h_i are non-associate irreducible polynomials in $F[X]$.

Example 17.15. It is important to keep in mind the distinction between factorization in $D[X]$ and $F[X]$. Consider the polynomial $2X^2 - 2 \in \mathbb{Z}[X]$. Over $\mathbb{Z}[X]$, this polynomial factors as $2(X - 1)(X + 1)$, where each of these three factors are irreducible in $\mathbb{Z}[X]$. Over $\mathbb{Q}[X]$, this polynomial has two irreducible factors, namely, $X - 1$ and $X + 1$. $\square$

The following theorem provides a useful criterion for establishing that a polynomial is irreducible.

Theorem 17.43 (Eisenstein's criterion). *Let D be a UFD and F its field of fractions. Let $f = f_n X^n + f_{n-1} X^{n-1} + \cdots + f_0 \in D[X]$. If there exists an irreducible $p \in D$ such that*

$$p \nmid f_n, \ p \mid f_{n-1}, \ \cdots, \ p \mid f_0, \ p^2 \nmid f_0,$$

then f is irreducible over F.

Proof. Let f be as above, and suppose it were not irreducible in $F[X]$. Then by Theorem 17.41, we could write $f = gh$, where $g, h \in D[X]$, both of degree strictly less than that of f. Let us write

$$g = g_r X^r + \cdots + g_0 \ \text{and} \ h = h_s X^s + \cdots + h_0,$$

where $g_r \neq 0$ and $h_s \neq 0$, so that $0 < r < n$ and $0 < s < n$. Now, since $f_n = g_r h_s$, and $p \nmid f_n$, it follows that $p \nmid g_r$ and $p \nmid h_s$. Further, since $f_0 = g_0 h_0$, and $p \mid f_0$ but $p^2 \nmid f_0$, it follows that p divides one of g_0 or h_0, but not both—for concreteness, let us assume that $p \mid g_0$ but $p \nmid h_0$. Also, let t be the smallest positive integer such that $p \nmid g_t$—note that $0 < t \leq r < n$.

Now consider the natural map that sends $c \in D$ to $\bar{c} \in D/pD$, which we can extend coefficient-wise to the map that sends $a \in D[X]$ to $\bar{a} \in (D/pD)[X]$. Because D is a UFD and p is irreducible, both D/pD and $(D/pD)[X]$ are integral domains. Since $f = gh$, we have

$$\bar{f}_n X^n = \bar{f} = \bar{g}\bar{h} = (\bar{g}_r X^r + \cdots + \bar{g}_t X^t)(\bar{h}_s X^s + \cdots + \bar{h}_0). \quad (17.12)$$

But notice that when we multiply out the two polynomials on the right-hand side of (17.12), the coefficient of X^t is $\bar{g}_t \bar{h}_0 \neq 0$, and as $t < n$, this clearly contradicts the fact that the coefficient of X^t in the polynomial on the left-hand side of (17.12) is zero. $\square$

As an application of Eisenstein's criterion, we have:

Theorem 17.44. *For any prime number q, the qth cyclotomic polynomial*

$$\Phi_q := \frac{X^q - 1}{X - 1} = X^{q-1} + X^{q-2} + \cdots + 1$$

is irreducible over $\mathbb{Q}$.

Proof. Let

$$f := \Phi_q[\, X + 1\,] = \frac{(X + 1)^q - 1}{(X + 1) - 1}.$$

It is easy to see that

$$f = \sum_{i=0}^{q-1} a_i X_i, \quad \text{where} \quad a_i = \binom{q}{i+1} \quad (i = 0, \ldots, q - 1).$$

Thus, $a_{q-1} = 1$, $a_0 = q$, and for $0 < i < q - 1$, we have $q \mid a_i$ (see Exercise 1.12). Theorem 17.43 therefore applies, and we conclude that f is irreducible over $\mathbb{Q}$. It follows that Φ_q is irreducible over $\mathbb{Q}$, since if $\Phi_q = gh$ were a non-trivial factorization of Φ_q, then $f = \Phi_q[\, X + 1\,] = g[\, X + 1\,] \cdot h[\, X + 1\,]$ would be a non-trivial factorization of f. $\square$

EXERCISE 17.36. Show that neither $\mathbb{Z}[X]$ nor $F[X, Y]$ (where F is a field) are PIDs (even though they are UFDs).

EXERCISE 17.37. Let $f \in \mathbb{Z}[X]$ be a monic polynomial. Show that if f has a root $\alpha \in \mathbb{Q}$, then $\alpha \in \mathbb{Z}$, and α divides the constant term of f.

EXERCISE 17.38. Let a be a non-zero, square-free integer, with $a \notin \{\pm 1\}$. For integer $n \geq 1$, show that the polynomial $X^n - a$ is irreducible in $\mathbb{Q}[X]$.

EXERCISE 17.39. Show that the polynomial $X^4 + 1$ is irreducible in $\mathbb{Q}[X]$.

EXERCISE 17.40. Let F be a field, and consider the ring of bivariate polynomials $F[X, Y]$. Show that in this ring, the polynomial $X^2 + Y^2 - 1$ is irreducible, provided F does not have characteristic 2. What happens if F has characteristic 2?

EXERCISE 17.41. Design and analyze an efficient algorithm for the following problem. The input is a pair of polynomials $a, b \in \mathbb{Z}[\mathtt{X}]$, along with their greatest common divisor d in the ring $\mathbb{Q}[\mathtt{X}]$. The output is the greatest common divisor of a and b the ring $\mathbb{Z}[\mathtt{X}]$.

EXERCISE 17.42. Let $a, b \in \mathbb{Z}[\mathtt{X}]$ be non-zero polynomials with $d :=$ $\gcd(a, b) \in \mathbb{Z}[\mathtt{X}]$. Show that for any prime p not dividing $\mathrm{lc}(a)\,\mathrm{lc}(b)$, we have $\bar{d} \mid \gcd(\bar{a}, \bar{b})$, and except for finitely many primes p, we have $\bar{d} = \gcd(\bar{a}, \bar{b})$. Here, $\bar{d}$, $\bar{a}$, and $\bar{b}$ denote the images of d, a, and b in $\mathbb{Z}_p[\mathtt{X}]$.

EXERCISE 17.43. Let F be a field, and let $f, g \in F[\mathtt{X}, \mathtt{Y}]$. Define $V(f, g) :=$ $\{(x, y) \in F \times F : f(x, y) = g(x, y) = 0_F\}$. Show that if f and g are relatively prime, then $V(f, g)$ is a finite set. Hint: consider the rings $F(\mathtt{X})[\mathtt{Y}]$ and $F(\mathtt{Y})[\mathtt{X}]$.

17.9 Notes

The "$(1 + i)$-ary gcd algorithm" in Exercise 17.33 for computing greatest common divisors of Gaussian integers is based on algorithms in Weilert [100] and Damgård and Frandsen [31]. The latter paper also develops a corresponding algorithm for Eisenstein integers (see Exercise 17.26). Weilert [101] presents an asymptotically fast algorithm that computes the greatest common divisor of ℓ-bit Gaussian integers in time $O(\ell^{1+o(1)})$.

18

Polynomial arithmetic and applications

In this chapter, we study algorithms for performing arithmetic on polynomials. Initially, we shall adopt a very general point of view, discussing polynomials whose coefficients lie in an arbitrary ring R, and then specialize to the case where the coefficient ring is a field F.

There are many similarities between arithmetic in $\mathbb{Z}$ and in $R[X]$, and the similarities between $\mathbb{Z}$ and $F[X]$ run even deeper. Many of the algorithms we discuss in this chapter are quite similar to the corresponding algorithms for integers.

As we did in Chapter 15 for matrices, we shall treat R as an "abstract data type," and measure the complexity of algorithms for polynomials over a ring R by counting "operations in R."

18.1 Basic arithmetic

Throughout this section, R denotes a non-trivial ring.

For computational purposes, we assume that a polynomial $a = \sum_{i=0}^{k-1} a_i X^i \in R[X]$ is represented as a coefficient vector $(a_0, a_1, \ldots, a_{k-1})$. Further, when a is non-zero, the coefficient a_{k-1} should be non-zero.

The basic algorithms for addition, subtraction, multiplication, and division of polynomials are quite straightforward adaptations of the corresponding algorithms for integers. In fact, because of the lack of "carries," these algorithms are actually much simpler in the polynomial case. We briefly discuss these algorithms here—analogous to our treatment of integer arithmetic, we do not discuss the details of "stripping" leading zero coefficients.

For addition and subtraction, all we need to do is to add or subtract coefficient vectors.

For multiplication, let $a = \sum_{i=0}^{k-1} a_i X^i \in R[X]$ and $b = \sum_{i=0}^{\ell-1} b_i X^i \in R[X]$, where $k \geq 1$ and $\ell \geq 1$. The product $c := a \cdot b$ is of the form $c = \sum_{i=0}^{k+\ell-2} c_i X^i$, and can be computed using $O(k\ell)$ operations in R as follows:

> for $i \leftarrow 0$ to $k + \ell - 2$ do $c_i \leftarrow 0$
> for $i \leftarrow 0$ to $k - 1$ do
>   for $j \leftarrow 0$ to $\ell - 1$ do
> $c_{i+j} \leftarrow c_{i+j} + a_i \cdot b_j$

For division, let $a = \sum_{i=0}^{k-1} a_i X^i \in R[X]$ and $b = \sum_{i=0}^{\ell-1} b_i X^i \in R[X]$, where $b_{\ell-1} \in R^*$. We want to compute polynomials $q, r \in R[X]$ such that $a = bq + r$, where $\deg(r) < \ell - 1$. If $k < \ell$, we can simply set $q \leftarrow 0$ and $r \leftarrow a$; otherwise, we can compute q and r using $O(\ell \cdot (k - \ell + 1))$ operations in R using the following algorithm:

> $t \leftarrow b_{\ell-1}^{-1} \in R$
> for $i \leftarrow 0$ to $k - 1$ do $r_i \leftarrow a_i$
> for $i \leftarrow k - \ell$ down to 0 do
> $q_i \leftarrow t \cdot r_{i+\ell-1}$
>   for $j \leftarrow 0$ to $\ell - 1$ do
> $r_{i+j} \leftarrow r_{i+j} - q_i \cdot b_j$
> $q \leftarrow \sum_{i=0}^{k-\ell} q_i X^i, \quad r \leftarrow \sum_{i=0}^{\ell-2} r_i X^i$

With these simple algorithms, we obtain the polynomial analog of Theorem 3.3. Let us define the **length** of $a \in R[X]$, denoted $\mathrm{len}(a)$, to be the length of its coefficient vector; more precisely, we define

$$\mathrm{len}(a) := \begin{cases} \deg(a) + 1 & \text{if } a \neq 0, \\ 1 & \text{if } a = 0. \end{cases}$$

It is sometimes more convenient to state the running times of algorithms in terms of $\mathrm{len}(a)$, rather than $\deg(a)$ (the latter has the inconvenient habit of taking on the value 0, or worse, $-\infty$).

Theorem 18.1. *Let a and b be arbitrary polynomials in $R[X]$.*

    (i) We can compute $a \pm b$ with $O(\mathrm{len}(a) + \mathrm{len}(b))$ operations in R.

    (ii) We can compute $a \cdot b$ with $O(\mathrm{len}(a)\,\mathrm{len}(b))$ operations in R.

    (iii) If $b \neq 0$ and $\mathrm{lc}(b)$ is a unit in R, we can compute $q, r \in R[X]$ such that $a = bq + r$ and $\deg(r) < \deg(b)$ with $O(\mathrm{len}(b)\,\mathrm{len}(q))$ operations in R.

Analogous to algorithms for modular integer arithmetic, we can also do arithmetic in the residue class ring $R[X]/(n)$, where $n \in R[X]$ is a polynomial of degree $\ell > 0$ whose leading coefficient $\mathrm{lc}(n)$ is a unit (in most applications, we may in fact assume that n is monic). For $\alpha \in R[\mathtt{X}]/(n)$, there exists a unique polynomial $a \in R[\mathtt{X}]$ with $\deg(a) < \ell$ and $\alpha = [a]_n$; we call this polynomial a the **canonical representative of** α, and denote it by $\mathrm{rep}(\alpha)$. For computational purposes, we represent elements of $R[\mathtt{X}]/(n)$ by their canonical representatives.

With this representation, addition and subtraction in $R[\mathtt{X}]/(n)$ can be performed using $O(\ell)$ operations in R, while multiplication takes $O(\ell^2)$ operations in R.

The repeated-squaring algorithm for computing powers works equally well in this setting: given $\alpha \in R[\mathtt{X}]/(n)$ and a non-negative exponent e, we can compute α^e using $O(\mathrm{len}(e))$ multiplications in $R[\mathtt{X}]/(n)$, and so a total of $O(\mathrm{len}(e)\,\ell^2)$ operations in R.

The following exercises deal with arithmetic with polynomials $R[\mathtt{X}]$ over a ring R.

EXERCISE 18.1. State and re-work the polynomial analog of Exercise 3.22.

EXERCISE 18.2. State and re-work the polynomial analog of Exercise 3.23. Assume $n_1, \ldots, n_k$ are monic polynomials.

EXERCISE 18.3. Given a polynomial $g \in R[\mathtt{X}]$ and an element $\alpha \in E$, where R is a subring of E, we may wish to compute $g(\alpha) \in E$. A particularly elegant and efficient way of doing this is called **Horner's rule**. Suppose $g = \sum_{i=0}^{k-1} g_i \mathtt{X}^i$, where $k \geq 0$ and $g_i \in R$ for $i = 0, \ldots, k-1$. Horner's rule computes $g(\alpha)$ as follows:

$\beta \leftarrow 0_E$
for $i \leftarrow k-1$ down to 0 do
$\quad \beta \leftarrow \beta \cdot \alpha + a_i$
output β

Show that this algorithm correctly computes $g(\alpha)$ using k multiplications in E and k additions in E.

EXERCISE 18.4. Let $f \in R[\mathtt{X}]$ be a monic polynomial of degree $\ell > 0$, and let $E := R[\mathtt{X}]/(f)$. Suppose that in addition to f, we are given a polynomial $g \in R[\mathtt{X}]$ of degree less than k and an element $\alpha \in E$, and we want to compute $g(\alpha) \in E$.

   (a) Show that a straightforward application of Horner's rule yields an algorithm that uses $O(k\ell^2)$ operations in R, and requires space for storing $O(\ell)$ elements of R.

(b) Show how to compute $g(\alpha)$ using just $O(k\ell + k^{1/2}\ell^2)$ operations in R, at the expense of requiring space for storing $O(k^{1/2}\ell)$ elements of R. Hint: first compute a table of powers $1, \alpha, \ldots, \alpha^m$, for $m \approx k^{1/2}$.

EXERCISE 18.5. Given polynomials $g, h \in R[X]$, show how to compute the composition $g(h) \in R[X]$ using $O(\operatorname{len}(g)^2 \operatorname{len}(h)^2)$ operations in R.

EXERCISE 18.6. Suppose you are given three polynomials $f, g, h \in \mathbb{Z}_p[X]$, where p is a large prime, in particular, $p \geq 2\deg(g)\deg(h)$. Design an efficient probabilistic algorithm that tests if $f = g(h)$ (i.e., if f equals g composed with h). Your algorithm should have the following properties: if $f = g(h)$, it should always output "true," and otherwise, it should output "false" with probability at least 0.999. The expected running time of your algorithm should be $O((\operatorname{len}(f) + \operatorname{len}(g) + \operatorname{len}(h)) \operatorname{len}(p)^2)$.

18.2 Computing minimal polynomials in $F[X]/(f)$ **(I)**

In this section, we shall examine a computational problem to which we shall return on several occasions, as it will serve to illustrate a number of interesting algebraic and algorithmic concepts.

Let F be a field, $f \in F[X]$ a monic polynomial of degree $\ell > 0$, and let $E := F[X]/(f)$. E is an F-algebra, and in particular, an F-vector space. As an F-vector space, it has dimension ℓ. Suppose we are given an element $\alpha \in E$, and want to efficiently compute the minimal polynomial of α over F, that is, the monic polynomial $\phi \in F[X]$ of least degree such that $\phi(\alpha) = 0$, which we know has degree at most ℓ (see §17.5).

We can solve this problem using polynomial arithmetic and Gaussian elimination, as follows. Consider the F-linear map $\rho : F[X]_{\leq \ell} \to E$ that sends a polynomial $h \in F[X]$ of degree at most ℓ to $h(\alpha)$. Let us fix ordered bases for $F[X]_{\leq \ell}$ and E: for $F[X]_{\leq \ell}$, let us take $X^\ell, X^{\ell-1}, \ldots, 1$, and for E, let us take $1, \eta, \ldots, \eta^{\ell-1}$, where $\eta := [X]_f \in E$. The matrix A representing the map ρ (via multiplication on the right by A), is the $(\ell+1) \times \ell$ matrix A whose ith row, for $i = 1, \ldots, \ell+1$, is the coordinate vector of $\alpha^{\ell+1-i}$.

We apply Gaussian elimination to A to find a set of row vectors $v_1, \ldots, v_s$ that are coordinate vectors for a basis for the kernel of ρ. Now, the coordinate vector of the minimal polynomial of α is a linear combination of $v_1, \ldots, v_s$. To find it, we form the $s \times (\ell+1)$ matrix B whose rows consist of $v_1, \ldots, v_s$, and apply Gaussian elimination to B, obtaining an $s \times (\ell+1)$ matrix B' in reduced row echelon form whose row space is the same as that of B. Let g be the polynomial whose coordinate vector is the last row of B'. Because of the choice of ordered basis for $F[X]_{\leq \ell}$, and because B' is in reduced row echelon form, it is clear that no non-zero polynomial in $\ker(\rho)$ has degree less than that of g. Moreover, as g is already monic (again, by the fact that B' is in reduced row echelon form), it follows that g is in fact the minimal polynomial of α over F.

The total amount of work performed by this algorithm is $O(\ell^3)$ operations in F to build the matrix A (this just amounts to computing ℓ successive powers of α, that is, $O(\ell)$ multiplications in E, each of which takes $O(\ell^2)$ operations in F), and $O(\ell^3)$ operations in F to perform both Gaussian elimination steps.

18.3 Euclid's algorithm

In this section, F denotes a field, and we consider the computation of greatest common divisors in $F[X]$.

The basic Euclidean algorithm for integers is easily adapted to compute $\gcd(a, b)$, for polynomials $a, b \in F[X]$. Analogous to the integer case, we assume that $\deg(a) \geq \deg(b)$; however, we shall also assume that $a \neq 0$. This is not a serious restriction, of course, as $\gcd(0, 0) = 0$, and making this restriction will simplify the presentation a bit. Recall that we defined $\gcd(a, b)$ to be either zero or monic, and the assumption that $a \neq 0$ means that $\gcd(a, b)$ is non-zero, and hence monic.

The following is the analog of Theorem 4.1.

Theorem 18.2. *Let $a, b \in F[X]$, with $\deg(a) \geq \deg(b)$ and $a \neq 0$. Define the polynomials $r_0, r_1, \ldots, r_{\ell+1} \in F[X]$, and $q_1, \ldots, q_\ell \in F[X]$, where $\ell \geq 0$, as follows:*

$$a = r_0,$$
$$b = r_1,$$
$$r_0 = r_1 q_1 + r_2 \quad (0 \leq \deg(r_2) < \deg(r_1)),$$
$$\vdots$$
$$r_{i-1} = r_i q_i + r_{i+1} \quad (0 \leq \deg(r_{i+1}) < \deg(r_i)),$$
$$\vdots$$
$$r_{\ell-2} = r_{\ell-1} q_{\ell-1} + r_\ell \quad (0 \leq \deg(r_\ell) < \deg(r_{\ell-1})),$$
$$r_{\ell-1} = r_\ell q_\ell \quad (r_{\ell+1} = 0).$$

Note that by definition, $\ell = 0$ if $b = 0$, and $\ell > 0$ otherwise; moreover, $r_\ell \neq 0$.

Then we have $r_\ell / \operatorname{lc}(r_\ell) = \gcd(a, b)$, and if $b \neq 0$, then $\ell \leq \deg(b) + 1$.

Proof. Arguing as in the proof of Theorem 4.1, one sees that

$$\gcd(a, b) = \gcd(r_0, r_1) = \gcd(r_\ell, r_{\ell+1}) = \gcd(r_\ell, 0) = r_\ell / \operatorname{lc}(r_\ell).$$

That proves the first statement.

For the second statement, if $b \neq 0$, then the degree sequence

$$\deg(r_1), \deg(r_2), \ldots, \deg(r_\ell)$$

is strictly decreasing, with $\deg(r_\ell) \geq 0$, from which it follows that $\deg(b) = \deg(r_1) \geq \ell - 1$. $\square$

This gives us the following Euclidean algorithm for polynomials, which takes as input polynomials $a, b \in F[\mathsf{X}]$ with $\deg(a) \geq \deg(b)$ and $a \neq 0$, and which produces as output $d = \gcd(a, b) \in F[\mathsf{X}]$.

> $r \leftarrow a, \ r' \leftarrow b$
> while $r' \neq 0$ do
> $r'' \leftarrow r \bmod r'$
> $(r, r') \leftarrow (r', r'')$
> $d \leftarrow r / \operatorname{lc}(r) \quad // \ make \ monic$
> output d

Theorem 18.3. *Euclid's algorithm for polynomials uses $O(\operatorname{len}(a) \operatorname{len}(b))$ operations in F.*

Proof. The proof is almost identical to that of Theorem 4.2. Details are left to the reader. $\square$

Just as for integers, if $d = \gcd(a, b)$, then $aF[\mathsf{X}] + bF[\mathsf{X}] = dF[\mathsf{X}]$, and so there exist polynomials s and t such that $as + bt = d$. The procedure to calculate s and t is precisely the same as in the integer case; however, in the polynomial case, we can be much more precise about the relative sizes of the objects involved in the calculation.

Theorem 18.4. *Let a, b, $r_0, r_1, \ldots, r_{\ell+1}$ and $q_1, \ldots, q_\ell$ be as in Theorem 18.2. Define polynomials $s_0, s_1, \ldots, s_{\ell+1} \in F[\mathsf{X}]$ and $t_0, t_1, \ldots, t_{\ell+1} \in F[\mathsf{X}]$ as follows:*

$$s_0 := 1, \quad t_0 := 0,$$
$$s_1 := 0, \quad t_1 := 1,$$

and for $i = 1, \ldots, \ell$,

$$s_{i+1} := s_{i-1} - s_i q_i, \quad t_{i+1} := t_{i-1} - t_i q_i.$$

Then:

(i) *for* $i = 0, \ldots, \ell+1$, *we have* $s_i a + t_i b = r_i$; *in particular,* $s_\ell a + t_\ell b = \mathrm{lc}(r_\ell) \gcd(a, b)$;

(ii) *for* $i = 0, \ldots, \ell$, *we have* $s_i t_{i+1} - t_i s_{i+1} = (-1)^i$;

(iii) *for* $i = 0, \ldots, \ell+1$, *we have* $\gcd(s_i, t_i) = 1$;

(iv) *for* $i = 1, \ldots, \ell+1$, *we have*

$$\deg(t_i) = \deg(a) - \deg(r_{i-1}),$$

and for $i = 2, \ldots, \ell+1$, *we have*

$$\deg(s_i) = \deg(b) - \deg(r_{i-1}).$$

Proof. (i), (ii), and (iii) are proved just as in the corresponding parts of Theorem 4.3.

For (iv), the proof will hinge on the following facts:

- For $i = 1, \ldots, \ell$, we have $\deg(r_{i-1}) \geq \deg(r_i)$, and since q_i is the quotient in dividing r_{i-1} by r_i, we have $\deg(q_i) = \deg(r_{i-1}) - \deg(r_i)$.
- For $i = 2, \ldots, \ell$, we have $\deg(r_{i-1}) > \deg(r_i)$.

We prove the statement involving the t_i by induction on i, and leave the proof of the statement involving the s_i to the reader.

One can see by inspection that this statement holds for $i = 1$, since $\deg(t_1) = 0$ and $r_0 = a$. If $\ell = 0$, there is nothing more to prove, so assume that $\ell > 0$ and $b \neq 0$.

Now, for $i = 2$, we have $t_2 = 0 - 1 \cdot q_1 = -q_1$. Thus, $\deg(t_2) = \deg(q_1) = \deg(r_0) - \deg(r_1) = \deg(a) - \deg(r_1)$.

Now for the induction step. Assume $i \geq 3$. Then we have

$$\begin{aligned}
\deg(t_{i-1} q_{i-1}) &= \deg(t_{i-1}) + \deg(q_{i-1}) \\
&= \deg(a) - \deg(r_{i-2}) + \deg(q_{i-1}) \quad \text{(by induction)} \\
&= \deg(a) - \deg(r_{i-1}) \\
&\quad (\text{since } \deg(q_{i-1}) = \deg(r_{i-2}) - \deg(r_{i-1})) \\
&> \deg(a) - \deg(r_{i-3}) \quad (\text{since } \deg(r_{i-3}) > \deg(r_{i-1})) \\
&= \deg(t_{i-2}) \quad \text{(by induction)}.
\end{aligned}$$

By definition, $t_i = t_{i-2} - t_{i-1} q_{i-1}$, and from the above reasoning, we see that

$$\deg(a) - \deg(r_{i-1}) = \deg(t_{i-1} q_{i-1}) > \deg(t_{i-2}),$$

from which it follows that $\deg(t_i) = \deg(a) - \deg(r_{i-1})$. $\square$

Note that part (iv) of the theorem implies that for $i = 1, \ldots, \ell + 1$, we have $\deg(t_i) \leq \deg(a)$ and $\deg(s_i) \leq \deg(b)$. Moreover, if $\deg(a) > 0$ and $b \neq 0$, then $\ell > 0$ and $\deg(r_{\ell-1}) > 0$, and hence $\deg(t_\ell) < \deg(a)$ and $\deg(s_\ell) < \deg(b)$.

We can easily turn the scheme described in Theorem 18.4 into a simple algorithm, taking as input polynomials $a, b \in F[X]$, such that $\deg(a) \geq \deg(b)$ and $a \neq 0$, and producing as output polynomials $d, s, t \in F[X]$ such that $d = \gcd(a, b)$ and $as + bt = d$:

$\quad r \leftarrow a, \; r' \leftarrow b$
$\quad s \leftarrow 1, \; s' \leftarrow 0$
$\quad t \leftarrow 0, \; t' \leftarrow 1$
$\quad$ while $r' \neq 0$ do
$\qquad$ Compute q, r'' such that $r = r'q + r''$, with $\deg(r'') < \deg(r')$
$\qquad (r, s, t, r', s', t') \leftarrow (r', s', t', r'', s - s'q, t - t'q)$
$\quad c \leftarrow \mathrm{lc}(r)$
$\quad d \leftarrow r/c, \; s \leftarrow s/c, \; t \leftarrow t/c \quad // \; make\ monic$
$\quad$ output d, s, t

Theorem 18.5. *The extended Euclidean algorithm for polynomials uses* $O(\mathrm{len}(a)\,\mathrm{len}(b))$ *operations in* F.

Proof. Exercise. $\square$

18.4 Computing modular inverses and Chinese remaindering

In this and the remaining sections of this chapter, we explore various applications of Euclid's algorithm for polynomials. Most of these applications are analogous to their integer counterparts, although there are some differences to watch for. Throughout this section, F denotes a field.

We begin with the obvious application of the extended Euclidean algorithm for polynomials to the problem of computing multiplicative inverses in $F[X]/(n)$, where $n \in F[X]$ with $\ell := \deg(n) > 0$.

Given $y \in F[X]$ with $\deg(y) < \ell$, using $O(\ell^2)$ operations in F, we can determine if y is relatively prime to n, and if so, compute $y^{-1} \bmod n$ as follows. We run the extended Euclidean algorithm on inputs $a := n$ and $b := y$, obtaining polynomials d, s, t such that $d = \gcd(n, y)$ and $ns + yt = d$. If $d \neq 1$, then y does not have a multiplicative inverse modulo n. Otherwise, if $d = 1$, then t is a multiplicative inverse of y modulo n. Moreover, by Theorem 18.4, and the discussion immediately following, $\deg(t) < \ell$, and so $t = y^{-1} \bmod n$.

If the polynomial n is irreducible, then $F[X]/(n)$ is a field, and the extended Euclidean algorithm, together with the basic algorithms for addition, subtraction, and multiplication modulo n, yield efficient algorithms for performing addition, subtraction, multiplication and division in the extension field $F[X]/(n)$.

We also observe that the Chinese remainder theorem for polynomials (Theorem 17.17) can be made computationally effective as well:

Theorem 18.6. *Given polynomials $n_1, \ldots, n_k \in F[X]$ and $a_1, \ldots, a_k \in F[X]$, where $n_1, \ldots, n_k$ are pairwise relatively prime, and where $\deg(n_i) > 0$ and $\deg(a_i) < \deg(n_i)$ for $i = 1, \ldots, k$, we can compute the polynomial $z \in F[X]$, such that $\deg(z) < \deg(n)$ and $z \equiv a_i \pmod{n_i}$ for $i = 1, \ldots, k$, where $n := \prod_i n_i$, using $O(\operatorname{len}(n)^2)$ operations in F.*

Proof. Exercise (just use the formulas in the proof of Theorem 2.8, which are repeated below the statement of Theorem 17.17). $\square$

18.4.1 Chinese remaindering and polynomial interpolation

We remind the reader of the discussion following Theorem 17.17, where the point was made that when $n_i = (X - b_i)$ for $i = 1, \ldots, k$, then the Chinese remainder theorem for polynomials reduces to Lagrange interpolation. Thus, Theorem 18.6 says that given distinct elements $b_1, \ldots, b_k \in F$, along with elements $a_1, \ldots, a_k \in F$, we can compute the unique polynomial $z \in F[X]$ of degree less than k such that

$$z(b_i) = a_i \quad (i = 1, \ldots, k),$$

using $O(k^2)$ operations in F.

It is perhaps worth noting that we could also solve the polynomial interpolation problem using Gaussian elimination, by inverting the corresponding Vandermonde matrix. However, this algorithm would use $O(k^3)$ operations in F. This is a specific instance of a more general phenomenon: there are many computational problems involving polynomials over fields that can be solved using Gaussian elimination, but which can be solved more efficiently using more specialized algorithmic techniques.

EXERCISE 18.7. State and re-work the polynomial analog of Exercises 4.3 and 4.4. In the special case of polynomial interpolation, this algorithm is called **Newton interpolation**.

18.4.2 Mutual independence and secret sharing

As we also saw in the discussion following Theorem 17.17, for $\ell \leq k$ and fixed and distinct $b_1, \ldots, b_\ell \in F$, the "multi-point evaluation" map $\sigma : F[X]_{<k} \to F^{\times \ell}$ that sends a polynomial $z \in F[X]$ of degree less than k to $(z(b_1), \ldots, z(b_\ell)) \in F^{\times \ell}$ is a surjective F-linear map.

If F is a finite field, then this has the following probabilistic interpretation: if the coefficient vector $(z_0, \ldots, z_{k-1})$ of z is a random variable, uniformly distributed over $F^{\times k}$, then the random variable $(z(b_1), \ldots, z(b_\ell))$ is uniformly distributed over $F^{\times \ell}$ (see part (a) of Exercise 8.22). Put another way, the collection $\{z(b) : b \in F\}$ of random variables is ℓ-wise independent, where each individual $z(b)$ is uniformly distributed over F. Clearly, given z and b, we can efficiently compute the value of $z(b)$, so this construction gives us a nice way to build effectively constructible, ℓ-wise independent collections of random variables for any ℓ, thus generalizing the constructions in Example 6.17 and Exercise 6.16 of pairwise and 3-wise independent collections.

As a particular application of this idea, we describe a simple **secret sharing scheme**. Suppose Alice wants to share a secret among some number m of parties, call them $P_1, \ldots, P_m$, in such a way that if less than k parties share their individual secret shares with one another, then Alice's secret is still well hidden, while any subset of k parties can reconstruct Alice's secret.

She can do this as follows. Suppose her secret s is (or can be encoded as) an element of a finite field F, and that $b_0, b_1, \ldots, b_m$ are some fixed, distinct elements of F, where $b_0 = 0$. This presumes, of course, that $|F| \geq m+1$. To share her secret s, Alice chooses $z_1, \ldots, z_{k-1} \in F$ at random, and sets $z_0 := s$. Let $z \in F[X]$ be the polynomial whose coefficient vector is $(z_0, \ldots, z_{k-1})$; that is,

$$z = \sum_{i=0}^{k-1} z_i X^i.$$

For $i = 1, \ldots, m$, Alice gives party P_i its share

$$a_i := z(b_i).$$

For the purposes of analysis, it is convenient to define

$$a_0 := z(b_0) = z(0) = z_0 = s.$$

Clearly, if any k parties pool their shares, they can reconstruct Alice's secret by interpolating a polynomial of degree less than k at k points—the constant term of this polynomial is equal to Alice's secret s.

It remains to show that Alice's secret remains well hidden provided less than k parties pool their shares. To do this, first assume that Alice's secret s is uniformly distributed over F, independently of $z_1, \ldots, z_{k-1}$ (we will relax this assumption below). With this assumption, $z_0, z_1, \ldots, z_{k-1}$ are independently and uniformly distributed over F. Now consider any subset of $k-1$ parties; to simplify notation, assume the parties are $P_1, \ldots, P_{k-1}$. Then the random variables $a_0, a_1, \ldots, a_{k-1}$ are mutually independent. The variables $a_1, \ldots, a_{k-1}$ are of course the shares of $P_1, \ldots, P_{k-1}$, while a_0 is equal to Alice's secret (the fact that a_0 has two interpretations, one as the value of z at a point, and one as a coefficient of z, plays a crucial role in the analysis). Because of mutual independence, the distribution of a_0, conditioned on fixed values of the shares $a_1, \ldots, a_{k-1}$, is still uniform over F, and so even by pooling their shares, these $k-1$ parties would have no better chance of guessing Alice's secret than they would have without pooling their shares.

Continuing the analysis of the previous paragraph, consider the conditional probability distribution in which we condition on the event that $a_0 = s$ for some specific, fixed value of $s \in F$. Because the $z_0, z_1, \ldots, z_{k-1}$ were initially independently and uniformly distributed over F, and because $z_0 = a_0$, in this conditional probability distribution, we have $z_0 = s$ and $z_1, \ldots, z_{k-1}$ are independently and uniformly distributed over F. So this conditional probability distribution perfectly models the secret sharing algorithm performed by Alice for a specific secret s, without presuming that s is drawn from any particular distribution. Moreover, because the $a_0, a_1, \ldots, a_{k-1}$ were initially independently and uniformly distributed over F, when we condition on the event $a_0 = s$, the variables $a_1, \ldots, a_{k-1}$ are still independently and uniformly distributed over F.

The argument in the previous two paragraphs shows that

> *for any fixed secret s, the shares $a_1, \ldots, a_m$ are $(k-1)$-wise independent, with each individual share a_i uniformly distributed over F.*

This property ensures that Alice's secret is *perfectly* hidden, provided that less than k parties pool their shares: for any secret s, these parties just see a bunch of random values in F, with no particular bias that would give any hint whatsoever as to the actual value of s.

Secret sharing has a number of cryptographic applications, but one simple motivation is the following. Alice may have some data that she wants to "back up" on some file servers, who play the role of the parties $P_1, \ldots, P_m$.

To do this, Alice gives each server a share of her secret data (if she has a lot of data, she can break it up into many small blocks, and process each block separately). If at a later time, Alice wants to restore her data, she contacts any k servers who will give Alice their shares, from which Alice can reconstruct the original data. In using a secret sharing scheme in this way, Alice trusts that the servers are reliable to the extent that they do not modify the value of their shares (as otherwise, this would cause Alice to reconstruct the wrong data). We shall discuss later in this chapter how one can relax this trust assumption. But even with this trust assumption, Alice does gain something above and beyond the simpler solution of just backing up her data on a single server, namely:

- even if some of the servers crash, or are otherwise unreachable, she can still recover her data, as long as at least k are available at the time she wants to do the recovery;

- even if the data on some (but strictly less than k) of the servers is "leaked" to some outside attacker, the attacker gains no information about Alice's data.

EXERCISE 18.8. Suppose that Alice shares secrets $s_1, \ldots, s_t \in F$ with parties $P_1, \ldots, P_m$, so that each P_i has one share of each s_j. At a later time, Alice obtains all the shares held by k of the parties. Show how Alice can reconstruct all of the secrets $s_1, \ldots, s_t$ using $O(k^2 + tk)$ operations in F.

EXERCISE 18.9. Suppose that Alice shares secrets $s_1, \ldots, s_t \in F$ with parties $P_1, \ldots, P_m$, so that each P_i has one share of each s_j. Moreover, Alice does not want to trust that the parties do not maliciously (or accidentally) modify their shares. Show that if Alice has a small amount of secure storage, namely, space for $O(m)$ elements of F that cannot be read or modified by the other parties, then she can effectively protect herself from malicious parties, so that if any particular party tries to give her modified shares, Alice will fail to detect this with probability at most $t/|F|$. If $|F|$ is very large (say, $|F| = 2^{128}$), and t is any realistic value (say, $t \leq 2^{40}$), this failure probability will be acceptably small for all practical purposes. Hint: see Exercise 9.12.

18.4.3 Speeding up algorithms via modular computation

In §4.4, we discussed how the Chinese remainder theorem could be used to speed up certain types of computations involving integers. The example we gave was the multiplication of integer matrices. We can use the same idea to speed up certain types of computations involving polynomials. For example, if one wants to multiply two matrices whose entries are elements of $F[X]$, one can use the Chinese remainder theorem for polynomials to speed things up. This strategy is most easily implemented if F is sufficiently large, so that we can use polynomial evaluation and interpolation directly, and do not have to worry about constructing irreducible polynomials. We leave the details as an exercise.

EXERCISE 18.10. You are give two matrices $A, B \in F[X]^{\ell \times \ell}$. All entries of A and B are polynomials of degree at most M. Assume that $|F| \geq 2M + 1$. Using polynomial evaluation and interpolation, show how to compute the product matrix $C = A \cdot B$ using $O(\ell^2 M^2 + \ell^3 M)$ operations in F. Compare this to the cost of computing C directly, which would be $O(\ell^3 M^2)$.

18.5 Rational function reconstruction and applications

We next state and prove the polynomial analog of Theorem 4.6. As we are now "reconstituting" a rational function, rather than a rational number, we call this procedure **rational function reconstruction**. Because of the relative simplicity of polynomials compared to integers, the rational reconstruction theorem for polynomials is a bit "sharper" than the rational reconstruction theorem for integers. Throughout this section, F denotes a field.

Theorem 18.7. *Let r^*, t^* be non-negative integers, and let $n, y \in F[X]$ be polynomials such that $r^* + t^* \leq \deg(n)$ and $\deg(y) < \deg(n)$. Suppose we run the extended Euclidean algorithm with inputs $a := n$ and $b := y$. Then, adopting the notation of Theorem 18.4, the following hold:*

(i) There exists a unique index $i = 1, \ldots, \ell+1$, such that $\deg(r_i) < r^* \leq \deg(r_{i-1})$, and for this i, we have $t_i \neq 0$.

  Let $r' := r_i$, $s' := s_i$, and $t' := t_i$.

(ii) Furthermore, for any polynomials $r, s, t \in F[X]$ such that

$$r = sn + ty, \quad \deg(r) < r^*, \quad 0 \leq \deg(t) \leq t^*, \qquad (18.1)$$

  we have

$$r = r'\alpha, \ s = s'\alpha, \ t = t'\alpha,$$

  for some non-zero polynomial $\alpha \in F[X]$.

Proof. By hypothesis, $0 \leq r^* \leq \deg(n) = \deg(r_0)$. Moreover, since

$$\deg(r_0), \ldots, \deg(r_\ell), \deg(r_{\ell+1}) = -\infty$$

is a decreasing sequence, and $t_i \neq 0$ for $i = 1, \ldots, \ell + 1$, the first statement of the theorem is clear.

Now let i be defined as in the first statement of the theorem. Also, let r, s, t be as in (18.1).

From part (iv) of Theorem 18.4 and the inequality $r^* \leq \deg(r_{i-1})$, we have

$$\deg(t_i) = \deg(n) - \deg(r_{i-1}) \leq \deg(n) - r^*.$$

From the equalities $r_i = s_i n + t_i y$ and $r = sn + ty$, we have the two congruences:

$$r \equiv ty \pmod{n},$$
$$r_i \equiv t_i y \pmod{n}.$$

Subtracting t_i times the first from t times the second, we obtain

$$rt_i \equiv r_i t \pmod{n}.$$

This says that n divides $rt_i - r_i t$; however, using the bounds $\deg(r) < r^*$ and $\deg(t_i) \leq \deg(n) - r^*$, we see that $\deg(rt_i) < \deg(n)$, and using the bounds $\deg(r_i) < r^*$, $\deg(t) \leq t^*$, and $r^* + t^* \leq \deg(n)$, we see that $\deg(r_i t) < \deg(n)$; it immediately follows that

$$\deg(rt_i - r_i t) < \deg(n).$$

Since n divides $rt_i - r_i t$ and $\deg(rt_i - r_i t) < \deg(n)$, the only possibility is that

$$rt_i - r_i t = 0.$$

The rest of the proof runs *exactly* the same as the corresponding part of the proof of Theorem 4.6, as the reader may easily verify. $\square$

18.5.1 Application: polynomial interpolation with errors

We now discuss the polynomial analog of the application in §4.5.1.

If we "encode" a polynomial $z \in F[X]$, with $\deg(z) < k$, as the sequence $(a_1, \ldots, a_k) \in F^{\times k}$, where $a_i = z(b_i)$, then we can efficiently recover z from this encoding, using an algorithm for polynomial interpolation. Here, of course, the b_i are distinct elements of F, and F is a finite field (which must have at least k elements, of course).

Now suppose that Alice encodes z as $(a_1, \ldots, a_k)$, and sends this encoding to Bob, but that some, say at most ℓ, of the a_i may be corrupted during transmission. Let $(\tilde{a}_1, \ldots, \tilde{a}_k)$ denote the vector actually received by Bob.

Here is how we can use Theorem 18.7 to recover the original value of z from $(\tilde{a}_1, \ldots, \tilde{a}_k)$, assuming:

- the original polynomial z has degree less than k',
- at most ℓ errors occur in transmission, and
- $k \geq 2\ell + k'$.

Let us set $n_i := (\mathtt{X} - b_i)$ for $i = 1, \ldots, k$, and $n := n_1 \cdots n_k$. Now, suppose Bob obtains the corrupted encoding $(\tilde{a}_1, \ldots, \tilde{a}_k)$. Here is what Bob does to recover z:

1. Interpolate, obtaining a polynomial y, with $\deg(y) < k$ and $y(b_i) = \tilde{a}_i$ for $i = 1, \ldots, k$.

2. Run the extended Euclidean algorithm on $a := n$ and $b := y$, and let r', t' be the values obtained from Theorem 18.7 applied with $r^* := k' + \ell$ and $t^* := \ell$.

3. If $t' \mid r'$, output r'/t'; otherwise, output "error."

We claim that the above procedure outputs z, under the assumptions listed above. To see this, let t be the product of the n_i for those values of i where an error occurred. Now, assuming at most ℓ errors occurred, we have $\deg(t) \leq \ell$. Also, let $r := tz$, and note that $\deg(r) < k' + \ell$. We claim that

$$r \equiv ty \pmod{n}. \tag{18.2}$$

To show that (18.2) holds, it suffices to show that

$$tz \equiv ty \pmod{n_i} \tag{18.3}$$

for all $i = 1, \ldots, k$. To show this, consider first an index i at which no error occurred, so that $a_i = \tilde{a}_i$. Then $tz \equiv ta_i \pmod{n_i}$ and $ty \equiv t\tilde{a}_i \equiv ta_i \pmod{n_i}$, and so (18.3) holds for this i. Next, consider an index i for which an error occurred. Then by construction, $tz \equiv 0 \pmod{n_i}$ and $ty \equiv 0 \pmod{n_i}$, and so (18.3) holds for this i. Thus, (18.2) holds, from which it follows that the values r', t' obtained from Theorem 18.7 satisfy

$$\frac{r'}{t'} = \frac{r}{t} = \frac{tz}{t} = z.$$

One easily checks that both the procedures to encode and decode a value z run in time $O(k^2)$. The above scheme is an example of an **error correcting code** called a **Reed–Solomon code**. Note that we are completely free to choose the finite field F however we want, just so long as it is big enough. An attractive choice in some settings is to choose $F = \mathbb{Z}_2[\mathtt{Y}]/(f)$, where $f \in \mathbb{Z}_2[\mathtt{Y}]$ is an irreducible polynomial; with this choice, elements of F may be encoded as bit strings of length $\deg(f)$.

One can combine the above error correction technique with the idea of secret sharing (see §18.4.2) to obtain a secret sharing scheme that is robust, even in the presence of erroneous (as opposed to just missing) shares. More precisely, Alice can share a secret $s \in F$ among parties $P_1, \ldots, P_m$, in such a way that (1) if less than k' parties pool their shares, Alice's secret remains well hidden, and (2) from any k shares, we can correctly reconstruct Alice's secret, provided at most ℓ of the shares are incorrect, and $k \geq 2\ell + k'$. To do this, Alice chooses $z_1, \ldots, z_{k'-1} \in F$ at random, sets $z_0 := s$, and $z := \sum_{i=0}^{k'-1} z_i X^i \in F[X]$, and computes the ith share as $a_i := z(b_i)$, for $i = 1, \ldots, m$. Here, we assume that the b_i are distinct, non-zero elements of F. Now, just as in §18.4.2, as long as less than k' parties pool their shares, Alice's secret remains well hidden; however, provided $k \geq 2\ell + k'$, we can correctly and efficiently reconstruct Alice's secret given any k values $\tilde{a}_i$, as long as at most ℓ of the $\tilde{a}_i$ differ from the corresponding value of a_i.

18.5.2 Application: recovering rational functions from their reversed formal Laurent series

We now discuss the polynomial analog of the application in §4.5.2. This is an entirely straightforward translation of the results in §4.5.2, but we shall see in the next chapter that this problem has its own interesting applications.

Suppose Alice knows a rational function $z = s/t \in F(X)$, where s and t are polynomials with $\deg(s) < \deg(t)$, and tells Bob some of the high-order coefficients of the reversed formal Laurent series (see §17.7) representing z in $F((X^{-1}))$. We shall show that if $\deg(t) \leq M$ and Bob is given the bound M on $\deg(t)$, along with the high-order $2M$ coefficients of z, then Bob can determine z, expressed as a rational function in lowest terms.

So suppose that $z = s/t = \sum_{i=1}^{\infty} z_i X^{-i}$, and that Alice tells Bob the coefficients $z_1, \ldots, z_{2M}$. Equivalently, Alice gives Bob the polynomial

$$y := z_1 X^{2M-1} + \cdots + z_{2M-1} X + z_{2M} = \lfloor z X^{2M} \rfloor.$$

Let us define $n := X^{2M}$, so that $y = \lfloor zn \rfloor$. Here is Bob's algorithm for recovering z:

1. Run the extended Euclidean algorithm on inputs $a := n$ and $b := y$, and let s', t' be as in Theorem 18.7, using $r^* := M$ and $t^* := M$.

2. Output s', t'.

We claim that $z = -s'/t'$. To prove this, observe that since $y = \lfloor zn \rfloor = \lfloor (ns)/t \rfloor$, if we set $r := (ns) \bmod t$, then we have

$$r = sn - ty, \ \deg(r) < r^*, \ 0 \leq \deg(t) \leq t^*, \ \text{and} \ r^* + t^* \leq \deg(n).$$

It follows that the polynomials s', t' from Theorem 18.7 satisfy $s = s'\alpha$ and $-t = t'\alpha$ for some non-zero polynomial α. Thus, $s'/t' = -s/t$, which proves the claim.

We may further observe that since the extended Euclidean algorithm guarantees that $\gcd(s', t') = 1$, not only do we obtain z, but we obtain z expressed as a fraction in lowest terms.

It is clear that this algorithm takes $O(M^2)$ operations in F.

The following exercises are the polynomial analogs of Exercises 4.7, 4.9, and 4.10.

EXERCISE 18.11. Let F be a field. Show that given polynomials $s, t \in F[X]$ and integer k, with $\deg(s) < \deg(t)$ and $k > 0$, we can compute the kth coefficient in the reversed formal Laurent series representing s/t using $O(\operatorname{len}(k)\operatorname{len}(t)^2)$ operations in F.

EXERCISE 18.12. Let F be a field. Let $z \in F((X^{-1}))$ be a reversed formal Laurent series whose coefficient sequence is ultimately periodic. Show that $z \in F(X)$.

EXERCISE 18.13. Let F be a field. Let $z = s/t$, where $s, t \in F[X]$, $\deg(s) < \deg(t)$, and $\gcd(s, t) = 1$. Let $d > 1$ be an integer.

(a) Show that if F is finite, there exist integers k, k' such that $0 \le k < k'$ and $sd^k \equiv sd^{k'} \pmod{t}$.

(b) Show that for integers k, k' with $0 \le k < k'$, the sequence of coefficients of the reversed Laurent series representing z is $(k, k' - k)$-periodic if and only if $sd^k \equiv sd^{k'} \pmod{t}$.

(c) Show that if F is finite and $X \nmid t$, then the reversed Laurent series representing z is purely periodic with period equal to the multiplicative order of $[X]_t \in (F[X]/(t))^*$.

(d) More generally, show that if F is finite and $t = X^k t'$, with $X \nmid t'$, then the reversed Laurent series representing z is ultimately periodic with pre-period k and period equal to the multiplicative order of $[X]_{t'} \in (F[X]/(t'))^*$.

18.5.3 *Applications to symbolic algebra*

Rational function reconstruction has applications in symbolic algebra, analogous to those discussed in §4.5.3. In that section, we discussed the application of solving systems of linear equations over the integers using rational reconstruction. In exactly the same way, one can use rational function re-construction to solve systems of linear equations over $F[X]$—the solution to such a system of equations will be a vector whose entries are elements of $F(X)$, the field of rational functions.

18.6 Faster polynomial arithmetic (∗)

The algorithms discussed in §3.5 for faster integer arithmetic are easily adapted to polynomials over a ring. Throughout this section, R denotes a non-trivial ring.

EXERCISE 18.14. State and re-work the analog of Exercise 3.32 for $R[X]$. Your algorithm should multiply two polynomials over R of length at most ℓ using $O(\ell^{\log_2 3})$ operations in R.

It is in fact possible to multiply polynomials over R of length at most ℓ using $O(\ell \operatorname{len}(\ell) \operatorname{len}(\operatorname{len}(\ell)))$ operations in R—we shall develop some of the ideas that lead to such a result below in Exercises 18.23–18.26 (see also the discussion in §18.7).

In Exercises 18.15–18.21 below, assume that we have an algorithm that multiplies two polynomials over R of length at most ℓ using at most $M(\ell)$ operations in R, where M is a well-behaved complexity function (as defined in §3.5).

EXERCISE 18.15. State and re-work the analog of Exercise 3.34 for $R[X]$.

EXERCISE 18.16. This problem is the analog of Exercise 3.35 for $R[X]$. Let us first define the notion of a "floating point" reversed formal Laurent series $\hat{z}$, which is represented as a pair (a, e), where $a \in R[X]$ and $e \in \mathbb{Z}$—the value of $\hat{z}$ is $aX^e \in R((X^{-1}))$, and we call $\operatorname{len}(a)$ the **precision** of $\hat{z}$. We say that $\hat{z}$ is a **length k approximation** of $z \in R((X^{-1}))$ if $\hat{z}$ has precision k and $\hat{z} = (1 + \epsilon)z$ for $\epsilon \in R((X^{-1}))$ with $\deg(\epsilon) \leq -k$, which is the same as saying that the high-order k coefficients of $\hat{z}$ and z are equal. Show how to compute—given monic $b \in R[X]$ and positive integer k—a length k approximation of $1/b \in R((X^{-1}))$ using $O(M(k))$ operations in R. Hint: using Newton iteration, show how to go from a length t approximation of $1/b$ to a length $2t$ approximation, making use of just the high-order $2t$ coefficients of b, and using $O(M(t))$ operations in R.

EXERCISE 18.17. State and re-work the analog of Exercise 3.36 for $R[X]$. Assume that b is a monic polynomial.

EXERCISE 18.18. State and re-work the analog of Exercise 3.37 for $R[X]$.

Conclude that a polynomial of length ℓ can be evaluated at ℓ points using $O(M(\ell)\operatorname{len}(\ell))$ operations in R.

EXERCISE 18.19. State and re-work the analog of Exercise 3.38 for $R[X]$, assuming that R is a field of odd characteristic.

EXERCISE 18.20. State and re-work the analog of Exercise 3.40 for $R[X]$. Assume that $2_R \in R^*$.

The next two exercises develop a useful technique known as **Kronecker substitution**.

EXERCISE 18.21. Let $E := R[X]$. Let $a, b \in E[Y]$ with $a = \sum_{i=0}^{m-1} a_i Y^i$ and $b = \sum_{i=0}^{m-1} b_i Y^i$, where each a_i and b_i is a polynomial in X of degree less than k. The product $c := ab \in E[Y]$ may be written $c = \sum_{i=0}^{2m-2} c_i Y^i$, where each c_i is a polynomial in X. Show how to compute c, given a and b, using $O(M(km))$ operations in R. Hint: for an appropriately chosen integer $t > 0$, first convert a, b to $\tilde{a}, \tilde{b} \in R[X]$, where $\tilde{a} := \sum_{i=0}^{m-1} a_i X^{ti}$ and $\tilde{b} := \sum_{i=0}^{m-1} b_i X^{ti}$; next, compute $\tilde{c} := \tilde{a}\tilde{b} \in R[X]$; finally, "read off" the values c_i from the coefficients of $\tilde{c}$.

EXERCISE 18.22. Assume that ℓ-bit integers can be multiplied in time $\bar{M}(\ell)$, where $\bar{M}$ is a well-behaved complexity function. Let $a, b \in \mathbb{Z}[X]$ with $a = \sum_{i=0}^{m-1} a_i X^i$ and $b = \sum_{i=0}^{m-1} b_i X^i$, where each a_i and b_i is a non-negative integer, strictly less than 2^k. The product $c := ab \in \mathbb{Z}[X]$ may be written $c = \sum_{i=0}^{2m-2} c_i X^i$, where each c_i is a non-negative integer. Show how to compute c, given a and b, using $O(\bar{M}((k + \operatorname{len}(m))m))$ operations in R. Hint: for an appropriately chosen integer $t > 0$, first convert a, b to $\tilde{a}, \tilde{b} \in \mathbb{Z}$, where $\tilde{a} := \sum_{i=0}^{m-1} a_i 2^{ti}$ and $\tilde{b} := \sum_{i=0}^{m-1} b_i 2^{ti}$; next, compute $\tilde{c} := \tilde{a}\tilde{b} \in \mathbb{Z}$; finally, "read off" the values c_i from the bits of $\tilde{c}$.

The following exercises develop an important algorithm for multiplying polynomials in almost-linear time. For integer $n \geq 0$, let us call $\omega \in R$ a **primitive 2^nth root of unity** if $n \geq 1$ and $\omega^{2^{n-1}} = -1_R$, or $n = 0$ and $\omega = 1_R$; if $2_R \neq 0_R$, then in particular, ω has multiplicative order 2^n. For $n \geq 0$, and $\omega \in R$ a primitive 2^nth root of unity, let us define the R-linear map $\mathcal{E}_{n,\omega} : R^{\times 2^n} \to R^{\times 2^n}$ that sends the vector $(g_0, \ldots, g_{2^n-1})$ to the vector $(g(1_R), g(\omega), \ldots, g(\omega^{2^n-1}))$, where $g := \sum_{i=0}^{2^n-1} g_i X^i \in R[X]$.

EXERCISE 18.23. Suppose $2_R \in R^*$ and $\omega \in R$ is a primitive 2^nth root of unity.

(a) Let k be any integer, and consider $\gcd(k, 2^n)$, which must be of the form 2^m for some $m = 0, \ldots, n$. Show that ω^k is a primitive 2^{n-m}th root of unity.

(b) Show that if $n \geq 1$, then $\omega - 1_R \in R^*$.

(c) Show that $\omega^k - 1_R \in R^*$ for all integers $k \not\equiv 0 \pmod{2^n}$.

(d) Show that for any integer k, we have

$$\sum_{i=0}^{2^n - 1} \omega^{ki} = \begin{cases} 2_R^n & \text{if } k \equiv 0 \pmod{2^n}, \\ 0_R & \text{if } k \not\equiv 0 \pmod{2^n}. \end{cases}$$

(e) Let M_2 be the 2-multiplication map on $R^{\times 2^n}$, which is a bijective, R-linear map. Show that

$$\mathcal{E}_{n,\omega} \circ \mathcal{E}_{n,\omega^{-1}} = M_2^n = \mathcal{E}_{n,\omega^{-1}} \circ \mathcal{E}_{n,\omega},$$

and conclude that $\mathcal{E}_{n,\omega}$ is bijective, with $M_2^{-n} \circ \mathcal{E}_{n,\omega^{-1}}$ being its inverse. Hint: write down the matrices representing the maps $\mathcal{E}_{n,\omega}$ and $\mathcal{E}_{n,\omega^{-1}}$.

EXERCISE 18.24. This exercise develops a fast algorithm, called the **fast Fourier transform** or **FFT**, for computing the function $\mathcal{E}_{n,\omega}$. This is a recursive algorithm $FFT(n, \omega; g_0, \ldots, g_{2^n-1})$ that takes as inputs integer $n \geq 0$, a primitive 2^nth root of unity $\omega \in R$, and elements $g_0, \ldots, g_{2^n-1} \in R$, and runs as follows:

> if $n = 0$ then
>> return g_0
>
> else
>> $(\alpha_0, \ldots, \alpha_{2^{n-1}-1}) \leftarrow FFT(n - 1, \omega^2; g_0, g_2, \ldots, g_{2^n-2})$
>> $(\beta_0, \ldots, \beta_{2^{n-1}-1}) \leftarrow FFT(n - 1, \omega^2; g_1, g_3, \ldots, g_{2^n-1})$
>> for $i \leftarrow 0$ to $2^{n-1} - 1$ do
>>> $\gamma_i \leftarrow \alpha_i + \beta_i \omega^i, \quad \gamma_{i+2^{n-1}} \leftarrow \alpha_i - \beta_i \omega^i$
>> return $(\gamma_0, \ldots, \gamma_{2^n-1})$

Show that this algorithm correctly computes $\mathcal{E}_{n,\omega}(g_0, \ldots, g_{2^n-1})$ using $O(2^n n)$ operations in R.

EXERCISE 18.25. Assume $2_R \in R^*$. Suppose that we are given two polynomials $a, b \in R[X]$ of length at most ℓ, along with a primitive 2^nth root of unity $\omega \in R$, where $2\ell \leq 2^n < 4\ell$. Let us "pad" a and b, writing $a = \sum_{i=0}^{2^n-1} a_i X_i$ and $b = \sum_{i=0}^{2^n-1} b_i X_i$, where a_i and b_i are zero for $i \geq \ell$. Show that the following algorithm correctly computes the product of a and b using $O(\ell \operatorname{len}(\ell))$ operations in R:

$$(\alpha_0, \ldots, \alpha_{2^n-1}) \leftarrow FFT(n, \omega; a_0, \ldots, a_{2^n-1})$$
$$(\beta_0, \ldots, \beta_{2^n-1}) \leftarrow FFT(n, \omega; b_0, \ldots, b_{2^n-1})$$
$$(\gamma_0, \ldots, \gamma_{2^n-1}) \leftarrow (\alpha_0\beta_0, \ldots, \alpha_{2^n-1}\beta_{2^n-1})$$
$$(c_0, \ldots, c_{2^n-1}) \leftarrow 2_R^{-n} FFT(n, \omega^{-1}; \gamma_0, \ldots, \gamma_{2^n-1})$$
output $\sum_{i=0}^{2\ell-2} c_i \mathtt{X}^i$

Also, argue more carefully that the algorithm performs $O(\ell \operatorname{len}(\ell))$ additions/subtractions in R, $O(\ell \operatorname{len}(\ell))$ multiplications in R by powers of ω, and $O(\ell)$ other multiplications in R.

EXERCISE 18.26. Assume $2_R \in R^*$. In this exercise, we use the FFT to develop an algorithm that multiplies polynomials over R of length at most ℓ using $O(\ell \operatorname{len}(\ell)^\beta)$ operations in R, where β is a constant. Unlike as in the previous exercise, we do not assume that R contains any particular primitive roots of unity; rather, the algorithm will create them "out of thin air." Suppose that $a, b \in R[\mathtt{X}]$ are of length at most ℓ. Set $k := \lfloor \sqrt{\ell/2} \rfloor$, $m := \lceil \ell/k \rceil$. We may write $a = \sum_{i=0}^{m-1} a_i \mathtt{X}^{ki}$ and $b = \sum_{i=0}^{m-1} b_i \mathtt{X}^{ki}$, where the a_i and b_i are polynomials of length at most k. Let n be the integer determined by $2m \le 2^n < 4m$. Let $f := \mathtt{X}^{2^{n-1}} + 1_R \in R[\mathtt{X}]$, $E := R[\mathtt{X}]/(f)$, and $\omega := [\mathtt{X}]_f \in E$.

(a) Show that ω is a primitive 2^nth root of unity in E, and that given an element $\delta \in E$ and an integer i between 0 and $2^n - 1$, we can compute $\delta \omega^i \in E$ using $O(\ell^{1/2})$ operations in R.

(b) Let $\bar{a} := \sum_{i=0}^{m-1}[a_i]_f \mathtt{Y}^i \in E[\mathtt{Y}]$ and $\bar{b} := \sum_{i=0}^{m-1}[b_i]_f \mathtt{Y}^i \in E[\mathtt{Y}]$. Using the FFT (over E), show how to compute $\bar{c} := \bar{a}\bar{b} \in E[\mathtt{Y}]$ by computing $O(\ell^{1/2})$ products in $R[\mathtt{X}]$ of polynomials of length $O(\ell^{1/2})$, along with $O(\ell \operatorname{len}(\ell))$ additional operations in R.

(c) Show how to compute the coefficients of $c := ab \in R[\mathtt{X}]$ from the value $\bar{c} \in E[\mathtt{Y}]$ computed in part (b), using $O(\ell)$ operations in R.

(d) Based on parts (a)–(c), we obtain a recursive multiplication algorithm: on inputs of length at most ℓ, it performs at most $\alpha_0 \ell \operatorname{len}(\ell)$ operations in R, and calls itself recursively on at most $\alpha_1 \ell^{1/2}$ subproblems, each of length at most $\alpha_2 \ell^{1/2}$; here, α_0, α_1 and α_2 are constants. If we just perform one level of recursion, and immediately switch to a quadratic multiplication algorithm, we obtain an algorithm whose operation count is $O(\ell^{1.5})$. If we perform two levels of recursion, this is reduced to $O(\ell^{1.25})$. For practical purposes, this is probably enough; however, to get an asymptotically better complexity bound, we can let the algorithm recurse all the way down to inputs of some (appropriately chosen) constant length. Show that if we do this, the operation count of the recursive algorithm is $O(\ell \operatorname{len}(\ell)^\beta)$ for some constant β (whose value depends on α_1 and α_2).

The approach used in the previous exercise was a bit sloppy. With a bit more care, one can use the same ideas to get an algorithm that multiplies polynomials over R of length at most ℓ using $O(\ell \operatorname{len}(\ell) \operatorname{len}(\operatorname{len}(\ell)))$ operations in R, assuming $2_R \in R^*$. The next exercise applies similar ideas, but with a few twists, to the problem of *integer* multiplication.

EXERCISE 18.27. This exercise uses the FFT to develop a linear-time algorithm for integer multiplication; however, a rigorous analysis depends on an unproven conjecture (which follows from a generalization of the Riemann hypothesis). Suppose we want to multiply two ℓ-bit, positive integers a and b (represented internally using the data structure described in §3.3). Throughout this exercise, assume that all computations are done on a RAM, and that arithmetic on integers of length $O(\operatorname{len}(\ell))$ takes time $O(1)$. Let k be an integer parameter with $k = \Theta(\operatorname{len}(\ell))$, and let $m := \lceil \ell/k \rceil$. We may write $a = \sum_{i=0}^{m-1} a_i 2^{ki}$ and $b = \sum_{i=0}^{m-1} b_i 2^{ki}$, where $0 \le a_i < 2^k$ and $0 \le b_i < 2^k$. Let n be the integer determined by $2m \le 2^n < 4m$.

(a) Assuming Conjecture 5.24 (and the result of Exercise 5.22), and assuming a deterministic, polynomial-time primality test (such as the one to be presented in Chapter 22), show how to efficiently generate a prime $p \equiv 1 \pmod{2^n}$ and an element $\omega \in \mathbb{Z}_p^*$ of multiplicative order 2^n, such that

$$2^{2k} m < p \le \ell^{O(1)}.$$

Your algorithm should be probabilistic, and run in expected time polynomial in $\operatorname{len}(\ell)$.

(b) Assuming you have computed p and ω as in part (a), let $\bar{a} := \sum_{i=0}^{m-1} [a_i]_p \mathsf{X}^i \in \mathbb{Z}_p[\mathsf{X}]$ and $\bar{b} := \sum_{i=0}^{m-1} [b_i]_p \mathsf{X}^i \in \mathbb{Z}_p[\mathsf{X}]$, and show how to compute $\bar{c} := \bar{a}\bar{b} \in \mathbb{Z}_p[\mathsf{X}]$ in time $O(\ell)$ using the FFT (over $\mathbb{Z}_p$). Here, you may store elements of $\mathbb{Z}_p$ in single memory cells, so that operations in $\mathbb{Z}_p$ take time $O(1)$.

(c) Assuming you have computed $\bar{c} \in \mathbb{Z}_p[\mathsf{X}]$ as in part (b), show how to obtain $c := ab$ in time $O(\ell)$.

(d) Conclude that assuming Conjecture 5.24, we can multiply two ℓ-bit integers on a RAM in time $O(\ell)$.

Note that even if one objects to our accounting practices, and insists on charging $O(\operatorname{len}(\ell)^2)$ time units for arithmetic on numbers of length $O(\operatorname{len}(\ell))$, the algorithm in the previous exercise runs in time $O(\ell \operatorname{len}(\ell)^2)$, which is "almost" linear time.

EXERCISE 18.28. Continuing with the previous exercise:

(a) Show how the algorithm presented there can be implemented on a RAM that has only built-in addition, subtraction, and branching instructions, but no multiplication or division instructions, and still run in time $O(\ell)$. Also, memory cells should store numbers of length at most $\operatorname{len}(\ell) + O(1)$. Hint: represent elements of $\mathbb{Z}_p$ as sequences of base-2^t digits, where $t \approx \alpha \operatorname{len}(\ell)$ for some constant $\alpha < 1$; use table lookup to multiply t-bit numbers, and to perform $2t$-by-t-bit divisions—for α sufficiently small, you can build these tables in time $o(\ell)$.

(b) Using Theorem 5.25, show how to make this algorithm fully deterministic and rigorous, provided that on inputs of length ℓ, it is provided with a certain bit string σ_ℓ of length $O(\operatorname{len}(\ell))$ (this is called a *non-uniform* algorithm).

EXERCISE 18.29. This exercise shows how the algorithm in Exercise 18.27 can be made quite concrete, and fairly practical, as well.

(a) The number $p := 2^{59} 27 + 1$ is a 64-bit prime. Show how to use this value of p in conjunction with the algorithm in Exercise 18.27 with $k = 20$ and any value of ℓ up to 2^{27}.

(b) The numbers $p_1 := 2^{30} 3 + 1$, $p_2 := 2^{28} 13 + 1$, and $p_3 := 2^{27} 29 + 1$ are 32-bit primes. Show how to use the Chinese remainder theorem to modify the algorithm in Exercise 18.27, so that it uses the three primes p_1, p_2, p_3, and so that it works with $k = 32$ and any value of ℓ up to 2^{31}. This variant may be quite practical on a 32-bit machine with built-in instructions for 32-bit multiplication and 64-by-32-bit division.

The previous three exercises indicate that we can multiply integers in essentially linear time, both in theory and in practice. As mentioned in §3.6, there is a different, fully deterministic and rigorously analyzed algorithm that multiplies integers in linear time on a RAM. In fact, that algorithm works on a very restricted type of machine called a "pointer machine," which can be simulated in "real time" on a RAM with a very restricted instruction set (including the type in the previous exercise). That algorithm works with finite approximations to complex roots of unity, rather than roots of unity in a finite field.

We close this section with a cute application of fast polynomial multiplication to the problem of factoring integers.

EXERCISE 18.30. Let n be a large, positive integer. We can factor n using trial division in time $n^{1/2+o(1)}$; however, using fast polynomial arithmetic in $\mathbb{Z}_n[\mathsf{X}]$, one can get a simple, deterministic, and rigorous algorithm that factors n in time $n^{1/4+o(1)}$. Note that all of the factoring algorithms discussed in Chapter 16, while faster, are either probabilistic, or deterministic but heuristic. Assume that we can multiply polynomials in $\mathbb{Z}_n[\mathsf{X}]$ of length at most ℓ using $M(\ell)$ operations in $\mathbb{Z}_n$, where M is a well-behaved complexity function, and $M(\ell) = \ell^{1+o(1)}$ (the algorithm from Exercise 18.26 would suffice).

(a) Let ℓ be a positive integer, and for $i = 1, \ldots, \ell$, let

$$a_i := \prod_{j=0}^{\ell-1} (i\ell - j) \bmod n.$$

Using fast polynomial arithmetic, show how to compute all of the integers $a_1, \ldots, a_\ell$ in time $\ell^{1+o(1)} \operatorname{len}(n)^{O(1)}$.

(b) Using the result of part (a), show how to factor n in time $n^{1/4+o(1)}$ using a deterministic algorithm.

18.7 Notes

Exercise 18.4 is based on an algorithm of Brent and Kung [20]. Using fast matrix arithmetic, Brent and Kung show how this problem can be solved using $O(\ell^{(\omega+1)/2})$ operations in R, where ω is the exponent for matrix multiplication (see §15.6), and so $(\omega + 1)/2 < 1.7$.

The interpretation of Lagrange interpolation as "secret sharing" (see §18.4.2), and its application to cryptography, was made by Shamir [85].

Reed–Solomon codes were first proposed by Reed and Solomon [77], although the decoder presented here was developed later. Theorem 18.7 was proved by Mills [64]. The Reed–Solomon code is just one way of detecting and correcting errors—we have barely scratched the surface of this subject.

Just as in the case of integer arithmetic, the basic "pencil and paper" quadratic-time algorithms discussed in this chapter for polynomial arithmetic are not the best possible. The fastest known algorithms for multiplication of polynomials of length ℓ over a ring R take $O(\ell \operatorname{len}(\ell) \operatorname{len}(\operatorname{len}(\ell)))$ operations in R. These algorithms are all variations on the basic FFT algorithm (see Exercise 18.25), but work without assuming that $2_R \in R^*$ or that R contains any particular primitive roots of unity (we developed some of the ideas in Exercise 18.26). The Euclidean and extended Euclidean algorithms for polynomials over a field F can be implemented so as to take $O(\ell \operatorname{len}(\ell)^2 \operatorname{len}(\operatorname{len}(\ell)))$ operations in F, as can the algorithms for Chinese remaindering and rational function reconstruction. See the book by von zur Gathen and Gerhard [37] for details (as well for an analysis of the Euclidean algorithm for polynomials over the field of rational numbers and over function fields). Depending on the setting and many implementation details, such asymptotically fast algorithms for multiplication and division can be significantly faster than the quadratic-time algorithms, even for quite moderately sized inputs of practical interest. However, the fast Euclidean algorithms are only useful for significantly larger inputs.

19

Linearly generated sequences and applications

In this chapter, we develop some of the theory of linearly generated sequences. As an application, we develop an efficient algorithm for solving sparse systems of linear equations, such as those that arise in the subexponential-time algorithms for discrete logarithms and factoring in Chapter 16. These topics illustrate the beautiful interplay between the arithmetic of polynomials, linear algebra, and the use of randomization in the design of algorithms.

19.1 Basic definitions and properties

Let F be a field, let V be an F-vector space, and consider an infinite sequence

$$S = (\alpha_0, \alpha_1, \alpha_2, \ldots),$$

where $\alpha_i \in V$ for $i = 0, 1, 2 \ldots$. We say that S is **linearly generated (over F)** if there exist scalars $a_0, \ldots, a_{k-1} \in F$ such that the following recurrence relation holds:

$$\alpha_{k+i} = \sum_{j=0}^{k-1} a_j \alpha_{j+i} \quad (\text{for } i = 0, 1, 2, \ldots).$$

In this case, all of the elements of the sequence S are determined by the initial segment $\alpha_0, \ldots, \alpha_{k-1}$, together with the coefficients $a_0, \ldots, a_{k-1}$ defining the recurrence relation.

The general problem we consider is this: how to determine the coefficients defining such a recurrence relation, given a sufficiently long initial segment of S. To study this problem, it turns out to be very useful to rephrase the problem slightly. Let $g \in F[X]$ be a polynomial of degree, say, k, and write

$g = \sum_{j=0}^{k} g_j \mathbf{X}^j$. Next, define

$$g \star S := \sum_{j=0}^{k} g_j \alpha_j.$$

Then it is clear that S is linearly generated if and only if there exists a non-zero polynomial g such that

$$(\mathbf{X}^i g) \star S = 0 \quad (\text{for } i = 0, 1, 2, \ldots). \tag{19.1}$$

Indeed, if there is such a non-zero polynomial g, then we can take

$$a_0 := -(g_0/g_k), \; a_1 := -(g_1/g_k), \; \ldots, \; a_{k-1} := -(g_{k-1}/g_k)$$

as coefficients defining the recurrence relation for S. We call a polynomial g satisfying (19.1) a **generating polynomial** for S. The sequence S will in general have many generating polynomials. Note that the zero polynomial is technically considered a generating polynomial, but is not a very interesting one.

Let $G(S)$ be the set of all generating polynomials for S.

Theorem 19.1. $G(S)$ *is an ideal of* $F[\mathbf{X}]$.

Proof. First, note that for any two polynomials f, g, we have $(f + g) \star S = (f \star S) + (g \star S)$ — this is clear from the definitions. It is also clear that for any $c \in F$ and $f \in F[\mathbf{X}]$, we have $(cf) \star S = c \cdot (f \star S)$. From these two observations, it is immediately clear that $G(S)$ is closed under addition and scalar multiplication. It is also clear from the definition that $G(S)$ is closed under multiplication by $\mathbf{X}$; indeed, if $(\mathbf{X}^i f) \star S = 0$ for all $i \geq 0$, then certainly, $(\mathbf{X}^i (\mathbf{X} f)) \star S = (\mathbf{X}^{i+1} f) \star S = 0$ for all $i \geq 0$. But any non-empty subset of $F[\mathbf{X}]$ that is closed under addition, multiplication by elements of F, and multiplication by $\mathbf{X}$ is an ideal of $F[\mathbf{X}]$ (see Exercise 9.27). $\square$

Since all ideals of $F[\mathbf{X}]$ are principal, it follows that $G(S)$ is the ideal of $F[\mathbf{X}]$ generated by some polynomial $\phi \in F[\mathbf{X}]$ — we can make this polynomial unique by choosing the monic associate (if it is non-zero), and we call this polynomial the **minimal polynomial of** S. Note that S is linearly generated if and only if $\phi \neq 0$.

We can now restate our main objective as follows: given a sufficiently long initial segment of a linearly generated sequence, determine its minimal polynomial.

***Example* 19.1.** Of course, one can always define a linearly generated sequence by simply choosing an initial sequence $\alpha_0, \alpha_1, \ldots, \alpha_{k-1}$, along with the coefficients $g_0, \ldots, g_{k-1}$ of a generating polynomial $g := g_0 + g_1 \mathsf{X} + \cdots + g_{k-1}\mathsf{X}^{k-1} + \mathsf{X}^k$. One can enumerate as many elements of the sequence as one wants by using storage for k elements of V, along with storage for the coefficients of g, as follows:

> $(\beta_0, \ldots, \beta_{k-1}) \leftarrow (\alpha_0, \ldots, \alpha_{k-1})$
> repeat
> > output β_0
> > $\beta' \leftarrow - \sum_{j=0}^{k-1} g_j \beta_j$
> > $(\beta_0, \ldots, \beta_{k-1}) \leftarrow (\beta_1, \ldots, \beta_{k-1}, \beta')$
> forever

Because of the structure of the above algorithm, linearly generated sequences are sometimes also called **shift register sequences**. Also observe that if F is a finite field, and V is finite dimensional, the value stored in the "register" $(\beta_0, \ldots, \beta_{k-1})$ must repeat at some point, from which it follows that the linearly generated sequence must be ultimately periodic (see definitions above Exercise 4.8). $\square$

Example 19.2. Linearly generated sequences can also arise in a natural way, as this example and the next illustrate. Let $E := F[\mathsf{X}]/(f)$, where $f \in F[\mathsf{X}]$ is a monic polynomial of degree $\ell > 0$, and let α be an element of E. Consider the sequence $S := (1, \alpha, \alpha^2, \cdots)$ of powers of α. For any polynomial $g = \sum_{j=0}^{k} g_j \mathsf{X}^j \in F[\mathsf{X}]$, we have

$$g \star S = \sum_{j=0}^{k} g_j \alpha^j = g(\alpha).$$

Now, if $g(\alpha) = 0$, then clearly $(\mathsf{X}^i g) \star S = \alpha^i g(\alpha) = 0$ for all $i \geq 0$. Conversely, if $(\mathsf{X}^i g) \star S = 0$ for all $i \geq 0$, then in particular, $g(\alpha) = 0$. Thus, g is a generating polynomial for S if and only if $g(\alpha) = 0$. It follows that the minimal polynomial ϕ of S is the same as the minimal polynomial of α over F, as defined in §17.5. Furthermore, $\phi \neq 0$, and the degree m of ϕ may be characterized as the smallest positive integer m such that $1, \alpha, \ldots, \alpha^m$ are linearly dependent; moreover, as E has dimension ℓ over F, we must have $m \leq \ell$. $\square$

Example 19.3. Let V be a vector space over F of dimension $\ell > 0$, and let $\tau : V \to V$ be an F-linear map. Let $\beta \in V$, and consider the sequence $S := (\alpha_0, \alpha_1, \ldots)$, where $\alpha_i = \tau^i(\beta)$; that is, $\alpha_0 = \beta$, $\alpha_1 = \tau(\beta)$, $\alpha_2 = \tau(\tau(\beta))$, and so on. For any polynomial $g = \sum_{j=0}^{k} g_j X^j \in F[X]$, we have

$$g \star S = \sum_{j=0}^{k} g_j \tau^j(\beta),$$

and for any $i \geq 0$, we have

$$(X^i g) \star S = \sum_{j=0}^{k} g_j \tau^{i+j}(\beta) = \tau^i \left(\sum_{j=0}^{k} g_j \tau^j(\beta) \right) = \tau^i (g \star S).$$

Thus, if $g \star S = 0$, then clearly $(X^i g) \star S = \tau^i(g \star S) = \tau^i(0) = 0$ for all $i \geq 0$. Conversely, if $(X^i g) \star S = 0$ for all $i \geq 0$, then in particular, $g \star S = 0$. Thus, g is a generating polynomial for S if and only if $g \star S = 0$. The minimal polynomial ϕ of S is non-zero and its degree m is at most ℓ; indeed, m may be characterized as the least non-negative integer such that $\beta, \tau(\beta), \ldots, \tau^m(\beta)$ are linearly dependent, and since V has dimension ℓ over F, we must have $m \leq \ell$.

The previous example can be seen as a special case of this one, by taking V to be E, τ to be the α-multiplication map on E, and setting β to 1. $\square$

The problem of computing the minimal polynomial of a linearly generated sequence can always be solved by means of Gaussian elimination. For example, the minimal polynomial of the sequence discussed in Example 19.2 can be computed using the algorithm described in §18.2. The minimal polynomial of the sequence discussed in Example 19.3 can be computed in a similar manner. Also, Exercise 19.3 below shows how one can reformulate another special case of the problem so that it is easily solved by Gaussian elimination. However, in the following sections, we will present algorithms for computing minimal polynomials for certain types of linearly generated sequences that are much more efficient than any algorithm based on Gaussian elimination.

EXERCISE 19.1. Show that the only sequence for which 1 is a generating polynomial is the "all zero" sequence.

EXERCISE 19.2. Let $S = (\alpha_0, \alpha_1, \ldots)$ be a sequence of elements of an F-vector space V. Further, suppose that S has non-zero minimal polynomial ϕ.

(a) Show that for any polynomials $g, h \in F[X]$, if $g \equiv h \pmod{\phi}$, then $g \star S = h \star S$.

(b) Let $m := \deg(\phi)$. Show that if $g \in F[X]$ and $(X^i g) \star S = 0$ for $i = 0, \ldots, m-1$, then g is a generating polynomial for S.

EXERCISE 19.3. This exercise develops an alternative characterization linearly generated sequences. Let $S = (z_0, z_1, \ldots)$ be a sequence of elements of F. Further, suppose that S has minimal polynomial $\phi = \sum_{j=0}^{m} c_j \mathsf{X}^j$ with $m > 0$ and $c_m = 1$. Define the matrix

$$A := \begin{pmatrix} z_0 & z_1 & \cdots & z_{m-1} \\ z_1 & z_2 & \cdots & z_m \\ \vdots & \vdots & \ddots & \vdots \\ z_{m-1} & z_m & \cdots & z_{2m-2} \end{pmatrix} \in F^{m \times m}$$

and the vector

$$w := (z_m, \ldots, z_{2m-1}) \in F^{1 \times m}.$$

Show that

$$v = (-c_0, \ldots, -c_{m-1}) \in F^{1 \times m}$$

is the *unique* solution to the equation

$$vA = w.$$

Hint: show that the rows of A are linearly independent by making use of Exercise 19.2 and the fact that no polynomial of degree less than m is a generating polynomial for S.

EXERCISE 19.4. Suppose that you are given $a_0, \ldots, a_{k-1} \in F$ and $z_0, \ldots, z_{k-1} \in F$. Suppose that for all $i \geq 0$, we define

$$z_{k+i} := \sum_{j=0}^{k-1} a_j z_{j+i}.$$

Given $n \geq 0$, show how to compute z_n using $O(\operatorname{len}(n)k^2)$ operations in F.

EXERCISE 19.5. Let V be a vector space over F, and consider the set $V^{\times \infty}$ of all infinite sequences $(\alpha_0, \alpha_1, \ldots)$, where the α_i are in V. Let us define the scalar product of $g \in F[\mathsf{X}]$ and $S \in V^{\times \infty}$ as

$$g \cdot S = (g \star S, (\mathsf{X}g) \star S, (\mathsf{X}^2 g) \star S, \ldots) \in V^{\times \infty}.$$

Show that with this scalar product, $V^{\times \infty}$ is an $F[\mathsf{X}]$-module, and that a polynomial $g \in F[\mathsf{X}]$ is a generating polynomial for $S \in V^{\times \infty}$ if and only if $g \cdot S = 0$.

19.2 Computing minimal polynomials: a special case

We now tackle the problem of computing the minimal polynomial of a linearly generated sequence from a sufficiently long initial segment.

We shall first address a special case of this problem, namely, the case where the vector space V is just the field F. In this case, we have

$$S = (z_0, z_1, z_2, \ldots),$$

where $z_i \in F$ for $i = 0, 1, 2, \ldots$.

Suppose that we do not know the minimal polynomial ϕ of S, but we know an upper bound $M \geq 0$ on its degree. Then it turns out that the initial segment $z_0, z_1, \ldots z_{2M-1}$ completely determines ϕ, and moreover, we can very efficiently compute ϕ given the bound M and this initial segment. The following theorem provides the essential ingredient.

Theorem 19.2. *Let $S = (z_0, z_1, \ldots)$ be a sequence of elements of F, and define the reversed formal Laurent series*

$$z := \sum_{i=0}^{\infty} z_i X^{-(i+1)} \in F((X^{-1})),$$

whose coefficients are the elements of the sequence S. Then for any $g \in F[X]$, we have $g \in G(S)$ if and only if $gz \in F[X]$. In particular, S is linearly generated if and only if z is a rational function, in which case, its minimal polynomial is the denominator of z when expressed as a fraction in lowest terms.

Proof. Observe that for any polynomial $g \in F[X]$ and any integer $i \geq 0$, the coefficient of $X^{-(i+1)}$ in the product gz is equal to $X^i g \star S$—just look at the formulas defining these expressions! It follows that g is a generating polynomial for S if and only if the coefficients of the negative powers of X in gz are all zero, which is the same as saying that $gz \in F[X]$. Further, if $g \neq 0$ and $h := gz \in F[X]$, then $\deg(h) < \deg(g)$—this follows simply from the fact that $\deg(z) < 0$ (together with the fact that $\deg(h) = \deg(g) + \deg(z)$). All the statements in the theorem follow immediately from these observations. $\square$

By virtue of Theorem 19.2, we can compute the minimal polynomial ϕ of S using the algorithm in §18.5.2 for computing the numerator and denominator of a rational function from its reversed Laurent series expansion. More precisely, we can compute ϕ given the bound M on its degree, along with the first $2M$ elements $z_0, \ldots, z_{2M-1}$ of S, using $O(M^2)$ operations in F. Just for completeness, we write down this algorithm:

1. Run the extended Euclidean algorithm on inputs

$$a := \mathbf{X}^{2M} \quad \text{and} \quad b := z_0 \mathbf{X}^{2M-1} + z_1 \mathbf{X}^{2M-2} + \cdots + z_{2M-1},$$

and let s', t' be as in Theorem 18.7, using $r^* := M$ and $t^* := M$.

2. Output $\phi := t' / \mathrm{lc}(t')$.

The characterization of linearly generated sequences provided by Theorem 19.2 is also very useful in other ways. For example, suppose the field F is finite. As we already saw in Example 19.1, any linearly generated sequence $S := (z_0, z_1, \ldots)$, where the z_i are in F, must be ultimately periodic. However, Theorem 19.2, together with the result of Exercise 18.13, tells us much more; for example, if the minimal polynomial ϕ of S is not divisible by $\mathbf{X}$, then S is purely periodic with period equal to the multiplicative order of $[\mathbf{X}]_\phi \in (F[\mathbf{X}]/(\phi))^*$.

19.3 Computing minimal polynomials: a more general case

Having dealt with the problem of finding the minimal polynomial of a sequence S of elements of F, we address the more general problem, where the elements of S lie in a vector space V over F. We shall only deal with a special case of this problem, but it is one which has useful applications:

- First, we shall assume that V has finite dimension $\ell > 0$ over F.

- Second, we shall assume that the sequence $S = (\alpha_0, \alpha_1, \ldots)$ has **full rank**, by which we mean the following: if the minimal polynomial ϕ of S over F has degree m, then the vectors $\alpha_0, \ldots, \alpha_{m-1}$ are linearly independent. The sequences considered in Examples 19.2 and 19.3 are of this type.

- Third, we shall assume that F is a finite field.

The Dual Space. To develop the theory behind the approach we are going to present, we need to discuss the **dual space** $\mathcal{D}_F(V)$ of V (over F), which consists of all F-linear maps from V into F. We may sometimes refer to elements of $\mathcal{D}_F(V)$ as **projections**. Now, as was discussed in §15.2, if we fix an ordered basis $\gamma_1, \ldots, \gamma_\ell$ for V, the elements of V are in one-to-one correspondence with the coordinate vectors $F^{1 \times \ell}$, where the element $a_1 \gamma_1 + \ldots + a_\ell \gamma_\ell \in V$ corresponds to the coordinate vector $(a_1, \ldots, a_\ell) \in F^{1 \times \ell}$. The elements of $\mathcal{D}_F(V)$ are in one-to-one correspondence with $F^{\ell \times 1}$, where the map $\pi \in \mathcal{D}_F(V)$ corresponds to the column vector whose jth coordinate is $\pi(\gamma_j)$, for $j = 1, \ldots, \ell$. It is natural to call the column vector corresponding to π its **coordinate vector**. A projection $\pi \in \mathcal{D}_F(V)$ may be evaluated at a point $\delta \in V$ by taking the product of the coordinate vector of δ with the coordinate vector of π.

One may also impose a vector space structure on $\mathcal{D}_F(V)$, in a very natural way: for $\pi, \pi' \in \mathcal{D}_F(V)$, the map $\pi + \pi'$ sends $\delta \in V$ to $\pi(\delta) + \pi'(\delta)$, and for $c \in F$, the map $c\pi$ sends $\delta \in V$ to $c\pi(\delta)$. By the observations in the previous paragraph, $\mathcal{D}_F(V)$ is an F-vector space of dimension ℓ; indeed, the sum and scalar multiplication operations on $\mathcal{D}_F(V)$ correspond to analogous operations on coordinate vectors.

One last fact we need about the dual space is the following:

Theorem 19.3. *Let V be an F-vector space of finite dimension $\ell > 0$. For any linearly independent vectors $\delta_1, \ldots, \delta_m \in V$, and any $a_1, \ldots, a_m \in F$, there exists $\pi \in \mathcal{D}_F(V)$ such that $\pi(\delta_i) = a_i$ for $i = 1, \ldots, m$.*

Proof. Fix any ordered basis for V, and let M be the $m \times \ell$ matrix whose ith row is the coordinate vector of δ_i with respect to this ordered basis. Let v be the $m \times 1$ column vector whose ith coordinate is a_i. As the δ_i are linearly independent, the rows of M must also be linearly independent. Therefore, the F-linear map that sends $w \in F^{\ell \times 1}$ to $Mw \in F^{m \times 1}$ is surjective. It follows that any solution w to the equation $v = Mw$ is the coordinate vector of a map $\pi \in \mathcal{D}_F(V)$ that satisfies the requirements of the theorem. $\square$

That completes our digression on the dual space. We now return to the problem of computing the minimal polynomial ϕ of the linearly generated sequence $S = (\alpha_0, \alpha_1, \ldots)$. Assume we have a bound M on the degree of ϕ. As we are assuming S has full rank, we may assume that $M \leq \ell$. For any $\pi \in \mathcal{D}_F(V)$, we may consider the projected sequence $S_\pi = (\pi(\alpha_0), \pi(\alpha_1), \ldots)$. Observe that ϕ is a generating polynomial for S_π; indeed, for any polynomial $g \in F[X]$, we have $g \star S_\pi = \pi(g \star S)$, and hence, for all $i \geq 0$, we have $(X^i \phi) \star S_\pi = \pi((X^i \phi) \star S) = \pi(0) = 0$. Let $\phi_\pi \in F[X]$ denote the minimal polynomial of S_π. Since ϕ_π divides any generating polynomial of S_π, and since ϕ is a generating polynomial for S_π, it follows that ϕ_π is a divisor of ϕ.

This suggests the following algorithm for efficiently computing the minimal polynomial of S:

Algorithm MP:

$g \leftarrow 1 \in F[\mathsf{X}]$
repeat
       choose $\pi \in \mathcal{D}_F(V)$ at random
       compute the first $2M$ terms of the projected sequence S_π
       use the algorithm in §19.2 to compute the minimal polynomial
           ϕ_π of S_π
       $g \leftarrow \mathrm{lcm}(g, \phi_\pi)$
until $g \star S = 0$
output g

A few remarks on the above procedure are in order:

- in every iteration of the main loop, g is the least common multiple of a number of divisors of ϕ, and hence is itself a divisor of ϕ;

- under our assumption that S has full rank, and since g is a monic divisor of ϕ, if $g \star S = 0$, we may safely conclude that $g = \phi$;

- under our assumption that F is finite, choosing a random element π of $\mathcal{D}_F(V)$ amounts to simply choosing at random the entries of the coordinate vector of π, relative to some ordered basis for V;

- we also assume that elements of V are represented as coordinate vectors, so that applying a projection $\pi \in \mathcal{D}_F(V)$ to a vector in V takes $O(\ell)$ operations in F;

- similarly, adding two elements of V, or multiplying an element of V times a scalar, takes $O(\ell)$ operations in F.

Based on the above observations, it follows that when the algorithm halts, its output is correct, and that the cost of each loop iteration is $O(M\ell)$ operations in F. The remaining question to be answered is this: what is the expected number of iterations of the main loop? The answer to this question is $O(1)$, which leads to a total expected cost of Algorithm MP of $O(M\ell)$ operations in F.

The key to establishing that the expected number of iterations of the main loop is constant is provided by the following theorem.

Theorem 19.4. *Let $S = (\alpha_0, \alpha_1, \ldots)$ be a linearly generated sequence over the field F, where the α_i are elements of a vector space V of finite dimension $\ell > 0$. Let ϕ be the minimal polynomial of S over F, let $m := \deg(\phi)$, and assume that S has full rank (i.e., $\alpha_0, \ldots, \alpha_{m-1}$ are linearly independent).*

Under the above assumptions, there exists a surjective F-linear map $\sigma :$ $\mathcal{D}_F(V) \to F[\mathsf{X}]_{<m}$ such that for all $\pi \in \mathcal{D}_F(V)$, the minimal polynomial ϕ_π

of the projected sequence $S_\pi := (\pi(\alpha_0), \pi(\alpha_1), \dots)$ satisfies

$$\phi_\pi = \frac{\phi}{\gcd(\sigma(\pi), \phi)}.$$

Recall that $F[X]_{<m}$ denotes the m-dimensional vector space of polynomials in $F[X]$ of degree less than m.

Proof. While the statement of this theorem looks a bit complicated, its proof is quite straightforward, given our characterization of linearly generated sequences in Theorem 19.2 in terms of rational functions. We build the linear map σ as the composition of two linear maps, σ_0 and σ_1.

Let us define the map

$$\sigma_0 : \ \mathcal{D}_F(V) \to F((X^{-1}))$$

$$\pi \mapsto \sum_{i=0}^{\infty} \pi(\alpha_i) X^{-(i+1)}.$$

We also define the map σ_1 to be the ϕ-multiplication map on $F((X^{-1}))$, that is, the map that sends $z \in F((X^{-1}))$ to $\phi \cdot z \in F((X^{-1}))$. The map σ is just the composition $\sigma = \sigma_1 \circ \sigma_0$. It is clear that both σ_0 and σ_1 are F-linear maps, and hence, so is σ.

First, observe that for $\pi \in \mathcal{D}_F(V)$, the series $z := \sigma_0(\pi)$ is the series associated with the projected sequence S_π, as in Theorem 19.2. Let ϕ_π be the minimal polynomial of S_π. Since ϕ is a generating polynomial for S, it is also a generating polynomial for S_π. Therefore, Theorem 19.2 tells us that

$$h := \sigma(\pi) = \phi \cdot z \in F[X]_{<m},$$

and that ϕ_π is the denominator of z when expressed as a fraction in lowest terms. Now, we have $z = h/\phi$, and it follows that $\phi_\pi = \phi/\gcd(h, \phi)$ is this denominator.

Second, the hypothesis that $\alpha_0, \dots, \alpha_{m-1}$ are linearly independent, together with Theorem 19.3, implies that $\dim_F(\mathrm{img}(\sigma_0)) \geq m$. Also, observe that σ_1 is an injective map (indeed, it is surjective as well). Therefore, $\dim_F(\mathrm{img}(\sigma)) \geq m$. In the previous paragraph, we observed that $\mathrm{img}(\sigma) \subseteq F[X]_{<m}$, and since $\dim_F(F[X]_{<m}) = m$, we may conclude that $\mathrm{img}(\sigma) = F[X]_{<m}$. That proves the theorem. $\square$

Given the above theorem, we can analyze the expected number of iterations of the main loop of Algorithm MP.

First of all, we may as well assume that the degree m of ϕ is greater than 0, as otherwise, we are sure to get ϕ in the very first iteration. Let $\pi_1, \dots, \pi_s$

be the random projections chosen in the first s iterations of Algorithm MP. By Theorem 19.4, the polynomials $\sigma(\pi_1), \ldots, \sigma(\pi_s)$ are uniformly and independently distributed over $F[X]_{<m}$, and we have $g = \phi$ at the end of loop iteration s if and only if $\gcd(\phi, \sigma(\pi_1), \ldots, \sigma(\pi_s)) = 1$.

Let us define $\Lambda_F^{\phi}(s)$ to be the probability that $\gcd(\phi, f_1, \ldots, f_s) = 1$, where $f_1, \ldots, f_s$ are randomly chosen from $F[X]_{<m}$. Thus, the probability that we have $g = \phi$ at the end of loop iteration s is equal to $\Lambda_F^{\phi}(s)$. While one can analyze the quantity $\Lambda_F^{\phi}(s)$, it turns out to be easier, and sufficient for our purposes, to analyze a different quantity. Let us define $\Lambda_F^{m}(s)$ to be the probability that $\gcd(f_1, \ldots, f_s) = 1$, where $f_1, \ldots, f_s$ are randomly chosen from $F[X]_{<m}$. Clearly, $\Lambda_F^{\phi}(s) \geq \Lambda_F^{m}(s)$.

Theorem 19.5. *If F is a finite field of cardinality q, and m and s are positive integers, then we have*

$$\Lambda_F^{m}(s) = 1 - 1/q^{s-1} + (q-1)/q^{sm}.$$

Proof. For any positive integer n, let U_n be the set of all tuples of polynomials $(f_1, \ldots, f_s) \in F[X]_{<n}^{\times s}$ with $\gcd(f_1, \ldots, f_s) = 1$, and let $u_n = |U_n|$. First, let h be any monic polynomial with $k := \deg(h) < n$. The set $U_{n,h}$ of all s-tuples of polynomials of degree less than n whose gcd is h is in one-to-one correspondence with U_{n-k}, via the map that sends $(f_1, \ldots, f_s) \in U_{n,h}$ to $(f_1/h, \ldots, f_s/h) \in U_{n-k}$. As there are q^k possible choices for h of degree k, we see that the set $V_{n,k}$, consisting of tuples $(f_1, \ldots, f_s) \in F[X]_{<n}^{\times s}$ with $\deg(\gcd(f_1, \ldots, f_s)) = k$, has cardinality $q^k u_{n-k}$. Every non-zero element of $F[X]_{<n}^{\times s}$ appears in exactly one of the sets $V_{n,k}$, for $k = 0, \ldots, n-1$. Taking into account the zero polynomial, it follows that

$$q^{sn} = 1 + \sum_{k=0}^{n-1} q^k u_{n-k}, \qquad (19.2)$$

which holds for all $n \geq 1$. Replacing n by $n-1$ in (19.2), we obtain

$$q^{s(n-1)} = 1 + \sum_{k=0}^{n-2} q^k u_{n-1-k}, \qquad (19.3)$$

which holds for all $n \geq 2$, and indeed, holds for $n = 1$ as well. Subtracting q times (19.3) from (19.2), we deduce that for $n \geq 1$,

$$q^{sn} - q^{sn-s+1} = 1 + u_n - q,$$

and rearranging terms:

$$u_n = q^{sn} - q^{sn-s+1} + q - 1.$$

Therefore,

$$\Lambda_F^m(s) = u_m/q^{sm} = 1 - 1/q^{s-1} + (q-1)/q^{sm}. \quad \square$$

From the above theorem, it follows that for $s \geq 1$, the probability P_s that Algorithm MP runs for more than s loop iterations is at most $1/q^{s-1}$. If T is the total number of loop iterations, then

$$\mathsf{E}[T] = \sum_{i \geq 1} \mathsf{P}[T \geq i] = 1 + \sum_{s \geq 1} P_s \leq 1 + \sum_{s \geq 1} 1/q^{s-1} = 1 + \frac{q}{q-1} = O(1).$$

Let us summarize all of the above analysis with the following:

Theorem 19.6. *Let S be a sequence of elements of an F-vector space V of finite dimension $\ell > 0$ over F, where F is a finite field. Assume that S is linearly generated over F with minimal polynomial $\phi \in F[\mathtt{X}]$ of degree m, and that S has full rank (i.e., the first m elements of S are linearly independent). Then given an upper bound M on m, along with the first $2M$ elements of S, Algorithm MP correctly computes ϕ using an expected number of $O(M\ell)$ operations in F.*

We close this section with the following observation. Suppose the sequence S is of the form $(\beta, \tau(\beta), \tau^2(\beta), \ldots)$, where $\beta \in V$ and $\tau : V \to V$ is an F-linear map. Suppose that with respect to some ordered basis for V, elements of V are represented as elements of $F^{1 \times \ell}$, and elements of $\mathcal{D}_F(V)$ are represented as elements of $F^{\ell \times 1}$. The linear map τ also has a corresponding representation as a matrix $A \in F^{\ell \times \ell}$, so that evaluating τ at a point α in V corresponds to multiplying the coordinate vector of α on the right by A. Now, suppose $\beta \in V$ has coordinate vector $b \in F^{1 \times \ell}$ and that $\pi \in \mathcal{D}_F(V)$ has coordinate vector $c^\top \in F^{\ell \times 1}$. Then if $\tilde{S}$ is the sequence of coordinate vectors of the elements of S, we have

$$\tilde{S} = (bA^i)_{i=0}^{\infty} \quad \text{and} \quad S_\pi = (bA^i c^\top)_{i=0}^{\infty}.$$

This more concrete, matrix-oriented point of view is sometimes useful; in particular, it makes quite transparent the symmetry of the roles played by β and π in forming the projected sequence.

EXERCISE 19.6. If $|F| = q$ and $\phi \in F[\mathtt{X}]$ is monic and factors into monic irreducible polynomials in $F[\mathtt{X}]$ as $\phi = p_1^{e_1} \cdots p_r^{e_r}$, show that

$$\Lambda_F^\phi(1) = \prod_{i=1}^{r} (1 - q^{-\deg(p_i)}) \geq 1 - \sum_{i=1}^{r} q^{-\deg(p_i)}.$$

From this, conclude that the probability that Algorithm MP terminates after just one loop iteration is $1 - O(m/q)$, where $m = \deg(\phi)$. Thus, if q is very large relative to m, it is highly likely that Algorithm MP terminates after just one iteration of the main loop.

19.4 Solving sparse linear systems

Let V be a vector space of finite dimension $\ell > 0$ over a finite field F, and let $\tau : V \to V$ be an F-linear map. The goal of this section is to develop time- and space-efficient algorithms for solving equations of the form

$$\tau(\gamma) = \delta; \tag{19.4}$$

that is, given τ and $\delta \in V$, find $\gamma \in V$ satisfying (19.4). The algorithms we develop will have the following properties: they will be probabilistic, and will use an expected number of $O(\ell^2)$ operations in F, an expected number of $O(\ell)$ evaluations of τ, and space for $O(\ell)$ elements of F. By an "evaluation of τ," we mean the computation of $\tau(\alpha)$ for some $\alpha \in V$.

We shall assume that elements of V are represented as coordinate vectors with respect to some fixed ordered basis for V. Now, if the matrix representing τ with respect to the given ordered basis is sparse, having, say, $\ell^{1+o(1)}$ non-zero entries, then the space required to represent τ is $\ell^{1+o(1)}$ elements of F, and the time required to evaluate τ is $\ell^{1+o(1)}$ operations in F. Under these assumptions, our algorithms to solve (19.4) use an expected number of $\ell^{2+o(1)}$ operations in F, and space for $\ell^{1+o(1)}$ elements of F. This is to be compared with standard Gaussian elimination: even if the original matrix is sparse, during the execution of the algorithm, most of the entries in the matrix may eventually be "filled in" with non-zero field elements, leading to a running time of $\Omega(\ell^3)$ operations in F, and a space requirement of $\Omega(\ell^2)$ elements of F. Thus, the algorithms presented here will be much more efficient than Gaussian elimination when the matrix representing τ is sparse.

We hasten to point out that the algorithms presented here may be more efficient than Gaussian elimination in other cases, as well. All that matters is that τ can be evaluated using $o(\ell^2)$ operations in F and/or represented using space for $o(\ell^2)$ elements of F—in either case, we obtain a time and/or space improvement over Gaussian elimination. Indeed, there are applications where the matrix of the linear map τ may not be sparse, but nevertheless has special structure that allows it to be represented and evaluated in subquadratic time and/or space.

We shall only present algorithms that work in two special, but important, cases:

- the first case is where τ is invertible,
- the second case is where τ is not invertible, $\delta = 0$, and a non-zero solution γ to (19.4) is required (i.e., we are looking for a non-zero element of $\ker(\tau)$).

In both cases, the key will be to use Algorithm MP in §19.3 to find the minimal polynomial ϕ of the linearly generated sequence

$$S := (\alpha_0, \alpha_1, \ldots), \quad (\alpha_i = \tau^i(\beta), \; i = 0, 1, \ldots), \tag{19.5}$$

where β is a suitably chosen element of V. From the discussion in Example 19.3, this sequence has full rank, and so we may use Algorithm MP. We may use $M := \ell$ as an upper bound on the degree of ϕ (assuming we know nothing more about τ and β that would allow us to use a smaller upper bound). In using Algorithm MP in this application, note that we do not want to store $\alpha_0, \ldots, \alpha_{2\ell-1}$—if we did, we would not satisfy our stated space bound. Instead of storing the α_i in a "warehouse," we use a "just in time" strategy for computing them, as follows:

- In the body of the main loop of Algorithm MP, where we calculate the values $a_i := \pi(\alpha_i)$, for $i = 0 \ldots 2\ell - 1$, we perform the computation as follows:

  $\alpha \leftarrow \beta$
  for $i \leftarrow 0$ to $2\ell - 1$ do
  $\quad a_i \leftarrow \pi(\alpha), \;\; \alpha \leftarrow \tau(\alpha)$

- In the test at the bottom of the main loop of Algorithm MP, if $g = \sum_{j=0}^{k} g_j \mathsf{X}^j$, we compute $\nu := g \star S \in V$ as follows:

  $\nu \leftarrow 0, \;\; \alpha \leftarrow \beta$
  for $j \leftarrow 0$ to k do
  $\quad \nu \leftarrow \nu + g_j \cdot \alpha, \;\; \alpha \leftarrow \tau(\alpha)$

Alternatively, one could use a Horner-like algorithm:

  $\nu \leftarrow 0$
  for $j \leftarrow k$ down to 0 do
  $\quad \nu \leftarrow \tau(\nu) + g_j \cdot \beta$

With this implementation, Algorithm MP uses an expected number of $O(\ell^2)$ operations in F, an expected number of $O(\ell)$ evaluations of τ, and space for $O(\ell)$ elements of F. Of course, the "warehouse" strategy is faster than the "just in time" strategy by a constant factor, but it uses about ℓ times as much space; thus, for large ℓ, using the "just in time" strategy is a very good time/space trade-off.

The invertible case. Now consider the case where τ is invertible, and we want to solve (19.4) for a given $\delta \in V$. We may as well assume that $\delta \neq 0$, since otherwise, $\gamma = 0$ is the unique solution to (19.4). We proceed as follows. First, using Algorithm MP as discussed above, compute the minimal polynomial ϕ of the sequence S defined in (19.5), using $\beta := \delta$. Let $\phi = \sum_{j=0}^{m} c_j X^j$, where $c_m = 1$ and $m > 0$. Then we have

$$c_0 \delta + c_1 \tau(\delta) + \cdots + c_m \tau^m(\delta) = 0. \tag{19.6}$$

We claim that $c_0 \neq 0$. To prove the claim, suppose that $c_0 = 0$. Then applying τ^{-1} to (19.6), we would obtain

$$c_1 \delta + \cdots + c_m \tau^{m-1}(\delta) = 0,$$

which would imply that ϕ/X is a generating polynomial for S, contradicting the minimality of ϕ. That proves the claim.

Since $c_0 \neq 0$, we can apply τ^{-1} to (19.6), and solve for $\gamma = \tau^{-1}(\delta)$ as follows:

$$\gamma = -c_0^{-1}(c_1 \delta + \cdots + c_m \tau^{m-1}(\delta)).$$

To actually compute γ, we use the same "just in time" strategy as was used in the implementation of the computation of $g \star S$ in Algorithm MP, which costs $O(\ell^2)$ operations in F, $O(\ell)$ evaluations of τ, and space for $O(\ell)$ elements of F.

The non-invertible case. Now consider the case where τ is not invertible, and we want to find non-zero vector $\gamma \in V$ such that $\tau(\gamma) = 0$. The idea is this. Suppose we choose an arbitrary, non-zero element β of V, and use Algorithm MP to compute the minimal polynomial ϕ of the sequence S defined in (19.5), using this value of β. Let $\phi = \sum_{j=0}^{m} c_j X^j$, where $m > 0$ and $c_m = 1$. Then we have

$$c_0 \beta + c_1 \tau(\beta) + \cdots + c_m \tau^m(\beta) = 0. \tag{19.7}$$

Let

$$\gamma := c_1 \beta + \cdots c_m \tau^{m-1}(\beta).$$

We must have $\gamma \neq 0$, since $\gamma = 0$ would imply that $\lfloor \phi/X \rfloor$ is a non-zero generating polynomial for S, contradicting the minimality of ϕ. If it happens that $c_0 = 0$, then equation (19.7) implies that $\tau(\gamma) = 0$, and we are done. As before, to actually compute γ, we use the same "just in time" strategy as was used in the implementation of the computation of $g \star S$ in Algorithm MP, which costs $O(\ell^2)$ operations in F, $O(\ell)$ evaluations of τ, and space for $O(\ell)$ elements of F.

The above approach fails if $c_0 \neq 0$. However, in this "bad" case, equation (19.7) implies that $\beta = -c_0^{-1}\tau(\gamma)$; that is, $\beta \in \mathrm{img}(\tau)$. One way to avoid such a "bad" β is to randomize: as τ is not surjective, the image of τ is a subspace of V of dimension strictly less than ℓ, and therefore, a *randomly* chosen β lies in the image of τ with probability at most $1/|F|$. So a simple technique is to choose repeatedly β at random until we get a "good" β. The overall complexity of the resulting algorithm will be as required: $O(\ell^2)$ expected operations in F, $O(\ell)$ expected evaluations of τ, and space for $O(\ell)$ elements of F.

As a special case of this situation, consider the problem that arose in Chapter 16 in connection with algorithms for computing discrete logarithms and factoring. We had to solve the following problem: given an $\ell \times (\ell - 1)$ matrix M with entries in a finite field F, containing $\ell^{1+o(1)}$ non-zero entries, find a non-zero vector $v \in F^{1 \times \ell}$ such that $vM = 0$. To solve this problem, we can augment the matrix M, adding an extra column of zeros, to get an $\ell \times \ell$ matrix M'. Now, let $V = F^{1 \times \ell}$ and let τ be the F-linear map on V that sends $\gamma \in V$ to $\gamma M'$. A non-zero solution γ to the equation $\tau(\gamma) = 0$ will provide us with the solution to our original problem; thus, we can apply the above technique directly, solving this problem using $\ell^{2+o(1)}$ expected operations in F, and space for $\ell^{1+o(1)}$ elements of F. As a side remark, in this particular application, we can choose a "good" β in the above algorithm without randomization: just choose $\beta := (0, \ldots, 0, 1)$, which is clearly not in the image of τ.

19.5 Computing minimal polynomials in $F[\mathrm{X}]/(f)$ (II)

Let us return to the problem discussed in §18.2: F is a field, $f \in F[\mathrm{X}]$ is a monic polynomial of degree $\ell > 0$, and $E := F[\mathrm{X}]/(f) = F[\eta]$, where $\eta := [\mathrm{X}]_f$; we are given an element $\alpha \in E$, and want to compute the minimal polynomial $\phi \in F[\mathrm{X}]$ of α over F. As discussed in Example 19.2, this problem is equivalent to the problem of computing the minimal polynomial of the sequence

$$S := (\alpha_0, \alpha_1, \ldots) \quad (\alpha_i := \alpha^i, \ i = 0, 1, \ldots),$$

and the sequence has full rank; therefore, we can use Algorithm MP in §19.3 directly to solve this problem, assuming F is a finite field.

If we use the "just in time" strategy in the implementation of Algorithm MP, as was used in §19.4, we get an algorithm that computes the minimal polynomial of α using $O(\ell^3)$ expected operations in F, but space for just $O(\ell^2)$ elements of F. Thus, in terms of space, this approach is far superior to the algorithm in §18.2, based on Gaussian elimination. In terms of time complexity, the algorithm based on linearly generated sequences is a bit slower than the one based on Gaussian elimination (but only by a constant factor). However, if we use any subquadratic-time algorithm for polynomial arithmetic (see §18.6 and §18.7), we immediately get an algorithm that runs in subcubic time, while still using linear space. In the exercises below, you are asked to develop an algorithm that computes the minimal polynomial of α using just $O(\ell^{2.5})$ operations in F, at the expense of requiring space for $O(\ell^{1.5})$ elements of F—this algorithm does not rely on fast polynomial arithmetic, and can be made even faster if such arithmetic is used.

EXERCISE 19.7. Let $f \in F[X]$ be a monic polynomial of degree $\ell > 0$ over a field F, and let $E := F[X]/(f)$. Also, let $\eta := [X]_f \in E$. For computational purposes, we assume that elements of E and $\mathcal{D}_F(E)$ are represented as co-ordinate vectors with respect to the usual "polynomial" basis $1, \eta, \dots, \eta^{\ell-1}$. For $\beta \in E$, let M_β denote the β-multiplication map on E that sends $\alpha \in E$ to $\alpha\beta \in E$, which is an F-linear map from E into E.

(a) Show how to compute—given as input the polynomial f defining E, along with a projection $\pi \in \mathcal{D}_F(E)$ and an element $\beta \in E$—the projection $\pi \circ M_\beta \in \mathcal{D}_F(E)$, using $O(\ell^2)$ operations in F.

(b) Show how to compute—given as input the polynomial f defining E, along with a projection $\pi \in \mathcal{D}_F(E)$, an element $\alpha \in E$, and a parameter $k > 0$—all of the k values

$$\pi(1), \pi(\alpha), \dots, \pi(\alpha^{k-1})$$

using just $O(k\ell + k^{1/2}\ell^2)$ operations in F, and space for $O(k^{1/2}\ell)$ elements of F. Hint: use the same hint as in Exercise 18.4.

EXERCISE 19.8. Let $f \in F[X]$ be a monic polynomial over a finite field F of degree $\ell > 0$, and let $E := F[X]/(f)$. Show how to use the result of the previous exercise, as well as Exercise 18.4, to get an algorithm that computes the minimal polynomial of $\alpha \in E$ over F using $O(\ell^{2.5})$ expected operations in F, and space for $O(\ell^{1.5})$ operations in F.

EXERCISE 19.9. Let $f \in F[X]$ be a monic polynomial of degree $\ell > 0$ over a field F (not necessarily finite), and let $E := F[X]/(f)$. Further, suppose that f is irreducible, so that E is itself a field. Show how to compute the minimal polynomial of $\alpha \in E$ over F *deterministically*, satisfying the following complexity bounds:

(a) $O(\ell^3)$ operations in F and space for $O(\ell)$ elements of F;

(b) $O(\ell^{2.5})$ operations in F and space for $O(\ell^{1.5})$ elements of F.

19.6 The algebra of linear transformations (∗)

Throughout this chapter, one could hear the whispers of the algebra of linear transformations. We develop some of the aspects of this theory here, leaving a number of details as exercises. It will not play a role in any material that follows, but it serves to provide the reader with a "bigger picture."

Let F be a field and V be a non-trivial F-vector space. We denote by $\mathcal{L}_F(V)$ the set of all F-linear maps from V into V. Elements of $\mathcal{L}_F(V)$ are called **linear transformations**. We can make $\mathcal{L}_F(V)$ into an F-vector space by defining addition and scalar multiplication as follows: for $\tau, \tau' \in \mathcal{L}_F(V)$, define $\tau + \tau'$ to be the map that sends $\alpha \in V$ to $\tau(\alpha) + \tau'(\alpha)$; for $c \in F$ and $\tau \in \mathcal{L}_F(V)$, define $c\tau$ to be the map that sends $\alpha \in V$ to $c\tau(\alpha)$.

EXERCISE 19.10. (a) Verify that with addition and scalar multiplication defined as above, $\mathcal{L}_F(V)$ is an F-vector space.

(b) Suppose that V has finite dimension $\ell > 0$. By identifying elements of $\mathcal{L}_F(V)$ with $\ell \times \ell$ matrices over F, show that $\mathcal{L}_F(V)$ has dimension ℓ^2.

As usual, for $\tau, \tau' \in \mathcal{L}_F(V)$, the composed map, $\tau \circ \tau'$ that sends $\alpha \in V$ to $\tau(\tau'(\alpha))$ is also an element of $\mathcal{L}_F(V)$ (verify). As always, function composition is associative (i.e., for $\tau, \tau', \tau'' \in \mathcal{L}_F(V)$, we have $\tau \circ (\tau' \circ \tau'') = (\tau \circ \tau') \circ \tau''$); however, function composition is not in general commutative (i.e., we may have $\tau \circ \tau' \neq \tau' \circ \tau$ for some $\tau, \tau' \in \mathcal{L}_F(V)$). For any $\tau \in \mathcal{L}_F(V)$ and an integer $i \geq 0$, the map τ^i (i.e., the i-fold composition of τ) is also an element of $\mathcal{L}_F(V)$. Note that for any $\tau \in \mathcal{L}_F(V)$, the map τ^0 is by definition just the identity map on V.

For any $\tau \in \mathcal{L}_F(V)$, and for any polynomial $f \in F[\mathsf{X}]$, with $f = \sum_i a_i \mathsf{X}_i$, we denote by $f(\tau)$ the linear transformation

$$f(\tau) := \sum_i a_i \tau^i.$$

EXERCISE 19.11. Verify the following properties of $\mathcal{L}_F(V)$. For all $\tau, \tau', \tau'' \in \mathcal{L}_F(V)$, for all $c \in F$, and all $f, g \in F[\mathsf{X}]$:

(a) $\tau \circ (\tau' + \tau'') = \tau \circ \tau' + \tau \circ \tau''$;

(b) $(\tau' + \tau'') \circ \tau = \tau' \circ \tau + \tau'' \circ \tau$;

(c) $c(\tau \circ \tau') = (c\tau) \circ \tau' = \tau \circ (c\tau')$;

(d) $f(\tau) \circ g(\tau) = (fg)(\tau) = g(\tau) \circ f(\tau)$;

(e) $f(\tau) + g(\tau) = (f + g)(\tau)$.

Under the addition operation of the vector space $\mathcal{L}_F(V)$, and defining multiplication on $\mathcal{L}_F(V)$ using the "∘" operation, we get an algebraic structure that satisfies all the properties of Definition 9.1, with the exception of property (v) of that definition (commutativity). Thus, we can view $\mathcal{L}_F(V)$ as a *non-commutative* ring with unity (the identity map acts as the multiplicative identity).

For a fixed $\tau \in \mathcal{L}_F(V)$, we may consider the subset of $\mathcal{L}_F(V)$,

$$F[\tau] := \{f(\tau) : f \in F[X]\},$$

which does in fact satisfy all the properties of Definition 9.1. Moreover, we can view F as a subring of $F[\tau]$ by identifying $c \in F$ with $c\tau^0 \in F[\tau]$. With this convention, for $f \in F[X]$, the expression $f(\tau)$ has its usual meaning as the value of f evaluated at the point τ in the extension ring $F[\tau]$ of F. Let ϕ_τ is the minimal polynomial of τ over F, so that $F[\tau]$ is isomorphic as an F-algebra to $F[X]/(\phi_\tau)$. We can also characterize ϕ_τ as follows (verify):

> if there exists a non-zero polynomial $f \in F[X]$ such that $f(\tau) = 0$, then ϕ_τ is the monic polynomial of least degree with this property; otherwise, $\phi_\tau = 0$.

Another way to characterize ϕ is as follows (verify):

> ϕ_τ is the minimal polynomial of the sequence $(1, \tau, \tau^2, \ldots)$.

Note that ϕ_τ is never 1 — this follows from the assumption that V is non-trivial.

It is easy to see that if V happens to be finite dimensional, with $\ell := \dim_F(V)$, then by Exercise 19.10, $\mathcal{L}_F(V)$ has dimension ℓ^2. Therefore, there must be a linear dependence among $1, \tau, \ldots, \tau^{\ell^2}$, which implies that the minimal polynomial of τ is non-zero with degree at most ℓ^2. We shall show below that in this case, the minimal polynomial of τ actually has degree at most ℓ.

For a fixed $\tau \in \mathcal{L}_F(V)$, we can define a "scalar multiplication" operation $\odot$, that maps $f \in F[X]$ and $\alpha \in V$ to

$$f \odot \alpha := f(\tau)(\alpha) \in V;$$

that is, if $f = \sum_i a_i X^i$, then

$$f \odot \alpha = \sum_i a_i \tau^i(\alpha).$$

EXERCISE 19.12. Show that the scalar multiplication $\odot$, together with the usual addition operation on V, makes V into an $F[X]$-module; that is, show that for all $f, g \in F[X]$ and $\alpha, \beta \in V$, we have

$$f \odot (g \odot \alpha) = (fg) \odot \alpha, \ (f+g) \odot \alpha = f \odot \alpha + g \odot \alpha,$$
$$f \odot (\alpha + \beta) = f \odot \alpha + f \odot \beta, \ 1 \odot \alpha = \alpha.$$

Note that each choice of τ gives rise to a different $F[X]$-module structure, but all of these structures are extensions of the usual vector space structure, in the sense that for all $c \in F$ and $\alpha \in V$, we have $c \odot \alpha = c\alpha$.

Now, for fixed $\tau \in \mathcal{L}_F(V)$ and $\alpha \in V$, consider the $F[X]$-linear map $\rho_{\tau,\alpha} : F[X] \to V$ that sends $f \in F[X]$ to $f \odot \alpha = f(\tau)(\alpha)$. The kernel of this map must be a submodule, and hence an ideal, of $F[X]$; since every ideal of $F[X]$ is principal, it follows that $\ker(\rho_{\tau,\alpha})$ is the ideal of $F[X]$ generated by some polynomial $\phi_{\tau,\alpha}$, which we can make unique by insisting that it is monic or zero. We call $\phi_{\tau,\alpha}$ the **minimal polynomial of α under** τ. We can also characterize $\phi_{\tau,\alpha}$ as follows (verify):

> if there exists a non-zero polynomial $f \in F[X]$ such that $f(\tau)(\alpha) = 0$, then $\phi_{\tau,\alpha}$ the monic polynomial of least degree with this property; otherwise, $\phi_{\tau,\alpha} = 0$.

Another way to characterize $\phi_{\tau,\alpha}$ is as follows (verify):

> $\phi_{\tau,\alpha}$ is the minimal polynomial of the sequence
> $$(\alpha, \tau(\alpha), \tau^2(\alpha), \ldots).$$

Note that since $\phi_\tau(\tau)$ is the zero map, we have

$$\phi_\tau \odot \alpha = \phi_\tau(\tau)(\alpha) = 0,$$

and hence $\phi_\tau \in \ker(\rho_{\tau,\alpha})$, which means that $\phi_{\tau,\alpha} \mid \phi_\tau$.

Now consider the image of $\rho_{\tau,\alpha}$, which we shall denote by $\langle \alpha \rangle_\tau$. As an $F[X]$-module, $\langle \alpha \rangle_\tau$ is isomorphic to $F[X]/(\phi_{\tau,\alpha})$. In particular, if $\phi_{\tau,\alpha}$ is non-zero and has degree m, then $\langle \alpha \rangle_\tau$ is a vector space of dimension m over F; indeed, the vectors $\alpha, \tau(\alpha), \ldots, \tau^{m-1}(\alpha)$ form a basis for $\langle \alpha \rangle_\tau$ over F; moreover, m is the smallest non-negative integer such that $\alpha, \tau(\alpha), \ldots, \tau^m(\alpha)$ are linearly dependent.

Observe that for any $\beta \in \langle \alpha \rangle_\tau$, we have $\phi_{\tau,\alpha} \odot \beta = 0$; indeed, if $\beta = f \odot \alpha$, then

$$\phi_{\tau,\alpha} \odot (f \odot \alpha) = (\phi_{\tau,\alpha} f) \odot \alpha = f \odot (\phi_{\tau,\alpha} \odot \alpha) = f \odot 0 = 0.$$

In the following three exercises, τ is an element of $\mathcal{L}_F(V)$, and $\odot$ is the associated scalar multiplication that makes V into an $F[X]$-module.

EXERCISE 19.13. Let $\alpha \in V$ have minimal polynomial $f \in F[X]$ under τ, and let $\beta \in V$ have minimal polynomial $g \in F[X]$ under τ. Show that if $\gcd(f, g) = 1$, then

(a) $\langle \alpha \rangle_\tau \cap \langle \beta \rangle_\tau = \{0\}$, and

(b) $\alpha + \beta$ has minimal polynomial $f \cdot g$ under τ.

EXERCISE 19.14. Let $\alpha \in V$. Let $q \in F[X]$ be a monic irreducible polynomial such that $q^e \odot \alpha = 0$ but $q^{e-1} \odot \alpha \neq 0$ for some integer $e \geq 1$. Show that q^e is the minimal polynomial of α under τ.

EXERCISE 19.15. Let $\alpha \in V$, and suppose that α has minimal polynomial $f \in F[X]$ under τ, with $f \neq 0$. Let $g \in F[X]$. Show that $g \odot \alpha$ has minimal polynomial $f / \gcd(f, g)$ under τ.

We are now ready to state the main result of this section, whose statement and proof are analogous to that of Theorem 8.40:

Theorem 19.7. *Let $\tau \in \mathcal{L}_F(V)$, and suppose that τ has non-zero minimal polynomial ϕ. Then there exists $\beta \in V$ such that the minimal polynomial of β under τ is ϕ.*

Proof. Let $\odot$ be the scalar multiplication associated with τ. Let $\phi = p_1^{e_1} \cdots p_r^{e_r}$ be the factorization of ϕ into monic irreducible polynomials in $F[X]$.

First, we claim that for each $i = 1, \ldots, r$, there exists $\alpha_i \in V$ such that $\phi/p_i \odot \alpha_i \neq 0$. Suppose the claim were false: then for some i, we would have $\phi/p_i \odot \alpha = 0$ for all $\alpha \in V$; however, this means that $(\phi/p_i)(\tau) = 0$, contradicting the minimality property in the definition of the minimal polynomial ϕ. That proves the claim.

Let $\alpha_1, \ldots, \alpha_r$ be as in the above claim. Then by Exercise 19.14, each $\phi/p_i^{e_i} \odot \alpha_i$ has minimal polynomial $p_i^{e_i}$ under τ. Finally, by part (b) of Exercise 19.13, the vector

$$\beta := \phi/p_1^{e_1} \odot \alpha_1 + \cdots + \phi/p_r^{e_r} \odot \alpha_r$$

has minimal polynomial ϕ under τ. □

Theorem 19.7 says that if τ has minimal polynomial ϕ of degree $m \geq 0$, then there exists $\beta \in V$ such that

$$\beta, \tau(\beta), \ldots, \tau^{m-1}(\beta)$$

are linearly independent. From this, it immediately follows that:

Theorem 19.8. *If V has finite dimension $\ell > 0$, then for any $\tau \in \mathcal{L}_F(V)$, the minimal polynomial of τ is non-zero of degree at most ℓ.*

We close this section a simple observation. Let V be an arbitrary, non-trivial $F[X]$-module with scalar multiplication $\odot$. Restricting the scalar multiplication from $F[X]$ to F, we can naturally view V as an F-vector space. Let $\tau : V \to V$ be the map that sends $\alpha \in V$ to $X \odot \alpha$. It is easy to see that $\tau \in \mathcal{L}_F(V)$, and that for all polynomials $f \in F[X]$, and all $\alpha \in V$, we have $f \odot \alpha = f(\tau)(\alpha)$. Thus, instead of starting with a vector space and defining an $F[X]$-module structure in terms of a given linear map, we can go the other direction, starting from an $F[X]$-module and obtaining a corresponding linear map. Furthermore, using the language introduced in Examples 14.14 and 14.15, we see that the $F[X]$-exponent of V is the ideal of $F[X]$ generated by the minimal polynomial of τ, and the $F[X]$-order of any element $\alpha \in V$ is the ideal of $F[X]$ generated by the minimal polynomial of α under τ. Theorem 19.7 says that there exists an element in V whose $F[X]$-order is equal to the $F[X]$-exponent of V, assuming the latter is non-zero.

So depending on one's mood, one can place emphasis either on the linear map τ, or just talk about $F[X]$-modules without mentioning any linear maps.

EXERCISE 19.16. Let $\tau \in \mathcal{L}_F(V)$ have non-zero minimal polynomial ϕ of degree m, and let $\phi = p_1^{e_1} \cdots p_r^{e_r}$ be the factorization of ϕ into monic irreducible polynomials in $F[X]$. Let $\odot$ be the scalar multiplication associated with τ. Show that $\beta \in V$ has minimal polynomial ϕ under τ if and only if $\phi/p_i \odot \beta \neq 0$ for $i = 1, \ldots, r$.

EXERCISE 19.17. Let $\tau \in \mathcal{L}_F(V)$ have non-zero minimal polynomial ϕ. Show that τ is an invertible map if and only if $X \nmid \phi$.

EXERCISE 19.18. Let F be a finite field, and let V have finite dimension $\ell > 0$ over F. Let $\tau \in \mathcal{L}_F(V)$ have minimal polynomial ϕ, with $\deg(\phi) = m$ (and of course, by Theorem 19.8, we have $m \leq \ell$). Suppose that $\alpha_1, \ldots, \alpha_s$ are randomly chosen elements of V. Let g_j be the minimal polynomial of α_j under τ, for $j = 1, \ldots, s$. Let Q be the probability that $\mathrm{lcm}(g_1, \ldots, g_s) = \phi$. The goal of this exercise is to show that $Q \geq \Lambda_F^\phi(s)$, where $\Lambda_F^\phi(s)$ is as defined in §19.3.

  (a) Using Theorem 19.7 and Exercise 19.15, show that if $m = \ell$, then $Q = \Lambda_F^\phi(s)$.

  (b) Without the assumption that $m = \ell$, things are a bit more challenging. Adopting the matrix-oriented point of view discussed at the end of §19.3, and transposing everything, show that

    – there exists $\pi \in \mathcal{D}_F(V)$ such that the sequence $(\pi \circ \tau^i)_{i=0}^{\infty}$ has minimal polynomial ϕ, and

    – if, for $j = 1, \ldots, s$, we define h_j to be the minimal polynomial of the sequence $(\pi(\tau^i(\alpha_j)))_{i=0}^{\infty}$, then the probability that $\mathrm{lcm}(h_1, \ldots, h_s) = \phi$ is equal to $\Lambda_F^{\phi}(s)$.

(c) Show that $h_j \mid g_j$, for $j = 1, \ldots, s$, and conclude that $Q \geq \Lambda_F^{\phi}(s)$.

EXERCISE 19.19. Let $f, g \in F[\mathsf{X}]$ with $f \neq 0$, and let $h := f / \gcd(f, g)$. Show that $g \cdot F[\mathsf{X}]/(f)$ and $F[\mathsf{X}]/(h)$ are isomorphic as $F[\mathsf{X}]$-modules.

EXERCISE 19.20. In this exercise, you are to derive the **fundamental theorem of finite dimensional $F[\mathsf{X}]$-modules**, which is completely analogous to the fundamental theorem of finite abelian groups. Both of these results are really special cases of a more general decomposition theorem for modules over a principal ideal domain. Let V be an $F[\mathsf{X}]$-module. Assume that as an F-vector space, V has finite dimension $\ell > 0$, and that the $F[\mathsf{X}]$-exponent of V is generated by the monic polynomial $\phi \in F[\mathsf{X}]$ (note that $1 \leq \deg(\phi) \leq \ell$). Show that there exist monic, non-constant polynomials $\phi_1, \ldots, \phi_t \in F[\mathsf{X}]$ such that

- $\phi_i \mid \phi_{i+1}$ for $i = 1, \ldots, t - 1$, and
- V is isomorphic, as an $F[\mathsf{X}]$-module, to the direct product of $F[\mathsf{X}]$-modules

$$V' := F[\mathsf{X}]/(\phi_1) \times \cdots \times F[\mathsf{X}]/(\phi_t).$$

Moreover, show that the polynomials $\phi_1, \ldots, \phi_t$ satisfying these conditions are uniquely determined, and that $\phi_t = \phi$. Hint: one can just mimic the proof of Theorem 8.44, where the exponent of a group corresponds to the $F[\mathsf{X}]$-exponent of an $F[\mathsf{X}]$-module, and the order of a group element corresponds to the $F[\mathsf{X}]$-order of an element of an $F[\mathsf{X}]$-module—everything translates rather directly, with just a few minor, technical differences, and the previous exercise is useful in proving the uniqueness part of the theorem.

EXERCISE 19.21. Let us adopt the same assumptions and notation as in Exercise 19.20, and let $\tau \in \mathcal{L}_F(V)$ be the map that sends $\alpha \in V$ to $\mathsf{X} \odot \alpha$. Further, let $\sigma : V \to V'$ be the isomorphism of that exercise, and let $\tau' \in \mathcal{L}_F(V')$ be the X-multiplication map on V'.

(a) Show that $\sigma \circ \tau = \tau' \circ \sigma$.

(b) From part (a), derive the following: there exists an ordered basis for V over F, with respect to which the matrix representing τ is the "block diagonal" matrix

$$T = \begin{pmatrix} C_1 & & & \\ & C_2 & & \\ & & \ddots & \\ & & & C_t \end{pmatrix},$$

where each C_i is the companion matrix of ϕ_i (see Example 15.1).

EXERCISE 19.22. Let us adopt the same assumptions and notation as in Exercise 19.20.

(a) Using the result of that exercise, show that V is isomorphic, as an $F[X]$-module, to a direct product of $F[X]$-modules

$$F[X]/(p_1^{e_1}) \times \cdots \times F[X]/(p_r^{e_r}),$$

where the p_i are monic irreducible polynomials (not necessarily distinct) and the e_i are positive integers, and this direct product is unique up to the order of the factors.

(b) Using part (a), show that there exists an ordered basis for V over F, with respect to which the matrix representing τ is the "block diagonal" matrix

$$T' = \begin{pmatrix} C'_1 & & & \\ & C'_2 & & \\ & & \ddots & \\ & & & C'_r \end{pmatrix},$$

where each C'_i is the companion matrix of $p_i^{e_i}$.

EXERCISE 19.23. Let us adopt the same assumptions and notation as in Exercise 19.20.

(a) Suppose $\alpha \in V$ corresponds to $([f_1]_{\phi_1}, \ldots, [f_t]_{\phi_t}) \in V'$ under the isomorphism of that exercise. Show that the $F[X]$-order of α is generated by the polynomial

$$\mathrm{lcm}(\phi_1/\gcd(f_1, \phi_1), \ldots, \phi_t/\gcd(f_t, \phi_t)).$$

(b) Using part (a), give a short and simple proof of the result of Exercise 19.18.

19.7 Notes

Berlekamp [15] and Massey [60] discuss an algorithm for finding the minimal polynomial of a linearly generated sequence that is closely related to the one presented in §19.2, and which has a similar complexity. This connection between Euclid's algorithm and finding minimal polynomials of linearly generated sequences has been observed by many authors, including Mills [64], Welch and Scholtz [102], and Dornstetter [35].

The algorithm presented in §19.3, is due to Wiedemann [103], as are the algorithms for solving sparse linear systems in §19.4, as well as the statement and proof outline of the result in Exercise 19.18.

Our proof of Theorem 19.5 is based on an exposition by Morrison [65].

Using fast matrix and polynomial arithmetic, Shoup [91] shows how to implement the algorithms in §19.5 so as to use just $O(\ell^{(\omega+1)/2})$ operations in F, where ω is the exponent for matrix multiplication (see §15.6), and so $(\omega + 1)/2 < 1.7$.

20

Finite fields

This chapter develops some of the basic theory of finite fields. As we already know (see Theorem 9.7), every finite field must be of cardinality p^w, for some prime p and positive integer w. The main results of this chapter are:

- for any prime p and positive integer w, there exists a finite field of cardinality p^w, and

- any two finite fields of the same cardinality are isomorphic.

20.1 Preliminaries

In this section, we prove a few simple facts that will be useful in this and later chapters; also, for the reader's convenience, we recall a few basic algebraic concepts that were discussed in previous chapters, but which will play important roles in this chapter.

Theorem 20.1. *Let F be a field, and let k, ℓ be positive integers. Then $\mathsf{X}^k - 1$ divides $\mathsf{X}^\ell - 1$ if and only if k divides ℓ.*

Proof. Let $\ell = kq + r$, with $0 \leq r < k$. We have

$$\mathsf{X}^\ell \equiv \mathsf{X}^{kq}\mathsf{X}^r \equiv \mathsf{X}^r \pmod{\mathsf{X}^k - 1},$$

and $\mathsf{X}^r \equiv 1 \pmod{\mathsf{X}^k - 1}$ if and only if $r = 0$. $\square$

Theorem 20.2. *Let $a \geq 2$ be an integer and let k, ℓ be positive integers. Then $a^k - 1$ divides $a^\ell - 1$ if and only if k divides ℓ.*

Proof. The proof is analogous to that of Theorem 20.1. We leave the details to the reader. $\square$

One may combine these two theorems, obtaining:

Theorem 20.3. *Let $a \geq 2$ be an integer, k, ℓ be positive integers, and F a field. Then $X^{a^k} - X$ divides $X^{a^\ell} - X$ if and only if k divides ℓ.*

Proof. We have $X^{a^k} - X$ divides $X^{a^\ell} - X$ iff $X^{a^k-1} - 1$ divides $X^{a^\ell-1} - 1$, and by Theorem 20.1, this happens iff $a^k - 1$ divides $a^\ell - 1$, which by Theorem 20.2 happens iff k divides ℓ. $\square$

Let F be a field. A polynomial $f \in F[X]$ is called **square-free** if it is not divisible by the square of any polynomial of degree greater than zero. Using formal derivatives, we obtain the following useful criterion for establishing that a polynomial is square-free:

Theorem 20.4. *If F is a field, and $f \in F[X]$ with $\gcd(f, \mathbf{D}(f)) = 1$, then f is square-free.*

Proof. Suppose f is not square-free, and write $f = g^2 h$, for $g, h \in F[X]$ with $\deg(g) > 0$. Taking formal derivatives, we have

$$\mathbf{D}(f) = 2g\mathbf{D}(g)h + g^2\mathbf{D}(h),$$

and so clearly, g is a common divisor of f and $\mathbf{D}(f)$. $\square$

We end this section by recalling some concepts discussed earlier, mainly in §17.1, §17.5, and §17.6.

Suppose F is a field, and E is an extension field of F; that is, F is a subfield of E, or F is embedded in E via some canonical embedding, and we identify elements of F with their images in E under this embedding. We may naturally view E as an F-vector space. Assume that as an F-vector space, E has finite dimension $\ell > 0$. This dimension ℓ is called the degree of E over F, and is denoted $(E : F)$; moreover, E is called a finite extension of F.

We may also naturally view E as an F-algebra, either via the inclusion map or via some canonical embedding. Let E' be another field extension of F, and let $\rho : E \to E'$ be a ring homomorphism (which in fact, must be injective). Then ρ is an F-algebra homomorphism if and only if $\rho(a) = a$ for all $a \in F$.

For any $\alpha \in E$, the set $F[\alpha] = \{g(\alpha) : g \in F[X]\}$ is a subfield of E containing F. Moreover, there exists a non-zero polynomial g of degree at most ℓ such that $g(\alpha) = 0$. The monic polynomial ϕ of least degree such that $\phi(\alpha) = 0$ is called the minimal polynomial of α over F, and this polynomial is irreducible over F. The field $F[X]/(\phi)$ is isomorphic, as an F-algebra, to $F[\alpha]$, via the map that sends $[g]_\phi \in F[X]/(\phi)$ to $g(\alpha) \in F[\alpha]$. We have $(F[\alpha] : F) = \deg(\phi)$, and this value is called the degree of α over F. If E' is an extension field of F, and if $\rho : F[\alpha] \rightarrow E'$ is an F-algebra homomorphism, then the action of ρ is completely determined by its action on α; indeed, for any $g \in F[\mathsf{X}]$, we have $\rho(g(\alpha)) = g(\rho(\alpha))$.

20.2 The existence of finite fields

Let F be a finite field. As we saw in Theorem 9.7, F must have cardinality p^w, where p is prime and w is a positive integer, and p is the characteristic of F. However, we can say a bit more than this. As discussed in Example 9.41, the field $\mathbb{Z}_p$ is embedded in F, and so we may simply view $\mathbb{Z}_p$ as a subfield of F. Moreover, it must be the case that w is equal to $(F : \mathbb{Z}_p)$.

We want to show that there exist finite fields of every prime-power cardinality. Actually, we shall prove a more general result:

> *If F is a finite field, then for every integer $\ell \geq 1$, there exists an extension field E of degree ℓ over F.*

For the remainder of this section, F denotes a finite field of cardinality $q = p^w$, where p is prime and $w \geq 1$.

Suppose for the moment that E is an extension of degree ℓ over F. Let us derive some basic facts about E. First, observe that E has cardinality q^ℓ. By Theorem 9.16, E^* is cyclic, and the order of E^* is $q^\ell - 1$. If $\gamma \in E^*$ is a generator for E^*, then every non-zero element of E can be expressed as a power of γ; in particular, every element of E can be expressed as a polynomial in γ with coefficients in F; that is, $E = F[\gamma]$. Let $\phi \in F[\mathsf{X}]$ be the minimal polynomial of γ over F, which is an irreducible polynomial of degree ℓ. It follows that F is isomorphic (as an F-algebra) to $F[\mathsf{X}]/(\phi)$.

So we have shown that any extension of F of degree ℓ must be isomorphic, as an F-algebra, to $F[\mathsf{X}]/(\phi)$ for some irreducible polynomial $\phi \in F[\mathsf{X}]$ of degree ℓ. Conversely, given any irreducible polynomial ϕ over F of degree ℓ, we can construct the finite field $F[\mathsf{X}]/(\phi)$, which has degree ℓ over F. Thus, the question of the existence of a finite fields of degree ℓ over F reduces to the question of the existence of an irreducible polynomial over F of degree ℓ.

We begin with a simple generalization Fermat's little theorem:

Theorem 20.5. *For any $a \in F^*$, we have $a^{q-1} = 1$, and for any $a \in F$, we have $a^q = a$.*

Proof. The multiplicative group of units F^* of F has order $q - 1$, and hence, every $a \in F^*$ satisfies the equation $a^{q-1} = 1$. Multiplying this equation by a yields $a^q = a$ for all $a \in F^*$, and this latter equation obviously holds for $a = 0$ as well. $\square$

Theorem 20.6. *We have*

$$X^q - X = \prod_{a \in F} (X - a).$$

Proof. The polynomial

$$(X^q - X) - \prod_{a \in F} (X - a)$$

has degree less than q, but has q distinct roots (namely, every element of F), and hence must be the zero polynomial. □

The following theorem generalizes Example 17.6:

Theorem 20.7. *Let E be an F-algebra. Then the map $\rho : E \to E$ that sends $\alpha \in E$ to α^q is an F-algebra homomorphism.*

Proof. Recall that E being an F-algebra simply means that E is a ring and that there is a ring homomorphism $\tau : F \to E$, and because F is a field, either τ is injective or E is trivial. Also, recall that ρ being an F-algebra homomorphism simply means that ρ is a ring homomorphism and $\rho(\tau(a)) = \tau(a)$ for all $a \in F$.

Now, if E is trivial, there is nothing to prove. Otherwise, as E contains a copy of F, it must have characteristic p. Since q is a power of the characteristic, the fact that ρ is a ring homomorphism follows from the discussion in Example 9.42. Moreover, by Theorem 20.5, we have $\tau(a)^q = \tau(a^q) = \tau(a)$ for all $a \in F$. □

Theorem 20.8. *Let E be a finite extension of F, and consider the map $\sigma : E \to E$ that sends $\alpha \in E$ to $\alpha^q \in E$. Then σ is an F-algebra automorphism on E. Moreover, if $\alpha \in E$ is such that $\sigma(\alpha) = \alpha$, then $\alpha \in F$.*

Proof. The fact that σ is an F-algebra homomorphism follows from the previous theorem. Any ring homomorphism from a field into a field is injective (see Exercise 9.38). Surjectivity follows from injectivity and finiteness.

For the second statement, observe that $\sigma(\alpha) = \alpha$ if and only if α is a root of the polynomial $X^q - X$, and since all q elements of F are already roots of this polynomial, there can be no other roots. □

The map σ defined in Theorem 20.8 is called the **Frobenius map on E over F**. As it plays a fundamental role in the study of finite fields, let us develop a few simple properties right away.

Since the composition of two F-algebra automorphisms is also an F-algebra automorphism, for any $i \geq 0$, the i-fold composition σ^i that sends $\alpha \in E$ to α^{q^i} is also an F-algebra automorphism.

Since σ is an F-algebra automorphism, the inverse function σ^{-1} is also an F-algebra automorphism. Hence, σ^i is an F-algebra automorphism for all $i \in \mathbb{Z}$. If E has degree ℓ over F, then applying Theorem 20.5 to the field E, we see that σ^ℓ is the identity map, from which it follows that $\sigma^{-1} = \sigma^{\ell-1}$. More generally, we see that for any $i \in \mathbb{Z}$, we have $\sigma^i = \sigma^j$, where $j = i \bmod \ell$.

Thus, in considering integer powers of σ, we need only consider the powers $\sigma^0, \sigma^1, \ldots, \sigma^{\ell-1}$. Furthermore, the powers $\sigma^0, \sigma^1, \ldots, \sigma^{\ell-1}$ are all distinct maps. To see this, assume that $\sigma^i = \sigma^j$ for some i, j with $0 \le i < j < \ell$. Then σ^{j-i} would be the identity map, which would imply that all of the q^ℓ elements of E were roots of the polynomial $\mathsf{X}^{q^{j-i}} - \mathsf{X}$, which is a non-zero polynomial of degree less that q^ℓ, and this yields a contradiction.

The following theorem generalizes Theorem 20.6:

Theorem 20.9. *For $k \ge 1$, let P_k denote the product of all the monic irreducible polynomials in $F[\mathsf{X}]$ of degree k. For all positive integers ℓ, we have*

$$\mathsf{X}^{q^\ell} - \mathsf{X} = \prod_{k \mid \ell} P_k,$$

where the product is over all positive divisors k of ℓ.

Proof. First, we claim that the polynomial $\mathsf{X}^{q^\ell} - \mathsf{X}$ is square-free. This follows immediately from Theorem 20.4, since $\mathbf{D}(\mathsf{X}^{q^\ell} - \mathsf{X}) = q^\ell \mathsf{X}^{q^\ell-1} - 1 = -1$.

So we have reduced the proof to showing that if f is a monic irreducible polynomial of degree k, then f divides $\mathsf{X}^{q^\ell} - \mathsf{X}$ if and only if $k \mid \ell$. Let $E := F[\mathsf{X}]/(f)$, and let $\eta := [\mathsf{X}]_f \in E$, which is a root of f.

For the first implication, assume that f divides $\mathsf{X}^{q^\ell} - \mathsf{X}$. We want to show that $k \mid \ell$. Now, if $\mathsf{X}^{q^\ell} - \mathsf{X} = fg$, then $\eta^{q^\ell} - \eta = f(\eta)g(\eta) = 0$, so $\eta^{q^\ell} = \eta$. Therefore, if σ is the Frobenius map on E over F, then we have $\sigma^\ell(\eta) = \eta$. We claim that $\sigma^\ell(\alpha) = \alpha$ for all $\alpha \in E$. To see this, recall from Theorem 17.1 that for all $h \in F[\mathsf{X}]$ and $\beta \in E$, we have $\sigma^\ell(h(\beta)) = h(\sigma^\ell(\beta))$. Moreover, any $\alpha \in E$ can be expressed as $h(\eta)$ for some $h \in F[\mathsf{X}]$, and so

$$\sigma^\ell(\alpha) = \sigma^\ell(h(\eta)) = h(\sigma^\ell(\eta)) = h(\eta) = \alpha.$$

That proves the claim.

From the claim, it follows that every element of E is a root of $\mathsf{X}^{q^\ell} - \mathsf{X}$. That is, $\prod_{\alpha \in E}(\mathsf{X} - \alpha)$ divides $\mathsf{X}^{q^\ell} - \mathsf{X}$. Applying Theorem 20.6 to the field E, we see that $\prod_{\alpha \in E}(\mathsf{X} - \alpha) = \mathsf{X}^{q^k} - \mathsf{X}$, and hence $\mathsf{X}^{q^k} - \mathsf{X}$ divides $\mathsf{X}^{q^\ell} - \mathsf{X}$. By Theorem 20.3, this implies k divides ℓ.

For the second implication, suppose that $k \mid \ell$. We want to show that $f \mid X^{q^\ell} - X$. Since f is the minimal polynomial of η, and since η is a root of $X^{q^k} - X$, we must have that f divides $X^{q^k} - X$. Since $k \mid \ell$, and applying Theorem 20.3 once more, we see that $X^{q^k} - X$ divides $X^{q^\ell} - X$. That proves the second implication, and hence, the theorem. $\square$

For $\ell \geq 1$, let $\Pi(\ell)$ denote the number of monic irreducible polynomials of degree ℓ in $F[X]$.

Theorem 20.10. *For all $\ell \geq 1$, we have*

$$q^\ell = \sum_{k \mid \ell} k\Pi(k). \tag{20.1}$$

Proof. Just equate the degrees of both sides of the identity in Theorem 20.9. $\square$

From Theorem 20.10 it is easy to deduce that $\Pi(\ell) > 0$ for all ℓ, and in fact, one can prove a density result—essentially a "prime number theorem" for polynomials over finite fields:

Theorem 20.11. *For all $\ell \geq 1$, we have*

$$\frac{q^\ell}{2\ell} \leq \Pi(\ell) \leq \frac{q^\ell}{\ell}, \tag{20.2}$$

and

$$\Pi(\ell) = \frac{q^\ell}{\ell} + O\left(\frac{q^{\ell/2}}{\ell}\right). \tag{20.3}$$

Proof. First, since all the terms in the sum on the right hand side of (20.1) are non-negative, and $\ell\Pi(\ell)$ is one of these terms, we may deduce that $\ell\Pi(\ell) \leq q^\ell$, which proves the second inequality in (20.2). Since this holds for all ℓ, we have

$$\ell\Pi(\ell) = q^\ell - \sum_{\substack{k \mid \ell \\ k < \ell}} k\Pi(k) \geq q^\ell - \sum_{\substack{k \mid \ell \\ k < \ell}} q^k \geq q^\ell - \sum_{k=1}^{\lfloor \ell/2 \rfloor} q^k.$$

Let us set

$$S(q, \ell) := \sum_{k=1}^{\lfloor \ell/2 \rfloor} q^k = \frac{q}{q-1}(q^{\lfloor \ell/2 \rfloor} - 1),$$

so that $\ell\Pi(\ell) \geq q^\ell - S(q, \ell)$. It is easy to see that $S(q, \ell) = O(q^{\ell/2})$, which proves (20.3). For the first inequality of (20.2), it suffices to show that

$S(q, \ell) \leq q^\ell/2$. One can check this directly for $\ell \in \{1, 2, 3\}$ (verify), and for $\ell \geq 4$, we have

$$S(q, \ell) \leq q^{\ell/2+1} \leq q^{\ell-1} \leq q^\ell/2. \quad \square$$

We note that the inequalities in (20.2) are tight, in the sense that $\Pi(\ell) = q^\ell/2\ell$ when $q = 2$ and $\ell = 2$, and $\Pi(\ell) = q^\ell$ when $\ell = 1$. The first inequality in (20.2) implies not only that $\Pi(\ell) > 0$, but that the fraction of all monic degree ℓ polynomials that are irreducible is at least $1/2\ell$, while (20.3) says that this fraction gets arbitrarily close to $1/\ell$ as either q or ℓ are sufficiently large.

EXERCISE 20.1. Starting from Theorem 20.10, show that

$$\Pi(\ell) = \ell^{-1} \sum_{k \mid \ell} \mu(k) q^{\ell/k},$$

where μ is the Möbius function (see §2.6).

EXERCISE 20.2. How many irreducible polynomials of degree 30 over $\mathbb{Z}_2$ are there?

20.3 The subfield structure and uniqueness of finite fields

We begin with a result that holds for field extensions in general.

Theorem 20.12. *Let E be an extension of a field F, and let σ be an F-algebra automorphism on E. Then the set $E' := \{\alpha \in E : \sigma(\alpha) = \alpha\}$ is a subfield of E containing F.*

Proof. By definition, σ acts as the identity function on F, and so $F \subseteq E'$. To show that E' is a subring of E, it suffices to show that E' is closed under addition and multiplication. To show that E' is closed under addition, let $\alpha, \beta \in E'$. Then $\sigma(\alpha + \beta) = \sigma(\alpha) + \sigma(\beta) = \alpha + \beta$, and hence $\alpha + \beta \in E'$. Replacing "+" by "·" in the above argument shows that E' is closed under multiplication. We conclude that E' is a subring of E.

To complete the proof that E' is a subfield of E, we need to show that if $0 \neq \alpha \in E'$ and $\beta \in E$ with $\alpha\beta = 1$, then $\beta \in E'$. We have

$$\alpha\beta = 1 = \sigma(1) = \sigma(\alpha\beta) = \sigma(\alpha)\sigma(\beta) = \alpha\sigma(\beta),$$

and hence $\alpha\beta = \alpha\sigma(\beta)$; canceling α, we obtain $\beta = \sigma(\beta)$, and so $\beta \in E'$. $\square$

The subfield E' in the above theorem is called **the subfield of E fixed** by σ. Turning our attention again to finite fields, the following theorem completely characterizes the subfield structure of a finite field.

Theorem 20.13. *Let E be an extension of degree ℓ of a finite field F, and let σ be the Frobenius map on E over F. Then the intermediate fields E', with $F \subseteq E' \subseteq E$, are in one-to-one correspondence with the divisors k of ℓ, where the divisor k corresponds to the subfield of E fixed by σ^k, which has degree k over F.*

Proof. Let q be the cardinality of F. Let k be a divisor of ℓ. Now, by Theorem 20.6, the polynomial $X^{q^\ell} - X$ splits into distinct linear factors over E, and by Theorem 20.3, the polynomial $X^{q^k} - X$ divides $X^{q^\ell} - X$. Hence, $X^{q^k} - X$ also splits into distinct linear factors over E. This says that the subfield of E fixed by σ^k, which consists of the roots of $X^{q^k} - X$, has precisely q^k elements, and hence is an extension of degree k over F. That proves the existence part of the theorem.

As for uniqueness, we have to show that any intermediate field is of this type. Let E' be an intermediate field of degree k over F. By Theorem 20.6, we have $X^{q^k} - X = \prod_{\alpha \in E'}(X - \alpha)$ and $X^{q^\ell} - X = \prod_{\alpha \in E}(X - \alpha)$, from which it follows that $X^{q^k} - X$ divides $X^{q^\ell} - X$, and so by Theorem 20.3, we must have $k \mid \ell$. There can be no other intermediate fields of the same degree k over F, since the elements of such a field would also be roots of $X^{q^k} - X$. $\square$

The next theorem shows that up to isomorphism, there is only one finite field of a given cardinality.

Theorem 20.14. *Let E, E' be extensions of the same degree over a finite field F. Then E and E' are isomorphic as F-algebras.*

Proof. Let q be of cardinality F, and let ℓ be the degree of the extensions. As we have argued before, we have $E' = F[\alpha']$ for some $\alpha' \in E'$, and so E' is isomorphic as an F-algebra to $F[X]/(\phi)$, where ϕ is the minimal polynomial of α' over F. As ϕ is an irreducible polynomial of degree ℓ, by Theorem 20.9, ϕ divides $X^{q^\ell} - X$, and by Theorem 20.6, $X^{q^\ell} - X = \prod_{\alpha \in E}(X - \alpha)$, from which it follows that ϕ has a root $\alpha \in E$. Since ϕ is irreducible, ϕ is the minimal polynomial of α over F, and hence $F[\alpha]$ is isomorphic as an F-algebra to $F[X]/(\phi)$. Since α has degree ℓ over F, we must have $E = F[\alpha]$. $\square$

EXERCISE 20.3. This exercise develops an alternative proof for the existence of finite fields—however, it does not yield a density result for irreducible polynomials. Let F be a finite field of cardinality q, and let $\ell \geq 1$ be an integer. Let E be a splitting field for the polynomial $X^{q^\ell} - X \in F[X]$ (see

Theorem 17.19), and let σ be the Frobenius map on E over F. Let E' be the subfield of E fixed by σ^ℓ. Show that E' is an extension of F of degree ℓ.

EXERCISE 20.4. Let E be an extension of degree ℓ over a finite field F of cardinality q. Show that at least half the elements of E have degree ℓ over F, and that the total number of elements of degree ℓ over F is $q^\ell + O(q^{\ell/2})$.

20.4 Conjugates, norms and traces

Throughout this section, F denotes a finite field of cardinality q, E denotes an extension over F of degree ℓ, and σ denotes the Frobenius map on E over F.

Consider an element $\alpha \in E$. We say that $\beta \in E$ is **conjugate to** α (**over** F) if $\beta = \sigma^i(\alpha)$ for some $i \in \mathbb{Z}$. The reader may verify that the "conjugate to" relation is an equivalence relation. We call the equivalence classes of this relation **conjugacy classes**, and we call the elements of the conjugacy class containing α the **conjugates of** α.

Starting with α, we can start listing conjugates:

$$\alpha, \sigma(\alpha), \sigma^2(\alpha), \ldots.$$

As σ^ℓ is the identity map, this list will eventually start repeating. Let k be the smallest positive integer such that $\sigma^k(\alpha) = \sigma^i(\alpha)$ for some $i = 0, \ldots, k-1$. It must be the case that $i = 0$ — otherwise, applying σ^{-1} to the equation $\sigma^k(\alpha) = \sigma^i(\alpha)$ would yield $\sigma^{k-1}(\alpha) = \sigma^{i-1}(\alpha)$, and since $0 \le i - 1 < k - 1$, this would contradict the minimality of k.

Thus, $\alpha, \sigma(\alpha), \ldots, \sigma^{k-1}(\alpha)$ are all distinct, and $\sigma^k(\alpha) = \alpha$. Moreover, for any $i \in \mathbb{Z}$, we have $\sigma^i(\alpha) = \sigma^j(\alpha)$, where $j = i \bmod k$, and so $\alpha, \sigma(\alpha), \ldots, \sigma^{k-1}(\alpha)$ are all the conjugates of α. Also, $\sigma^i(\alpha) = \alpha$ if and only if k divides i. Since $\sigma^\ell(\alpha) = \alpha$, it must be the case that k divides ℓ.

With α and k as above, consider the polynomial

$$\phi := \prod_{i=0}^{k-1} (\mathtt{X} - \sigma^i(\alpha)).$$

The coefficients of ϕ obviously lie in E, but we claim that in fact, they lie in F. This is easily seen as follows. Consider the extension of the map σ from E to $E[\mathtt{X}]$ that applies σ coefficient-wise to polynomials. This was discussed in Example 9.48, where we saw that the extended map, which we also denote by σ, is a ring homomorphism from $E[\mathtt{X}]$ into $E[\mathtt{X}]$. Applying σ

to ϕ, we obtain

$$\sigma(\phi) = \prod_{i=0}^{k-1} \sigma(\mathsf{X} - \sigma^i(\alpha)) = \prod_{i=0}^{k-1}(\mathsf{X} - \sigma^{i+1}(\alpha)) = \prod_{i=0}^{k-1}(\mathsf{X} - \sigma^i(\alpha)),$$

since $\sigma^k(\alpha) = \alpha$. Thus we see that $\sigma(\phi) = \phi$. Writing $\phi = \sum_i a_i \mathsf{X}^i$, we see that $\sigma(a_i) = a_i$ for all i, and hence by Theorem 20.8, $a_i \in F$ for all i. Hence $\phi \in F[\mathsf{X}]$. We further claim that ϕ is the minimal polynomial of α. To see this, let $f \in F[\mathsf{X}]$ be any polynomial over F for which α is a root. Then for any integer i, by Theorem 17.1, we have

$$0 = \sigma^i(0) = \sigma^i(f(\alpha)) = f(\sigma^i(\alpha)).$$

Thus, all the conjugates of α are also roots of f, and so ϕ divides f. That proves that ϕ is the minimal polynomial of α. Since ϕ is the minimal polynomial of α and $\deg(\phi) = k$, it follows that the number k is none other than the degree of α over F.

Let us summarize the above discussion as follows:

Theorem 20.15. *Let $\alpha \in E$ be of degree k over F, and let ϕ be the minimal polynomial of α over F. Then k is the smallest positive integer such that $\sigma^k(\alpha) = \alpha$, the distinct conjugates of α are $\alpha, \sigma(\alpha), \ldots, \sigma^{k-1}(\alpha)$, and ϕ factors over E (in fact, over $F[\alpha]$) as*

$$\phi = \prod_{i=0}^{k-1}(\mathsf{X} - \sigma^i(\alpha)).$$

Another useful way of reasoning about conjugates is as follows. First, if $\alpha = 0$, then the degree of α over F is 1, and there is nothing more to say, so let us assume that $\alpha \in E^*$. If r is the multiplicative order of α, then note that any conjugate $\sigma^i(\alpha)$ also has multiplicative order r — this follows from the fact that for any positive integer s, $\alpha^s = 1$ if and only if $(\sigma^i(\alpha))^s = 1$. Also, note that we must have $r \mid |E^*| = q^\ell - 1$, or equivalently, $q^\ell \equiv 1 \pmod{r}$. Focusing now on the fact that σ is the q-power map, we see that the degree k of α is the smallest positive integer such that $\alpha^{q^k} = \alpha$, which holds iff $\alpha^{q^k-1} = 1$, which holds iff $q^k \equiv 1 \pmod{r}$. Thus, the degree of α over F is simply the multiplicative order of q modulo r. Again, we summarize these observations as a theorem:

Theorem 20.16. *If $\alpha \in E^*$ has multiplicative order r, then the degree of α over F is equal to the multiplicative order of q modulo r.*

Let us define the polynomial

$$\chi := \prod_{i=0}^{\ell-1}(\mathtt{X} - \sigma^i(\alpha)).$$

It is easy to see, using the same type of argument as above, that $\chi \in F[\mathtt{X}]$, and indeed, that

$$\chi = \phi^{\ell/k}.$$

The polynomial χ is called the **characteristic polynomial of** α **(from** E **to** F**)**.

Two functions that are often useful are the "norm" and "trace." The **norm of** α **(from** E **to** F**)** is defined as

$$\mathbf{N}_{E/F}(\alpha) := \prod_{i=0}^{\ell-1}\sigma^i(\alpha),$$

while the **trace of** α **(from** E **to** F**)** is defined as

$$\mathbf{Tr}_{E/F}(\alpha) := \sum_{i=0}^{\ell-1}\sigma^i(\alpha).$$

It is easy to see that both the norm and trace of α are elements of F, as they are fixed by σ; alternatively, one can see this by observing that they appear, possibly with a minus sign, as coefficients of the characteristic polynomial χ—indeed, the constant term of χ is equal to $(-1)^{\ell}\mathbf{N}_{E/F}(\alpha)$, and the coefficient of $\mathtt{X}^{\ell-1}$ in χ is $-\mathbf{Tr}_{E/F}(\alpha)$.

The following two theorems summarize the most important facts about the norm and trace functions.

Theorem 20.17. *The function* $\mathbf{N}_{E/F}$*, restricted to* E^**, is a group homomorphism from* E^* *onto* F^**.*

Proof. We have

$$\mathbf{N}_{E/F}(\alpha) = \prod_{i=0}^{\ell-1}\alpha^{q^i} = \alpha^{\sum_{i=0}^{\ell-1}q^i} = \alpha^{(q^{\ell}-1)/(q-1)}.$$

Since E^* is a cyclic group of order $q^{\ell} - 1$, the image of the $(q^{\ell} - 1)/(q - 1)$-power map on E^* is the unique subgroup of E^* of order $q - 1$ (see Theorem 8.31). Since F^* is a subgroup of E^* of order $q - 1$, it follows that the image of this power map is F^*. $\square$

Theorem 20.18. *The function* $\mathbf{Tr}_{E/F}$ *is an* F-*linear map from* E *onto* F*.*

Proof. The fact that $\mathbf{Tr}_{E/F}$ is an F-linear map is a simple consequence of the fact that σ is an F-algebra automorphism (verify). As discussed above, $\mathbf{Tr}_{E/F}$ maps into F. Since the image of $\mathbf{Tr}_{E/F}$ is a subspace of F, the image is either $\{0\}$ or F, and so it suffices to show that $\mathbf{Tr}_{E/F}$ does not map all of E to zero. But an element $\alpha \in E$ is in the kernel of $\mathbf{Tr}_{E/F}$ if and only if α is a root of the polynomial

$$\mathsf{X} + \mathsf{X}^q + \cdots + \mathsf{X}^{q^{\ell-1}},$$

which has degree $q^{\ell-1}$. Since E contains q^ℓ elements, not all elements of E can lie in the kernel of $\mathbf{Tr}_{E/F}$. $\square$

***Example* 20.1.** As an application of some of the above theory, let us investigate the factorization of the polynomial $\mathsf{X}^r - 1$ over F, a finite field of cardinality q. Let us assume that $r > 0$ and is relatively prime to q. Let E be a splitting field of $\mathsf{X}^r - 1$ (see Theorem 17.19), so that E is a finite extension of F in which $\mathsf{X}^r - 1$ splits into linear factors:

$$\mathsf{X}^r - 1 = \prod_{i=1}^{r}(\mathsf{X} - \alpha_i).$$

We claim that the roots α_i of $\mathsf{X}^r - 1$ are distinct—this follows from the Theorem 20.4 and the fact that $\gcd(\mathsf{X}^r - 1, r\mathsf{X}^{r-1}) = 1$.

Next, observe that the r roots of $\mathsf{X}^r - 1$ in E actually form a subgroup of E^*, and since E^* is cyclic, this subgroup must be cyclic as well. So the roots of $\mathsf{X}^r - 1$ form a cyclic subgroup of E^* of order r. Let ζ be a generator for this group. Then all the roots of $\mathsf{X}^r - 1$ are contained in $F[\zeta]$, and so we may as well assume that $E = F[\zeta]$.

Let us compute the degree of ζ over F. By Theorem 20.16, the degree ℓ of ζ over F is the multiplicative order of q modulo r. Moreover, the $\phi(r)$ roots of $\mathsf{X}^r - 1$ of multiplicative order r are partitioned into $\phi(r)/\ell$ conjugacy classes, each of size ℓ; indeed, as the reader is urged to verify, these conjugacy classes are in one-to-one correspondence with the cosets of the subgroup of $\mathbb{Z}_r^*$ generated by $[q]_r$, where each such coset $C \subseteq \mathbb{Z}_r^*$ corresponds to the conjugacy class $\{\zeta^a : [a]_r \in C\}$.

More generally, for any $s \mid r$, any root of $\mathsf{X}^r - 1$ whose multiplicative order is s has degree k over F, where k is the multiplicative order of q modulo s. As above, the $\phi(s)$ roots of multiplicative order s are partitioned into $\phi(s)/k$ conjugacy classes, which are in one-to-one correspondence with the cosets of the subgroup of $\mathbb{Z}_s^*$ generated by $[q]_s$.

This tells us exactly how $\mathsf{X}^r - 1$ splits into irreducible factors over F. Things are a bit simpler when r is prime, in which case, from the above discussion, we see that

$$\mathsf{X}^r - 1 = (\mathsf{X} - 1) \prod_{i=1}^{(r-1)/\ell} f_i,$$

where each f_i is an irreducible polynomial of degree ℓ, and ℓ is the multiplicative order of q modulo r.

In the above analysis, instead of constructing the field E using Theorem 17.19, one could instead simply construct E as $F[\mathsf{X}]/(\phi)$, where ϕ is any irreducible polynomial of degree ℓ, and where ℓ is the multiplicative order of q modulo r. We know that such a polynomial ϕ exists by Theorem 20.11, and since E has cardinality q^ℓ, and $r \mid (q^\ell - 1) = |E^*|$, and E^* is cyclic, we know that E^* contains an element ζ of multiplicative order r, and each of the r distinct powers of ζ are roots of $\mathsf{X}^r - 1$, and so this E is a splitting field $\mathsf{X}^r - 1$ over F. $\square$

EXERCISE 20.5. Let E be a finite extension of a finite field F. Show that for $a \in F$, we have $\mathbf{N}_{E/F}(a) = a^\ell$ and $\mathbf{Tr}_{E/F}(a) = \ell a$.

EXERCISE 20.6. Let E be a finite extension of a finite field F. Let E' be an intermediate field, $F \subseteq E' \subseteq E$. Show that

(a) $\mathbf{N}_{E/F}(\alpha) = \mathbf{N}_{E'/F}(\mathbf{N}_{E/E'}(\alpha))$, and

(b) $\mathbf{Tr}_{E/F}(\alpha) = \mathbf{Tr}_{E'/F}(\mathbf{Tr}_{E/E'}(\alpha))$.

EXERCISE 20.7. Let F be a finite field, and let $f \in F[\mathsf{X}]$ be a monic irreducible polynomial of degree ℓ. Let $E = F[\mathsf{X}]/(f) = F[\eta]$, where $\eta := [\mathsf{X}]_f$.

(a) Show that

$$\frac{\mathbf{D}(f)}{f} = \sum_{j=1}^{\infty} \mathbf{Tr}_{E/F}(\eta^{j-1})\mathsf{X}^{-j}.$$

(b) From part (a), deduce that the sequence

$$\mathbf{Tr}_{E/F}(\eta^{j-1}) \quad (j = 1, 2, \ldots)$$

is linearly generated over F with minimal polynomial f.

(c) Show that one can always choose a polynomial f so that sequence in part (b) is purely periodic with period $q^\ell - 1$.

EXERCISE 20.8. Let F be a finite field, and $f \in F[\mathsf{X}]$ an irreducible polynomial of degree k over F. Let E be an extension of degree ℓ over F. Show that over E, f factors as the product of d distinct irreducible polynomials, each of degree k/d, where $d = \gcd(k, \ell)$.

EXERCISE 20.9. Let E be a finite extension of a finite field F of characteristic p. Show that if $\alpha \in E$ and $0 \neq a \in F$, and if α and $\alpha + a$ are conjugate over F, then p divides the degree of α over F.

EXERCISE 20.10. Let F be a finite field of characteristic p. For $a \in F$, consider the polynomial $f := X^q - X - a \in F[X]$.

(a) Show that if $F = \mathbb{Z}_p$ and $a \neq 0$, then f is irreducible.

(b) More generally, show that if $\mathbf{Tr}_{F/\mathbb{Z}_p}(a) \neq 0$, then f is irreducible, and otherwise, f splits into distinct linear factors over F.

EXERCISE 20.11. Let E be a finite extension of a finite field F. Let $\alpha, \beta \in E$, where α has degree a over F, β has degree b over F, and $\gcd(a, b) = 1$. Show that $\alpha + \beta$ has degree ab over F.

EXERCISE 20.12. Let E be a finite extension of a finite field F. Show that any F-algebra automorphism on E must be a power of a the Frobenius map on E over F.

EXERCISE 20.13. Show that for all primes p, the polynomial $X^4 + 1$ is reducible in $\mathbb{Z}_p[X]$. (Contrast this to the fact that this polynomial is irreducible in $\mathbb{Q}[X]$, as discussed in Exercise 17.39.)

EXERCISE 20.14. This exercise depends on the concepts and results in §19.6. Let F be a finite field and let E be an extension of degree ℓ. Let σ be the Frobenius map on E over F.

(a) Show that the minimal polynomial of σ over F is $X^\ell - 1$.

(b) Show that there exists $\beta \in E$ such that the minimal polynomial of β under σ is $X^\ell - 1$.

(c) Conclude that $\beta, \sigma(\beta), \ldots, \sigma^{\ell-1}(\beta)$ is a basis for E over F. This type of basis is called a **normal basis**.

21

Algorithms for finite fields

This chapter discusses efficient algorithms for factoring polynomials over finite fields, and related problems, such as testing if a given polynomial is irreducible, and generating an irreducible polynomial of given degree.

> *Throughout this chapter, F denotes a finite field of characteristic p and cardinality $q = p^w$.*

In addition to performing the usual arithmetic and comparison operations in F, we assume that our algorithms have access to the numbers p, w, and q, and have the ability to generate random elements of F. Generating such a random field element will count as one "operation in F," along with the usual arithmetic operations. Of course, the "standard" ways of representing F as either $\mathbb{Z}_p$ (if $w = 1$), or as the ring of polynomials modulo an irreducible polynomial over $\mathbb{Z}_p$ of degree w (if $w > 1$), satisfy the above requirements, and also allow for the implementation of arithmetic operations in F that take time $O(\operatorname{len}(q)^2)$ on a RAM (using simple, quadratic-time arithmetic for polynomials and integers).

21.1 Testing and constructing irreducible polynomials

Let $f \in F[X]$ be a monic polynomial of degree $\ell > 0$. We develop here an efficient algorithm that determines if f is irreducible.

The idea is a simple application of Theorem 20.9. That theorem says that for any integer $k \geq 1$, the polynomial $X^{q^k} - X$ is the product of all monic irreducibles whose degree divides k. Thus, $\gcd(X^q - X, f)$ is the product of all the distinct linear factors of f. If f has no linear factors, then $\gcd(X^{q^2} - X, f)$ is the product of all the distinct quadratic irreducible factors of f. And so on. Now, if f is not irreducible, it must be divisible by some irreducible polynomial of degree at most $\ell/2$, and if g is an irreducible factor of f

of minimal degree, say k, then we have $k \leq \ell/2$ and $\gcd(\mathsf{X}^{q^k} - \mathsf{X}, f) \neq 1$. Conversely, if f is irreducible, then $\gcd(\mathsf{X}^{q^k} - \mathsf{X}, f) = 1$ for all positive integers k up to $\ell/2$. So to test if f is irreducible, it suffices to check if $\gcd(\mathsf{X}^{q^k} - \mathsf{X}, f) = 1$ for all positive integers k up to $\ell/2$ — if so, we may conclude that f is irreducible, and otherwise, we may conclude that f is not irreducible. To carry out the computation efficiently, we note that if $h \equiv \mathsf{X}^{q^k} \pmod{f}$, then $\gcd(h - \mathsf{X}, f) = \gcd(\mathsf{X}^{q^k} - \mathsf{X}, f)$.

The above observations suggest the following algorithm, which takes as input a monic polynomial $f \in F[\mathsf{X}]$ of degree $\ell > 0$, and outputs *true* if f is irreducible, and *false* otherwise:

Algorithm IPT:

$h \leftarrow \mathsf{X} \bmod f$
for $k \leftarrow 1$ to $\lfloor \ell/2 \rfloor$ do
$\qquad h \leftarrow h^q \bmod f$
$\qquad$ if $\gcd(h - \mathsf{X}, f) \neq 1$ then return *false*
return *true*

The correctness of Algorithm IPT follows immediately from the above discussion. As for the running time, we have:

Theorem 21.1. *Algorithm IPT uses $O(\ell^3 \operatorname{len}(q))$ operations in F.*

Proof. Consider an execution of a single iteration of the main loop. The cost of the qth-powering step (using a standard repeated-squaring algorithm) is $O(\operatorname{len}(q))$ multiplications modulo f, and so $O(\ell^2 \operatorname{len}(q))$ operations in F. The cost of the gcd computation is $O(\ell^2)$ operations in F. Thus, the cost of a single loop iteration is $O(\ell^2 \operatorname{len}(q))$ operations in F, from which it follows that the cost of the entire algorithm is $O(\ell^3 \operatorname{len}(q))$ operations in F. $\square$

Algorithm IPT is a "polynomial time" algorithm, since the length of the binary encoding of the input is about $\ell \operatorname{len}(q)$, and so the algorithm runs in time polynomial in its input length, assuming that arithmetic operations in F take time polynomial in $\operatorname{len}(q)$. Indeed, using a standard representation for F, each operation in F takes time $O(\operatorname{len}(q)^2)$ on a RAM, and so the running time on a RAM for the above algorithm would be $O(\ell^3 \operatorname{len}(q)^3)$, that is, cubic in the bit-length of the input.

Let us now consider the related problem of constructing an irreducible polynomial of specified degree $\ell > 0$. To do this, we can simply use the result of Theorem 20.11, which has the following probabilistic interpretation: if we choose a random, monic polynomial f of degree ℓ over F, then the probability that f is irreducible is at least $1/2\ell$. This suggests the following probabilistic algorithm:

Algorithm RIP:

repeat
      choose $a_0, \ldots, a_{\ell-1} \in F$ at random
      set $f \leftarrow X^\ell + \sum_{i=0}^{\ell-1} a_i X^i$
      test if f is irreducible using Algorithm IPT
until f is irreducible
output f

Theorem 21.2. *Algorithm RIP uses an expected number of $O(\ell^4 \operatorname{len}(q))$ operations in F, and its output is uniformly distributed over all monic irreducibles of degree ℓ.*

Proof. Because of Theorem 20.11, the expected number of loop iterations of the above algorithm is $O(\ell)$. Since Algorithm IPT uses $O(\ell^3 \operatorname{len}(q))$ operations in F, the statement about the running time of Algorithm RIP is immediate. The statement about its output distribution is clear. $\square$

The expected running-time bound in Theorem 21.2 is actually a bit of an over-estimate. The reason is that if we generate a random polynomial of degree ℓ, it is likely to have a small irreducible factor, which will be discovered very quickly by Algorithm IPT. In fact, it is known (see §21.7) that the expected value of the degree of the least degree irreducible factor of a random monic polynomial of degree ℓ over F is $O(\operatorname{len}(\ell))$, from which it follows that the expected number of operations in F performed by Algorithm RIP is actually $O(\ell^3 \operatorname{len}(\ell) \operatorname{len}(q))$.

EXERCISE 21.1. Let $f \in F[X]$ be a monic polynomial of degree $\ell > 0$. Also, let $\eta := [X]_f \in E$, where E is the F-algebra $E := F[X]/(f)$.

(a) Show how to compute—given as input $\alpha \in E$ and $\eta^{q^m} \in E$ (for some integer $m > 0$)—the value $\alpha^{q^m} \in E$, using just $O(\ell^{2.5})$ operations in F, and space for $O(\ell^{1.5})$ elements of F. Hint: see Theorems 17.1 and 20.7, as well as Exercise 18.4.

(b) Show how to compute—given as input $\eta^{q^m} \in E$ and $\eta^{q^{m'}} \in E$, where m and m' are positive integers—the value $\eta^{q^{m+m'}} \in E$, using $O(\ell^{2.5})$ operations in F, and space for $O(\ell^{1.5})$ elements of F.

(c) Show how to compute—given as input $\eta^q \in E$ and a positive integer m—the value $\eta^{q^m} \in E$, using $O(\ell^{2.5} \operatorname{len}(m))$ operations in F, and space for $O(\ell^{1.5})$ elements of F. Hint: use a repeated-squaring-like algorithm.

EXERCISE 21.2. This exercise develops an alternative irreducibility test.

(a) Show that a monic polynomial $f \in F[X]$ of degree $\ell > 0$ is irreducible if and only if $X^{q^\ell} \equiv X \pmod{f}$ and $\gcd(X^{q^{\ell/s}} - X, f) = 1$ for all primes $s \mid \ell$.

(b) Using part (a) and the result of the previous exercise, show how to determine if f is irreducible using $O(\ell^{2.5} \operatorname{len}(\ell)\omega(\ell) + \ell^2 \operatorname{len}(q))$ operations in F, where $\omega(\ell)$ is the number of distinct prime factors of ℓ.

(c) Show that the operation count in part (b) can be reduced to $O(\ell^{2.5} \operatorname{len}(\ell) \operatorname{len}(\omega(\ell)) + \ell^2 \operatorname{len}(q))$. Hint: see Exercise 3.30.

EXERCISE 21.3. Design and analyze a *deterministic* algorithm that takes as input a list of irreducible polynomials $f_1, \ldots, f_r \in F[X]$, where $\ell_i := \deg(f_i)$ for $i = 1, \ldots, r$. Assuming that the degrees $\ell_1, \ldots, \ell_r$ are pairwise relatively prime, your algorithm should output an irreducible polynomial $f \in F[X]$ of degree $\ell := \prod_{i=1}^r \ell_i$ using $O(\ell^3)$ operations in F.

EXERCISE 21.4. Design and analyze a probabilistic algorithm that, given a monic irreducible polynomial $f \in F[X]$ of degree ℓ as input, generates as output a random monic irreducible polynomial $g \in F[X]$ of degree ℓ (i.e., g should be uniformly distributed over all such polynomials), using an expected number of $O(\ell^{2.5})$ operations in F. Hint: use Exercise 19.8 (or alternatively, Exercise 19.9).

EXERCISE 21.5. Let $f \in F[X]$ be a monic irreducible polynomial of degree ℓ, let $E := F[X]/(f)$, and let $\eta := [X]_f \in E$. Design and analyze a deterministic algorithm that takes as input the polynomial f defining the extension E, and outputs the values

$$s_j := \mathbf{Tr}_{E/F}(\eta^j) \in F \quad (j = 0, \ldots, \ell - 1),$$

using $O(\ell^2)$ operations in F. Here, $\mathbf{Tr}_{E/F}$ is the trace from E to F (see §20.4). Show that given an arbitrary $\alpha \in E$, along with the values $s_0, \ldots, s_{\ell-1}$, one can compute $\mathbf{Tr}_{E/F}(\alpha)$ using just $O(\ell)$ operations in F.

21.2 Computing minimal polynomials in $F[X]/(f)$ (III)

We consider, for the third and final time, the problem considered in §18.2 and §19.5: $f \in F[X]$ is a monic polynomial of degree $\ell > 0$, and $E :=$

$F[X]/(f) = F[\eta]$, where $\eta := [X]_f$; we are given an element $\alpha \in E$, and want to compute the minimal polynomial $\phi \in F[X]$ of α over F. We develop an alternative algorithm, based on the theory of finite fields. Unlike the algorithms in §18.2 and §19.5, this algorithm only works when F is finite and the polynomial f is irreducible, so that E is also a finite field.

From Theorem 20.15, we know that the degree of α over F is the smallest positive integer k such that $\alpha^{q^k} = \alpha$. By successive qth powering, we can compute the conjugates of α, and determine the degree k, using $O(k \operatorname{len}(q))$ operations in E, and hence $O(k\ell^2 \operatorname{len}(q))$ operations in F.

Now, we could simply compute the minimal polynomial ϕ by directly using the formula

$$\phi(Y) = \prod_{i=0}^{k-1} (Y - \alpha^{q^i}). \tag{21.1}$$

This would involve computations with polynomials in the variable Y whose coefficients lie in the extension field E, although at the end of the computation, we would end up with a polynomial all of whose coefficients lie in F. The cost of this approach would be $O(k^2)$ operations in E, and hence $O(k^2\ell^2)$ operations in F.

A more efficient approach is the following. Substituting η for Y in the identity (21.1), we have

$$\phi(\eta) = \prod_{i=0}^{k-1} (\eta - \alpha^{q^i}).$$

Using this formula, we can compute (given the conjugates of α) the value $\phi(\eta) \in E$ using $O(k)$ operations in E, and hence $O(k\ell^2)$ operations in F. Now, $\phi(\eta)$ is an element of E, and for computational purposes, it is represented as $[g]_f$ for some polynomial $g \in F[X]$ of degree less than ℓ. Moreover, $\phi(\eta) = [\phi]_f$, and hence $\phi \equiv g \pmod{f}$. In particular, if $k < \ell$, then $g = \phi$; otherwise, if $k = \ell$, then $g = \phi - f$. In either case, we can recover ϕ from g with an additional $O(\ell)$ operations in F.

Thus, given the conjugates of α, we can compute ϕ using $O(k\ell^2)$ operations in F. Adding in the cost of computing the conjugates, this gives rise to an algorithm that computes the minimal polynomial of α using $O(k\ell^2 \operatorname{len}(q))$ operations in F.

In the worst case, then, this algorithm uses $O(\ell^3 \operatorname{len}(q))$ operations in F. A reasonably careful implementation needs space for storing a constant number of elements of E, and hence $O(\ell)$ elements of F. For very small values of q, the efficiency of this algorithm will be comparable to that of the algorithm in §19.5, but for large q, it will be much less efficient. Thus, this approach does not really yield a better algorithm, but it does serve to illustrate some of the ideas of the theory of finite fields.

21.3 Factoring polynomials: the Cantor–Zassenhaus algorithm

In the remaining sections of this chapter, we develop efficient algorithms for factoring polynomials over the finite field F.

The algorithm we discuss in this section is due to Cantor and Zassenhaus. It has two stages:

Distinct Degree Factorization: The input polynomial is decomposed into factors so that each factor is a product of distinct irreducibles of the same degree (and the degree of those irreducibles is also determined).

Equal Degree Factorization: Each of the factors produced in the distinct degree factorization stage are further factored into their irreducible factors.

The algorithm we present for distinct degree factorization is a deterministic, polynomial-time algorithm. The algorithm we present for equal degree factorization is a *probabilistic* algorithm that runs in expected polynomial time (and whose output is always correct).

21.3.1 Distinct degree factorization

The problem, more precisely stated, is this: given a monic polynomial $f \in F[X]$ of degree $\ell > 0$, produce a list of polynomial/integer pairs (g, k), where

- each g is a product of distinct monic irreducible polynomials of degree k, and

- the product of all the polynomials g in the list is equal to f.

This problem can be easily solved using Theorem 20.9, using a simple variation of the algorithm we discussed in §21.1 for irreducibility testing. The basic idea is this. We can compute $g := \gcd(X^q - X, f)$, so that g is the product of all the distinct linear factors of f. We can remove the factor g from f, but after doing so, f may still contain some linear factors (if the original polynomial was not square-free), and so we have to repeat the above step until no linear factors are discovered. Having removed all linear factors from f, we next compute $\gcd(X^{q^2} - X, f)$, which will be the product of all the distinct quadratic irreducibles dividing f, and we can remove these from f—although $X^{q^2} - X$ is the product of all linear and quadratic irreducibles, since we have already removed the linear factors from f, the gcd will give us just the quadratic factors of f. As above, we may have to repeat this a few times to remove all the quadratic factors from f. In general, for $k = 1, \ldots, \ell$, having removed all the irreducible factors of degree less than k from f, we compute $\gcd(\mathrm{X}^{q^k} - \mathrm{X}, f)$ to obtain the product of all the distinct irreducible factors of f of degree k, repeating as necessary to remove all such factors.

The above discussion leads to the following algorithm for distinct degree factorization, which takes as input a monic polynomial $f \in F[\mathrm{X}]$ of degree $\ell > 0$:

Algorithm DDF:

$h \leftarrow \mathrm{X} \bmod f$
$k \leftarrow 1$
while $f \neq 1$ do
$\quad h \leftarrow h^q \bmod f$
$\quad g \leftarrow \gcd(h - \mathrm{X}, f)$
$\quad$ while $g \neq 1$ do
$\quad\quad$ output (g, k)
$\quad\quad f \leftarrow f/g$
$\quad\quad h \leftarrow h \bmod f$
$\quad\quad g \leftarrow \gcd(h - \mathrm{X}, f)$
$\quad k \leftarrow k + 1$

The correctness of Algorithm DDF follows from the discussion above. As for the running time:

Theorem 21.3. *Algorithm DDF uses $O(\ell^3 \operatorname{len}(q))$ operations in F.*

Proof. Note that the body of the outer loop is executed at most ℓ times, since after ℓ iterations, we will have removed all the factors of f. Thus, we perform at most ℓ qth-powering steps, each of which takes $O(\ell^2 \operatorname{len}(q))$ operations in F, and so the total contribution to the running time of these is $O(\ell^3 \operatorname{len}(q))$ operations in F. We also have to take into account the cost of the gcd computations. We perform one gcd computation in every iteration of the main loop, for a total of ℓ such computations. We also perform an "extra" gcd computation whenever we discover a non-trivial factor of f; however, since we only discover at most ℓ such non-trivial factors, we perform at most ℓ such "extra" gcd computations. So the total number of gcd computations is at most 2ℓ, and as each of these takes $O(\ell^2)$ operations in F, they contribute a term of $O(\ell^3)$ to the total operation count. This term is dominated by the cost of the qth-powering steps (as is the cost of the division step in the inner loop), and so the total cost of Algorithm DDF is $O(\ell^3 \operatorname{len}(q))$ operations in F. $\square$

21.3.2 Equal degree factorization

The problem, more precisely stated, is this: given a monic polynomial $g \in F[\mathsf{X}]$ of degree $\ell > 0$, and an integer $k > 0$, such that g is of the form

$$g = g_1 \cdots g_r$$

for distinct monic irreducible polynomials $g_1, \ldots, g_r$, each of degree k, compute these irreducible factors of g. Note that given g and k, the value of r is easily determined, since $r = \ell/k$.

We begin by discussing the basic mathematical ideas that will allow us to efficiently split g into two non-trivial factors, and then we present a somewhat more elaborate algorithm that completely factors g.

By the Chinese remainder theorem, we have an F-algebra isomorphism

$$\theta : E_1 \times \cdots \times E_r \to E,$$

where for $i = 1, \ldots, r$, E_i is the extension field $F[\mathsf{X}]/(g_i)$ of degree k over F, and E is the F-algebra $F[\mathsf{X}]/(g)$.

Recall that $q = p^w$. We have to treat the cases $p = 2$ and $p > 2$ separately. We first treat the case $p = 2$. Let us define the polynomial

$$M_k := \sum_{j=0}^{wk-1} \mathsf{X}^{2^j} \in F[\mathsf{X}]. \tag{21.2}$$

(The algorithm in the case $p > 2$ will only differ in the definition of M_k.)

For $\alpha \in E$, if $\alpha = \theta(\alpha_1, \ldots, \alpha_r)$, then we have

$$M_k(\alpha) = \theta(M_k(\alpha_1), \ldots, M_k(\alpha_r)).$$

Note that each E_i is an extension of $\mathbb{Z}_2$ of degree wk, and that

$$M_k(\alpha_i) = \sum_{j=0}^{wk-1} \alpha_i^{2^j} = \mathbf{Tr}_{E_i/\mathbb{Z}_2}(\alpha_i),$$

where $\mathbf{Tr}_{E_i/\mathbb{Z}_2} : E_i \to \mathbb{Z}_2$ is the trace from E_i to $\mathbb{Z}_2$, which is a surjective, $\mathbb{Z}_2$-linear map (see §20.4).

Now, suppose we choose $\alpha \in E$ at random. Then if $\alpha = \theta(\alpha_1, \ldots, \alpha_r)$, the α_i will be independently distributed, with each α_i uniformly distributed over E_i. It follows that the values $M_k(\alpha_i)$ will be independently and uniformly distributed over $\mathbb{Z}_2$. Thus, if $a := \text{rep}(M_k(\alpha))$ (i.e., $a \in F[\mathsf{X}]$ is the polynomial of degree less than ℓ such that $M_k(\alpha) = [a]_g$), then $\gcd(a, g)$ will be the product of those factors g_i of g such that $M_k(\alpha_i) = 0$. We will fail to get a non-trivial factorization only if the $M_k(\alpha_i)$ are either all 0 or all 1, which for $r \geq 2$ happens with probability at most $1/2$ (the worst case being when $r = 2$).

That is our basic splitting strategy. The algorithm for completely factoring g works as follows. The algorithm proceeds in stages. At any stage, we have a partial factorization $g = \prod_{h \in H} h$, where H is a set of non-constant, monic polynomials. Initially, $H = \{g\}$. With each stage, we attempt to get a finer factorization of g by trying to split each $h \in H$ using the above splitting strategy—if we succeed in splitting h into two non-trivial factors, then we replace h by these two factors. We continue in this way until $|H| = r$.

Here is the full equal degree factorization algorithm. It takes as input a monic polynomial $g \in F[\mathsf{X}]$ of degree $\ell > 0$, and an integer $k > 0$, such that g is the product of $r := \ell/k$ distinct monic irreducible polynomials, each of degree k. With M_k as defined in (21.2), the algorithm runs as follows:

Algorithm EDF:

$H \leftarrow \{g\}$
while $|H| < r$ do
$\quad H' \leftarrow \emptyset$
$\quad$ for each $h \in H$ do
$\quad\quad$ choose $\alpha \in F[\mathsf{X}]/(h)$ at random
$\quad\quad d \leftarrow \gcd(\text{rep}(M_k(\alpha)), h)$
$\quad\quad$ if $d = 1$ or $d = h$
$\quad\quad\quad$ then $H' \leftarrow H' \cup \{h\}$
$\quad\quad\quad$ else $\quad H' \leftarrow H' \cup \{d, h/d\}$
$\quad H \leftarrow H'$
output H

The correctness of the algorithm is clear from the above discussion. As for its expected running time, we can get a quick-and-dirty upper bound as follows:

- For a given h, the cost of computing $M_k(\alpha)$ for $\alpha \in F[\mathsf{X}]/(h)$ is $O(k \deg(h)^2 \operatorname{len}(q))$ operations in F, and so the number of operations in F performed in each iteration of the main loop is at most a constant times

$$k \operatorname{len}(q) \sum_{h \in H} \deg(h)^2 \leq k \operatorname{len}(q) \left(\sum_{h \in H} \deg(h) \right)^2 = k\ell^2 \operatorname{len}(q).$$

- The expected number of iterations of the main loop until we get some non-trivial split is $O(1)$.
- The algorithm finishes after getting $r - 1$ non-trivial splits.
- Therefore, the total expected cost is $O(rk\ell^2 \operatorname{len}(q))$, or $O(\ell^3 \operatorname{len}(q))$, operations in F.

This analysis gives a bit of an over-estimate—it does not take into account the fact that we expect to get fairly "balanced" splits. For the purposes of analyzing the overall running time of the Cantor–Zassenhaus algorithm, this bound suffices; however, the following analysis gives a tight bound on the complexity of Algorithm EDF.

Theorem 21.4. *In the case $p = 2$, Algorithm EDF uses an expected number of $O(k\ell^2 \operatorname{len}(q))$ operations in F.*

Proof. We may assume $r \geq 2$. Let L be a random variable that denotes the number of iterations of the main loop of the algorithm.

We claim that $E[L] = O(\operatorname{len}(r))$. To prove this claim, we make use of the fact (see Theorem 6.25) that

$$\mathsf{E}[L] = \sum_{t \geq 1} \mathsf{P}[L \geq t].$$

For $i = 1, \ldots, r$ and $j = i+1, \ldots, r$, define L_{ij} to be the number of iterations of the main loop in which the factors g_i and g_j remain unseparated at the beginning of the loop. Now, if g_i and g_j have not been separated at the beginning of one loop iteration, then they will be separated at the beginning of the next with probability $1/2$. It follows that

$$\mathsf{P}[L_{ij} \geq t] \leq 2^{-(t-1)}.$$

Also note that $L \geq t$ implies that $L_{ij} \geq t$ for some i, j, and hence

$$\mathsf{P}[L \geq t] \leq \sum_{i=1}^{r} \sum_{j=i+1}^{r} \mathsf{P}[L_{ij} \geq t] \leq r^2 2^{-t}.$$

So we have

$$E[L] = \sum_{t \geq 1} P[L \geq t]$$

$$= \sum_{t \leq 2 \log_2 r} P[L \geq t] + \sum_{t > 2 \log_2 r} P[L \geq t]$$

$$\leq 2 \log_2 r + \sum_{t > 2 \log_2 r} r^2 2^{-t}$$

$$\leq 2 \log_2 r + \sum_{t \geq 0} 2^{-t}$$

$$= 2 \log_2 r + 2.$$

That proves the claim.

As discussed in the paragraph above this theorem, the cost of each iteration of the main loop is $O(k\ell^2 \operatorname{len}(q))$ operations in F. Combining this with the fact that $E[L] = O(\operatorname{len}(r))$, it follows that the expected number of operations in F for the entire algorithm is $O(\operatorname{len}(r)k\ell^2 \operatorname{len}(q))$. This is significantly better than the above quick-and-dirty estimate, but is not quite the result we are after—we have to get rid of the factor $\operatorname{len}(r)$. There are a number of ways to do this. We sketch one such way, which is a bit ad hoc, but sufficient for our purposes.

Let us define

$$S := \sum_{i=1}^{r} \sum_{j=i+1}^{r} L_{ij}.$$

We claim that the total work performed by the algorithm in attempting to split non-irreducible factors of g is

$$O(Sk^3 \operatorname{len}(q)).$$

To see why this is so, consider one iteration of the inner loop of the algorithm, where we are trying to split a factor h of g, where h is the product of two or more irreducible factors of g. Let us write $h = g_{i_1} \cdots g_{i_n}$, where $2 \leq n \leq r$. On the one hand, the number of operations in F performed in this step is at most $ck \deg(h)^2 \operatorname{len}(q)$ for some constant c, which we may write as $cn^2 \cdot k^3 \operatorname{len}(q)$. On the other hand, each pair of indices $(i_j, i_{j'})$, with $1 \leq j < j' \leq n$, contributes 1 to the sum defining S, for a total contribution from pairs at this step of $n(n-1)/2 \geq n^2/4$. The claim now follows.

Algorithm EDF is a little silly in that it wastes time trying to split irreducible factors (and although it would be trivial to modify the algorithm to avoid this, the asymptotic running time would not be affected significantly).

It is easy to see that attempting to split a single irreducible factor takes $O(k^3 \operatorname{len}(q))$ operations in F, and hence the total amount of work wasted in this way is $O(Lrk^3 \operatorname{len}(q))$.

We next claim that $\mathsf{E}[L_{ij}] = O(1)$, for all i, j. Indeed,

$$\mathsf{E}[L_{ij}] = \sum_{t \geq 1} \mathsf{P}[L_{ij} \geq t] \leq \sum_{t \geq 1} 2^{-(t-1)} = 2.$$

It follows that

$$\mathsf{E}[S] = \sum_{ij} \mathsf{E}[L_{ij}] = O(r^2).$$

Therefore, the expected number of operations in F performed by the algorithm is at most a constant times

$$\mathsf{E}[S]k^3 \operatorname{len}(q) + \mathsf{E}[L]rk^3 \operatorname{len}(q) = O(r^2 k^3 \operatorname{len}(q) + r \operatorname{len}(r)k^3 \operatorname{len}(q)),$$

which is $O(k\ell^2 \operatorname{len}(q))$. $\square$

That completes the discussion of Algorithm EDF in the case $p = 2$.

The case $p > 2$

Now assume that $p > 2$, so that p, and hence also q, is odd. Algorithm EDF in this case is exactly the same as above, except that in this case, we define the polynomial M_k as

$$M_k := \mathsf{X}^{(q^k-1)/2} - 1 \in F[\mathsf{X}]. \tag{21.3}$$

Just as before, for $\alpha \in E$ with $\alpha = \theta(\alpha_1, \ldots, \alpha_r)$, we have

$$M_k(\alpha) = \theta(M_k(\alpha_1), \ldots, M_k(\alpha_r)).$$

Note that each group E_i^* is a cyclic group of order $q^k - 1$, and therefore, the image of the $(q^k - 1)/2$-power map on E_i^* is $\{\pm 1\}$.

Now, suppose we choose $\alpha \in E$ at random. Then if $\alpha = \theta(\alpha_1, \ldots, \alpha_r)$, the α_i will be independently distributed, with each α_i uniformly distributed over E_i. It follows that the values $M_k(\alpha_i)$ will be independently distributed. If $\alpha_i = 0$, which happens with probability $1/q^k$, then $M_k(\alpha_i) = -1$; otherwise, $\alpha_i^{(q^k-1)/2}$ is uniformly distributed over $\{\pm 1\}$, and so $M_k(\alpha_i)$ is uniformly distributed over $\{0, -2\}$. That is to say,

$$M_k(\alpha_i) = \begin{cases} 0 & \text{with probability } (q^k - 1)/2q^k, \\ -1 & \text{with probability } 1/q^k, \\ -2 & \text{with probability } (q^k - 1)/2q^k. \end{cases}$$

Thus, if $a := \operatorname{rep}(M_k(\alpha))$, then $\gcd(a, g)$ will be the product of those factors

g_i of g such that $M_k(\alpha_i) = 0$. We will fail to get a non-trivial factorization only if the $M_k(\alpha_i)$ are either all zero or all non-zero. Assume $r \geq 2$. Consider the worst case, namely, when $r = 2$. In this case, a simple calculation shows that the probability that we fail to split these two factors is

$$\left(\frac{q^k - 1}{2q^k}\right)^2 + \left(\frac{q^k + 1}{2q^k}\right)^2 = \frac{1}{2}(1 + 1/q^{2k}).$$

The (very) worst case is when $q^k = 3$, in which case the probability of failure is at most $5/9$.

The same quick-and-dirty analysis given just above Theorem 21.4 applies here as well, but just as before, we can do better:

Theorem 21.5. *In the case $p > 2$, Algorithm EDF uses an expected number of $O(k\ell^2 \operatorname{len}(q))$ operations in F.*

Proof. The analysis is essentially the same as in the case $p = 2$, except that now the probability that we fail to split a given pair of irreducible factors is at most $5/9$, rather than equal to $1/2$. The details are left as an exercise for the reader. □

21.3.3 Analysis of the whole algorithm

Given an arbitrary polynomial $f \in F[X]$ of degree $\ell > 0$, the distinct degree factorization step takes $O(\ell^3 \operatorname{len}(q))$ operations in F. This step produces a number of polynomials that must be further subjected to equal degree factorization. If there are s such polynomials, where the ith polynomial has degree ℓ_i, for $i = 1, \ldots, s$, then $\sum_{i=1}^{s} \ell_i = \ell$. Now, the equal degree factorization step for the ith polynomial takes an expected number of $O(\ell_i^3 \operatorname{len}(q))$ operations in F (actually, our initial, "quick and dirty" estimate is good enough here), and so it follows that the total expected cost of all the equal degree factorization steps is $O(\sum_i \ell_i^3 \operatorname{len}(q))$, which is $O(\ell^3 \operatorname{len}(q))$, operations in F. Putting this all together, we conclude:

Theorem 21.6. *The Cantor–Zassenhaus factoring algorithm uses an expected number of $O(\ell^3 \operatorname{len}(q))$ operations in F.*

This bound is tight, since in the worst case, when the input is irreducible, the algorithm really does do this much work.

EXERCISE 21.6. Show how to modify Algorithm DDF so that the main loop halts as soon as $2k > \deg(f)$.

EXERCISE 21.7. This exercise extends the techniques developed in Exercise 21.1. Let $f \in F[X]$ be a monic polynomial of degree $\ell > 0$, and let $\eta := [X]_f \in E$, where $E := F[X]/(f)$. For integer $m > 0$, define polynomials

$$T_m := X + X^q + \cdots + X^{q^{m-1}} \in F[X] \quad \text{and} \quad N_m := X \cdot X^q \cdots \cdots X^{q^{m-1}} \in F[X].$$

(a) Show how to compute—given as input $\eta^{q^m} \in E$ and $\eta^{q^{m'}}$, where m and m' are positive integers, along with $T_m(\alpha)$ and $T_{m'}(\alpha)$, for some $\alpha \in E$—the values $\eta^{q^{m+m'}}$ and $T_{m+m'}(\alpha)$, using $O(\ell^{2.5})$ operations in F, and space for $O(\ell^{1.5})$ elements of F.

(b) Using part (a), show how to compute—given as input $\eta^q \in E$, $\alpha \in E$, and a positive integer m—the value $T_m(\alpha)$, using $O(\ell^{2.5} \operatorname{len}(m))$ operations in F, and space for $O(\ell^{1.5})$ elements of F.

(c) Repeat parts (a) and (b), except with "N" in place of "T."

EXERCISE 21.8. Using the result of the previous exercise, show how to implement Algorithm EDF so that it uses an expected number of

$$O(\operatorname{len}(k)\ell^{2.5} + \ell^2 \operatorname{len}(q))$$

operations in F, and space for $O(\ell^{1.5})$ elements of F.

EXERCISE 21.9. This exercise depends on the concepts and results in §19.6. Let E be an extension field of degree ℓ over F, specified by an irreducible polynomial of degree ℓ over F. Design and analyze an efficient probabilistic algorithm that finds a normal basis for E over F (see Exercise 20.14). Hint: there are a number of approaches to solving this problem; one way is to start by factoring $X^\ell - 1$ over F, and then turn the construction in Theorem 19.7 into an efficient probabilistic procedure; if you mimic Exercise 11.2, your entire algorithm should use $O(\ell^3 \operatorname{len}(\ell) \operatorname{len}(q))$ operations in F (or $O(\operatorname{len}(r)\ell^3 \operatorname{len}(q))$ operations, where r is the number of distinct irreducible factors of $X^\ell - 1$ over F).

21.4 Factoring polynomials: Berlekamp's algorithm

We now develop an alternative algorithm, due to Berlekamp, for factoring a polynomial over the finite field F.

This algorithm usually starts with a pre-processing phase to reduce the problem to that of factoring square-free polynomials. There are a number of ways to carry out this step. We present a simple-minded method here that is sufficient for our purposes.

21.4.1 A simple square-free decomposition algorithm

Let $f \in F[X]$ be a monic polynomial of degree $\ell > 0$. Suppose that f is not square-free. According to Theorem 20.4, $d := \gcd(f, \mathbf{D}(f)) \neq 1$, and so we might hope to get a non-trivial factorization of f by computing d; however, we have to consider the possibility that $d = f$. Can this happen? The answer is "yes," but if it does happen that $d = f$, we can still get a non-trivial factorization of f by other means:

Theorem 21.7. *Suppose that $f \in F[X]$ is a polynomial of degree $\ell > 0$, and that $\gcd(f, \mathbf{D}(f)) = f$. Then $f = g(X^p)$ for some $g \in F[X]$. Moreover, if $g = \sum_i b_i X^i$, then $f = h^p$, where $h = \sum_i b_i^{p^{(w-1)}} X^i$.*

Proof. Since $\deg(\mathbf{D}(f)) < \deg(f)$, if $\gcd(f, \mathbf{D}(f)) = f$, then we must have $\mathbf{D}(f) = 0$. If $f = \sum_{i=0}^{\ell} a_i X^i$, then $\mathbf{D}(f) = \sum_{i=1}^{\ell} i a_i X^{i-1}$. Since this derivative must be zero, it follows that all the coefficients a_i with $i \not\equiv 0 \pmod{p}$ must be zero to begin with. That proves that $f = g(X^p)$ for some $g \in F[X]$. Furthermore, if h is defined as above, then

$$h^p = \left(\sum_i b_i^{p^{(w-1)}} X^i \right)^p = \sum_i b_i^{p^w} X^{ip} = \sum_i b_i (X^p)^i = g(X^p) = f. \quad \square$$

This suggests the following recursive algorithm. The input is the polynomial f as above, and a parameter s, which is set to 1 on the initial invocation. The output is a list of pairs (g_i, s_i) such that each g_i is a square-free, non-constant polynomial over F and $f = \prod_i g_i^{s_i}$.

Algorithm SFD:

$d \leftarrow \gcd(f, \mathbf{D}(f))$
if $d = 1$ then
      output (f, s)
else if $d \neq f$ then
      recursively process (d, s) and $(f/d, s)$
else
      let $f = X^\ell + \sum_{i=0}^{\ell-1} a_i X^i$ // *note that $a_i = 0$ except when $p \mid i$*
      set $h \leftarrow X^{\ell/p} + \sum_{i=0}^{\ell/p-1} (a_{pi})^{p^{w-1}} X^i$ // *note that $h = f^{1/p}$*
      recursively process (h, ps)

The correctness of Algorithm SFD follows from the discussion above. As for its running time:

Theorem 21.8. *Algorithm SFD uses $O(\ell^3 + \ell(w-1)\operatorname{len}(p)/p)$ operations in F.*

Proof. For input polynomial f with $\deg(f) > 0$, let $R(f)$ denote the number of recursive invocations of the algorithm, and let $P(f)$ denote the number of p^{w-1}th powers in F computed by the algorithm. It is easy to see that the number of operations in F performed by the algorithm is

$$O(R(f)\deg(f)^2 + P(f)(w-1)\operatorname{len}(p)).$$

The theorem will therefore follow from the following two inequalities:

$$R(f) \leq 2\deg(f) - 1 \tag{21.4}$$

and

$$P(f) \leq 2\deg(f)/p. \tag{21.5}$$

We prove (21.4) by induction of $\deg(f)$. We assume (21.4) holds for all input polynomials of degree less than that of f, and prove that it holds for f. Let $d := \gcd(f, \mathbf{D}(f))$. If $d = 1$, then $R(f) = 1 \leq 2\deg(f) - 1$. If $d \neq 1$ and $d \neq f$, then applying the induction hypothesis, we have

$$\begin{aligned}
R(f) &= 1 + R(d) + R(f/d) \leq 1 + (2\deg(d) - 1) + (2\deg(f/d) - 1) \\
&= 2\deg(f) - 1.
\end{aligned}$$

Finally, if $d = f$, then again applying the induction hypothesis, we have

$$R(f) = 1 + R(f^{1/p}) \leq 1 + (2\deg(f)/p - 1) \leq \deg(f) \leq 2\deg(f) - 1.$$

The inequality (21.5) is proved similarly by induction. We assume (21.5) holds for all input polynomials of degree less than that of f, and prove that it holds for f. Let $d := \gcd(f, \mathbf{D}(f))$. If $d = 1$, then $P(f) = 0 \leq 2\deg(f)/p$. If $d \neq 1$ and $d \neq f$, then applying the induction hypothesis, we have

$$P(f) = P(d) + P(f/d) \leq 2\deg(d)/p + 2\deg(f/d)/p = 2\deg(f)/p.$$

Finally, if $d = f$, then again applying the induction hypothesis, we have

$$P(f) = \deg(f)/p + P(f^{1/p}) \leq \deg(f)/p + 2\deg(f)/p^2 \leq 2\deg(f)/p. \quad \square$$

The running-time bound in Theorem 21.8 is essentially tight (see Exercise 21.10 below). Although it suffices for our immediate purpose as a preprocessing step in Berlekamp's factoring algorithm, Algorithm SFD is by no means the most efficient algorithm possible for square-free decomposition of polynomials. We return to this issue below, in §21.6.

21.4.2 The main factoring algorithm

Let us now assume we have a monic square-free polynomial f of degree $\ell > 0$ that we want to factor into irreducibles, such as is output by the square-free decomposition algorithm above. We first present the mathematical ideas underpinning the algorithm.

Let E be the F-algebra $F[X]/(f)$. We define a subset B of E as follows:

$$B := \{\alpha \in E : \alpha^q = \alpha\}.$$

It is easy to see that B is a subalgebra of E. Indeed, for $\alpha, \beta \in B$, we have $(\alpha+\beta)^q = \alpha^q + \beta^q = \alpha+\beta$, and similarly, $(\alpha\beta)^q = \alpha^q\beta^q = \alpha\beta$. Furthermore, one sees that $c^q = c$ for all $c \in F$, and hence B is a subalgebra.

The subalgebra B is called the **Berlekamp subalgebra of** E. Let us take a closer look at it. Suppose that f factors into irreducibles as

$$f = f_1 \cdots f_r,$$

and let

$$\theta : E_1 \times \cdots \times E_r \to E$$

be the F-algebra isomorphism from the Chinese remainder theorem, where $E_i := F[X]/(f_i)$ is an extension field of F of finite degree for $i = 1, \ldots, r$. Now, for $\alpha = \theta(\alpha_1, \ldots, \alpha_r) \in E$, we have $\alpha^q = \alpha$ if and only if $\alpha_i^q = \alpha_i$ for $i = 1, \ldots, r$; moreover, by Theorem 20.8, we know that for any $\alpha_i \in E_i$, we have $\alpha_i^q = \alpha_i$ if and only if $\alpha_i \in F$. Thus, we may characterize B as follows:

$$B = \{\theta(c_1, \ldots, c_r) : c_1, \ldots, c_r \in F\}.$$

Since B is a subalgebra of E, then as F-vector spaces, B is a subspace of E. Of course, E has dimension ℓ over F, with the natural basis $1, \eta, \ldots, \eta^{\ell-1}$, where $\eta := [X]_f$. As for the Berlekamp subalgebra, from the above characterization of B, it is evident that

$$\theta(1, 0, \ldots, 0), \ \theta(0, 1, 0, \ldots, 0), \ \ldots, \ \theta(0, \ldots, 0, 1)$$

is a basis for B over F, and hence, B has dimension r over F.

Now we come to the actual factoring algorithm.

Stage 1: Construct a basis for B

The first stage of Berlekamp's factoring algorithm constructs a basis for B over F. We can easily do this using Gaussian elimination, as follows. Let $\rho : E \to E$ be the map that sends $\alpha \in E$ to $\alpha^q - \alpha$. Since the qth power map on E is an F-algebra homomorphism (see Theorem 20.7)—and in particular, an F-linear map—the map ρ is also F-linear. Moreover, the kernel of ρ is none other than the Berlekamp subalgebra B. So to find a basis for B, we simply need to find a basis for the kernel of ρ using Gaussian elimination over F, as in §15.4.

To perform the Gaussian elimination, we need to choose an ordered basis for E over F, and construct a matrix $Q \in F^{\ell \times \ell}$ that represents ρ with respect to that ordered basis as in §15.2, so that evaluation of ρ corresponds to multiplying a row vector on the right by Q. We are free to choose an ordered basis in any convenient way, and the most convenient ordered basis, of course, is $(1, \eta, \ldots, \eta^{\ell-1})$, as this directly corresponds to the way we represent elements of E for computational purposes. Let us define the F-vector space isomorphism

$$
\begin{aligned}
\epsilon: \qquad F^{1 \times \ell} &\to E \\
(a_0, \ldots, a_{\ell-1}) &\mapsto a_0 + a_1 \eta + \cdots + a_{\ell-1} \eta^{\ell-1}.
\end{aligned}
\tag{21.6}
$$

The maps ϵ and ϵ^{-1} are best thought of as "type conversion operators" that require no actual computation to evaluate. The matrix Q, then, is the $\ell \times \ell$ matrix whose ith row, for $i = 1, \ldots, \ell$, is $\epsilon^{-1}(\rho(\eta^{i-1}))$. Note that if $\alpha := \eta^q$, then $\rho(\eta^{i-1}) = (\eta^{i-1})^q - \eta^{i-1} = (\eta^q)^{i-1} - \eta^{i-1} = \alpha^{i-1} - \eta^{i-1}$. This observation allows us to construct the rows of Q by first computing α as η^q via repeated squaring, and then just computing successive powers of α.

After we construct the matrix Q, we apply Gaussian elimination to get row vectors $v_1, \ldots, v_r$ that form a basis for the row null space of Q. It is at this point that our algorithm actually discovers the number r of irreducible factors of f. We can then set $\beta_i := \epsilon(v_i)$ for $i = 1, \ldots, r$ to get our basis for B.

Putting this altogether, we have the following algorithm to compute a basis for the Berlekamp subalgebra. It takes as input a monic square-free polynomial f of degree $\ell > 0$. With $E := F[X]/(f)$, $\eta := [X]_f \in E$, and ϵ as defined in (21.6), the algorithm runs as follows:

Algorithm B1:

let Q be an $\ell \times \ell$ matrix over F (initially with undefined entries)
compute $\alpha \leftarrow \eta^q$ using repeated squaring
$\beta \leftarrow 1_E$
for $i \leftarrow 1$ to ℓ do   //   *invariant:* $\beta = \alpha^{i-1} = (\eta^{i-1})^q$
       $Q(i) \leftarrow \epsilon^{-1}(\beta)$, $Q(i,i) \leftarrow Q(i,i) - 1$, $\beta \leftarrow \beta\alpha$
compute a basis $v_1, \ldots, v_r$ of the row null space of Q using
       Gaussian elimination
for $i = 1, \ldots, r$ do $\beta_i \leftarrow \epsilon(v_i)$
output $\beta_1, \ldots, \beta_r$

The correctness of Algorithm B1 is clear from the above discussion. As for the running time:

Theorem 21.9. *Algorithm B1 uses $O(\ell^3 + \ell^2 \operatorname{len}(q))$ operations in F.*

Proof. This is just a matter of counting. The computation of α takes $O(\operatorname{len}(q))$ operations in E using repeated squaring, and hence $O(\ell^2 \operatorname{len}(q))$ operations in F. To build the matrix Q, we have to perform an additional $O(\ell)$ operations in E to compute the successive powers of α, which translates into $O(\ell^3)$ operations in F. Finally, the cost of Gaussian elimination is an additional $O(\ell^3)$ operations in F. $\square$

Stage 2: Splitting with B

The second stage of Berlekamp's factoring algorithm is a probabilistic procedure that factors f using a basis $\beta_1, \ldots, \beta_r$ for B. As we did with Algorithm EDF in §21.3.2, we begin by discussing how to efficiently split f into two non-trivial factors, and then we present a somewhat more elaborate algorithm that completely factors f.

Let $M_1 \in F[X]$ be the polynomial defined by (21.2) and (21.3); that is,

$$M_1 := \begin{cases} \sum_{j=0}^{w-1} X^{2^j} & \text{if } p = 2, \\ X^{(q-1)/2} - 1 & \text{if } p > 2. \end{cases}$$

Using our basis for B, we can easily generate a random element β of B by simply choosing $c_1, \ldots, c_r$ at random, and computing $\beta := \sum_i c_i \beta_i$. If $\beta = \theta(b_1, \ldots, b_r)$, then the b_i will be uniformly and independently distributed over F. Just as in Algorithm EDF, $\gcd(\operatorname{rep}(M_1(\beta)), f)$ will be a non-trivial factor of f with probability at least $1/2$, if $p = 2$, and probability at least $4/9$, if $p > 2$.

That is the basic splitting strategy. We turn this into an algorithm to completely factor f using the same technique of iterative refinement that was used in Algorithm EDF. That is, at any stage of the algorithm, we have a partial factorization $f = \prod_{h \in H} h$, which we try to refine by attempting to split each $h \in H$ using the strategy outlined above. One technical difficulty is that to split such a polynomial h, we need to efficiently generate a random element of the Berlekamp subalgebra of $F[X]/(h)$. A particularly efficient way to do this is to use our basis for the Berlekamp subalgebra of $F[X]/(f)$ to generate a random element of the Berlekamp subalgebra of $F[X]/(h)$ for all $h \in H$ simultaneously. Let $g_i := \operatorname{rep}(\beta_i)$ for $i = 1, \ldots, r$. If we choose $c_1, \ldots, c_r \in F$ at random, and set $g := c_1 g_1 + \cdots + c_r g_r$, then $[g]_f$ is a random element of the Berlekamp subalgebra of $F[X]/(f)$, and by the Chinese remainder theorem, it follows that the values $[g]_h$ for $h \in H$ are independently distributed, with each $[g]_h$ uniformly distributed over the Berlekamp subalgebra of $F[X]/(h)$.

Here is the algorithm for completely factoring a polynomial, given a basis for the corresponding Berlekamp subalgebra. It takes as input a monic, square-free polynomial f of degree $\ell > 0$, together with a basis $\beta_1, \ldots, \beta_r$ for the Berlekamp subalgebra of $F[X]/(f)$. With $g_i := \text{rep}(\beta_i)$ for $i = 1, \ldots, r$, the algorithm runs as follows:

Algorithm B2:

$H \leftarrow \{f\}$
while $|H| < r$ do
        choose $c_1, \ldots, c_r \in F$ at random
        $g \leftarrow c_1 g_1 + \cdots + c_r g_r \in F[X]$
        $H' \leftarrow \emptyset$
        for each $h \in H$ do
            $\beta \leftarrow [g]_h \in F[X]/(h)$
            $d \leftarrow \gcd(\text{rep}(M_1(\beta)), h)$
            if $d = 1$ or $d = h$
                then $H' \leftarrow H' \cup \{h\}$
                else $H' \leftarrow H' \cup \{d, h/d\}$
        $H \leftarrow H'$
output H

The correctness of the algorithm is clear. As for its expected running time, we can get a quick-and-dirty upper bound as follows:

- The cost of generating g in each loop iteration is $O(r\ell)$ operations in F. For a given h, the cost of computing $\beta := [g]_h \in F[X]/(h)$ is $O(\ell \deg(h))$ operations in F, and the cost of computing $M_1(\beta)$ is $O(\deg(h)^2 \text{len}(q))$ operations in F. Therefore, the number of operations in F performed in each iteration of the main loop is at most a constant times

$$r\ell + \ell \sum_{h \in H} \deg(h) + \text{len}(q) \sum_{h \in H} \deg(h)^2$$

$$\leq 2\ell^2 + \text{len}(q) \left(\sum_{h \in H} \deg(h) \right)^2 = O(\ell^2 \text{len}(q)).$$

- The expected number of iterations of the main loop until we get some non-trivial split is $O(1)$.

- The algorithm finishes after getting $r - 1$ non-trivial splits.
- Therefore, the total expected cost is $O(r\ell^2 \operatorname{len}(q))$ operations in F.

A more careful analysis reveals:

Theorem 21.10. *Algorithm B2 uses an expected number of*

$$O(\operatorname{len}(r)\ell^2 \operatorname{len}(q))$$

operations in F.

Proof. The proof follows the same line of reasoning as the analysis of Algorithm EDF. Indeed, using the same argument as was used there, the expected number of iterations of the main loop is $O(\operatorname{len}(r))$. As discussed in the paragraph above this theorem, the cost per loop iteration is $O(\ell^2 \operatorname{len}(q))$ operations in F. The theorem follows. $\square$

The bound in the above theorem is tight (see Exercise 21.11 below): unlike Algorithm EDF, we cannot make the multiplicative factor of $\operatorname{len}(r)$ go away.

21.4.3 Analysis of the whole algorithm

Putting together Algorithm SFD with algorithms B1 and B2, we get Berlekamp's complete factoring algorithm. The running time bound is easily estimated from the results already proved:

Theorem 21.11. *Berlekamp's factoring algorithm uses an expected number of $O(\ell^3 + \ell^2 \operatorname{len}(\ell) \operatorname{len}(q))$ operations in F.*

So we see that Berlekamp's algorithm is in fact faster than the Cantor–Zassenhaus algorithm, whose expected operation count is $O(\ell^3 \operatorname{len}(q))$. The speed advantage of Berlekamp's algorithm grows as q gets large. The one disadvantage of Berlekamp's algorithm is space: it requires space for $\Theta(\ell^2)$ elements of F, while the Cantor–Zassenhaus algorithm requires space for only $O(\ell)$ elements of F. One can in fact implement the Cantor–Zassenhaus algorithm so that it uses $O(\ell^3 + \ell^2 \operatorname{len}(q))$ operations in F, while using space for only $O(\ell^{1.5})$ elements of F—see Exercise 21.13 below.

EXERCISE 21.10. Give an example of a family of input polynomials f that cause Algorithm SFD to use at least $\Omega(\ell^3)$ operations in F, where $\ell :=$ $\deg(f)$.

EXERCISE 21.11. Give an example of a family of input polynomials f that cause Algorithm B2 to use an expected number of at least $\Omega(\ell^2 \operatorname{len}(\ell) \operatorname{len}(q))$ operations in F, where $\ell := \deg(f)$.

EXERCISE 21.12. Using the ideas behind Berlekamp's factoring algorithm, devise a deterministic irreducibility test that, given a monic polynomial of degree ℓ over F, uses $O(\ell^3 + \ell^2 \operatorname{len}(q))$ operations in F.

EXERCISE 21.13. This exercise develops a variant of the Cantor–Zassenhaus algorithm that uses $O(\ell^3 + \ell^2 \operatorname{len}(q))$ operations in F, while using space for only $O(\ell^{1.5})$ elements of F. By making use of Algorithm SFD (which with a bit of care can be implemented so as to use space for $O(\ell)$ elements of F) and the variant of Algorithm EDF discussed in Exercise 21.8, our problem is reduced to that of implementing Algorithm DDF within the stated time and space bounds, assuming that the input polynomial is square-free.

(a) For non-negative integers i, j, with $i \neq j$, show that the irreducible polynomials in $F[X]$ that divide $X^{q^i} - X^{q^j}$ are precisely those whose degree divides $i - j$.

(b) Let $f \in F[X]$ be a monic polynomial of degree $\ell > 0$, and let $m \approx \ell^{1/2}$. Let $\eta := [X]_f \in E$, where $E := F[X]/(f)$. Show how to compute

$$\eta^q, \eta^{q^2}, \ldots, \eta^{q^{m-1}} \in E \quad \text{and} \quad \eta^{q^m}, \eta^{q^{2m}}, \ldots, \eta^{q^{(m-1)m}} \in E$$

using $O(\ell^3 + \ell^2 \operatorname{len}(q))$ operations in F, and space for $O(\ell^{1.5})$ elements of F.

(c) Combine the results of parts (a) and (b) to implement Algorithm DDF on square-free inputs of degree ℓ, so that it uses $O(\ell^3 + \ell^2 \operatorname{len}(q))$ operations in F, and space for $O(\ell^{1.5})$ elements of F.

21.5 Deterministic factorization algorithms (∗)

The algorithms of Cantor and Zassenhaus and of Berlekamp are probabilistic. The exercises below develop a deterministic variant of the Cantor–Zassenhaus algorithm. (One can also develop deterministic variants of Berlekamp's algorithm, with similar complexity.)

This algorithm is only practical for finite fields of small characteristic, and is anyway mainly of theoretical interest, since from a practical perspective, there is nothing wrong with the above probabilistic method. In all of these exercises, we assume that we have access to a basis $\epsilon_1, \ldots, \epsilon_w$ for F as a vector space over $\mathbb{Z}_p$.

To make the Cantor–Zassenhaus algorithm deterministic, we only need to develop a deterministic variant of Algorithm EDF, as Algorithm DDF is already deterministic.

EXERCISE 21.14. Let $g = g_1 \cdots g_r$, where the g_i are distinct monic irreducible polynomials in $F[X]$. Assume that $r > 1$, and let $\ell := \deg(g)$. For this exercise, the degrees of the g_i need not be the same. For an intermediate field F', with $\mathbb{Z}_p \subseteq F' \subseteq F$, let us call a set $S = \{\lambda_1, \ldots, \lambda_s\}$ of polynomials in $F[X]_{<\ell}$ a **separating set for** g **over** F' if the following conditions hold:

- for $i = 1, \ldots, r$ and $u = 1, \ldots, s$, there exists $c_{ui} \in F'$ such that $\lambda_u \equiv c_{ui} \pmod{g_i}$, and

- for any distinct pair of indices i, j, with $1 \le i < j \le r$, there exists $u = 1, \ldots, s$ such that $c_{ui} \ne c_{uj}$.

Show that if S is a separating set for g over $\mathbb{Z}_p$, then the following algorithm completely factors g using $O(p|S|\ell^2)$ operations in F.

$$H \leftarrow \{g\}$$
for each $\lambda \in S$ do
    for each $a \in \mathbb{Z}_p$ do
        $H' \leftarrow \emptyset$
        for each $h \in H$ do
            $d \leftarrow \gcd(\lambda - a, h)$
            if $d = 1$ or $d = h$
                then $H' \leftarrow H' \cup \{h\}$
                else $H' \leftarrow H' \cup \{d, h/d\}$
        $H \leftarrow H'$
output H

EXERCISE 21.15. Let g be as in the previous exercise. Show that if S is a separating set for g over F, then the set

$$S' := \{\sum_{i=0}^{w-1} (\epsilon_j \lambda)^{p^i} \bmod g : 1 \le j \le w, \ \lambda \in S\}$$

is a separating set for g over $\mathbb{Z}_p$. Show how to compute this set using $O(|S|\ell^2 \operatorname{len}(p)w(w-1))$ operations in F.

EXERCISE 21.16. Let g be as in the previous two exercises, but further suppose that each irreducible factor of g is of the same degree, say k. Let $E := F[X]/(g)$ and $\eta := [X]_g \in E$. Define the polynomial $\phi \in E[Y]$ as follows:

$$\phi := \prod_{i=0}^{k-1} (Y - \eta^{q^i}).$$

If

$$\phi = Y^k + \alpha_{k-1} Y^{k-1} + \cdots + \alpha_0,$$

with $\alpha_0, \ldots, \alpha_{k-1} \in E$, show that the set

$$S := \{\mathrm{rep}(\alpha_i) : 0 \leq i \leq k - 1\}$$

is a separating set for g over F, and can be computed deterministically using $O(k^2 + k\,\mathrm{len}(q))$ operations in E, and hence $O(k^2\ell^2 + k\ell^2\,\mathrm{len}(q))$ operations in F.

EXERCISE 21.17. Put together all of the above pieces, together with Algorithm DDF, so as to obtain a deterministic algorithm for factoring polynomials over F that runs in time at most p times a polynomial in the input length, and make a careful estimate of the running time of your algorithm.

EXERCISE 21.18. It is a fact that when our prime p is odd, then for all integers a, b, with $a \not\equiv b \pmod{p}$, there exists a non-negative integer $i \leq p^{1/2} \log_2 p$ such that $(a + i \mid p) \neq (b + i \mid p)$ (here, "$(\cdot \mid \cdot)$" is the Legendre symbol). Using this fact, design and analyze a deterministic algorithm for factoring polynomials over F that runs in time at most $p^{1/2}$ times a polynomial in the input length.

The following two exercises show that the problem of factoring polynomials over F reduces in deterministic polynomial time to the problem of finding roots of polynomials over $\mathbb{Z}_p$.

EXERCISE 21.19. Let g be as in Exercise 21.14. Suppose that $S = \{\lambda_1, \ldots, \lambda_s\}$ is a separating set for g over $\mathbb{Z}_p$, and $\phi_u \in F[X]$ is the minimal polynomial over F of $[\lambda_u]_g \in F[X]/(g)$ for $u = 1, \ldots, s$. Show that each ϕ_u is the product of linear factors over $\mathbb{Z}_p$, and that given S along with the roots of all the ϕ_u, we can deterministically factor g using $(|S| + \ell)^{O(1)}$ operations in F. Hint: see Exercise 17.9.

EXERCISE 21.20. Using the previous exercise, show that the problem of factoring a polynomial over a finite field F reduces in deterministic polynomial time to the problem of finding roots of polynomials over the prime field of F.

21.6 Faster square-free decomposition (∗)

The algorithm presented in §21.4.1 for square-free decomposition was simple and suitable for our immediate purposes, but is certainly not the most efficient algorithm possible. The following exercises develop a faster algorithm for this problem.

We begin with an exercise that more fully develops the connection between square-free polynomials and formal derivatives for polynomials over arbitrary fields:

EXERCISE 21.21. Let K be a field, and let $f \in K[X]$ with $\deg(f) > 0$.

(a) Show that if $\mathbf{D}(f) = 0$, then the characteristic of K must be a prime p, and f must be of the form $f = g(X^p)$ for some $g \in K[X]$.

(b) Show that if K is a finite field or a field of characteristic zero, then f is square-free if and only if $d := \gcd(f, \mathbf{D}(f)) = 1$; moreover, if $d \neq 1$, then either $\deg(d) < \deg(f)$, or K has prime characteristic p and $f = h^p$ for some $h \in K[X]$.

(c) Give an example of a field K of characteristic p and an irreducible polynomial $f \in K[X]$ such that $f = g(X^p)$ for some $g \in K[X]$.

Next, we consider the problem of square-free decomposition of polynomials over fields of characteristic zero, which is simpler than the corresponding problem over finite fields.

EXERCISE 21.22. Let $f \in K[X]$ be a monic polynomial over a field K of characteristic zero. Suppose that the factorization of f into irreducibles is

$$f = f_1^{e_1} \cdots f_r^{e_r}.$$

Show that

$$\frac{f}{\gcd(f, \mathbf{D}(f))} = f_1 \cdots f_r.$$

EXERCISE 21.23. Let K be a field of characteristic zero. Consider the following algorithm that takes as input a monic polynomial $f \in K[X]$ of degree $\ell > 0$:

$j \leftarrow 1, \ g \leftarrow f / \gcd(f, \mathbf{D}(f))$
repeat
    $f \leftarrow f/g, \ h \leftarrow \gcd(f, g), \ m \leftarrow g/h$
    if $m \neq 1$ then output (m, j)
    $g \leftarrow h, \ j \leftarrow j + 1$
until $g = 1$

Using the result of the previous exercise, show that this algorithm outputs a list of pairs (g_i, s_i), such that each g_i is square-free, $f = \prod_i g_i^{s_i}$, and the g_i are pairwise relatively prime. Furthermore, show that this algorithm uses $O(\ell^2)$ operations in K.

We now turn our attention to square-free decomposition over finite fields.

EXERCISE 21.24. Let $f \in F[X]$ be a monic polynomial over F (which, as usual, has characteristic p and cardinality $q = p^w$). Suppose that the factorization of f into irreducibles is

$$f = f_1^{e_1} \cdots f_r^{e_r}.$$

Show that

$$\frac{f}{\gcd(f, \mathbf{D}(f))} = \prod_{\substack{1 \le i \le r \\ e_i \not\equiv 0 \,(\mathrm{mod}\ p)}} f_i.$$

EXERCISE 21.25. Consider the following algorithm that takes as input a monic polynomial $f \in F[X]$ of degree $\ell > 0$:

> $s \leftarrow 1$
> repeat
> > $j \leftarrow 1, \; g \leftarrow f/\gcd(f, \mathbf{D}(f))$
> > repeat
> > > $f \leftarrow f/g, \; h \leftarrow \gcd(f, g), \; m \leftarrow g/h$
> > > if $m \neq 1$ then output (m, js)
> > > $g \leftarrow h, \; j \leftarrow j + 1$
> > until $g = 1$
> > if $f \neq 1$ then // f is a pth power
> > > // we compute a pth root as in Algorithm SFD
> > > $f \leftarrow f^{1/p}, \; s \leftarrow ps$
> until $f = 1$

Using the result of the previous exercise, show that this algorithm outputs a list of pairs (g_i, s_i), such that each g_i is square-free, $f = \prod_i g_i^{s_i}$, and the g_i are pairwise relatively prime. Furthermore, show that this algorithm uses $O(\ell^2 + \ell(w-1)\operatorname{len}(p)/p)$ operations in F.

21.7 Notes

The average-case analysis of Algorithm IPT, assuming its input is random, and the application to the analysis of Algorithm RIP, is essentially due to Ben-Or [14]. If one implements Algorithm RIP using fast polynomial arithmetic, one gets an expected cost of $O(\ell^{2+o(1)}\operatorname{len}(q))$ operations in F. Note that Ben-Or's analysis is a bit incomplete—see Exercise 32 in Chapter 7 of Bach and Shallit [12] for a complete analysis of Ben-Or's claims.

The asymptotically fastest probabilistic algorithm for constructing an irreducible polynomial over F of degree ℓ is due to Shoup [91]. That algorithm uses an expected number of $O(\ell^{2+o(1)} + \ell^{1+o(1)}\operatorname{len}(q))$ operations in F, and in fact does not follow the "generate and test" paradigm of Algorithm RIP, but uses a completely different approach. Exercise 21.2 is based on [91].

As far as *deterministic* algorithms for constructing irreducible polynomials of given degree over F, the only known methods are efficient when the characteristic p of F is small (see Chistov [26], Semaev [83], and Shoup [89]), or under a generalization of the Riemann hypothesis (see Adleman and Lenstra [4]). Shoup [89] in fact shows that the problem of constructing an irreducible polynomial of given degree over F is deterministic, polynomial-time reducible to the problem of factoring polynomials over F.

The algorithm in §21.2 for computing minimal polynomials over finite fields is due to Gordon [41].

The Cantor–Zassenhaus algorithm was initially developed by Cantor and Zassenhaus [24], although many of the basic ideas can be traced back quite a ways. A straightforward implementation of this algorithm using fast polynomial arithmetic uses an expected number of $O(\ell^{2+o(1)} \operatorname{len}(q))$ operations in F.

Berlekamp's algorithm was initially developed by Berlekamp [15, 16], but again, the basic ideas go back a long way. A straightforward implementation using fast polynomial arithmetic uses an expected number of $O(\ell^3 + \ell^{1+o(1)} \operatorname{len}(q))$ operations in F; the term ℓ^3 may be replaced by ℓ^ω, where ω is the exponent of matrix multiplication (see §15.6).

There are no known efficient, deterministic algorithms for factoring polynomials over F when the characteristic p of F is large (even under a generalization of the Riemann hypothesis, except in certain special cases).

The square-free decomposition of a polynomial over a field K of characteristic zero can be computed using an algorithm of Yun [105] using $O(\ell^{1+o(1)})$ operations in K. Yun's algorithm can be adapted to work over finite fields as well (see Exercise 14.30 in von zur Gathen and Gerhard [37]).

The asymptotically fastest algorithms for factoring polynomials over a finite field F are due to von zur Gathen, Kaltofen, and Shoup: the algorithm of von zur Gathen and Shoup [38] uses an expected number of $O(\ell^{2+o(1)} + \ell^{1+o(1)} \operatorname{len}(q))$ operations in F; the algorithm of Kaltofen and Shoup [51] has a cost that is subquadratic in the degree—it uses an expected number of $O(\ell^{1.815} \operatorname{len}(q)^{0.407})$ operations in F. Exercises 21.1, 21.7, and 21.8 are based on [38]. Although the "fast" algorithms in [38] and [51] are mainly of theoretical interest, a variant in [51], which uses $O(\ell^{2.5} + \ell^{1+o(1)} \operatorname{len}(q))$ operations in F, and space for $O(\ell^{1.5})$ elements of F, has proven to be quite practical (Exercise 21.13 develops some of these ideas; see also Shoup [92]).

22

Deterministic primality testing

For many years, despite much research in the area, there was no known deterministic, polynomial-time algorithm for testing whether a given integer $n > 1$ is a prime. However, that is no longer the case—the breakthrough algorithm of Agrawal, Kayal, and Saxena, or AKS algorithm for short, is just such an algorithm. Not only is the result itself remarkable, but the algorithm is striking in both its simplicity, and in the fact that the proof of its running time and correctness are completely elementary (though ingenious).

We should stress at the outset that although this result is an important theoretical result, as of yet, it has no real practical significance: probabilistic tests, such as the Miller–Rabin test discussed in Chapter 10, are *much* more efficient, and a practically minded person should not at all bothered by the fact that such algorithms may in theory make a mistake with an incredibly small probability.

22.1 The basic idea

The algorithm is based on the following fact:

Theorem 22.1. *Let $n > 1$ be an integer. If n is prime, then for all $a \in \mathbb{Z}_n$, we have the following identity in the ring $\mathbb{Z}_n[\mathrm{X}]$:*

$$(\mathrm{X} + a)^n = \mathrm{X}^n + a \qquad (22.1)$$

Conversely, if n is composite, then for all $a \in \mathbb{Z}_n^*$, the identity (22.1) does not hold.

Proof. Note that

$$(\mathrm{X} + a)^n = \mathrm{X}^n + a^n + \sum_{i=1}^{n-1} \binom{n}{i} a^i \mathrm{X}^{n-i}.$$

If n is prime, then by Fermat's little theorem (Theorem 2.16), we have $a^n = a$, and by Exercise 1.12, all of the binomial coefficients $\binom{n}{i}$, for $i = 1, \ldots, n-1$, are divisible by n, and hence their images in the ring $\mathbb{Z}_n$ vanish. That proves that the identity (22.1) holds when n is prime.

Conversely, suppose that n is composite and that $a \in \mathbb{Z}_n^*$. Consider any prime factor p of n, and suppose $n = p^k m$, where $p \nmid m$.

We claim that $p^k \nmid \binom{n}{p}$. To prove the claim, one simply observes that

$$\binom{n}{p} = \frac{n(n-1)\cdots(n-p+1)}{p!},$$

and the numerator of this fraction is an integer divisible by p^k, but no higher power of p, and the denominator is divisible by p, but no higher power of p. That proves the claim.

From the claim, and the fact that $a \in \mathbb{Z}_n^*$, it follows that the coefficient of X^{n-p} in $(\mathsf{X}+a)^n$ is not zero, and hence the identity (22.1) does not hold. $\square$

Of course, Theorem 22.1 does not immediately give rise to an efficient primality test, since just evaluating the left-hand side of the identity (22.1) takes time $\Omega(n)$ in the worst case. The key observation of Agrawal, Kayal, and Saxena is that if (22.1) holds modulo $\mathsf{X}^r - 1$ for a suitably chosen value of r, and for sufficiently many a, then n must be prime. To make this idea work, one must show that a suitable r exists that is bounded by a polynomial in $\mathrm{len}(n)$, and that the number of different values of a that must be tested is also bounded by a polynomial in $\mathrm{len}(n)$.

22.2 The algorithm and its analysis

The algorithm is shown in Fig. 22.1. It takes as input an integer $n > 1$.

A few remarks on implementation are in order:

- In step 1, we can use the algorithm for perfect-power testing discussed in §10.5, which is a deterministic, polynomial-time algorithm.

- The search for r in step 2 can just be done by brute-force search; likewise, the determination of the multiplicative order of $[n]_r \in \mathbb{Z}_r^*$ can be done by brute force: after verifying that $\gcd(n,r) = 1$, compute successive powers of n modulo r until we get 1.

We want to prove that Algorithm AKS runs in polynomial time and is correct. To prove that it runs in polynomial time, it clearly suffices to prove that there exists an integer r satisfying the condition in step 2 that is bounded by a polynomial in $\mathrm{len}(n)$, since all other computations can be

1. if n is of the form a^b for integers $a > 1$ and $b > 1$ then
    return *false*
2. find the smallest integer $r > 1$ such that either
    $$\gcd(n, r) > 1$$
    or
    $$\gcd(n, r) = 1 \text{ and}$$
    $$[n]_r \in \mathbb{Z}_r^* \text{ has multiplicative order} > 4\,\text{len}(n)^2$$
3. if $r = n$ then return *true*
4. if $\gcd(n, r) > 1$ then return *false*
5. for $j \leftarrow 1$ to $2\,\text{len}(n)\lfloor r^{1/2} \rfloor + 1$ do
    if $(\mathsf{X} + j)^n \not\equiv \mathsf{X}^n + j \pmod{\mathsf{X}^r - 1}$ in the ring $\mathbb{Z}_n[\mathsf{X}]$ then
        return *false*
6. return *true*

Fig. 22.1. Algorithm AKS

carried out in time $(r + \text{len}(n))^{O(1)}$. Correctness means that it outputs *true* if and only if n is prime.

22.2.1 Running time analysis

The question of the running time of Algorithm AKS is settled by the following fact:

Theorem 22.2. *For integers $n > 1$ and $m \geq 1$, the least prime r such that $r \nmid n$ and the multiplicative order of $[n]_r \in \mathbb{Z}_r^*$ is greater than m is $O(m^2\,\text{len}(n))$.*

Proof. Call a prime r "good" if $r \nmid n$ and the multiplicative order of $[n]_r \in \mathbb{Z}_r^*$ is greater than m, and otherwise call r "bad." If r is bad, then either $r \mid n$ or $r \mid (n^d - 1)$ for some $d = 1, \ldots, m$. Thus, any bad prime r satisfies

$$r \mid n \prod_{d=1}^{m} (n^d - 1).$$

If all primes r up to some given bound $x \geq 2$ are bad, then the product of all primes up to x divides $n \prod_{d=1}^{m}(n^d - 1)$, and so in particular,

$$\prod_{r \leq x} r \leq n \prod_{d=1}^{m} (n^d - 1),$$

where the first product is over all primes r up to x. Taking logarithms, we obtain

$$\sum_{r \leq x} \log r \leq \log\left(n \prod_{d=1}^{m} (n^d - 1)\right) \leq (\log n)\left(1 + \sum_{d=1}^{m} d\right)$$

$$= (\log n)(1 + m(m+1)/2).$$

But by Theorem 5.6, we have

$$\sum_{r \leq x} \log r \geq cx$$

for some constant $c > 0$, from which it follows that

$$x \leq c^{-1}(\log n)(1 + m(m+1)/2),$$

and the theorem follows. $\square$

From this theorem, it follows that the value of r found in step 2—which need not be prime—will be $O(\text{len}(n)^5)$. From this, we obtain:

Theorem 22.3. *Algorithm AKS can be implemented so as to run in time* $O(\text{len}(n)^{16.5})$.

Proof. As discussed above, the value of r determined in step 2 will be $O(\text{len}(n)^5)$. It is fairly straightforward to see that the running time of the algorithm is dominated by the running time of step 5. Here, we have to perform $O(r^{1/2}\text{len}(n))$ exponentiations to the power n in the ring $\mathbb{Z}_n[\mathsf{X}]/(\mathsf{X}^r - 1)$. Each of these exponentiations takes $O(\text{len}(n))$ operations in $\mathbb{Z}_n[\mathsf{X}]/(\mathsf{X}^r - 1)$, each of which takes $O(r^2)$ operations in $\mathbb{Z}_n$, each of which takes time $O(\text{len}(n)^2)$. This yields a running time bounded by a constant times

$$r^{1/2}\text{len}(n) \times \text{len}(n) \times r^2 \times \text{len}(n)^2 = r^{2.5}\text{len}(n)^4.$$

Substituting the bound $O(\text{len}(n)^5)$ for r, we obtain the stated bound in the theorem. $\square$

22.2.2 Correctness

As for the correctness of Algorithm AKS, we first show:

Theorem 22.4. *If the input to Algorithm AKS is prime, then the output is* true.

Proof. Assume that the input n is prime. The test in step 1 will certainly fail. If the algorithm does not return *true* in step 3, then certainly the test in step 4 will fail as well. If the algorithm reaches step 5, then all of the tests in the loop in step 5 will fail—this follows from Theorem 22.1. □

The interesting case is the following:

Theorem 22.5. *If the input to Algorithm AKS is composite, then the output is* false.

The proof of this theorem is rather long, and is the subject of the remainder of this section.

Suppose the input n is composite. If n is a prime power, then this will be detected in step 1, so we may assume that n is not a prime power. Assume that the algorithm has found a suitable value of r in step 2. Clearly, the test in 3 will fail. If the test in step 4 passes, we are done, so we may assume that this test fails; that is, we may assume that all prime factors of n are greater than r. Our goal now is to show that one of the tests in the loop in step 5 must pass. The proof will be by contradiction: we shall assume that none of the tests pass, and derive a contradiction.

The assumption that none of the tests in step 5 fail means that in the ring $\mathbb{Z}_n[\mathtt{X}]$, the following congruences hold:

$$(\mathtt{X} + j)^n \equiv \mathtt{X}^n + j \ (\mathrm{mod}\ \mathtt{X}^r - 1) \quad (j = 1, \ldots, 2\,\mathrm{len}(n)\lfloor r^{1/2}\rfloor + 1). \quad (22.2)$$

For the rest of the proof, we fix any particular prime divisor p of n—the choice does not matter. Since $p \mid n$, we have a natural ring homomorphism from $\mathbb{Z}_n[\mathtt{X}]$ to $\mathbb{Z}_p[\mathtt{X}]$ (see Example 9.48), which implies that the congruences (22.2) hold in the ring of polynomials over $\mathbb{Z}_p$ as well. *From now on, we shall work exclusively with polynomials over $\mathbb{Z}_p$.*

Let us state in somewhat more abstract terms the precise assumptions we are making in order to derive our contradiction:

(**A0**) $n > 1$, $r > 1$, *and* $\ell \geq 1$ *are integers*, p *is a prime dividing* n, *and* $\gcd(n, r) = 1$;

(**A1**) n *is not a prime power*;

(**A2**) $p > r$;

(**A3**) *the congruences*

$$(\mathtt{X} + j)^n \equiv \mathtt{X}^n + j \ (\mathrm{mod}\ \mathtt{X}^r - 1) \quad (j = 1, \ldots, \ell)$$

hold in the ring $\mathbb{Z}_p[\mathtt{X}]$;

(**A4**) *the multiplicative order of* $[n]_r \in \mathbb{Z}_r^*$ *is greater than* $4\,\mathrm{len}(n)^2$;

(**A5**) $\ell > 2\,\mathrm{len}(n)\lfloor r^{1/2}\rfloor$.

The rest of the proof will rely only on these assumptions, and not on any other details of Algorithm AKS. From now on, only assumption (A0) will be implicitly in force. The other assumptions will be explicitly invoked as necessary. Our goal is to show that assumptions (A1), (A2), (A3), (A4), and (A5) cannot all be true simultaneously.

Define the $\mathbb{Z}_p$-algebra $E := \mathbb{Z}_p[\mathsf{X}]/(\mathsf{X}^r - 1)$, and let $\eta := [\mathsf{X}]_{\mathsf{X}^r - 1} \in E$, so that $E = \mathbb{Z}_p[\eta]$. Every element of E can be expressed uniquely as $g(\eta) = [g]_{\mathsf{X}^r - 1}$, for $g \in \mathbb{Z}_p[\mathsf{X}]$ of degree less than r, and for an arbitrary polynomial $g \in \mathbb{Z}_p[\mathsf{X}]$, we have $g(\eta) = 0$ if and only if $(\mathsf{X}^r - 1) \mid g$. Note that $\eta \in E^*$ and has multiplicative order r: indeed, $\eta^r = 1$, and $\eta^s - 1$ cannot be zero for $s < r$, since $\mathsf{X}^s - 1$ has degree less than r.

Assumption (A3) implies that we have a number of interesting identities in the $\mathbb{Z}_p$-algebra E:

$$(\eta + j)^n = \eta^n + j \quad (j = 1, \ldots, \ell).$$

For the polynomials $g_j := \mathsf{X} + j \in \mathbb{Z}_p[\mathsf{X}]$, with j in the given range, these identities say that $g_j(\eta)^n = g_j(\eta^n)$.

In order to exploit these identities, we study more generally functions σ_k, for various integer values k, that send $g(\eta) \in E$ to $g(\eta^k)$, for arbitrary $g \in \mathbb{Z}_p[\mathsf{X}]$, and we investigate the implications of the assumption that such functions behave like the kth power map on certain inputs. To this end, let $\mathbb{Z}^{(r)}$ denote the set of all positive integers k such that $\gcd(r, k) = 1$. Note that the set $\mathbb{Z}^{(r)}$ is multiplicative; that is, $1 \in \mathbb{Z}^{(r)}$, and for all $k, k' \in \mathbb{Z}^{(r)}$, we have $kk' \in \mathbb{Z}^{(r)}$. Also note that because of our assumption (A0), both n and p are in $\mathbb{Z}^{(r)}$. For integer $k \in \mathbb{Z}^{(r)}$, let $\hat{\sigma}_k : \mathbb{Z}_p[\mathsf{X}] \to E$ be the polynomial evaluation map that sends $g \in \mathbb{Z}_p[\mathsf{X}]$ to $g(\eta^k)$. This is of course a $\mathbb{Z}_p$-algebra homomorphism, and we have:

Lemma 22.6. *For all $k \in \mathbb{Z}^{(r)}$, the kernel of $\hat{\sigma}_k$ is $(\mathsf{X}^r - 1)$, and the image of $\hat{\sigma}_k$ is E.*

Proof. Let $J := \ker(\hat{\sigma}_k)$, which is an ideal of $\mathbb{Z}_p[\mathsf{X}]$. Let k' be a positive integer such that $kk' \equiv 1 \pmod{r}$, which exists because $\gcd(r, k) = 1$.

To show that $J = (\mathsf{X}^r - 1)$, we first observe that

$$\hat{\sigma}_k(\mathsf{X}^r - 1) = (\eta^k)^r - 1 = (\eta^r)^k - 1 = 1^k - 1 = 0,$$

and hence $(\mathsf{X}^r - 1) \subseteq J$.

Next, we show that $J \subseteq (\mathsf{X}^r - 1)$. Let $g \in J$. We want to show that $(\mathsf{X}^r - 1) \mid g$. Now, $g \in J$ means that $g(\eta^k) = 0$. If we set $h := g(\mathsf{X}^k)$, this implies that $h(\eta) = 0$, which means that $(X^r - 1) \mid h$. So let us write $h = (X^r - 1)f$, for some $f \in \mathbb{Z}_p[X]$. Then

$$g(\eta) = g(\eta^{kk'}) = h(\eta^{k'}) = (\eta^{k'r} - 1)f(\eta^{k'}) = 0,$$

which implies that $(X^r - 1) \mid g$.

That finishes the proof that $J = (X^r - 1)$.

Finally, to show that $\hat{\sigma}_k$ is surjective, suppose we are given an arbitrary element of E, which we can express as $g(\eta)$ for some $g \in \mathbb{Z}_p[X]$. Now set $h := g(X^{k'})$, and observe that

$$\hat{\sigma}_k(h) = h(\eta^k) = g(\eta^{kk'}) = g(\eta). \quad \Box$$

Because of lemma 22.6, then by Theorem 9.26, the map $\sigma_k : E \to E$ that sends $g(\eta) \in E$ to $g(\eta^k)$, for $g \in \mathbb{Z}_p[X]$, is well defined, and is a ring automorphism—indeed, a $\mathbb{Z}_p$-*algebra* automorphism—on E. Note that for any $k, k' \in \mathbb{Z}^{(r)}$, we have

- $\sigma_k = \sigma_{k'}$ if and only if $\eta^k = \eta^{k'}$ if and only if $k \equiv k' \pmod{r}$, and

- $\sigma_k \circ \sigma_{k'} = \sigma_{k'} \circ \sigma_k = \sigma_{kk'}$.

So in fact, the set of all σ_k forms an abelian group (with respect to composition) that is isomorphic to $\mathbb{Z}_r^*$.

> **Remark.** It is perhaps helpful (but not necessary for the proof) to examine the behavior of the map σ_k in a bit more detail. Let $\alpha \in E$, and let
>
> $$\alpha = \sum_{i=0}^{r-1} g_i \eta^i$$
>
> be the canonical representation of α. Since $\gcd(r, k) = 1$, the map $\pi : \{0, \dots, r-1\} \to \{0, \dots, r-1\}$ that sends i to $ki \bmod r$ is a permutation whose inverse is the permutation π' that sends i to $k'i \bmod r$, where k' is a multiplicative inverse of k modulo r. Then we have
>
> $$\sigma_k(\alpha) = \sum_{i=0}^{r-1} g_i \eta^{ki} = \sum_{i=0}^{r-1} g_i \eta^{\pi(i)} = \sum_{i=0}^{r-1} g_{\pi'(i)} \eta^i.$$
>
> Thus, the action of σ_k is to permute the coordinate vector $(g_0, \dots, g_{r-1})$ of α, sending α to the element in E whose coordinate vector is $(g_{\pi'(0)}, \dots, g_{\pi'(r-1)})$. So we see that although we defined the maps σ_k in a rather "highbrow" algebraic fashion, their behavior in concrete terms is actually quite simple.

Recall that the pth power map on E is a $\mathbb{Z}_p$-algebra homomorphism (see Theorem 20.7), and so for all $\alpha \in E$, if $\alpha = g(\eta)$ for $g \in \mathbb{Z}_p[X]$, then (by

Theorem 17.1) we have

$$\alpha^p = g(\eta)^p = g(\eta^p) = \sigma_p(\alpha).$$

Thus, σ_p acts just like the pth power map on all elements of E.

We can restate assumption (A3) as follows:

$$\sigma_n(\eta + j) = (\eta + j)^n \quad (j = 1, \ldots, \ell).$$

That is to say, the map σ_n acts just like the nth power map on the elements $\eta + j$ for $j = 1, \ldots, \ell$.

Now, although the σ_p map must act like the pth power map on all of E, there is no good reason why the σ_n map should act like the nth power map on any particular element of E, and so the fact that it does so on all the elements $\eta + j$ for $j = 1, \ldots, \ell$ looks decidedly suspicious. To turn our suspicions into a contradiction, let us start by defining some notation. For $\alpha \in E$, let us define

$$C(\alpha) := \{k \in \mathbb{Z}^{(r)} : \sigma_k(\alpha) = \alpha^k\},$$

and for $k \in \mathbb{Z}^{(r)}$, let us define

$$D(k) := \{\alpha \in E : \sigma_k(\alpha) = \alpha^k\}.$$

In words: $C(\alpha)$ is the set of all k for which σ_k acts like the kth power map on α, and $D(k)$ is the set of all α for which σ_k acts like the kth power map on α. From the discussion above, we have $p \in C(\alpha)$ for all $\alpha \in E$, and it is also clear that $1 \in C(\alpha)$ for all $\alpha \in E$. Also, it is clear that $\alpha \in D(p)$ for all $\alpha \in E$, and $1_E \in D(k)$ for all $k \in \mathbb{Z}^{(r)}$.

The following two simple lemmas say that the sets $C(\alpha)$ and $D(k)$ are multiplicative.

Lemma 22.7. *For any $\alpha \in E$, if $k \in C(\alpha)$ and $k' \in C(\alpha)$, then $kk' \in C(\alpha)$.*

Proof. If $\sigma_k(\alpha) = \alpha^k$ and $\sigma_{k'}(\alpha) = \alpha^{k'}$, then

$$\sigma_{kk'}(\alpha) = \sigma_k(\sigma_{k'}(\alpha)) = \sigma_k(\alpha^{k'}) = (\sigma_k(\alpha))^{k'} = (\alpha^k)^{k'} = \alpha^{kk'},$$

where we have made use of the homomorphic property of σ_k. $\square$

Lemma 22.8. *For any $k \in \mathbb{Z}^{(r)}$, if $\alpha \in D(k)$ and $\beta \in D(k)$, then $\alpha\beta \in D(k)$.*

Proof. If $\sigma_k(\alpha) = \alpha^k$ and $\sigma_k(\beta) = \beta^k$, then

$$\sigma_k(\alpha\beta) = \sigma_k(\alpha)\sigma_k(\beta) = \alpha^k\beta^k = (\alpha\beta)^k,$$

where again, we have made use of the homomorphic property of σ_k. $\square$

Let us define

- s to be the multiplicative order of $[p]_r \in \mathbb{Z}_r^*$, and
- t to be the order of the subgroup of $\mathbb{Z}_r^*$ generated by $[p]_r$ and $[n]_r$.

Since $r \mid (p^s - 1)$, if we take any extension field F of degree s over $\mathbb{Z}_p$ (which we know exists by Theorem 20.11), then since F^* is cyclic (Theorem 9.15) and has order $p^s - 1$, we know that there exists an element $\zeta \in F^*$ of multiplicative order r (Theorem 8.31). Let us define the polynomial evaluation map $\hat{\tau} : \mathbb{Z}_p[\mathsf{X}] \to F$ that sends $g \in \mathbb{Z}_p[\mathsf{X}]$ to $g(\zeta) \in F$. Since $\mathsf{X}^r - 1$ is clearly in the kernel of $\hat{\tau}$, then by Theorem 9.27, the map $\tau : E \to F$ that sends $g(\eta)$ to $g(\zeta)$, for $g \in \mathbb{Z}_p[\mathsf{X}]$, is a well-defined ring homomorphism, and actually, it is a $\mathbb{Z}_p$-algebra homomorphism.

For concreteness, one could think of F as $\mathbb{Z}_p[\mathsf{X}]/(\phi)$, where ϕ is an irreducible factor of $\mathsf{X}^r - 1$ of degree s. In this case, we could simply take ζ to be $[\mathsf{X}]_\phi$ (see Example 20.1), and the map $\hat{\tau}$ above would be just the natural map from $\mathbb{Z}_p[\mathsf{X}]$ to $\mathbb{Z}_p[\mathsf{X}]/(\phi)$.

The key to deriving our contradiction is to examine the set $S := \tau(D(n))$, that is, the image under τ of the set $D(n)$ of all elements $\alpha \in E$ for which σ_n acts like the nth power map.

Lemma 22.9. *Under assumption (A1), we have*

$$|S| \leq n^{2\lfloor t^{1/2} \rfloor}.$$

Proof. Consider the set of integers

$$I := \{n^u p^v : u, v = 0, \ldots, \lfloor t^{1/2} \rfloor\}.$$

We first claim that $|I| > t$. To prove this, we first show that each distinct pair (u, v) gives rise to a distinct value $n^u p^v$. To this end, we make use of our assumption (A1) that n is not a prime power, and so is divisible by some prime q other than p. Thus, if $(u', v') \neq (u, v)$, then either

- $u \neq u'$, in which case the power of q in the prime factorization of $n^u p^v$ is different from that in $n^{u'} p^{v'}$, or
- $u = u'$ and $v \neq v'$, in which case the power of p in the prime factorization of $n^u p^v$ is different from that in $n^{u'} p^{v'}$.

The claim now follows from the fact that both u and v range over a set of size $\lfloor t^{1/2} \rfloor + 1 > t^{1/2}$, and so there are strictly more than t such pairs (u, v).

Next, recall that t was defined to be the order of the subgroup of $\mathbb{Z}_r^*$ generated by $[n]_r$ and $[p]_r$; equivalently, t is the number of distinct residue classes of the form $[n^u p^v]_r$, where u and v range over all non-negative integers. Since each element of I is of the form $n^u p^v$, and $|I| > t$, we may conclude that there must be two distinct elements of I, call them k and k', that are congruent modulo r. Furthermore, any element of I is a product of two positive integers each of which is at most $n^{\lfloor t^{1/2} \rfloor}$, and so both k and k' lie in the range $1, \ldots, n^{2\lfloor t^{1/2} \rfloor}$.

Now, let $\alpha \in D(n)$. This is equivalent to saying $n \in C(\alpha)$. We always have $1 \in C(\alpha)$ and $p \in C(\alpha)$, and so by lemma 22.7, we have $n^u p^v \in C(\alpha)$ for all non-negative integers u, v, and so in particular, $k, k' \in C(\alpha)$.

Since both k and k' are in $C(\alpha)$, we have

$$\sigma_k(\alpha) = \alpha^k \quad \text{and} \quad \sigma_{k'}(\alpha) = \alpha^{k'}.$$

Since $k \equiv k' \pmod{r}$, we have $\sigma_k = \sigma_{k'}$, and hence

$$\alpha^k = \alpha^{k'}.$$

Now apply the homomorphism τ, obtaining

$$\tau(\alpha)^k = \tau(\alpha)^{k'}.$$

Since this holds for all $\alpha \in D(n)$, we conclude that all elements of S are roots of the polynomial $\mathsf{X}^k - \mathsf{X}^{k'}$. Since $k \neq k'$, we see that $\mathsf{X}^k - \mathsf{X}^{k'}$ is a non-zero polynomial of degree at most $\max\{k, k'\} \leq n^{2\lfloor t^{1/2} \rfloor}$, and hence can have at most $n^{2\lfloor t^{1/2} \rfloor}$ roots in the field F (Theorem 9.14). $\square$

Lemma 22.10. *Under assumptions (A2) and (A3), we have*

$$|S| \geq 2^{\min(t,\ell)} - 1.$$

Proof. Let $m := \min(t, \ell)$. Under assumption (A3), we have $\eta + j \in D(n)$ for $j = 1, \ldots, m$. Under assumption (A2), we have $p > r > t \geq m$, and hence the integers $j = 1, \ldots, m$ are distinct modulo p. Define

$$P := \left\{ \prod_{j=1}^{m} (\mathsf{X} + j)^{e_j} \in \mathbb{Z}_p[\mathsf{X}] : e_j \in \{0, 1\} \text{ for } j = 1, \ldots, m, \text{ and } \sum_{j=1}^{m} e_j < m \right\}.$$

That is, we form P by taking products over all subsets $S \subsetneq \{\mathsf{X} + j : j = 1, \ldots, m\}$. Clearly, $|P| = 2^m - 1$.

Define $P(\eta) := \{f(\eta) \in E : f \in P\}$ and $P(\zeta) := \{f(\zeta) \in F : f \in P\}$. Note that $\tau(P(\eta)) = P(\zeta)$, and that by lemma 22.8, $P(\eta) \subseteq D(n)$.

Therefore, to prove the lemma, it suffices to show that $|P(\zeta)| = 2^m - 1$. Suppose that this is not the case. This would give rise to distinct polynomials $g, h \in \mathbb{Z}_p[\mathsf{X}]$, both of degree at most $t - 1$, such that

$$g(\eta) \in D(n), \; h(\eta) \in D(n), \; \text{and} \; \tau(g(\eta)) = \tau(h(\eta)).$$

So we have $n \in C(g(\eta))$ and (as always) $1, p \in C(g(\eta))$. Likewise, we have

$1, n, p \in C(h(\eta))$. By lemma 22.7, for all integers k of the form $n^u p^v$, where u and v range over all non-negative integers, we have

$$k \in C(g(\eta)) \quad \text{and} \quad k \in C(h(\eta)).$$

For any such k, since $\tau(g(\eta)) = \tau(h(\eta))$, we have $\tau(g(\eta))^k = \tau(h(\eta))^k$, and hence

$$
\begin{aligned}
0 &= \tau(g(\eta))^k - \tau(h(\eta))^k \\
&= \tau(g(\eta)^k) - \tau(h(\eta)^k) \quad (\tau \text{ is a homomorphism}) \\
&= \tau(g(\eta^k)) - \tau(h(\eta^k)) \quad (k \in C(g(\eta)) \text{ and } k \in C(h(\eta))) \\
&= g(\zeta^k) - h(\zeta^k) \quad (\text{definition of } \tau).
\end{aligned}
$$

Thus, the polynomial $f := g - h \in \mathbb{Z}_p[X]$ is a non-zero polynomial of degree at most $t - 1$, having roots ζ^k in the field F for all k of the form $n^u p^v$. Now, t is by definition the number of distinct residue classes of the form $[n^u p^v]_r \in \mathbb{Z}_r^*$. Also, since ζ has multiplicative order r, for integers k, k', we have $\zeta^k = \zeta^{k'}$ if and only if $k \equiv k' \pmod{r}$. Therefore, as k ranges over all integers of the form $n^u p^v$, ζ^k ranges over precisely t distinct values in F. But since all of these values are roots of the polynomial f, which is non-zero and of degree at most $t - 1$, this is impossible (Theorem 9.14). $\square$

We are now (finally!) in a position to complete the proof of Theorem 22.5. Under assumptions (A1), (A2), and (A3), Lemmas 22.9 and 22.10 imply that

$$2^{\min(t,\ell)} - 1 \le |S| \le n^{2\lfloor t^{1/2} \rfloor}. \tag{22.3}$$

The contradiction is provided by the following:

Lemma 22.11. *Under assumptions (A4) and (A5), we have*

$$2^{\min(t,\ell)} - 1 > n^{2\lfloor t^{1/2} \rfloor}.$$

Proof. Observe that $\log_2 n \le \text{len}(n)$, and so it suffices to show that

$$2^{\min(t,\ell)} - 1 > 2^{2\,\text{len}(n)\lfloor t^{1/2} \rfloor},$$

and for this, it suffices to show that

$$\min(t, \ell) > 2\,\text{len}(n)\lfloor t^{1/2} \rfloor,$$

since for any integers a, b with $a > b \ge 1$, we have $2^a > 2^b + 1$.

To show that $t > 2\,\text{len}(n)\lfloor t^{1/2} \rfloor$, it suffices to show that $t > 2\,\text{len}(n)t^{1/2}$, or equivalently, that $t > 4\,\text{len}(n)^2$. But observe that by definition, t is the order of the subgroup of $\mathbb{Z}_r^*$ generated by $[n]_r$ and $[p]_r$, which is at least as large as the multiplicative order of $[n]_r$ in $\mathbb{Z}_r^*$, and by assumption (A4), this is larger than $4 \operatorname{len}(n)^2$.

Finally, directly by assumption (A5), we have $\ell > 2 \operatorname{len}(n) \lfloor t^{1/2} \rfloor$. $\square$

That concludes the proof of Theorem 22.5.

EXERCISE 22.1. Show that if Conjecture 5.26 is true, then the value of r discovered in step 2 of Algorithm AKS satisfies $r = O(\operatorname{len}(n)^2)$.

22.3 Notes

The algorithm presented here is due to Agrawal, Kayal, and Saxena. The paper is currently available only on the Internet [6]. The analysis in the original version of the paper made use of a deep number-theoretic result of Fouvry [36], but it was subsequently noticed that the algorithm can be fully analyzed using just elementary arguments (as we have done here).

If fast algorithms for integer and polynomial arithmetic are used, then using the analysis presented here, it is easy to see that the algorithm runs in time $O(\operatorname{len}(n)^{10.5+o(1)})$. More generally, it is easy to see that the algorithm runs in time $O(r^{1.5+o(1)} \operatorname{len}(n)^{3+o(1)})$, where r is the value determined in step 2 of the algorithm. In our analysis of the algorithm, we were able to obtain the bound $r = O(\operatorname{len}(n)^5)$, leading to the running-time bound $O(\operatorname{len}(n)^{10.5+o(1)})$. Using Fouvry's result, one can show that $r = O(\operatorname{len}(n)^3)$, leading to a running-time bound of $O(\operatorname{len}(n)^{7.5+o(1)})$. Moreover, if Conjecture 5.26 on the density of Sophie Germain primes is true, then one could show that $r = O(\operatorname{len}(n)^2)$ (see Exercise 22.1), which would lead to a running-time bound of $O(\operatorname{len}(n)^{6+o(1)})$.

Prior to this algorithm, the fastest deterministic, rigorously proved primality test was one introduced by Adleman, Pomerance, and Rumely [5], called the **Jacobi sum test**, which runs in time

$$O(\operatorname{len}(n)^{c \operatorname{len}(\operatorname{len}(\operatorname{len}(n)))})$$

for some constant c. Note that for numbers n with less than 2^{256} bits, the value of $\operatorname{len}(\operatorname{len}(\operatorname{len}(n)))$ is at most 8, and so this algorithm runs in time $O(\operatorname{len}(n)^{8c})$ for any n that one could ever actually write down.

We also mention the earlier work of Adleman and Huang [3], who gave a probabilistic algorithm whose output is always correct, and which runs in expected polynomial time (i.e., a *Las Vegas* algorithm, in the parlance of §7.2).

Appendix: Some useful facts

A1. *Some handy inequalities.* The following inequalities involving exponentials and logarithms are very handy.

(i) For all real x, we have

$$1 + x \leq e^x,$$

or, taking logarithms,

$$\log(1 + x) \leq x.$$

(ii) For all real $x \geq 0$, we have

$$e^{-x} \leq 1 - x + x^2/2,$$

or, taking logarithms,

$$-x \leq \log(1 - x + x^2/2).$$

(iii) For all real x with $0 \leq x \leq 1/2$, we have

$$1 - x \geq e^{-x-x^2} \geq e^{-2x},$$

or, taking logarithms,

$$\log(1 - x) \geq -x - x^2 \geq -2x.$$

A2. *Estimating sums by integrals.* Using elementary calculus, it is easy to estimate sums over a monotone sequences in terms of a definite integral, by interpreting the integral as the area under a curve. Let f be a real-valued function that is continuous and monotone on the closed interval $[a, b]$, where a and b are integers. Then we have

$$\min(f(a), f(b)) \leq \sum_{i=a}^{b} f(i) - \int_a^b f(x)dx \leq \max(f(a), f(b)).$$

A3. *Integrating piece-wise continuous functions.* In discussing the Riemann integral $\int_a^b f(x)dx$, many introductory calculus texts only discuss in any detail the case where the integrand f is continuous on the closed interval $[a, b]$, in which case the integral is always well defined. However, the Riemann integral is well defined for much broader classes of functions. For our purposes in this text, it is convenient and sufficient to work with integrands that are **piece-wise continuous** on $[a, b]$, that is, there exist real numbers $x_0, x_1, \ldots, x_k$ and functions $f_1, \ldots, f_k$, such that $a = x_0 \leq x_1 \leq \cdots \leq x_k = b$, and for $i = 1, \ldots, k$, the function f_i is continuous on the *closed* interval $[x_{i-1}, x_i]$, and agrees with f on the *open* interval (x_{i-1}, x_i). In this case, f is integrable on $[a, b]$, and indeed

$$\int_a^b f(x)dx = \sum_{i=1}^{k} \int_{x_{i-1}}^{x_i} f_i(x)dx.$$

It is not hard to prove this equality, using the basic definition of the Riemann integral; however, for our purposes, we can also just take the value of the expression on the right-hand side as the definition of the integral on the left-hand side.

We also say that f is piece-wise continuous on $[a, \infty)$ if for all $b \geq a$, f is piece-wise continuous on $[a, b]$. In this case, we may define the improper integral $\int_a^\infty f(x)dx$ as the limit, as $b \to \infty$, of $\int_a^b f(x)dx$, provided the limit exists.

A4. *Infinite series.* It is a basic fact from calculus that if an infinite series $\sum_{i=1}^{\infty} x_i$ of non-negative terms converges to a value y, then any infinite series whose terms are a rearrangement of the x_i converges to the same value y.

An infinite series $\sum_{i=1}^{\infty} x_i$, where now some of the x_i may be negative, is called **absolutely convergent** if the series $\sum_{i=1}^{\infty} |x_i|$ is convergent. It is a basic fact from calculus that if an infinite series $\sum_{i=1}^{\infty} x_i$ is absolutely convergent, then not only does the series itself converge to some value y, but any infinite series whose terms are a rearrangement of the x_i also converges to the same value y.

A5. *Double infinite series.* The topic of **double infinite series** may not be discussed in a typical introductory calculus course; we summarize here the basic facts that we need. We state these facts without proof, but all of them are fairly straightforward applications of the definitions.

Suppose that $x_{ij}, i, j = 1, 2, \ldots$ are *non-negative* real numbers. The

ith row gives a series $\sum_j x_{ij}$, and if each of these converges, one can form the double infinite series $\sum_i \sum_j x_{ij}$. Similarly, one may form the double infinite series $\sum_j \sum_i x_{ij}$ One may also arrange the terms x_{ij} in a single infinite series $\sum_{ij} x_{ij}$, using some enumeration of the set of pairs (i, j). Then these three series either all diverge or all converge to the same value.

If we drop the requirement that the x_{ij} are non-negative, but instead require that the single infinite series $\sum_{ij} x_{ij}$ is absolutely convergent, then these three series all converge to the same value.

As a special application of the above discussion, if the series $\sum_i a_i$ is absolutely convergent and converges to A, and if the series $\sum_j b_j$ is absolutely convergent and converges to B, then if we arrange the terms $a_i b_j$ in any way in a single infinite series $\sum_{ij} a_i b_j$, this latter series is absolutely convergent and converges to AB.

Bibliography

[1] L. M. Adleman. A subexponential algorithm for the discrete logarithm problem with applications to cryptography. In *20th Annual Symposium on Foundations of Computer Science*, pages 55–60, 1979.

[2] L. M. Adleman. The function field sieve. In *Proc. 1st International Symposium on Algorithmic Number Theory (ANTS-I)*, pages 108–121, 1994.

[3] L. M. Adleman and M.-D. Huang. *Primality Testing and Two Dimensional Abelian Varieties over Finite Fields (Lecture Notes in Mathematics No. 1512)*. Springer-Verlag, 1992.

[4] L. M. Adleman and H. W. Lenstra, Jr. Finding irreducible polynomials over finite fields. In *18th Annual ACM Symposium on Theory of Computing*, pages 350–355, 1986.

[5] L. M. Adleman, C. Pomerance, and R. S. Rumely. On distinguishing prime numbers from composite numbers. *Annals of Mathematics*, 117:173–206, 1983.

[6] M. Agrawal, N. Kayal, and N. Saxena. PRIMES is in P. Manuscript, www.cse.iitk.ac.in/news/primality.html, 2002.

[7] W. Alford, A. Granville, and C. Pomerance. There are infintely many Carmichael numbers. *Annals of Mathematics*, 140:703–722, 1994.

[8] T. M. Apostol. *Introduction to Analytic Number Theory*. Springer-Verlag, 1973.

[9] E. Bach. How to generate factored random numbers. *SIAM Journal on Computing*, 17:179–193, 1988.

[10] E. Bach. Explicit bounds for primality testing and related problems. *Mathematics of Computation*, 55:355–380, 1990.

[11] E. Bach. Efficient prediction of Marsaglia-Zaman random number generators. *IEEE Transactions on Information Theory*, IT-44:1253–1257, 1998.

[12] E. Bach and J. Shallit. *Algorithmic Number Theory*, volume 1. MIT Press, 1996.

[13] M. Bellare and P. Rogaway. Random oracles are practical: a paradigm for designing efficient protocols. In *First ACM Conference on Computer and Communications Security*, pages 62–73, 1993.

[14] M. Ben-Or. Probabilistic algorithms in finite fields. In *22nd Annual Symposium on Foundations of Computer Science*, pages 394–398, 1981.

[15] E. R. Berlekamp. *Algebraic Coding Theory*. McGraw-Hill, 1968.

[16] E. R. Berlekamp. Factoring polynomials over large finite fields. *Mathematics of Computation*, 24(111):713–735, 1970.

[17] L. Blum, M. Blum, and M. Shub. A simple unpredictable pseudo-random number generator. *SIAM Journal on Computing*, 15:364–383, 1986.

[18] D. Boneh. The Decision Diffie-Hellman Problem. In *Proc. 3rd International Symposium on Algorithmic Number Theory (ANTS-III)*, pages 48–63, 1998. Springer LNCS 1423.

[19] D. Boneh and G. Durfee. Cryptanalysis of RSA with private key d less than $N^{0.292}$. *IEEE Transactions on Information Theory*, IT-46:1339–1349, 2000.

[20] R. P. Brent and H. T. Kung. Fast algorithms for manipulating formal power series. *Journal of the ACM*, 25:581–595, 1978.

[21] J. P. Buhler, H. W. Lenstra, Jr., and C. Pomerance. Factoring integers with the number field sieve. In A. K. Lenstra and H. W. Lenstra, Jr., editors, *The Development of the Number Field Sieve*, pages 50–94. Springer-Verlag, 1993.

[22] D. A. Burgess. The distribution of quadratic residues and non-residues. *Mathematika*, 4:106–112, 1957.

[23] E. Canfield, P. Erdős, and C. Pomerance. On a problem of Oppenheim concerning 'Factorisatio Numerorum'. *Journal of Number Theory*, 17:1–28, 1983.

[24] D. G. Cantor and E. Kaltofen. On fast multiplication of polynomials over arbitrary rings. *Acta Informatica*, 28:693–701, 1991.

[25] J. L. Carter and M. N. Wegman. Universal classes of hash functions. *Journal of Computer and System Sciences*, 18:143–154, 1979.

[26] A. L. Chistov. Polynomial time construction of a finite field. In *Abstracts of Lectures at 7th All-Union Conference in Mathematical Logic, Novosibirsk*, page 196, 1984. In Russian.

[27] D. Coppersmith. Modifications to the number field sieve. *Journal of Cryptology*, 6:169–180, 1993.

[28] D. Coppersmith and S. Winograd. Matrix multiplication via arithmetic progressions. *Journal of Symbolic Computation*, 9(3):23–52, 1990.

[29] T. H. Cormen, C. E. Leiserson, R. L. Rivest, and C. Stein. *Introduction to Algorithms*. MIT Press, second edition, 2001.

[30] R. Crandall and C. Pomerance. *Prime Numbers: A Computational Perspective*. Springer, 2001.

[31] I. Damgård and G. Frandsen. Efficient algorithms for gcd and cubic residuosity in the ring of Eisenstein integers. In *14th International Symposium on Fundamentals of Computation Theory, Springer LNCS 2751*, pages 109–117, 2003.

[32] I. Damgård, P. Landrock, and C. Pomerance. Average case error estimates for the strong probable prime test. *Mathematics of Computation*, 61:177–194, 1993.

[33] W. Diffie and M. E. Hellman. New directions in cryptography. *IEEE Transactions on Information Theory*, IT-22:644–654, 1976.

[34] J. Dixon. Asymptotically fast factorization of integers. *Mathematics of Computation*, 36:255–260, 1981.

[35] J. L. Dornstetter. On the equivalence between Berlekamp's and Euclid's algorithms. *IEEE Transactions on Information Theory*, IT-33:428–431, 1987.

[36] E. Fouvry. Théorème de Brun-Titchmarsh; application au théorème de Fermat. *Inventiones Mathematicae*, 79:383–407, 1985.

[37] J. von zur Gathen and J. Gerhard. *Modern Computer Algebra*. Cambridge University Press, 1999.

[38] J. von zur Gathen and V. Shoup. Computing Frobenius maps and factoring polynomials. *Computational Complexity*, 2:187–224, 1992.

[39] S. Goldwasser and S. Micali. Probabilistic encryption. *Journal of Computer and System Sciences*, 28:270–299, 1984.

[40] D. M. Gordon. Discrete logarithms in GF(p) using the number field sieve. *SIAM Journal on Discrete Mathematics*, 6:124–138, 1993.

[41] J. Gordon. Very simple method to find the minimal polynomial of an arbitrary non-zero element of a finite field. *Electronic Letters*, 12:663–664, 1976.

[42] H. Halberstam and H. Richert. *Sieve Methods*. Academic Press, 1974.

[43] G. H. Hardy and J. E. Littlewood. Some problems of partito numerorum. III. On the expression of a number as a sum of primes. *Acta Mathematica*, 44:1–70, 1923.

[44] G. H. Hardy and E. M. Wright. *An Introduction to the Theory of Numbers*. Oxford University Press, fifth edition, 1984.

[45] D. Heath-Brown. Zero-free regions for Dirichlet L-functions and the least prime in an arithmetic progression. *Proceedings of the London Mathematical Society*, 64:265–338, 1992.

[46] R. Impagliazzo, L. Levin, and M. Luby. Pseudo-random number generation from any one-way function. In *21st Annual ACM Symposium on Theory of Computing*, pages 12–24, 1989.

[47] R. Impagliazzo and D. Zuckermann. How to recycle random bits. In *30th Annual Symposium on Foundations of Computer Science*, pages 248–253, 1989.

[48] H. Iwaniec. On the error term in the linear sieve. *Acta Arithmetica*, 19:1–30, 1971.

[49] H. Iwaniec. On the problem of Jacobsthal. *Demonstratio Mathematica*, 11:225–231, 1978.

[50] A. Kalai. Generating random factored numbers, easily. In *Proc. 13th ACM-SIAM Symposium on Discrete Algorithms*, page 412, 2002.

[51] E. Kaltofen and V. Shoup. Subquadratic-time factoring of polynomials over finite fields. In *27th Annual ACM Symposium on Theory of Computing*, pages 398–406, 1995.

[52] A. A. Karatsuba and Y. Ofman. Multiplication of multidigit numbers on automata. *Soviet Physics Doklady*, 7:595–596, 1963.

[53] S. H. Kim and C. Pomerance. The probability that a random probable prime is composite. *Mathematics of Computation*, 53(188):721–741, 1989.

[54] D. E. Knuth. *The Art of Computer Programming*, volume 2. Addison-Wesley, second edition, 1981.

[55] D. Lehmann. On primality tests. *SIAM Journal on Computing*, 11:374–375, 1982.

[56] D. Lehmer and R. Powers. On factoring large numbers. *Bulletin of the AMS*, 37:770–776, 1931.

[57] H. W. Lenstra, Jr. Factoring integers with elliptic curves. *Annals of Mathematics*, 126:649–673, 1987.

[58] H. W. Lenstra, Jr. and C. Pomerance. A rigorous time bound for factoring integers. *Journal of the AMS*, 4:483–516, 1992.

[59] M. Luby. *Pseudorandomness and Cryptographic Applications*. Princeton University Press, 1996.

[60] J. Massey. Shift-register synthesis and BCH coding. *IEEE Transactions on Information Theory*, IT-15:122–127, 1969.

[61] U. Maurer. Fast generation of prime numbers and secure public-key cryptographic parameters. *Journal of Cryptology*, 8:123–155, 1995.

[62] A. Menezes, P. van Oorschot, and S. Vanstone. *Handbook of Applied Cryptography*. CRC Press, 1997.

[63] G. L. Miller. Riemann's hypothesis and tests for primality. *Journal of Computer and System Sciences*, 13:300–317, 1976.

[64] W. Mills. Continued fractions and linear recurrences. *Mathematics of Computation*, 29:173–180, 1975.

[65] K. Morrison. Random polynomials over finite fields. Manuscript, `www.calpoly.edu/~kmorriso/Research/RPFF.pdf`, 1999.

[66] M. Morrison and J. Brillhart. A method of factoring and the factorization of F_7. *Mathematics of Computation*, 29:183–205, 1975.

[67] V. I. Nechaev. Complexity of a determinate algorithm for the discrete logarithm. *Mathematical Notes*, 55(2):165–172, 1994. Translated from *Matematicheskie Zametki*, 55(2):91–101, 1994.

[68] I. Niven and H. Zuckerman. *An Introduction to the Theory of Numbers*. John Wiley and Sons, Inc., second edition, 1966.

[69] J. Oesterlé. Versions effectives du théorème de Chebotarev sous l'hypothèse de Riemann généralisée. *Astérisque*, 61:165–167, 1979.

[70] P. van Oorschot and M. Wiener. On Diffie-Hellman key agreement with short exponents. In *Advances in Cryptology–Eurocrypt '96, Springer LNCS 1070*, pages 332–343, 1996.

[71] S. Pohlig and M. Hellman. An improved algorithm for computing logarithms over $GF(p)$ and its cryptographic significance. *IEEE Transactions on Information Theory*, IT-24:106–110, 1978.

[72] J. M. Pollard. Monte Carlo methods for index computation mod p. *Mathematics of Computation*, 32:918–924, 1978.

[73] J. M. Pollard. Factoring with cubic integers. In A. K. Lenstra and H. W. Lenstra, Jr., editors, *The Development of the Number Field Sieve*, pages 4–10. Springer-Verlag, 1993.

[74] C. Pomerance. Analysis and comparison of some integer factoring algorithms. In H. W. Lenstra, Jr. and R. Tijdeman, editors, *Computational Methods in Number Theory, Part I*, pages 89–139. Mathematisch Centrum, 1982.

[75] M. O. Rabin. Probabilistic algorithms. In *Algorithms and Complexity, Recent Results and New Directions*, pages 21–39. Academic Press, 1976.

[76] D. Redmond. *Number Theory — An Introduction*. Marcel Dekker, 1996.

[77] I. Reed and G. Solomon. Polynomial codes over certain finite fields. *SIAM Journal on Applied Mathematics*, pages 300–304, 1960.

[78] R. L. Rivest, A. Shamir, and L. M. Adleman. A method for obtaining digital signatures and public-key cryptosystems. *Communications of the ACM*, 21(2):120–126, 1978.

[79] J. Rosser and L. Schoenfeld. Approximate formulas for some functions of prime numbers. *Illinois Journal of Mathematics*, 6:64–94, 1962.

[80] O. Schirokauer, D. Weber, and T. Denny. Discrete logarithms: the effectiveness of the index calculus method. In *Proc. 2nd International Symposium on Algorithmic Number Theory (ANTS-II)*, pages 337–361, 1996.

[81] A. Schönhage. Schnelle Berechnung von Kettenbruchentwicklungen. *Acta Informatica*, 1:139–144, 1971.

[82] A. Schönhage and V. Strassen. Schnelle Multiplikation grosser Zahlen. *Computing*, 7:281–282, 1971.

[83] I. A. Semaev. Construction of irreducible polynomials over finite fields with linearly independent roots. *Mat. Sbornik*, 135:520–532, 1988. In Russian; English translation in *Math. USSR–Sbornik*, 63(2):507–519, 1989.

[84] A. Shamir. Factoring numbers in $O(\log n)$ arithmetic steps. *Information Processing Letters*, 8:28–31, 1979.

[85] A. Shamir. How to share a secret. *Communications of the ACM*, 22:612–613, 1979.

[86] D. Shanks. Class number, a theory of factorization, and genera. In *Proceedings of Symposia in Pure Mathematics*, volume 20, pages 415–440, 1969.

[87] P. Shor. Algorithms for quantum computation: discrete logarithms and factoring. In *35th Annual Symposium on Foundations of Computer Science*, pages 124–134, 1994.

[88] P. Shor. Polynomial-time algorithms for prime factorization and discrete logarithms on a quantum computer. *SIAM Review*, 41:303–332, 1999.

[89] V. Shoup. New algorithms for finding irreducible polynomials over finite fields. *Mathematics of Computation*, 54(189):435–447, 1990.

[90] V. Shoup. Searching for primitive roots in finite fields. *Mathematics of Computation*, 58:369–380, 1992.

[91] V. Shoup. Fast construction of irreducible polynomials over finite fields. *Journal of Symbolic Computation*, 17(5):371–391, 1994.

[92] V. Shoup. A new polynomial factorization algorithm and its implementation. *Journal of Symbolic Computation*, 20(4):363–397, 1995.

[93] V. Shoup. Lower bounds for discrete logarithms and related problems. In *Advances in Cryptology–Eurocrypt '97*, pages 256–266, 1997.

[94] R. Solovay and V. Strassen. A fast Monte-Carlo test for primality. *SIAM Journal on Computing*, 6:84–85, 1977.

[95] J. Stein. Computational problems associated with Racah algebra. *Journal of Computational Physics*, 1:397–405, 1967.

[96] A. Walfisz. *Weylsche Exponentialsummen in der neueren Zahlentheorie*. VEB Deutscher Verlag der Wissenschaften, 1963.

[97] P. Wang, M. Guy, and J. Davenport. p-adic reconstruction of rational numbers. *SIGSAM Bulletin*, 16:2–3, 1982.

[98] Y. Wang. On the least primitive root of a prime. *Scientia Sinica*, 10(1):1–14, 1961.

[99] M. N. Wegman and J. L. Carter. New hash functions and their use in authentication and set equality. *Journal of Computer and System Sciences*, 22:265–279, 1981.

[100] A. Weilert. $(1+i)$-ary GCD computation in $\mathbf{Z}[i]$ as an analogue to the binary GCD algorithm. *Journal of Symbolic Computation*, 30:605–617, 2000.

[101] A. Weilert. Asymptotically fast GCD computation in $\mathbf{Z}[i]$. In *Proc. 4th International Symposium on Algorithmic Number Theory (ANTS-IV)*, pages 595–613, 2000.

[102] L. Welch and R. Scholtz. Continued fractions and Berlekamp's algorithm. *IEEE Transactions on Information Theory*, IT-25:19–27, 1979.

[103] D. Wiedemann. Solving sparse linear systems over finite fields. *IEEE Transactions on Information Theory*, IT-32:54–62, 1986.

[104] M. Wiener. Cryptanalysis of short RSA secret exponents. *IEEE Transactions on Information Theory*, IT-44:553–558, 1990.

[105] D. Y. Y. Yun. On square-free decomposition algorithms. In *Proc. ACM Symposium on Symbolic and Algebraic Computation*, pages 26–35, 1976.

Index of notation

Entries are listed in order of appearance.

510

Index